COMMERCIAL PROPERTY

COMMERCIAL PROPERTY

Editor

Anne Rodell MA (Cantab), Solicitor

Contributors

Stephen Allinson, Simon Barnett, Michael Feeney,
Simon Halliwell, Clare Harris, Stephanie McGuiness,
Mark O'Brien O'Reilly, Gareth Richards and Anne Rodell

Published by

The University of Law,
2 Bunhill Row, London EC1Y 8HQ

© The University of Law 2025

All rights reserved. No part of this publication may be reproduced, stored in a retrieval system, or transmitted in any way or by any means, including photocopying or recording, without the written permission of the copyright holder, application for which should be addressed to the publisher.

Crown copyright material is licensed under the Open Government Licence v3.0.

British Library Cataloguing-in-Publication Data
A catalogue record for this book is available from the British Library.

ISBN 978 1 80502 109 4

Typeset by Style Photosetting Ltd, Mayfield, East Sussex
Tables and index by Moira Greenhalgh, Arnside, Cumbria

Preface

The aim of this book is to provide law students with a comprehensive introduction to the areas of property law particularly relevant to commercial property.

Part I of the book deals with areas relevant to property acquisition and development. These include structures for joint ownership, arrangements for funding, contractual arrangements with the seller, the need for planning permission, environmental considerations, contractual arrangements with members of the construction team and taxation. Part II takes the reader through the grant of a commercial lease, the assignment of that lease and its termination. Part III deals with the law relating to property and insolvency.

Although we hope that this book will provide a useful guide to trainee solicitors and others involved in commercial property work, it is primarily intended to complement the Stage 2 Advanced Real Estate Law and Practice elective. This elective is only undertaken once the Stage 1 Real Estate Law and Practice course has been completed. Apart from the matters specifically mentioned in Part I of this book, the conveyancing process for the transfer and leasing of commercial property is as described in the Legal Practice Guide entitled *Property Law and Practice* accompanying the Stage 1 course, so the conveyancing process is not dealt with in this book.

The University of Law would like to thank Practical Law for authorising the use of the following documents in this book:

- Practice note on Overage Payments <http://uk.practicallaw.thomsonreuters.com/4-200-2514> (Chapter 3)
- Lease of part: office (complies with Lease Code 2020) (Appendix 4)
- Diagrams on procurement <http://uk.practicallaw.thomsonreuters.com/0-367-5966> and linked documents (Chapter 10)

The current team of authors would like to acknowledge the valuable contributions made by Paul Butt, Flora Curtis, Neil Duckworth, John Grimbley, Susannah Herbert, Sue Highmore, Leona Mason, Lucy Morton, Vanessa Ralph, Michael Rhimes, Fiona Sawyer, Hayley Tam, Robert Tam, Julie Vaughan, Helen Watson and Matthew White to earlier editions of this book. The current team of authors bears responsibility for any failings in this edition.

The law is as stated as at 1 September 2024.

Anne Rodell
The University of Law
Moorgate

About the Contributors

Stephen Allinson is a solicitor and Licensed Insolvency Practitioner and a Visiting Lecturer at the University of Law in business and commercial law. He is Chairman of The Joint Insolvency Examination Board and also the former Chairman of the Board of The Insolvency Service and currently Head of Legal at Apex Litigation Finance.

Simon Barnett is a Senior Lecturer at the University of Hertfordshire and has served as Programme and Deputy Programme Leader of the Legal Practice Course. He qualified as a barrister in 1991 and was a Senior Lecturer at the Royal Agricultural College, Cirencester. He has also worked as an in-house legal adviser to several registered charities and as a sole practitioner. He has advised on legal matters in Nigeria, Kenya, Estonia, Lithuania, Malta, the United States and France. He has authored a book on Equity and Trusts and also teaches Wills and Administration, Property Law and Practice and the Private Client elective on the Legal Practice Course.

Michael Feeney is a barrister at Francis Taylor Building specialising in planning, public and environmental law. Michael has acted for and advised a wide range of clients, including developers, residents' groups and public authorities. Michael is also currently seconded part-time to Westminster City Council and the Royal Borough of Kensington and Chelsea, where he advises on a broad range of planning issues.

Simon Halliwell is a leading non-contentious construction law specialist who has worked on some of the largest construction projects both in the UK and internationally, acting for major developers, investment banks, blue-chip commercial organisations and governmental institutions. He founded *www.constructionlawexpert.com* as a niche construction law practice in November 2012 after over a decade of working at major global law firms in the City of London. After graduating with a law degree from Trinity Hall, Cambridge University, he joined 'magic circle' law firm, Linklaters LLP, and qualified into the non-contentious construction law department in 2003. Following moves to leading US law firm King & Spalding International LLP and Herbert Smith Freehills LLP, Simon set up *www.constructionlawexpert.com* in 2012 and later established Simon B Halliwell Solicitors in 2024.

Clare Harris is a Senior Lecturer at the University of Law. She qualified as a solicitor in 1994, working as a commercial property lawyer for Edge Ellison (now Squire Patton Boggs) and NatWest Bank. In 2001 she moved to the University of Law where she currently teaches property law and advanced property law. Clare is co-author of *Property Law and Practice*.

Stephanie McGuiness was a Senior Lecturer at the University of Law from 2006, having trained and practised at Herbert Smith. At the University, she has taught on both the LPC (Property Law and Practice) and GDL (Contract) programmes and now teaches, as a visiting lecturer, on the Professional Skills courses and Professional Development courses.

Mark O'Brien O'Reilly is a barrister at Francis Taylor Building specialising in planning, public and environmental law. He is a First Class Honours graduate of University College Dublin (BCL Law with History) and the University of Cambridge (LLM). He was awarded the Baroness Hale of Richmond BPTC Scholarship, and the Reid Senior Scholarship for Pupillage, by Gray's Inn and was elected by the Governing Body of Queens' College, Cambridge to a Foundation Scholarship. He has acted for, and advised, developers as well as local planning authorities and local residents. He has appeared before several planning inquiries as well as in the High Court. He is a member of the Attorney General's 'Junior' Junior Scheme and is regularly instructed to advise several government departments.

Gareth Richards trained and qualified as a solicitor at Linklaters in the City of London, specialising on qualification in commercial property and planning and environmental law. In 1997 he joined the then College (now University) of Law. At the University he has designed and taught real estate modules on the Legal Practice Course and taught real estate on the SQE, land and EU law on the GDL and environment law on the LLM. He is a Senior Lecturer and now heads up the Real Estate Professional Development team at the University, designing and delivering course to trainees and qualified solicitors.

Anne Rodell is an Associate Professor at the University of Law. She qualified as a solicitor in 1989 and was an assistant solicitor in the Real Estate Department of Linklaters LLP until 1998. At the University, she is a tutor for Professional Development Courses in Real Estate and is co-author of *Property Law and Practice*. She is also a Consultant Editor to The Law Society's *Conveyancing Handbook*.

Contents

PREFACE	v
ABOUT THE CONTRIBUTORS	vii
TABLE OF CASES	xv
TABLE OF STATUTES	xxiii
TABLE OF SECONDARY LEGISLATION	xxix
LIST OF ABBREVIATIONS	xxxiii

Part I   SITE ACQUISITIONS — 1

Chapter 1   THE COMMERCIAL CONTEXT   *Anne Rodell* — 3
1.1 What is commercial property? — 3
1.2 Who buys commercial property? — 4
1.3 Buying commercial property jointly — 6
1.4 Methods of structuring a property joint venture — 6
Review activity — 9

Chapter 2   OBTAINING PROPERTY FINANCE   *Anne Rodell* — 11
2.1 Methods of finance — 11
2.2 Debt finance — 12
Review activity — 17

Chapter 3   MATTERS OF CONTRACT   *Anne Rodell* — 19
3.1 The contract of sale — 19
3.2 Different types of contract — 20
3.3 Overage — 25
3.4 Future developments — 27
Review activity — 28

Chapter 4   PLANNING CONTROL   *Mark O'Brien O'Reilly* — 29
4.1 The planning system — 29
4.2 When is planning permission needed? — 35
4.3 Planning permission — 46
4.4 Application to the local planning authority — 53
4.5 Appeals against adverse planning determinations — 59
Review activity — 63

Chapter 5   PLANNING OBLIGATIONS AND COMMUNITY INFRASTRUCTURE LEVY   *Michael Feeney* — 65
5.1 Introduction — 65
5.2 Planning obligations — 66
5.3 Government policy — 68
5.4 Unilateral undertakings — 68
5.5 Modification and discharge of planning obligations — 69
5.6 Community Infrastructure Levy — 69
5.7 Community Infrastructure Levy and planning obligations — 76
5.8 Practical points — 77
Review activity — 79

Chapter 6   ENFORCEMENT OF PLANNING CONTROL   *Mark O'Brien O'Reilly* — 81
6.1 Introduction — 81
6.2 Definitions and time limits — 81
6.3 Certificates of lawful use or development (ss 191–192) — 82

	6.4	Right of entry for enforcement purposes (ss 196A–196C)	84
	6.5	Planning contravention notice (ss 171C–171D)	85
	6.6	Breach of condition notice (s 187A)	86
	6.7	Enforcement notice (ss 172–182)	87
	6.8	Stop notice and temporary stop notice (ss 183–187 and ss 171E–171G)	91
	6.9	Injunctions (s 187B)	93
	6.10	Appeals against enforcement notices (ss 174–177)	94
		Review activity	96
Chapter 7		COMPULSORY PURCHASE AND COMPENSATION *Simon Barnett*	97
	7.1	Introduction	97
	7.2	Inverse compulsory purchase	98
	7.3	Compulsory purchase procedure – the stages of compulsory purchase	101
	7.4	Compulsory purchase compensation	104
	7.5	Injurious affection	108
	7.6	Disturbance compensation and additional payments	110
		Review activity	112
Chapter 8		ENVIRONMENTAL ISSUES *Gareth Richards*	115
	8.1	Introduction to environmental law	115
	8.2	Environmental risk management	118
	8.3	Contaminated land	120
	8.4	Nuisance	130
	8.5	Environmental permitting and regulation	133
	8.6	Climate change law and energy performance	136
	8.7	Asbestos	141
	8.8	Japanese knotweed	143
	8.9	Flood risks	143
		Review activity	144
Chapter 9		SEARCHES AND ENQUIRIES *Anne Rodell*	145
	9.1	Local search and enquiries	145
	9.2	Planning matters	145
	9.3	Drainage	146
	9.4	Highways	146
	9.5	Railways	146
	9.6	Utilities	146
	9.7	Contaminated land	147
	9.8	Commons registration	147
	9.9	Rights of way and access land	147
	9.10	Enquiries of the seller	147
	9.11	Flood searches	147
	9.12	Survey and inspection	148
	9.13	Investigation of title	148
		Review activity	149
Chapter 10		CONSTRUCTION PROJECTS *Simon Halliwell*	151
	10.1	Introduction	151
	10.2	Who will be involved? The design and construction team	151
	10.3	Different forms of procurement	154
	10.4	Duties owed to third parties	162
	10.5	Protecting third parties	165
	10.6	Dispute resolution	169
		Review activity	170
Chapter 11		AN OUTLINE OF TAXATION OF COMMERCIAL PROPERTIES *Anne Rodell*	173
	11.1	Value added tax	173
	11.2	Stamp duty land tax on leases	179
		Review activity	179

Part II	**COMMERCIAL LEASES**	**181**
Chapter 12	LANDLORD AND TENANT LAW *Stephanie McGuiness*	183
	12.1 Introduction	183
	12.2 Lease/licence distinction	183
	12.3 Security of tenure	184
	12.4 Liability of the parties on the covenants in the lease	184
	Review activity	185
Chapter 13	AGREEMENTS FOR LEASE *Stephanie McGuiness*	187
	13.1 Introduction	187
	13.2 A typical agreement	188
	Review activity	192
Chapter 14	LEASE CONTENTS *Stephanie McGuiness*	193
	14.1 Introduction	193
	14.2 The 2020 Code for Leasing Business Premises in England and Wales	193
	14.3 Model Commercial Lease	195
	14.4 Drafting leases	196
	14.5 Prescribed clauses leases	197
	14.6 The structure of the lease	197
	Review activity	202
Chapter 15	THE PARTIES TO THE LEASE AND THEIR LIABILITIES *Clare Harris*	203
	15.1 Introduction	203
	15.2 The landlord	203
	15.3 The tenant	205
	15.4 The guarantor	209
	Review activity	213
Chapter 16	THE PARCELS CLAUSE *Anne Rodell*	215
	16.1 Purpose	215
	16.2 Airspace and underground	215
	16.3 Fixtures	215
	16.4 Rights to be granted and reserved	217
	Review activity	217
Chapter 17	TERM *Anne Rodell*	219
	17.1 Introduction	219
	17.2 Break clauses	220
	17.3 Options to renew	222
	17.4 Impact of SDLT	222
	Review activity	222
Chapter 18	RENT *Anne Rodell*	223
	18.1 Introduction	223
	18.2 Amount	224
	18.3 Time for payment	224
	18.4 Other payments reserved as rent	224
	18.5 Suspension of rent	224
	18.6 Interest	224
	18.7 VAT	225
	Review activity	225
Chapter 19	THE RENT REVIEW CLAUSE *Clare Harris*	227
	19.1 The need for review	227
	19.2 Types of rent review clause	227
	19.3 The dates for review	230
	19.4 Working out the open market rent	230
	19.5 The assumptions	231

	19.6	The disregards	238
	19.7	The mechanism for determining the rent	239
	19.8	The late review	241
	19.9	Recording the review	241
		Review activity	241

Chapter 20 REPAIR Stephanie McGuiness 243

20.1	Introduction	243
20.2	Tenant's covenant to repair	244
20.3	Definition of the subject matter of the covenant	244
20.4	Extent of liability	245
20.5	Tenant's concerns and amendments	248
20.6	Enforcement of covenant by landlord	250
20.7	Covenant to yield up in repair	250
20.8	Decorating	250
20.9	Landlord's covenant to repair	251
	Review activity	251

Chapter 21 ALIENATION Clare Harris 253

21.1	Dealings with the premises	253
21.2	Restrictions on alienation	255
21.3	The 2020 Code for Leasing Business Premises	259
21.4	Seeking consent from the landlord	260
21.5	Notice of assignment or sub-letting	263
21.6	Virtual assignments	264
	Review activity	264

Chapter 22 USER Clare Harris 265

22.1	The need for a user covenant	265
22.2	The permitted use	267
22.3	The extent of the landlord's control	268
22.4	Ancillary clauses	269
22.5	Impact of competition legislation on user covenants	270
	Review activity	272

Chapter 23 ALTERATIONS Stephanie McGuiness 273

23.1	Introduction	273
23.2	Lease controls	274
23.3	Restrictions outside the lease	277
23.4	Compensation for improvements	278
23.5	The 2020 Code for Leasing Business Premises	278
23.6	The Alterations Protocol	279
	Review activity	279

Chapter 24 THE LANDLORD'S COVENANT FOR QUIET ENJOYMENT Anne Rodell 281

24.1	Nature of the covenant	281
24.2	Negotiating the covenant	281
24.3	Acts constituting a breach	282
	Review activity	283

Chapter 25 INSURANCE Clare Harris 285

25.1	Introduction	285
25.2	The obligation to insure	286
25.3	The obligation to pay for the insurance	288
25.4	Compliance with the terms of the insurance	289
25.5	The obligation to reinstate	289
25.6	Rent suspension	291
25.7	Termination	292
25.8	Damage by uninsured risks	293

	25.9	Additional provisions	294
	25.10	Insurance by the tenant	294
		Review activity	294

Chapter 26 — FORFEITURE *Stephanie McGuiness* 295

	26.1	Introduction	295
	26.2	Express reservation of the right	295
	26.3	Waiver of the right to forfeit	296
	26.4	Strict procedural rules and relief against forfeiture	296
	26.5	Additional rules in special cases	300
	26.6	Position of sub-tenants and mortgagees on forfeiture	302
	26.7	The 2020 Code for Leasing Business Premises	302
	26.8	Reform	302
		Review activity	302

Chapter 27 — LEASE OF PART *Clare Harris* 305

	27.1	Introduction	305
	27.2	Defining the demised premises	305
	27.3	Rights granted and reserved	306
	27.4	Repairs	306
	27.5	Service charges	307
	27.6	Sinking and reserve funds	312
	27.7	Insurance	312
	27.8	RICS Professional Statement: Service Charges	312
		Review activity	313

Chapter 28 — SELLING THE LEASE *Clare Harris* 315

	28.1	Applications for consent to assign	315
	28.2	The landlord's licence	317
	28.3	Authorised guarantee agreements	318
		Review activity	319

Chapter 29 — SUB-LEASES *Clare Harris* 321

	29.1	The nature of a sub-lease	321
	29.2	Reasons for sub-letting	321
	29.3	Consent to the sub-letting	322
	29.4	Liability to the head-landlord	323
	29.5	Drafting the sub-lease	323
		Review activity	326

Chapter 30 — REMEDIES FOR BREACH OF COVENANT *Anne Rodell* 327

	30.1	Landlord's remedies	327
	30.2	Tenant's remedies	333

Chapter 31 — METHODS OF TERMINATION *Stephanie McGuiness* 337

	31.1	Introduction	337
	31.2	Expiry	337
	31.3	Notice to quit	337
	31.4	Operation of break clause	338
	31.5	Surrender	338
	31.6	Merger	339
		Review activity	339

Chapter 32 — THE LANDLORD AND TENANT ACT 1954, PART II *Anne Rodell* 341

	32.1	Introductory matters	341
	32.2	Termination under the Act	347
	32.3	The application to court	351
	32.4	Interim rents	352
	32.5	Grounds of opposition	353

	32.6	Compensation for failure to obtain a new tenancy	358
	32.7	The renewal lease	359
	32.8	The order for the new lease	361
	32.9	Procedural flowchart – s 25 notice	362
	32.10	Future developments	362
		Review activity	363

Part III PROPERTY AND INSOLVENCY 365

Chapter 33 INSOLVENCY AND ITS EFFECT ON COMMERCIAL PROPERTY *Stephen Allinson* 367

33.1	Why insolvency matters	367
33.2	Measures to reduce the perceived risk of insolvency	370
33.3	Always establish the type of insolvency regime	370
33.4	Identify the type of contract	372
33.5	The different types of insolvency regime	373
33.6	Setting aside transactions which have already been completed	380
33.7	The effect of a tenant becoming insolvent	382
33.8	Requiring the insolvency official to pay rent	389
33.9	Requiring the insolvency official to observe the lease covenants	390
33.10	Disclaimer and its effects	391

Appendix 1	Review Activity Answers	395
Appendix 2	Prescribed forms of notice under the Landlord and Tenant Act 1954	415
Appendix 3	Code for Leasing Business Premises, England and Wales 2020	427
Appendix 4	Lease of part: office (complies with Lease Code 2020)	439
Appendix 5	Specimen Authorised Guarantee Agreement	489
Appendix 6	Extracts from the Landlord and Tenant Act 1954, Part II	493
Appendix 7	Use classes prior to 1 September 2020	507
Appendix 8	Use classes from 1 September 2020	509

INDEX 511

Table of Cases

A

ABC Coupler and Engineering Co Ltd (No 3) [1970] 1 All ER 650	393
Aberdeen CC v Sim [1982] 2 EGLR 22	110
Aberdeen City and Shire Strategic Development Planning Authority v Elsick Development Co Ltd [2017] PTSR 1413	49
Actionstrength Ltd v International Glass Engineering [2003] 2 AC 541	212
Active Estates Ltd v Parness [2002] EWHC 893	393
Addiscombe Garden Estates v Crabbe [1958] 1 QB 513	342
Akasuc Enterprise Ltd v Farmar & Shirreff [2003] EWHC 1275 (Ch)	27
Akici v LR Butlin Ltd [2006] 1 WLR 201	298
Albany Holdings Ltd v Crown Estate Commissioners [2003] EWHC 1480	299
Allen v Corporation of the City of London [1981] JPL 685	48
Allied Dunbar Assurance plc v Homebase Ltd [2002] EWCA Civ 666, [2002] 27 EG 144, [2002] 2 EGLR 23	262, 324
Allied Dunbar Pension Services Ltd v Baker [2001] All ER (D) 46	323
Allnatt London Properties Ltd v Newton [1984] 1 All ER 423	339
American Cyanamid v Ethicon Ltd [1975] AC 396	93
Anglia Building Society v Secretary of State for the Environment and Another [1984] JPL 175	48
Anixter Ltd v Secretary of State for Transport [2020] EWCA Civ 43	103
Anstruther-Gough-Calthorpe v McOscar and Another [1924] 1 KB 716	247, 248
Arnold v Britton and Others [2015] UKSC 36	196
Artworld Financial Corporation v Safaryan [2009] 23 EG 94	339
Arundel Corporation v The Financial Training Co Ltd [2000] 3 All ER 456	338, 347
Ashburn Anstalt v Arnold [1989] Ch 1	183
Ashworth Frazer Ltd v Gloucester City Council [2002] 05 EG 133	262
Associated Picture Houses v Wednesbury Corporation [1947] 1 All ER 680	102
Atlantic Computer Systems plc, Re [1990] EWCA Civ 20	389
Attorney General of Belize and others v Belize Telecom Ltd [2009] UKPC 10	196
Attorney-General v PYA Quarries Ltd [1957] 2 QB 169	131
Aubergine Enterprises Ltd v Lakewood International Ltd [2002] EWCA Civ 177	317
Avocet Industrial Estates LLP v Merol and Another [2011] EWHC 3422 (Ch)	221
Avonridge Property Co Ltd v Mashru [2005] UKHL 70	204

B

B&Q plc v Liverpool and Lancashire Properties Ltd [2000] EGCS 101	306
Bacchiocci v Academic Agency Ltd [1998] 1 WLR 1313	347
Bairstow Eves (Securities) Ltd v Ripley [1992] 2 EGLR 47	221, 406
Barclays Bank plc v Daejan Investments (Grove Hall) Ltd [1995] 18 EG 117	269
Barclays Wealth Trustees (Jersey) Ltd v Erimus Housing Ltd [2014] EWCA Civ 303	343
Barnes v City of London Real Property Co [1918] 2 Ch 18	309
Barr and Others v Biffa Waste Services Ltd [2012] EWCA Civ 312	131
Barrett v Morgan [2000] 2 AC 264	338
Barth v Pritchard [1990] 1 EGLR 109	356
Barton Park Estates v SHCLG [2022] EWCA Civ 833	84
Basildon BC v Anderson [2020] EWHC 3382 (QB)	93
Bates v Donaldson [1896] 2 QB 241	262
Bayliss v Secretary of State for Communities and Local Government 2013] EWHC 1612 (Admin)	34
Bede Distributors v Newcastle Corporation (1973) 26 P & CR 298	110
Belcourt Estates Ltd v Adesina [2005] EWCA Civ 208	338
Berkley v Poulett (1976) 242 EG 39	216
Bernstein v Skyviews & General Ltd [1978] QB 479	215
Betty's Cafes Ltd v Phillips Furnishing Stores Ltd [1959] AC 20	355
BHP Great Britain Petroleum Ltd v Chesterfield Properties Ltd [2001] EWCA Civ 1797, [2002] 2 WLR 672	204
Bibby v Merseyside CC (1980) 251 EG 757	111
Bickerton's Aerodromes v Young (1958) 108 LJ 217	299
Billson v Residential Apartments Ltd [1992] 1 AC 494	299
Blockbuster Entertainment Ltd v Barnsdale Properties Ltd [2003] EWHC 2912	316
Blue Manchester Ltd v North West Ground Rents Ltd [2019] EWHC 142 (TCC)	333

Case	Page
Boland v Bridgend CBC [2017] EWCA Civ 1004	107
Bolton (HL) Engineering Co Ltd v Graham & Sons Ltd [1957] 1 QB 159	357
Booth v Thomas [1926] Ch 397	282
Bourne Leisure (Hopton) Ltd v Great Yarmouth Port Authority [2016] UKUT 44 (LC)	109
Broadgate Square plc v Lehman Brothers Ltd [1995] 1 EGLR 97, [1995] 01 EG 111	235
Bromilow v Greater Manchester Council (1975) 29 P & CR 517	107
Brown & Root Technology v Sun Alliance [1997] 18 EG 123	220
Burdle and Another v Secretary of State for the Environment and Another [1972] 3 All ER 240	37
Burn v North Yorkshire County Council [1992] EGCS 91	99
Burt v British Transport Commission (1955) 166 EG 4	331

C

Case	Page
C&A Pension Trustees Ltd v British Vita Investments Ltd [1984] 2 EGLR 75, (1984) 272 EG 63	266
Cambridge Water Company v Eastern Counties Leather plc [1994] 1 All ER 53	130, 132
Campbell v Daejan Properties Ltd [2012] EWCA Civ 1503	307
Canary Wharf (BP4) T1 Ltd v European Medicines Agency [2019] EWHC 335 (Ch)	224, 292
Caparo Industries plc v Dickman [1990] 2 AC 605	165
Capitol Park Leeds plc v Global Radio Services Ltd [2021] EWCA Civ 995	220
Cavendish Square Holding BV v Talal El Makdessi [2015] UKSC 767	196
Central Estates (Belgravia) Ltd v Woolgar (No 2) [1972] 1 WLR 1048	296
Central Estates Ltd v Secretary of State for the Environment [1997] 1 EGLR 239	240
Chartbrook Ltd v Persimmon Homes [2009] UKHL 38	196
Chartered Trust plc v Davies [1997] 49 EG 135	335
Cheryl Investments Ltd v Saldhana [1978] 1 WLR 1329	342
Cheverell Estates Ltd v Harris [1998] 02 EG 127	327
Church Commissioners for England v Secretary of State for the Environment (1996) 7 P & CR 73	37
Circular Facilities (London) Ltd v Sevenoaks District Council [2005] EWHC 865 (Admin)	120, 126
City of London Corporation v Fell [1993] 49 EG 113	206
Civil Service Co-operative Society v McGrigor's Trustee [1923] 2 Ch 347	299
Claire's Accessories v Kensington High Street [2001] PLSCS 112	221
Clarence House Ltd v National Westminster Bank plc [2009] EWHC 77 (Ch); [2009] EWCA Civ 1311	264
Claridge [2011] EWHC 2047 (Ch)	382
Clear Channel UK Ltd v Manchester City Council [2005] EWCA Civ 1304	184
Clowes v Staffordshire Potteries Waterworks (1872) LR 8 Ch 125	108
Colman v Secretary of State for Communities and Local Government and RWE Npower [2013] EWHC 1138 (Admin)	34
Commercial Union Life Assurance Co v Label Ink Ltd [2001] L & TR 29	247
Cook v Shoesmith [1951] 1 KB 752	256
Cooper's Lease, Re (1968) 19 P & CR 541	262
Cooperative Bank PLC v Hayes Freehold Limited (In Liquidation) [2017] EWHC 1820 (Ch)	339
Co-operative Insurance Society Ltd v Argyll Stores (Holdings) Ltd [1997] 23 EG 137	332
Coppin v Bruce-Smith [1998] EGCS 45	355
Corby Group Litigation v Corby District Council [2009] EWHC 1944	131
Coventry v Lawrence [2014] All ER (D) 245 (Feb)	131
Crane v Secretary of State for Communities and Local Government [2015] EWHC 425 (Admin)	34
Credit Suisse v Beegas Nominees Ltd [1994] 11 EG 151	248
Creska Ltd v Hammersmith and Fulham London Borough Council (No 2) (1999) 78 P & CR D46	331
Cricket Ltd v Shaftesbury plc [1999] 3 All ER 283	343
Crown Estate Commissioners v Town Investments Ltd [1992] 08 EG 111	361
Cunliffe v Goodman [1950] 2 KB 237	355

D

Case	Page
D&F Estates Ltd v Church Commissioners for England [1989] AC 177	164
Daiches v Bluelake Investments Ltd [1985] 2 EGLR 67	334
Davies v Bridgend County Borough Council [2023] EWCA Civ 80	143
Davies v Yadegar [1990] 1 EGLR 71	406
DB Symmetry Ltd v Swindon BC [2020] EWCA Civ 1331	67
DB Symmetry Ltd v Swindon BC [2022] UKSC 33	67
Dennis v Ministry of Defence [2003] EWHC 793 (QB)	130
Department of the Environment v Allied Freehold Property Trust Ltd [1992] 45 EG 156	353
Discovery (Northampton) Ltd and others v Debenhams Retail Ltd and others [2019] EWHC 2441 (Ch)	373
Doleman v Shaw [2009] EWCA Civ 283	393
Dolgellau Golf Club v Hett [1998] 2 EGLR 75, CA	357
Dong Bang Minerva (UK) Ltd v Davina Ltd [1996] 31 EG 87	317

Case	Page
Donoghue v Stevenson [1932] AC 562	164
Duke of Buccleuch v Metropolitan Board of Works (1872) LR 5 HL 418	108
Duval v 11-13 Randolph Crescent Ltd [2020] UKSC 18	274

E

Case	Page
Earl of Camrose v Basingstoke Corporation (1966) 64 LGR 337, CA	105
East Staffordshire Borough Council v Secretary of State for Communities and Local Government [2017] EWCA Civ 893	34
Elliott-Smith v Secretary of State for Business, Energy and Industrial Strategy [2021] EWHC 1633 (Admin)	137
English Exporters (London) Ltd v Eldonwall Ltd [1973] Ch 415	353
Envirocor Waste Holdings v Secretary of State for the Environment [1995] EG 60 CS, QB	48
Esselte AB v Pearl Assurance plc [1997] 1 WLR 891	347
Essexcrest Ltd v Evenlex Ltd [1988] 1 EGLR 69	344
Esso Petroleum Co Ltd v Fumegrange Ltd [1994] 46 EG 199	183
Esso Petroleum v Southport Corporation [1956] AC 218	133
Expert Clothing Service & Sales Ltd v Hillgate House Ltd [1986] Ch 340	298

F

Case	Page
Faiz v Burnley Borough Council [2021] EWCA Civ 55	296
Family Management v Grey (1979) 253 EG 369	236
Farr v Ginnings (1928) 44 TLR 249	262
Fawke v Viscount Chelsea [1980] QB 441	361
First Property Growth Partnership v Royal & Sun Alliance Services Ltd [2002] EWHC 305 (Ch), [2002] 22 EG 140	240
Fitzroy House Epworth Street (No 1) v The Financial Times Ltd [2006] EWCA Civ 329	221
Fivaz v Marlborough Knightsbridge Management Ltd [2020] UKUT 138 (LC)	216
Flairline Properties Ltd v Hassan [1997] 1 EGLR 138	342
Footwear Corporation Ltd v Amplight Properties Ltd [1999] 1 WLR 551	262, 263
Forbuoys plc v Newport Borough Council [1994] 24 EG 156	361
Fouladi v Darout Ltd and others [2018] EWHC 3501 (Ch)	282
Fowles v Heathrow Airport Ltd [2008] EWCA Civ 1270	354
Freifield v West Kensington Court Limited [2015] EWCA Civ 806	300
Friends Life Ltd v Siemens Hearing Instruments Ltd [2014] EWCA Civ 382	221
Friends Provident Life Office v British Railways Board [1995] 1 All ER 336	205, 208, 209, 211
FW Woolworth v Charlwood Alliance Properties [1987] 1 EGLR 53	262

G

Case	Page
G & K Ladenbau (UK) Ltd v Crawley and de Reya [1978] 1 All ER 682	147
Gardiner v Hertsmere BC [2022] EWCA Civ 1162	70
Gateshead Metropolitan Borough Council v Secretary of State for the Environment [1995] JPL 432, CA	48
Gemini Press Ltd v Cheryl Lindsay Parsons [2012] EWHC 1608 (QB)	220
General Estates v Minister for Housing and Local Government (1965) 194 Estates Gazette 201	100
Gibson v Lakeside Developments Ltd [2018] EWCA Civ 2874	298
Glass v Kencakes Ltd [1966] 1 QB 611	299, 410
Globe Motors Inc and others v TRW Lucas Varity Electric Steering Ltd Globe Motors, Inc and another [2016] EWCA Civ 396	196
Go West Ltd v Spigarolo [2003] EWCA Civ 17, [2003] 07 EG 136	316
Goldacre (Offices) Ltd v Nortel Networks (UK) Ltd (in administration) [2009] EWHC 3389 (Ch)	390
Goldmile Properties Ltd v Lechouritis [2003] EWCA Civ 49, [2003] 15 EG 143	282
Good Harvest LLP v Centaur Services Limited [2010] EWHC 330 (Ch)	210, 212, 213, 259
Graysim Holdings Ltd v P&O Property Holdings Ltd [1995] 3 WLR 854	342
Great Portland Estates plc v Westminster City Council [1985] AC 661, HL	48
Gurton v Parrot [1991] 1 EGLR 98	343

H

Case	Page
Hadley v Baxendale (1854) 9 Exch 341	163, 331
Hancock & Willis v GMS Syndicate Ltd (1982) 265 EG 473	342
Harmer v Jumbil (Nigeria) Tin Areas Ltd [1921] 1 Ch 200	334
Harvey v Crawley Development Corporation [1957] 1 All ER 504, CA	110
Havant International Holdings Ltd v Lionsgate (H) Investments Ltd [1999] EGCS 144	221
Havenridge Ltd v Boston Dyers Ltd [1994] 49 EG 111	289
Hazel v Akhtar [2002] EWCA Civ 1883, [2002] 07 EG 124	354
Hedley Byrne & Co Ltd v Heller & Partners Ltd [1964] AC 465	164
Henderson & Jones Ltd v Ross and others [2023] EWHC 1276 (Ch)	382

Herbert Duncan Ltd v Cluttons [1992] 1 EGLR 101	206, 223
Heronslea (Mill Hill) Ltd v Kwik-Fit Properties Ltd [2009] EWHC 295	409
Herts County Council v Ozanne [1991] 1 WLR 105, HL	105
Hills (Patents) Ltd v University College Hospital Board of Governors [1956] 1 QB 90	342
Hindcastle v Barbara Attenborough Associates [1997] AC 70	393
Historic Hotels Ltd v Cadogan Estates [1995] 1 EGLR 117	239
Hockley Engineering Ltd v V & P Midlands Ltd [1993] 1 EGLR 76	301
Holme v Brunskill (1877) 3 QBD 495	211
Homes and Communities Agency v JS Bloor (Wilmslow) Ltd [2017] UKSC 12	105
Hopkins Homes Ltd v Secretary of State for Communities and Local Government [2017] UKSC 37	34
Hopley v Tarvin Parish Council (1910) 54 JP 209	299
Horn v Sunderland Corporation [1941] 2 KB 26	104, 110, 400
Horne & Meredith Properties v Cox, Billingsley [2014] EWCA Civ 423	354
Horsey Estate Limited v Steiger [1899] 2 QB 79	254
Hotgroup plc v Royal Bank of Scotland plc [2010] EWHC 1193	221
Hughes v Doncaster Corporation [1990] 2 WLR 16	105
Hunt & Others v Optima (Cambridge) Ltd & Others [2014] EWCA Civ 714	165
Hunter v Canary Wharf Ltd [1997] 2 WLR 684	130
Hyman v Rose [1912] AC 623	300

I

International Drilling Fluids Ltd v Louisville Investments (Uxbridge) Ltd [1986] Ch 513, [1986] 1 All ER 321	261, 275
Investment Bank PSC v El-Husseini and others [2023] EWCA Civ 555	382
Ipswich v Borough Council v Fairview Hotels [2022] EWHC 2868 (KB)	93
Iqbal v Thakrar [2004] All ER (D) 304	275

J

Janmohamed v Hassam (1976) 241 EG 609	21
Javad v Aqil [1991] 1 WLR 1007	343
Jelson v Blaby District Council (1977) 34 P & CR 77	101
Jolley v Carmel [2000] 43 EG 185	22
Jon Harding and Sarah Clements v Secretary of State for Transport (2017) BNO/37/2016	99
Junction Estates Ltd v Cope (1974) 27 P & CR 482	210
Junior Books v Veitchi [1983] 1 AC 520	164

K

K/S Victoria Street v House of Fraser (Stores Management) Limited [2011] EWCA Civ 904	210, 213
Kalford Ltd v Peterborough City Council [2001] EGCS 42	275
Kent CC v Brockman [1996] 1 PLR 1, [1994] Crim LR 296	91
Keshwala and another v Bhalsod [2021] EWCA Civ 492	297
Khatun v United Kingdom, European Commission of Human Rights, 1 July 1998	130
Kissel v Secretary of State for the Environment and Another [1994] JPL 819	48

L

Lambert v FW Woolworth & Co Ltd (No 2) [1938] 2 All ER 664	275
Lambert v Keymood Ltd [1997] 43 EG 131	287
Landmaster Properties Ltd v Thackeray Property Services [2003] 35 EG 83	330
Law Land Co Ltd v Consumers Association Ltd (1980) 255 EG 617	267
Lazari GP Ltd v Jervis [2012] EWHC 1466	378
Lazari Properties 2 Ltd & Ors v New Look Retailers Ltd & Ors [2021] EWHC 1209 (Ch)	374
Leech Homes Ltd v Northumberland County Council [2021] EWCA Civ 198	107
Lee-Parker and Another v Izzet and Others (No 2) [1972] 2 All ER 800	21
Lee-Parker v Izzet [1971] 1 WLR 1688	333
Leeward Securties v Lilyheath (1983) 17 HLR 35	300
Leisure Norwich (II) Ltd v Luminar Lava Ignite Ltd & Others [2012] EWHC 951 (Ch)	390
Lemmerbell Ltd v Britannia LAS Direct Ltd [1998] 3 EGLR 67	221
Leschallas v Woolf [1908] 1 Ch 641	216
Linden Garden Trust Ltd v Lenesta Sludge Disposals Ltd; St Martins Property Corporation Ltd v Sir Robert McAlpine & Sons Ltd [1993] 3 WLR 408	167
Linden Print v West Midlands CC [1987] 2 EGLR 200	110
Lister v Lane & Nesham [1893] 2 QB 212	246
Lock v Pearce [1893] 2 Ch 271	299
London and Ilford Ltd v Sovereign Property Holdings Ltd [2018] EWCA Civ 1618	26

Case	Page
London Baggage Co (Charing Cross) Ltd v Railtrack plc [2000] EGCS 57	343
London Borough of Newham v Thomas-Van Staden [2008] EWCA Civ 1414	219
London College of Business Ltd v Tareem Ltd & Another [2018] EWHC 437 (Ch)	184
London Hilton Jewellers Ltd v Hilton International Hotels Ltd [1990] 1 EGLR 112	356
London Historic Parks and Gardens Trust v Minister of State for Housing [2022] EWHC 829 (Admin)	49
London Residuary Body v Lambeth Borough Council [1990] 2 All ER 309, HL	48
Lurcott v Wakeley & Wheeler [1911] 1 KB 905	246

M

Case	Page
M&P Enterprises (London) Ltd v Norfolk Square Hotels Ltd [1994] 1 EGLR 129	349
Magnic Ltd v Ul-Hassan & Another [2015] EWCA Civ 224	300
Maidstone BC v Beck and Others [2021] EWHC 509 (QB)	93
Malvern Hills DC v Secretary of State for the Environment [1982] JPL 439	53
Manchester City Council v Secretary of State for Housing, Communities and Local Government [2021] EWCA Civ 1920	36
Mannai Investment Co Ltd v Eagle Star Life Assurance Co Ltd [1997] AC 749	221, 406
Mark Rowlands Ltd v Berni Inns Ltd [1986] 1 QB 211	287
Marks and Spencer plc v BNP Paribas Securities Services Trust Company (Jersey) Ltd [2015] UKSC 72	196, 221
Martin Retail Group Ltd v Crawley Borough Council (CC (Central London), 24 December 2013)	271
McCaw v City of Westminster Magistrates' Court (D) and Middlesex SARL [2008] EWHC 1504	132
McDonald's Restaurants Ltd v Shirayama Shokusan Company Ltd [2024] EWHC 1133 (Ch)	356
McDougall v Easington DC (1989) 58 P & CR 201, CA	246
Meadfield Properties Ltd v Secretary of State for the Environment [1995] 03 EG 128	219, 406
Mears Ltd v Costplan Services (South East) Ltd & Others [2019] EWCA Civ 502	191
Mellor v Watkins (1874) LR 9 QBD 400	339
Metropolitan Board of Works v McCarthy (1874) LR 7 HL 243	108
Michael v Salford City Council [2016] UKUT 370 (LC)	108
Mintblue Properties Ltd, Re Car Park of Former E-Mag Factory [2016] UKUT 172 (LC)	107
Mira v Aylmer Square Investments Ltd [1990] 1 EGLR 45	282
Mizen Design/Build Ltd (in company voluntary arrangement), Re [2023] EWHC 127 (Ch)	373
Monsolar IQ Ltd v Woden Park Ltd [2021] EWCA Civ 961	196
Moore v Secretary of State for Communities and Local Government [2012] EWCA Civ 1202	36
Morcom v Campbell-Johnson [1955] 3 All ER 264	247
Morgan Sindall v Sawston Farms (Cambs) Ltd [1999] 1 EGLR 90	312
Moss Bros Group plc v CSC Properties Ltd [1999] EGCS 47	262
Moule v Garrett and Others (1872) LR 7 Exch 101	206
Mount Eden Land Ltd v Folia Ltd [2003] EWHC 1815	316
Mourant & Co Trustees Ltd v Sixty UK Ltd (in administration) [2010] EWHC 1890	373
Mullaney v Maybourne Grange (Croydon) Ltd [1986] 1 EGLR 70	309
Mumford Hotels Ltd v Wheler and Another [1964] Ch 117	290
Murphy v Brentwood District Council [1990] 2 All ER 908	164
Myers v Milton Keynes Development Corporation [1974] 1 WLR 696	106

N

Case	Page
National Car Parks Ltd v The Paternoster Consortium Ltd [1990] 15 EG 53	360
National Car Parks Ltd v Trinity Development Co (Banbury) Ltd [2001] EWCA Civ 1686, [2001] 28 EG 144	183
National Carriers Ltd v Panalpina (Northern) Ltd [1981] AC 675	224, 292
National Grid Co plc v M25 Group Ltd [1999] 08 EG 169	312
National Westminster Bank plc v Arthur Young McClelland Moores & Co [1985] 1 WLR 1123	234
Newbury District Council v Secretary of State for the Environment; Newbury District Council v International Synthetic Rubber Co [1981] AC 578	49
Next plc v National Farmers Union Mutual Insurance Co Ltd [1997] EGCS 181	317, 412
Northways Flats Management Co v Wimpey Pension Trustees [1992] 31 EG 65	308
Norwich Union Life Insurance Society v Low Profile Fashions Ltd (1992) 21 EG 104	316
Norwich Union Life Insurance Society v Shopmoor Ltd [1999] 1 WLR 531	262
Nynehead Developments Ltd v RH Fibreboard Containers Ltd and Others [1999] 9 EG 174	335

O

Case	Page
O'May v City of London Real Property Co Ltd [1983] AC 726	361
Oceanfill Ltd v Nuffield Health Wellbeing Ltd, Cannons Group Ltd [2022] EWHC 2178 (Ch). In	369
Oceanic Village Ltd v Shirayama Shokusan Co Ltd [2001] All ER (D) 62 (Feb)	335
Orlando Investments v Grosvenor Estate Belgravia [1989] 2 EGLR 74	261
Osibanjo v Seahive Investments Ltd [2008] EWCA Civ 1282	296

Owen v Gadd [1956] 2 QB 99 — 282

P

P&A Swift Investments v Combined English Stores Group plc [1983] 3 WLR 313 — 204
Padwick Properties Ltd v Punj Lloyd [2016] 502 (Ch) — 338
Palisade Investments Ltd v Secretary of State for the Environment [1995] 69 P & CR 638, CA — 39
Patel, Patel v K & J Restaurants Ltd, MP Catering Ltd [2010] ECWA Civ 1211 — 299, 410
Payne v Haine (1847) 153 ER 1304 — 245
Pearson v Alyo [1990] 1 EGLR 114 — 349
Peel Land & Property (Ports No 3) Ltd v TS Sheerness Steel Ltd [2013] EWHC 1658 (Ch); [2014] EWCA Civ 100 — 216
Peires v Bickerton's Aerodromes Ltd [2017] EWCA Civ 273 — 131
Penny and South Eastern Railway, Re (1851) 26 LJ QB 225 — 109
Pepper v City of Worcester (1971) Lands Tribunal — 105
Petra Investments Ltd v Jeffrey Rogers plc [2000] 3 EGLR 120 — 334
Pick v Chief Land Registrar [2011] EWHC 206 — 377
Pillar Denton Ltd and Others v Jervis and Others [2014] EWCA Civ 180 (24 February 2014) — 390
Pineport v Grangeglen [2016] EWHC 1318 (Ch); [2016] EWHC 2170 (Ch) — 298
Platt v London Underground [2001] 20 EG 227 — 334
Plinth Property Investments Ltd v Mott, Hay & Anderson [1979] 1 EGLR 17 — 266
Pointe Gourde v Sub-Intendent of Crown Lands [1947] AC 565 — 101, 105
Pointon York Group plc v Poulton [2006] EWCA Civ 1001 — 342
Ponderosa International Development v Pengap Securities [1986] 1 EGLR 66 — 262
Port v Griffith [1938] 1 All ER 295 — 335
Post Office Counters Ltd v Harlow District Council [1991] 2 EGLR 121 — 267
Post Office v Aquarius Properties Ltd [1987] 1 All ER 1055 — 245
Poundland Ltd v Toplain Ltd (unreported, 7 April 2021) — 361
Powys County Council v Price [2017] EWCA Civ 1133 — 127
Prasad v Wolverhampton BC [1983] Ch 333 — 110
Prezzo Investco Ltd, Re [2023] EWHC 1679 (Ch) — 369
Price v West London Investment Building Society [1964] 2 All ER 318 — 351
Proudfoot v Hart (1890) 25 QBD 42 — 245, 247
Prudential Assurance Co Ltd v Exel UK Ltd [2009] EWHC 1350 (Ch) — 406
Prudential Assurance Co Ltd v Grand Metropolitan Estate Ltd [1993] 32 EG 74 — 238
Prudential Assurance Co Ltd v London Residuary Body [1992] 2 AC 386 — 219
Prudential Assurance Company Ltd & Others v PRG Powerhouse Ltd & Others [2007] EWHC 1002 — 373
Pullman Foods Ltd v Welsh Ministers and another [2020] EWHC 2521 (TCC) — 248

Q

Qdime Ltd v various leaseholders at Bath Building (Swindon) [2014] UKUT 0261 (LC) — 288
QFS Scaffolding Limited v Sable and Another [2010] EWCA Civ 682 — 338
Quick v Taff-Ely Borough Council [1986] QB 809 — 245

R

R (Ardagh Glass Ltd) v Chester CC [2009] Env LR 34 — 87
R (Dawes) v Birmingham City Council [2021] EWHC 1676 (Admin) — 103
R (on the application of Crest Nicholson Residential Ltd) v SSEFRA & Others [2010] EWHC 561 (Admin) — 127
R (on the application of Fidler) v Secretary of State for Communities and Local Government [2011] EWCA Civ 1159 — 82
R (on the application of Hampton Bishop PC) v Herefordshire Council [2014] EWCA Civ 878 — 34
R (on the application of Harris) v Haringey LBC [2010] EWCA Civ 703 — 48
R (on the application of Mansfield DC) v SSHCLG [2018] EWHC 1794 (Admin) — 69
R (on the application of National Grid Gas plc) v Environment Agency [2007] UKHL 30 — 126
R (on the application of Redland Minerals Ltd) v SSEFRA & Others [2010] EWHC 913 (Admin) — 124, 127
R (on the application of Trent) v Hertsmere Borough Council [2021] EWHC 907 (Admin) — 72
R (on the application of Wright) v (1) Resilient Energy Severndale Ltd (2) Forest of Dean District Council [2019] UKSC 53 — 49
R (Rights: Community: Action) v Secretary of State for Housing, Communities and Local Government [2021] EWCA Civ 1954 — 39
R v Del Basso and Another [2010] EWCA Crim 1119 — 91
R v Greenwich London Borough Council, ex p Patel [1985] JPL 851, CA — 89
R v Hillingdon London Borough Council, ex p Royco Homes Ltd [1974] QB 720 — 50
R v Kuxhaus [1988] 2 WLR 1005, [1988] 2 All ER 705, CA — 95
R v Minister for Housing and Local Government ex parte Chichester RDC [1960] 1 WLR 587 — 100
R v Rochester upon Medway CC, ex p Hobday [1989] 2 PLR 28, (1989) 58 P&CR 424 — 87

Case	Page
R v Secretary of State for the Environment, ex p Collins [1989] EG 15 (CS)	37
R v West Oxfordshire District Council, ex p CH Pearce Homes [1986] JPL 523	57
Railtrack plc v Gojra [1998] 08 EG 158	351
Rainbow Estates Ltd v Tokenhold Ltd [1999] Ch 64	331
Ravenseft Properties Ltd v Davstone (Holdings) Ltd [1980] QB 12	245, 246
Ravensgate Estates Ltd v Horizon Housing Group Ltd [2007] All ER (D) 294	329
Receiver for Metropolitan Police District v Palacegate Properties Ltd [2001] 2 Ch 131	344
Rees v Windsor-Clive [2020] EWCA Civ 816	334
Riverside CREM 3 Ltd v Virgin Active Health Clubs Ltd [2021] EWHC 746 (Ch)	369
Riverside Park Ltd v NHS Property Services Ltd [2016] EWHC 1313 (Ch)	220
Roberts v Coventry Corporation [1947] 1 All ER 308	110
Romulus Trading Co Ltd v Comet Properties Ltd [1996] 2 EGLR 70	335
Romulus Trading Co Ltd v Henry Smith's Charity Trustees [1990] 2 EGLR 75	356
Royal Bank of Scotland plc v Jennings and Others [1997] 19 EG 152	196
Rugby Football Union v Secretary of State for Transport, Local Government and the Regions [2002] EWCA Civ 1169	39
Rugby School (Governors) v Tannahill [1935] 1 KB 87	298
Rushmer v Polsue and Alfieri Ltd [1906] 1 Ch 234	130
Rylands v Fletcher [1868] UKHL 1	132

S

Case	Page
S Frances Ltd v The Cavendish Hotel (London) Ltd [2018] UKSC 62	355
Sabella Ltd v Montgomery [1998] 09 EG 153	348
Sage v SSETR [2003] 1 WLR 983	82
Savva v Hussein (1997) 73 P & CR 150	298
Scala House & District Property Co Ltd v Forbes [1974] QB 575	298
Scholl Manufacturing Ltd v Clifton (Slim-Line) Ltd [1967] Ch 41	348
Scottish & Newcastle plc v Raguz [2007] EWCA Civ 150	327
Sea & Land Power & Energy v Secretary of State for Communities and Local Government [2012] EWHC 1419 (Admin)	34
Secretary of State for Transport v Curzon Park Ltd and others [2023] UKSC 30	107
Segal Securities Ltd v Thoseby [1963] 1 QB 887	296
Shanley v Ward (1913) 29 TLR 714	261
SHB Realisations Ltd v Cribbs Mall Nominee (1) Ltd [2019] 3 WLUK 588	332, 380, 389
Sight and Sound Education Ltd v Books etc Ltd [1999] 43 EG 61	347
Simpson v Stoke on Trent (1982) 44 P & CR 226	111
Skilleter v Charles [1992] 13 EG 113	308
Smiley v Townshend [1950] 2 KB 311	329
Smith v Draper [1990] 2 EGLR 69	348
Somerfield Stores Ltd v Spring (Sutton Coldfield) Ltd [2009] EWHC 2384	378
South Bucks DC v Porter [2003] 2 AC 558	93
South Northamptonshire Council & Ward v Secretary of State for Communities and Local Government [2013] EWHC 11 (Admin)	34
Southampton City Council v Hallyard Ltd [2009] 1 P&CR 5	67
Southport Old Links Ltd v Naylor [1985] 1 EGLR 66	349
Southwark London Borough Council v Mills and Others; Baxter v Camden London Borough Council [1999] 3 WLR 939	282
Sovmots v Secretary of State for the Environment; Brompton Securities Ltd v Secretary of State for the Environment [1977] 2 WLR 951	48
Sparks v Biden [2017] EWHC 1994 (Ch)	26
Spire Property Development LLP & Anor v Withers LLP [2021] EWHC 2400 (Comm)	147
St Helens Smelting Company v Tipping [1865] UKHL J81	109
St Mowden Developments v Secretary of State for Communities and Local Government [2017] EWCA Civ 1643	34
Starmark Enterprises Ltd v CPL Distribution Ltd [2001] 32 EG 89 (CS)	240
Sterling Land Office Developments Ltd v Lloyds Bank plc (1984) 271 EG 894	267
Stevens v Bromley London Borough Council [1972] 2 WLR 605, CA	89
Stile Hall Properties Ltd v Gooch [1979] 3 All ER 848	350
Stonecrest Marble Ltd v Shepherds Bush Housing Association Ltd [2021] EWHC 2621 (Ch)	282, 333
Straudley Investments Ltd v Barpress Ltd [1987] 1 EGLR 69	406
Street v Mountford [1985] AC 809, [1985] 2 All ER 289	183, 254
Stringer v Minister for Housing and Local Government [1971] 1 All ER 65	47
Sunberry Properties Limited v Innovate Logistics Ltd (in administration) [2008] EWCA Civ 1261	390
Surrey County Council v Single Horse Properties Ltd [2002] EWCA Civ 367, [2002] 1 WLR 2106	347
Swish Estates v Secretary of State for Communities and Local Government [2017] EWHC 3331 (Admin)	102

T

Tamplins Brewery v County Borough of Brighton (1970) 22 P & CR 746	111
Taylor and Taylor v Stockport Metropolitan Borough Council [2022] UKUT 00142 (LC)	106
Tesco Stores Limited v Dundee CC [2012] UKSC 13	47
Tesco Stores Ltd v Dundee City Council [2012] UKSC 13	34
Thames Heliport plc v Tower Hamlets LBC [1997] 2 PLR 72	37
Thirunavukkrasu v Brar [2018] EWHC 2461 (Ch)	329
Timothy Taylor Ltd v Mayfair House Corporation and another [2016] EWHC 1075 (Ch)	282
Tindall Cobham 1 Ltd & Others v Adda Hotels (an unlimited company) & Others [2014] EWCA Civ 1215	259
Toms v Ruberry [2017] EWHC 2970 (QB)	298
Topland Portfolio No 1 Ltd v Smiths New Trading Ltd [2014] EWCA Civ 18	211
Transco v Stockport MBC [2003] UKHL 61	132
Transport for London (London Underground Ltd) v Spirerose Ltd (in administration) [2009] UKHL 44	106, 108
Transworld Land Co Ltd v J Sainsbury plc [1990] 2 EGLR 255	332
Tyco Fire & Integrated Solutions (UK) Ltd v Rolls Royce Motor Cars Ltd [2008] EWCA Civ 286	287

U

Ultraworth Ltd v General Accident Fire and Life Assurance Corporation [2000] 2 EGLR 115	329
United Dominion Trust Ltd v Shellpoint Trustees [1993] EGCS 57	302
United Scientific Holdings v Burnley Borough Council [1978] AC 904, [1972] 2 All ER 62	221, 240
URT Group Ltd and Others v Dowers and Others [2018] EWHC 3195 (Ch)	216

V

Van Dal Footwear v Ryman Ltd [2009] EWCA Civ 1478	329
Virgin Active Holdings Ltd & Ors, Re [2021] EWHC 1246 (Ch)	369

W

Waistell v Network Rail Infrastructure Ltd; Williams v Network Rail Infrastructure Ltd [2018] EWCA Civ 1514	143
Wallington v Secretary of State for Wales [1991] JPL 942, CA	37
Wallis Fashion Group Ltd v General Accident Life Assurance Ltd [2000] EGCS 45	361
Ward Construction Medway v Barclays Bank (1994) 68 P&CR 391, CA	105
Waters v Welsh Development Agency [2004] UKHL 19	105
Watts v Stewart [2016] EWCA Civ 1247	183
Webber (CA) Transport Ltd v Railtrack plc [2004] 1 WLR 320	351
Welsh v Greenwich London Borough Council [2000] PLSCS 149	248
Welwyn Hatfield Council v Secretary of State for Communities and Local Government [2011] 4 All ER 851, SC	82
Wembley National Stadium Limited v Wembley (London) Limited [2007] EWHC 756 (Ch)	204
Western Fish Products Limited v Penwith DC and Another (1979) 38 P & CR 7	55
WH Smith Retail Holdings Ltd v Commerz Real Investmentgesellshaft mbH (unreported, 25 March 2021)	361
Whiteminster Estates v Hodges Menswear (1974) 232 EG 715	261
Williams v Cumbria County Council (1994) Lands Tribunal	109
Willis v Derwentside District Council [2013] All ER (D) 70 (Apr)	130
Willison v Cheverell Estates Ltd [1996] 26 EG 133	353
Winfrey and Chatterton's Agreement, Re [1921] 2 Ch 7	262
Wood v Capita Insurance Services Ltd [2017] UKSC 24	196
Wood v Secretary of State for the Environment [1973] 1 WLR 707, HL	37
Woodcock Holdings v Secretary of State for Communities and Local Government [2015] EWHC 1173 (Admin)	33

Y

Young v Nero Holdings Ltd [2021] EWHC 2600 (Ch)	374
Youssefi v Musselwhite [2014] EWCA Civ 885	354

Z

Zarvos v Pradhan [2003] 2 P & CR 9, [2003] EWCA Civ 208	355, 357

Table of Statutes

Acquisition of Land Act 1981
   s 11(2) 102
   s 12 102
Agricultural Holdings Act 1986 343
Alkali Act 1863 116
Arbitration Act 1996 170, 240

Building Safety Act 2022 154

Civil Aviation Act 1982
   s 76(1) 131
   s 77(2) 131
Clean Air Act 1956 116
Climate Change Act 2008 136, 137
   s 13 137
   s 14 137
   s 44 137
Commercial Rent (Coronavirus) Act 2022 329, 379
Common Law Procedure Act 1852
   s 210 297
Companies Act 2006 7, 8, 369
   s 172 139
   s 859A 15
   Part 26A (ss 901A–901L) 369
   s 1139 351
Competition Act 1998 271
   s 2 270, 271
   s 9 270, 271
Compulsory Purchase Act 1965
   s 4 101
   s 7 108
   s 10 103
   s 11 103
   s 23 111, 112
   Sch 2A
      para 5 103
Compulsory Purchase (Vesting Declarations) Act 1981 103
Contracts (Rights of Third Parties) Act 1999 163, 323
Corporate Insolvency and Governance Act 2020 368–70, 371, 374, 379
Countryside and Rights of Way Act 2000 147
County Courts Act 1984
   s 139(1) 297
Criminal Law Act 1977
   s 6 295

Defective Premises Act 1972 250

Enterprise and Regulatory Reform Act 2013 30, 40, 52
Environment Act 1995 121
Environment Act 2021 117, 140
   Pt 7 (ss 117–138) 141
   s 113 117
Environmental Protection Act 1990 127, 143
   s 33 135
   s 34 132, 135
   s 34(1A) 135

Environmental Protection Act 1990 – *continued*
   s 37 142
   s 75 135
   Part IIA (s 78A–78YC) 118, 120, 121, 122, 126, 127, 128, 129
   s 78A(2) 121
   s 78A(4) 121
   s 78A(9) 122, 123
   s 78B 121, 123
   s 78C 123
   s 78E 123
   s 78F 123
   s 78F(2) 123
   s 78F(4) 123
   s 78M 128
   s 78M(5) 128
   s 78P(2) 126
   s 78U 129
   ss 79-80 132
   s 79H(5) 127
   s 82 132
   s 157 128
Equality Act 2010 48, 256, 262, 278
   s 149 48
European Union (Withdrawal) Act 2018 117
   s 16 117

Growth and Infrastructure Act 2013 30, 31, 53
   s 6 55
   Sch 1 48

Health and Safety at Work etc Act 1974
   s 33(1)(c) 142
Highways Act 1980 77
Housing Act 1985
   s 17 103
Housing Grants, Construction and Regeneration Act 1996
   Part II 170
Housing and Planning Act 2016 7, 30, 31, 445
   ss 203–205 97
Human Rights Act 1998 46, 102, 109
   s 6 131

Infrastructure Act 2015 30
Insolvency Act 1986 212, 367, 368, 373, 377, 378
   ss 1–7 373
   s 28 375
   s 44 376
   s 112 380
   s 126 388
   s 130 388
   s 145 212
   s 178 387, 388
   s 178(3) 392
   s 178(3)(a) 380
   s 178(4) 393

Insolvency Act 1986 – *continued*
   s 178(5) 392
   s 238 381
   s 239 381
   s 241 382
   s 252 373, 374
   s 253 373
   s 254 373, 374
   ss 255–263 373
   s 284(1) 377
   s 285(1) 377, 385
   s 285(3) 377, 385
   s 285(4) 377
   s 316 385
   s 316(1) 392
   s 339 381
   s 340 381
   s 342 382
   s 423 382
   Sch B1
      para 3(1) 377
      para 43 378
Insolvency Act 2006
   s 178 391
   s 315 391

Land Charges Act 1972 352
Land Compensation Act 1961
   Part 1 400
   s 5 104
      r 2 104, 110, 111, 400
      r 4 105, 401
      r 6 110
   ss 6A–6E 105
   s 9 101
   s 14 105, 106, 108
   s 15 105
   s 16 105, 106
   s 16(5) 106
   s 17 105, 107–8, 400
   s 31 103
Land Compensation Act 1973
   Part 1 (ss 1–19) 109
   ss 29–33 112
   s 33A 112
   s 33C 112
   s 41 112
   s 46 111, 401
   s 47 104
   s 52 104, 111, 401
Land Registration Act 2002 197
   s 86 376
   Sch 3 352
   Sch 12 206, 207, 208
Landlord and Tenant Act 1927 250, 275, 278, 351
   Part I (ss 1–17) 278
   s 18 329, 330, 333
   s 19(1)(a) 256, 257, 258, 261, 315, 322
   s 19(1A) 257, 260, 261, 263, 315, 318
   s 19(1C) 257
   s 19(2) 275–6
   s 19(3) 269
   s 23(1) 350

Landlord and Tenant Act 1954 184, 191, 198, 213, 255, 259, 271, 318, 322, 324, 341, 412
   Part II (ss 23–46) 104, 179, 184, 201, 219–23, 254, 262, 293, 323, 326, 337–9, 341–63, 362, 378, **493–506**
   s 23 342, 343
   s 23(1) 341
   s 23(1A)–(1B) 342
   s 23(3) 344
   s 24 206, 210, 223, 341, 347, 349
   s 24(2) 221
   s 24(3) 343
   s 24A 198, 206, 223, 230, 347, 353
   s 25 342, 347–53, 355, 357–8, 362, 413, **415–18**
   s 26 347–53, 355, 357–8, 413, **419–21**
   s 27 347
   s 27(1) 347, 413
   s 27(1A) 347
   s 27(2) 347
   s 29A 352
   s 29A(2) 351
   s 29B 352
   s 30 348, 351, 353, 359
   s 30(1) 353
   s 30(1)(f)–(g) 222
   s 30(2)–(3) 357
   s 31A 356, 360
   s 34 230
   s 34(3) 361
   s 37 201
   s 38 339
   s 38(1) 344
   s 38(2) 359
   s 38(4) 344
   s 40 344
   s 40(1) **421–3**
   s 40(3) **423–5**
   s 41 342, 357
   s 41A 342
   s 42 357
   s 43ZA 343
   s 44 344
   s 46 342
   s 46(2) 342
   Part III (ss 47–50) 278
Landlord and Tenant Act 1988 260, 262, 263, 269, 315, 316, 317
   s 1 315, 317, 322
   s 1(3)(b) 263
Landlord and Tenant (Covenants) Act 1995 185, 203–5, 207, 208, 213, 257, 258, 315, 316–18, 323, 327, 332, 334, 361, 376, 391
   s 6 204
   s 8 204
   s 17 205–6, 210, 327, 407
   s 18 205, 208, 211
   s 24(2) 210
   s 25 210, 212
   s 28 406
   s 28(1) 192
Law of Property Act 1925 199, 370
   s 44 323
   s 52 338
   s 61 199

Law of Property Act 1925 – *continued*
   s 77 206, 207, 208
   s 101 375
   s 139 339
   s 141 205
   s 141(1) 204
   s 142 205
   s 142(1) 204
   s 144 260, 263
   s 146 198, 202, 224, 298–301, 326, 330, 389
   s 146(2) 299–300
   s 146(4) 302
   s 146(9) 301
   s 147 301
   s 150 339
   s 196 24, 201
   s 196(3)–(4) 201
   s 205(1) 183
Law of Property (Miscellaneous Provisions) Act 1989
   s 2 187
Leasehold Property (Repairs) Act 1938 250, 300, 301, 330
   s 1(5) 300
Levelling-up and Regeneration Act 2023 29, 66, 82, 107
   s 182 102
   s 183 102
   s 185 101
   s 186 103
   s 189 107, 108
   s 190 107
Limitation Act 1980 163, 328
Limited Partnership Act 1907 8
Local Democracy, Economic Development and Construction Act 2009 170
Local Government Act 1972 55
   s 250(5) 63
Local Government Act 2003
   s 93 55
Local Government (Miscellaneous Provisions) Act 1976
   s 13 102
Localism Act 2011 30, 32, 45, 82, 107
   s 109 32
   s 232 105, 106
London County Council (Improvements) Act 1900 49

Mental Health Act 1983
   s 99 212
Misrepresentation Act 1967
   s 3 201

Neighbourhood Planning Act 2017 30, 33, 51, 97
   s 14 51
   s 32 101, 105
   s 33 106

Partnership Act 1890 8
Planning Act 2008 30, 53, 70, 72
   s 56 397
   s 73 397
   Part 11 (ss 205–225) 65
   s 212 71
Planning and Compensation Act 1991 30
   s 66 106

Planning and Compulsory Purchase Act 2004 30, 52, 112
   s 38(6) 32, 33, 34, 397
   s 43 56
   s 103 103
Planning (Hazardous Substances) Act 1990
   s 4 135
Proceeds of Crime Act 2002 90
Public Health Act 1848 116

Recorded Delivery Service Act 1962 201
Retained EU Law (Revocation and Reform) Act 2023 118
   s 1(1) 118

Senior Courts Act 1981
   s 37 334
Supply of Goods and Services Act 1982 310
   s 4 152
   s 13 152

Town and Country Planning Act 1947 29
Town and Country Planning Act 1990 30, 45, 46, 53, 81–2, 99
   s 52 65
   s 55 277
   s 55(1) 35, 36
   s 55(1A) 35
   s 55(2) 35, 37–9
   s 55(2)(a) 35
   s 55(2)(d) 37
   s 55(2)(e) 37
   s 55(2)(f) 38
   s 55(2)(g) 36
   s 55(3) 37
   s 55(5) 37
   s 56 52
   s 56(4) 73
   s 57(1) 35
   s 57(2) 39, 43, 51
   s 57(3)–(6) 39
   ss 59–61 39
   s 61W 55
   s 62A 48
   ss 62–65 55
   s 65(8) 56
   ss 66–68 55
   s 69 55, 56, 57, 84
   s 70 33
   s 70(1) 47, 49
   s 70B 56, 57
   s 70C 57
   s 72(1) 49
   s 73 50, 53, 55, 58, 59, 72, 74, 78
   s 73A 58, 59, 78, 90
   s 75(1) 51
   s 75(2) 51
   s 75(3) 51
   s 77 48
   s 78 57, 59, 62
   s 92 51
   s 96A 58
   s 97 52
   s 106 57, 66, 67, 68, 70, 76, 77
   s 106(1) 66, 68

Town and Country Planning Act 1990 – *continued*
- s 106(2) 66
- s 106(3) 66, 67
- s 106(4) 66, 67
- s 106(5)–(6) 68
- s 106(9) 67
- s 106(11) 67
- s 106(12) 68
- s 106A 69
- s 106A(1) 69
- s 106A(3)–(4) 69
- s 106B 69
- s 106BC 69
- s 107 52
- Part VI (ss 137–171) 98
- s 137 98, 100–1
- s 140 101
- s 143 101
- s 149 99
- s 150 99
- s 151(4) 99
- Part VII (ss 171–196) 81
- s 171A 81–2, 89
- s 171A(1) 88
- s 171B 82, 88, 89
- s 171B(4)(b) 82, 88
- s 171BA 82, 88
- s 171C 85, 93
- s 171C(1) 86
- s 171C(5) 86
- s 171D 85
- s 171D(2)–(6) 86
- ss 171E–171G 91
- s 172 87, 89, 94
- s 172(1) 87
- s 173 87, 88, 89
- s 173(1) 88
- s 173(2) 88, 91
- s 173(3)–(7) 88
- s 173(8) 88
- s 173(9) 88
- s 173(11)–(12) 90
- s 174 87, 89, 90, 94
- s 174(1) 95
- s 174(2) 94
- s 174(2)(a) 92, 93
- s 174(3) 94
- s 174(3)(b) 95
- s 174(4) 95
- s 174(6) 95
- s 175 87, 89, 94
- s 175(5) 94
- s 176 87, 89, 94
- s 176(1) 94
- s 176(2) 90
- s 177 87, 89, 94
- s 177(1C) 94
- s 178 87
- s 178(1) 91
- s 179 87
- s 179(1)–(2) 90
- s 179(3) 91
- s 179(4)–(5) 90

Town and Country Planning Act 1990 – *continued*
- s 179(7) 91
- s 179(8)–(9) 90
- ss 180–182 87
- s 183 91
- s 183(1) 92
- s 183(2) 92
- s 183(3) 92
- s 183(6) 92
- s 183(7) 92
- s 184 91
- s 184(1)–(2) 92
- s 184(3) 92
- s 184(7) 92
- s 185 91, 92
- s 186 91
- s 187 91
- s 187A 86
- s 187B 91, 93–4
- s 188 91, 92
- s 191 82, 83
- s 191(1) 83
- s 191(4) 84
- s 192 82, 83
- s 193(4) 84
- s 193(6) 84
- ss 196A–196C 84–5
- s 284 63
- s 285 90
- s 285(1) 89
- s 288 63, 84
- s 289 91, 95, 96
- s 289(4A) 87, 95
- s 289(6) 95
- s 320 95
- s 320(2) 63
- s 322 63, 95
- s 329 89
- s 336 59, 72
- s 336(1) 35, 89
- Sch 1
  - para 1 31
- Sch 7A
  - para 13 49

Town and Country Planning (Listed Buildings) Act 1990 36
Tribunals, Courts and Enforcement Act 2007
- Part 3 (ss 62–90) 328
- s 77 328
- s 81 329, 382, 383, 385–9
- Sch 12 328

Unfair Contracts Terms Act 1977 201
- s 8 201

Value Added Tax Act 1994
- s 49 178
- s 89 177

Water Acts 48
Water Act 2014
- Pt 4 (ss 64–84) 143
Water Industry Act 1991
- s 118 134

Water Resources Act 1991
    s 24 134
    s 25 134
    s 104 122
Wildlife and Countryside Act 1981 143

International legislation
European Convention on Human Rights 46, 87
    Art 8 109, 130
UN Framework Convention on Climate Change 136
    Kyoto Protocol 1997 136
    Paris Agreement 117, 136, 137

Table of Secondary Legislation

Building Regulations 2010 (SI 2010/2214) 138, 139–40, 188, 277

Civil Procedure Rules 1998 (SI 1998/3132) 298
　Part 54 59
Community Infrastructure Levy Regulations 2010 (SI 2010/948) 65–77, 70
　reg 4(2) 72
　reg 5 72
　reg 5(2) 72
　reg 6(2) 72
　reg 7 73
　reg 8 73
　reg 9(4) 73
　Part 3 (regs 11–30) 71
　reg 20 71
　reg 28A 71
　reg 32 72
　reg 36 72
　Part 5, reg 40 71
　reg 42(1) 71
　reg 44 74
　reg 49 74
　reg 55 75
　reg 59A 74
　reg 65(1) 72
　reg 69B 73
　reg 73 73
　reg 80 76
　reg 81 76
　reg 83 76
　reg 83(1A) 75, 76
　reg 87 76
　reg 89 76
　reg 90 76
　regs 98–99 76
　reg 100 76
　Part 10 (regs 112–121) 73
　reg 113 73
　reg 121A 77
　reg 121B 77
　reg 121C 71
　reg 122 68
　reg 122(2) 67
　reg 123 76
　Sch 1 71
　　para 1(2) 73
Community Infrastructure Levy (Amendment) (England) Regulations 2019 (SI 2019/966) (Cross Rail funding) 69
Community Infrastructure Levy (Amendment) (England) Regulations 2020 (SI 2020/781) 69
Community Infrastructure Levy (Amendment) (England) Regulations 2020 (SI 2020/1226) 69
Community Infrastructure Levy (Amendment) (England) Regulations 2021 (SI 2021/337) 69

Community Infrastructure Levy (Amendment) (England) Regulations (No 2) 2019 (SI 2019/1103) (2019 CIL Regs) 66, 69, 70, 71, 72, 73–4, 75, 77
Community Infrastructure Levy (Amendment) Regulations 2011 (SI 2011/987) 66, 69
Community Infrastructure Levy (Amendment) Regulations 2012 (SI 2012/98) 66, 69
Community Infrastructure Levy (Amendment) Regulations 2013 (SI 2013/382) 66
Community Infrastructure Levy (Amendment) Regulations 2013 (SI 2013/982) 69
Community Infrastructure Levy (Amendment) Regulations 2014 (SI 2014/395) 66, 69, 72, 76
Community Infrastructure Levy (Amendment) Regulations 2015 (SI 2015/836) 66, 69
Community Infrastructure Levy (Amendment) Regulations 2018 (SI 2018/172) 69
Conservation of Habitats and Species Regulations 1972 (SI 2017/1012) (Habitats Regulations) 117
　Part 6 117
Construction (Design and Management) Regulations 2015 (SI 2015/51) 153
Contaminated Land (England) Regulations 2006 (SI 2006/1380) 123, 128
Control of Asbestos Regulations 2012 (SI 2012/632) 142–3
　reg 4 142, 143
　reg 4(1) 142
Control of Major Accident Hazard Regulations 2015 (SI 2015/483) (COMAH) 135
　reg 4 135
Control of Substances Hazardous to Health Regulations 2002 (SI 2002/2677) 135, 136
Controlled Waste (England and Wales) Regulations 2012 (SI 2012/811) 143

Energy Efficiency (Private Rented Property) (England and Wales) Regulations 2015 (SI 2015/962) 139
Energy Performance of Buildings (England and Wales) Regulations 2012 (SI 2012/3118) 138
　regs 5–7 138
　reg 7A 138
　reg 9 138
　reg 14 138
　Part 4 (regs 17–21) 138
Environmental Permitting (England and Wales) Regulations 2010 (SI 2010/675) 133, 135
Environmental Permitting (England and Wales) Regulations 2016 (SI 2016/1154) 133–5
　reg 7 133
　reg 12 133, 134
　reg 12(1) 133, 134
　reg 38 134
　reg 38(1) 134
　Sch 3 135
　Sch 9 135
　Sch 21 134
　Sch 22 134

Greenhouse Gas Emissions Trading Scheme Order 2020 (SI 2020/1265) 137

Home Loss Payments (Prescribed Amounts) (England) Regulations 2015 (SI 2015/1514) 112

Insolvency Rules 2016 (SI 2016/1024) 367–8, 379
   r 15.34 373
   r 19.9 388

Land Registration Rules 2005 (SI 2005/1766)
   Sch 1A 197
Land Registration (Amendment) (No 2) Rules 2005 (SI 2005/1982) 197
Landlord and Tenant Act 1954 Part II (Notices) (England and Wales) Regulations 2004 (SI 2004/1005) 348, 349
Local Land Charges Rules 2018 (SI 2018/273) 145

Planning (Hazardous Substances) Regulations 2015 (SI 2015/627) 135

Scheme for Construction Contracts (England and Wales) Regulations 1998 (Amendment) (England) Regulations 2011 (SI 2011/2333) 170
Scheme for Construction Contracts (England and Wales) Regulations 1998 (SI 1998/649) 170

Town and Country Planning (Appeals) (Written Representations Procedure) (England) Regulations 2009 (SI 2009/452) 61
Town and Country Planning (Determination by Inspectors) (Inquiries Procedure) (England) Rules 2000 (SI 2000/1625) 62
Town and Country Planning (Development Management Procedure) (England) Order 2015 (SI 2015/595) 30, 46, 55
   art 2 46
   art 5 46
   art 7 46
   art 12 55
   art 13 56
   art 13(9) 56
   art 14 56
   art 15 56
   art 34 57, 84
   art 35 57
   art 36 60
   art 37 59, 60
   art 39 84
   art 40 57
Town and Country Planning (Enforcement Notices and Appeals) (England) Regulations 2002 (SI 2002/2682)
   regs 4–5 88
   reg 6 95
Town and Country Planning (Enforcement Notices and Appeals) (Wales) Regulations 2017 (SI 2017/530) 88
Town and Country Planning (Environmental Impact Assessment) Regulations 2017 (SI 2017/571) 56
Town and Country Planning (General Permitted Development) (England) Order 2015 (SI 2015/596) 26, 30, 35, 39–45, 63, 72, 75, 82, 105, 272, 397, 398, 408
   art 2(3) 41, 43
   art 3(5) 44

Town and Country Planning (General Permitted Development) (England) Order 2015 – *continued*
   art 3(6) 44
   art 3(10) 36, 44
   art 4 45, 63, 397
   Sch 2 36, 39, 41, 44
Town and Country Planning (General Permitted Development) (England) (Amendment) (No 2) Order 2020 (SI 2020/755) 105
Town and Country Planning (General Permitted Development) Order 1995 (SI 1995/418) 39
Town and Country Planning (Hearings and Inquiries Procedure) (Amendment) (England) Rules 2009 (SI 2009/455) 62
Town and Country Planning (Hearings and Inquiries Procedure) (Amendment) (England) Rules 2013 (SI 2013/2137) 62
Town and Country Planning (Hearings and Inquiries Procedure) (England) (Amendment and Revocation) Rules 2015 (SI 2015/316) 62
Town and Country Planning (Hearings Procedure) (England) Rules 2000 (SI 2000/1626) 62
Town and Country Planning (Inquiries Procedure) (England) Rules 2000 (SI 2000/1624) 62
Town and Country Planning (Local Planning) (England) Regulations 2012 (SI 2012/767) 34
   reg 10A 32
Town and Country Planning (Permission in Principle) Order 2017 (SI 2017/402) 47, 72
Town and Country Planning (Precommencement Conditions) Regulations 2018 (SI 2018/566) 53
Town and Country Planning (Use Classes) Order 1987 (SI 1987/764) 30, 35, 38–9, 41, 105, 234, 267, 272
   Sch 43
Town and Country Planning (Use Classes) (Amendment) (England) Regulations 2020 (SI 2020/757) 105–6

Value Added Tax (Land) Order 1995 (SI 1995/282) 178

Waste Electrical and Electronic Equipment Regulations 2013 (SI 2013/3113) 135

Circulars
DCLG Circular 11/95 50–1
   Appendix A 50–1
DCLG Circular 5/2005 67

Codes of Practice and Arbitration Rules
Code for Leasing Business Premises in England and Wales 2007 194, 195, 196
   see also RICS Code for Leasing Business Premises in England and Wales 2020
Institution of Civil Engineers Arbitration Rules 170
International Chamber of Commerce (ICC) Arbitration Rules 170
London Court of International Arbitration Rules 170
DCLG Model Planning Conditions for Contaminated Land 2008 128
RICS Code for Leasing Business Premises in England and Wales 2020 193–5, 220, 229, 242, 248, 254, 255, 257, 259–60, 285–7, 289, 291, 293, 294, 302, 318, 324, 407–8, 409, **427–37**
   Part 1 194

RICS Code for Leasing Business Premises in England and Wales 2020 – *continued*
  Part 2 194–5
  Part 3 195, 220
  paras 1.1–1.4 194
  para 4 229
  para 4.1–4.4 229
  para 6.1 259–60
  para 6.2–6.3 260
  para 6.4 259, 260
  para 6.5–6.6 260
  para 7.1 249
  para 7.2 249
  para 7.3 249
  para 8.1-8.2 266
  para 8.1–8.2 278
  para 8.3 278–9
  para 8.4–8.6 279
  para 9.1–9.4 285
  para 10 302
  Part 4
    Appendix A 195
    Appendix B 195, 302
      para 8 249
      para 9 279
      para 14 279
RICS Professional Statement: Service Charges in Commercial Property 2006 195, 312–13
  s 2 313
  s 3 313
  s 4 313

Direction
Town and Country Planning (Demolition–Descriptions of Buildings) Direction 2021 36

Guidance
Better Buildings Partnership Green Lease Toolkit 2024 140
Central Government Guidance on the Acceptability of Conditions 50–1
Contaminated Land Statutory Guidance 2012 121, 124
  s 3.8 122
  s 4 121
  s 4.1 121
  s 4.3 122
  s 4.19 122
  s 4.33 122
  s 7 125
  s 7(c) 124
  s 7(d) 125
  s 7(e) 124
  s 7(f) 125
  s 7.30 126
  s 7.3.2(b) 124
  s 7.32 124
  s 7.67 125

Contaminated Land Statutory Guidance 2012 – *continued*
  s 7.68–7.72 125
  s 7.79 124
  s 7.80–7.86 126
Law Society Guidance on The Impact of Climate Change on Solicitors 141
Law Society Practice Note on Contaminated Land 119, 121
Law Society Practice Note on Flood Risk 144
Ministry of Housing, Communities and Local Government guidance on compulsory purchase matters with regard to the Covid-19 situation 98, 102
PINS Procedural Guide 60, 61, 62
Planning Practice Guidance (PPG) 30, 31, 37, 50–1, 52, 55, 58, 61, 68, 70, 72, 85, 87, 88, 128, 129, 398
  para 21 78

National Planning Policy Framework 30, 31, 33–4, 37, 52, 60, 78, 87, 128, 398
  para 7 33
  para 10 33
  para 11 33
  para 11(b) 33
  para 11(d) 33
  para 12 34
  para 17 32
  para 30 32
  para 33 33
  para 44 46
  para 55 49, 68
  para 56 51
  para 57 67, 68
  para 58 68
  para 59 87
  para 77 52
  para 219 33
National Planning Practice Guidance *see* Planning Practice Guidance (PPG)

Producer Responsibility Obligations (Packaging Waste) Regulations 2007 (SI 2007/871) 135

Property Protocols
Protocol for Applications for Consent to Assign or Sublet (Alienation Protocol) 263, 317
Protocol for Applications for Consent to Carry Out Alterations (Alterations Protocol) 279

EU secondary legislation
Directive 2003/87/EC Emissions Trading Scheme 136
Directive 2006/21/EC Mining Waste
  Art 2 135
Directive 2008/98/EC Water Framework
  Art 3(1) 135
Directive 2010/31/EU Energy Performance of Buildings 137
  Art 8 138
  Art 9 138

List of Abbreviations

The following abbreviations are used throughout this book.

ADR	alternative dispute resolution
AGA	Authorised Guarantee Agreement
AMP	Asbestos Management Plan
BCN	breach of condition notice
CA 1998	Competition Act 1998
CGT	capital gains tax
CIGA	Corporate Insolvency and Governance Act 2020
CIL	Community Infrastructure Levy
CLEUD	certificate of lawful use or development
CRAR	Commercial Rent Arrears Recovery
CRC Energy Efficiency Scheme	Carbon Reduction Commitment Energy Efficiency Scheme
CVA	company voluntary arrangement
DAS	designs and access statement
DEC	Display Energy Certificate
Defra	Department for Environment, Food and Rural Affairs
DMPO	Town and Country Planning (Development Management Procedure) Order 2015
EA	Environment Agency
EIA	environmental impact assessment
EPA 1990	Environmental Protection Act 1990
EPB Regulations 2012	Energy Performance of Buildings (England and Wales) Regulations 2012
EPC	Energy Performance Certificate
EPR 2016	Environmental Permitting (England and Wales) Regulations 2016
ERRA 2013	Enterprise and Regulatory Reform Act 2013
ES	environmental statement
EU ETS	European Union Emission Trading System
GAIA 2013	Growth and Infrastructure Act 2013
GHG	greenhouse gas
GIA	gross internal area
GPDO	Town and Country Planning (General Permitted Development) Order 2015
HMRC	HM Revenue & Customs
HPA 2016	Housing and Planning Act 2016
HSE	Health and Safety Executive
IA 1986	Insolvency Act 1986
IVA	individual voluntary arrangement
LA 2011	Localism Act 2011

LDF	local development framework
LPA	local planning authority
LPA 1925	Law of Property Act 1925
LP(R)A 1938	Leasehold Property (Repairs) Act 1938
LRA 2002	Land Registration Act 2002
LTA 1927	Landlord and Tenant Act 1927
LTA 1954	Landlord and Tenant Act 1954
LTA 1988	Landlord and Tenant Act 1988
LT(C)A 1995	Landlord and Tenant (Covenants) Act 1995
MHCLG	Ministry of Housing, Communities and Local Government
NPA 2017	Neighbourhood Planning Act 2017
NPPF	National Planning Policy Framework
NSIP	nationally significant infrastructure project
NPV	net present value
OMR	open market rent
PA 2008	Planning Act 2008
PCN	planning contravention notice
PCPA 2004	Planning and Compulsory Purchase Act 2004
PINS	Planning Inspectorate
PPG	Planning Policy Guidance
RESA 2008	Regulatory Enforcement and Sanctions Act 2008
RICS	Royal Institution of Chartered Surveyors
SCPC	Standard Commercial Property Condition
SDLT	stamp duty land tax
SDO	special development order
SOS	Secretary of State for Housing, Communities and Local Government
SPV	special purpose vehicle
SPZ	simplified planning zone
SSSI	site of special scientific interest
TCEA 2007	Tribunals, Courts and Enforcement Act 2007
TCPA 1990	Town and Country Planning Act 1990
UCO	Town and Country Planning (Use Classes) Order 1987
VATA 1994	Value Added Tax Act 1994

PART I

SITE ACQUISITIONS

CHAPTER 1

The Commercial Context

1.1	What is commercial property?	3
1.2	Who buys commercial property?	4
1.3	Buying commercial property jointly	6
1.4	Methods of structuring a property joint venture	6
	Review activity	9

1.1 WHAT IS COMMERCIAL PROPERTY?

Commercial property is property that is not designed or used for residential purposes, or for purposes associated with the primary industries such as agriculture and mining. The three main types of commercial property are offices (single office buildings and business parks), retail (individual shops, shopping centres, retail warehouses and supermarkets) and industrial (factories, warehouses and distribution centres). The remaining properties are those used for leisure (pubs, restaurants and hotels), sport, education, the provision of utilities and healthcare (hospitals and nursing homes).

The total value of UK commercial property at the end of 2022 was £887 billion, about 7.5% of the value of all land, buildings and structures in the UK. The long-term effects of Brexit and the Covid-19 pandemic on the UK property market have yet to become clear, but in 2022 the commercial property industry directly contributed approximately £74 billion (3.3%) to the UK economy from the development, construction and funding of new buildings and the management, refurbishment, renovation, retrofit, repurposing and maintenance of existing buildings, for retailers, wholesalers/distributors, business and financial services firms, hoteliers, industrial firms and for the public sector. Taxes paid by the commercial property industry were over £18 billion, with a further £26 billion in business rates in 2022, and there were over 1.1 million people employed. (These figures are from the PIA Property Data Report 2023 published by the Property Industry Alliance.)

In terms of value, the breakdown of the different types of commercial property at the end of 2020 was industrial 31%, retail 29%, offices 29% and other commercial properties 11%. The industrial sector became the largest commercial property sector for the first time, retail having fallen in value by over 20% since 2018. (These figures are from the IPF report, 'The Size and Structure of the UK Property Market: End-2020 Update', published in January 2022, and have been rounded.)

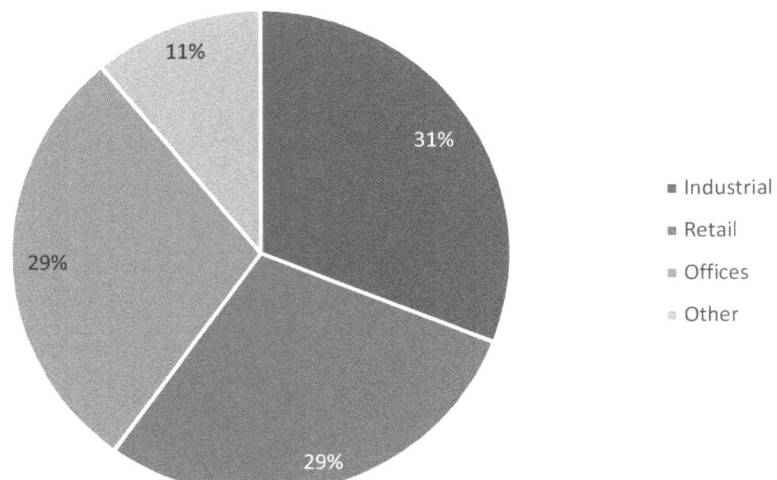

Figure 1.1 Value of UK commercial property at the end of 2020

This book will concentrate on two of the main types of commercial property, offices and retail, although most of what is covered in it will also be relevant to the other types of commercial property.

1.2 WHO BUYS COMMERCIAL PROPERTY?

1.2.1 Occupiers

About 45% of all commercial property is bought by owner-occupiers, who need land and buildings from which to conduct their business. Some of these occupiers want to buy a freehold or long leasehold interest in the property because they need certainty and complete freedom to deal with the property as the business dictates, but it does means that a lot of capital is tied up in the building. Other occupiers prefer to take a so-called 'rack rent lease', where the occupation cost is paid, usually quarterly, over the period of the lease by way of rent, rather than all at the beginning. In recent years, particularly among the large food retailers, there has been a move away from freehold ownership through 'sale and leaseback', where the freehold interest in the property is sold to an investor (thus releasing capital for use in the operating part of the business) and the occupier takes a rack rent lease instead.

1.2.2 Investors

The other 55% of all commercial property is bought by investors, who buy property to let out to others so that they can make an income from the rent and a profit from any increase in the capital value of the property. Although the capital value of commercial property suffered considerable falls in 2007–08 and 2020, it remains popular with certain types of investor because the average lease offers an income stream of about seven years. So the income return (or 'yield') from commercial property is reasonable: over the 46 years prior to 2022, commercial property produced annualised returns of around 10%, higher than UK government bonds but lower than equities (see PIA *Property Data Report* 2023, p 18). Commercial property has tended not to track the performance of gilts and equities particularly closely, so including some commercial property in your investment portfolio is a way of diversifying and spreading risk. Moreover, by good management of tenants and/or refurbishment of a tired building, a property investor may be able to enhance the value of the asset, even in times of economic downturn.

There are two ways to invest in commercial property, directly or indirectly. Direct property investment involves buying a property in your own name or in the name of a group company, letting it out, taking responsibility for managing it and selling it on when you no longer require it. Although you can employ surveyors and other professionals to assist you, this still uses up a considerable amount of time and effort. It also means that you have to find a considerable amount of cash, or a loan, or a combination of both, to fund the initial purchase. An alternative way is to buy shares or units in a company that invests in a range of commercial and residential property, such as a real estate investment trust (REIT) or an offshore property unit trust (PUT). These indirect property investment vehicles offer opportunities for smaller levels of investment, some taxation advantages, less management responsibility and, arguably, greater flexibility as it may be easier to trade units than to sell a property. However, indirect property investment is beyond the scope of this book.

So who invests in commercial property? According to figures in the *PIA Property Data Report 2023*, at the end of 2022 overseas investors held the largest block of directly-owned investment property (31%); UK insurance companies and pension funds held 16%; UK collective investment schemes held 16%; UK REITs and listed property companies held 15%; and UK private companies and private individuals held 11%. Traditional estates and charities held 4% and UK others held 6%. The share of the market held by overseas investors has doubled since 2006. Some of the units in the UK collective investment schemes are bought by private individuals, but many are bought by the investors who also buy property directly. For example, in 2022 the UK insurance companies and pension funds invested £80 billion (2.2% of their total investments) in directly owned property, £71 billion (2.0%) in indirect property and £45 billion (1.3%) in property equities/REITs.

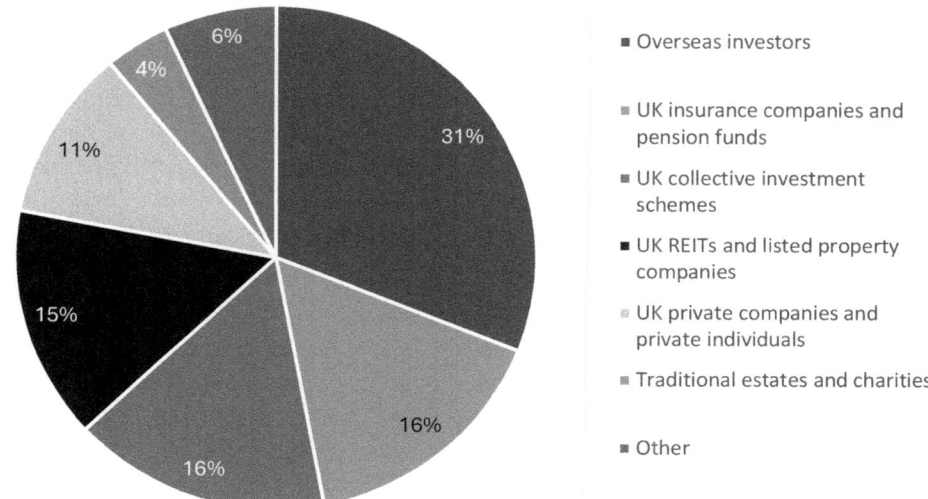

Figure 1.2   Investors in UK commercial property

1.2.3   Developers

Another way to make a profit from commercial property is to buy a property that is not being used to its full potential, construct some new buildings on the site, let at least some of the new buildings to quality tenants so that there is good income flow, and then sell the completed development to an occupier or an investor at a price greater than you have spent on the purchase and development of the property. Commercial property development stalled after the credit crunch of 2007 because of the difficulties developers experienced in obtaining loans to fund what is still seen as a risky activity, but in times of economic growth, when there is a shortage in the supply of new buildings, commercial property development returns.

Of course, the aims of occupation, investment and development are not mutually exclusive. For example, some larger investors develop property themselves, or participate in joint ventures with developers so as to spread the risks (see **1.3**). Some potential occupiers, particularly those looking for prestige headquarters buildings, may prefer to develop their own building or work alongside a developer in order to achieve a high degree of customisation.

1.3 BUYING COMMERCIAL PROPERTY JOINTLY

Both property investment and property development involve substantial financial risks. For example, between the summer of 2007 and the autumn of 2008, commercial property lost, on average, about 40% of its value. Investment into UK commercial property peaked in 2015 but has declined since. In 2020 the commercial property investment market saw the lowest value since 2012. The retail sector has been struggling since the middle of 2018 and it is anticipated that a large number of office buildings will need to be repurposed in the aftermath of the Covid-19 pandemic. The growth of hybrid working and online shopping has shifted attention away from offices and on to industrial and logistics buildings. Property development is particularly risky because the economic conditions can worsen considerably in the months, sometimes years, between the purchase of the site and completion of the development. So, although it is sometimes the case that a developer will purchase a site and develop the site itself, this normally occurs only in the case of small-scale developments. In larger developments it is usual to find that the development will be a joint venture between two or more parties.

Joint ventures enable the cost and potential risks, and profits (if any), of a development scheme to be shared. So a developer might find it easier to obtain funding, and those wishing to invest funds (eg banks, pension funds, etc) can share in the profits of a development rather than just obtaining a fixed return. They may also have more control over the nature of the development.

Joint ventures also enable landowners and those without particular skills in a particular aspect of property development to undertake them competently. So, for example, the cleaning up of a seriously contaminated site would need the involvement of specialists. This service could always be purchased, ie a contractor is employed to clean up the site, but if the landowner/developer does not understand the issues involved it can be very difficult to manage outside contractors properly. If the contractor is involved as a party to the venture, such problems should be avoided.

Property joint ventures are not always carried out purely for profit. For example, a local authority might enter into a joint venture as a way of bringing about urban regeneration or other social benefits. Other landowning public bodies that have historically entered into joint ventures include Transport for London, the National Health Service, Sport England, the Ministry of Defence, housing associations, registered social landlords and the Olympic Delivery Authority. Indeed, the Home and Communities Agency was specifically set up to assist these types of landowner to get their surplus or under-utilised land redeveloped.

Before entering into any kind of joint venture, various matters need careful consideration. A detailed business plan will need to be put together, along with possible exit strategies. The duration of the venture will need to be agreed, including terms of dissolution. The arrangements for the management of the venture will also need to be agreed.

The financial credentials of the proposed joint venturers will need to be confirmed. The profit share (or share of the loss) and financial contributions of each party will have to be agreed, along with each party's involvement in the development works themselves. The form the joint venture will take will also need to be established.

1.4 METHODS OF STRUCTURING A PROPERTY JOINT VENTURE

A joint venture set up for development purposes might involve, for example, the landowner, the developer, the funder and the ultimate occupier of the completed development. There are various ways in which such a joint venture can be structured. No one scheme is always appropriate, and the advantages and disadvantages of each option should be considered carefully. Often taxation will be of prime consideration, and specialist advice should be obtained with regard to the tax implications of the chosen scheme.

1.4.1 Contractual joint venture

This, in essence, involves the parties entering into a contract which sets out the terms of their agreement. These will include each party's financial commitment and duties in relation to the development, so the arrangement is very flexible and responsive to the parties' individual needs. If one of the parties already owns the property, there is no need to transfer the ownership of the site at the start of the joint venture as there is no setting up of a separate legal entity, so a charge to stamp duty land tax (SDLT) is avoided. The joint venture contract arrangement is 'tax transparent', so each party will be responsible for payment of income tax on its profits and capital gains tax (CGT) on its capital gains, and will get the direct benefit of any tax deductions and reliefs. Moreover, as the parties are in a mere contract together, it is less likely that one party would be liable for the actions of another (subject to the terms of the agreement). On the other hand, as there is no separate legal entity, there will be unlimited liability in relation to any losses. Thus the failure of the joint venture could result in threats to the continued existence of the contracting parties.

1.4.2 Special purpose vehicle companies

This is a limited company set up for a particular purpose, eg to develop a particular site. The special purpose vehicle company (SPV) may be a subsidiary of just one company, but it can also be a jointly-owned subsidiary of several companies. The companies that set up the SPV are shareholders in it and have all of the usual rights of a shareholder. Different companies can invest different amounts in the property that the SPV purchases and receive differing profit shares. Although certain matters can be customised in a shareholders agreement, in default the arrangements will be governed by company law, which is a tried and tested framework with which the parties are likely to be familiar.

A key advantage of using an SPV is that the shareholders in the SPV will have limited liability (ie the liability of each shareholder will be capped at the amount of capital put in). This means that the risk of a particular business venture can be capped for the shareholders at a quantifiable amount. If the property investment turns out to be a very bad one and the SPV becomes insolvent, the other interests of the shareholders are protected.

Another good reason for choosing an SPV is that on completion of the development, it is possible to transfer ownership of the property by selling the shares in the SPV company, rather than by transferring the property itself. The benefit of this comes from the way stamp duty is charged. Stamp duty land tax is paid using a separate rate of tax on each portion of the purchase price, but at 5% on that part which exceeds £250,000. However, if you sell shares in a company, stamp duty is paid at the rate of 0.5% on the consideration. There are, however, special anti-avoidance SDLT rules which need to be considered in this context. As always, specialist taxation advice will be needed. Note also that although it is the buyer, rather than the seller, who pays the SDLT and who therefore benefits from the saving, as the buyer will be making an SDLT saving it may be prepared to pay a higher purchase price for the SPV than for the property, so the seller benefits too.

The most significant disadvantage of this structure is that the SPV itself will be assessed to corporation tax on the rental income and on capital gains from the property held as an investment, and the shareholder companies will pay corporation tax on the dividends issued by the SPV. This is sometimes referred to as 'double taxation'. For this reason, an SPV is perhaps more suited to a development that is to be disposed of within a short period of its completion rather than held as a long-term investment. Also, as a limited company governed by the Companies Acts, annual returns must be filed, which will result in administrative expense and a lack of privacy as to the company's structure and finances. A third disadvantage is that if the property is owned by a third party and has to be transferred to the SPV when the joint venture is formed, a charge to SDLT will arise when the property transfer takes place.

Nevertheless, the SPV is a popular option, particularly where the joint venture involves only one property.

1.4.3 Traditional unlimited liability partnership

In this type of partnership, the joint venture partners will enter into a partnership agreement to purchase the property. This agreement will regulate the way in which risk and profits are shared and the roles and responsibilities of each partner. A joint venture partnership, like the joint venture contract, is very flexible and can be tailored to suit the needs of the partners. However, unlike a joint venture contract, a partnership is a legally recognised structure, governed by a statutory code in the Partnership Act 1890, so there is a default position when unexpected events occur.

The property will be held in the name of the partnership, so if the property is being acquired from a third party, a charge to SDLT will arise when the property is transferred from the third party to the joint venture partners. Alternatively, one of the joint venture parties might already own the property, in which case a charge to SDLT will arise when the property is transferred to the joint venture partnership (something that can be avoided by using a contractual joint venture instead). In either case, as the legal interest in property can only be held by up to four people, if there are more than four partners the legal interest will be held in the names of some of those partners, with the beneficial interest vesting in all of the partners, in specified shares.

As far as tax is concerned, a partnership is tax transparent, so each partner is taxed on its own share of the profits and capital gains separately, and each is able to choose how best to use its tax deductions and reliefs. As a partnership, there is no requirement to file an annual return, and the accounts will remain private.

The main disadvantage is that in the traditional unlimited liability partnership, each partner will be wholly liable for the debts and obligations of the partnership, so the partners have to know and trust each other to a very high degree. Moreover, each partner will have the authority to bind the partnership and its co-partners when dealing with third parties.

Joint venture partnerships have been commonly used to acquire property, and are preferable to a simple contractual relationship where a long-term, complex project is contemplated.

1.4.4 Limited partnership

Under a limited partnership, established under the Limited Partnerships Act 1907, there are one or more general partners and one or more limited partners. A general partner is liable for all of the debts of the partnership, although the general partner can be a limited liability company. A limited partner is only liable up to the limit of its capital subscribed to the partnership.

The limited partnership is registered under the name of the general partner. The property would commonly be held by the general partner and a nominee of the limited partners, acting as trustees for the partnership.

The limited partnership has the advantage of being tax transparent; there is no tax liability on income or capital gains of the partnership itself, before distribution of returns to the partners. The disadvantage is that the partnership can only be managed by the general partner. If a limited partner participates in the management of the partnership, then it will lose its limited liability status (although a limited partner can exercise negative control through a power of veto over actions proposed by the general partner). A limited partnership is most suitable for a joint venture development where there are parties content to be passive investors.

1.4.5 Limited liability partnership

An LLP is a hybrid between a partnership under the Partnership Act 1890 and a limited company under the Companies Act 2006. An LLP shares many of the features of a traditional partnership (including tax transparency), but it also offers reduced personal responsibility for business debts. The LLP is a corporate body with a separate identity from the members, and the LLP itself is responsible for any debts that it incurs, rather than the individual members. The accounting and filing requirements for an LLP are similar to those for a company, but the members' agreement is private and does not need to be filed. An LLP therefore offers the flexibility and tax transparency of a partnership with limited liability for its members.

REVIEW ACTIVITY

1. What are the three main types of commercial property?
2. When choosing a commercial property from which to conduct its business, why might a business organisation prefer to rent a property than buy a freehold property?
3. How do investors hope to make a profit from commercial property?
4. How do developers hope to make a profit from commercial property?
5. Why might an investor enter into a joint venture with others to develop a commercial property?
6. Why might a contractual joint venture or a joint venture partnership be more tax-efficient for the parties than an SPV?
7. In terms of reducing financial risk to the joint venture parties, which joint venture structures are most advantageous?
8. Which joint venture structure is most efficient in terms of SDLT?

Answers to this Review activity may be found in Appendix 1.

CHAPTER 2

Obtaining Property Finance

2.1	Methods of finance	11
2.2	Debt finance	12
	Review activity	17

2.1 METHODS OF FINANCE

One of the first considerations of any buyer of commercial property, whether the buyer is a developer, an institutional investor or simply a company looking to acquire premises from which to operate, is how to fund the acquisition. Even the largest commercial organisation is unlikely to have sufficient funds to buy the property without recourse to outside funding; and even if it does have the funds readily available, it may not make financial sense to use them. There may be tax advantages to borrowing the necessary funds, as discussed at **2.1.4**. There are a number of ways in which a company may finance an acquisition and/or development. These are considered below.

2.1.1 Share capital

Where the buyer is a company, it may consider issuing further shares to raise additional capital to invest in property. This method of raising funds may not be popular with the current shareholders of the company. Depending on the method used, a new issue of shares may result in reduced dividends as a current shareholder's percentage shareholding may be diluted, which will also affect voting power and capital rights. Further, if the company is a publicly listed company there will be additional regulations to consider before any such fund-raising may be considered. Details of these regulations are dealt with in **Public Companies and Equity Finance.**

2.1.2 Forward funding and equity funding

Institutional investors such as pension and life insurance funds have substantial sums of money at their disposal for investment. These investors will usually invest in property in addition to shares and bonds, in order to maintain a balanced investment portfolio. This investment may take the form of a simple purchase of an established commercial property (an office block or shopping centre) which has been let. The investor will receive the rental income stream from the tenants, and it will also hope that, over time, the capital value of the property will increase.

As an alternative to purchasing a property that has already been let, such investors may also take an active part in the development of suitable property. Examples of ways of doing this are discussed below.

2.1.2.1 Forward funding

In this instance, the institutional investor finances the development from the outset, acquiring the land and paying all the construction costs, including architects' fees, etc. The developer is paid a fee for its work and, once the development has been completed and let (to tenants with an agreed covenant strength), is paid a profit share. The developer may be prepared to accept a lower profit because there is less risk to the developer than if it had developed the property using its own funds. The investor will hope to have paid less for the completed and let property than if it had waited to buy the property until after the developer had built and let it.

2.1.2.2 Equity funding

In the case of equity funding, an investor and a developer will form a joint venture company to acquire the development site and undertake the development. The investor takes preference shares in order to be assured of a priority return on its investment. This way, the investor is participating in the profits and losses of the development.

2.1.3 Sale and leaseback

It is possible for the owner-occupier of a freehold property to raise funds against the value of its property and remain in occupation by entering into a sale and leaseback arrangement. The freehold interest in the property is sold; immediately following completion of the sale, the buyer leases it back to the seller/former owner, usually at a market rent. In this way the former owner can raise capital for whatever purpose it requires, eg working capital to acquire further premises for investment or development, etc. The buyer will see a return on its capital investment in the form of the rent paid by the former owner.

2.1.4 Debt finance

One of the most common ways of raising finance is to borrow, usually from banks or 'alternative credit providers' such as insurance companies or debt funds. These alternative lenders have filled a funding gap, left when banks tightened their lending criteria following the financial crisis of 2007–08. Where the debt requirement is large, eg a sum exceeding £50,000,000, the debt package will often consist of senior debt, provided by a single lender or syndicate of lenders that will participate in the senior debt, and mezzanine debt (which will be more expensive and only be repaid once the senior debt has been repaid), provided by a different lender or lenders.

The attraction of borrowing for UK tax resident corporate borrowers is that they may be entitled to tax relief on any loan interest paid. Further, even if the buyer has sufficient cash to purchase the property without recourse to borrowing, the return it will get from investing the cash may be higher than the rate of interest it will pay on a loan. It is not uncommon for commercial property to be acquired by a new company, a single (or special) purpose vehicle (SPV), incorporated offshore. There may be tax benefits to proceeding in this manner.

The remainder of this chapter will concentrate on debt finance, as this is probably the method you will encounter most often in practice.

2.2 DEBT FINANCE

2.2.1 Term sheet

A term sheet is a document that sets out the principal terms on which the lender is prepared to lend. It is produced following initial negotiations between the lender and the borrower, and is not usually intended to be legally binding as it is based on the limited information the lender has about the borrower and the property at this early stage. The term sheet will often be attached to a commitment letter or mandate letter that contains any terms which are intended to be legally binding at that stage, including provisions relating to payment of the lender's fees and expenses. Alternatively, it may be produced as a stand-alone document that clearly states that the parties do not intend the document to bind them legally, save in respect of the payment of fees and confidentiality.

Typically a term sheet will include brief details of the following:

(a) the borrower;
(b) the lender;

(c) the amount of the loan and the period during which the borrower can request release of the loan monies;

(d) any provisions relating to the release of the loan in stage payments, called tranches, which may be the case where the loan is to finance a development project;

(e) the purpose of the loan;

(f) the interest rate;

(g) the date for repayment of the loan in full and any repayment schedule;

(h) any provisions relating to repayment of the whole or part of the loan prior to the scheduled date for repayment (called prepayment);

(i) the security required for the loan;

(j) the conditions precedent that must be satisfied by the borrower prior to the loan being made;

(k) the representations and warranties that the borrower must make as to both its status and the property, many of which will be deemed repeated throughout the period of the loan;

(l) the undertakings and financial covenants to be given by the borrower, with which the borrower must comply throughout the period of the loan;

(m) the events which will constitute events of default under the loan agreement;

(n) the costs to be paid by the borrower.

If the loan is to be guaranteed, the identity of the guarantor will be included. If the loan is to be syndicated, the identity of the parties involved in the syndication will also be included, eg the arranging bank, facility agent and security trustee.

2.2.2 Due diligence

Prior to issuing the term sheet the lender will have undertaken a certain amount of due diligence in respect of the borrower and the property to assess the risk that the borrower will be unable to meet the payments due under the loan. Where the borrower is an SPV, the lender's only source of repayment will be the property and the projected income from the property, which will derive, generally, from an occupational lease or leases. Once the terms of the loan have been accepted by the borrower, by signing and returning either the commitment letter, or the term sheet itself if it has been produced as a stand-alone document, the next phase of the due diligence process can commence. The lender will undertake a more detailed analysis of the borrower, its constitution and powers if it is a corporate borrower, and of the property to be purchased. At this stage the lender will also instruct its solicitors to prepare a first draft of the loan agreement, sometimes referred to as the facility agreement or credit agreement.

2.2.3 Loan agreement

The term sheet and any commitment letter are the starting point for negotiation of the loan agreement. It is not uncommon for the term sheet to use generic language such as 'The Loan Agreement will contain the usual conditions precedent applicable to this type of facility'. The loan agreement will incorporate the provisions outlined in the term sheet, but the brief outline of conditions precedent, representations and warranties, undertakings and financial covenants will become detailed provisions. The precise nature and number of these clauses will depend upon the nature of the borrower and its business, and the extent of any issues identified during the continuing due diligence process.

The borrower needs to consider the provisions in the loan agreement carefully, as it needs to be satisfied that it can comply with the provisions in order to obtain the loan and, further, that any repeating representations and warranties and any undertakings and financial covenants are not drafted in such a way that they restrict the borrower's ability to run its business or may easily trigger a default on the part of the borrower.

Part of the due diligence process to be undertaken at this stage will be the investigation of title to the property. This will often result either in changes to the terms outlined in the term sheet, or in additional terms.

For example, a satisfactory valuation of the property will generally be a condition precedent that must be satisfied prior to the release of the funds. The lender will have proposed a loan-to-value ratio when negotiating the terms of the loan. If the property is valued at less than anticipated, this can affect the proposed loan. Generally, the property is the principal security for the lender. The lender will need to be satisfied that a sale of the property by the lender as mortgagee, in the event of a default by the borrower, will achieve sufficient funds to repay the loan, any accrued interest, and the legal costs and charges incurred by the lender in recovering the loan. The loan-to-value ratio is intended to ensure that there is a margin by which the value of the property exceeds the amount of the loan. The margin should be sufficient to cover accrued interest, etc and to alleviate the possibility of the lender suffering a shortfall in recovering the loan either due to a decline in property values generally, or due to the property simply being sold for less than anticipated. In order to meet the loan-to-value ratio a lower valuation will result in a reduction in the amount the lender is willing to lend.

In addition to being concerned with the valuation of the property, the lender will also wish to be satisfied that the property has good and marketable title. As mentioned above, on a default by the borrower the lender will wish to enforce its security to repay the loan, interest, costs and charges. If there are any defects in the title, this could cause a delay in the sale, thereby causing further interest to accrue, or enable a buyer to renegotiate the price. This increases the risk of the lender suffering a shortfall. For example, if investigation of title reveals a subsisting breach of covenant, the lender may require restrictive covenant indemnity insurance to be put in place prior to the release of funds. This would be added as a further condition precedent.

The loan agreement will also include the detail of provisions such as events of default. If a borrower breaches a term of the loan agreement, the lender will want the ability to terminate the loan and demand repayment of all outstanding principal and interest (known as 'acceleration'). The most common events of default are as follows:

(a) failure to pay any capital, interest, fees or expenses;
(b) breach of any representation or warranty, undertaking or covenant in the loan agreement or the security documents;
(c) the insolvency of the borrower;
(d) the borrower becoming involved in any litigation or similar proceedings;
(e) it becomes unlawful for the borrower to continue to perform its obligations under the loan agreement;
(f) a material adverse change in the borrower's position or circumstances;
(g) cross-default if the borrower defaults under another contract, eg another loan agreement in favour of this or any other lender.

Each of the above may be an indication that the borrower is, or may soon be, in some financial difficulty and unable to comply with its obligations under the loan agreement. Once an event of default has occurred, depending on the seriousness of the breach, the lender may decide to accelerate the loan. Alternatively, if the breach is minor or technical in nature, the lender may permit the loan to continue but may take this opportunity to renegotiate the terms of the loan, for example increasing the interest rate to compensate the lender for any increased risk the lender perceives in continuing.

2.2.4 Security

2.2.4.1 Need for security

It may be the case that the loan will be unsecured. This is likely to be the case only where the borrower is in a very strong financial position. An example would be a developer, with a national reputation, building a housing estate, financed by lenders with whom it had an established relationship. In the majority of other cases, however, the loan agreement will provide that prior to the release of any funds, the security specified in the loan agreement must be in place. A loan agreement relating to the acquisition or re-financing of commercial property will generally require the following:

(a) a charge by way of legal mortgage over the property. The lender has the same protection, powers and remedies as if it had a 3,000-year lease (or for a leasehold property a term of one day less than the lease). Any fixtures affixed to the property may be included in this security automatically;

(b) a fixed charge over any plant and machinery that is not affixed to the property;

(c) an assignment of any rental income generated by the property;

(d) a floating charge over all the assets and undertaking of any corporate borrower as a catch-all to cover anything not specifically charged by the security listed above and incorporating a negative pledge. The importance of a negative pledge is discussed at **2.2.4.2**.

Clearly, the borrower will not be in a position to complete the security prior to acquisition of the property, and cannot complete the acquisition of the property without the release of funds. In a commercial property transaction it is likely that the lender and borrower will be separately represented. The solicitors acting for the lender will expect to have the security executed, but undated, and in their possession prior to the release of funds. The security will then be completed immediately following completion of the acquisition.

2.2.4.2 Perfection of security

It is essential that any steps required to perfect the security are taken to ensure that the security is valid against third parties and to achieve priority over other security interests.

Since 6 April 2013, all charges created by a UK company are registrable at Companies House (unless they fall into one of the exceptions) (Companies Act 2006, s 859A). 'Charges' includes a charge by way of legal mortgage over land. Registration of a charge is made using Form MR01. Form MR01 must be sent to the Registrar of Companies, together with a certified copy of the charge and the relevant fee, within 21 days beginning with the day after the date of creation of the charge.

If the security is not registered at Companies House it will be void against any administrator, liquidator and creditors of the borrower, and the debt it secures becomes immediately repayable.

Priority between floating charges is governed by their date of creation if properly registered. However, a charge by way of legal mortgage and a fixed charge will rank in priority to a floating charge. It is for this reason that most lenders will stipulate that a floating charge in the lender's favour must contain a negative pledge on the part of the borrower not to grant any further security. If the borrower then acts in breach of the negative pledge, this will be an event of default enabling the lender to accelerate the loan. Although a negative pledge acts as a constraint on the borrower in terms of granting further security, the negative pledge does not amount to a security interest and so is not binding on the subsequent lender. Any new mortgage or charge would be effective security as between the borrower and the subsequent lender. Any such security will have priority over the floating charge, unless the subsequent lender has notice of the negative pledge at the time it takes its security. In this case, priority is reversed and the subsequent lender's new security, although valid, will rank behind the floating charge. In addition, it is arguable that the subsequent lender may be subject to an action for the tort of interfering with contractual relations and should hold any new security on trust for the original lender. Since 6 April 2013, details of any negative pledge must be given on Form MR01, and therefore a subsequent lender who searches the register will have actual notice of the negative pledge and be bound by it.

Once registration of the security at Companies House has been completed, any charge by way of legal mortgage must be registered at Land Registry. If the transaction involves an acquisition of land, registered or unregistered, the application for registration of the borrower's title, either as a dealing with registered land or as a first registration, will also include an application to register the charge. If the transaction involves a re-finance of existing borrowing secured on a registered property, an application will be made to register the discharge of any existing security and register the new charge. If the transaction involves the re-finance of unregistered land, completion of the charge will trigger first registration of the land.

Where the transaction involves registered land, the application for registration of the dealing must be made on the appropriate application form, accompanied by the correct documentation and fee, and must be received by Land Registry within the priority period afforded by the land registry search made prior to completion of the transaction.

Where the application is for first registration of title, this must be made within two months of the transaction that induces first registration.

Priority of charges relating to registered land is generally governed by the date of registration. First registered in time will rank ahead of charges subsequently registered, irrespective of the date of creation. The order of priority can be altered by the lenders entering into a contractual arrangement, called a deed of priority or intercreditor agreement, and applying to have this noted on the register.

It is common for the lender to require registration of a restriction on the title at Land Registry providing that no disposition of the property will be registered without a written consent signed by the lender. This restriction prevents the borrower creating a further charge in favour of a subsequent lender without the consent of the original lender. The original lender will have first-ranking security and, on a sale by a mortgagee, the sale proceeds will first be applied in discharging the original loan. Nevertheless, the lender may prefer that the borrower does not create a subsequent charge. The reason for this is that on completion of a subsequent charge, the lender will lose a degree of control in respect of the property. A subsequent lender may seek to exercise its power of sale on a default by the borrower under the subsequent loan (or on a cross-default), whereas the original lender may not wish to take this step but to give the borrower time. Further, once notice of a subsequent charge has been given, the original lender can make further advances with first-ranking security only if the steps detailed at **2.2.4.3** have been taken.

2.2.4.3 Further advances

Where the loan relates to the acquisition or re-finance of an existing commercial property or a development site, the loan agreement will generally provide for the loan to be released by the lender in one sum, on request, once all conditions precedent have been satisfied.

Where the loan relates to a development project, however, the loan agreement may provide for the loan to be released in tranches, as the development progresses. The loan agreement will usually specify that an independent monitoring surveyor's or project monitor's certificate, certifying that the development has reached a certain stage, must be produced to the lender prior to the release of the next tranche required to finance the next stage of the development.

The charge by way of legal mortgage will secure the whole loan. However, it is necessary to protect the first-ranking security of the further tranches which will be classed as further advances.

If the property is registered, an application can be made to Land Registry to note the lender's obligation to make further advances, ie release the further tranches. Alternatively, the parties may agree that the original charge secures a maximum amount, and an application can be made to Land Registry to note this on the register. Registration of the obligation or the agreement preserves the priority of the original charge. It puts any subsequent lender on notice that there may be further advances to be released pursuant to the original charge, and those further monies will, on default by the borrower, be repaid to the original lender, together with the original loan, prior to any monies due to the subsequent lender.

If the property is unregistered, any further advance by the original lender will rank ahead of any monies secured by a subsequent charge if the original lender has no notice of the subsequent charge at the time of the further advance or the original charge imposes an obligation to make further advances, in which case the further advances have priority, whether or not the original lender has notice of the subsequent charge.

REVIEW ACTIVITY

Scenario

Ross Developments (Spice Quay) Limited ('Ross') has negotiated the purchase of a former warehouse building (Unit 3) in Spice Quay, an area adjacent to Canary Wharf, for a sum of £10,000,000. Unit 3 was constructed in 1925, and was used for the storage of spices and fruits until 2020. It has been empty since that date. Ross intends to convert the warehouse into offices, adding a large glass and steel extension in the process, and is in discussion with an institutional investor, which has expressed an interest in buying the property once it has been fully developed and let.

Ross is financing the acquisition and development with a loan from Western Bank plc ('Western'), and has received a commitment letter and term sheet confirming a proposed loan of £7,000,000 towards the acquisition of Unit 3 and a further £7,000,000 towards the development costs, to be released in tranches of no less than £500,000 against monitoring surveyor's certificates certifying completion of certain stages of the development. The term sheet contains only brief details of the agreed terms.

Western has instructed your firm to act on its behalf in connection with the preparation and perfection of its security. Ross is separately represented.

You have received a copy of the valuation report in respect of Unit 3. The surveyor has noted:

(a) The rear wall of the building is bowing, and there are some diagonal cracks running between the windows on the first and second floors. It is not clear whether these cracks relate to settlement that took place many years ago, or whether any movement is recent.

The solicitors acting for Ross have investigated title to the property and have reported the following issues to you:

(b) The sellers are currently in dispute with the owners of an adjoining property (Unit 4) regarding a right of way over Unit 3 to access Unit 4 (which is also in the course of development). The right of way runs over the proposed site of the extension to Unit 3.

(c) Three years ago Unit 3 and the surrounding area suffered severe flooding.

Question

Western and Ross are negotiating the provisions of the loan agreement. Western is keen to proceed with the loan, but does not want to release the loan if there are any risks in doing so. Explain the risks to Western and, in the light of the issues arising from the valuation and investigation of title, suggest provisions to be included in the loan agreement that will give Western the protection it needs.

Answers to this Review activity may be found in Appendix 1.

CHAPTER 3

MATTERS OF CONTRACT

3.1	The contract of sale	19
3.2	Different types of contract	20
3.3	Overage	25
3.4	Future developments	27
	Review activity	28

3.1 THE CONTRACT OF SALE

As in residential conveyancing, it is the seller's solicitor who will draft the contract of sale for the purchase of a commercial property for submission to the buyer's solicitor for approval. The seller's solicitor will probably use a form of contract incorporating the Standard Commercial Property Conditions (SCPCs), and will draft the contract adopting the same drafting principles applicable in residential conveyancing. Further, on the sale of a green field site, where the seller's main interest is in the receipt of money and the buyer's in obtaining vacant possession, the solicitor will include clauses similar to those used in residential conveyancing. It is only where matters are complicated (eg by the need to obtain planning permission before completion) that drafting techniques will differ from residential conveyancing.

The following points are particularly relevant to the sale of a commercial property:

(a) The seller is likely to insist upon the payment of a full 10% deposit on exchange of contracts and is unlikely to agree to accept a reduced deposit. The buyer, being in business, should be able to pay the usual contractual deposit, but it is likely to insist that the deposit is to be held by the seller's solicitor as stakeholder, and it may insist that the interest on the deposit (which may itself amount to a sizeable sum) is to be paid to the buyer at completion. However, some larger organisations will be able to agree a reduced deposit, or even to dispense with the payment of a deposit altogether, on the basis that the size and reputation of the organisation is a sufficient guarantee that completion will take place.

(b) It will be very important to the commercial buyer of a development site to ensure that the contract provides for vacant possession of the whole of the site at completion so that the buyer's development plans are not frustrated.

(c) Value added tax (VAT) must be dealt with clearly in the agreement. The danger for the buyer is that if the contract is silent as to VAT, and after exchange of contracts the seller (being a person registered for VAT) elects to charge VAT on the purchase price, the buyer will have to add VAT to the purchase price. A buyer that has difficulty recovering the VAT it pays may want to ensure that the contract contains an express warranty by the seller that it has not, before exchange, elected to charge VAT on the purchase price, and that it will not do so thereafter, or that the purchase price is paid inclusive of VAT. In any case, the buyer will want to make enquiries of the seller to ascertain its intentions regarding VAT on the purchase price. VAT on property is dealt with more fully at **11.1**.

(d) The seller, having entered into a bargain with a chosen buyer, will usually want to deal with the chosen buyer alone and will, therefore, want to ensure there is a clause in the contract that prevents the buyer from assigning the benefit of the contract to a third party. Further, the seller will often attempt to prevent the buyer from entering into a sub-sale of the property, by stipulating that the seller cannot be required by the buyer to execute a transfer of the property to anyone other than the buyer. (This last clause does not prevent a sub-sale but makes it less attractive to the buyers, since SDLT will be payable both on the transfer to the buyer and on the buyer's transfer to the sub-buyer.)

(e) Frequently, the seller will deal with the possibility of the buyer becoming bankrupt, or going into liquidation or becoming subject to other insolvency proceedings before completion of the sale, by giving itself the right to rescind the contract upon any such event. This frees the seller to arrange a sale to another buyer without the delay of having to await completion and the expiry of a notice to complete.

(f) If the buyer has agreed to pay all or part of the seller's legal and other expenses in connection with the sale, the contract should so provide.

(g) Express provision should be made, where appropriate, for the grant and reservation of easements and the imposition of covenants. If the seller is retaining some adjoining or neighbouring land, it will be anxious to retain some control over the future development of the property.

(h) Where the property already has the benefit of planning permission obtained by the seller, the benefit of that permission will automatically pass to the buyer, since planning permission enures for the benefit of the land concerned (unless it states otherwise). The buyer will no doubt want to develop in accordance with the plans and specifications upon which the application for permission was based, but copyright in those plans and specifications will be retained by the architect who drew them up in the first place. The buyer should therefore ensure that the contract provides for the seller to assign to it, or procure the grant to it of, of a valid licence to use the plans and specifications.

(i) If the land is sold without the benefit of planning permission, the seller may wish to make provision for the payment of 'overage' should planning permission for development be granted in the future. Where land is sold without planning permission for development, the price would have been fixed on the basis of its current use, eg agricultural. If planning permission for development is granted, its value will increase considerably. The seller may wish to share in that increase, and so the contract may provide for the buyer to make an additional payment (the overage payment) should planning permission be granted (see **3.3.3**).

3.2 DIFFERENT TYPES OF CONTRACT

Sometimes the sale will be by simple private treaty; sometimes it will be by way of auction or tender; and sometimes the nature of the transaction may justify a departure altogether from the straightforward kind of sale and purchase contract. There are many types of commercial contracts that can be entered into by a seller and buyer of a commercial site, catering for widely different circumstances, and the agreement between the seller and buyer will need to reflect the bargain they have struck. This section of this chapter considers the four most common alternative forms of agreement: conditional agreements, call options, put options and pre-emption agreements.

3.2.1 Conditional agreements

There will be occasions when one of the parties to the contract will be either unable, or unwilling, immediately to enter into an unconditional agreement for the sale or purchase of the property, and so arrangements may be made to effect a conditional exchange of contracts. The seller is usually reluctant to agree to a conditional exchange, since what the seller ordinarily seeks is the security of knowing that its buyer is firmly committed to paying over money on a specified date for completion.

A conditional contract rarely serves a useful purpose for the seller. It is normally the buyer who suggests a conditional exchange of contracts, in a situation where the buyer is anxious to avoid losing the property to another buyer but is not yet in a position to commit itself irrevocably to the purchase.

3.2.1.1 Types of conditional agreements

A conditional agreement may be useful in the following situations:

(a) where planning permission for development of the site has not yet been obtained;

(b) where the results of the buyer's local search and enquiries of the local authority have not yet been received;

(c) where vacant possession of the site is not yet available owing to the existence of a tenancy agreement in respect of all or part of the site, which the buyer requires to be terminated;

(d) where the property is leasehold, and the consent of the landlord is required but has not yet been obtained for the proposed assignment to the buyer (see also SCPC 11.3), or for alterations to the property, or for a change in the use of the property proposed by the buyer.

Great care must be taken to distinguish between a contract that contains a condition precedent to the formation of the contract itself (in which case no contract exists unless and until the condition is performed), and a contract that contains a condition precedent to the performance of certain specified obligations (in which case a binding contract is immediately created, but if the condition is not fulfilled the specified obligations, typically the obligations to complete the sale and purchase, never come into effect). In drafting the contract, the seller's solicitor should make it expressly clear which type of agreement is intended. If the former type of contract is used then, despite the fact that the parties have entered into a written agreement, effectively they will still be in the same position as if negotiations were continuing since, until the condition has been satisfied, no binding contract exists and either party is free to back out. The condition must be fulfilled before any part of the contract comes into effect. If the latter type of contract is used (and in order to obtain a degree of certainty and commitment, both of the parties are likely to favour this type), a binding contract immediately comes into effect so that neither party can back out without the other's consent while the condition still remains to be performed, and the parties must comply with any obligations they have taken on to work toward fulfilment of the condition. If the condition is not ultimately fulfilled, the contract terminates, unless the party for whose sole benefit the condition was inserted waives the benefit of the condition and elects to proceed.

3.2.1.2 The condition

Certainty is required with conditional agreements. If the court cannot judge with certainty whether the conditionality of the contract has been removed, the court will reluctantly declare the entire contract void. Hence, in *Lee-Parker and Another v Izzet and Others (No 2)* [1972] 2 All ER 800, a contract that was stated to be conditional upon the buyer obtaining a satisfactory mortgage was held to be void, since the concept of a satisfactory mortgage was too vague and indefinite. By way of contrast, in *Janmohamed v Hassam* (1976) 241 EG 609, a contract that was conditional upon the receipt of a mortgage offer satisfactory to the buyer was held to be valid, since the court was prepared to imply an obligation upon the buyer to act reasonably in deciding whether the mortgage offer was satisfactory to him.

In drafting the conditional clause, the seller's solicitor should clearly set out what is required to be done, by whom, and by when, in order for the contract to become unconditional. Consider the following situations by way of example:

(a) If the buyer has not yet received the results of its local search and replies to enquiries of the local authority, the contract can be made conditional upon the buyer receiving what it considers to be satisfactory results and replies, by a stipulated date. The contract should contain an obligation upon the buyer to submit the correct forms to the local authority and to pay the fees (in case it has not already done so). Upon receipt of the search certificate and replies, the buyer should be obliged to notify the seller of receipt, indicating one of three things:

(i) that the buyer considers the results and replies to be satisfactory, in which case the contract proceeds to completion; or

(ii) that the buyer considers them to be unsatisfactory, in which case the contract becomes unenforceable, and the contract should provide for the return of the deposit to the buyer and of the evidence of title to the seller; or

(iii) that the buyer is prepared to waive the benefit of the condition.

Such a contract is heavily weighted in favour of the buyer, since it is up to it to determine whether or not the condition has been satisfied. A more neutral and objectively based conditional clause could make the contract conditional upon the receipt by the buyer of a set of results and replies to the local search and enquiries which disclose no adverse matters of a kind that would materially affect the value or beneficial use or occupation of the property by the buyer. This type of clause may not be favoured by the buyer since it leaves scope for argument.

(b) If the buyer is not prepared to complete without the benefit of planning permission for the type of development it proposes to carry out on the property, the contract could be made conditional upon the receipt of an 'acceptable' planning permission by a stipulated date. Again, the buyer should be obliged by the contract to submit a valid planning application without delay, to serve the correct statutory notices, and to pay the fees for the application. Consideration ought to be given as to whether provision should be made so that, upon refusal of permission (which ordinarily would render the contract unenforceable), the buyer may be allowed or, perhaps, obliged to pursue an appeal.

Particular consideration must be given to the definition of an 'acceptable' planning permission. It ought to be one that is granted pursuant to an application, precise details of which are set out in the contract and which is subject only to the usual planning conditions imposed by statute (eg conditions imposing time limits for the commencement of development), or which relate simply to the materials to be used or the provision of works of landscaping, or which are conditions which the buyer should reasonably accept. If this clause appears to be too objectively based for a developer's liking, it can be given control over the conditionality of the contract (in the same way as above) by having a clause that allows it to accept or reject the suitability of the permission, or to waive the benefit of the clause.

3.2.1.3 Time for performance

The condition must be satisfied either by a stipulated date, or, if none is stated, by the contractual completion date or, if neither, within a reasonable time. It is good practice to stipulate in the contract a long-stop date by which the condition must be satisfied. The contract can then provide that if the condition is fulfilled by that date, completion is to take place within 14 or 21 days of the contract becoming unconditional. The contract should be drafted to oblige one party to notify the other that the contract has become unconditional (eg if the buyer receives the outstanding local search then, unless the seller is notified, the seller will not know that the contract has become unconditional and that a completion date has been triggered).

If fulfilment of the condition depends upon action by one of the parties (eg the submission of a local search, or the making of an application for planning permission by the buyer), that party should not be able to rely upon its own inaction to argue that the contract has become unenforceable due to the non-fulfilment of the condition. To avoid this situation arising, the contract should place a contractual obligation upon the party of whom action is required to act diligently/with all reasonable speed and best/reasonable endeavours, and to pay the costs of the action required (eg search fees, planning application fees). However, in *Jolley v Carmel*

[2000] 43 EG 185, the Court of Appeal was prepared to adopt a construction of a conditional contract that was commercially realistic and practical, and to imply terms into it to that end. In particular, terms were implied that the buyer would use reasonable efforts to obtain planning permission within a reasonable time. What was reasonable would depend upon the circumstances that actually existed and would not be judged by an objective test. It was also implied that the seller would do nothing to hinder the grant of the planning permission. It was held that the buyer would not be in breach of the implied term to obtain planning permission so long as any delay in obtaining the permission was attributable to causes beyond the buyer's control and so long as the buyer had not acted negligently or unreasonably.

3.2.2 Option agreements

3.2.2.1 Call options

The usual form of option agreement entered into with a landowner (referred to as a 'call' option) gives the buyer, as grantee of the option, the right within a specified time to serve notice upon the landowner requiring it to transfer the property either at an agreed price, or at the market value of the property at the time the option notice is served. Whilst a conditional agreement is useful to a buyer who is trying to commit a landowner to a sale of land at a time when the buyer is not able unconditionally to commit itself, call options have many more varying uses for the buyer, and are particularly useful for a developer buyer attempting to piece together a development site. Under a conditional contract, unless the contract is drafted in a manner that favours the buyer, the buyer is usually obliged to complete the purchase at the contract price once the condition has been fulfilled, even though in the meantime market conditions have caused it to rethink the development. With a call option, the buyer can exercise the option if it wants to, or it can let it lapse if market conditions are no longer in its favour. While this is clearly not ideal for the seller, call options are usually granted for a non-returnable option fee. So the buyer is purchasing the right to require the seller to sell, and is compensating the seller for the uncertainty as to whether the sale will actually proceed and the inconvenience of not being able to dispose of the property elsewhere in the meantime.

Once the call option has been entered into, the buyer acquires an immediate equitable interest in the land, which the buyer must protect by registration of a Class C(iv) land charge, in the case of unregistered land, or by a notice, in the case of registered land.

3.2.2.2 Put options

A 'put' option is a contract that enables a landowner to require the potential buyer to buy the property, subject to the terms of the contract as to price, time limits, etc. There is no obligation on the seller to sell. Again, the option is often granted in return for a non-returnable fee; but in the case of a put option, it will be the seller who pays the buyer to take the risk that it may be required to purchase the property. Put options, while offering maximum flexibility to landowners, confer little benefit on developers so are much less common than call options.

Put options do not create an interest in land and so cannot be protected by registration at Land Registry.

3.2.2.3 Uses of options

An option agreement may be useful in the following situations:

(a) Where planning permission for development proposed by the developer has not yet been applied for, the developer may consider securing a call option over the land before investing resources into making an application for permission. Once the application succeeds, the call option can be exercised by the developer. This is very similar to a conditional agreement, but with a call option, the developer may be able to delay the exercise of the option until it is prepared to part with its money and commence development, whereas under a conditional agreement, as soon as the condition has been satisfied, the developer will have to complete.

(b) Moreover, with a call option the developer can decide not to exercise the option at all if economic conditions are no longer right for the development.

(c) Where the land proposed as the site for development is sub-divided amongst landowners and there is no guarantee that all of them will sell, the developer can assemble the development site gradually, by acquiring call options over each parcel of land. Once the entire site is under call option, the developer can then apply for planning permission (it would not make financial sense to do so beforehand), and then once permission has been obtained, it could exercise each call option.

(d) Where a developer developing a site feels that there is some prospect of being able to expand the development at some future date, it may attempt to acquire a call option over adjacent land which can be exercised when the prospect becomes a reality.

A speculator may attempt to acquire call options over land where there is little immediate prospect of obtaining planning permission (eg because the land forms part of the green belt, or is land not allocated for any particular purpose in the local planning authority development plan). The speculator may either adopt a wait-and-see approach, in the hope that planning policy in the area changes, or (as is more likely to be the case) may invest time and resources in seeking to influence planning policy to get the land released for development purposes when the next draft development plan is being prepared. In this way, developers build up considerable land banks, to be drawn upon when conditions are right.

3.2.2.4 Terms of an option

An option will grant the one party the right to call for the property, or require the purchase of the property, by serving a written notice on the other within a specified period. Regardless of whether it is a put option or a call option, time limits are construed by the courts to be of the essence of the agreement. The option agreement should set out the correct method of serving the option notice, or alternatively incorporate the provisions of s 196 of the Law of Property Act 1925 (LPA 1925) into the agreement.

The option will usually be granted in consideration of an option fee, which can be nominal but is more likely to be a considerable sum, depending upon the development potential of the land. When the option is exercised, the agreement will usually require the land to be transferred to the buyer for a further consideration (a credit or discount sometimes being given for the option fee already paid) which may be fixed by the agreement at the outset, or may be determined at the time of the exercise of the option either by reference to the market value of the land at that time or by reference to the development value of the land as ascertained by a valuation formula set out in the agreement. It should be noted that both the option agreement and the subsequent transfer of the land are subject to SDLT. Further, because of the VAT implications of the transaction, the buyer should ensure that the agreement clearly states that any option fee it has to pay and the purchase price is inclusive of VAT. There may also be capital gains tax (CGT) implications for the landowner, since an option is treated as an asset for CGT purposes, separate from the land itself, which is disposed of in consideration of the option fee.

Provision should be made in the agreement for the deduction of title and the raising of requisitions on title after the option notice is served, and for the other usual conveyancing steps which need to be taken before completion. It is usual for the option agreement to incorporate a set of conditions of sale (eg, the SCPCs current at the time of the option agreement). In many cases, the developer will want title to be deduced before the option agreement is entered into (requisitions on title then being barred), and it will then require the seller to enter into a condition in the agreement not to incumber the land any further without the developer's consent.

3.2.3 Pre-emption agreements

A right of pre-emption, sometimes known as a right of 'first refusal', obliges a seller who wishes to sell its property within an agreed pre-emption period to offer it first to the developer. The pre-emption agreement will provide that if the landowner decides to sell the property, it must first serve a notice offering it to the developer. If the developer wishes to buy the property on the terms set out in the landowner's notice, it must serve an acceptance notice, whereupon a binding contract for sale will come into existence. If the developer does not serve an acceptance notice within the agreed timescale then the landowner is free to sell the property to a third party. The key point to note is that unlike a call option (see **3.2.2.1**), a right of pre-emption does not oblige the seller to sell the property to the developer, or indeed to sell it at all.

3.3 OVERAGE

> The University of Law would like to thank Practical Law for authorising the adaptation in this publication of the following section on 'Overage Payments' – see <http://uk.practicallaw.thomsonreuters.com/4-200-2514>. For further information about Practical Law, visit <http://uk.practicallaw.thomsonreuters.com/> or call 0345 600 9355. © Thomson Reuters 2025.

Many contracts for the sale of development land will include provisions for the possible payment by the buyer of 'overage'. Overage provisions are generally used where a seller wishes to share in any potential development value in a property that might be realised after completion of a sale. So, a seller is likely to require an overage payment from the buyer where there is a reasonable belief that value will be added when the land is redeveloped, or when permission for change of use is granted in the future, or when a proposed development produces more profit than expected due to a rise in sale prices or an increase in the number of units authorised by the planning consent. An overage obligation requires the buyer to make a further payment to the seller, representing a share of the increased market value of the property after the occurrence of an agreed event. The seller can therefore maximise its return from the sale by realising the current market value of the property immediately, without losing out on future increases in value by having sold the property before the full development potential is actually realised.

It is sometimes said that the existence of overage should not affect the initial sale price, but this is not always true. The insistence on overage provisions in a deal may well affect the initial purchase price that the buyer is willing to pay for the land. It will certainly involve more legal work, and the greater costs and potential delays associated with it. It will thus always be a question of judgement of the commercial issues involved as to whether the provision is justified.

3.3.1 'Positive' or 'negative' overage

Overage provisions are sometimes described as being either positive or negative in character.

'Positive overage' methods involve the seller extracting an express promise from the buyer to make a further payment if a particular specified event (such as redevelopment) should occur in the future. The way in which the payment will be calculated and the trigger event for payment must be carefully defined in advance.

'Negative overage' methods, however, occur when the seller imposes a restrictive covenant, or another mechanism such as retaining a ransom strip, that *prevents* a particular development or change of use from taking place. In such a case there is no need for a specific promise to pay overage, as the seller has control over the situation. The development cannot take place without the seller's consent, and the seller can then require payment of an additional sum in return for the release of the covenant or the sale of the ransom strip.

3.3.2 Drafting considerations

As overage provisions usually reflect complex arrangements, the parties and their solicitors must take particular care to ensure that the documentation reflects precisely what has been agreed. This is obvious, but the problem with overage is that this can be very difficult to achieve. It is not enough just to have an agreement in place which provides for the payment of overage; it is also necessary for the seller's solicitor to ensure that the payment will actually be made – to secure the payment of the amount due. So, as well as setting out how the overage payment is to be calculated and when it is to be payable, both parties' solicitors need to consider carefully all the various combinations of events which might happen over the period of the overage being potentially payable. This can be problematic given the difficulty in predicting future events and the state of the property market over what may be many years. Obviously, issues such as the possible liquidation or insolvency of the buyer must be considered. What if the liquidator then exercises the right to disclaim onerous contracts? How might all these events impact on the payment of the overage? And the more complex the provisions, the greater the risk that mistakes, oversights and omissions will occur.

In *Sparks v Biden* [2017] EWHC 1994 (Ch), the High Court was prepared to imply an obligation to sell into an agreement containing overage provisions as a matter of business efficacy, but the parties should not have to rely on the courts to do this. In *London and Ilford Ltd v Sovereign Property Holdings Ltd* [2018] EWCA Civ 1618, the Court of Appeal held that the developer must make the overage payment as the trigger event (prior approval for the development being granted under the Town and Country Planning (General Permitted Development) (England) Order 2015) had occurred, despite the fact that the development could not go ahead as it would have breached building regulations. The Court took the view that if the parties had intended the satisfaction of building regulations to be a requirement for the overage payment, they would have included this expressly in the drafting as both parties were experienced developers and had been professionally advised.

3.3.2.1 The trigger event

The first thing that will need to be agreed between the parties – and clearly stated in the contract – is precisely when the overage payment will become payable. This 'trigger' event for payment could be, for example:

(a) the grant of planning permission for specified development or change of use;
(b) the implementation of such planning permission;
(c) the practical completion of a development;
(d) the disposal of the property with the benefit of planning permission;
(e) the disposal of the completed development;
(f) the disposal of individual units (eg houses) at more than a stated price;
(g) the amount of profit on the completion of a development exceeding a stated amount.

Ideally, a seller would like the payment to be triggered when the increase in value actually occurs, eg on the grant of planning permission. Equally, a buyer would prefer to have to make the payment only when it has actually realised that increase in value, eg on the sale of the completed development. And often the buyer will wish to impose a time limit on the period during which it is at risk of having to pay overage – five years, 10 years or whatever.

3.3.2.2 The amount of the overage payment

Of equal importance to both seller and buyer is the amount of the payment to be made. This could be, for example:

(a) a percentage of the increase in value of the land;
(b) a percentage of the profit made on the development;

(c) a percentage of the profit made on the development if it exceeds a specified amount;

(d) a percentage of the sale price of units if that exceeds a specified amount.

The amount of negotiation that might be necessary before agreement is reached on precise figures in relation to any of these can well be imagined.

3.3.2.3 Securing the overage payment

It is the seller's solicitor's responsibility to ensure that adequate security is given to the seller to protect the future payment and ensure that it will be made if the appropriate trigger event occurs. Without adequate security, overage provisions may be virtually worthless. In *Akasuc Enterprise Ltd v Farmar & Shirreff* [2003] EWHC 1275 (Ch), the defendant firm failed to incorporate appropriate provisions in an agreement to protect an overage payment. As a result, the claimant lost an opportunity to obtain a further £250,000. The court considered that it was the firm's responsibility to ensure that the documentation contained an appropriate mechanism to secure the overage payment and that it had been negligent.

There are various ways in which overage obligations can be drafted and secured, and the most appropriate method should be chosen to suit the particular circumstances. The methods differ according to whether a negative or positive overage provision has been agreed. Normally, the seller will need recourse in some form or other against either the land itself or the buyer's successors in title. For example:

(a) a positive covenant by the buyer to make a further payment to the seller on the occurrence of a specified event, perhaps supported by a guarantee or bond from a third party, combined with a buyer's covenant to ensure that any successor in title will enter into a similar commitment to the seller;

(b) a legal charge over the property following completion, enabling the seller to sell the land and recover the overage from the sale proceeds if the overage payment is not made as agreed;

(c) a seller's lien over the property for unpaid purchase price, enabling the seller to apply to court for an order of sale if the overage payment is not made as agreed;

(d) a freehold right of re-entry, whereby the property reverts to the seller if the overage payment is not made as agreed;

(e) a restrictive covenant against building on the land or using it for specified purposes, which will be released by the seller only when the overage payment is made;

(f) the seller retains ownership of a piece of land (a 'ransom strip') so that the buyer cannot develop the land until the overage payment is made and the seller sells the ransom strip to the buyer or grants a right of way over it.

These methods are not exhaustive, and each has its own advantages and disadvantages which are outside the scope of this book. Further information on overage agreements may be obtained from the Practical Law Company at <http://uk.practicallaw.thomsonreuters.com/4-200-2514>.

3.4 FUTURE DEVELOPMENTS

In January 2024 the Government published a consultation ('Contractual controls on land') on a proposal to create a publicly available dataset that would show who holds conditional contracts, options, rights of pre-emption and promotion agreements over registered land, with a view to making it easier to establish the ownership of land available for development. (A promotion agreement allows a developer to promote the land through the planning process, obtain planning permission for the development and receive a fee once the land is sold whilst regulating how the proprietor of the land can dispose of it during the period of the agreement.) Under the proposal, the beneficiary of such a 'contractual control agreement' would have to supply details to HM Land Registry within 60 days of the contractual control agreement being entered into. Updated information would need to be provided within 60 days of an assignment of the contractual control agreement, any variation in writing to a contractual control agreement that altered any of the required information and the termination or expiry of the whole or any part of the contractual control agreement.

The proposed implementation date for the proposal was 6 April 2026, but the requirement to notify would apply to contractual control agreements entered into after 6 April 2021 and the requirement to provide updated information would also include contractual control agreements created before 6 April 2021.

The consultation closed on 20 March 2024.

REVIEW ACTIVITY

1. ABC Developments Ltd ('ABC') is interested in buying a plot of former agricultural land in Dorset that already has the benefit of planning permission for the conversion of three existing barns to light industrial units. However, given the current economic climate, ABC is unlikely to be able to obtain funding for the conversion on acceptable financial terms in the next couple of years. While ABC has been deliberating, the seller has become impatient and is threatening to sell the land to a rival developer.

   What type(s) of contract with the seller would you recommend to ABC in this situation?

2. You act for Mulcaster Borough Council ('MBC'), which is looking to dispose of some land that is surplus to requirements since the privatisation of the refuse collection service. Its preferred option is to sell the land to a local housing association, which would build much-needed social housing, but the housing association is constantly prevaricating whilst it waits to see if its funding will be renewed. In the meantime, a national house building chain has expressed an interest in buying the site for private residential development. MBC would like to give the housing association more time to make a decision, but cannot allow the situation to drag on indefinitely.

   What type(s) of contract with the housing association would you recommend to MBC in this situation?

Answers to this Review activity may be found in Appendix 1.

CHAPTER 4

Planning Control

4.1	The planning system	29
4.2	When is planning permission needed?	35
4.3	Planning permission	46
4.4	Application to the local planning authority	53
4.5	Appeals against adverse planning determinations	59
	Review activity	63

4.1 THE PLANNING SYSTEM

The town and country planning system is designed to ensure that land is used in a planned and appropriate manner. It was first introduced by the Town and Country Planning Act 1947. Prior to that, such controls had been imposed by local bye-laws and by private arrangements such as the use of restrictive covenants. The planning system is a creature of statute, and as such is governed by statute and detailed regulations, but planning policies at both the central and local government level, such as the policies in the local development plan, also play an extremely important part of the planning system. Accordingly, planning is governed by public law principles rather than private law.

The planning system has been in a state of flux for some years. Successive Governments have focused on planning as a means to bring forward economic growth and, in particular, housing that people can afford in the places where it is needed. There has been a focus on giving the 'power to plan' back to local communities, in part to help local communities accept housing development in their areas. The need to tackle the climate emergency is also driving change. The result has meant significant changes to the planning system, including the introduction of a raft of measures intended to remove uncertainty from, and to speed up, the planning process and to help increase housing supply. Significant changes to policy guidance and secondary legislation have been made since July 2018. The present Government has earmarked the planning system as needing reform and has said that the planning system requires modernisation so as to support economic growth. In particular, the Government has said that it wants to streamline and speed up the planning system so as to improve the delivery of infrastructure. In May 2022, the Levelling Up and Regeneration Bill, which proposes a number of widespread reforms to the planning system, was introduced into Parliament. The Levelling-up and Regeneration Act 2023 received Royal Assent on 26 October 2023. The new Labour Government published a draft revised version of the National Planning Policy Framework in July 2024 which, if adopted, will make significant changes, including the introduction of a new classification of 'Grey Belt'. The aim is to increase the delivery of housing, and affordable housing in particular.

This chapter will begin with an overview of the structure of the town and country planning system. It will then consider the key trigger of the system, namely that for certain kinds of development, planning permission is required before that development can take place. Next it will look at planning permission in its own right, including what types of planning permission can be obtained, what factors influence whether planning permission will be obtained (and subject to what conditions) and the effect of planning permission once obtained. The chapter will conclude by looking at how that permission, if needed, can be obtained either directly from the local planning authority (LPA) (or, in certain circumstances, the Secretary of State) or on appeal.

For the sake of brevity, the following abbreviations have been used:

MHCLG   Ministry of Housing, Communities and Local Government (formally the Department for Levelling Up, Housing and Communities)

SOS   Secretary of State for Housing, Communities and Local Government

DMPO   Town and Country Planning (Development Management Procedure) (England) Order 2015

GPDO   Town and Country Planning (General Permitted Development) (England) Order 2015

NPPF   National Planning Policy Framework

PPG   National Planning Practice Guidance

UCO   Town and Country Planning (Use Classes) Order 1987

Note that the MHCLG website (<www.gov.uk/government/organisations/ministry-of-housing-communities-local-government>) (a section within the Government's website, <www.gov.uk>) and the Planning Portal (<www.planningportal.co.uk>) are useful resources where many of the policy and other documents mentioned below can be found.

The NPPF and PPG are available online (<www.gov.uk/government/publications/national-planning-policy-framework--2> and <www.gov.uk/government/collections/planning-practice-guidance>).

4.1.1 Legislation

The principal Act is the Town and Country Planning Act 1990 (TCPA 1990). This has been substantially amended by the Planning and Compensation Act 1991 (PCA 1991), the Planning and Compulsory Purchase Act 2004 (PCPA 2004), the Planning Act 2008 (PA 2008), the Localism Act 2011 (LA 2011), the Growth and Infrastructure Act 2013 (GAIA 2013), the Enterprise and Regulatory Reform Act 2013 (ERRA 2013), the Infrastructure Act 2015 (IA 2015), the Housing and Planning Act 2016 (HPA 2016) and the Neighbourhood Planning Act 2017 (NPA 2017). All references in this and the following two chapters to 'the Act' are to the 1990 Act as amended, unless the contrary is stated. The Act sets out the main framework of the planning system. The majority of the detail (including procedural rules and regulations, prescribed forms and many more substantive matters) is provided by a vast body of delegated legislation.

4.1.2 Central and local government

4.1.2.1 The Ministry for Housing, Communities and Local Government

The Ministry for Housing, Communities and Local Government (MHCLG) (formally the Department for Levelling Up, Housing and Communities (DLUHC)) is the central government department with responsibility for town and country planning. It has three broad classes of function under the Act, namely legislative, administrative and quasi-judicial.

As regards legislative powers, the Act contains many powers for the SOS to make orders, rules and regulations, usually by statutory instrument. Examples include the UCO 1987, the DMPO 2015 and the GPDO 2015, all of which will be considered below.

The SOS's administrative powers include the dissemination of policy guidance that, until 2012, came through a variety of documents such as circulars, planning policy guidance and planning policy statements. With effect from 27 March 2012, the Government replaced many of these separate documents with a single National Planning Policy Framework (NPPF). This was revised and republished for the first time on 24 July 2018, and then again with minor clarifications on 19 February 2019. It was then updated on 19 June 2019. The NPPF was again revised on 20 July 2021. The Government indicated that a fuller review of the NPPF was needed to reflect the Government's proposals for wider planning reforms. A revised form of the NPPF was published in September 2023 and December 2023. It will be considered further below. Unless otherwise indicated, references to 'the NPPF' are to the December 2023 version. Note that the NPPF should be read as a whole, including its footnotes and annexes. A new consultation draft of the NPPF was published in July 2024 but has not yet been formally adopted. It should also be read alongside government planning policy for traveller sites and for waste.

The Government also published simplified planning guidance to replace the 6,000 or so pages of previous existing planning guidance. The national Planning Practice Guidance (PPG) was launched online on 6 March 2014 (see website link above) and is updated on an ongoing basis.

In terms of quasi-judicial functions, the SOS has powers to 'call in' a wide variety of matters for the SOS's own consideration (such as development plan documents and applications for planning permission). In a recent expansion to the jurisdiction, the GAIA 2013 now also permits applicants for prescribed types of development to make planning applications and certain other applications directly to the SOS with a view to development being brought forward more quickly. In cases where the relevant LPA has been designated by the SOS as not performing its function of determining applications adequately, the SOS will therefore take on the LPA's role (this originally only applied to major development, but from 26 October 2016 the rules were amended to include non-major development (HPA 2016)).

Lastly, as regards quasi-judicial powers, the SOS is the person to whom an appeal is made in the first instance against most decisions of a planning authority. In particular, appeals lie to the SOS in respect of a refusal of, or unsatisfactory conditions imposed on, a planning permission or the service of an enforcement notice by an LPA. Those appeals will be considered by an Inspector appointed by the SOS.

4.1.2.2 Local government

The LPA administers much of the planning system, preparing development plans, determining planning applications and carrying out enforcement where there has been a breach of planning control. Subject to any express provision to the contrary, all references in the Act to an LPA should be construed as a reference to both the county planning authority and district planning authority in which the development is located. The county council is the county planning authority, and the district council is the district planning authority. The county planning authority normally has exclusive jurisdiction over mineral planning, and development control and enforcement that relate to 'county matters'. 'County matters' are defined in Sch 1, para 1 to the Act, as being concerned with minerals and operational development falling partly within and partly outside a national park. The district planning authority has exclusive jurisdiction over development control (ie managing the extent and nature of growth in the local area) and enforcement that does not concern a county matter, and hazardous substances. Responsibility for the preparation of the development plan is considered below (see **4.1.3**).

Where unitary councils have been established (ie there is just one tier of local government), those councils will normally be the LPAs for all purposes.

Note that, since devolution, the Welsh Assembly has had responsibility for the overall planning system in Wales. Differences will increasingly arise when dealing with properties in Wales. In London, some town and country planning functions are undertaken by the Mayor.

4.1.3 'The development plan'

4.1.3.1 Meaning of 'development plan'

Historically, the development plan was made up of two documents: the 'structure plan' (normally prepared by the county planning authority, which detailed the broad, strategic development policy for the regional area); and the 'local plan' (prepared by the district planning authority, which contained more detailed policies for the specific area of that district). In the case of unitary authorities, the development plan was a single document, the unitary development plan, which covered both issues in one document.

The structure plan and local plan system was then gradually replaced by a system of regional strategies (prepared by Regional Development Agencies) and local development frameworks (LDFs) (prepared by the LPAs). There were detailed transitional provisions; pending adoption of an LDF, former local plans were allowed to continue in operation and are referred to as 'saved' plans. All regional strategies have now been revoked by the SOS pursuant to the power in s 109 of the LA 2011, but LDFs remain. The LDF is a portfolio of documents, including a core strategy and proposals map (essentially the replacement of the old 'local plan') but also documents covering ongoing monitoring of the implementation of the core strategy and other matters. The LDF must specify which documents are development plan documents.

In short, the statutory 'development plan' means the policies in any development plan document that has been adopted within an LDF and any 'saved' local plan policies, and any neighbourhood development plans (see below) that have been adopted. Paragraph 17 of the NPPF provides that the development plan must include strategic policies which can be contained either in joint or individual local plans, produced by local authorities working together or independently, and/or a 'spatial development strategy' produced by an elected Mayor or combined authority where plan-making powers have been conferred. Enquiry should be made on a case-by-case basis to determine the current position. The development plan is effectively given primacy in planning decisions by s 38(6) of the PCPA 2004: see **4.1.3.3**.

Policies in local plans and spatial development strategies should now be reviewed at least once every five years and updated as necessary (para 33 of the NPPF and reg 10A of the Town and Country Planning (Local Planning) (England) Regulations 2012 (SI 2012/767) (which came into force on 6 April 2018)).

See **4.1.2.2** regarding the planning system in Wales.

In the case of London, the Mayor's London Plan is the spatial development strategy which forms part of the local plan and therefore provides the planning framework for London Boroughs alongside each individual LPA's own LDF.

Neighbourhood development plans

The LA 2011 introduced new rights and powers for local communities to establish general planning policies for the development and use of land in a neighbourhood. These policies are called 'neighbourhood development plans', which must focus on enabling, not restricting, development. LPAs must set out their policies for assisting with neighbourhood planning in a statement of community involvement ('SCI').

The creation of neighbourhood development plans can be led by town and parish councils or 'neighbourhood forums', which are community groups designated to take forward neighbourhood planning in areas without parishes. Town and parish councils and neighbourhood forums are required to apply to the LPA to be designated a 'qualifying body' to produce a neighbourhood development plan. A neighbourhood development plan must also be approved, and adopted as soon as reasonably practicable by an LPA, if more than half those voting have voted in favour of adopting the plan at a referendum held for that purpose.

Neighbourhood development plans must have regard to national policy, be in general conformity with strategic policies in the adopted local plan for the area (and any other strategic policies that form part of the statutory development plan where relevant), and be compatible with EU obligations and human rights requirements. Once adopted, a neighbourhood development plan will become part of the development plan for the purposes of s 38(6) of the PCPA 2004, and its policies will take precedence over existing non-strategic policies in a local plan covering the neighbourhood area unless superseded by strategic or non-strategic policies adopted subsequently (para 30 of the NPPF).

The first neighbourhood plan was adopted by Eden District Council on 11 April 2013. There have been numerous neighbourhood plans adopted since, and these are an important planning consideration with statutory weight and as part of the wider development plan. They attract, therefore, the same legal status as a local plan once it has been approved and becomes part of the statutory development plan. Those areas with a neighbourhood plan in place receive a greater portion of CIL funding (see **Chapter 5**). There have been several cases involving the weight to be given to an emerging neighbourhood plan (eg *Woodcock Holdings v Secretary of State for Communities and Local Government* [2015] EWHC 1173 (Admin)). The NPA 2017 amended s 70 of the TCPA 1990 to provide that post-examination draft neighbourhood development plans are also material considerations to be taken into account by the LPA.

4.1.3.2 The NPPF

Although the NPPF does not form part of the development plan, it nevertheless has a significant role in both plan-making and planning decisions.

At the heart of the NPPF is a presumption in favour of sustainable development (see para 10 of the NPPF). The meaning of sustainable development is summarised in para 7 of the NPPF as meeting the needs of the present without compromising the ability of future generations to meet their own needs. Paragraph 7 of the NPPF makes clear that the purpose of the planning system is to contribute to the achievement of sustainable development. Paragraph 11 of the NPPF states that plans and decisions should apply the presumption in favour of sustainable development. Paragraph 11 sets out what this presumption means in each context. First, for plan-making, the presumption means that plans should promote a sustainable pattern of development that seeks to meet the development needs of the area; align growth and infrastructure; improve the environment; mitigate climate change (including by making effective use of land in urban areas) and adapt to its effects. The presumption also means that strategic policies should, as a minimum and subject to certain exceptions (set out in para 11(b) of the NPPF), provide for objectively assessed needs for housing and other uses, as well as any needs that cannot be met within neighbouring areas. Second, for decision-taking, the presumption in favour of sustainable development means approving development proposals that accord with an up-to-date development plan without delay; or, where there are no relevant development plan policies, or the policies which are most important for determining the application are out of date, granting permission unless certain exceptions apply (as set out in para 11(d) of the NPPF). For both plan-making and decision-taking, exceptions to the presumption include where there are adverse impacts which demonstrably outweigh the benefits of the proposal, when assessed against the policies in the NPPF taken as a whole.

The NPPF does not affect the statutory duty in s 38(6) of the PCPA 2004 for LPAs to determine planning applications in accordance with the development plan unless material considerations indicate otherwise. However, the policies contained in the NPPF must be taken into account as material considerations in planning decisions. Local plans and spatial development strategies must also be assessed against the NPPF and other statements of national planning policy while they are being prepared and examined for adoption. Paragraph 219 of the NPPF provides guidance regarding the weight that should be given to local plan policies which were prepared and published under previous versions of the NPPF:

> ... existing policies should not be considered out-of-date simply because they were adopted or made prior to the publication of this Framework. Due weight should be given to them, according to their degree of consistency with this Framework (the closer the policies in the plan to the policies in the Framework, the greater the weight that may be given).

The role of s 38(6), and the weight to be given to development plan policies in decision-making, has been the subject of a number of cases. These cases have confirmed that primacy must be given to development plan policies when determining planning applications, albeit the NPPF is capable of being a material consideration that can outweigh policies in the local development plan. (See *Sea & Land Power & Energy v Secretary of State for Communities and Local Government* [2012] EWHC 1419 (Admin), *South Northamptonshire Council & Ward v Secretary of State for Communities and Local Government* [2013] EWHC 11 (Admin), *Colman v Secretary of State for Communities and Local Government and RWE Npower* [2013] EWHC 1138 (Admin), *Bayliss v Secretary of State for Communities and Local Government* [2013] EWHC 1612 (Admin), *R (on the application of Hampton Bishop PC) v Herefordshire Council* [2014] EWCA Civ 878 and *Hopkins Homes Ltd v Secretary of State for Communities and Local Government* [2017] UKSC 37.) The weight to be given to conflict or compliance with the policies of the NPPF is a matter for decision makers, and the court will not interfere except on established public law grounds (*St Mowden Developments v Secretary of State for Communities and Local Government* [2017] EWCA Civ 1643). The NPPF does not stipulate how much weight should be given to 'out of date' policies; this is also a matter for the decision maker (*Crane v Secretary of State for Communities and Local Government* [2015] EWHC 425 (Admin)).

It is settled law that the interpretation of planning policy is a question of law and not, therefore, a matter of planning judgment for the LPA (see *Tesco Stores Ltd v Dundee City Council* [2012] UKSC 13, [35]). Where there is a dispute, it will be 'for the court to determine as a matter of law what the words were capable of meaning' (*Tesco* at [15]). The test is that 'policy statements should be interpreted objectively in accordance with the language used, read as always in its proper context' (see *Tesco* at [18]).

Moreover, while the interpretation of policy is a task for the court, the application of that policy is for the decision maker and is a matter of planning judgment and may only be challenged on public law grounds (*East Staffordshire Borough Council v Secretary of State for Communities and Local Government* [2017] EWCA Civ 893).

4.1.3.3 The importance of the development plan

The development plan sits at the heart of the town and country planning system. The Town and Country Planning (Local Planning) (England) Regulations 2012 set out the requirements for plan making. The special weight attributed to the development plan derives from the fact that it has been subjected to a lengthy statutory procedure for adoption; it is publicised for consultation so that representations from the public and interested parties can be made, submitted to the MHCLG, independently examined by an inspector appointed by the SOS at a public hearing, considered in an inspector's report, and finally adopted after a review of any modifications proposed by the inspector. When applying for planning permission (and in other instances, such as the service of an enforcement notice – see **6.7**), it is the development plan that is the main document for determining the outcome of the application or any appeal against an enforcement notice. The development plan aims to ensure that land is used in a planned and appropriate fashion by setting out a framework of policies to govern the future development of a given area. Development plans seek to address needs and opportunities in relation to housing, the economy, community facilities and infrastructure, and to provide a basis for conserving and enhancing the natural and historic environment, mitigating and adapting to climate change, and achieving well designed places. By s 38(6) of the PCPA 2004:

> If regard is to be had to the development plan for the purpose of any determination to be made under the planning Acts the determination must be made in accordance with the plan unless material considerations indicate otherwise.

Policy guidance on the importance of the development plan, reflecting the statutory requirements, can be found at para 12 of the NPPF, which states that:

> ... Where a planning application conflicts with an up-to-date development plan (including any neighbourhood plans that form part of the development plan), permission should not usually be granted. Local planning authorities may take decisions that depart from an up-to-date development plan, but only if material considerations in a particular case indicate that the plan should not be followed.

Developers therefore will need to look very carefully at the development plan as a starting point to see if it contains any policy on the development proposed; if it does so and the proposal is not in accordance with the plan, any planning application is unlikely to succeed unless material considerations indicate that the plan should not be followed.

The development plan is not the sole factor, however (despite its pre-eminent position): any local finance considerations, so far as material to the application, and any other material considerations must also be taken into account including, crucially, the NPPF. Material considerations can indicate that the development plan, even where it is up to date, should not be followed such that planning permission can be granted for developments which conflict with the development plan. Material considerations will be considered further at **4.3.2** below.

4.2 WHEN IS PLANNING PERMISSION NEEDED?

The basic rule is to be found in s 57(1) of the Act, which states that planning permission is required for the carrying out of any 'development' of land. The term 'development' is defined in s 55(1) as

> the carrying out of building, engineering, mining or other operations in, on, over or under land, or the making of any material change in the use of any buildings or other land.

The term 'development' is considered to have two limbs, the first being the carrying out of operations and, the second, the making of a material change of use. Depending on the type of development proposed, a planning application may seek authorisation for one or both of these types of development.

It is possible to apply to the LPA for certification that any current or proposed use or operation is lawful and therefore does not require an application for planning permission. This is considered at **6.3**. Also considered below are the exclusions from the definition of development in s 55(2) of the Act (**4.2.2.1**) and matters for which permission is automatically granted, such as permitted development rights under the UCO (**4.2.3**) or the GPDO.

4.2.1 Operations

4.2.1.1 Operational development

Operational development is defined in ss 55(1A) and 336(1) of the Act. 'Building operations' include rebuilding, structural alterations of or additions to buildings, and other operations normally undertaken by a person carrying on business as a builder. 'Engineering operations' include the formation or laying out of means of access to highways. 'Mining operations' and 'other operations' are not defined in the Act but relate to physical changes to the land and/or buildings on which they are to be carried out. The demolition of buildings can fall within the definition of operational development and will be considered separately at **4.2.1.2**.

Works for the maintenance, improvement or other alteration of a building which affect only the interior of the building, or which do not materially affect its external appearance, and which do not provide additional space underground do not constitute development (s 55(2)(a)). However, increasing retail floor space by internal works (eg the construction of a mezzanine floor) will require planning permission in England if the increase is more than 200m2, and the building is used for the retail sale of goods other than hot food.

4.2.1.2 Demolition

Demolition falls within the definition of operational development (s 55(1A)). However, as a result of some complicated provisions elsewhere in the planning legislation, much demolition will not require a grant of planning permission.

First, under s 55(2)(g), the SOS has the power to identify works of demolition which can be excepted from operational development. Pursuant to this power, the Town and Country Planning (Demolition – Descriptions of Buildings) Direction 2021 excepts the demolitions of:

(a) any building the cubic content of which, measured externally, does not exceed 50 cubic metres; and

(b) the whole or any part of any gate, fence, wall or other means of enclosure (where not in a conservation area),

unless the building described by (a) or (b) is a statue, monument or memorial.

Secondly, Class B of Part 11 of Sch 2 to the GPDO grants a very wide permitted development right to carry out 'any building operation consisting of demolition' without the need for a grant of planning permission. This extensive right is, however, qualified in a number of respects and does not include the demolition of drinking establishments, buildings rendered unsafe by the action or inaction of an owner, the demolition of unlisted buildings in a conservation area, and the demolition of statues, memorials or monuments in place for a period of at least 10 years (save in certain excepted circumstances, such as statues within the grounds of museums or art galleries). Where the permitted development right applies, the carrying out of the demolition operation will normally be subject to conditions as imposed by para B2 of Class B of Part 11 of Sch 2 to the GPDO, which generally require the prior approval of the LPA to the method of demolition and the carrying out of the operation in accordance with that prior approval within five years. The prior approval requirement does not apply in cases where demolition is required in order to undertake development which has been granted planning permission on an application.

It should be noted that the right under Class B cannot apply if the demolition is required in order to undertake development for which an EIA is required (art 3(10) of the GPDO). In that case an application for planning permission must be made.

Note that also, as regards demolition of listed buildings and scheduled monuments, whatever the requirement for planning permission, consents under the separate legislation dealing with the historic environment will also be needed, eg listed buildings consent under the Town and Country Planning (Listed Buildings) Act 1990.

4.2.2 Material change of use

In order to constitute development, a change of use must be material. The Act does not define what is meant by 'material'.

Case law makes it clear that the question as to whether a change of use is material is one of fact and degree in each case. The question of whether there has been a material change of use 'is a question of fact and degree and is decided by reference to the planning unit' (*Manchester City Council v Secretary of State for Housing, Communities and Local Government* [2021] EWCA Civ 1920 at [16]). The answer will always depend upon the particular characteristics of the use in question (*Moore v Secretary of State for Communities and Local Government* [2012] EWCA Civ 1202 at [27]). A change of use must be material in planning terms for it to constitute a material change of use. It follows, therefore, that the courts will not normally interfere with a planning decision on the question of the materiality of a particular change of use unless the decision is totally unreasonable on the facts, or the deciding body has misdirected itself as to the relevant law. Note, however, the following general points decided by case law:

(a) It is necessary to look at the change in the use of the relevant 'planning unit'. In many cases this will be the whole of the land concerned, ie the land in the same ownership and occupation. Occasionally, particularly with larger sites, a single occupation may comprise two or more physically distinct and separate areas that are occupied for substantially different and unrelated purposes, in which case each area (with its own main or primary use) should be considered as a separate planning unit (see Burdle and Another v Secretary of State for the Environment and Another [1972] 3 All ER 240 and Thames Heliport plc v Tower Hamlets LBC [1997] 2 PLR 72). In a mall-type development, each shop unit will be a separate planning unit (Church Commissioners for England v Secretary of State for the Environment (1996) 7 P & CR 73).

(b) The use of a planning unit may involve various (and possibly fluctuating) ancillary uses that do not need planning permission provided that they remain ancillary to, and retain their ancillary connection with, the primary use. For instance, where produce grown on an agricultural unit is sold on a limited scale from the farmhouse, this retail use is ancillary to the primary agricultural use; however, the ancillary status is lost if, for example, produce is subsequently bought in for the purposes of resale (see Wood v Secretary of State for the Environment [1973] 1 WLR 707, HL).

As the courts will not normally interfere with LPAs' decisions on questions of fact and degree, it will generally be the SOS or one of the SOS's inspectors who will be the final arbiter of the question as to whether a particular change of use is material. Thus, their views in similar cases will be important, and guidance may be found in particular in relevant MHCLG circulars, the NPPF and PPG and in Ministerial Decisions.

4.2.2.1 Statutory clarifications

As noted above, the determination of what is a material change of use will normally be a judgment made on the basis of fact and degree, but there are certain cases in which the legislation expressly includes and excludes changes of use.

Section 55(3) and (5) of the Act declares the following to be material changes of use:

(a) the use as two or more separate dwelling houses of any building previously used as a single dwelling house;

(b) (generally) the deposit of refuse or waste materials; and

(c) (subject to any regulations) the use for display of advertisements of any external part of a building which is not normally used for that purpose.

Certain changes of use are also expressly excluded from amounting to development. These are set out in s 55(2) and include the following:

(a) The use of any building or other land within the curtilage of a dwelling house for any purpose incidental to the enjoyment of the dwelling house as such (s 55(2)(d)).

Factors to be considered in deciding whether the use is 'incidental to the enjoyment of the dwelling house as such' include the nature and scale of the use, and whether it is one that could reasonably be expected to be carried out in or around the house for domestic needs or incidental to the personal enjoyment of the house by its occupants: see Ministerial Decision [1977] JPL 116. Thus, for example, in Wallington v Secretary of State for Wales [1991] JPL 942, CA, the keeping of 44 dogs as pets was held not to be an incidental use. Enjoyment of the dwelling house must be distinguished from the enjoyment of the particular occupier (ie the test for enjoyment is objective, not subjective).

Land will not form part of the curtilage of a dwelling house simply because it adjoins and is in the same ownership as the dwelling house (R v Secretary of State for the Environment, ex p Collins [1989] EG 15 (CS)).

(b) The use of any land or buildings occupied with it for the purposes of agriculture or forestry (s 55(2)(e)).

38 Commercial Property

(c) In the case of buildings or other land that are used for a purpose of any class specified in the UCO 1987, the use of the buildings or other land for any other purpose of the same class (s 55(2)(f)). This very important exception will now be considered in detail.

4.2.2.2 The Town and Country Planning (Use Classes) Order 1987

Section 55(2)(f) of the Act enables the SOS to make an order that groups different uses of land and buildings into classes, known as 'use classes' and provide that a change from one type of use within these classes will not constitute development (but see the UCO 1987 checklist at 4.2.2.3). Consequently, a change from one type of use to another within the same class will not require planning permission. This is an important element of the planning system as it carries with it the flexibility to make changes to the purpose for which land can be used and dispenses with the time and expense associated with securing individual planning permissions. The order made under this provision is the UCO.

The use class groupings have been amended on a number of occasions, but have recently undergone major changes a result of significant amendments to the UCO which took effect on 1 September 2020 as part of the Government's efforts to streamline, and simplify, the planning system. The Government's reasons for the overhaul of the use classes were expressed to be 'to better reflect the diversity of uses found on the high street and in town centres and to provide flexibility for businesses to adapt and diversify to meet changing demands'.

The details of the main use classes as they stood prior to 1 September 2020 and the main use classes from 1 September 2020 are set out at **Appendices** 7 and **8** respectively.

Prior to the 2020 changes, use classes were divided into four main groups, namely:

- Group A: which different classes of use generally found in shopping areas and town centres;
- Group B: containing certain types of offices, business, industrial and distribution use classes;
- Group C: containing various classes of residential uses;
- Group D: containing various classes of non-residential uses.

For any planning applications submitted before 1 September 2020, the use classes in effect when the application was submitted will be used to determine the application.

Following the changes, the main groups now include:

- Group B: general industrial and distribution uses;
- Group C: continues to include various types of residential uses;
- Group E: this contains a single and very broad new use class including retail shops, financial and professional services, offices, research and development, cafes, 'light' industrial uses suitable for a residential area, clinics, health centres, gyms, recreational and indoor sport;
- Group F: this includes various classes including schools, non-residential learning, places of worship, local community uses.

Some of the groups (both in the former and amended use classes) include several classes, such as A1, A2, A3 etc. A change of use class would not be considered as development if it took place within the specific use class, ie a change within the types of uses within Class A1 would not rank as development, but a change from a use in Class A1 to a use in Class A2 would constitute development (but see **4.2.3** on permitted development for cases where certain changes from one use class to another are granted planning permission automatically and a planning application is not required).

It should be noted that not every type of use is found within a use class. There are also certain types of uses which the UCO states do not fall within use classes ('sui generis uses'). These include uses which could potentially have particular adverse effects on their locality. By way of example, a hostel use is considered to be a sui generis use. It is therefore a requirement that planning permission for these changes of use, including a change from a sui generis use to another sui generis use, must be the subject of a planning application.

4.2.2.3 UCO 1987 checklist

Although a change of use within a class does not amount to development, it does not necessarily follow that a change of use from one class to another will constitute development. Whether it will constitute development depends on the basic rule, ie is that change of use 'material'? However, *Palisade Investments Ltd v Secretary of State for the Environment* [1995] 69 P & CR 638, CA, suggests that it will be extremely rare for this not to be the case. In *Rugby Football Union v Secretary of State for Transport, Local Government and the Regions* [2002] EWCA Civ 1169, the Court of Appeal, at para 4, said that the correct way of approaching the Order 'is to establish the use class in which the current activity is to be found ... and then see whether the proposed activity can be found in the same use class'. The Court of Appeal went on to say, at para 5, that it is 'necessary to ask the question in the form set out in the relevant use class' and that, for example, 'Class C1 poses the question "is the land used as a hotel?"'.

A change of use within a class may be accompanied by building operations, which could amount to development in their own right (remember that development has two parts to it – see **4.2** above).

A change of use within a class may have been validly restricted by a condition attached to a previous planning permission, in which case a new permission will be needed to change to a use restricted by a previous condition.

4.2.3 Permitted development

Once it has been established that a proposal amounts to development, the basic rule is that planning permission will be required. However, it is not always necessary to make an application for planning permission, for the reasons given below.

4.2.3.1 Resumption of previous use

By s 57(2)–(6), certain changes of use do not require planning permission even though they may amount to development, for example the resumption of a previous lawful use after service of an enforcement notice or the expiration of a temporary planning permission.

4.2.3.2 The Town and Country Planning (General Permitted Development) (England) Order 2015

By ss 59–61 of the Act, the SOS may provide by statutory instrument for the automatic grant of planning permission by means of development orders. The most important of these orders is the GPDO 2015. Note that the GPDO 2015 applies to England only; in Wales, the relevant order is the Town and Country Planning (General Permitted Development) Order 1995 as amended. This chapter considers the GPDO 2015 as it applies to England. In *R (Rights: Community: Action) v Secretary of State for Housing, Communities and Local Government* [2021] EWCA Civ 1954, the Court of Appeal, at para 63, said that a grant of planning permission by the GPDO 2015 for each of the permitted development rights it provides for is a 'statutory process by which development consent is actually granted for a project of development' and the GPDO sets out 'the restrictions imposed on that planning permission by way of exceptions, limitations and conditions'. It is not the case, therefore, that development which has the benefit of a permitted development right is exempt from the need for planning permission; rather it is the case that planning permission for that development was granted by the GPDO.

The GPDO 2015 lists, in Sch 2, numerous categories of development for which planning permission has been automatically granted, ie although the activity amounts to development, planning permission has been granted for it subject to any exceptions, limitations and conditions set out in the GPDO 2015 itself (but see the GPDO 2015 checklist at **4.2.3.3**). The

GPDO 2015 consolidates the GPDO 1995 and the many subsequent amendments to that Order, as well as making some additional changes to permitted development rights. The GPDO 2015 itself has been amended since it came into force.

Similar principles will apply in relation to works to listed buildings. Following provisions in the ERRA 2013, 'listed building consent orders' may be made, which will grant listed building consent for specific categories of work, subject to conditions and limitations. This will remove the need to obtain an express grant of listed building consent except in cases where, as a matter of policy, that should be required.

As to the development permitted by the GPDO 2015, note in particular the following six categories:

Part 1: development within the curtilage of a dwelling house

Part 1 is divided into classes as follows:

- Class A: the enlargement, improvement or other alteration of the dwelling house;
- Class AA: enlargement of a dwelling house by construction of additional storeys;
- Classes B and C: additions or alterations to its roof;
- Class D: the erection of a porch;
- Class E: the provision within the curtilage of the dwelling house of any building, enclosure or pool for a purpose incidental to the enjoyment of the dwelling house as such, or the maintenance, improvement or alteration of such a building or enclosure; or the provision of a container for the storage of domestic heating oil or liquefied petroleum gas;
- Classes F and G: the provision or replacement of a hard surface for any purpose incidental to the enjoyment of a dwelling house, and the installation, alteration or replacement of a chimney, flue or soil and vent pipe; and
- Class H: the installation, alteration or replacement of microwave antenna on a dwelling house.

All of these classes of permitted development are, however, subject to certain restrictions, limitations or conditions (see below).

There may occasionally be problems in determining the extent of the 'curtilage' of the dwelling house. It is the small area forming part of the land on which the house stands and used for the purposes of the enjoyment of the house. Its extent is a question of fact and degree in each case. It is not necessarily synonymous with 'garden'.

Restrictions on Class A development (enlargement, improvement, etc) include:

(a) a limit on the increase in the cubic content of the dwelling house;
(b) height limits;
(c) specified limits on distances from the rear wall of the original dwelling and to a neighbouring dwelling;
(d) limits on extending beyond a wall that fronts a highway and forms either the principal elevation or a side elevation of the original dwelling house; and
(e) limits on extending beyond a wall forming a side elevation of the original dwelling house.

There are also conditions set out in para AA.2 of Class A, eg an application for prior approval must be made to the LPA (a different process from applying for planning permission). Prior approval means that a developer has to seek approval from the local planning authority that specified elements of the development are acceptable before work can proceed. The matters for prior approval vary depending on the type of development, and these are set out in full in the relevant Parts in Sch 2 to the Order. An LPA cannot consider any other matters when determining a prior approval application.

Restrictions on Class E development (the provision of buildings within the curtilage, etc) include restrictions (a) and (b) above. Additional restrictions include:

(a) the building must not have more than one storey; and
(b) the development must not be situated within the curtilage of a listed building.

Note that for a dwelling house on 'article 2(3) land' (ie within a National Park, an area of outstanding natural beauty or conservation area) there are further restrictions.

Restrictions on Class H development (satellite antennae) include dish size, height and siting.

Part 2: minor operations

Part 2 permits:

(a) the erection, construction, maintenance, improvement or alteration of a gate, fence, wall or other means of enclosure (Class A);
(b) the construction of a means of access to a highway which is not a trunk or classified road (Class B);
(c) the painting of the exterior of a building (Class C);
(d) electrical outlets and upstands for recharging electric vehicles (Classes D and E);
(e) the installation, alteration or replacement on a building of CCTV cameras for security purposes (Class F); and
(f) moveable structures for pubs, restaurants etc (Class G).

In Class A, any gates, fences, etc must be for the purpose of enclosure. They must not exceed 1 metre in height (2 metres in the case of a school) if they adjoin a highway, or 2 metres in any other case. Development within the curtilage of, or to enclosures surrounding, a listed building is not permitted.

In Class C, painting of the exterior is not permitted if it is for the purpose of advertisement, announcement or direction.

In Classes D and E, the outlets and upstands must not be in certain locations (eg within 2 metres of a highway) and must meet certain criteria, for example as to height.

In Class F, CCTV cameras may not be installed on listed buildings or scheduled monuments, and must meet certain dimensions.

In Class G, inter alia, the height must not exceed 3 meters and must not be on land which is or forms part of a scheduled monument or land within its curtilage or a listed building or land within its curtilage.

Part 3: changes of use

The UCO contains a transitional provision that preserves the right to change certain uses within the use classes as they existed prior to the amendments which took effect on 1 September 2020. These rights remained in force until 31 July 2021, when new revised permitted development rights were introduced. Applications for planning submitted prior to 1 September 2020 should, however, be determined by reference to the previous use classes.

Part 3 permits certain changes of use within and between Classes A, B, C and D and others of the UCO 1987, including but not limited to:

(a) from casino, betting office, pay day loan shop or hot food takeaway to commercial, business and service (Class E) (Class A);
(b) from public house, wine bar or drinking establishment to drinking establishment with expanded food provision or vice versa (Class AA);

(c) from B2 (general industrial) to B8 (storage and distribution) (Class I);

(d) from Class C4 (small houses in multiple occupation) to Class C3 (dwellinghouses) (Class L);

(e) from a launderette, betting office, pay day loan shop or a hot food takeaway, or a mixed use combining use as a dwellinghouse with a use falling within one of those uses, to Class C3 (dwellinghouse) (Class M);

(f) from B1(a) (offices) to C3 (dwelling houses), subject to the limitations in para O1, eg the building is a listed building or is within the curtilage of a listed building (Class O);

(g) from an agricultural building to C3 (dwelling houses) (Class Q); and

(h) from C1 (hotels), C2 (residential institutions), C2A (secure residential institutions) or Class E (commercial, business or service) to use as a state-funded school (Class F.1(a)) (Class T).

It should be noted that the permitted development rights in Part 3 are subject to certain restrictions if the asset has been listed as an Asset of Community Value (ACV).

In some cases, changes permitted under Part 3 are subject to obtaining prior approval (or a determination that prior approval is not required) from the LPA. The procedure to be followed is set out in para W of Part 3. The LPA can impose conditions or refuse to grant prior approval, but planning permission is not required.

Part 4: temporary buildings and uses

Part 4 permits, inter alia:

(a) the provision of buildings, structures, plant, machinery etc required temporarily in connection with authorised operations (Class A);

(b) the use of open land for any purpose for not more than 28 days in any calendar year of which not more than 14 days may be used for holding a market or motor racing/trials (Class B);

(c) the use of any land, in addition to that permitted by Class B of Part 4, for any purposes for not more than 21 days in total during the period from 1 January 2021 to 31 December 2021, of which no more than 14 days in total may be for the purposes of holding a market, motor car and motorcycle racing or practising for those activities (Class BA, which was added in August 2020 to deal with the specific challenges presented by the Covid-19 pandemic);

(d) the provision of one moveable structure within the curtilage, and for the purposes, of a drinking establishment, a building used for the sale of food and drink, or a historic visitor attraction (Class BB, also added as a response to the Covid-19 pandemic but since amended);

(e) the use of a building and any land within its curtilage as a state-funded school for two academic years (Class C) and provision of temporary school buildings on vacant commercial land and the use of that land as a state-funded school falling for up to three academic years (Class CA);

(f) various flexible uses for a single continuous period of up to three years (Class D). In May 2019 these uses were widened, and the temporary period extended from two years, to encourage the revitalisation of town centres; and

(g) the temporary use of any land or buildings for no more than 12 months in any 27 month period for the purpose of commercial film-making; and the provision on such land of any temporary structures, works, plant or machinery required in connection with that use during the filming period (Class E which was introduced in July 2023).

In terms of limitation and conditions applying to Part 4 rights, these include:

- Class A rights are subject to conditions requiring removal of the buildings, etc or reinstatement of land at the end of the operations.
- Class C rights apply only if the existing use of the site is specified in the Schedule to the UCO 1987. This means that 'sui generis' uses do not benefit from the rights conferred by Class C. Class C rights do not apply to listed buildings and building on certain, specified types of land. The use of the land must be approved by the relevant Minister and may be used only once in relation to a particular site. The land may not be used for any other purpose and will revert to its previous use at the end of the second academic year.
- Class D rights apply to a maximum of 150 square metres of floorspace. At some point during the three-year period, there must be only one use ongoing from the list of flexible uses. Class D rights do not apply if they have already been exercised in respect of the site, and do not apply for certain types of buildings and land (for example, military explosives storage areas). A site will revert to its previous lawful use at the end of the period of flexible use.

The developer may also be required to make an application to the LPA for a determination as to whether the prior approval of the authority will be required.

The right to revert to the previous use of the land after the expiry of the temporary use is permitted by s 57(2) (see **4.2.3.1**).

Part 5: caravan sites and recreational campsites

Part 5 permits, inter alia, the use of land as a caravan site (in some circumstances) and the use of land by members of a recreational organisation for the purposes of recreation or instruction, and the erection or placing of tents on the land for the purposes of the use.

Part 6: agricultural buildings and operations

Part 6 permits, inter alia, the carrying out on agricultural land of certain operations (in particular the erection, extension or alteration of buildings or excavation or engineering operations) that are reasonably necessary for the purposes of agriculture on that unit. These are subject to many exceptions and conditions.

Part 7: non-domestic extensions, alterations etc

Part 7 Class A: commercial, business or service establishments

Part 7 Class A permits the extension or alteration of a commercial, business or service establishment, subject to various limitations and conditions. Extensions on article 2(3) land or within an SSSI are only permitted where the gross floorspace would be increased by up to 25% of the original floorspace, or 50 square metres (whichever is the lesser). All other developments may be extended by up to 50% or 100 square metres, whichever is the lesser. In the case of residential buildings, article 2(3) land and development within an SSSI, a minimum distance of two metres from the boundary must be maintained. Listed buildings (and their curtilage) do not benefit from these rights. Alterations are not permitted on article 2(3) land. A number of other limitations apply.

Under Part 7, Classes B, C and D were introduced in the GPDO 2015 to give further rights of alteration and extensions of shops in order to provide for the construction of shop trolley stores, collection facilities and the modification of shop loading bays.

Part 8: transport related development

Part 9: development relating to roads

Part 10: repairs to services

Part 11: heritage and demolition of buildings

Class B permits any building operation consisting of the demolition of a building, except, inter alia, where the building has been made unsafe or uninhabitable by the fault of anyone who owns the relevant land, or where it is practicable to secure health or safety by works of repair or temporary support. This is also subject to prior approval unless certain exemptions apply. As noted above at **4.2.1.2**, demolition in a conservation area without planning permission is a criminal offence.

The remaining Parts, which warrant close consideration, grant permitted development rights to a number of bodies including, in particular, LPAs, statutory undertakers, highway authorities and educational institutions.

Part 12: development by local authorities

Part 12A: development by local authorities and health service bodies

Part 13: water and sewerage

Part 14: renewable energy

Part 15: power related development

Part 16: communications

Part 17: mining and mineral exploration

Part 18: miscellaneous development

Part 19: development by the Crown or for national security purposes

Part 20: construction of new dwellinghouses

4.2.3.3 GPDO 2015 checklist

If the proposed development is permitted by the GPDO 2015, there should, prima facie, be no need to make an express application for planning permission. However, before deciding, the following other matters should also be checked.

Limitations, etc

Confirm that all the limitations, restrictions and conditions imposed by the GPDO 2015 will be complied with. There are two categories of these. First, there is a general restriction in art 3(6), which applies to all the Parts in Sch 2 and which states that (subject to limited exceptions) the making or altering of an access to a trunk or classified road, or any development which obstructs the view of road users so as to cause them danger, is not permitted. Secondly, there are specific limitations, conditions, etc in almost all of the Parts of Sch 2 which must be observed (see above). Note also art 3(5), which provides that:

> The permission granted by Schedule 2 does not apply if—
>
> (a) in the case of permission granted in connection with an existing building, the building operations involved in the construction of that building are unlawful;
>
> (b) in the case of permission granted in connection with an existing use, that use is unlawful.

If the limitations, etc are not complied with then, as a general rule, the whole development will be unauthorised by the GPDO 2015 and not merely the excess. This, though, is subject to the LPA's power to under-enforce if it thinks fit (see **Chapter 6** and in particular **6.1**). If the excess is *de minimis* it can be ignored.

Where the development is (or as a result of case law on environmental impact assessment (EIA) forms part of) a wider development for which EIA is required, most permitted development rights are not available and a planning application will be necessary (see art 3(10) of the GPDO 2015 and **4.4.2.1** below).

The HPA 2016 broadened the types of permitted development right which can be made subject to prior approvals by the LPA, to include those rights allowing building operations and other development orders so that LPAs can take local sensitivities into account.

Conditions on existing planning permission

Check any existing planning permission to see whether it contains a condition excluding or restricting relevant permitted development rights. Such conditions can be imposed in appropriate cases (see **4.3.3**).

Article 4 direction

Ascertain by means of an appropriate inquiry of the local authority whether an Article 4 direction is in force which may affect the proposed development.

Article 4 of the GPDO 2015 empowers the SOS or an LPA (usually with the SOS's approval) to make a direction removing permitted development rights normally enjoyed under the GPDO 2015 on the area of land specified in the direction. Such directions are quite common in conservation areas.

The making of an Article 4 direction will not affect the lawfulness of any permitted development commenced before the direction was made.

Compensation may be payable if an LPA introduces an Article 4 direction as the direction has the effect of removing vested rights to develop the property within permitted development limitations.

Special development orders

Check whether the land is in an area covered by a special development order (SDO).

Some SDOs restrict the provisions of the GPDO 2015 which would otherwise apply in the relevant area; others (especially those made for urban development areas) confer wider permitted development rights. It is therefore important to be aware of what SDOs exist and, where relevant, their provisions. The Manston Airport SDO is a recent example, which was granted in order to extend the scale and scope of the use of Manston Airport to act as a contingency for the stationing, transit and processing of goods vehicles in response to potential traffic congestion caused by post-Brexit disruption to cross-channel services at the Port of Dover.

Local development orders and simplified planning zones

As part of the LDF (see **4.1.3.2**), the LPA is able to introduce local development orders (LDOs) and simplified planning zones (SPZs). Local development orders operate to give permitted development rights, but are granted at local rather than national level. They can apply over the whole or part of an LPA's geographical area. Whilst in the past they were rarely adopted, recent evidence suggests their introduction has become more widespread as a result of the Government's localism agenda. Local planning authorities have seen an opportunity to encourage investment in their areas in a difficult economic climate by introducing LDOs, which enable businesses to carry out development without express planning permission.

In practice, LDOs complement the introduction of SPZs. An SPZ is an area in which an LPA wishes to stimulate development and encourage investment. It operates by granting a specified planning permission in the zone without the need for a formal application or the payment of planning fees.

Neighbourhood development orders

The LA 2011 amended the TCPA 1990 to introduce a right for communities to draw up 'neighbourhood development orders', which permit development without the need for planning applications. The creation of neighbourhood development orders is led by parish and town councils or neighbourhood forums, which first need to apply to the LPA to be designated a 'qualifying body' to produce a neighbourhood development order.

The TCPA 1990 now sets out the basic conditions for neighbourhood development orders, including that they must:

(a) be appropriate having regard to national policy and advice contained in guidance issued by the Secretary of State;

(b) be in general conformity with the strategic policies contained in the development plan for the area; and

(c) not breach, nor otherwise be incompatible with, retained EU obligations and Convention rights under the Human Rights Act 1998.

4.3 PLANNING PERMISSION

4.3.1 Types of planning permission

There are two main types of planning permission under the Act: full and outline. Relevant law and procedures are set out in the DMPO 2015.

Applicants for full planning permission will submit all the details of the proposed development at the time they make their application, including the size, layout and appearance of the development, as well as the landscaping and access arrangements.

By art 5 of the DMPO 2015, the applicant may, instead, apply for outline planning permission. If the applicant elects to submit an outline application, the application need only contain a description of the proposed development sufficient to indicate its major features (eg, for residential developments, the number and type of dwellings). A plan is also required of sufficient detail to identify the boundaries of the site and the nearest classified public highway. These basic requirements have been supplemented by additional case law and regulations, which have defined the minimum thresholds of information that must be provided more precisely (see the DMPO 2015, art 7 which sets out the general requirements for applications for planning permission including outline planning permission). However, the application need not contain the considerable amount of detail that is required for a full application for permission. Paragraph 44 of the NPPF highlights the need for LPAs to keep their information requirements for planning applications to a minimum needed to make decisions, and only request supporting information that is relevant, necessary and material to the application in question. An application for outline planning permission can only be submitted if the development involves buildings; it cannot be made for a pure change of use.

If outline planning permission is granted, it will be subject to a condition setting out certain matters for which the subsequent approval of the LPA is required. The only matters that can be so specified ('reserved matters') are defined in the DMPO 2015, art 2 as those concerned with access, appearance, landscaping, layout and scale of the development. The definition of reserved matters is exclusive but the LPA can still impose a condition on a grant of outline planning permission to require the authority's approval of other matters in addition to the 'reserved matters' defined in the DMPO 2015.

The effect of outline planning permission is that the LPA is committed to allowing the development in principle, subject to approval of any reserved matters and the discharge of any other planning conditions. This is because it is the grant of the outline permission that constitutes the grant of planning permission for the proposed development, ie no further planning permission is required. The LPA cannot revoke the outline permission except on payment of compensation (see revocation of planning permissions at **4.3.4.2**), neither can it impose additional conditions subsequently, except in respect of the approvals of reserved matters.

Applications for the approval of the reserved matters can be made in stages, but must be made within the timeframe specified in the decision notice, usually three years from the grant of the original outline permission, but sometimes longer in the case of larger, multi-phase developments.

It is also common for developers to make outline planning applications and at the same time ask the LPA to approve certain details at the permission stage rather than reserving them for subsequent approval. This approach is known as making a 'hybrid' application. It is a useful way for a developer to retain flexibility over the development to be brought forward on a particular site and provide extra information on the impact of the development if, for example, it would affect the setting of a listed building.

The HPA 2016 introduced another type of planning permission, 'permission in principle' ('PiP') for housing-led development. Development that qualifies for PiP will have deemed consent, with only a few technical details to be approved by the LPA at a later date (a 'technical details consent'). PiP applies to sites (usually a previously developed 'brownfield' site) which have been identified for housing-led development by the LPA. An LPA may also grant PiP for housing-led development on receipt of a valid application. Once the technical details consent has been obtained, the PiP will be equivalent to a full planning permission. Land can be identified for housing-led development in certain publicly available documents, for example brownfield land registers, development plan documents or neighbourhood plans. Sites which are entered in Part 2 of an LPA's brownfield land register will be granted PiP under the Town and Country Planning (Permission in Principle) Order 2017 (SI 2017/402). PiPs under this Order last for five years (or three years where the PiP was granted following an application), during which time technical details consent must be obtained. Other types of PiPs, including for housing-led development allocated in development plan documents and neighbourhood plans, are not yet in force as at the time of writing.

It should be noted that certain types of development cannot be granted PiP. These include EIA development (see **4.4.2.1**), habitats development and householder developments.

4.3.2 The basis for decision

An application for planning permission is made initially to the LPA, unless an applicant is able to make an application direct to the SOS (see **4.1.2.1**). By s 70(1), the LPA may grant planning permission either unconditionally or subject to such conditions as it thinks fit, or it may refuse planning permission.

In reaching its decision the LPA must have regard to the provisions of the development plan, if it is relevant to the application, and to any other material considerations. The importance of this 'plan-led' system was considered at **4.1.3**, and its importance should be acknowledged, as it is this test that will determine whether planning permission is granted at all and, if so, on what terms. Note, as set out above, the case of *Tesco Stores Limited v Dundee CC* [2012] UKSC 13, in which the Supreme Court confirmed that the interpretation of planning policy is a matter for the courts. Prior to *Tesco*, the courts had largely left the interpretation of planning policy to decision-makers, subject to *Wednesbury* reasonableness. Now, its interpretation is a matter of law. If the court decides that the LPA or SOS has not interpreted a policy correctly, there will be an error of law which could result in the decision being quashed. The application of planning policy, by contrast, is still a matter for decision-makers, and is a matter of planning judgment which can only be challenged on public law grounds. *Tesco* has undoubtedly expanded the court's role in interpreting planning policy, which will be of particular importance in deciding whether or not to appeal or judicially review a refusal of permission.

For considerations other than the development plan to be 'material', they must reasonably relate to the proposed development, and must be *planning* considerations. A 'planning consideration' is one which relates to the use and development of land (see *Stringer v Minister* for Housing and Local Government [1971] 1 All ER 65). Matters which the courts have held to be capable of being 'material planning considerations' include:

(a) an emerging development plan, ie one which is in the course of preparation (see, eg, *Allen v Corporation of the City of London* [1981] JPL 685 and *Kissel v Secretary of State for the Environment and Another* [1994] JPL 819). The closer the new plan gets to adoption, the greater the weight that should be given to it;

(b) financial considerations associated with the proposed development (see, eg, *Sovmots v Secretary of State for the Environment; Brompton Securities Ltd v Secretary of State for the Environment* [1977] 2 WLR 951);

(c) planning obligations (see **Chapter 5**);

(d) retention of an existing use (see, eg, *London Residuary Body v Lambeth Borough Council* [1990] 2 All ER 309, HL);

(e) the previous planning history of the site;

(f) a real danger of setting an undesirable precedent (see, eg, *Anglia Building Society v Secretary of State for the Environment and Another* [1984] JPL 175);

(g) planning policies of the MHCLG;

(h) policies of other government departments where relevant (eg, transport, energy, etc);

(i) policies of the LPA concerned (as evidenced in its own policy statements and non-statutory plans);

(j) environmental considerations. It is likely that environmental pollution from a proposed development is a material consideration, but it is not the function of the planning system to duplicate statutory pollution controls (see *Gateshead Metropolitan Borough Council v Secretary of State for the Environment* [1995] JPL 432, CA; and *Envirocor Waste Holdings v Secretary of State for the Environment* [1995] EG 60 CS, QB). The loss of environmentally important habitats and species will usually be an important consideration. However, if a type of environmental effect, such as water pollution, might arise but can be controlled by other statutory regimes (such as under discharge consents to watercourses under the Water Acts), the LPA should not exercise its powers to duplicate that regime by, for example, imposing its own condition controlling discharges; and

(k) the protection of private interests in a proper case and, in exceptional circumstances, personal hardship (see eg *Great Portland Estates plc v Westminster City Council* [1985] AC 661, HL).

Note that in making planning decisions, LPAs must comply with the public sector equality duty set out in s 149 of the Equality Act 2010 (see *R (on the application of Harris) v Haringey LBC* [2010] EWCA Civ 703). This imposes a duty on LPAs to have 'due regard' to the need to:

(a) eliminate unlawful discrimination, harassment and victimisation and other conduct prohibited by the Equality Act 2010;

(b) advance equality of opportunity between people who share a protected characteristic and those who do not; and

(c) foster good relations between people who share a protected characteristic and those who do not.

The SOS has the power to recover jurisdiction and consider and determine certain planning applications in place of a poorly performing planning authority if the application made to the SOS seeks permission for specific kinds of development, and the local planning authority has been designated by the SOS for that purpose (see s 62A of the TCPA 1990). The SOS also has power under s 77 of the TCPA 1990 to recover jurisdiction to determine a planning application under the call-in procedure. Current policy provides that the SOS will only call in an application when it is of more than local importance. The general powers and duties that apply to LPAs in determining applications also apply in general terms to the SOS (see TCPA 1990, s 62A and the amendments to the TCPA set out in the GAIA 2013, Sch 1). The SOS will in general, therefore, be subject to the same restrictions and guidance in exercising planning functions normally exercised by LPAs.

An example of an application for planning permission which was called in by the SOS was the application relating to the United Kingdom Holocaust Memorial and Learning Centre next to the Houses of Parliament. That grant of planning permission was, however, the subject of a successful challenge – *London Historic Parks and Gardens Trust v Minister of State for Housing* [2022] EWHC 829 (Admin). The King's Speech in November 2023 included a commitment to introduce a Holocaust Memorial Bill which will disapply the relevant sections of the London County Council (Improvements) Act 1900.

4.3.3 Planning permissions subject to conditions

The power in s 70(1) for an LPA to impose such conditions as it thinks fit (see **4.3.2**) is supplemented by s 72(1), which provides that, without prejudice to the generality of s 70(1), conditions may be imposed on the grant of planning permission for the purpose of:

(a) regulating the development or use of any land under the control of the applicant (whether or not it is land in respect of which the application was made), or requiring the carrying out of works on any such land, so far as appears to the LPA to be expedient for the purposes of or in connection with the development authorised by the permission; or

(b) requiring the removal of any buildings or works authorised by the permission, or the discontinuance of any use of land so authorised, at the end of a specified period, and the carrying out of any works required for the reinstatement of land at the end of that period.

Whether an applicant has 'control' of the relevant land is a question of fact and degree in each case.

The NPPF, para 55, sets out that LPAs 'should consider whether otherwise unacceptable development could be made acceptable through the use of conditions' and says that planning obligations should only be used where it is not possible to address unacceptable impacts through a planning condition.

Some conditions may also be imposed by virtue of legislation. One example is the biodiversity net gain condition imposed by para 13 of Sch 7A to the Act, which provides that 'Every planning permission granted for the development of land in England shall be deemed to have been granted subject to the condition' that 'a biodiversity net gain [BNG] plan has been submitted' and 'the planning authority has approved the plan'. Unless exempt, developers in England are required to provide 10% BNG on all habitats within the redline boundary of their development, whether or not they are impacted.

4.3.3.1 Judicial restrictions on the power

The general power to impose conditions in s 70(1) is not as wide or unfettered as it appears, because over the years the courts have imposed restraints on it.

The leading case on judicial control of the power is *Newbury District Council v Secretary of State for the Environment; Newbury District Council v International Synthetic Rubber Co* [1981] AC 578, where Viscount Dilhorne (at p 599) said:

> The conditions imposed must be for a planning purpose and not for any ulterior one and ... they must fairly and reasonably relate to the development permitted. Also they must not be so unreasonable that no reasonable planning authority could have imposed them.

The three elements of the test in *Newbury* were considered and approved by the Supreme Court in *Aberdeen City and Shire Strategic Development Planning Authority v Elsick Development Co Ltd* [2017] PTSR 1413 and in *R (on the application of Wright) v (1) Resilient Energy Severndale Ltd (2) Forest of Dean District Council* [2019] UKSC 53.

It is important to bear in mind that the majority of conditions imposed on planning permissions do not fall foul of the test in Newbury. In the very few cases where a condition does fail, it will normally breach more than one of the elements in the test. This is because there are potentially considerable areas of overlap between the three elements of the test.

Planning purpose

There are many cases illustrating the first limb of the above test (ie that conditions must be imposed for a planning purpose). For example, in R v Hillingdon London Borough Council, ex p Royco Homes Ltd [1974] QB 720, outline permission for a residential development was granted subject to a condition that the dwellings constructed should first be occupied by persons on the local authority's housing waiting list with security of tenure for 10 years. The court held that the principal purpose of the condition was to require the developer to assume, at its own expense, a significant part of the authority's statutory duties as a housing authority, thereby relieving the authority of that burden. This was not a planning purpose, and the condition was therefore ultra vires.

'Fairly and reasonably related to the development permitted'

The second part of the test in Newbury is probably the most difficult one to understand and apply. In Newbury the facts were that planning permission was granted for a change of use of aircraft hangars to warehouses, subject to a condition requiring removal of the hangars at the end of 10 years. The House of Lords held that although this condition satisfied the first test, in that the removal of unsightly old buildings was a proper planning purpose, the condition was not sufficiently related to the change of use of the hangars to warehouses, and was therefore void.

'Manifestly unreasonable'

The final part of the test in Newbury is that the condition must not be manifestly unreasonable in the sense that no reasonable LPA would have imposed the condition in question.

Under this element, a condition may not require the applicant to pay money or provide other consideration for the granting of planning permission (but see **Chapter 5**, where a similar practical result can be achieved by means of a planning obligation). A condition may not require the ceding of land owned by the applicant for public purposes (eg a highway) either, even if the applicant consents.

Severability of void conditions

If the condition in question is fundamental to the permission (ie if the permission would not have been granted without the condition), the court will not sever the offending condition. Most conditions are considered to be fundamental to their permissions. In those circumstances, if the condition is quashed, the whole permission will fail, ie the applicant will be left with no permission at all. A condition imposed by an LPA can be challenged by appealing the whole permission to the SOS, but this risks a refusal. It may therefore be better to apply for a modified permission under s 73 of the TCPA 1990 (see **4.4.3.1**).

4.3.3.2 Central Government Guidance on the Acceptability of Conditions

The PPG contains a section on the 'Use of Planning Conditions', which gives detailed guidance to planning authorities on the imposition of conditions. This guidance replaces the previous guidance on use of conditions in planning permission, Circular 11/95, which has been cancelled save for Appendix A (model conditions) which is retained and referred to in the PPG.

The PPG section on the Use of Planning Conditions sets out six criteria ('the 6 tests') that conditions must satisfy, namely that they should be imposed only where they are:

(a) necessary;

(b) relevant to planning;
(c) relevant to the development to be permitted;
(d) enforceable;
(e) precise; and
(f) reasonable in all other respects.

Paragraph 56 of the NPPF says that 'Planning conditions should be kept to a minimum and only imposed where they are necessary, relevant to planning and to the development to be permitted, enforceable, precise and reasonable in all other respects'.

These basic principles (which are clearly based on the court's criteria, above) are further explained in the PPG Use of Planning Conditions section, which sets out guidance on key considerations for the LPA to take into account with respect to each of the six tests. Model conditions are recommended, which are contained in the retained Appendix A to Circular 11/95.

The NPA 2017 amended the TCPA 1990 to empower the Secretary of State to make regulations restricting the imposition of certain types of conditions, so as to ensure that planning conditions meet the policy test in the NPPF. Section 14 of the NPA 2017 also prevents the imposition of pre-commencement conditions to which the applicant does not agree in writing. Regulations restricting the imposition of pre-commencement conditions came into force on 1 October 2018. A pre-commencement condition must not be imposed on the grant of permission (other than a grant of outline planning permission within the meaning of s 92 of the Act) without the written agreement of the applicant except in the circumstances set out in the regulations.

4.3.4 The effect of planning permission

4.3.4.1 General

By s 75(1) of the TCPA 1990, without prejudice to the provisions of the Act on duration, revocation or modification (for all of which, see below), planning permission shall (except in so far as the permission otherwise provides) enure for the benefit of the land and of all persons for the time being interested in it. As a general rule, therefore, the benefit of planning permission runs with the land concerned and, once implemented (see **4.3.4.3**), runs forever. This is (as indicated) subject to contrary conditions in the permission, and it is possible for planning permission to be granted for a limited period or be made personal to the applicant, but this is rare and must be justified on planning grounds. Once a temporary permission lapses, the right to revert to the previous use of the land is permitted by s 57(2) (see **4.2.3.1**).

Note that any conditions attached to the planning permission will also run with the land, ie will burden the relevant land.

It follows from the provisions in s 75(1) that the doctrine of abandonment cannot apply to express planning permissions (in other words, once implemented, the permission will not lapse if the activity ceases). Note, however, that once a permission has been fully implemented its effect is spent, ie it does not authorise the re-carrying out of that development. Thus if a building is destroyed, a new planning permission will be required to authorise its re-erection.

Where planning permission is granted for the erection of a building, the grant of permission may specify the purposes for which the building may be used (s 75(2)). If no purpose is so specified, the permission shall be construed as including permission to use the building for the purpose for which it is designed (s 75(3)).

The grant of planning permission is effective for planning purposes only. At the time of writing, it does not confer, for example, listed building consent, building regulation approval or any consent required under any other enactment (except conservation area consent, see below); nor does it confer the right to break any enforceable covenant affecting the land.

The ERRA 2013 introduced changes which, from 1 October 2013, removed the need to obtain conservation area consent when demolishing unlisted buildings in a conservation area. Consent for demolition is instead conferred by the grant of planning permission for the development including the demolition of the building. The enforcement regime has been amended to take into account this change (see **Chapter 6**).

4.3.4.2 Revocation and modification of planning permissions

By s 97, the LPA may, if it thinks it expedient to do so, revoke or modify (to the extent the LPA considers necessary) any planning permission, provided that the LPA does so before the development authorised by the permission is completed. Under s 107, the LPA may have to pay compensation in respect of abortive expenditure (such as preparation of plans) or for any other loss or damage directly attributable to the revocation or modification.

4.3.4.3 Implementation

Although generally, once implemented, the benefit of a planning permission lasts forever, there are statutory time limits governing implementation itself. If the time limit expires without the development having been started, the permission effectively lapses. Any further development will be unauthorised and subject to possible enforcement proceedings.

For full permissions granted before 24 August 2005, this time limit is five years. For full permissions granted on or after 24 August 2005, the PCPA 2004 has reduced the default period to three years. In the case of outline permissions, the time limit for implementation is within two years of approval of the last of the reserved matters (see **4.3.1**).

Note also that the LPA may substitute longer or shorter time limits if it thinks it appropriate on planning grounds. If an LPA does this, it must give its reasons for doing so in case the applicant should wish to appeal against it. The NPPF and PPG encourage shorter time limits for housing developments; para 77 of the NPPF says:

> To help ensure that proposals for housing development are implemented in a timely manner, local planning authorities should consider imposing a planning condition providing that development must begin within a timescale shorter than the relevant default period, where this would expedite the development without threatening its deliverability or viability.

The TCPA 1990 (s 56) defines the steps that must be taken to implement the permission. It provides that development is taken to be begun (ie implemented) on the earliest date on which any of the following 'material' operations begin to be carried out:

(a) any work of construction in the course of erection of a building;
(b) any work of demolition of a building;
(c) the digging of a trench for the foundations of a building;
(d) the laying of an underground main or pipe to the foundations;
(e) any operation in the course of laying out or constructing a road;
(f) any material change in the use of any land.

If a planning permission is lawfully implemented, the permission will be preserved and will not expire. Consequently, there is much case law considering how a planning permission may be 'lawfully implemented'. The court's consideration has focused on two main issues.

The first issue is whether the works carried out are significant enough in themselves to 'implement' the permission lawfully. Works that are more than *de minimis* will be sufficient to implement a planning permission and can include, for example, merely digging a trench for the foundations of the building. A number of court decisions have confirmed that, in practice, the threshold of operation required to establish that development has begun is very low (see, for example, *Malvern Hills DC v Secretary of State for the Environment* [1982] JPL 439).

The second issue is whether the work carried out to implement the permission has been carried out 'lawfully'. This will turn on, for example, whether the 'pre-commencement conditions' listed on the permission have been discharged before any substantive works of development have been carried out. If all pre-commencement conditions are discharged, any kind of building work subsequently carried out on site will lawfully implement the development. Work carried out in breach of a pre-commencement condition may lawfully implement development if the condition is subsequently discharged. The *Whitley* principle provides that works which contravene a true condition precedent cannot lawfully have commenced a development. Note that the Town and Country Planning (Pre-commencement Conditions) Regulations 2018 (SI 2018/566), which came into force on 1 October 2018, prevent the grant of planning permission subject to a pre-commencement condition which the applicant has not agreed to, save in the circumstances set out in the regulations.

4.3.4.4 Renewal of a planning permission

What if a developer cannot start the development within the time limit because of, for instance, financial problems? It used to be that the implementation time limit could be extended using s 73 of the Act, but a planning permission cannot now be renewed. Where a permission has expired without being implemented, the whole permission will lapse and a fresh application for planning permission will therefore have to be made.

4.3.4.5 Completion notice

Once a developer starts the development, there is generally no time limit in which the development must be completed. However, if the LPA is of the opinion that the development will not be completed within a reasonable period, it may serve a completion notice on the owner and any occupier of the land stating that the permission will cease to have effect at the expiration of a further period specified in the notice (being not less than 12 months after the notice takes effect). The notice is subject to confirmation by the SOS. Any part of the development carried out before a confirmed completion notice takes effect remains lawful and cannot be the subject of an enforcement notice requiring demolition (however unsightly). The service of completion notices is rare, however.

4.4 APPLICATION TO THE LOCAL PLANNING AUTHORITY

An application for planning permission is, in the first instance, usually made to the LPA, which will consider and determine the application in accordance with the principles referred to throughout this chapter. There are exceptions to this. As already mentioned, the Government introduced a power for an applicant to make an application directly to the Planning Inspectorate (PINS) on behalf of the SOS, provided that the application is within a specified description and the SOS has designated the relevant LPA as performing inadequately in respect of making planning decisions. The criteria that must be met for an LPA to be designated are set out in guidance prepared by the MHCLG and cover both major and non-major development. Adequacy will be judged on the basis of: (i) the speed with which applications are dealt with by LPAs; and (ii) the quality of decisions, measured by the proportion of planning decisions overturned at appeal. An assessment of the speed and quality of decisions will be made (and regularly reviewed) using the tests also found in the guidance. Other exceptions include applications for the development of 'nationally significant infrastructure projects' (NSIPs) and applications for urgent Crown development.

In the case of NSIPs (such as, for example, in respect of power stations or gas pipelines exceeding a certain threshold in terms of scale), the PA 2008 requires applications for development consent to be made directly to the SOS. A recent extension to this regime introduced by the GAIA 2013 means that certain business or commercial projects now fall within the definition of an NSIP. However, these may only be determined by the SOS pursuant to a formal request from the applicant. This means that the vast majority of commercial and business projects remain likely to be considered and determined under the 1990 Act planning regime. The consideration of NSIPs is outside the scope of this book.

4.4.1 Preliminary steps

It makes sense at this stage in the chapter to consider what steps should be undertaken in advance of applying to the LPA for permission. It is unusual for a solicitor to make this original application, but it is common for a legal audit to be undertaken prior to submission to ensure that all statutory requirements have been complied with. Further, should the LPA refuse planning permission (or impose adverse conditions), a solicitor may become involved in advising on any appeal. As an appeal takes the form of a total rehearing of the merits of the original application, the solicitor will therefore in effect need to review the matter as if from the outset at the appeal stage. A barrister will often be appointed to act as an advocate at the hearing of that appeal.

Steps to be taken include the following:

(a) Considering whether planning permission is required at all, ie whether the proposals amount to development and, if so, whether they are permitted development (see **4.2** and **4.3**).

(b) Considering whether the development requires an EIA; failure to identify this at an early stage will cause very considerable delays while the EIA is prepared.

(c) Ensuring that areas of land which are not owned by the applicant are included if works need to be carried out to make the development acceptable, eg including areas of the public highway that will require junction improvements.

(d) Undertaking a site visit. A site visit can be very valuable as it may:
 (i) clarify the client's maps, diagrams and plans;
 (ii) provide information about the immediate environment; and
 (iii) alert the solicitor to potential problems with the application.

(e) Obtaining copies of the relevant parts of the development plan and any non-statutory plans that may affect the proposed development. This could be vital in many cases because, for the application to stand a chance of succeeding, the development proposed will usually have to be in accordance with the development plan (see **4.1.3**).

(f) Investigating the title to the land concerned. This is necessary for two main reasons: first, to check whether the proposed development is in breach of an enforceable covenant affecting the land concerned; secondly, to identify any other 'owners' who will need to be given notice of the application (see further **4.4.2**). A failure to provide notice in the correct way can cause difficulties even following the grant of planning permission, eg a judicial review by an aggrieved party.

(g) Obtaining the relevant application form from the LPA, which is in prescribed form, and obtaining the LPA's list of documents to be provided with a planning application (requirements may vary depending on the nature of the development to be permitted).

(h) Considering whether a pre-application discussion with the appropriate case officer might be beneficial. This is encouraged by the MHCLG in order to reduce uncertainty and delay in processing applications. Such discussions can be particularly helpful in the case of large-scale or potentially controversial development proposals, to enable the developer to find out in what respects the proposals may not be acceptable and in what ways chances of success can be improved; they also enable the LPA to advise the developer of probable objections to the development which, if remedied, should lead to a quicker determination.

Note that LPAs have no statutory duty to enter into such discussions, although in practice they do so regularly. It follows, therefore, that any advice, etc given in such discussions is merely informal and advisory, and ultimately cannot normally bind the LPA (see *Western Fish Products Limited v Penwith DC and Another* (1979) 38 P & CR 7).

A developer and the LPA may use a Planning Performance Agreement (PPA) to agree a timeframe for pre-application discussions to take place and to fund provision of LPA resources to determine the application. More information can be found in the 'Before submitting an application' section of the PPG. A PPA is not intended to be a legally binding contract but instead a 'memorandum of understanding'. A PPA may be completed by an LPA under its general powers under the Local Government Act 1972. An LPA also has the power to charge for pre-application discussions under s 93 of the Local Government Act 2003.

(i) Considering whether there is a statutory requirement to carry out pre-application community consultation under s 61W of the TCPA 1990. Note that this duty is separate from the duty on the LPA to publicise the application (see **4.4.2.3**).

4.4.2 The procedure

Procedure is governed mainly by ss 62 to 69 of the Act and the DMPO 2015.

4.4.2.1 What is submitted to whom?

The application form and such other documents, plans, drawings, etc as are prescribed by the LPA should be submitted (usually in triplicate) to the district planning authority, London borough or metropolitan district council or unitary council (as the case may be). The application will require the applicant to detail its proposals. Since 25 June 2013, a design and access statement (DAS) has been required in limited circumstances; a DAS must be submitted with applications for 'major development', or applications for development to be carried out in a conservation area or to property designated as a World Heritage Site where one or more dwelling is provided, or where 100 square metres of floorspace or more would be created. A DAS need not be provided alongside applications for permission made under s 73 of the Act, for engineering or mining operations, for changes of use, for waste development or for applications to renew permissions (see **4.3.4.4**).

Whilst LPAs have a power to require submission of a number of documents, s 6 of the GAIA 2013 imposes a limit on this power. It must be reasonable to request the document(s) sought (having regard to the nature and scale of development in particular), and an applicant may be required to provide such document or evidence only if it is reasonable to think that the matter addressed in that document or evidence will be a material consideration in the determination of the application.

In addition, the Government has reduced the amount of detail that must be provided as part of an outline planning application. Since 31 January 2013 there is no longer a requirement to provide minimum information about layout and scale. Note, however, the need to provide sufficient information in order to be able to carry out a robust EIA (see below).

If the LPA is satisfied that the appropriate documents have been submitted, it will 'validate' the application, after which the LPA will commence the consultation process (see **4.4.2.2**). This step had been the subject of disputes between the applicant and an LPA. In some cases, LPAs required an unreasonable number of documents or made unreasonable requests for additional information but refused to validate the application until the additional information was provided. Alongside the introduction of the 'reasonableness' criterion, the Government introduced measures designed to avoid such an impasse. Article 12 of the DPMO 2015 sets out the procedure that an applicant must follow if he considers that an LPA is requiring particulars or evidence that do not meet the tests outlined above.

In cases where the development to be permitted exceeds particular thresholds and where the impacts of the development are likely to have significant effects on the environment, an EIA must be undertaken and an environmental statement (ES) provided to the LPA as part of the application (see the Town and Country Planning (Environmental Impact Assessment) Regulations 2017 (EIA Regulations) (SI 2017/571)). If an EIA is legally required, it will be unlawful for the LPA (or SOS on appeal) to grant planning permission unless one has been undertaken. The EIA must identify, describe and assess the direct and indirect significant effects of the proposed development on a specific list of factors set out in the EIA Regulations. The ES sets out the results of the EIA. If an ES should have been provided but has not been supplied, the LPA must not determine the planning application. The need to carry out the assessment and its scope are significant areas for legal challenge, and considerable care must therefore be taken to ensure that an EIA is carried out in compliance with the EIA Regulations. This will include not only considering whether EIA is required but, if it is, the scope of the EIA to be undertaken. It is usual for an EIA to be carried out using a set of parameters, within which the development if carried out would be within the bounds of the EIA undertaken. The EIA process will need to take into account not only the legal requirement to provide specific information in detailed (and to a lesser extent, outline) applications, but also the need to prepare a robust EIA (and ES) that seeks to minimise the risk of judicial challenge.

The application must be accompanied by the appropriate fee. The fee will vary according to the type of application and the scale of development involved.

4.4.2.2 Notification of persons by the applicant

It is not necessary for the applicant to have any interest in the land that is the subject of the planning application. It is not uncommon for a person who is not an owner or tenant to make a planning application for a site, for example where a developer wishes to develop land of a third party and enters into a conditional contract to acquire the land if a satisfactory planning permission is granted.

By the DMPO 2015, art 13, where the applicant is not the sole owner of the application site, they must give notice to all persons who are 'owners' or 'tenants' of the land.

'Owner' is defined by s 65(8) of the Act as meaning any person who owns the fee simple, or a tenancy granted or extended for a term certain of which not less than seven years remain unexpired.

'Tenant' is defined by the DMPO 2015, art 13(9) as meaning the tenant of an agricultural holding any part of which is comprised in the application site.

The application must also be accompanied by a certificate under art 14 of the DMPO 2015 and an agricultural holdings certificate. These certificates have to be given to certify compliance with the DMPO 2015, art 13.

4.4.2.3 Action by the LPA

By s 69 of the Act, the LPA must enter certain particulars of the application in the register that it is required to keep by that section. The register is open to public inspection.

By the DMPO 2015, art 15, the LPA must publicise the application. This publicity may consist of a site notice, notifying neighbours, or a local advertisement, depending upon the type of development proposed.

4.4.2.4 Power to decline to determine applications

Section 70B of the TCPA 1990 (inserted by s 43 of the PCPA 2004) gives LPAs the power to decline to determine:

(a) repeat planning applications;
(b) overlapping planning applications.

Repeat planning applications are applications that are submitted repeatedly with the intention that, over time, opposition to a controversial proposed development is reduced and permission granted. This process may result in undesirable developments being built.

Section 70B allows the LPA to decline to determine an application that is similar to one refused by the authority or by the Secretary of State on appeal within the preceding two years, and where the LPA thinks there has been no significant change in the relevant considerations since such refusal. The LPA may also decline to determine an application where another application relating to the same or substantially the same land is still under consideration. These powers are not intended to prevent submission of a new application that is similar to an earlier one but altered to address objections raised in relation to the earlier application.

Section 70C also permits an LPA to decline to determine an application if granting planning permission for the development would involve granting, whether in relation to the whole or any part of the land to which a pre-existing enforcement notice relates, planning permission in respect of the whole or any part of the matters specified in the enforcement notice as constituting a breach of planning control.

4.4.2.5 The making of the decision

The decision should be made within eight weeks of the submission of the application, or such longer period as may have been agreed in writing with the applicant (DMPO 2015, art 34). However, in the case of major developments, the time limit is 13 weeks; and if an EIA of the development is required, so that an ES accompanies the application, then the period is 16 weeks. If no decision has been made in time, the applicant can appeal to the SOS. Section 78 provides a right of appeal against a failure to take a decision.

The LPA should make its decision in line with the plan-led principle (see **4.1.3**).

If the LPA does not make its decision within the relevant time limit, this is treated as a deemed refusal of planning permission and entitles the applicant to appeal to the SOS. This is referred to as an appeal against non-determination.

Decisions are taken by members of the LPA at a committee meeting or by officers under delegated powers through the LPA's scheme of delegation (or 'standing orders'). It is important that decisions are made in accordance with the LPA's scheme of delegation as otherwise the decision may be quashed as an unlawful decision.

4.4.2.6 Procedure after the decision

After making the decision, the LPA must register it in its planning register (s 69 of the Act and the DMPO 2015, art 40). In addition, the applicant must be given written notification of the decision and full reasons for each condition imposed, and in the case of pre-commencement conditions full reasons for the condition being a pre-commencement condition, or a clear and precise statement of the full reasons for refusal, specifying all policies and proposals in the development plan which are relevant to the decision (see the DMPO 2015, art 35). If full reasons are not given, the decision could be challenged by judicial review or dealt with by way of appeal.

It is the written notification (or 'decision notice') that constitutes the grant of planning permission (see *R v West Oxfordshire District Council, ex p CH Pearce Homes* [1986] JPL 523). Planning permission is not granted, therefore, until a decision notice is given to the applicant. Where a deed of planning obligations under s 106 of the Act is required to be entered into as a prerequisite to the grant of planning permission, the notification may follow some time after a resolution to grant is made.

4.4.3 Amendments to planning permissions

If an LPA imposes conditions, it is open to the applicant to appeal. However, as the appeal takes effect as a total rehearing of the matter, it is possible that the original grant (admittedly subject to adverse conditions) might be reversed altogether, leaving the appellant worse off. A number of procedures are available to reduce this risk, and to give greater flexibility in relation to planning permissions that have been granted.

4.4.3.1 Section 73

Section 73 of the Act entitles a person to apply for planning permission to develop land without complying with conditions subject to which a previous planning permission was granted. Such an application must be made before the previous permission expires.

The application has to be made in writing and give sufficient information to enable the LPA to identify the previous grant of planning permission and the condition or conditions in question.

The important feature of a s 73 application is that in determining the application, the planning authority may consider only the question of the conditions subject to which the permission should be granted, and thus may only:

(a) grant unconditional permission;
(b) grant permission subject to different conditions; or
(c) refuse the application.

In the first two cases above, the applicant will then have the benefit of two permissions (ie the original one and the one obtained as a result of the s 73 application). In cases (b) and (c), the applicant can appeal to the SOS in the usual way. Thus, whatever happens on the s 73 application, the applicant will always retain the benefit of the original planning permission.

This is the only procedure available for challenging a condition where the time limit for appealing the grant of permission has passed.

Section 73 cannot be used to extend, or have the effect of extending, the time within which a development must be started or an application for approval of reserved matters must be made.

A streamlined procedure under s 73 also exists. This enables 'minor material' changes to be made to a planning permission. The procedure was introduced following the Killian Pretty Review, which recommended that 'Government should take steps to allow a more proportionate approach to minor material changes in development proposals after permission has been granted'. This procedure can be used where the original planning permission included a condition specifying that the development should be carried out in accordance with certain plans. If the developer wishes to change details of design, it can apply to modify the condition so that it will refer to the new plans. The procedure cannot, however, be used to expand the scope of the original permission, eg by raising the number of houses to be built from, say, 450 to 500. A minor material amendment is defined in the 'Flexible options for planning permissions' section of the PPG as 'likely to include any amendment where its scale and/or nature results in a development which is not substantially different from the one which has been approved'. The guidance recommends that a developer seeking to rely on the streamlined procedure engages in pre-application discussions with the relevant LPA to determine that using the procedure is appropriate in the circumstances.

4.4.3.2 Section 73A

Section 73 applies only to applications for the removal, etc of a condition before it is breached. However, under s 73A of the Act, an application may be made for planning permission for, inter alia, development carried out before the date of the application in breach of a condition subject to which planning permission was previously granted.

Permission for such development may be granted to have effect from the date on which the development was carried out, thereby rendering it retrospectively lawful.

4.4.3.3 Section 96A

There is also a mechanism under s 96A of the Act that enables a person with an interest in the land to apply for approval of non-material changes to a planning permission. The scope of the power given to the LPA is necessarily limited. It may only make a change to the planning permission if it is satisfied that the change is not material. In deciding whether the change is material, the LPA must have regard to the effect of the change (cumulatively with any others approved under the section) on the planning permission originally granted. However, where the LPA is so satisfied, the procedure provides a quicker and more desirable route for a change to be permitted, which would formerly have to have been made under the s 73 procedure.

Unlike a s 73 application, a successful amendment under s 96A will not result in the grant of a new planning permission. Instead, it takes effect as a modification to the original permission. The applicant for a s 96A amendment must have an interest in the land that is the subject of the proposed modification.

4.5 APPEALS AGAINST ADVERSE PLANNING DETERMINATIONS

Where an LPA has:

(a) refused to grant planning permission; or
(b) granted planning permission subject to conditions to which the applicant objects; or
(c) refused approval of reserved matters on an outline permission; or
(d) refused an application or granted a permission subject to conditions under s 73 or s 73A; or
(e) failed to notify its decision within the prescribed period (normally eight weeks),

the applicant may appeal to the SOS. This right to appeal is subject to certain time limits, themselves dependent on the nature of the appeal (s 78 of the Act; DMPO 2015, art 37). In the case of appeals not being brought by a householder, the time limit is six months from the date of the relevant notice from the LPA or expiry of the prescribed period.

4.5.1 Who may appeal?

Only the applicant may appeal; this is so even though the applicant may not be the owner of an interest in the land. Third parties, such as local objectors to a new housing estate being built in their vicinity, have no right of appeal and neither does the owner of the freehold have an independent right of appeal. However, third parties may challenge a planning decision by way of judicial review where there has been a substantive error of law or a procedural error which has prejudiced the third parties; judicial review is not an appeal on the merits of the decision but a challenge to the way in which the decision was made. A third party who objects to the grant of planning permission may challenge the grant of that permission by way of judicial review in the High Court within six weeks of the decision to grant planning permission.

The Ministry of Justice introduced the Planning Court, as a separate part of the High Court, with effect from 6 April 2014, in which specialist planning judges hear planning cases. This was done to speed up the system by freeing up the burdened court system and ensuring that the most appropriate judges hear planning cases.

The time limit for making a challenge by way of judicial review is normally three months. However, a six-week time limit applies to statutory and judicial reviews brought under 'the Planning Acts' (as defined by s 336 of the Act; see Part 54 of the Civil Procedure Rules 1998). The change is intended to permit developers to commence development more quickly, since they may be reluctant to implement planning permission during the challenge period. This also brings the limit in line with the six-week period for bringing a statutory challenge to the grant of a planning permission by the SOS on appeal.

4.5.2 Initial procedure (DMPO 2015, arts 36, 37)

Guidance regarding the appeals procedure to be followed can be found on the PINS website or in the PPG online guidance. This guidance was updated in 2019 following the conclusion of the Independent Review of Planning Appeal Inquiries, which was chaired by Bridget Rosewell OBE (the 'Rosewell Review'). The procedure is set out in PINS' 'Planning appeals: Procedural guide', updated most recently in April 2022 (<www.gov.uk/government/publications/planning-appeals-procedural-guide>) (the 'PINS Procedural Guide').

4.5.2.1 The appeal form

An appeal must be made in a standard form. The completed form, together with all relevant documents, must be submitted to PINS in good time to reach it within the time limit. Wherever possible, the appeal should be made online through PINS' Appeals Casework Portal (<acp.planninginspectorate.gov.uk/>). Copies must also be sent to the LPA, together with copies of any documents sent to PINS which the LPA has not yet seen (DMPO 2015, art 37).

4.5.2.2 Statement of case and statement of common ground

Guidance regarding statements of case and statements of common ground was updated in October 2021 to implement the recommendations of the Rosewell Review.

When the appeal is made, a full 'statement of case' must be provided containing the full particulars of the case and copies of any documents which the appellant intends to rely on. The appellant's statement of case must be set out on the appeal form. As a general guide, the statement should:

(a) contain quotations from relevant policies in the development plan, the NPPF and other policy documents which support the appellant's case;

(b) consider each of the reasons given (where relevant) for the refusal, etc, and analyse and refute them by logical argument. In this part, any precedent (eg showing that the LPA has granted a similar application) should be mentioned, as should any policies of the LPA that contradict the LPA's reasons;

(c) justify the appellant's case. Here there should be a brief description of the development proposed, together with additional plans, photographs, etc if desired. The local environment may be described (although the inspector will visit the site). Any material considerations and special circumstances should be set out, and any objections from third parties should be addressed. Any relevant previous decisions (whether by the LPA or on appeal) should be set out as being 'material considerations'. Potential planning obligations should also be outlined; and

(d) conclude with a general statement in support of the appellant's case.

There will be no opportunity to add to the statement of case at a later stage.

A draft 'statement of common ground' must also be submitted where the appeal is to be heard by a hearing or an inquiry. This identifies what matters are agreed between the appellant and the LPA and what matters are not agreed. This assists the efficient running of the hearing or inquiry.

4.5.3 Types of appeal

As well as setting out the grounds of appeal, the appellant must indicate whether it would like the appeal to be determined by the written representations procedure, whether it wishes it to be heard by an inspector at a hearing, or whether it wishes the appeal to be determined at a public inquiry. Note, however, that it is PINS that will choose the procedure; it will not necessarily adopt the method desired by the appellant. The LPA's views as to the choice of procedure will also be taken into account.

PPG notes that the procedure to be followed at the appeal will depend on the complexity of the planning matters to be considered. The PINS Procedural Guide notes that the majority of appeals are determined via written representations but that, for more complex cases, hearings provide an opportunity for the inspector to ask questions, and inquiries provide an opportunity for evidence to be tested. PINS' decision will be made in the light of published criteria approved by Ministers. These criteria are as follows:

Written representations - written representations would be appropriate if:
- the planning issues raised or, in an enforcement appeal, the grounds of appeal, can be clearly understood from the appeal documents and a site inspection (if required); or
- the issues are not complex and the Inspector is not likely to need to test the evidence by questioning or to clarify any other matters; or
- in an enforcement appeal the alleged breach, and the requirements of the notice, are clear.

Hearing - a hearing would be appropriate if:
- the Inspector is likely to need to test the evidence by questioning or to clarify matters; or
- the status or personal circumstances of the appellant are at issue; or
- there is no need for evidence to be tested through formal questioning by an advocate or given on oath; or
- the case has generated a level of local interest such as to warrant a hearing; or
- it can reasonably be expected that the parties will be able to present their own cases (supported by professional witnesses if required) without the need for an advocate to represent them; or
- in an enforcement appeal, the grounds of appeal, the alleged breach, and the requirements of the notice, are relatively straight forward.

Inquiry - an inquiry would be appropriate if:
- there is a clearly explained need for the evidence to be tested through formal questioning by an advocate; or
- the issues are complex; or
- the appeal has generated substantial local interest to warrant an inquiry as opposed to dealing with the case by a hearing; or
- in an enforcement appeal, evidence needs to be given on oath; or
- in an enforcement appeal, the alleged breach, or the requirements of the notice, are unusual and particularly contentious.

Note. It is considered that the prospect of legal submissions being made is not, on its own, a reason why a case would need to be conducted by inquiry. Where a party considers that legal submissions will be required (and are considered to be complex such as to warrant being made orally), PINS requires that the matters on which submissions will be made are fully explained – including why they may require an inquiry – at the outset of the appeal or otherwise at the earliest opportunity.

There is also an expedited process based on written representations where a householder is appealing through the Householder Appeals Service. This covers appeals in relation to minor developments affecting existing dwellings, eg extensions, garages, etc.

4.5.3.1 Written representations

Under the written representations procedure the appeal is decided, as its name suggests, almost entirely on the basis of written representations submitted to PINS by the appellant, the LPA and any other interested parties. No oral evidence is permitted, and that includes evidence by way of video or audio tape; maps, plans and photographs are acceptable, however, and in many cases will be necessary. At some point before a decision is made, the inspector will visit the site either unaccompanied, if the site can be seen sufficiently well from a public road or place, or accompanied by the appellant or its representative and a representative from the LPA.

The procedure is governed by the Town and Country Planning (Appeals) (Written Representations Procedure) (England) Regulations 2009 (SI 2009/452). It is speedy and cost-effective, and is recommended by the MHCLG for simple or non-controversial cases. It is by far the most common appeal procedure in England, accounting for about 92% of current appeals (see Planning Inspectorate, Statistics: England; Table 2.1 s 78 received planning appeals (2021/22) <www.gov.uk/government/statistics/planning-inspectorate-statistics>). Because of its nature, it also offers less scope for third parties to influence the eventual decision.

4.5.3.2 Inquiry

This is the most formal of the appeal procedures and is reserved for larger and more controversial developments. Inquiries are usually held in LPA offices, village halls or community centres. The procedure is governed by the Town and Country Planning (Inquiries Procedure) (England) Rules 2000 (SI 2000/1624) and the Town and Country Planning (Determination by Inspectors) (Inquiries Procedure) (England) Rules 2000 (SI 2000/1625) as amended by the Town and Country Planning (Hearings and Inquiries Procedure) (Amendment) (England) Rules 2009 (SI 2009/455), the Town and Country Planning (Hearings and Inquiries Procedure) (Amendment) (England) Rules 2013 (SI 2013/2137) and the Town and Country Planning (Hearings and Inquiries Procedure) (England) (Amendment and Revocation) Rules 2015 (SI 2015/316).

An inquiry may last for several days, weeks or even months. It is not a court of law, but the proceedings will often seem to be quite similar, with expert evidence presented and witnesses cross-examined. The appellant and the LPA usually have legal representatives, normally barristers, as may other parties to the proceedings. It is thus a much slower and more costly procedure.

PINS sets out the following guidance in its 'Guide to taking part in enforcement appeals and lawful development certificate appeals proceeding by an inquiry – England' (June 2022):

> Local people are encouraged to take part in the inquiry process. Local knowledge and opinion can often be a valuable addition to the evidence given by the appellant and the LPA ... Inquiries are open to members of the public, and although [they] do not have a legal right to speak, the Inspector will normally allow [them] to do so. ...
>
> The Inspector will then usually give an outline of what the case is about and what the main issues are that need to be covered/dealt with. ...
>
> The Inspector has the discretion to decide the order of appearances at the inquiry but normally the appellant will be asked whether they wish to make a brief opening statement, followed by the LPA. Whether the parties make an opening statement or not, the appellant will usually present his/her case first; the witnesses will give their evidence and the opposing side will be allowed to cross-examine (question) them. ... This is followed by the other side presenting its case with witnesses being cross examined by the opposing side. Similarly, those who registered that they wished to speak and who oppose the case just put forward, will be asked if they have any questions to put to the witnesses. ...
>
> Finally ... there are closing statements which are an opportunity for [the parties] to sum up their case ... The Inspector will then hear any applications for costs.

Following the Rosewell Review, an appellant must now give the LPA at least 10 working days' notice of the appellant's intention to submit a planning appeal where the inquiry procedure is requested.

4.5.3.3 Hearing

This is less formal than a public inquiry. The hearing is an inquisitorial process led by the Inspector, who identifies the issues for discussion based on the evidence submitted and any representations made. The hearing may include a discussion at the site, or the site may be inspected, without discussion, on an accompanied or unaccompanied basis.

The procedure is governed by the Town and Country Planning (Hearings Procedure) (England) Rules 2000 (SI 2000/1626), as amended. The procedure is intended to save time and money for the parties. In essence, it will be an informal hearing before an inspector, who will try to stimulate a discussion on the main issues between the parties. It is not appropriate for complex or controversial appeals, but where it is appropriate it is quicker and more cost-effective than an inquiry.

4.5.4 Costs in appeals

By ss 320(2) and 322 of the TCPA 1990, the SOS is given the powers set out in s 250(5) of the Local Government Act 1972 to award costs in planning appeals. Inspectors, who are appointed by the SOS, may exercise the SOS's powers. An award may be made irrespective of the procedure for deciding the appeal.

Detailed guidance on the exercise of the power to award costs is contained in the PPG online guidance. The basic principle is that, unlike in civil cases, costs do not 'follow the event', ie normally, each party will bear its own costs. Costs may be awarded against one party in favour of another, however, where there has been unreasonable behaviour which has directly caused the other party unnecessary and wasted expense.

The Government intends to amend this guidance, to give PINS more power to initiate an award of costs in planning appeal proceedings 'where it is clear that an application has not been handled as it should have been with due process'.

4.5.5 Challenging the appeal decision

By s 284 of the Act the validity of an appeal decision may not be challenged in any legal proceedings. However, by s 288, a 'person aggrieved' may question the decision by appeal to the High Court if the decision was not within the powers of the Act, or if any relevant procedural requirements have not been complied with.

In certain limited cases, a challenge may alternatively be mounted by way of judicial review.

REVIEW ACTIVITY

1. 'When determining an application for planning permission, there are no criteria with which LPAs are required to comply.'

   Do you agree with this statement?

2. An individual has bought a house for investment purposes. He plans to sub-divide the building and create three self-contained flats which he will then sell. The exterior of the building will be unaffected apart from the installation of a window in the roof (which is permitted by the GPDO).

   'He will not need planning permission for his proposals.'

   Do you agree with this statement?

3. Would change of use from a clothing store to a bookshop require planning permission (ignore any building works that might need to be undertaken)?

4. What is the effect of an Article 4 Direction?

5. Does the GPDO give an individual who currently has permission for use of premises under use Class A2 an unqualified right to change to a use under use Class A1?

6. 'The longest an outline planning permission can last before implementation is three years.'

   Do you agree with this statement?

7. A full planning permission has been granted for the erection of an office block. Is there a time limit within which the office block must be completed?

8. On appeal against an adverse planning decision by an LPA, what is the basis on which the matter is heard?
9. What is the time limit within which an appeal against an adverse planning decision by an LPA must be made?
10. A farmer plans to convert a disused barn into a row of cottages. The LPA has granted planning permission and has imposed conditions limiting occupation to agricultural workers only. In the farmer's opinion, this outcome is better than nothing, but he would like to challenge the decision.

    How would you advise the farmer?

Answers to this Review activity may be found in Appendix 1.

CHAPTER 5

Planning Obligations and Community Infrastructure Levy

5.1	Introduction	65
5.2	Planning obligations	66
5.3	Government policy	68
5.4	Unilateral undertakings	68
5.5	Modification and discharge of planning obligations	69
5.6	Community Infrastructure Levy	69
5.7	Community Infrastructure Levy and planning obligations	76
5.8	Practical points	77
	Review activity	79

5.1 INTRODUCTION

The limitations discussed in **Chapter 4** (see **4.3.3**) on what matters can be dealt with by way of a condition attached to a planning permission provide certainty and clarity. There will, however, be situations where these limitations prove problematic. An example might be where a development proposal gives rise to the need for additional infrastructure provision (such as roads or schools). A condition cannot be imposed requiring the developer to make a financial contribution towards this because the power to impose conditions does not specifically authorise the LPA or SOS (on appeal) to require the payment of money. The use of planning obligations in section 106 agreements under the TCPA 1990 (and previously their predecessors, usually referred to as 'section 52 agreements') provides an alternative means to secure mitigation measures when planning conditions cannot be used. They also bind successors in title to the land and can thus avoid the need to engage with the complex common law and statutory provisions on covenants (discussed in **Part II**).

In simple terms, a planning obligation is a separate agreement or undertaking made by deed that runs alongside the planning permission, and which can be used to deal with issues (such as provision of affordable housing) that cannot be dealt with in the planning permission itself. It can therefore make development which would otherwise be unacceptable in planning terms (eg because the population increase from the development would have an adverse impact on local schools) acceptable (eg by the provision of money to fund school expansion). The planning obligation may be treated as a 'material consideration' in determining whether the planning permission should be granted and on what terms (see **4.3.2**). Planning obligations have not, however, been without criticism. First, because obligations tend to be negotiated on a case-by-case basis, it can be difficult for LPAs to manage their infrastructure spending strategically and for developers to predict the costs of development. Second, costs can fall disproportionately on developers promoting larger projects.

For these reasons, among others, the Planning Act (PA) 2008, in Part 11, provided for a Community Infrastructure Levy, which was then spelled out in the Community Infrastructure

Levy Regulations 2010 (SI 2010/948) (as amended) (CIL Regulations). This introduced an additional optional mechanism for developer contributions, the Community Infrastructure Levy (CIL). The introduction of CIL was intended to reduce the use of planning obligations, the idea being – in very broad terms – to impose a consistent and transparent levy on developers by taxing the creation of new floorspace, rather than rely on individually negotiated and *ad hoc* planning obligations with particular developers. The CIL regime has since been the subject of many amendments, in particular in 2019 (see **5.6**).

The CIL regime has also been the subject of criticism. To address this, the Levelling-up and Regeneration Act 2023 (LURA 2023) that was passed under the Conservative Government provided that a new non-negotiable locally determined Infrastructure Levy (IL) would be rolled out across England. The intention was for the IL to largely (though not entirely) replace CIL and financial contributions secured via section 106 agreements. LURA 2023 set out the broad framework for delivering the new IL, but much of the detail was left to be provided through secondary legislation. However, following the General Election on 4 July 2024, the new Labour Government announced that it would not be bringing forward the IL through secondary legislation. The IL has, for now, been effectively dropped. Planning obligations and CIL will therefore continue to operate for the foreseeable future.

5.2 PLANNING OBLIGATIONS

The terms of each planning obligation will depend on the individual needs of the development proposal, but a model form of planning obligation (which may be accessed on the MHCLG section of the Government's website and on The Law Society's website) is available as a starting point.

Unless stated otherwise, all references to section numbers in this chapter are to the TCPA 1990.

5.2.1 Meaning of 'planning obligation'

Any person interested in land in the area of an LPA may, by agreement or otherwise, enter into a planning obligation, which may (s 106(1)):

(a) restrict the development or use of the land in a specified way; or
(b) require specified operations or activities to be carried out in, on, over or under the land; or
(c) require the land to be used in a specified way; or
(d) require money to be paid to the LPA on a specified date or dates, or periodically.

Note the following points:

(a) 'Person interested in land' means a person with any legal or equitable interest in the land.
(b) 'Agreement or otherwise' indicates that a planning obligation may be created either by agreement between the LPA and the developer, or by means of a unilateral undertaking offered by the developer or a combination of both (as to the potential use of unilateral undertakings, see **5.4**).
(c) A planning obligation may impose both restrictive covenants (eg restricting the development or use of the land) and positive obligations (eg requiring works to be done or money to be paid). These covenants and obligations will then be enforceable against successors in title of the developer (s 106(3)) (see **5.2.4**).
(d) A planning obligation may be unconditional or subject to conditions, and may impose restrictions and requirements either indefinitely or for a specified period. It may also provide that a person will be bound by the obligation only while they have an interest in the land (s 106(2) and (4)).

(e) A planning obligation can require a change in ownership, eg require a developer to cede rights in land to a third party such as Highways England. It does not appear that this could be achieved by planning condition (see *DB Symmetry Ltd v Swindon BC* [2020] EWCA Civ 1331, [52]). The Court of Appeal's judgment was upheld in the Supreme Court; see *DB Symmetry Ltd v Swindon BC* [2022] UKSC 33.

5.2.2 When can a planning obligation be used?

It is important to distinguish between (i) when a planning obligation can be *used*, and (ii) when a planning obligation will be a *material consideration* in the grant of planning permission. A planning obligation may be used when the statutory conditions in s 106 are met (see (i)). As to when a planning obligation will be a material consideration, that is a matter governed by the CIL Regulations, reg 122(2). Under that provision, a planning obligation may only constitute a reason to grant planning permission if it is:

(a) necessary to make the development acceptable in planning terms;
(b) directly related to the proposed development; and
(c) fairly and reasonably related in scale and kind to the proposed development.

This test was introduced by the CIL Regulations in April 2011. It enshrines in legislation a similar test previously found in Circular 05/05 and now contained in para 57 of the National Planning Policy Framework (NPPF) (see **5.3** below) which restricts what type of planning obligations an LPA can seek. Planning obligations that do not meet these criteria cannot be reasons to grant planning permission but will still be enforceable by the LPA against the developer and (usually) those deriving title from the developer.

5.2.3 Formalities

A planning obligation must be made by a deed that states that it is a planning obligation for the purposes of s 106, and which identifies the land and the parties concerned (including the interest of the developer) (s 106(9)). It is registrable by the LPA as a local land charge (s 106(11)).

Since 1 September 2019, local authorities can include provisions in section 106 agreements for charging proportionate and reasonable monitoring fees.

5.2.4 Enforceability

By s 106(3) and (4), a planning obligation is enforceable by the LPA against the original person entering into the obligation (the 'developer') and any person deriving title from that person. A failure to follow the requisite formalities (see **5.2.3**) will result in the section 106 agreement not being binding upon successors-in-title (see *Southampton City Council v Hallyard Ltd* [2009] 1 P&CR 5).

Note the following points:

(a) The obligation will bind only the interest or estate of the developer and those deriving title from the developer (s 106(3)). It cannot bind a superior title. Thus, for example, if a tenant enters into a planning obligation, it cannot bind the landlord of that tenant.

(b) A planning obligation cannot bind parties who have an interest in the land existing at the time the obligation is entered into unless they are parties to that obligation. Thus, for example, existing mortgagees of the land will not be bound (unless they consent), so that if they subsequently sell under their statutory power, the purchaser will take the land free from the obligation which will be enforceable only against the original party to the planning obligation.

For these reasons, the LPA will generally insist on all parties with an interest in the relevant land entering into a planning obligation.

5.2.5 Enforcement by the LPA

Section 106 provides three main methods of enforcement, as follows:

(a) Injunction to restrain a breach or enforce a requirement in the obligation (s 106(5)).

(b) By s 106(6), where there is a failure to carry out any operations required by a planning obligation, the LPA may enter upon the land, carry out the operations and recover its expenses from the person or persons against whom the obligation is enforceable.

(c) Any sums due under the planning obligation (including any expenses recoverable under s 106(6) above) may be charged on the land in accordance with regulations yet to be made (s 106(12)). Until regulations have been made, it is unclear whether such a charge will be registrable as a local land charge or as a private charge (and therefore registrable as a land charge or by notice, etc on the register of title).

5.3 GOVERNMENT POLICY

Government policy on planning obligations is currently set out in the NPPF and also in national Planning Practice Guidance (PPG). Paragraphs 55, 57 and 58 of the NPPF set out the following:

> 55. Local planning authorities should consider whether otherwise unacceptable development could be made acceptable through the use of conditions or planning obligations. Planning obligations should only be used where it is not possible to address unacceptable impacts through a planning condition.
>
> 57. Planning obligations must only be sought where they meet all of the following tests:
>   a) necessary to make the development acceptable in planning terms;
>   b) directly related to the development; and
>   c) fairly and reasonably related in scale and kind to the development.
>
> 58. Where up-to-date policies have set out the contributions expected from development, planning applications that comply with them should be assumed to be viable. It is up to the applicant to demonstrate whether particular circumstances justify the need for a viability assessment at the application stage. The weight to be given to a viability assessment is a matter for the decision maker, having regard to all the circumstances in the case, including whether the plan and the viability evidence underpinning it is up to date, and any change in site circumstances since the plan was brought into force. All viability assessments, including any undertaken at the plan-making stage, should reflect the recommended approach in national planning guidance, including standardised inputs, and should be made publicly available.

5.4 UNILATERAL UNDERTAKINGS

By s 106(1), planning obligations may be entered into 'by agreement or otherwise'; 'or otherwise' indicates that a fully enforceable obligation may be offered unilaterally by the developer. The rules as to the contents and formalities of such 'unilateral undertakings' are the same as those that apply to ordinary planning obligations entered into by agreement, except that the agreement of the LPA is not needed. They are also binding and enforceable in the same way.

The unilateral undertaking is designed to deal with the situation where the LPA and developer do not agree as to what should be covered by way of a planning obligation, and allows a developer to break the deadlock by offering what it believes to be acceptable terms in a unilateral undertaking. If the LPA refuses the developer's application, the developer can then appeal to the SOS against the refusal or deemed refusal of planning permission. At the appeal the unilateral undertaking will (subject to compliance with the CIL Regulations, reg 122) be taken into consideration by the inspector, which, if they consider it appropriate, may result in the grant of planning permission. Indeed, a unilateral undertaking (if given at the time of the original planning application) may dissuade the LPA from refusing planning permission in the first place.

5.5 MODIFICATION AND DISCHARGE OF PLANNING OBLIGATIONS

5.5.1 The power to modify or discharge

A planning obligation may not be modified or discharged except either, first, by agreement between the LPA and the person(s) against whom it is then enforceable or, second, by application by such person to the LPA or an appeal to the SOS (see s 106A(1)).

5.5.2 Application for modification or discharge

A person against whom a planning obligation is enforceable may, at any time after the expiry of five years from the date of the planning obligation, apply to the LPA for the obligation to have effect subject to such modifications as may be specified in the application, or to be discharged (s 106A(3)–(4)). If the LPA considers the planning obligation to no longer serve a useful purpose, then it must be discharged.

The critical question is whether the objection serves some useful function, the absence of which makes the maintenance of the obligation pointless (R (on the application of Mansfield DC) v SSHCLG [2018] EWHC 1794 (Admin), [38]). It is not necessary to consider whether the condition has some useful *planning* purpose; only a useful purpose.

5.5.3 Determination of application by the LPA

In the case of an application made under s 106A, the LPA must notify the applicant of its decision within eight weeks, or such longer period as may be agreed in writing between the parties. Where the application is refused, the notification must state clearly and precisely the LPA's full reasons for its decision, and tell the applicant of its rights of appeal (see **5.5.4** below).

5.5.4 Appeal against determination (s 106B and s 106BC)

Where the LPA fails to reach a decision on a s 106A application in the eight-week period, or determines that the planning obligation shall continue to have effect without modification, the applicant may appeal to the SOS within six months of the date of the notice or deemed refusal, or such longer period as the SOS may allow.

The appeal procedure is closely modelled on that for ordinary planning appeals (see **Chapter 4**).

5.6 COMMUNITY INFRASTRUCTURE LEVY

5.6.1 Fundamentals

The Community Infrastructure Levy (CIL) is a fixed charge levied on development in order to fund the provision of infrastructure. The purpose of CIL is to ensure that infrastructure necessary to support development within an area can be provided by the local authority. Infrastructure is widely defined in the CIL Regulations. It includes roads and transport facilities, educational facilities and recreational facilities.

The Government's continuing focus on economic growth and housing provision, along with negative feedback from developers, has resulted in the CIL regime undergoing significant changes since it was first introduced. The CIL Regulations have been amended multiple times, in 2011, 2012, 2013, 2014, 2015 and 2018 (SI 2011/987, SI 2012/98, SI 2013/982, SI 2014/395, SI 2015/836 and SI 2018/172), significantly changed twice in 2019 by the Community Infrastructure Levy (Amendment) (England) Regulations 2019 (SI 2019/966) (relating to Crossrail funding) and, importantly, the Community Infrastructure Levy (Amendment) (England) Regulations (No 2) 2019 (SI 2019/1103) (2019 CIL Regs), and further changed subsequently (SI 2020/781, SI 2020/1226 and SI 2021/337). Amendments range from the rectification of errors in the formulas used to calculate CIL, to taking certain planning applications outside the scope of CIL liability all together. This section focuses on the arrangements relating to CIL contained in the CIL Regulations in force at the time of writing. These are principally found in the CIL Regulations as amended by the 2019 CIL Regs.

The changes made in the 2019 CIL Regs were the result of a lengthy review and consultation process lasting several years. The Government's aim was to make the system of developer contributions (both CIL and section 106 obligations) 'more effective, fairer and more transparent to local communities and developers'. It was expected that there would be a wholesale reform of the system of developer contributions, potentially moving towards a system of land value capture. Instead, the CIL Regulations were once again amended rather than replaced, although arguably an element of land value capture could be creeping in, for example through the return of the potential for 'double-dipping' (see **5.7**).

The 2019 CIL Regs came into force on 1 September 2019. Note that, as they relate to England only, some provisions in the previous version of the CIL Regulations (as amended) still apply to Wales. The previous version of the CIL Regulations (as amended) also still applies to permissions granted before 1 September 2019, or liability notices issued or reissued before that date. The PPG relating to developer contributions and planning obligations has also been updated to reflect and expand on the 2019 CIL Regs.

A high-level summary of CIL can be offered as follows. CIL seeks to institute a transparent means of levying contributions for infrastructure from developers based on the floorspace of new development, rather than having to negotiate such contributions from developers through individually negotiated planning obligations. CIL is thus, in the broadest terms, a tax (or *charge*) on developers for the creation of certain new floorspace in certain development (called *chargeable development*). Authorities – called *charging authorities* – levy this tax in accordance with a *charging schedule*. That charging schedule will set out fixed rates per square meter of floorspace which may depend on the nature and size of the development. The liability itself is then calculated based on formulas provided in the Regulations.

The interpretation of the CIL Regulations has given rise to a number of cases, chiefly concerning the situations in which a person may lose an entitlement to a relief from CIL where they fail to submit a commencement notice for the relevant development. It should be noted that since the 2019 Amendments the consequence of failing to submit a commencement notice is not that the relief is totally lost, rather, generally speaking, there is a tailored financial penalty instead. The cases emphasise that CIL is to be interpreted as a comprehensive code for funding local infrastructure needs. The regulatory scheme for CIL is 'self-contained and carefully constructed' (see *Gardiner v Hertsmere BC* [2022] EWCA Civ 1162 at [45] per Sir Keith Lindblom, Senior President of Tribunals). It is not therefore appropriate or desirable to add glosses to the text of the CIL Regulations (ibid at [48]–[49]).

It is important to note that the PA 2008 did not require all authorities to adopt and levy CIL. They have the power to charge CIL if they choose to do so.

5.6.1.1 Charging authorities

CIL is imposed by charging authorities. In England, these are district and metropolitan district councils, London borough councils, unitary authorities, national park authorities, the Broads Authority and the Mayor of London. In Wales, the county and county borough councils and the national park authorities have the power to charge CIL. In Greater London, the Mayor can charge CIL in addition to the LPA, meaning that a developer may be liable to pay two CIL charges: one imposed by the Mayor of London and one by the LPA for the area in which the development will be situated. No CIL will be payable if there is no CIL 'charging schedule' (which sets the rates payable) in force when planning permission is granted.

5.6.1.2 Rate payable – charging schedules and indexation

The rates payable are set out in charging schedules, governed by Part 3 of the CIL Regulations. The rate payable will vary between charging authorities, which may apply different rates to different use classes of development and even different parts of their local area. For example, the Mayor of London has imposed tiered CIL charges (so that more CIL is payable in more affluent boroughs) for the purpose of funding the Crossrail development in London. Other authorities have applied different rates to different use classes of development in different areas across their districts. Charging authorities may also set differential rates by reference to the scale of development as well as use. A charging schedule must be subject to examination in public before it can be adopted (PA 2008, s 212).

The lengthy consultation process for introducing or revising charging schedules was seen by the Government as a block against authorities adopting CIL. The 2019 CIL Regs therefore reduced the requirement for consultation prior to introducing or revising a charging schedule from two rounds to one (although authorities may exceed the minimum requirement if they wish). Charging authorities are, however, obliged to demonstrate how they have taken representations on the draft charging schedule into account (reg 20), and they should also consider consulting residents, businesses, voluntary bodies and bodies representing businesses in the area.

The 2019 CIL Regs also introduced a requirement that, prior to determining that a charging schedule shall cease to have effect, a charging authority must consult for four weeks and must issue a statement confirming what measures it is putting in place to fund the infrastructure needs of the area (reg 28A).

Local authorities must now publish an 'annual CIL rate summary' for the next calendar year, setting out when each charging schedule or revised charging schedule took effect, the chargeable rates and the development to which they apply, and the current rates indexed in accordance with the CIL Regulations (reg 121C).

All CIL payments are indexed from the date that the relevant charging schedule took effect. The indexation method was changed by the 2019 CIL Regs with effect from 1 September 2019. It is now contained in the formulas provided in Sch 1, entitled 'Calculation of chargeable amount'. To link CIL rates 'more closely with the value of development, rather than the cost of building infrastructure', the Government proposed that residential development should be indexed to the annual local House Price Index and that non-residential development should be indexed to the national Consumer Price Index. Arguably, this would have been a form of land value capture. A simpler indexation method was instead adopted, linked to a new bespoke index published by the Royal Institution of Chartered Surveyors (RICS).

5.6.1.3 Calculating the area subject to a CIL charge

CIL is charged, in accordance with reg 40 and Sch 1, based on pounds per square metre of gross internal area (GIA) on the net additional increase in floor space of any chargeable development. Chargeable development is the development authorised by the planning permission. There are minimum thresholds for liability, which means that CIL will not be payable unless the GIA of the new build comprising the development is at least 100 square metres or a new dwelling is created (reg 42(1)).

In calculating the area in respect of which CIL payments will be charged, the GIA of existing buildings that are either to be demolished and redeveloped, or which will be retained as part of the development on completion may be deducted from the GIA of the proposed development. The existing buildings must have been in lawful use for a continuous period of at least six months in the three years before the date on which planning permission first permits development where the use is not abandoned (see **5.6.1.6**). The test was designed so that CIL is not required where infrastructure supporting a development is already in place. The levy will be payable in full if the previous use of the existing buildings has been abandoned, because the infrastructure required to support the development may not be in place in these circumstances.

The CIL Regulations do not adopt the definition of 'building' found in the TCPA 1990, s 336. They only set out what a building does not include. The result is that the meaning of 'building' for the purposes of the CIL Regulations is any building capable of having a GIA, except for buildings that people do not normally go into and buildings into which people go only intermittently for the purpose of inspecting or maintaining fixed plant or machinery (reg 6(2)).

5.6.1.4 Liability

The liability to pay CIL is triggered on the grant of most types of planning permission, including planning permission that is deemed granted under the Town and Country Planning (General Permitted Development) Order 2015 (as amended) (permitted development), permission granted under a neighbourhood development order and 'development consent' granted under the PA 2008 (reg 5). CIL may also apply to development granted by permission in principle if technical details consent has been obtained; the levy will become due from the date that a chargeable development is commenced (see the Permission in Principle section of the PPG). An important exception to CIL liability is where planning permission is granted for a limited period (reg 5(2)). A charging authority is required to serve a liability notice as soon as practicable after the date that planning permission first permits development (reg 65(1)). In R (on the application of Trent) v Hertsmere Borough Council [2021] EWHC 907 (Admin), Lang J held (at [67]) that this meant weeks or months, not years.

Following changes to the CIL regime made by the Government in 2012, planning permissions granted pursuant to a s 73 application no longer trigger CIL liability, except where they grant permission for an increase in floorspace or amend the proposed planning uses permitted. Anomalies that arose from these and subsequent changes to the CIL Regulations have been addressed in the 2019 CIL Regs, which have extended abatement provisions to s 73 permissions, provide that indexation is now applied where planning permission is amended, and have redefined the term 'new build' to ensure that floorspace constructed under an earlier permission is correctly assessed in the overall CIL calculation.

Following the amendments made to the CIL Regulations in 2014, new applications bringing forward only design changes to an existing scheme prior to or during its construction will not trigger a new full CIL liability for the whole development. The amount payable will be reduced by the levy already paid under the earlier permission.

5.6.1.5 Party liable to pay CIL

As with planning obligations, liability for payment of CIL runs with the land. Every person with a material interest in the land on the day planning permission first permits development (see **5.6.1.6**) is liable to pay CIL in proportion to the value of their land (where there is a chargeable development) (see reg 4(2)). However, the legislation envisages that in the normal course of events liability will be assumed by one person, and there is a procedure for this. Indeed, assumption of liability is a prerequisite to claiming certain exemptions and reliefs (see **5.6.2**). There is also provision allowing authorities to transfer liability to landowners in the event of non-payment (reg 36). Lastly, there is provision for the transfer of liability between willing parties, and liability may be shared, although only on a joint and several basis (reg 32). This means that any party may be pursued by the collecting authority in the event of non-payment.

5.6.1.6 Date on which rate payable is fixed

If CIL liability arises, the amount of CIL payable will be calculated on the date that planning permission first permits development. This date is a defined term in the CIL Regulations, and currently its meaning depends on the nature of the permission granted (reg 8).

If an outline planning permission is granted, the amount of CIL payable will be calculated on the date of final approval of the last reserved matter associated with the permission or relevant phase of development (if the planning permission allows phasing).

If a full permission is granted, the amount of CIL liability will be calculated on the date the last planning condition that must be discharged to allow development to commence is discharged for that permission or that phase (where the permission allows phasing). Where there are no pre-commencement conditions, the relevant time for calculating CIL for a full permission will be the date of the grant of the permission.

5.6.1.7 Figure

The figure payable will be set out by the charging authority in a notice in prescribed form. The figure will be indexed from the date the charging schedule came into effect until the date planning permission is granted. There is an appeal mechanism for resolving certain disputes, but this is limited in scope (see Part 10, reg 113).

If, when calculated, the CIL payable is less than £50 it is deemed to be zero (Sch 1, para 1(2)).

5.6.1.8 Payment

Payment must be made to the collecting authority on commencement of the scheme in question.

Commencement is defined as the carrying out of a material operation in accordance with s 56(4) of the TCPA 1990 (see **4.3.4.2**) (reg 7). Payment of CIL may become due if planning permission is commenced by the demolition of buildings on the site (where demolition is not set out as a separate phase in the permission; see below). Note that the material operation does not have to be lawful to trigger CIL liability.

Payment may be made in instalments where a charging authority has an instalment policy in place (reg 69B). A 60-day grace period for payment to be made is permitted in cases where a party has assumed liability for CIL. In London, special arrangements apply if either the Mayor or a London borough has an instalment policy in place.

The CIL Regulations allow payment of CIL in phases in respect of outline or full planning permissions, where such permission requires or expressly permits development to be carried out in phases; each phase is treated as a separate phase of development (reg 9(4)). This enables a developer to manage its payments and does not require it to discharge its entire liability on commencement. These arrangements allow developers to avoid paying CIL in relation to site preparation (including demolition) works, where these are carried out as a separate phase. Liability to pay would arise only when a phase that involves erecting buildings (new floorspace) commences.

The CIL Regulations allow a charging authority to accept a payment in kind (eg a developer transferring land to the charging authority as payment or part payment of CIL liability) (reg 73). In-kind payments can include provision of land or infrastructure (on-site or off-site), or a combination of both. The inclusion of infrastructure as an in-kind payment is intended to permit a developer to deliver infrastructure that it may be best placed to bring forward itself and reflect the cost in a reduction to the levy charge.

Under the current CIL Regulations, a charging authority may collect CIL on its own behalf and also on behalf of other charging authorities, eg London borough councils collect Mayoral CIL of behalf of the Mayor of London. The CIL Regulations also provide for the transfer of CIL collected by a charging authority to a third party in some circumstances. In England, where a development is in an area where a neighbourhood plan is in place, or permission for it was granted by a neighbourhood development order, the charging authority must pass 25% of the CIL receipts to the parish council (reg 59A). In other circumstances, the charging authority must pass 15% of the CIL receipts to the parish council.

5.6.2 Exemptions and reliefs

As previously explained, CIL is a levy payable at a rate determined in accordance with the charging schedule(s) in effect in the area in which the development is located. This means that the principle and amount of liability cannot in general be disputed, and exemptions and reliefs are only available in the limited circumstances specified in the CIL Regulations.

Some exemptions and reliefs are available provided that certain conditions are met. If an exemption applies, CIL will not be chargeable. A relief may be applied at the charging authority's discretion. In all cases, the claimant must be an owner of a material interest in the relevant land that is earmarked for development in order to claim the exemption or relief.

Note that, following the 2019 CIL Regs, the CIL Regulations now enable certain exemptions and reliefs to be carried over or taken into account in calculating the amount of CIL payable following s 73 variations of planning permission. Subsequent s 73 variations also benefit from these new provisions.

5.6.2.1 Charitable exemption

An owner of a material interest in the relevant land will be exempt from liability to pay CIL in respect of chargeable development, if that owner is a charitable institution and the chargeable development will be used wholly or mainly for charitable purposes (as defined in the CIL Regulations). The part of the development to be used for such purposes must be occupied by or under the control of a charitable institution. The owner cannot benefit from the exemption if its material interest is jointly owned with another person who is not a charitable institution.

5.6.2.2 Discretionary charitable relief (reg 44)

Charitable relief relates to development held by a charitable institution as an investment (investment relief). An owner may be eligible for the investment relief if such relief has been made available by the charging authority in the area in which the development will be situated; the owner is a charitable institution; and the whole or greater part of the development will be held by the owner, or it and other charitable institutions, as an investment from which the profits will be applied for charitable purposes.

Neither relief can be applied if the owner of a material interest will occupy that part of the development and use it for ineligible activities (defined in the CIL Regulations).

5.6.2.3 Social housing relief (reg 49)

The CIL Regulations give full relief from paying the levy on a part of the chargeable development intended for social housing. In short, chargeable development that does or will comprise 'qualifying dwellings', in whole or in part, is eligible for the relief. Qualifying dwellings are those that are let by registered housing providers, social landlords or a local housing authority on a specified basis (eg an assured tenancy), or those occupied under shared ownership arrangements (provided certain terms are met). Since 1 April 2015 qualifying dwellings also include houses let by landlords that are not registered housing providers, social landlords or a local housing authority, if the dwellings are let at no more than 80% of market rent (including service charge) and let to people whose needs are not adequately served by the commercial housing market.

In order to claim social housing relief, the claimant must own the land in respect of which the planning permission has been granted. It must also have assumed liability to pay CIL.

5.6.2.4 Exceptional circumstances relief (reg 55)

Exceptional circumstances relief is available only where a charging authority has chosen to make it available and where a planning obligation has been entered into in respect of the development, the value of which is greater than the CIL charge that would be payable, meaning that having to pay the CIL charge too would have an unacceptable impact on the economic viability of the development.

The Mayor of London has decided not to make this relief available. Other charging authorities have varied in their approach or decided to keep their position under review.

5.6.2.5 Management and recovery of exempted or relieved sums

The CIL Regulations contain provisions that manage liability in particular circumstances (eg if land to which social housing relief has been applied is subsequently transferred to another party).

The amount by which any CIL liability has been reduced on application of an exemption or relief may be clawed back by the charging authority in certain circumstances (eg where a social housing product later falls outside the definition of 'qualifying dwellings') for a period of seven years after commencement of the chargeable development to which the relief is applied.

5.6.3 Procedure

Strict procedures must be followed when paying CIL, or in claiming an exemption or relief.

5.6.3.1 General

Assumption of liability must be made using a prescribed form. Where CIL is payable because planning permission has been granted under a general consent (such as the GPDO 2015), the collecting authority must be notified of that fact on a prescribed form. Various surcharges may be payable if procedural requirements are not complied with (see **5.6.4.1**).

5.6.3.2 Exemptions and reliefs

Claims for exemptions or reliefs must also be made on a prescribed form. Claims will lapse if the claimant carries out any activity that is inconsistent with such a claim (eg commencing development before the claim is determined by the charging authority).

The CIL Regulations contain provisions on when and how an exemption or relief may be applied to reduce CIL liability. In general, the CIL charge should be calculated in full before an exemption or relief is applied.

Developers qualifying for CIL exemptions or reliefs are required to submit a 'Commencement Notice' prior to starting works. Prior to the 2019 CIL Regs, failure to do so would result in the entire benefit being lost. Since 1 September 2019, where the 2019 CIL Regs apply, claimants for certain exemptions or reliefs will no longer lose the benefit of the exemption or relief if the chargeable development commences before a Commencement Notice is submitted; instead, the collecting authority must impose a surcharge (equal to 20% of the notional chargeable amount or £2,500, capped at whichever is the lower amount) (reg 83(1A)). The exemptions and reliefs covered by this are the residential annexes and self-build exemptions, and the charitable and social housing reliefs. Note that this amendment does not apply to the relief for exceptional circumstances; claimants for this relief must still submit a Commencement Notice prior to commencing chargeable development to avoid losing the relief.

5.6.4 Enforcement

The CIL Regulations impose serious penalties for non-compliance with the procedures relating to, or failure to make, payment of CIL to the collecting authority.

5.6.4.1 Surcharges and interest

Surcharges are payable in a number of circumstances, including where:

(a) development has commenced without anyone assuming liability to pay CIL (£50, which increases to £500 if the CIL is to be apportioned between different interests) (regs 80 and 81); or

(b) a notice of commencement of development has not been served (the lower of 20% of the chargeable amount payable in respect of that development or £2,500) (reg 83).

Interest will be payable on any amount payable under the CIL Regulations that is not paid on the date it is due. The imposition of late payment interest is mandatory (reg 87), whereas the imposition of surcharges is discretionary (with the exception of reg 83(1A) identified above).

5.6.4.2 Penalties for non-payment of CIL and other amounts payable in respect of chargeable development

In circumstances where the collecting authority thinks it is expedient to do so, it may serve notice requiring a development to stop if an amount that is payable in respect of chargeable development has not been paid (regs 89 and 90). The collecting authority must first serve a notice warning of its intention to serve a CIL stop notice. A CIL stop notice must be noted on the public register.

In cases where CIL remains unpaid, the collecting authority may pursue a number of ways to recover the sum. These include by levying distress (selling goods), which it may do if a liability order has been made by the magistrates' court in respect of the sum payable, or by application for a charging order (regs 98–99). Where a collecting authority is unable to recover the sum by means of a charging order, a debtor may be committed to prison (reg 100).

Following a person's death, their liability to pay CIL will lie with their executor, to be paid out of the estate.

5.7 COMMUNITY INFRASTRUCTURE LEVY AND PLANNING OBLIGATIONS

One supposed advantage of the CIL regime is that it allows parties to identify, at an early stage, what contributions will be required and in what sums. However, because CIL charges are not calculated or capable of being calculated until the time planning permission first permits development, a developer will in practice be required to estimate its actual CIL liability. The time when CIL is calculated may be some way in the future (especially in the case of phased planning permissions), by which time a CIL charging schedule may have been amended or replaced. This can make assessing the viability of a development difficult.

The Government had hoped that CIL would replace the use of the planning obligation in the majority of cases. However, for certain contributions, the section 106 obligation remains the appropriate mechanism. This is the case for some site-specific impact mitigation requirements, and for all affordable housing. Note that the charging authority may recalculate CIL when the provision of affordable housing is varied (since the 2014 amendments) (see **5.5.2**).

Until 1 September 2019, reg 123 of the CIL Regulations provided that no more than five planning obligations entered into on or after 6 April 2010 could be used to fund a single infrastructure project or type of infrastructure. This was known as the 'pooling restriction'. It was designed to encourage local authorities to adopt CIL, rather than rely on multiple and overlapping planning obligations to fund infrastructure. Regulation 123 also provided that a planning obligation could not constitute a reason for granting planning permission for development to the extent that the obligation provided for the funding or provision of 'relevant infrastructure', identified by the charging authority in a list. This prevented the practice of 'double dipping', where a development could be required to contribute twice to the same item of infrastructure through both a planning obligation and CIL. However, the pooling restriction caused problems, including that necessary infrastructure was not delivered or that planning permission had to be refused as planning obligations could not be entered into. The pooling restriction was removed by the 2019 CIL Regs with effect from 1 September 2019. Therefore development can now be required to contribute towards infrastructure both through planning obligations and through CIL.

To make authorities accountable for how CIL and section 106 obligation receipts are spent, so that the developer contribution process is more transparent, the 2019 CIL Regs introduced the mandatory publication of annual Infrastructure Funding Statements (IFSs) by 'contribution receiving authorities'. Regulation 121A of the CIL Regulations provides that IFSs must set out how much CIL has been collected for the area over the previous financial year, how much has been spent and on what, and the same information for planning obligations. Summary details of non-monetary section 106 contributions must also be recorded. Details of funding through highways agreements may also be included. 'Contribution receiving authorities' include any charging authority which issues a liability notice and any local planning authority which is to receive a monetary or non-monetary contribution during the reported year, including county councils. Parish councils must also produce and publish similar reports pursuant to reg 121B of the CIL Regulations.

The relationship between CIL and section 106 obligations has attracted critical comment from the developer community. The CIL Regulations require the charging authority to use CIL to fund infrastructure specified in the CIL charging schedule. However, the charging schedule may be changed by the charging authority, subject to complying with consultation requirements. In addition, there is no obligation to bring forward any infrastructure within a particular period. This leaves developers with the risk that infrastructure necessary for their development may not be provided. Moreover, developers to date have not perceived much significant change in the way LPAs negotiate section 106 agreements to take account of CIL, which leaves developers in a difficult negotiating position and ultimately increases the financial burden for any development to bear.

5.8 PRACTICAL POINTS

In view of the law and guidance above, the following points should be borne in mind when drafting and negotiating a planning obligation.

5.8.1 By the LPA

(a) It is important that the title to the land is thoroughly investigated before the LPA enters into the planning obligation. All parties with a legal interest in the land should be made parties to it, including any persons with existing interests (such as a prior mortgagee); otherwise the obligation may not be enforceable against a successor in title to that interest.

(b) The future exercise of any of the LPA's statutory powers should not be fettered by the obligation. If this does occur and the obligation is later challenged in court, it could invalidate the planning obligation (see *Royal Borough of Windsor and Maidenhead v Brandrose Investments* [1983] 1 WLR 509).

(c) The planning obligation should be executed either before, or simultaneously with, the grant of the planning permission, otherwise the developer may have the benefit of the permission without being bound by the obligation.

(d) The timing of related infrastructure agreements should be considered carefully. It will normally be preferable, where possible, to have all related agreements (eg agreements under the Highways Act 1980) executed at the same time as the planning obligation.

(e) Consideration should be given as to whether the obligation ought, in the circumstances of the case, to provide that liability under the obligation will cease once the owner of the interest parts with it. In the absence of such a provision, liability will continue against the original covenantor(s).

(f) If there is a disagreement about the inclusion of a particular term in the planning obligation, the LPA should consider whether it is within the policy guidance contained in the NPPF. If it is doubtful, or may be considered excessive, the LPA may find that the developer will appeal and offer a unilateral undertaking on the appeal (see further **5.6**).

(g) Consideration should also be given as to whether a clause should be included providing for payment of the LPA's costs in connection with the negotiation, drafting and execution of the planning obligation. If there is no such clause, the LPA will have to bear its own costs.

(h) Consideration should be given to the amount of any CIL charge to be paid in respect of the proposed development.

5.8.2 By the developer

(a) The draft planning permission should be included in one of the schedules to the obligation so that it is clear from the terms of the obligation what conditions, etc will be attached to the planning permission.

(b) The developer should try to ensure that the terms of the obligation do not continue to bind after it has sold its interest to a successor. This is particularly important where positive covenants in the obligation are likely to continue well into the future, and if lenders are involved in the transaction.

(c) The developer should attempt to have a clause inserted to the effect that the planning obligation will be discharged or cease to have effect if the planning permission expires or is revoked, or if planning permission is later granted for some other development. In addition, the developer should also ensure that any sums paid under the planning obligation that are not used by the local authority on expenses relating to the development should be returned to the developer after a certain period of time (as contemplated in the PPG on planning obligations, para 21).

(d) The obligation should not contain a covenant to comply with the conditions attached to the related planning permission. If there is such a covenant and the conditions on the planning permission are subsequently varied (under s 73 or s 73A, see **4.4.3**), or the permission lapses or is revoked, the conditions will continue to bind the land by virtue of the covenant in the planning obligation; such a covenant is in any case unnecessary since conditions can be enforced directly.

(e) Covenants should be avoided that impose obligations (in particular, positive ones) that take effect as soon as the planning obligation is executed (as opposed to when the planning permission is implemented). There may be a gap of quite a few months, if not a few years, between the developer obtaining the permission and being in a position to implement it, and in some cases the permission may never be implemented, so the developer should not be bound to perform the obligations.

(f) The developer should consider its potential CIL liability and whether it can lawfully restrict payment of planning obligations to reflect such liability.

(g) Should the obligations bind certain classes of successors? For example, it will be a disincentive to purchasers of individual houses or flats if they are bound by obligations to build a new school on a future phase of development. That is an obligation that should remain with the developer and bind its interests only.

REVIEW ACTIVITY

1. An LPA intends to require a developer to contribute to the construction costs of a new roundabout that will be needed as a result of the developer's proposals. Could the LPA do this by way of a condition attached to the planning permission?
2. Assume that the LPA intends instead to embody the obligation to contribute towards the cost of the roundabout mentioned in Question 1 in a planning obligation. What are the relevant factors to consider if acting for a developer?
3. Do you think the LPA would be acting reasonably if the background to the situation in Question 1 is that local traffic is already busy and the roundabout is already really needed: the developer's proposal has merely made the need particularly pressing?
4. The developer mentioned in Question 1 currently has an option to buy the land he wishes to develop. Does this mean that there needs to be another party to the planning obligation?
5. What steps would you take to protect any additional party identified in answer to Question 4 in respect of the obligation to contribute towards the costs of the roundabout?

Answers to this Review activity may be found in Appendix 1.

CHAPTER 6

Enforcement of Planning Control

6.1	Introduction	81
6.2	Definitions and time limits	81
6.3	Certificates of lawful use or development (ss 191–192)	82
6.4	Right of entry for enforcement purposes (ss 196A–196C)	84
6.5	Planning contravention notice (ss 171C–171D)	85
6.6	Breach of condition notice (s 187A)	86
6.7	Enforcement notice (ss 172–182)	87
6.8	Stop notice and temporary stop notice (ss 183–187 and ss 171E–171G)	91
6.9	Injunctions (s 187B)	93
6.10	Appeals against enforcement notices (ss 174–177)	94
	Review activity	96

6.1 INTRODUCTION

There are two central themes that run through enforcement under the TCPA 1990 (which is, broadly speaking, the steps taken to enforce against unauthorised development, ie development without the benefit of planning permission, and to ensure the conditions imposed upon the grant of planning permission). First, the TCPA 1990 provides that carrying out development of land requires planning permission; but that Act does not criminalise undertaking development without planning permission. Rather, it is only if an LPA takes enforcement action which is not complied with that criminal offences may be committed. Second, an LPA is not generally required to take enforcement action in respect of a breach of planning control. It has a broad discretion whether to act (which usually requires the LPA to consider whether enforcement action is 'expedient'), but it may choose not to do so. If it does, Part VII of the TCPA 1990 (ss 171–196) gives LPAs wide powers as follows:

(a) a right of entry for enforcement purposes;
(b) service of a planning contravention notice;
(c) service of a breach of condition notice;
(d) service of an enforcement notice;
(e) service of a stop notice or temporary stop notice; and
(f) injunction.

Each of these powers will be considered in turn, but first it is necessary to set out some basic definitions and time limits which apply to enforcement generally, and to consider applications for certificates of lawful existing use or development which can provide that a use or development is immune from enforcement action. (Unless stated otherwise, references in this chapter are to the TCPA 1990.)

6.2 DEFINITIONS AND TIME LIMITS

6.2.1 Definitions (s 171A)

For the purposes of the Act:

(a) a 'breach of planning control' occurs when development is carried out without the requisite planning permission, or when any condition or limitation attached to a permission is not complied with; and

(b) 'taking enforcement action' means the issue of an enforcement notice or the service of a breach of condition notice.

6.2.2 Time limits (s 171B)

The LPA normally can only take enforcement action if it does so within the time limits set out in the TCPA 1990. The effect of the amendments made by the Levelling-up and Regeneration Act 2023 is that within England, the applicable time limit for operational development carried out without planning permission, the change of use to any building to use as a single dwelling house or any other breach of planning control is now 10 years. This time limit applies, however, from 25 April 2024.

The transitional arrangements provide that for developments substantially completed before 25 April 2024, or where the change of use to a dwelling took place prior to that date, there are two relevant limits:

(a) Where the breach of planning control consists of:
   (i) operational development carried out without planning permission; or
   (ii) a change of use of any building to use as a single dwelling house;
   the LPA may not take enforcement action after four years from the date on which the operations were substantially completed or the change of use occurred (as the case may be). Note the case of *Sage v SSETR* [2003] 1 WLR 983 for its commentary on the meaning of 'substantially completed'.

(b) With all other breaches (ie any material change of use other than to use as a single dwelling house and any breach of condition or limitation attached to a planning permission) no enforcement action may be brought after the expiry of 10 years from the date of the breach.

As regards both of the above time limits, see the provisions of s 171B(4)(b) at **6.7.3**.

Provisions in the LA 2011 that came into force on 6 April 2012 affect the strict time limits set out above. Section 171BA of the TCPA 1990 permits an LPA to take enforcement action for an apparent breach of planning control even if the periods specified in s 171B have expired. An LPA must apply, however, to the magistrates' court for an order (a 'planning enforcement order') entitling the LPA to take such action. The order may be made by the court only if it is satisfied on a balance of probabilities that the apparent breach has been 'deliberately concealed', which is a term that is not defined. The enactment of these provisions follows cases such as *Welwyn Hatfield Council v Secretary of State for Communities and Local Government* [2011] 4 All ER 851, SC and *R (on the application of Fidler) v Secretary of State for Communities and Local Government* [2011] EWCA Civ 1159, where in each case the development was deliberately concealed.

The ability of an LPA to take enforcement action outside the limits defined in s 171B is a factor that may need to be considered when advising the purchaser of a property.

6.3 CERTIFICATES OF LAWFUL USE OR DEVELOPMENT (ss 191–192)

Historically, expiry of the time limit for enforcement rendered the breach of planning control immune from enforcement but it did not make the development 'lawful' per se. This meant that rights (such as those given by the GPDO 2015) that depend on lawfulness (as opposed to mere immunity) could not be enjoyed. This is no longer the case. It is now provided that development is lawful if:

(a) the relevant time limit for enforcement has passed; and

(b) the use, operation or breach of condition is not being carried on in contravention of a current enforcement notice.

It will make a property more marketable if a seller is able to provide proof of such lawfulness to a buyer. The Act provides mechanisms to obtain proof that an existing or proposed use or development is lawful. One of those ways is to seek a Certificate of Lawful Existing Use or Development from an LPA.

6.3.1 Existing development (s 191)

'Any person' (which could include a prospective buyer) who wishes to ascertain the lawfulness of any existing use, operation or breach of a condition or limitation may apply to the LPA, which will specify the land and describe the lawful use, operations or other matter (s 191(1)) in question. This is a 'certificate of lawful existing use or development' (CLEUD).

6.3.1.1 Onus of proof

The onus of proof is on the applicant, who must prove the lawfulness on a balance of probabilities. The planning merits of the case (ie whether or not the development is desirable or whether it contravenes policies in the development plan) are irrelevant as a CLEUD application is not an application for planning permission; the sole question in issue is whether, as a matter of evidence and law, the use or development described in the application is, or is not, lawful. The development may be lawful for a variety of reasons, such as (a) the time limit for enforcement action has expired, (b) the development has the benefit of a permitted development right, or (c) that on a proper construction of an existing planning permission, the development was already authorised. A CLEUD can, therefore, be extremely useful.

6.3.1.2 Issue of CLEUD

If the LPA is satisfied of the lawfulness at the time of the application of the use, etc, it must issue a certificate. In any other case it must refuse one; note, though, that a refusal merely indicates that the matter has not been proved on a balance of probabilities, rather than a determination that the use is now lawful.

6.3.1.3 Effect of CLEUD

The lawfulness of any use, operations, etc for which a certificate is in force shall be conclusively presumed. Thus, no enforcement action may be brought in respect of the matters stated as lawful in the certificate.

6.3.2 Proposed development (s 192)

Any person who wishes to ascertain the lawfulness of any proposed use or operational development of land can apply to the LPA, specifying the land and describing the proposed use or operational development in question.

The lawfulness of any use or operations stated in the certificate shall be conclusively presumed unless there is a material change, before the proposed use or operations are started, in any of the matters relevant to the determination. As with a CLEUD, there are a number of reasons why the proposed development might be lawful. They include where the development would have the benefit of a permitted development right; that on a proper construction of an existing planning permission, the development would be already authorised; or that no permission would be required as the relevant matters would not constitute development. The latter point is of particular importance where, for example, there is an existing lawful use and the applicant wants to intensify that existing use. That intensification would only require planning permission if it were a material change in use, and a certificate of lawfulness of proposed use or development (CLOPUD) can be a useful mechanism to determine the legality of the intensification (see eg *Barton Park Estates v SHCLG* [2022] EWCA Civ 833).

6.3.3 General provisions applying to certificates of lawful use or development

Applicants should refer to the specific requirements as to the form and manner of applications for a CLEUD as set out in art 39 of the Town and Country Planning (Development Management Procedure) (England) Order 2015.

A certificate may be issued in respect of part only of the land or just some of the matters specified in the application (s 193(4)), or, with existing development, may be issued in terms which differ from those specified in the application (s 191(4)).

The LPA must enter prescribed details of any applications and decisions in its s 69 register (s 193(6)), and must notify the applicant of its decision within eight weeks or such longer period as may be agreed in writing between the parties (DMPO 2015, art 34).

6.3.3.1 Appeals

The applicant can appeal to the Secretary of State for Levelling Up, Housing and Communities (SOS) against a refusal, a refusal in part or a deemed refusal (ie where the LPA fails to determine the application within the relevant time). The time limit for such an appeal is six months from the date of notification of the decision or the deemed refusal.

A further legal challenge can be made to the High Court within six weeks of the decision of the SOS under s 288 of the Act. The grounds of challenge are limited to judicial review grounds. The High Court will not, therefore, consider the planning merits.

6.3.3.2 Offences

It is an offence for any person to procure a particular decision on an application by knowingly or recklessly making a statement which is misleading or false in a material particular, or (with intent to deceive) using a document which is false or misleading in a material particular or withholding any material information.

If a statement was made or a document was used which was false or misleading in a material particular, or if any material information was withheld (whether or not this was done knowingly or recklessly or with intent to deceive), the LPA may revoke the certificate without payment of compensation.

6.4 RIGHT OF ENTRY FOR ENFORCEMENT PURPOSES (ss 196A–196C)

6.4.1 Right of entry without a warrant

Any person duly authorised in writing by the LPA may enter any land at any reasonable hour without a warrant to:

(a) ascertain whether there is or has been any breach of planning control on that or any other land; or

(b) determine whether any enforcement power should be exercised and, if so, how; or

(c) ascertain whether there has been compliance with any enforcement power that has been exercised.

There must, however, be 'reasonable grounds' for doing so, ie entry must be the logical means of obtaining the information in question.

In the case of a dwelling house (which includes any residential accommodation in, say, a commercial building), 24 hours' notice of the intended entry must be given to the occupier. This requirement does not apply, however, to land or outbuildings in the curtilage of the house.

6.4.2 Power to enter under a warrant

A justice of the peace may issue a warrant to any person duly authorised as stated at **6.4.1** for any of the purposes listed above, if they are satisfied on sworn information in writing that:

(a) there are reasonable grounds for entering for the purpose in question; and

(b) admission has been refused, or it is reasonably apprehended that it will be refused, or it is an urgent case. Entry is deemed to be refused if no reply is received within a reasonable time to a request for admission.

Entry under a warrant must be at a reasonable hour (except in cases of urgency) and must be within one month from the date of issue of the warrant. Each warrant authorises one entry only.

6.4.3 Restrictions and offences

The person entering the land must produce their authority and state the purpose of their entry, if requested, and may take with them such other persons as may be necessary (eg police officer, expert, etc). On leaving the land, if the owner or occupier is not then present, the person must ensure that the land is as secured against trespassers as when they entered.

Anyone who wilfully obstructs a person exercising a lawful right of entry is guilty of an offence.

6.5 PLANNING CONTRAVENTION NOTICE (ss 171C–171D)

A planning contravention notice (PCN) (rather than the right of entry) is the principal power available to an LPA for obtaining information needed for enforcement purposes. An LPA may serve a planning contravention notice on any person who is the owner or occupier of the land or has any other interest in it or who is carrying out operations on the land or using it where it appears to the LPA that there may have been a breach of planning control.

6.5.1 Contents of a PCN

There is no prescribed form of PCN, although a model is suggested in the 'enforcement and post-permission matters' section of the online national Planning Practice Guidance (PPG) (available online).

Section 171C states that a PCN may require the person on whom it is served to give any information specified in the notice in respect of any operations, use or activities being carried out on the land and any matter relating to conditions or limitations attached to an existing permission. In particular, it may require the person served, so far as they are able, to:

(a) state whether the land is being used as alleged in the notice, or whether alleged operations or activities are or have been carried out;

(b) state when any use, operation or activity began;

(c) give particulars of any person known to use or have used the land for any purpose, or to be carrying out or have carried out any operations or activities;

(d) give any information they hold about any relevant planning permission, or to state why planning permission is not required;

(e) state their interest (if any) in the land and the name and address of any person they know to have an interest in the land.

A PCN may also give notice of a time and place at which the LPA will consider:

(a) any offer from the person served to apply for planning permission, or to refrain from operations or activities, or to undertake remedial work; and

(b) any representations they may wish to make about the notice.

If the notice states this, the LPA must give them the opportunity to make the offer or representations at that time and place.

By s 171C(5), a PCN must warn the person served that if they fail to reply, enforcement action may be taken and they may be deprived of compensation if a stop notice is served.

6.5.2 The person served

A PCN may be served on anyone who is the owner or occupier of the land to which the notice relates, or who has any other interest in it, or on anyone who is carrying out operations on the land or using it for any purpose (s 171C(1)).

It is an offence for any person served with a PCN to fail to reply to it within 21 days unless they have a reasonable excuse. The offence is a continuing one, even after conviction (s 171D(2)–(4)).

It is also an offence knowingly or recklessly to make a statement in a purported reply which is false or misleading in a material particular (s 171D(5)–(6)).

6.5.3 Effect of a PCN

Apart from the consequences mentioned above, service of a PCN does not affect the exercise of any other enforcement power available to the LPA.

6.6 BREACH OF CONDITION NOTICE (s 187A)

A breach of condition notice (BCN) is primarily intended as an alternative remedy to an enforcement notice where the LPA desires to secure compliance with conditions or limitations attached to an existing planning permission. It has a considerable advantage to the LPA that, unlike an enforcement notice, there is no right of appeal against the service of such a notice (see **6.7.1**).

6.6.1 When and on whom a BCN may be served

Where there has been a breach of condition attached to an existing permission, the LPA may serve a BCN on any person who is carrying out or has carried out the development, or on any person having control of the land.

6.6.2 Contents of a BCN

The BCN must specify the steps which the LPA considers ought to be taken or the activities which ought to cease in order to secure compliance with the conditions, etc specified in the notice. Where, however, a notice is served on a person who has control of the land but who is not carrying (or has not carried) out the development, it can only require compliance with any conditions regulating the use of the land.

The notice must also specify a period for compliance, which must not be less than 28 days from the date of service of the notice.

6.6.3 Effect of a BCN

Unlike an enforcement notice, there is no right of appeal against service of a BCN (although there may be a possibility of judicial review on public law grounds).

If the person served has not remedied the breach by the time specified in the notice (or by the time specified in any further notice served by the LPA), they are guilty of an offence: the offence is a continuing one. It is a defence, however, for the person served to prove that they took all reasonable measures to ensure compliance with the conditions specified in the notice or, if they were served as the person having control of the land, that they did not have control at the time they were served.

6.7 ENFORCEMENT NOTICE (ss 172–182)

6.7.1 Introduction

The enforcement notice was intended as the primary method of enforcement of breaches of planning control, and it is the most flexible in that it can be used to address any kind of breach, including a breach of condition. It is possible to appeal against the service of an enforcement notice, the detail of which is considered at the end of this chapter. For the moment it should be noted that if an enforcement notice is appealed, it ceases to take effect until the appeal is finally determined. In principle, an enforcement notice appeal could then be further challenged in the High Court, during which period it will still not take effect (see s 289(4A)). As the determination of an appeal against an enforcement notice may take some time and may be costly, this is worth bearing in mind when considering the effectiveness of enforcement notices.

6.7.2 Issue of enforcement notice

By s 172(1), an LPA may issue an enforcement notice where it appears to the LPA that there has been a breach of planning control and that it is expedient to issue the notice having regard to the provisions of its development plan and any other material considerations.

6.7.2.1 Prerequisites to issue

There must be an apparent breach of planning control and it must be expedient to issue an enforcement notice.

Apparent breach of planning control

The requirement of an apparent breach of planning control means that an enforcement notice cannot be issued prospectively, ie before there is such a breach (see *R v Rochester upon Medway CC, ex p Hobday* [1989] 2 PLR 28, (1989) 58 P&CR 424).

It must be expedient to issue an enforcement notice

The LPA should not automatically issue an enforcement notice whenever there appears to be a breach of planning control. It must consider whether it is expedient to do so, and consider, to that end, its development plan and any other material considerations (which will include advice in the National Planning Policy Framework (NPPF) and PPG). The provisions of the European Convention on Human Rights will also be relevant, as will the Public Sector Equality Duty. The test of expediency is, in essence, a balancing of the advantages and disadvantages of an enforcement action: *R (Ardagh Glass Ltd) v Chester CC* [2009] Env LR 34, [47].

Paragraph 59 of the NPPF provides guidance to LPAs on this matter, accepting that enforcement action is important as a means of maintaining public confidence in the planning system. It also states that enforcement action is discretionary and LPAs should act proportionately in responding to suspected breaches. The PPG advises that, when deciding whether enforcement action should be taken, the LPA should have regard (where relevant) to the potential impact of the proposed action on the health, housing needs and welfare of those affected by the proposed action and those affected by the breach of planning control.

It should also be noted that individual local planning authorities may have their own policy on when to enforce against breach of planning control. That will be a material consideration in any decision whether to enforce. Paragraph 59 of the NPPF encourages LPAs to have a local enforcement plan which should set out how they will monitor the implementation of planning permissions, investigate alleged cases of unauthorised development and take action where appropriate.

6.7.2.2 Challenging the issue or failure to issue an enforcement notice

There are precedents for challenging a local authority's decision to issue – or not to issue – an enforcement notice. However, there are statutory rights of appeal against the notice itself, and these will normally form the most likely means of recourse against an enforcement notice. It should be noted that an application for judicial review may be refused where there is an adequate alternative remedy which has not been exhausted.

6.7.3 Time limits

An enforcement notice must be issued (though not necessarily served) within the relevant time limit as defined in s 171B. Failure to do so will render the breach lawful, subject to any action the LPA may take under s 171BA (see **6.2.2**).

However, by s 171B(4)(b), an LPA is not prevented from taking further enforcement action in respect of a breach of planning control if, during the four years prior to the new action being taken, the LPA has taken or purported to take enforcement action in respect of that breach. This would enable an LPA, for example, to serve another enforcement notice within four years of one which had been withdrawn or set aside on an appeal (see **6.7.8** and **6.10**).

6.7.4 Contents of an enforcement notice (s 173)

No statutory form is prescribed, but the notice must comply with the following:

(a) it must state the matters alleged to constitute the breach of planning control in such a way as to enable the person served to know what those matters are, and must state the paragraph of s 171A(1) (development without permission or breach of condition/limitation – see **6.2.1**) within which, in the opinion of the LPA, the breach falls (s 173(1) and (2));

(b) it must specify the steps to be taken or the activities to be discontinued in order to achieve wholly or partly the remedying of the breach or of any injury to amenity caused by the breach (s 173(3) and (4)). Examples of requirements that may be included are given in s 173(5)–(7) and include:
   (i) alteration or removal of buildings or works,
   (ii) carrying out of any building or other operations,
   (iii) cessation of any activity except to the extent permitted by the notice,
   (iv) modification of the contour of any deposit of refuse or waste,
   (v) construction of a replacement building after unauthorised demolition;

(c) it must state the calendar date on which the notice is to take effect, which must be at least 28 days from service of the notice (s 173(8));

(d) it must state the period within which any steps specified in the notice are to be taken and may specify different periods for different steps (s 173(9));

(e) it must state such additional matters as may be prescribed. These are set out in the Town and Country Planning (Enforcement Notices and Appeals) (England) Regulations 2002 (SI 2002/2682), regs 4 and 5, which require that the notice:
   (i) states the reasons why the LPA considered it expedient to issue the enforcement notice. This is intended to enable appellants to direct their minds to relevant issues (see online PPG);
   (ii) specifies all policies and proposals in the development plan which are relevant to the decision to issue an enforcement notice; and
   (iii) defines the precise boundaries of the site by reference to a plan or otherwise (see online PPG).

The relevant regulations in Wales are the Town and Country Planning (Enforcement Notices and Appeals) (Wales) Regulations 2017 (SI 2017/530).

The notice must be accompanied by an explanatory note, which must include the following:

(a) a copy of ss 171A, 171B and 172 to 177, or a summary of those sections including the following information—
   (i) that there is a right to appeal to the SOS;
   (ii) details of how to make the appeal by sending notice to the SOS, including the deadlines;
   (iii) the grounds on which an appeal may be brought under s 174;
   (iv) the fee payable in relation to the deemed application for planning permission for the development alleged to be in breach of planning control in the enforcement notice (see **6.10.4.1** below);

(b) notification that an appellant must submit a statement in writing specifying the grounds on which they are appealing and stating briefly the facts on which they propose to rely, and that this must be submitted with the notice of appeal or within 14 days from the date on which the SOS sends a notice requiring this;

(c) a list of the names and addresses of the persons on whom a copy of the enforcement notice has been served.

6.7.5 Service

6.7.5.1 Persons to be served

The enforcement notice must be served on:

(a) the owner – this term is defined in s 336(1) as being the person (other than a mortgagee not in possession) who is entitled to receive a rack (ie full) rent, or who would be so entitled if the land were let; and

(b) the occupier – this includes any person occupying by virtue of a lease or tenancy, but may also extend to licensees if their occupation resembles that of a tenant (see *Stevens v Bromley London Borough Council* [1972] 2 WLR 605, CA); and

(c) any other person having an interest in the land, being an interest which, in the opinion of the LPA, is likely to be materially affected by the notice – this would include, in particular, known mortgagees.

The methods of service for the purpose of the TCPA 1990 are defined in s 329.

6.7.5.2 Time for service

The notice must be served not more than 28 days after its issue and not less than 28 days before the date specified in the notice as the date on which it is to take effect. Failure to comply with these provisions is a ground for appeal to the SOS and, in general, is challengeable only in that way (s 285(1) and see *R v Greenwich London Borough Council, ex p Patel* [1985] JPL 851, CA; see also **6.10**).

6.7.6 Validity of notice

An error or defect in an enforcement notice may render it either a nullity or invalid. It is extremely important, therefore, to consider the way in which the enforcement notice has been granted.

6.7.6.1 Nullity

The notice will be a nullity only where there is a major defect on the face of it, for example where it does not state what the alleged breach is, what must be done to put it right or on what date the notice takes effect. The notice will also be a nullity if it does not fairly and reasonably tell the recipient what they must do to remedy the breach.

If the notice is a nullity it is of no effect. This is therefore a complete defence to any prosecution brought for non-compliance with it. In addition, there is technically no right of appeal to the SOS under s 174, although in practice, an appeal will normally be made at which the SOS may find as a preliminary issue that the notice is a nullity and that they therefore have no jurisdiction to hear the appeal. Any such finding may be challenged by the LPA by way of judicial review.

6.7.6.2 Invalidity

Other defects, errors or misdescriptions in an enforcement notice do not render it a nullity. In such a case, it can be challenged only by way of appeal under s 174 (see s 285 and **6.10**).

On a s 174 appeal, the SOS may correct such defects, etc, or vary the terms of the notice if satisfied that this will not cause injustice to either the appellant or the LPA (s 176(2)). This means that defects in a notice that might otherwise have resulted in its being quashed may be overcome and the notice upheld.

6.7.7 Effect of enforcement notice

An enforcement notice does not have to require restoration of the status quo, ie under-enforcement is possible. For example, in a case where a house has been constructed without planning permission, the LPA does not have to require the total demolition of the property and might only require the removal of certain features. Where a notice could have required buildings or works to be removed or an activity to cease but does not do so, and the notice is complied with, then planning permission is deemed to have been given under s 73A (see **4.4.3**) for those buildings, works or activities (s 173(11)).

Similarly, where an enforcement notice requires construction of a replacement building and is complied with, planning permission is deemed to have been given (s 173(12)).

Where a notice has become effective and has not been complied with, the then owner is guilty of an offence. In addition, the LPA may enter the land and take the steps required by the notice, and recover its expenses of so doing.

6.7.8 Variation and withdrawal

The LPA may withdraw, or waive or relax any requirement of an enforcement notice whether or not it has become effective. If it does so, it must immediately notify everyone who was served with the enforcement notice, or who would have been served if it had been re-issued.

Note that the withdrawal of the notice (but not the waiver or relaxation of any requirement in it) does not affect the power of the LPA to issue a further enforcement notice in respect of the same breach.

6.7.9 Non-compliance with notice

6.7.9.1 Offences

Where the notice has become effective and any step required by the notice has not been taken or any activity required to cease is being carried on, the then owner is in breach and is liable on summary conviction or on conviction on indictment to a fine. The court in assessing any fine must take into account any financial benefit or potential benefit accruing or likely to accrue as a result of the offence (s 179(1), (2), (8) and (9)). Note that the burden of proving ownership is on the prosecutor.

Any person (other than the owner) who has control of, or an interest in, the land must not carry on, or permit to be carried on, any activity required by the notice to cease. If they do so, they are guilty of an offence (s 179(4) and (5)).

Where a conviction for breach of an enforcement notice is secured, local authorities may also use the Proceeds of Crime Act 2002 to bring confiscation proceedings to recover an amount equivalent to the value of the benefit the offender has obtained from the criminal conduct. See

R v Del Basso and Another [2010] EWCA Crim 1119. The resulting confiscation order could exceed the cost of the fine.

6.7.9.2 Defences

It is a defence for the owner to show that they did everything they could reasonably be expected to do to secure compliance (s 179(3)). The characteristics of the recipient of the notice are relevant. A person who does nothing to comply with a notice may have a defence if they were genuinely incapacitated and had no money to get a third party to carry out the works: *Kent CC v Brockman* [1996] 1 PLR 1, [1994] Crim LR 296.

It is also a defence for the person charged to show that they were not served with the enforcement notice, and that it was not entered in the s 188 register (in which LPAs are required to note all enforcement and stop notices) and that they did not know of the existence of the notice (s 179(7)).

It is no defence to show that the notice was defective because it failed to comply with s 173(2) (see **6.7.4**), although it would be a defence to show that the notice was a nullity (see **6.7.6.1**).

6.7.9.3 Action by the LPA

After any period for compliance with an enforcement notice has passed and the notice has not been fully complied with, the LPA, in addition to prosecuting, may enter the land and take any steps required by the notice. It may then recover any reasonable expenses incurred from the owner of the land at that time (s 178(1)).

Where the breach is a continuing one, the LPA may seek an injunction, whether or not after any conviction (s 187B, see **6.9**).

6.8 STOP NOTICE AND TEMPORARY STOP NOTICE (ss 183–187 AND ss 171E–171G)

6.8.1 Introduction

An enforcement notice cannot become effective earlier than 28 days after service, and its effect is suspended until final determination of any appeal (and, if forthcoming, challenge to the High Court under the TCPA 1990, s 289). As such, it may be many months before the LPA can take steps to enforce it other than by way of an injunction. In the meantime, local amenity may suffer detriment because of the continuing breach. Accordingly, the Act provides for the possibility of a stop notice to be served, to bring activities in breach of planning control to an end before the enforcement notice takes effect.

A stop notice cannot be served as a method of enforcement action in its own right, which effectively forces an LPA to serve an enforcement notice before doing so. The temporary stop notice procedure was introduced to deal with this issue. It is a free-standing form of stop notice (ie does not require the issue of an enforcement notice) but it lasts for no more than 28 days. This will give the LPA time to investigate the matter further and decide what, if any, action it wishes to take.

Stop notices and temporary stop notices will be considered in turn, but in both cases it should be noted that they cannot be used to stop use as a dwelling house or any activity that has been carried out (whether continuously or not) for a period of more than four years prior to the date of the service of the notice. It should also be noted that a stop notice cannot be served where the enforcement notice has already taken effect.

6.8.2 Stop notice

6.8.2.1 General

Where an LPA considers it expedient that any relevant activity should cease before the expiry of the period for compliance with an enforcement notice, it may serve a stop notice (s 183(1) and (2)). Details of this should be entered in the register of enforcement and stop notices kept under s 188. The SOS also has power to serve a stop notice if the SOS considers it expedient (s 185).

6.8.2.2 Contents

The stop notice must refer to the enforcement notice and must have a copy of it annexed. It must also state the date on which it will take effect, being at least three days and not more than 28 days after service of the notice. An earlier date may be specified if the LPA considers that there are special reasons and a statement of those reasons is served with the notice (s 184(1)–(3)).

6.8.2.3 Service

A stop notice may be served with the enforcement notice or subsequently, but must be served before the enforcement notice takes effect (s 183(1) and (3)).

It must be served on any person who appears to have an interest in the land or to be engaged in any activity prohibited by the enforcement notice (s 183(6)).

Where a stop notice has been served, the LPA may also display a 'site notice' on the land concerned, stating that a stop notice has been served, giving its details and stating that any person contravening it may be prosecuted.

6.8.2.4 Offences

Any person who contravenes a stop notice (or causes or permits its contravention) after a site notice has been displayed or after they have been served with the stop notice is guilty of an offence which is punishable in the same way as for enforcement notices (including the taking into account of any financial benefit, see **6.7.9.1**).

It is a defence to prove that the stop notice was not served on them and that they did not know, and could not reasonably be expected to know, of its existence.

6.8.2.5 Withdrawal

By ss 183(7) and 184(7), the LPA may at any time withdraw a stop notice without prejudice to its power to serve another one. If it does withdraw a stop notice, it must serve notice of this on everyone who was served with the original stop notice and, if a site notice was displayed, display a notice of withdrawal in place of the site notice. Compensation may then become payable (see **6.8.2.6**).

6.8.2.6 Compensation

The LPA is liable to pay compensation in respect of any prohibition in a stop notice if:

(a) the enforcement notice is quashed on any ground other than that in s 174(2)(a) (see **6.10.1**); or
(b) the enforcement notice is varied other than under s 174(2)(a) so that the activity would no longer have fallen within the stop notice; or
(c) the enforcement notice is withdrawn otherwise than in consequence of a grant of planning permission or of permission to retain or continue the development without complying with a condition or limitation attached to a previous permission; or
(d) the stop notice is withdrawn.

No compensation is payable:

(a) if the enforcement notice is quashed or varied on the ground in s 174(2)(a); or

(b) in respect of any activity which, when the stop notice was in effect, constituted or contributed to a breach of planning control; or

(c) in respect of any loss or damage which could have been avoided if the claimant had provided the information when required to do so under s 171C (ie a PCN, see **6.5**).

Compensation is payable to the person who, when the stop notice was first served, had an interest in or occupied the relevant land. The amount payable is that loss or damage which is directly attributable to the prohibition in the notice, and can include any sum payable for breach of contract caused by compliance with the stop notice.

Any claim must be made within 12 months of the date compensation became payable (ie the date on which the enforcement notice was quashed, varied, etc). In the event of a dispute as to the amount, the matter must be referred to the Lands Tribunal.

6.8.3 Temporary stop notice

A temporary stop notice may be served where the LPA thinks there has been a breach of planning control and that it is expedient that the activity or any part of it should be stopped immediately. Any person who contravenes a stop notice (or causes or permits its contravention) after a site notice has been displayed or after they have been served with the stop notice is guilty of an offence which is punishable in the same way as for enforcement notices (including the taking into account of any financial benefit, see **6.7.9.1**).

Compensation is payable by the LPA if a temporary stop notice is served in respect of any activity which is authorised by a planning permission or development order, or in respect of which a CLEUD (see **6.3**) is issued or if the LPA withdraws the notice. The latter is not available if the LPA grants planning permission in respect of the alleged breach.

6.9 INJUNCTIONS (s 187B)

An LPA may apply to the High Court or county court for an injunction if it considers it necessary or expedient to restrain an actual or apprehended breach of planning control. It may do this whether or not it has used, or proposes to use, any of its other enforcement powers under the Act.

Whether an injunction is granted and, if so, its terms are entirely a matter for the discretion of the court as the remedy is an equitable one. The general principles for interim injunctions laid down in *American Cyanamid v Ethicon Ltd* [1975] AC 396 will apply where an interim injunction is sought. Thus, an LPA will need to show a *prima facie* case of a breach of planning control; that any harm cannot be adequately compensated in damages (this will normally be the case as the LPA is enforcing planning control in the public interest); and that the balance of convenience is in favour of the injunction. Given the planning context, the LPA will be required to show not only that the remedy is expedient and necessary, but also that it has taken into account all relevant considerations in coming to that decision, that there is a clear breach or a clear likelihood of a breach, and that the remedy is the most appropriate one in the circumstances of the case: *South Bucks DC v Porter* [2003] 2 AC 558, [29] which is the leading case on the power to grant a section 187B injunction. Injunctions are often sought to preserve areas of particular public amenity from harmful development, such as green belts or areas of outstanding natural beauty: *Maidstone BC v Beck and Others* [2021] EWHC 509 (QB) (AONB); *Basildon BC v Anderson* [2020] EWHC 3382 (QB) (Green Belt). The High Court in *Ipswich v Borough Council v Fairview Hotels* [2022] EWHC 2868 (KB) reaffirmed the principles to be applied to an application for a section 187B injunction.

It is important to bear in mind that injunctions carry with them the potential for imprisonment if they are breached. They are, therefore, very serious. While it is an offence to breach an enforcement notice and an injunction, the Act gives the developer a right of appeal to the SOS against that enforcement notice where they may (for example) argue that the development would have been given planning permission. By contrast, in an injunction, the court will be reluctant to consider the planning merits of the development in line with the case law. For that reason, an LPA should carefully consider alternative enforcement methods and will have to show to the court why an injunction is necessary, eg other enforcement methods may be ineffective.

A section 187B injunction may be sought where there has been an actual breach of planning control as well as where there is an apprehended breach of planning control, ie the breach has not yet happened. An example of the latter is the attempts by several LPAs to seek injunctions preventing the use of hotels as hostels for asylum seekers.

6.10 APPEALS AGAINST ENFORCEMENT NOTICES (ss 174–177)

6.10.1 Grounds of appeal

Section 174(2) lists seven grounds of appeal, as follows:

(a) Planning permission ought to be granted, or any condition or limitation attached to an existing permission ought to be discharged (as the case may be) in respect of the matters alleged to be a breach of planning control in the enforcement notice.

(b) The matters alleged have not occurred.

(c) The matters, if they occurred, do not amount to a breach of planning control.

(d) No enforcement action could be taken at the date the notice was issued as regards the matters alleged in it (ie the LPA was out of time, see **6.2.2**).

(e) Copies of the enforcement notice were not served as required by s 172 (see **6.7.5**).

(f) The steps required by the notice or the activities required to cease exceed what is necessary to remedy any breach of planning control or injury to amenity (as the case may be).

(g) The period specified in the notice for the taking of steps, etc falls short of what should reasonably be allowed.

Note also the following points:

(i) If ground (a) is expressly made a ground of appeal, the SOS may grant planning permission in determining the appeal (as if a planning application had been made to the SOS), but this is the only circumstance in which they may do so (s 177(1C)).

(ii) As regards ground (e), the SOS may disregard failure to serve any person if that failure has not caused substantial prejudice to that person or to the appellant (s 175(5)).

(iii) Grounds (f) and (g) do not go to the validity of the enforcement notice and the SOS may vary the requirements of the original notice (s 176(1)).

6.10.2 Time limit (s 174(3))

Written notice of appeal (which can be by letter, although the standard form supplied by the MHCLG is normally used) must be given to the SOS before the date on which the enforcement notice takes effect. There is no power for the SOS or the court to extend the time limit for appealing. In practice, this is a significant point as the failure to appeal before the enforcement notice comes into effect means that the failure to comply with it will result in criminal liability.

Note that if the notice is sent to the proper address by pre-paid post at such time that, in the ordinary course of post (two working days in the case of first-class post), it would have been delivered before the enforcement notice takes effect, the appeal will be in time even if it is delayed in the post (s 174(3)(b)).

6.10.3 Who may appeal? (s 174(1) and (6))

Any person having an interest in the land (whether served with the enforcement notice or not) may appeal, as may any person who was occupying the land under a licence at the time the notice was issued and continues to occupy the land when the appeal is brought.

6.10.4 Procedure

6.10.4.1 Documentation and fees to be submitted

By s 174(4), and reg 6 of the Town and Country Planning (Enforcement Notices and Appeals) (England) Regulations 2002, the applicant may submit with the notice of appeal a statement in writing specifying the grounds on which they are appealing and stating briefly the facts in support of those grounds. If they do not submit this with the appeal, they must do so within 14 days of being required to do so by notice from the SOS. It is important for the appellant to specify all the grounds on which they wish to rely as amendments adding additional grounds are unlikely to be allowed subsequently.

Where there is a deemed application for planning permission, a fee is payable for that deemed application.

The appeal fee is refundable in certain circumstances (eg if the appeal is allowed on grounds (b) to (e), or if the enforcement notice is quashed or found to be invalid).

6.10.4.2 Appeal forum

There are three possible procedures for the determination of an appeal: written representations, hearings and inquiries. PINS will decide which procedure an appeal should follow, but will take into account the views of the appellant and the LPA. Its decision will be based on indicative criteria issued by the SOS. See **Chapter 4** for detailed consideration of this topic.

6.10.4.3 Effect of appeal

Until the final determination or withdrawal of the appeal, the enforcement notice is of no effect. According to the Court of Appeal in R v Kuxhaus [1988] 2 WLR 1005, [1988] 2 All ER 705, CA, 'final determination' means when all rights of appeal have been exhausted, including appeals to the High Court under s 289. However, note that the High Court can, in any appeal under s 289, order that the notice takes effect while the appeal is being determined (s 289(4A)).

6.10.4.4 Written representations and informal hearings

As mentioned above, the SOS may suggest these alternatives in appropriate cases, but they can be used only with the consent of both parties.

6.10.5 Costs

The SOS or their inspector has power to award costs in all cases, even where the appeal was by way of written representations or even where the inquiry was not held (ss 320 and 322). Again, costs will only be awarded where there has been unreasonable behaviour (either substantive or procedural) and where that unreasonable behaviour has caused a party to incur unnecessary or wasted expense.

6.10.6 Further appeals (s 289)

A further appeal may be made to the High Court, but only on a point of law or procedure, against any decision made by the SOS in proceedings on an enforcement appeal. By s 289(6), leave of the court to bring such proceedings is required. No such appeal lies, though, under s 289 if the SOS declined to entertain the appeal or set the enforcement notice aside as being a nullity; in these cases the appropriate way to proceed is by way of judicial review.

REVIEW ACTIVITY

1. An individual has completed building an extension on the rear of his house. Has he committed an offence under the law governing planning control?
2. Assuming the same facts as Question 1, does the LPA have an automatic right to issue an enforcement notice in respect of any breach?
3. Assuming the same facts as Question 1, how long would the individual have to respond to any planning contravention notice served by the LPA investigating the matter?
4. Would your answer to Question 1 differ if the individual had completed the work five years ago?
5. Assuming the same facts as in Question 4, how would you advise the individual should he decide to sell the house given that he is concerned that any breach of planning control might deter a purchaser?
6. You are a planning enforcement officer at an LPA. You have received a report that a coffee shop has started operating as a wine bar. How might you confirm whether this is the case?
7. It turns out that the coffee shop considered in Question 6 is indeed operating as a wine bar. There is a planning permission allowing the property to be used as a shop within use Class A1 but it is subject to a condition that no alcohol be served. What enforcement options are available?
8. Assuming the same facts as for Questions 6 and 7, why can you not just serve a stop notice to force the owner to stop its activities?
9. What is the time limit for appealing against the service of an enforcement notice?
10. A firm of accountants is operating in a property that has planning permission for any use within use Class A2. The property is in an area identified in the Local Development Framework as one where mixed retail and business use should be encouraged. An enforcement notice has been issued requiring the firm to cease trading within six weeks. What grounds of appeal do you think the firm could rely on should it decide to challenge the service of the enforcement notice?

Answers to this Review activity may be found in Appendix 1.

CHAPTER 7

Compulsory Purchase and Compensation

7.1	Introduction	97
7.2	Inverse compulsory purchase	98
7.3	Compulsory purchase procedure – the stages of compulsory purchase	101
7.4	Compulsory purchase compensation	104
7.5	Injurious affection	108
7.6	Disturbance compensation and additional payments	110
	Review activity	112

7.1 INTRODUCTION

Sometimes public bodies require real property in order to carry out their functions, such as highway, housing or industrial development. The proposed high-speed rail link (HS2) would be a further example. These functions cannot be carried out without significant powers relating to compulsory purchase. As the name suggests, the purchase is compulsory; the land owner cannot refuse the purchase, whether they are willing to consent to the purchase or not. The public body that is undertaking the compulsory purchase is known as the 'acquiring authority'. When a compulsory purchase takes place, the owner or occupier of the property will have to be compensated for its loss. Usually, compensation will be based on the market value of the property – what a willing seller would expect to realise for the property when sold on the open market. Note that there are other factors that do not directly relate to the value of the land, such as loss of goodwill (if the land is a business), moving and legal costs and adapting new premises. These latter factors are known as 'disturbance' (see **7.6**).

Other factors to consider are the loss of rights to third parties, such as those enjoying the benefit of an easement or restrictive covenant over the acquired property. The Housing and Planning Act 2016, ss 203 to 205 came into force on 13 July 2016. These sections give broad powers to specified authorities to override third party rights, subject to the appropriate payment of compensation. The land need not have been compulsory acquired by the relevant authority, but the authority must have compulsory purchase powers in order to override the third party interests. It is irrelevant who undertakes the works. So an authority could transfer the land to a private developer and the authority can still override any third party rights on the land, even though it no longer owns the property. A lender who has advanced money to the landowner under a mortgage would likewise have to be compensated, as would a tenant of the property that has lost its tenancy. The effect of 'Brexit' on compulsory purchase is as yet unknown.

The Neighbourhood Planning Act 2017, when fully in force, will give a right for an acquiring authority to take *temporary* possession (rather than ownership) of property. This temporary possession can be compulsorily or by agreement with the landowner. An example might be where land is being compulsorily acquired and the authority needs storage facilities for, say, construction equipment on nearby land. An owner of freehold or leasehold land that is affected by this temporary possession can serve a counter-notice on the acquiring authority limiting the temporary possession to 12 months where the land is or includes a dwelling. The period is six years in all other cases.

Compulsory purchase can occur either by the acquiring authority taking the necessary steps to compulsorily acquire the property, or by the property owner itself compelling the authority to purchase its property – a form of 'inverse compulsory purchase'. This inverse compulsory purchase will be considered first.

In May 2020, the Ministry of Housing, Communities and Local Government published guidance on compulsory purchase matters with regard to the Covid-19 situation (see <www.gov.uk/guidance/coronavirus-covid-19-compulsory-purchase-guidance>). It deals predominantly with procedural matters such as service of documents, time limits for serving documents, inspection and how to deal with claimants. Acquiring authorities must exercise particular caution regarding residential evictions where these are as a result of compulsory purchase. Strong emphasis was placed in the guidance on acquiring authorities paying compulsory purchase compensation promptly to claimants.

7.2 INVERSE COMPULSORY PURCHASE

7.2.1 Introduction

Here the claimant is able to compel the relevant authority to purchase the property or the interest in the property. Compensation will be assessed as if the property or interest had been compulsorily purchased. There are two main forms of inverse compulsory purchase – the blight notice and the purchase notice.

The blight notice is suitable where the property or interest has a high or reasonable existing use value but is failing to appreciate or is depreciating because of the 'blight'. The blight is caused by the existence of the compulsory purchase order over the property, meaning that potential buyers or tenants are immediately put off from purchasing or renting. The main requirement for service of a blight notice is that the land in question must be in an area designated for compulsory purchase. (However, this strict requirement has been relaxed for those affected by the new high-speed network HS2. See below for more information.) A reduction in value of one's property merely due to proximity (because, for example, a sewage works is being built nearby) does *not* entitle a blight notice to be served.

The purchase notice applies where the property's existing use value is virtually zero. Planning permission to develop must have been refused and hence the land is 'incapable of reasonably beneficial use in its existing state' (Town and Country Planning Act (TCPA) 1990, s 137).

7.2.2 The blight notice

As stated, the essence of a blight notice is that the land involved has a reasonable existing use value but fails to appreciate or depreciates due to the 'blight', the blight being the threat of compulsory purchase. The blight notice is to speed up the process of compulsory purchase so that the claimant is not left for long with a depreciating asset. Note that, as a result of HS2, many properties are now blighted. The Government has created special rules to allow the owners of such properties to have their land compulsorily acquired. See <www.gov.uk/claim-compensation-if-affected-by-hs2/homeowner-payment-scheme>.

The conditions for service of a blight notice are as follows:

(a) *The land must be within a 'specified description'* (TCPA 1990, Pt VI). This, for our purposes, means that the claimant's land *must* be in an area designated for compulsory purchase itself and is usually on the development plan. Thus, as stated above, merely living near public works that causes depreciation in a claimant's land *does not* entitle a blight notice to be served. Instead the claimant should pursue a claim for injurious affection compensation (see **7.5** below). As stated above, this requirement has been relaxed somewhat for those affected by HS2.

(b) *The claimant must have a 'qualifying interest'.* TCPA 1990, s 149 defines this to include:

    (i) the resident owner-occupier of any hereditament. This refers to anyone who is a freeholder or leaseholder (with at least three years unexpired) of a dwelling (a residential property) at the date of service of the blight notice. The word 'hereditament' simply means land that is on the valuation list for rating purposes;

    (ii) the owner-occupier of any hereditament with a net annual value of £36,000 or less (the net annual value is the rating for business rates determined by the local authority and is only applicable to non-domestic properties – it is generally based on what a yearly business tenant would pay in rent for the property in question).

(c) *The claimant must make a reasonable attempt to sell the property on the open market* unless the compulsory purchase order has already been confirmed by the relevant minister (TCPA 1990, s 150).

7.2.2.1 Procedure

The following procedure must be followed for proper service of the blight notice.

(1) The claimant serves the blight notice over the whole unit (this still applies even if only part of the claimant's land is blighted) on the 'appropriate authority' (usually the county or district council). Difficulties can arise in determining what is 'the unit'. If a landowner owns two plots of land that are close to each other or contiguous, that does not per se make the two properties one unit. In *Jon Harding and Sarah Clements v Secretary of State for Transport* (2017) BNO/37/2016 the Lands Chamber of the Upper Tribunal adopted a threefold test. First, were the plots geographically a visual or cartographic unit; secondly, whether the two plots could reasonably be let separately or was one plot necessary for the enjoyment of the other plot; thirdly, the test is objective as to whether a reasonable person would regard the two plots as separate units. If the units are separate then two blight notices would have to be served.

(2) That authority then has two months to either accept the notice and acquire the land or issue a counter-notice giving reasons for refusal. If the authority does not accept or issue a counter-notice within the two-month period, the blight notice is then deemed to be accepted.

(3) The claimant, on receipt of the counter-notice, can refer the matter to a statutory body called the Lands Chamber of the Upper Tribunal.

(4) The Lands Chamber of the Upper Tribunal can then direct that the authority acquires the land or uphold the counter-notice.

7.2.2.2 The counter-notice

The authority must give reasons in the counter-notice as to why it does not accept the blight notice. These reasons are contained in s 151(4) of the TCPA 1990 and are:

(a) the land is not in the blight (not within the compulsory purchase order);

(b) the authority does not propose to acquire the land at all;

(c) the authority only intends to acquire part of the land;

(d) the authority does not intend to acquire the land within the next 15 years;

(e) the claimant does not have sufficient interest in the land.

Measures are available to prevent abuse of the system by a public authority, for example, claiming say (b) or (d) above and then later serving a compulsory purchase order when it suits it. The TCPA 1990 provides that such a later compulsory purchase order would be invalid. The authority also cannot amend the counter-notice, in that it cannot raise a further objection that was not in the original counter-notice (*Burn v North Yorkshire County Council* [1992] EGCS 91).

If the authority argues that it intends to acquire part only, the claimant can demand that the remainder be acquired, provided the latter is suffering 'material detriment'. In *Burn v North Yorkshire County Council*, the claimant's land included a shop and a large area at the rear that could be used for car parking. The car-parking area was shown on the development plan as being designated for compulsory purchase for the purpose of building a relief road. In 1989 the claimant obtained planning permission for the car-parking area to be developed for office use. However, the development plan had the effect of blighting the property. The claimant put the property on the open market for sale, but no one would purchase it due to the threat of compulsory purchase. The claimant issued a blight notice and the authority served a counter-notice, stating that it was only going to acquire the car-parking area. The claimant argued that the remainder of his property would suffer material detriment on its own. The Lands Tribunal (now the Lands Chamber of the Upper Tribunal) upheld the claimant's contention; acquisition only of the car-parking area would make the use and manageability of the shop very difficult. Hence the authority had to acquire the whole of the property.

7.2.3 Purchase notice

7.2.3.1 Introduction

As stated above, this involves the situation where the land has negligible existing use value, and restrictions on development leave the land virtually useless.

The essential characteristic is that the land must have become *incapable of reasonably beneficial use in its existing state* due to a refusal of planning permission or permission subject to conditions (TCPA 1990, s 137). There are therefore two primary conditions:

(a) planning permission to redevelop must have been refused or granted subject to conditions;
(b) the land is incapable of reasonably beneficial use in its existing state.

Note that there is no requirement that the land must already be in an area designated for compulsory purchase, as is the case with a blight notice.

The meaning of the phrase 'incapable of reasonably beneficial use' has been the subject of litigation and, generally speaking, a restrictive interpretation has been favoured by the courts. In *General Estates v Minister for Housing and Local Government* (1965) 194 *Estates Gazette* 201, the claimant's land was used partly for a sports club at a rent of £52 per year and partly for grazing at £12 per year. The claimant applied to redevelop the land, which was refused, and so the claimant served a purchase notice. The court held that the existing uses were beneficial and hence the notice was refused. Accordingly, the word 'beneficial' does not mean 'profitable' but merely means that the land does have some use in its existing state. In *Hudscott Estates v Secretary of State for the Environment, Transport and the Regions* [2000] 82 P & CR 71, the court held that 'incapable of' bore its ordinary dictionary meaning of 'not susceptible of'. Thus it will be rare that a purchase notice is successful.

Nor is it acceptable to compare existing use values with values the land would have had if permission had been granted. In *R v Minister for Housing and Local Government ex parte Chichester RDC* [1960] 1 WLR 587, the land in question was used for caravans; planning permission for housing was refused. The Minister allowed the claimant's purchase notice on the ground that there was considerable difference between the value of the land with planning permission and the value without it. The Court of Appeal quashed the Minister's decision, stating that he had applied the wrong test. The test was simply whether the land was incapable of reasonably beneficial use in its existing state. A comparison of existing use and development values is incorrect.

7.2.3.2 Procedure

Under s 137 of the TCPA 1990:

(1) The owner serves the purchase notice on the district council within 12 months of the refusal of development.

(2) The district council can accept the notice and purchase the land or refuse and submit the notice to the relevant Minister. The council notifies the owner within three months.

(3) The Minister will then arrange a hearing, giving the parties 28 days' notice. The Minister has power to confirm, reject or modify the notice or the planning permissions that led to the notice being served (TCPA 1990, s 140).

(4) The Minister's decision is to be given within nine months of service by the owner, or within six months of the council's submission to the Minister (TCPA 1990, s 143).

Even if the purchase notice is accepted, difficulties can arise in the assessment of compensation. In valuing the land, the general rule is the open market value of the property. As planning permission has been refused then, generally, the property will have no development potential and hence only existing use value is payable. As the purchase notice was issued because the land is virtually worthless, it means that little compensation is payable.

As stated above, there is no need, where a purchase notice is concerned, for the claimant's land to be designated for compulsory purchase for an acquiring authority's scheme. If such a scheme exists, the claimant can be in a more advantageous position than if there were no scheme. If the planning permission was refused due to the authority's scheme then statutory and common law rules can allow the effect of the scheme to be disregarded when assessing compensation. In other words, the value is what the land is worth had there not been the scheme to prevent the planning permission being granted.

In *Jelson v Blaby District Council* (1977) 34 P & CR 77, the claimant was able to obtain permission to build a housing development in Leicester on his land, except for a small strip that was to be later compulsory purchased for a road scheme. The scheme was later abandoned and the claimant applied to develop the strip. This was refused on the ground that the strip was too small. Its existing use value was about £9,000, but had planning permission been granted its value would be about £67,000. The claimant relied on s 9 of the Land Compensation Act 1961, which states that depreciation caused by the threat of compulsory purchase is to be disregarded in assessing compensation. A comparative common law principle is derived from the case of *Pointe Gourde v Sub-Intendent of Crown Lands* [1947] AC 565. Here, it was held that increases or decreases in the land acquired due to the scheme are (with exceptions) to be disregarded in assessing compensation (note that the *Pointe Gourde* principle has now been inserted into statute – see Neighbourhood Planning Act 2017, s 32). In applying s 9 and the *Pointe Gourde* principle to the *Jelson* case, the court held that the scheme to build the road caused the initial refusal of planning permission. Hence the claimant achieved £67,000 in compensation, rather than £9,000. Had there been no scheme, s 9 and the *Pointe Gourde* principle could not have been applied to the case.

7.3 COMPULSORY PURCHASE PROCEDURE – THE STAGES OF COMPULSORY PURCHASE

These stages are, first, the compulsory purchase order, secondly, the notice to treat and, thirdly, expropriation (the unilateral vesting of the legal title of the property in the acquiring authority). Any disputes as to compensation are referred to the Lands Chamber of the Upper Tribunal.

7.3.1 The compulsory purchase order

A compulsory purchase commences with the issue of a compulsory purchase order by the acquiring authority. This has a life of three years (Compulsory Purchase Act 1965, s 4). Note that the Levelling-up and Regeneration Act 2023, s 185 permits acquiring authorities to increase this time limit to more than three years. The procedure for the issue of such an order is as follows.

7.3.1.1 Notification stage

Notice has to be served for at least two weeks in one or more newspapers (Acquisition of Land Act 1981, s 11(2)). Personal notice has to be served on 'every owner, lessee or occupier' of any land covered by the order (Acquisition of Land Act 1981, s 12). Tenants of one month or less need not be served, nor those with third party rights such as easements. However, if the acquiring authority wishes to acquire third party rights over neighbouring land (such as easements) then such landowners are entitled to personal notice (Local Government (Miscellaneous Provisions) Act 1976, s 13).

Note that the Government has issued updated guidance in line with Covid-19 measures as to how acquiring authorities should act in the compulsory purchase process. In particular, they should extend time limits for objections and service of documents (see 'Compulsory Purchase Guidance', updated July 2021 at <www.gov.uk/guidance/coronavirus-covid-19-compulsory-purchase-guidance>.

7.3.1.2 Objections stage

Any person may object. Such objections tend to relate to the visual or noise impact of a scheme, or to the possibility of an alternative route if, say, a highway is involved. Sometimes a claimant might put forward an alternative method of undertaking the scheme, with the claimant itself doing the work proposed by the scheme. In this instance, the inspector, and on appeal the Secretary of State, should give full consideration to the time and cost involved and also the expertise of the claimant when considering whether to allow the claimant to undertake the relevant work instead of through the compulsory purchase mechanism (*Swish Estates v Secretary of State for Communities and Local Government* [2017] EWHC 3331 (Admin)).

7.3.1.3 Inquiry stage

If any person served with a personal notice objects, the relevant Government Minister must hold an inquiry, where the normal rules of natural justice apply. However, from 31 January 2025, the relevant Minister will have power to direct that an inquiry need not be held (Levelling-up and Regeneration Act 2023, s 182). An inspector appointed by the Minister will oversee the inquiry and make a report to the Minister. After the inquiry, the Minister, subject to rights of appeal, can refuse or confirm the order. As stated, the authority has three years in which to exercise the order.

If there are no objections, the relevant Minister can then confirm, reject or modify the compulsory purchase order without an inquiry. Note that the Levelling-up and Regeneration Act 2023, s 183 permits conditional confirmation where, for example, planning permission still needs to be obtained for the proposed works or there are still funding issues.

7.3.1.4 Challenging the compulsory purchase order

If any person interested wishes to challenge the order, they must do so usually under normal public law grounds – breach of the *Wednesbury* principles of unreasonableness (*Associated Picture Houses v Wednesbury Corporation* [1947] 1 All ER 680) or the rules of natural justice, or, since the Human Rights Act 1998, any relevant grounds in the statute.

7.3.2 The notice to treat

The notice to treat is basically the first formal step towards the actual acquisition of the relevant property. It is analogous to a contract for the sale of land, though it is not legally binding until compensation is agreed. It is, though, registrable as a local land charge. After it becomes legally binding, either party can then obtain an order of specific performance. Occupiers of the property, except those with leases of less than one year, are entitled to a notice to treat. The notice to treat extends the life of the compulsory purchase order for a further three years.

Under the Compulsory Purchase Act 1965, Sch 2A, para 5, if only part of the land is to be taken, the claimant can serve a counter-notice that the remaining land is suffering 'material detriment' and hence all the land should be compulsory purchased (see **7.2.2** for the meaning of 'material detriment'). The claimant has 28 days to issue a counter-notice from the date of service of the notice to treat. The Court of Appeal in *Anixter Ltd v Secretary of State for Transport* [2020] EWCA Civ 43 held that 'service' meant 'delivery'. The claimant in that case had claimed that service meant the date the claimant had knowledge of the notice to treat, which was rejected by the Court.

The interests in the land are said to be 'fixed' as at the date of the notice to treat. Thus whatever interests (leasehold/freehold, etc) exist at the date of the notice are to be valued. Hence, for example, tenancies *created* after the date of the notice to treat are not compensatable. A freehold that is subject to a lease as at the date of the notice to treat will therefore be valued as such, even if the tenancy has expired by the date of the assessment of compensation. The relevant date of valuation is the date of the assessment itself or the date the acquiring authority takes possession, whichever is the sooner (Planning and Compulsory Purchase Act 2004, s 103).

After service of the notice to treat, the acquiring authority can take early possession (even before vesting the legal title in itself). This is by means of serving a notice of entry on the occupier (Compulsory Purchase Act 1965, s 11), giving a minimum of 14 days' notice.

The acquiring authority may withdraw from the notice to treat within six weeks of receiving the landowner's claim for compensation or six weeks from the Lands Chamber of the Upper Tribunal's decision (Land Compensation Act 1961, s 31).

7.3.3 Expropriation

This refers to the vesting of the entire legal interest of the property in the acquiring authority and is normally undertaken by the owner of the land. Note that the Levelling-up and Regeneration Act 2023, s 186 permits the acquiring authority and the owner to vary in writing the vesting date (as to when the authority becomes the legal owner of the acquired property). If the owner is unwilling or there are problems with identifying ownership under the notice to treat procedure, there is an alternative procedure called the general vesting declaration, which combines the notice to treat and expropriation into one stage. The authority will unilaterally vest legal title in itself using this procedure (Compulsory Purchase (Vesting Declarations) Act 1981).

A primary ground of challenge against a general vesting declaration is through judicial review. In R (*Dawes*) *v Birmingham City Council* [2021] EWHC 1676 (Admin), the Council executed a general vesting declaration against the claimant on the ground of s 17 of the Housing Act 1985. This allows an empty property to be acquired for housing purposes. The Council, however, had made no recent attempt to assess the internal condition of the property or its current occupation status, making the process procedurally unfair. The general vesting declaration was therefore quashed by the High Court by order of certiorari.

If expropriation takes place in accordance with the notice to treat, third parties with interests over the land (such as mortgagees) will be compensated by the acquiring authority. Usually, persons with easements over the acquired land will lose their interest and be compensated for the loss under s 10 of the Compulsory Purchase Act 1965.

Lessees of over one year who were served with a notice to treat will likewise be expropriated and compensation paid to them. However, those with less than one year do not receive a notice to treat, and hence the acquiring authority can act as an ordinary landlord and give a notice to quit. Alternatively, if the land is required early, a notice of entry can also be given to the short leaseholder (even though it did not receive a notice to treat) and compensation then becomes payable.

7.4 COMPULSORY PURCHASE COMPENSATION

The actual mechanism for compensation assessment will now be considered.

Compensation for compulsory purchase involves the following elements:

(a) market value of the property, including the full development potential;
(b) severance factors where only part of the land is taken;
(c) disturbance, which is *not* based on market value but relates to the loss suffered on having to vacate or move. This will include losses such as goodwill, loss of existing profits, and legal and surveyor costs in selling the property and purchasing another property.

In the leading case of *Horn v Sunderland Corporation* [1941] 2 KB 26, the Court of Appeal held that the compensation claimed should represent the claimant's true loss, no more, no less. To be able to claim both full market value with development potential (which pre-supposes the landowner remaining and developing the land) and disturbance (which pre-supposes the landowner leaving the land) would over-compensate the landowner. Therefore a landowner whose land is compulsorily purchased has the choice of claiming either:

(a) the value of the property with full development potential; or
(b) existing use value of the property only (without development potential) plus disturbance.

7.4.1 Market value compensation

As stated, this will comprise the value of the interest, including full development potential. Generally, payment will be made on completion of the vesting of the legal title in the acquiring authority (known as expropriation). However, s 52 of the Land Compensation Act 1973 permits an advanced payment of compensation to be made if the authority takes possession before compensation is paid. The amount is 90% of the agreed compensation or 90% of the acquiring authority's estimate if compensation has not been agreed.

The Land Compensation Act 1961, s 5 contains six rules of valuation. For commercial property purposes, the most important rule is rule 2, which states that the market value assessment is to be that value if sold in the open market by a willing seller. As well as development potential, which will be considered below, this will include such factors as:

(a) *Existing use value.* This can be the land as a whole, or 'lotting' can be assessed where the land is valued in individual plots and may on aggregate give the claimant more compensation than if sold as a whole. Note that, with a protected business tenancy under Part II of the Landlord and Tenant Act 1954, the rights of renewal of the business tenant under that Act are to be taken into account when valuing the tenancy and the freehold for compulsory purchase compensation assessment (Land Compensation Act 1973, s 47).

(b) *Marriage and ransom values.* A sitting tenant might be prepared to pay more to merge with the freehold ('marriage value') and if so would increase the value of the property. Or if, for example, a plot of land is severed, the two plots may be worth less than the whole plot (the marriage value of the two plots as one).

Alternatively, the claimant might have land that is necessary to 'unlock' the development potential of nearby land that is acquired for, say, housing development. The amount of compensation payable for such a 'ransom value' can be staggering.

In *Ward Construction Medway v Barclays Bank* (1994) 68 P&CR 391, CA, a strip of land worth about £3,000 and owned by the Bank was to be compulsorily purchased to widen the road leading to a proposed housing development. The developers, Ward Construction, agreed to meet the costs of the acquiring authority when the latter compulsorily purchased the Bank's land. The cost of land to 'unlock' the development was put at £2,150,000, which the Bank naturally claimed. The developers argued that increases due to the scheme should be disregarded when assessing compensation (relying on the principle in *Pointe Gourde v Sub-Intendent of Crown Lands* [1947] AC 565, PC – now contained in s 32 of the Neighbourhood Planning Act 2017); hence the value should be only £3,000. The Court of Appeal disagreed, stating that provided a private developer could do road-widening work, the increase could be taken into account. Thus the developers had to pay £2,150,000 (see also *Herts County Council v Ozanne* [1991] 1 WLR 105, HL).

(c) *Disregards.* In general terms, any increases or decreases due to the scheme (or the threat of the scheme) are disregarded when assessing compensation (Land Compensation Act 1961, ss 6A–6E; *Pointe Gourde v Sub-Intendent of Crown Lands*; *Waters v Welsh Development Agency* [2004] UKHL 19). The Supreme Court has clarified that it is only increases and decreases due to the scheme that are disregarded. Past and present planning policies which support development can still be used to the landowner's advantage to increase the compensation payable. Likewise, the scheme will not prevent any of the planning assumptions stated in 'Development potential' below from applying where relevant (*Homes and Communities Agency v JS Bloor (Wilmslow) Ltd* [2017] UKSC 12). The exception, as stated, is when a private developer could do the work in the 'no-scheme' world. Likewise, if the claimant is carrying on a business in breach of planning control or doing anything illegal on the land, any increase in the value of the property caused by the breach or illegality is disregarded (Land Compensation Act 1961, s 5, rule 4; *Hughes v Doncaster Corporation* [1990] 2 WLR 16).

(d) *Betterment.* Sometimes a claimant might have other land in the vicinity that appreciates due to the works, as opposed to depreciates. For example, the land retained might now benefit from a key access route to the highway, which causes that land to appreciate (*Pepper v City of Worcester* (1971) Lands Tribunal). As the claimant is only entitled to its true loss then any increase in value of retained land is 'set off' against the compensation payable for the land taken (Land Compensation Act 1961, ss 6A–6E). Thus in *Pepper*, above, the key access route increased the claimant's retained land by £500. This led to a reduction of that amount in the compensation for the land taken.

7.4.2 Development potential

In order to claim for development potential, there must be two elements: first, market demand for the development and, secondly, planning permission (*Earl of Camrose v Basingstoke Corporation* (1966) 64 LGR 337, CA). Generally, market demand is determined by whether a private developer would be able and willing to gain planning permission to undertake the desired works. The second element of the *Camrose* principle is the availability of planning permission. Planning permission for compulsory purchase compensation principles can be either actual or assumed. Actual and assumed planning permissions are governed by the important ss 14 to 17 of the Land Compensation Act 1961, as amended by s 232 of the Localism Act 2011.

When valuing the land, the following planning assumptions can be taken into account:

(a) *Existing planning permission.* Any existing planning permission, including any permitted development under the Town and Country Planning (General Development) (England) Order 2015 (as amended by the Town and Country Planning (General Permitted Development) (England) (Amendment) (No 2) Order 2020) and the Town and Country Planning (Use Classes Order) 1987 (as amended by the Town and Country Planning

(Use Classes) (Amendment) (England) Regulations 2020), of the claimant must be taken into account in assessing compensation, including any conditions or restrictions on that permission (Land Compensation Act 1961, s 14).

(b) *Acquiring authority's planning permission.* Any planning permission of the authority is treated as planning permission of the claimant (Land Compensation Act 1961, s 16(5)). Thus if the authority has planning permission for a motorway, so does the claimant. However, such permission is not of much use as, according to the *Camrose* case (above), market demand (ie a private developer must be able to get the permission and do the work) must also be available. Only an acquiring authority could get planning permission for a motorway, etc (see *Myers v Milton Keynes Development Corporation* [1974] 1 WLR 696, where the acquiring authority gained planning permission for a new town but this was not compensatable as a private developer could not gain such permission).

(c) *Development under the current development plan* (s 16). Generally, if the development plan permits development of the claimant's land then this can be taken into account.

(d) *Subsequent planning permission.* Sometimes an acquiring authority (or its successor in title) gains additional planning permission after acquisition. For example, an authority acquires land for a particular scheme and later abandons the scheme and sells the land to a private developer who gains new planning permissions. According to s 66 of the Planning and Compensation Act 1991, if the acquiring authority (or a successor in title) within 10 years of the notice to treat gains further planning permission then this is treated as if it existed at the time of the original claim. However, this only applies now to claims made before 29 September 2017 as s 33 of the Neighbourhood Planning Act 2017 has repealed s 66 of the 1991 Act.

(e) *Hope value.* This applies to a situation where the land is likely to gain planning permission some time in the future. Consideration of the planning background, the emergence of new development plans and comparable land in the vicinity may give some idea of future planning permission (*Myers v Milton Keynes Development Corporation* [1974] 1 WLR 696; see also *Taylor and Taylor v Stockport Metropolitan Borough Council* [2022] UKUT 00142 (LC) where hope value was refused as the land was firmly in the green belt with no prospect of planning permission). However, assessment for hope value is not to be based on a certainty of the permission being granted. Under general civil law principles, if a matter has a 51% chance or more of occurring then 100% compensatory damages are payable ('on a balance of probabilities'). According to the House of Lords in *Transport for London (London Underground Ltd) v Spirerose Ltd (in administration)* [2009] UKHL 44, however, valuation for hope value is based on the 'loss of a chance principle'. In other words, what percentage chance would the claimant have of obtaining planning permission, or what is the value of the hope of obtaining the permission? If the claimant had a 60% chance of obtaining the permission, they would be able to claim not the full 100% compensation but 60% of what the permission would be worth.

The Localism Act 2011, s 232, which inserted a new s 14 into the Land Compensation Act 1961, appears to have partly changed the *Spirerose* method of valuation of hope value. According to the amended s 14, at the valuation date it has to be determined whether the planning permission 'could at that date be reasonably expected to have been granted'. The phrase 'reasonable expectation' suggests at least, or more than, a 50% chance. If this is the case then anything above 50% is to be based not on the loss of a chance valuation but on the full balance of probabilities valuation – 100% certainty of the permission being granted.

Where the hope of obtaining planning permission is less than 50% then there is no 'reasonable expectation', and hence the value will have to be determined on the loss of a chance valuation. To give an example, a house has an existing use value of £2m. There is a 60% chance of obtaining planning permission for redevelopment, which, if granted, would have caused the value to double to £4m. According to the new s 14 of the Land

Compensation Act 1961, there is a reasonable expectation of gaining the permission and hence the full £4m can be claimed. If, however, there was only a 40% chance of obtaining the planning permission, there is not a reasonable expectation and hence the prospective planning permission will have to be valued using the loss of a chance principles. So the value will be £2m existing use plus 40% of the additional £2m (£800,000), the total value being £2,800,000.

So it appears that the law on hope value since the Localism Act 2011 is that where the 'hope' of obtaining planning permission is at least or more than 50%, the full 100% value is taken into account. If the 'hope' is less than 50%, valuation is based on the loss of a chance principle.

Note that the Levelling-up and Regeneration Act 2023 removes the right to hope value in schemes that enable affordable and social housing, or education- and health-related development (see s 190).

(f) *Section 17 certificate*. Sometimes it is not clear what development would be allowed. If so, a certificate under s 17 of the Land Compensation Act 1961 can be served (known as a 's 17 certificate'). Note that the Levelling-up and Regeneration Act 2023, s 189 now makes it compulsory for the claimant to serve this certificate if alternative development potential is to be claimed. Here the applicant states on the application what classes of development it thinks are appropriate and encloses a map of the land. The application should be made before the notice to treat is served (it may be made afterwards with the consent of the authority and Upper Tribunal if the matter has been referred to it). The local planning authority can then either reject the application or give a 'positive certificate' permitting the permissions in whole or in part. Note again that the scheme of the acquiring authority is to be ignored in determining what planning permission might be available on the land in question (*Boland v Bridgend CBC* [2017] EWCA Civ 1004). The Supreme Court in *Secretary of State for Transport v Curzon Park Ltd and others* [2023] UKSC 30 held that the compensating authority can take into account a Certificate of Appropriate Development given on other land not belonging to the claimant regarding the same scheme. In that case, four landowners had served Certificates of Appropriate Alternative Assessment under the same scheme. Each landowner could have their compensation assessed taking into account the certificates given to the other three landowners.

There is a right of appeal against a rejection or a partially positive certificate to the Lands Chamber of the Upper Tribunal within one month of the certificate's issue. In the recent Court of Appeal case of *Leech Homes Ltd v Northumberland County Council* [2021] EWCA Civ 198, the Court held that the Upper Tribunal had rightly rejected the s 17 certificate application of the claimant. The claimant had claimed that without the scheme 135 houses could have been built. However, the land was in part of the green belt area and there was no suggestion or prospect of obtaining such planning permission. In *Mintblue Properties Ltd, Re Car Park of Former E-Mag Factory* [2016] UKUT 172 (LC), the claimants had received a positive certificate but only for 'affordable housing', which greatly depreciated the value of the land. However, the local planning authority had failed to take account of the existence of planning permission for general housing on adjoining land, which the Upper Tribunal stated was a material consideration, and therefore it deleted the word 'affordable' from the s 17 certificate. Note that the right to serve a s 17 application is available to all claimants, not just to those who are not clear what development might be permitted. Note also that the *Camrose* principle still applies – there must be market demand even if a positive certificate is granted. In *Bromilow v Greater Manchester Council* (1975) 29 P & CR 517, a positive certificate was granted giving permission for offices to be built. However, the claimant's land was adjacent to an 'offensive' trade, and thus no market demand existed for offices in that area. Consequently, no compensation was payable for this planning permission for offices, even though a positive certificate was given.

It should be noted that if an appeal is made to the Upper Tribunal (Lands Chamber) and the tribunal finds against the claimant, there is no jurisdiction for the tribunal to award costs against the claimant. The Court of Appeal held that the Certificate of Appropriate Alternative Development is part of the overall compensation assessment, and the compensation process is not to be sub-divided into separate divisions (see *Leech Homes Ltd* (above)).

Note: According to *Transport for London (London Underground Ltd) v Spirerose Ltd (in administration)* (above), where a s 17 notice has not been served but all the parties believe that planning permission is likely to have been granted for certain development, this must not be assessed as a certainty. Rather, assessment should be based on 'hope value', which is the percentage chance of attaining the planning permission. (This is now subject to the amended s 14 of the Land Compensation Act 1961 (see (e) above).) Note that, as from 31 January 2025, it will be compulsory to serve a s 17 certification if the landowner is claiming for alternative development (Levelling-up and Regeneration Act 2023, s 189).

Sometimes it can be difficult to assess the increase in value due to the existence of development potential, such as through planning permission, especially if there are no similar comparable properties. To meet this difficulty, the Residual Method of valuation is used. Here the valuer values the property as if the development had already been carried out and then deducts from this value the costs of the development plus fees and profits. The net figure is the compensation claimable by the land owner. (See *Michael v Salford City Council* [2016] UKUT 370 (LC).)

Note that some additional payments are also claimable that are not directly based on the market value of the land (see **7.6.6** below).

7.5 INJURIOUS AFFECTION

This relates only to land remaining, not to land that has been compulsory purchased, and involves two main areas. First, where only some of the claimant's land is acquired, leaving a plot that is reduced in value on its own. Secondly, where none of the claimant's land is taken but, due to the scheme, it is now depreciating. In both examples, the land remaining is said to be 'injuriously affected'.

It is much more beneficial for compensation purposes for a claimant to have just a tiny fraction of land taken, rather than none at all. This is because s 7 of the Compulsory Purchase Act 1965 states that regard must be had not only to the severance but also to the injurious affection of the land remaining (in other words the depreciation in the market value of the land left). In *Duke of Buccleuch v Metropolitan Board of Works* (1872) LR 5 HL 418, part of the Duke's land by the River Thames was acquired for building the Victoria Embankment. This led to the retained land being affected by the noise, dust and smell of the works, and a consequential loss of privacy after the works were completed. The full market value loss of the retained land (which included loss of privacy) was claimable, as well as the market value of the land taken.

Matters are very different when no land is taken from the claimant. Rights to compensation are very limited, and a distinction is made between losses caused by the works themselves and the later use of the works. In *Metropolitan Board of Works v McCarthy* (1874) LR 7 HL 243, four principles were necessary to claim for losses caused by the building of the works (known as the *McCarthy* rules):

(a) The action causing the depreciation must have been authorised by statute. The acquiring authority must therefore be acting in harmony with its powers. If not, the claim must be in tort. In *Clowes v Staffordshire Potteries Waterworks* (1872) LR 8 Ch 125, the authority wrongfully discharged chemicals into the nearby river, polluting the claimant's river. The claimant sought injurious affection compensation, which was rejected, as the authority had no power to discharge the chemicals under statute. The claim should thus have been in tort.

(b) The cause of the depreciation must be actionable at law but for the statutory authority. In other words, the acquiring authority must be committing what would be actionable as a tort – usually that of nuisance. Therefore such things as loss of privacy (which can considerably devalue a property) are not actionable, as this is not an independent tort (*Re Penny and South Eastern Railway* (1851) 26 LJ QB 225). Also, it is very difficult to prove nuisance from common effects of public works, such as noise, dust and smell – everyone has to put up with such factors, and they tend not to amount to a nuisance unless actually damaging the land itself (*St Helens Smelting Company v Tipping* [1865] UKHL J81). Contrast this with the *Duke of Buccleuch* case (above) – where only some land is taken, full depreciation can be claimed regardless of how it was caused. A further point is whilst the Human Rights Act 1998 has incorporated Article 8 of the European Convention on Human Rights into English law (right to respect for private and family life), it appears that the Article does not create freestanding rights, ie there is no new tort of loss of privacy. For privacy to be applicable in this context, the courts would have to extend the tort of nuisance to include privacy – something that has not been done.

(c) Compensation can only be claimed for depreciation of rights in land. Thus there must generally be a permanent devaluation in the value of the legal estate. A mere temporary loss of profits, for example, will not result in the value of the land or interest diminishing. Thus only if the claimant's land or business had been permanently affected would there be a right to compensation. In *Bourne Leisure (Hopton) Ltd v Great Yarmouth Port Authority* [2016] UKUT 44 (LC), the Upper Tribunal held that the cost of remedial work to remedy the damage caused would also be claimable under this head. It should be noted, however, that where the cost of remedy is greater than the reduction in the value of the land, it is only the latter sum that is likely to be awarded.

(d) The loss must be caused by the execution of the works, rather than their use. In other words, these principles only apply to when the works are being built (eg when the motorway is being constructed), not to when they are in use.

Consequently, successful claims under the *McCarthy* rules are rare and are only likely to succeed where, for example, the claimant is in the process of selling the property and the building of the works is decreasing the market value.

There is some 'light at the end of tunnel' for a claimant who has had no land taken. Part 1 of the Land Compensation Act 1973 permits a claim for depreciation caused by the use of public works. The depreciation must have been caused by 'physical factors' (such as noise, dust, smoke, vibration and smell), hence loss of privacy is still not claimable, nor is mere proximity (*Williams v Cumbria County Council* (1994) Lands Tribunal).

To make a claim, the applicant must have a qualifying interest, that is, for dwellings, to be the freeholder or leaseholder with at least three years unexpired when the works were first used or open to the public. For businesses, the applicant must have the same interest as with the dwelling, but the business's rateable value must be less than the net annual value of £34,800.

The time of assessment is one year after the day following when the works were open to the public. Therefore if the works were first used on 1 January 2017, the relevant date is 2 January 2018. The compensation is based on the decrease in existing use value only, caused by the physical factors.

7.6 DISTURBANCE COMPENSATION AND ADDITIONAL PAYMENTS

7.6.1 Introduction

Disturbance applies only to *land taken*, not to land remaining. It includes those losses an occupier incurs in having to quit the property, such as fees, loss of existing profits, loss of goodwill, costs of moving and adapting new premises.

The right to this compensation emanates from s 5, rule 6 of the Land Compensation Act 1961. This states that the provisions of rule 2 (which is the open market valuation principle) shall not affect a claim for disturbance or any other claim not related to the value of the land.

7.6.2 General principles relating to a claim for disturbance

7.6.2.1 The claimant must be in occupation or be a property investor

This criterion means that a hardship arises for shareholders where a company is in occupation and, as a result of the compulsory purchase, shares in the company fall in value. As the shareholders are not in occupation, they cannot claim disturbance compensation (*Roberts v Coventry Corporation* [1947] 1 All ER 308).

7.6.2.2 The type of loss claimable

Disturbance can include any loss sustained that flows from the acquisition, provided it is not too remote and is the natural and reasonable consequence of the dispossession of the owner (*Harvey v Crawley Development Corporation* [1957] 1 All ER 504, CA). This has been interpreted generously by the courts. In *Aberdeen CC v Sim* [1982] 2 EGLR 22, the claimant vacated his land after the notice to treat had been served but five years before the actual acquisition. The court said that this met the *Harvey* criteria and disturbance compensation was awarded.

However, a danger of vacating before acquisition was highlighted in *Prasad v Wolverhampton BC* [1983] Ch 333. Here the claimant vacated after the notice to treat, but the acquiring authority never acquired the land and hence no disturbance compensation was payable.

7.6.2.3 Mitigation of losses

The claimant has a legal duty to mitigate its losses. In *Bede Distributors v Newcastle Corporation* (1973) 26 P & CR 298, the claimant could have moved into a building of similar standard to the previous one with similar costs, but chose instead to move to a more expensive area with much higher costs. The claim for disturbance was restricted to the amount that the claimant would have received had the first building been used instead.

Note that the duty to mitigate only demands that reasonable efforts be made. Thus if only a very short time is given between notice to treat and expropriation, and the claimant does not move into suitable premises, no deduction will be made (*Linden Print v West Midlands CC* [1987] 2 EGLR 200).

7.6.3 Where only part is acquired

Disturbance only relates to *land taken*. Therefore a claim for disturbance compensation could be made for the part taken, but only injurious affection compensation could be claimed for the part remaining.

7.6.4 Disturbance and development potential

The leading case of *Horn v Sunderland Corporation* (see **7.4**) states that a claimant can only claim its true loss. The claimant therefore has two choices; it can *either* claim the value of the property with full development potential, or it can claim existing use value plus disturbance. A claimant cannot claim both; thus a valuation will have to take place and the greater amount claimed.

7.6.5 Compensatable losses under disturbance

Goodwill

A payment to reflect loss of goodwill is available if relocation is impossible, or if relocation is possible and the value of goodwill falls. For older business occupiers, s 46 of the Land Compensation Act 1973 permits a goodwill payment to be made where:

(a) the claimant is 60 or over, plus an undertaking to retire;
(b) the rateable value of the premises is not greater than £36,000 (£42,200 in Greater London);
(c) the claimant has not disposed of the goodwill and *undertakes* not to dispose of it; and
(d) the claimant has no other interest of the same kind.

If the claimant is a partnership then all the partners have to be over 60 and give similar undertakings; if the claimant is a company, all the shareholders have to be over 60 and give similar undertakings.

Profits

Loss of existing profits is claimable under disturbance, as they are not reflected in rule 2 of s 5 of the Land Compensation Act 1961.

Removal costs and travelling expenses

Legal costs

This refers to the legal costs of the claimant when acquiring another property. Legal costs of the compulsory purchase are payable by the acquiring authority anyway under s 23 of the Compulsory Purchase Act 1965.

Adaptation of new premises

The adaptation must represent the facilities originally in the premises that were expropriated. If the adaptation can be seen as an improvement then a deduction will be made. In *Tamplins Brewery v County Borough of Brighton* (1970) 22 P & CR 746, the claimant installed in the new premises a brand new plant system, which led to savings on running costs over a 10-year period, and hence a disturbance payment was not available for such 'value for money'. Likewise, if the claimant incurs higher rent or rates due to having to move, this is not compensatable if the higher expenditure represents value for money (*Bibby v Merseyside CC* (1980) 251 EG 757).

Interests and charges

Bank loans might have to be incurred by the claimant in moving. If so then a disturbance payment can be made to reflect this. However, if the claimant obtained 'value for money' or did not reasonably mitigate its losses, no payment is available. In *Simpson v Stoke on Trent* (1982) 44 P & CR 226, the authority wanted early possession of the premises before compensation was paid. This gave the claimant an automatic right to claim an advance payment of compensation of 90% of the agreed amount, or 90% of the acquiring authority's estimate if not agreed (Land Compensation Act 1973, s 52). However, the claimant, for some unknown reason, declined the advance payment, took out a bridging loan and claimed a disturbance payment for the interest incurred. This was rejected since the loss could have been mitigated by accepting the advance payment.

7.6.6 Additional payments

These payments are *not* subject to the *Horn v Sunderland* restriction (see **7.4**). They are therefore claimable regardless of whether the claimant has chosen the value of the property with full development potential, or existing use plus disturbance.

7.6.6.1 The basic loss payment and the occupier's loss payment

In the context of commercial property, there have been some fundamental additions to the compensatory scheme made by the Planning and Compulsory Purchase Act 2004.

The basic loss payment (Land Compensation Act 1973, s 33A) is equal to 7.5% of the value of the claimant's interest or £75,000, whichever is the lower. This is claimable by a business freeholder or leaseholder with at least one year or more unexpired on the date when compensation is agreed or the acquiring authority takes possession of the land, whichever is the earlier.

The occupier's loss payment (Land Compensation Act 1973, s 33C) has the same conditions as for the basic loss payment, with the additional requirement that the claimant must have been in occupation of the land. The amount is, in general terms, 2.5% of the claimant's interest, with a ceiling of £25,000.

7.6.6.2 The home loss payment

If the occupier has their home at the property expropriated, they can claim a home loss payment. If the occupier is the freeholder or has a lease with at least three years unexpired, they can claim 10% of the market value as a home loss payment, which since 1 October 2016 is subject to a maximum of £58,000 and a minimum of £5,800. Any other claimant is entitled to a flat rate of £5,800 (Land Compensation Act 1973, ss 29–33; Home Loss Payments (Prescribed Amounts) (England) Regulations 2015).

However, if the claimant qualifies for a home loss payment, they cannot also claim the basic or occupier's loss payments above.

7.6.6.3 Legal and other costs

As stated previously, s 23 of the Compulsory Purchase Act 1965 states that the acquiring authority is required to pay all costs incurred relating to the conveyance of the claimant's land to the ownership of the authority. Such costs will also include surveyors' costs and legal costs relating to advice on the acquisition.

7.6.6.4 Loans for acquiring new premises

Under s 41 of the Land Compensation Act 1973, provided the claimant is a freeholder or has a lease with at least three years unexpired at the date of displacement, such a loan may be claimed from the acquiring authority.

REVIEW ACTIVITY

1. In what circumstances can a blight notice and a purchase notice be served?
2. Explain the legal basis of compulsory purchase compensation.
3. How is compulsory purchase compensation assessed for market value purposes?
4. In terms of severance and injurious affection, explain why it is more advantageous for a landowner to have only a small portion of its land compulsorily purchased, rather than no land being acquired at all.
5. Explain the principles relating to compensation for disturbance and additional payments.
6. You have been contacted by Orchard Tailors Ltd, a firm that specialises in selling clothes to retailers. Orchard Tailors Ltd owns a number of properties that have been subject to compulsory purchase and requests your advice.

(a) Property 1 is based in Leeds, West Yorkshire. Part only of this property is set to be compulsorily acquired in late 2017 for a new housing development. As a result, the remaining part of Orchard Tailors Ltd's land has increased in value. Orchard Tailors Ltd wonders what effect this will have on its compensation for the part acquired.

(b) Property 2 is based near Buckingham and is set to be compulsorily acquired by Buckingham County Water Corporation for building a sewage works. Currently the land only has planning permission for retail use, though according to information obtained from an officer at the local planning authority, the new development plan will most likely have permission for industrial use. Apparently, for the last two years, the premises have been used for selling hot food. Orchard Tailors Ltd wants to know the possible effect on compensation of the acquisition and the selling of hot food.

(c) Property 3 is based in Hertford and is set to be compulsorily acquired by Hertfordshire County Council later this year. Orchard Tailors Ltd has recently been served with a notice of entry, which permits the acquiring authority to take possession early before compensation is paid. Orchard Tailors Ltd wants to know what effect this will have on when compensation is paid.

Chapter 8

Environmental Issues

8.1	Introduction to environmental law	115
8.2	Environmental risk management	118
8.3	Contaminated land	120
8.4	Nuisance	130
8.5	Environmental permitting and regulation	133
8.6	Climate change law and energy performance	136
8.7	Asbestos	141
8.8	Japanese knotweed	143
8.9	Flood risks	143
	Review activity	144

8.1 INTRODUCTION TO ENVIRONMENTAL LAW

Environmental law is an established specialisation and one of the fastest expanding areas of law. It applies not only by imposing liabilities with regard to the environmental condition of a specific parcel of land and contamination escaping from it, but also by placing restrictions on operators of certain polluting activities there. Further, much domestic environmental law does not exist in splendid isolation but results from obligations imposed at the EU or international level. It is a mixture of tort and statute, including both criminal and civil liabilities, and to an increasing amount of expected best practice driven by investors, bankers and environmental campaigning groups.

Environmental issues are increasingly part of our socio-economic consciousness. How we build, heat or cool our homes is regulated by increasingly strict standards of a low carbon existence. In the space of a generation, our global environmental awareness has moved from singular campaigns to save endangered species to the regulation of our everyday lives.

This recent emphasis is mostly due to anthropogenic climate change. The rise in extreme weather events and global warming now gain economic quantification, as well as mainstream media and political coverage. Beyond economics, climate change remains the greatest threat to our existence as a species. The Intergovernmental Panel on Climate Change (IPCC) published a 'special' report in October 2018 which estimates that human activities have caused approximately 1.0°C of global warming above pre-industrial levels, with a likely range of 0.8°C to 1.2°C. Furthermore, global warming is likely to reach 1.5°C between 2030 and 2052 if it continues to increase at the current rate. The report states that limiting global warming to 1.5°C with no or limited overshoot would require rapid and far-reaching transitions in energy generation, infrastructure (including transport and buildings), and industrial systems. In 2021, the IPCC published its Sixth Assessment Report, which reiterated the unprecedented scale of change across the climate system, and the role that humans have played in accelerating that change. The report stated, among other things, that temperatures would reach 1.5°C above 1850–1900 levels by 2040 under all modelled emissions scenarios, that the Arctic would likely be practically ice free in all scenarios assessed, and that there would be an increasing occurrence of unprecedented extreme events. UN Secretary General António Guterres described the report as 'code red for humanity'.

Accordingly, the wealth of environmental laws and issues in practice and academia now overlaps with planning and construction, health and safety, energy and projects, conservation, climate change, carbon markets, sustainable international development, corporate responsibility and human rights.

This chapter focuses on the core environmental issues that arise in commercial property practice, namely:

(a) *Environmental risk management* (see **8.2**). Environmental risks and liabilities should be considered as part of the legal due diligence of any transaction. Environmental liabilities could arise from various sources, including remediation of contaminated land, compliance with permit requirements and mitigating flood risks. Some risk management tools are universal, such as enquiries of the seller, contractual warranties and indemnities. However, environmental desktop studies, Phase I and II Reports, and environmental insurance are peculiar to this area of practice.

(b) *Contaminated land* (see **8.3**). The Contaminated Land Regime is based on 'the polluter pays' principle and may impose retrospective liability. It remains a core environmental concern in property acquisition, particularly as an innocent owner or occupier of contaminated land may be liable if the original polluter cannot be found.

(c) *Nuisance* (see **8.4**). Anything emanating from land may cause a nuisance – from methane emissions to oil spills to noise – and liability may arise in tort (including under the rule in *Rylands v Fletcher*) or pursuant to statute.

(d) *Environmental regulation and permitting* (see **8.5**). Most non-residential properties will require an environmental permit or exemption of some sort, whether it is a restaurant discharging waste or a factory emitting industrial pollutants. Failure to comply can lead to significant criminal penalties and civil sanctions.

(e) *Climate change and energy performance* (see **8.6**). This area represents the legal and practical ramifications of the universal drive towards reducing greenhouse gas (GHG) emissions. It includes Energy Performance Certificates (EPCs) and Green Leases.

(f) *Asbestos* (see **8.7**). Responsible for more cancer-related deaths than any product in history, asbestos could be present in any UK building built before 2000. The responsible person (who could be the owner or occupier) must monitor and manage its existence.

This chapter also briefly Japanese knotweed (see **8.8**) and flood risks (see **8.9**). It concludes with some review activities addressing the main environmental issues along with some related areas of property law.

8.1.1 Sources of environmental law in the United Kingdom

Environmental law is the body of law that seeks to protect or enhance the environment. It evolved out of the Industrial Revolution where rapid urbanisation led to public health problems. The Public Health Act 1848 arose in response to sanitation issues and outbreaks of typhoid and cholera from contaminated water. Intense industrial production and the use of coal led to further regulation to address air and water pollution, starting with the Alkali Act 1863 which regulated atmospheric emissions. Almost a century later, the Clean Air Act 1956 was developed in response to 'The Great Smog of London' in 1952.

Since then, the body of environmental law in the UK has continued to grow to address new and ever more challenging issues, from land contamination to complex waste issues and more recently greenhouse gas emissions.

Environmental law in the UK comes from three main sources:

International law

Given the transboundary nature of many environmental problems, such as climate change and ozone depletion, various international conventions and agreements have been negotiated to address global environmental issues. The UK is signatory to a number of these agreements, for example the Paris Agreement. Due to the dualist system of the UK constitution, the international agreements to which it is a signatory require implementation into domestic law through Acts of Parliament or secondary legislation.

Retained European Union law

A substantial proportion of UK environmental law is derived from EU law. Since joining the European Community in 1972, environmental law in the UK has developed rapidly. EU environmental law touches on a range of subjects, from air pollution to waste management, to environmental impact assessment, to habitats and biodiversity, and climate change and sustainable development.

Following Britain's exit from the EU, the status of EU-derived environmental law has been governed by the European Union (Withdrawal) Act 2018 ('Withdrawal Act'), which received royal assent on 26 June 2018. Pursuant to the Withdrawal Act, EU-derived domestic legislation (including environmental legislation) continues to have effect in domestic law on and after exit day. So, for example, secondary legislation, enacted to implement environmental Directives, continues to have effect in domestic law unless and until it is amended. Direct EU legislation, operative immediately before exit day, also forms part of domestic law by way of the Withdrawal Act.

English and Welsh courts and tribunals are bound by the decisions of the Court of Justice of the European Union made before exit day ('retained EU case law'), but are only required to 'have regard' to decisions of the CJEU made after 31 December 2020. Furthermore, the Court of Appeal and the Supreme Court are able to depart from retained EU case law, applying the same test that the Supreme Court would apply in deciding whether to depart from its own decisions.

Despite an amendment approved by the House of Lords, the final version of the Withdrawal Act placed no duty on the Secretary of State to prevent the 'removal or diminution' of EU environmental law. Section 16 of the Withdrawal Act did, however, require the Secretary of State to publish, within six months, a draft bill including the following matters:

- a list of 'environmental principles';
- a duty that the Secretary of State publish a statement of policy in relation to the application and interpretation of those principles;
- a requirement that Ministers have regard to the statement of policy;
- provisions for the establishment of a public authority with functions for taking proportionate enforcement action (including legal proceedings if necessary) where the authority considers that a Minister of the Crown is not complying with environmental law (commonly referred to as an 'independent environmental watchdog').

Those requirements were ultimately included in the Environment Bill, introduced to Parliament on 28 October 2019. After a long passage through Parliament, the Bill was given royal assent on 9 November 2021. The Environment Act 2021 sets out the UK's framework for environmental protection post-Brexit. The Act provides the framework for (among other things) the setting of UK-wide environmental targets, environmental monitoring, the creation of the new Office of Environmental Protection (OEP), and makes provision for waste, air quality, water, biodiversity, and conservation covenants. The Environment Act 2021 confers powers on the Secretary of State to amend certain provisions of retained EU law. For example, s 113 of the Act empowers the Secretary of State to amend Pt 6 of the Conservation of Habitats and Species Regulations 2017 ('the Habitats Regulations'), the main piece of domestic legislation transposing the Habitats Directive.

The Retained EU Law (Revocation and Reform) Act 2023 includes a 'sunset clause' for both EU-derived subordinate legislation and retained direct EU legislation. Section 1(1) of the Act provides that such legislation will be revoked at the end of 2023. The Act will force the Government to review and replace retained EU environmental legislation rapidly in order to avoid any lacunae developing in UK environmental law and protection.

Domestic law

In addition to international and EU sources, environmental law has developed at the domestic level. Devolution has led to a divergence in some areas of environmental law between England, Northern Ireland, Scotland and Wales. Brexit may lead to a divergence in environmental protection between the UK and the EU. Domestic environmental legislation is likely to become increasingly distinctive and important.

8.2 ENVIRONMENTAL RISK MANAGEMENT

8.2.1 Introduction

In accordance with the principle 'caveat emptor' (let the buyer beware), a seller is not under a duty to disclose material facts to a prospective buyer in a property transaction. Therefore, the buyer must undertake its own searches, enquiries and inspections to identify the risk of inheriting environmental liabilities.

If significant risks or existing issues are identified, the buyer's solicitor may then consider a variety of tools to limit the buyer's potential liability. For example, where contaminated land is a risk, these may include:

(a) specific environmental provisions in the sale contract, eg a 'sold with information' clause and/or a 'payments for remediation' clause, which are intended to exclude liability for remediation under Pt IIA of the Environmental Protection Act 1990 (EPA 1990);

(b) an agreement on liabilities, ie for the purposes of determining who is liable for the remediation of contaminated land under Pt IIA of the EPA 1990;

(c) an indemnity in relation to any environmental losses incurred;

(d) environmental insurance.

In addition, where the risk is more certain, the following methods may be pursued:

(e) positive obligations on either party, eg to undertake remediation;

(f) carving out the land, so as to purchase only the 'non-risky' section, eg a 'pie-crust' lease;

(g) negotiate a price reduction;

(h) in the worst-case scenario, decline the deal.

We look at pre-contract searches, enquiries of the seller, environmental searches and investigations and insurance at **8.2.2–8.2.5**.

Precedent clauses are normally available from law firm know-how databases and legal service providers such as LexisPSL Environment and Practical Law Environment.

8.2.2 Pre-contract searches

The first step in identifying any significant environmental risks in a property transaction is to conduct pre-contract searches.

The Law Society's Practice Note on contaminated land states that in 'all purchases, leases or mortgages', solicitors should (unless otherwise instructed) undertake enquiries of the local authority using Standard Form CON29 and a local land charges search using form LLC1 to ascertain whether the land has been designated by the local authority as contaminated.

Standard Form CON29O includes a number of optional enquiries relevant to environmental matters, such as noise abatement actions and environmental and pollution notices.

Additional pre-contract searches relevant to environmental issues include a search of the Coal Authority's mining records to identify subsidence risks.

8.2.3 Enquiries of the seller

In addition to the standard queries made in a property transaction, a buyer should request specific environmental information from the seller, such as details of any:

(a) historic, present or potential pollution incidents, hazardous substances, enforcement actions, or complaints by third parties in relation to environmental matters at the property; and

(b) environmental permits, licences, consents held or required for the property or any activity at the property.

In commercial property transactions, most practitioners use the Commercial Property Standard Enquiries (CPSEs). These are industry standard pre-contract enquiries endorsed by the British Property Federation. The main environmental enquiries are set out at enquiry 15, although other enquiries will also be relevant to environmental matters, for example enquiries 8.3–8.7 deal with asbestos.

8.2.4 Environmental searches and investigations

The Law Society's Practice Note on contaminated land advises solicitors to consider whether land contamination is an issue in all conveyancing transactions. It notes that land contamination may be a significant issue in a small number of transactions, and states that solicitors should be aware that environmental liabilities may arise and should consider what enquiries and specialist assistance their clients may require. The Practice Note provides further guidance on the searches and investigations that should be undertaken where contamination appears to be an issue.

In all transactions, a prudent solicitor should commission an environmental desktop screening study. Specialist environmental consultants provide basic desktop studies for around £50–300 (depending on the size of the property) – the turnaround time is usually 1–2 days. As the name suggests, a desktop study does not entail a physical inspection of the site but a trawl through databases and maps of present and historical land use, pollution incidents, flood risks, regulatory enforcement and neighbouring uses, amongst other things. The reports are often automated, or partly automated. Although some of the information is derived from public sources, such as the Environment Agency (EA), the speed, breadth and analysis in consultants' reports warrants their use over free searches.

Where actual or potential liabilities have been identified in the desktop report, the consultant will normally recommend further action that can be taken to reduce or mitigate the risk, such as:

- making specific enquiries of a regulator;
- carrying out a site inspection (Phase I Report); or
- undertaking a detailed site investigation, including testing and analysis of the soil, water, etc (Phase II Report).

The results of the desktop study and the reports should clarify and quantify any concerns flagged by the enquiries or desktop study. If a major issue is identified at any stage, it may become a bargaining point or remedial condition of the transaction. Remediation may also be statutorily required (see **8.3.4**).

For a summary of the range of different environmental searches available, see LexisPSL Environment *Practice Note: Environmental investigations – types of searches and investigations*.

8.2.5 Insurance

Environmental insurance in the UK has grown from a nascent to a competitive market in 20 years. There are several providers, which generally offer up to 10 years' protection for historical contamination and up to 5 years' protection for ongoing operations. Insurance cover may be provided for a range of environmental liabilities, including:

- historical pollution
- operational liabilities
- contractor's pollution liabilities
- remediation costs overrun (known as costcap/step loss policies).

Environmental insurance will usually cover on-site and off-site clean-up costs to the extent *required* by environmental law, as well as property damage. Typically, the insurer will exclude cover for losses arising from known pollution conditions where a liability to remediate or compensate a third party is active or likely.

As this market develops, environmental insurance is increasingly seen as a valuable tool in risk management, for both buyer and seller. It can often be the last 'comfort' required for a risky site transfer.

8.3 CONTAMINATED LAND

8.3.1 Introduction

Contaminated land remains one of the single biggest environmental issues facing property lawyers in the UK. This is due to centuries of environmentally harmful progress: a legacy of the Industrial Revolution and many unsound agricultural, construction and development practices.

Land which is 'contaminated' is, essentially, land on which there is a significant risk of harm being caused as a result of substances in, on or under the land. The Department for International Trade stated in May 2015 that the UK has over 400,000 hectares of contaminated land.

Contamination can severely impact any acquisition of property, as liability for contamination can be extremely costly.

8.3.2 The risks in summary: legal and practical

Like most environmental liability, the law is intended to ensure that 'the polluter pays'. This is clearly an important principle – the clean-up bill for dealing with something seemingly as innocuous as waste vegetables could amount to millions of pounds due to associated methane emissions (*Circular Facilities (London) Ltd v Sevenoaks District Council* [2005] EWHC 865 (Admin)).

Under the current contaminated land regime, authorities will in the first instance seek to hold the original polluter liable for any contamination. However, if that polluter cannot be identified, authorities may hold the incumbent owner or occupier liable for contamination. Liability is strict and may be retrospective. This element of the contaminated land regime is clearly of great concern to landowners and occupiers.

Most issues associated with contaminated land are dealt with by the planning regime, rather than by Pt IIA of the EPA 1990 (see **8.3.3**). Remediation of contaminated land may also, for example, be required upon the relinquishment of environmental permits for polluting activity (see **8.5**). However, a client should be warned of the risks in any case. In 2000, given the risks of contaminated land, The Law Society saw fit to issue a (rare) Warning Card setting out what it regards as 'best practice' for solicitors in conveyances. The Warning Card was replaced by the Law Society's Practice Note on contaminated land in December 2014, updated most recently on 28 January 2020.

8.3.3 The Contaminated Land Regime

The Environment Act 1995 amended the EPA 1990 and introduced a new Pt IIA, dealing with contamination. In summary, Pt IIA requires local authorities to identify contaminated land and then require the 'appropriate person' to clean it up. A variety of exclusion and apportionment tests apply if there is more than one appropriate person. In practice, a local authority is more likely to use a planning permission condition to ensure clean up, rather than the imposition of a statutory remediation notice.

Defra reissued its Contaminated Land Statutory Guidance (Guidance) in April 2012. The Guidance remains of pivotal importance, particularly in elaborating on the statutory definitions set out in the Act, exclusion tests, and the apportionment of liability.

8.3.3.1 Local authority: duty to investigate and require remediation

Local authorities have a duty to investigate land in their area to identify any contaminated land (EPA 1990, s 78B). Where the authority does identify any contamination, it must notify a number of persons, including the owners and any occupiers of the land (EPA 1990, s 78B).

In practice, local authorities have limited resources at their disposal, and many have therefore prioritised the investigation of higher-risk sites. Most local authorities have used the planning regime, rather than Pt IIA, to ensure remediation. This is because development proposals will often require an environmental assessment, which effectively outsources the investigation of contamination to the developer or an environmental consultant. The local authority can then require a remediation scheme for any contamination identified, so as to ensure the property is suitable for the proposed use.

8.3.3.2 Contaminated land and contaminant linkages

Local authorities have a duty to investigate and identify contaminated land, and to require remediation where any contamination is identified. The precise meaning of 'contaminated land' in the legislation is, therefore, important.

Contaminated land

Part IIA of the EPA 1990 sets out four key definitions, which are crucial to understanding the contaminated land regime. Italicised words appearing below have been added by the authors for emphasis:

(a) 'Contaminated land' is defined in s 78A(2) of the EPA 1990 as:

any land which appears to the local authority in whose area it is situated to be in such a condition, by reason of substances in, on or under the land, that (a) *significant harm* is being caused or there is a *significant possibility of such harm* being caused; or (b) significant pollution of controlled waters is being caused or there is a significant possibility of such pollution being caused.

(b) 'Harm' is defined (EPA 1990, s 78A(4)) as:

harm to the *health of living organisms* or other interference with the *ecological systems* of which they form part, and in the case of man, includes harm to his *property*.

The Guidance (Section 4) explains 'harm' as follows:

(i) *human health* – harm to human health includes death, life-threatening diseases, serious injury, birth defects and the impairment of reproductive functions. In deciding whether other health effects constitute significant harm, the local authority must consider the impact on health, quality of life, and the scale of harm (Section 4.1);

(ii) *ecological systems* – harm to ecological systems includes irreversible adverse change, or some other substantial adverse change, in the functioning of the ecological system. However, ecological systems comprise only recognised protected nature areas, eg SSSIs, National Nature Reserves, or Marine Nature Reserves (Section 4.3);

(iii) *property* – harm to property includes crops, livestock and buildings, and includes substantial damage, disease and diminution in yield or value to these (Section 4.3).

(c) '*Significant possibility*' is defined depending on one of the four categories of human health affected, and separately again for ecological systems and property. Very broadly, the tests used include 'unacceptably high probability' (Section 4.19, Category 1: Human Health), and 'more likely than not to result' and 'reasonable possibility' (Section 4.33, Table 1: Ecological system effects). You should consult the Guidance for more detail.

(d) '*Controlled waters*' takes the meaning from s 104 of the Water Resources Act 1991, namely all territorial (to three nautical miles) coastal, inland and ground waters (EPA 1990, s 78A(9)).

Local authorities must investigate land for contamination where there is a reasonable possibility that a 'significant contaminant linkage' exists. A 'significant contaminant linkage' is a linkage which gives rise to a level of risk of harm that is sufficient to justify a piece of land being determined as contaminated land.

Contaminant linkage

A contaminant linkage requires a contaminant, a pathway and a receptor. A 'contaminant' is a substance which is in, on or under the land, and which has the potential to cause significant harm to a relevant receptor, or to cause significant pollution of controlled waters. A 'receptor' is something that could be adversely affected by a contaminant, such as a person, an ecosystem, property, or waters. A 'pathway' is the route by which a receptor is (or might be) affected by a contaminant (Guidance, Section 3.8).

For example, the elements of the *Sevenoaks* case (see **8.3.2**) were as follows:

(a) rotting vegetation (organic waste – a *contaminant* by methane emissions);
(b) excavations, as part of construction work for residential development (creating drains and soil *pathways* for the contaminant); and
(c) housing residents (*receptors* who could become ill due to the emissions).

Pathways can be as simple as the air, earth, soil, water table or rivers and streams.

Receptors will often be human beings, but they could also include buildings, livestock, or protected areas.

Figure 8.1 below illustrates some typical pollution linkages. Note that the term 'source' is often used instead of 'contaminant'. Removing one of the elements would break the chain, such that the land would no longer come under Pt IIA of the EPA 1990.

Figure 8.1 Contaminant linkages

(*Source*: Canterbury Regional Council, New Zealand)

Special Sites and further guidance

Local authorities may also designate Special Sites (EPA 1990, s 78C). Special Sites are sites which meet one of the definitions set out in the Contaminated Land (England) Regulations 2006. Generally, they are sites where a particular risk of harm is present (eg land that is contaminated by waste, acid, tars, or radioactivity), and which require regulation by the EA.

Often, in order to establish whether the relevant definitions are met, a process of data analysis and scientific assessment must be carried out. The Guidance and further Defra and EA reports provide some information for these purposes, for example through Soil Guideline Values and Contaminated Land Exposure Assessment Models, from which consultants can make meaningful evaluations of risk. The detail of that guidance is beyond the scope of this book.

8.3.3.3 Who is liable? Responsibility, exclusion and apportionment

Where a local authority has identified land as being contaminated, the relevant enforcing authority has a *duty* to require remediation (EPA 1990, s 78E).

Responsibility

The local authority must notify all 'interested persons' (including the site owner) that land has been identified as contaminated under s 78B.

The enforcing authority must under s 78E identify and serve a *remediation notice* on each *'appropriate person'*, specifying what that person must do by way of remediation, and the timescale by which they must do each of the things specified. In the first instance, an authority will seek to identify the original polluter and/or a knowing permitter of the contamination (a 'Class A' person) as liable for any remediation. However, if the original polluter cannot be found then the owner or occupier or the land (a 'Class B' person) could be the appropriate person. This understandably causes some concern for landowners and occupiers.

A 'Class A' person is defined as:

> the person, or any of the persons, who *caused or knowingly permitted* the substance, or any of the substances, by reason of which the contaminated land in question is such land to be in, on or under that land. (EPA 1990, s 78F(2))

The precise meaning of 'knowingly permitted' is unclear in terms of the minimum level of knowledge that a person must have to fall within the scope of s 78F(2). Parliamentary debates from the passage of s 78F indicate that the intention was that a person must have both knowledge of the substances, and the power to prevent those substances from being present on, in or under the land (Hansard, HL Deb vol 565, coll 1495–501 (11 July 1995), at 1497). In the *Sevenoaks* case, Newman J concluded that 'knowledge' means knowledge of the relevant substance, not knowledge of the risk of harm posed by the substance.

A 'Class B' person is defined as 'the *owner or occupier* of the land for the time being' (EPA 1990, s 78F(4)). An *'owner'* means:

> a person (other than a mortgagee not in possession) who, whether in his own right or as trustee for any other person, is entitled to receive the rack rent of the land, or, where the land is not let at a rack rent, would be so entitled if it were so let. (EPA 1990, s 78A(9))

This definition would therefore cover a lessor.

Procedure for determining liability

Enforcing authorities should follow the five-step procedure set out in the Guidance for determining liability under the EPA 1990, s 78F:

Step 1: identify appropriate persons and liability groups for each significant pollutant linkage
Step 2: characterise remediation actions
Step 3: attribute responsibility between liability groups
Step 4: should any members of a liability group be excluded?
Step 5: apportion liability between members of a liability group

Not all stages of the procedure will be relevant in all cases. In practice, legal practitioners advising in the context of property transactions will be concerned with Steps 4 and 5.

Exclusion tests

Where the enforcing authority identifies two or more 'appropriate persons' within a liability group, those persons may take advantage of one of the exclusion tests provided in the Guidance (Sections 7(c) Class A Persons, and Section 7(e) Class B Persons). Importantly, however, a person will not be excluded if the effect is to exclude everyone in their group from liability (Guidance, Sections 7.32, 7.79). The tests are summarised below – see the Guidance for more detail, as this is a particularly important area of the Contaminated Land Regime.

Class A person exclusion tests

The enforcing authority must apply these six tests sequentially, from 1 to 6 (Guidance, Section 7.3.2(b)).

A Class A person will be excluded from liability in the following circumstances:

- *Test 1: Excluded activities*

    The person's *supporting* or *advisory* role is of such limited scope and responsibility that even if they could be said to have knowingly permitted contamination, they should still be excluded. The activities include lending, insuring, advising, licensing, consigning waste, consenting to activities or leasing land to the actual polluter.

- *Test 2: Payments made for remediation*

    The person made a sufficient payment for remediation to a responsible party, but remediation is not carried out properly or at all. A reduction in the purchase price due to estimated remediation costs could constitute such a payment. However, they must not retain control of the land.

- *Test 3: Sold with information*

    The person sold the land at arm's length and provided sufficient information to enable the buyer to be aware of the risk. Note that this exception was not relied upon successfully in the case of R (*on the application of Redland Minerals Ltd*) v SSEFRA & Others [2010] EWHC 913 (Admin). The Court emphasised that a polluter could not evade liability to pay for remedial works as a result of only partial disclosure of information regarding relevant pollution. If the buyer is a large commercial organisation or public body, however, and the seller permits the buyer to investigate the land, this will constitute constructive knowledge of any risks.

- *Test 4: Changes to substances*

    Person 1 deposits substance A in, on or under the land. Person 2 in the liability group later introduces substance B, which reacts with substance A, creating a significant contaminant linkage. Person 1 will be excluded if, before the date on which substance B was introduced, (i) they could not reasonably have foreseen that substance B would be introduced, (ii) they could not reasonably have foreseen that substance B would cause a chemical reaction, biological process, or radioactive decay, or (iii) they took what were, at that date, reasonable precautions to prevent the introduction of the later substances or the occurrence of the intervening change. After the introduction of substance B, person 1 must not (i) cause or knowingly permit any more of substance A to be in, on or under the land in question, (ii) do anything which has contributed to the conditions that brought about the intervening change, or (iii) fail to do something which they could reasonably have been expected to do to prevent the intervening change happening.

- Test 5: *Escaped substances*

    Persons are excluded where they would otherwise be liable for contamination as a result of the escape of substances from other land, where it can be shown that another member of the liability group was actually responsible for the escape.

- Test 6: *Introduction of pathways or receptors*

    The person caused or knowingly permitted the contaminant that created a significant contaminant linkage, but only because another person later introduced a pathway or receptor. The first person should be excluded. These were the facts of the *Sevenoaks* case (see **8.3.2**).

Class B person exclusion tests

A Class B person will be excluded from liability if:

(a) they occupy the land under a licence with no marketable value; or

(b) they pay a market rent with no beneficial ownership other than the tenancy itself.

The latter will normally exclude a tenant.

Apportionment of liability

If there is more than one appropriate person remaining within a class, liability will be apportioned between them (Guidance, Section 7).

For *Class A appropriate persons* (Section 7(d)), the enforcing authority should apportion liability as summarised below:

(1) Apportion according to relative responsibility (per steps 2–4 below), or otherwise in equal shares.

(2) Where one person *caused the entry of a contaminant* into, onto or under land, and another person *permitted its continued presence*, the two should share responsibility if the latter had the necessary 'means and opportunity' to deal with the contaminant.

    Where the second person did not have, or had insufficient, means and opportunity to deal with the presence of the contaminant, their responsibility should be reduced. See Section 7.67 for more detail.

(3) Where more than one person has *caused or knowingly permitted the entry of the contaminant*:

    (a) If there is a clear delineation of responsibility for remediation, liability should be apportioned according to that responsibility. This is particularly relevant if different persons were responsible for different areas of land, each requiring separate remediation.

    (b) If no such position is clear, liability should be apportioned according to the relative amounts of contaminant referable to different persons.

    (c) If neither (a) nor (b) applies, apportionment will depend on a broader consideration of the appropriate persons' activities and periods of control.

    See Sections 7.68–7.72 for more detail.

(4) Where more than one person has *knowingly permitted the continued presence of a contaminant*, liability should be apportioned according to their control in terms of:

    (a) time;

    (b) area;

    (c) means and reasonable opportunity to deal with the contaminant; or

    (d) a combination of (a) to (c).

For *Class B appropriate persons* (Section 7(f)), liability is apportioned within this group:

(a) to the Class B member who owns or occupies a particular area of land, where all or part of the remediation action clearly relates to it;
(b) according to the capital values of the respective Class B members; or
(c) equally, if the capital values of the Class B members cannot be ascertained.

See Sections 7.80–7.86 for more detail.

Agreement on liabilities

Appropriate persons may have agreed to divide responsibility for the contamination. If they provide the enforcing authority with a copy of such an agreement, the enforcing authority should give effect to it, unless it would place a party under hardship (see Guidance, Section 7.30, and EPA 1990, s 78P(2)).

8.3.3.4 Case law

The application of Pt IIA of the EPA 1990 is not an exact science. The four cases discussed below demonstrate the complexity of the case law in this area. Despite the apparently simple starting point that the 'original polluter pays', the reality can be more complex.

Circular Facilities (London) Ltd v Sevenoaks District Council [2005] EWHC 865 (Admin) was the first case involving an appeal against a remediation notice issued under Pt IIA. In *Circular Facilities*, the previous owner of the land had filled in clay pits with biodegradable waste, leading to the production of significant concentrations of methane and carbon dioxide. Circular Facilities London (CFL) bought the land and redeveloped it, constructing a housing development. Mr Justice Newman allowed CFL's appeal against a District Judge's refusal to quash a remediation notice, and remitted the appeal back to the magistrates' court to be reheard on the basis that it was unclear whether the District Judge had properly concluded that CFL had 'knowingly permitted' the contaminant to remain on the site. In his judgment, Newman J commented on the meaning of 'knowingly permitted' in the statute, indicating that what was needed was knowledge of the presence of the contaminant itself, rather than knowledge of the risk of harm posed by the contaminant. Newman J also appeared to accept that it was the act of development itself that had created the relevant contaminant linkage, by installing service entry points and concrete slab floors on the site that allowed methane and carbon dioxide to reach the relevant receptors. Liability under the contaminated land regime is therefore strict, and a person may be classed as a 'Class A' person even though they have not introduced a contaminant onto a site.

In the second reported remediation appeal (*R (on the application of National Grid Gas plc) v Environment Agency* [2007] UKHL 30, the '*Transco* case') black coal tar residue had been left in containers beneath the earth on a site that was later redeveloped into a housing estate consisting of 11 properties. The presence of coal tar beneath the gardens of the properties constituted contamination that was potentially harmful to health. The EA formed the opinion that remediation works were necessary, and imposed liability on the current statutory successor (National Grid Gas) to the gas companies that had disposed of the coal tar on the site. This was despite the fact that it was the redevelopment of the site that had created the necessary contaminant linkage, by introducing the necessary pathways and receptors that could be harmed by the contaminant. The House of Lords allowed National Grid's appeal against the EA's decision. The gas companies that had originally polluted the land were no longer in existence. Both companies that had redeveloped the site had also been dissolved. The House of Lords rejected the EA's argument that a 'person ... who caused or knowingly permitted' a contaminant to remain under land should be interpreted to include every person who became by statute the successor to the liabilities of the original polluters, even where the successor no longer owned or had any interest in the land in question. This was particularly so on the facts of the *Transco* case, where the statutory successors had assumed liability before the EPA 1990 was even passed. The emphasis in the statute is on the actual polluter. The 'polluter pays' principle did not extend as far as the EA had sought to argue.

In *Powys County Council v Price* [2017] EWCA Civ 1133, the Court of Appeal went on to confirm that Pt IIA could not be construed as operating retrospectively so as to deem a statutory predecessor to have been liable for historic contamination on land, when liability was only imposed by legislation which came into force after the predecessor ceased to exist. In *Price*, the appellant local authority's predecessor had operated a landfill site on a farm owned by the respondents. The appellant had been created in 1996 as part of a Welsh local government reorganisation. The remediation regime under Pt IIA had only come into force in Wales in 2001. The Court of Appeal concluded that very clear wording would have been needed for Pt IIA to impose remediation liability on the appellant as successor to the previous local authority in circumstances where such liabilities had been non-existent at the date of succession.

Two further examples of the courts considering the correct apportionment of liability and the validity of remediation notices can be found in the related cases of R (*on the application of Crest Nicholson Residential Ltd*) v SSEFRA & Others [2010] EWHC 561 (Admin) and R (*on the application of Redland Minerals Ltd*) v SSEFRA & Others [2010] EWHC 913 (Admin). The background to those claims was that Redland Minerals had operated a chemical production site from the 1950s until 1980. The chemical production process had led to leakage of bromide and bromate. Redland sold the site to Crest Nicholson, a developer. Crest Nicholson demolished existing buildings on the site, leaving it exposed and allowing the rain to wash contaminants into the soil. Remediation notices were issued to both Redland and Crest. The Secretary of State imposed liability on both parties, with 85% of remediation costs to be paid by Redland, and 15% by Crest. Redland sought to argue that it should not be liable, on the basis that it had supplied Crest with information on the contamination before selling the site. The Court rejected this on the basis that Redland had sold the site to Crest without information that would reasonably have allowed them to be aware of the *extent* of bromide contamination, in particular that contamination was already present in the groundwater at the site. The Court also rejected Crest's suggestion that it should not be held liable, as it had accelerated the process by which contamination descended into the ground at the site. In terms of the apportionment of liability, the High Court agreed that while the Secretary of State had identified no simple quantitative causative mechanism for measuring apportionment, he had adopted a broad *evaluative judgement* reflecting the length of ownership and use of the land. This approach was acceptable.

There have been further examples of statutory appeals against remediation notices that have not reached the High Court. For example, in April 2017 a remediation notice issued by Walsall MBC on the developer of a former gasworks site was quashed by the Secretary of State on the basis that Walsall MBC had not followed the 2006 statutory guidance correctly when identifying the land as contaminated land.

8.3.3.5 Enforcement

Overall, very few remediation notices have been served since the regime commenced. By 2013, only 19 remediation notices had been served in England: see the EA's report, *Dealing with contaminated land in England*, published in April 2016. Instead, most contaminated land is addressed voluntarily or through the planning system. The regulator may also carry out works itself, at the expense of the 'appropriate person'.

Remediation notices

There are certain circumstances in which a remediation notice cannot be served (see s 79H(5)), including the following:

(a) the contamination is being or will be remediated voluntarily, and the enforcing authority is satisfied that this approach will adequately deal with the problem;
(b) the act causing the contamination is licensed under another regime;
(c) if the enforcing authority were to do the works itself, it would not recover the costs from the person concerned on grounds of hardship.

If none of these circumstances applies then the enforcing authority must serve a remediation notice on the appropriate person(s).

A remediation notice must specify what the recipient must do and the periods within which the work must be carried out.

Sanctions

Failure to comply with a remediation notice is an offence (EPA 1990, s 78M). The level of fine depends on whether an offender is an individual or a corporate entity. More importantly, the enforcing authority may seek an injunction in the High Court to secure compliance with the notice (EPA 1990, s 78M(5)). If an order is obtained and breached, the company and its officers may be held personally criminally liable (EPA 1990, s 157).

Appeals

A person who has been served with a remediation notice may appeal to the magistrates' court (if the local authority is the enforcing authority) or to the Secretary of State (if the EA is the enforcing authority). The Contaminated Land (England) Regulations 2006 (SI 2006/1380) identify the grounds for appeal, which, along with other matters, include:

(a) the enforcing authority failed to comply with the guidance notes (Guidance);
(b) the enforcing authority acted unreasonably in determining that the appellant was an appropriate person;
(c) disagreement with the requirements of what is to be done by way of remediation.

8.3.4 Planning and contaminated land

Despite the detailed regime set out in Pt IIA of the EPA 1990, in practice the main tool for dealing with contaminated land is the planning regime.

Most contaminated land is identified during the process of developing or redeveloping land. Where a developer applies for planning permission and it becomes apparent that the land in question is contaminated, the relevant local planning authority will attach conditions to the grant of planning permission requiring the remediation of any contamination.

In 2008, the Department for Communities and Local Government (DCLG) issued Model Planning Conditions for Contaminated Land, which recommended that developers be required to undertake and submit the following:

(a) site investigation and risk assessment;
(b) proposed remediation scheme;
(c) remediation;
(d) reporting of unexpected contamination;
(e) long-term monitoring.

Development could not take place until conditions (a) to (d) were satisfied. The first iteration of the NPPF (March 2012) revoked these Model Conditions, but it is likely that councils will continue to use similar conditions to require the remediation of contaminated land.

The current version of the NPPF, last updated in December 2023, requires planning authorities to take into account the possibility that land will be contaminated when preparing local plans and determining planning applications. Local planning authorities must consider whether sites are suitable for their proposed use by developers, taking into account any risks associated with contamination. Planning authorities must, where appropriate, determine planning applications in a way which supports and contributes to the remediation of contaminated land. The National Planning Practice Guidance sets out further guidance, and continues to recommend that planning authorities consider using planning conditions to address contaminated land.

8.3.5 Landlord and tenant issues

Landlords will be anxious to ensure that the tenant will be responsible for the clean-up of any contamination discovered during the term of the lease, particularly where it is caused or knowingly permitted by the tenant, or where existing contamination is disturbed by the tenant. It is doubtful whether clean-up works would fall within a tenant's general repairing covenant unless the pollution caused some physical damage to the building. However, a tenant's covenant to comply with all statutory obligations may be sufficiently broad to extend to environmental clean-up requirements. Furthermore, where there is a service charge in a lease, the landlord may be able to recover sums expended on the necessary clean-up. Even where not expressly mentioned in the list of services to be provided, a 'sweeping-up' clause may be wide enough to embrace such work.

Most modern commercial leases, however, deal expressly with environmental issues. Either party may negotiate a clause protecting them from liability for existing contamination. Alternatively, the parties may agree that the landlord will be liable for any existing contamination, and the tenant liable for any new contamination.

8.3.6 Report: Review of the Contaminated Land Regime

The EA is under a statutory duty to 'from time to time … prepare and publish a report on the state of contaminated land in England [and] Wales' (EPA 1990, s 78U). The most recent Reports, published in April 2016 by the EA in relation to England, and by Natural Resources Wales in relation to Wales, covered the period from 2000 to 2013. Some of the EA's findings in relation to England are summarised in **Table 8.1**.

Table 8.1   Environment Agency: Summary of findings

Environment Agency, *Dealing with contaminated land in England: A review of progress from April 2000 to December 2013 with Part 2A of the Environmental Protection Act 1990*

- More than 511 sites had been determined under Pt 2A, including 54 Special Sites.
- At least another 10,000 sites identified by preliminary inspection require further investigation to establish the risks they pose.
- The majority of individual remedial actions were completed within a year, although a significant number of sites took more than one year.
- Remediation was mostly secured by voluntary agreement or regulatory notice and less than 5% used a combination of both. Statutory notices (including remediation statements and notices) were issued at 159 sites and voluntary remediation was agreed at 296 sites.
- Only 19 remediation notices have been served since the legislation was introduced (including one for a Special Site).
- Class A polluters and knowing permitters were pursued to bear the costs of remediation at 61% of sites, and Class B owners and occupiers were pursued at 26% of sites. However, at the majority of remediated sites, the responsibility for carrying out remediation fell to either the local council or the EA. Whilst the Class A polluters were often pursued, in the majority of cases they could either not be found or made to pay.

130   Commercial Property

For further practical guidance on the contaminated land regime, see LexisPSL Environment's series of practice notes, precedents, checklists, Q&As and multimedia in the 'contaminated land regime' topic, and Practical Law Environment's practice notes, standard documents and checklists in the 'contaminated land' topic.

8.4 NUISANCE

8.4.1 Introduction

Private nuisance, public nuisance, statutory nuisance and the rule in *Rylands v Fletcher* combine to provide a wide ambit of potential liability for interference with land, people's enjoyment of it, or people's health. Liability is strict in each case; there is no requirement to establish carelessness on the part of the defendant. Remedies may lie in damages or injunction.

8.4.2 Private nuisance

8.4.2.1 Introduction

Private nuisance is the 'unlawful interference with a person's use or enjoyment of land, or of some right over or in connection with that land'. Private nuisance may cover anything from:

(a) aircraft noise and turbulence affecting nearby residents (*Dennis v Ministry of Defence* [2003] EWHC 793 (QB)); to

(b) a particularly loud printing press affecting residents on Fleet Street (*Rushmer v Polsue and Alfieri Ltd* [1906] 1 Ch 234); to

(c) solvents from a leather works seeping into an aquifer (*Cambridge Water Company v Eastern Counties Leather plc* [1994] 1 All ER 53). Though note that, on the facts of the claim, the court found that the solvent leakage was not a nuisance. The claimant's case had rested on changes that had been made to drinking water regulations which had come into force long after the defendant's practices had stopped. The claimant was, however, successful in its *Rylands v Fletcher* claim (see **8.4.5**); to

(d) gas escaping from land and passing through a property in underground pipes (*Willis v Derwentside District Council* [2013] All ER (D) 70 (Apr)); to

(e) Japanese knotweed (see **8.8.3**).

8.4.2.2 Standing

In *Hunter v Canary Wharf Ltd* [1997] 2 WLR 684, the House of Lords confirmed that only people with rights to the land affected have standing to bring a private nuisance action. In *Hunter*, the tenants and freehold owners in London's Docklands had successfully sued the developers of Canary Wharf and the London Docklands Development Corporation in nuisance for dust caused by construction work and interference with television signals from the Canary Wharf Tower.

Certain of the claimants in *Hunter*, who had not had the relevant property rights and so had not been successful, took their case to the European Commission of Human Rights. They claimed that the construction works breached their right to respect for their homes and family life under Article 8 of the European Convention on Human Rights (ECHR) (*Khatun v United Kingdom*, European Commission of Human Rights, 1 July 1998). The Commission rejected the claimants' substantive claim as inadmissible, finding that their Article 8 rights had not been violated by the construction dust. The Commission did, however, comment that the claimants could bring an Article 8 claim without having to establish any proprietary interest in land. It is indeed well established in the case law of the European Court of Human Rights that 'home' under Article 8 is an autonomous concept and is not limited to property of which a person is the owner or tenant.

This leaves open the possibility that the courts will, pursuant to their duty under s 6 of the Human Rights Act 1998, in future extend the tort of nuisance so as to make it available to persons who do not have proprietary interests in affected land.

Many environmental matters, particularly emissions, can found a claim in nuisance. The breadth of legitimate claimants may increase.

8.4.2.3 Interaction with planning permission

The case of *Coventry v Lawrence* [2014] All ER (D) 245 (Feb) ('Fen Tigers' case) concerned a claim in nuisance brought by a neighbour in relation to noise from a motorcross stadium and speedway. The activities and noise existed long before the claimant moved to the property. In summary, the Supreme Court held that:

- it was possible to obtain by prescription a right to commit what would otherwise be a nuisance by noise (however, the defendant had not established such a right in this case);
- it is no defence that the claimant had come to the nuisance;
- activities that give rise to a nuisance could constitute part of the character of the locality, but only to the extent that those activities did not constitute a nuisance;
- the mere fact that an activity had the benefit of planning permission was normally of no assistance to the defendant in a claim that the activity caused a nuisance; and
- the power to award damages in lieu of an injunction was a discretion, which should not, as a matter of principle, be fettered.

8.4.2.4 Interaction with environmental permitting

In *Barr and Others v Biffa Waste Services Ltd* [2012] EWCA Civ 312, a group of residents in a mixed-use area successfully sued Biffa for odours emanating from its waste disposal site. Biffa was not entitled to rely on compliance with its Environmental Permit (see **8.5**), which did not expressly or impliedly authorise committing any nuisance. Biffa was therefore liable in nuisance.

8.4.2.5 Statutory immunity

In *Peires v Bickerton's Aerodromes Ltd* [2017] EWCA Civ 273, the Court of Appeal confirmed that an aerodrome enjoyed statutory immunity against claims for nuisance caused by aircraft either in flight or on an aerodrome under the Civil Aviation Act 1982, ss 76(1) and 77(2). The Court held that the helicopter activity was clearly 'flight', and there was 'no proper basis' for the judge's conclusion that the activities fell outside the immunity because they were carried out in an unreasonable way.

8.4.3 Public nuisance

Historically, public nuisance included a wide range of activities, from dumping sewage into a river to playing loud music in a public park. The Court of Appeal in *Corby Group Litigation v Corby District Council* [2009] EWHC 1944 referred to the following definition of public nuisance (at [686]):

> A person is guilty of public nuisance ... who (a) does an act not warranted by law or (b) omits to discharge a legal duty, if the effect of the act or omission is to endanger the life, health, property, morals or comfort of the public, or to obstruct the public in the exercise or enjoyment of rights common to all Her Majesty's subjects.

Although an established common law offence, public nuisance is used sparingly. This is because most public nuisance activities are now addressed by statute. Furthermore, while the 'public' can mean a class of Her Majesty's subjects, in *Attorney-General v PYA Quarries Ltd* [1957] 2 QB 169, a case on dust and tremor nuisance by a quarry, Denning LJ also stated (at 191) that a public nuisance is a nuisance which is so widespread in its range or so indiscriminate in its effect that it would not be reasonable to expect one person to take proceedings on his own responsibility to put a stop to it, but that it should be taken on the responsibility of the community at large.

Consequently, such a stand-alone claim would need both a large number of people to be affected and the breach of relevant statutory liability. However, public nuisance could still comprise part of a suite of claims. This was used in the *Corby* case, where the council was successfully sued in negligence, public nuisance and under s 34 of the EPA 1990, for birth defects caused by its poor reclamation of a former steelworks site.

8.4.4 Statutory nuisance

8.4.4.1 Introduction

In statutory nuisance, the claimant does not need to have a property interest. Statutory nuisance is actionable pursuant to s 79 of the EPA 1990 and includes smoke, fumes, gases, dust, odours, insects, artificial light and noise emitted from premises that are 'prejudicial to health or a nuisance'. 'Nuisance' is given either its private or public nuisance meaning, whereas 'prejudicial to health' is assessed objectively, ie one would consider the impact on the health of the average traveller on the Clapham omnibus.

8.4.4.2 Enforcement

Local authorities are under an express duty to inspect their areas periodically for statutory nuisance (EPA 1990, ss 79–80), and must serve an abatement notice on persons who are responsible for it. As in the Contaminated Land Regime, if that person cannot be found, the abatement notice will be served on the owner or occupier of the relevant premises. Otherwise, an aggrieved individual may seek an abatement order through the courts (EPA 1990, s 82) (see *McCaw v City of Westminster Magistrates' Court (D) and Middlesex SARL* [2008] EWHC 1504).

There is a defence of 'best practicable means' for some of the categories of public nuisance. Essentially, the defence will be available where the defendant can show that they did what is currently best practice in order to prevent or counteract the nuisance, having regard to the local circumstances, current technical knowledge, and financial means.

8.4.5 The Rule in *Rylands v Fletcher*

The rule in *Rylands v Fletcher* [1868] UKHL 1 is essentially a subspecies of nuisance. Where an occupier of land brings or keeps something on the land that is likely to do mischief if it escapes, the rule makes that occupier liable for any damage that is the natural consequence of its escape. As reformulated in *Transco v Stockport MBC* [2003] UKHL 61, the elements of liability are that:

(a) the defendant must bring or keep an exceptionally dangerous or mischievous thing on their land;

(b) they ought reasonably to have recognised that there is an exceptionally high risk of danger or mischief if that thing should escape, however unlikely an escape may be;

(c) their use of their land must, having regard to all the circumstances of time and place, be extraordinary and unusual;

(d) the thing must escape from their property into or onto the property of another;

(e) damages for death or personal injury are not recoverable;

(f) an Act of God or the act of a stranger will provide a defence.

In *Cambridge Water v Eastern Counties Leather* [1994] 1 All ER 53, the House of Lords held that the foreseeability of damage (of the relevant type) is a prerequisite of liability. Strict liability for the escape from land of things likely to do mischief only arose if the defendant knew, or ought reasonably to have foreseen, that those things might cause damage if they escaped. The defendant will be liable where there is an escape occurring in the course of the non-natural use of land, even if they had exercised all due care to prevent the escape from occurring.

Traditionally the hardest element to satisfy was 'non-natural use'. However, in *Cambridge Water*, Lord Goff stated that:

> the storage of substantial quantities of chemicals on industrial premises should be regarded as an almost classic case of non-natural use; and I find it very difficult to think that it should be thought objectionable to impose strict liability for damage caused in the event of their escape.

In light of this judgment, and considering the range of non-natural uses to be found on a given property (from solvents to industrial cleaning agents), the rule in *Rylands v Fletcher* continues to pose an environmental liability risk.

8.4.6 Trespass

Trespass requires an intentional or a negligent act which interferes directly with a person or their rights in land. The emphasis is on direct interference. In the case of *Esso Petroleum v Southport Corporation* [1956] AC 218, the defendant's tanker jettisoned oil into an estuary; the oil eventually polluted the foreshore. This was not an actionable trespass as there was no certainty the oil would end up on the foreshore – it was indirect. As with nuisance and the rule in *Rylands v Fletcher*, trespass is also a potential claim for environmental incidents.

8.5 ENVIRONMENTAL PERMITTING AND REGULATION

8.5.1 Introduction

This is a vast area, covering permits and regulations for activities ranging from running a dry cleaners to dealing with radioactive substances. A variety of environmental authorisations could be required under different regimes for activities undertaken at any one site (see **Table 8.2** below).

The Environmental Permitting (England and Wales) Regulations 2016 (SI 2016/1154) (EPR 2016) (as amended) is the main environmental permitting regime in England and Wales. It came into force on 1 January 2017, consolidating and replacing the Environmental Permitting (England and Wales) Regulations 2010 (SI 2010/675) without making any substantive changes. Environmental permitting brings together the licences previously managed under a number of different regulatory regimes (eg former pollution prevention and control permits, water discharge consents, groundwater authorisations, waste management licences, radioactive substances authorisations etc). Previously this constituted 41 different statutory instruments. These regimes now appear as schedules to the Regulations.

8.5.2 Requirement for an environmental permit

Principally, reg 12 of EPR 2016 requires the following:

(1) A person must not, except under and to the extent authorised by an environmental permit—
    (a) operate a regulated facility; or
    (b) cause or knowingly permit a water discharge activity or groundwater activity.
...

Regulation 7 defines 'operate a regulated facility' as:

(a) operate an installation, mobile plant, a medium combustion plant or a specified generator, or
(b) carry on a waste operation, mining waste operation, radioactive substances activity, water discharge activity, groundwater activity, small waste incineration plant operation, solvent emission activity or flood risk activity;
...

8.5.3 Enforcement

Subject to certain exceptions listed in reg 38, it is an offence under EPR 2016 to operate a regulated facility, or cause or knowingly permit a water discharge activity or groundwater activity, without the necessary environmental permit. It is also an offence to cause or knowingly permit a person to operate a regulated facility without an environmental permit.

8.5.4 Transfer of permits

Where a buyer of land intends to carry out the same activities on the site as the seller, the seller may need to transfer its environmental permits and other authorisations to the buyer. If the buyer is instead buying shares in a company which operates the business at the property, the environmental permit should already be held in the company's name and hence no transfer will be necessary.

Different requirements apply in respect of transfers, depending on the type of permit. For example, an application to transfer an environmental permit governed by the EPR 2016 must be made jointly by the buyer and the seller and can take at least two months. By contrast, there is no statutory mechanism for the transfer of a trade effluent consent, and the buyer will usually need to make a new application to the local sewage undertaker.

Table 8.2 Common authorisations, offences and duties in environmental regulation

---

Industry and installations

Pollution prevention

It is an offence to operate a heavy industrial installation or listed activity without a licence (Environmental Permitting (England and Wales) Regulations 2016 (SI 2016/1154) (EPR 2016), regs 12 and 38). These include energy, mining, chemical or waste industries and lighter industries where emissions may be harmful. Together these are referred to as Part A(1) (regulated by the EA) and Part A(2) and Part B activities (regulated by local authorities). There are thresholds of activity before a permit is required.

Water

(1) *Pollution*

It is an offence, except pursuant to an environmental permit, to 'cause or knowingly permit a water discharge activity or groundwater activity' (EPR 2016, regs 12(1) and 38(1)).

A 'water discharge activity' includes the discharge or entry into inland freshwaters, coastal waters or territorial waters of any: (i) poisonous, noxious or polluting matter, (ii) waste matter, or (iii) trade effluent or sewage effluent, as well as certain other discharge activities (Sch 21).

A 'groundwater activity' includes the discharge of pollutants directly or indirectly into groundwater, as well as certain other discharge activities (Sch 22).

(2) *Abstraction*

It is an offence to abstract or impound water without an abstraction or impoundment licence or in contravention of one (Water Resources Act 1991, ss 24 and 25).

(3) *Trade effluent*

It is an offence to discharge trade effluent to a public sewer without a consent or authorisation from the relevant water or sewerage undertaker (Water Industry Act 1991, s 118).

Waste

(1) *Keeping or disposing*

Pursuant to s 33 of the EPA 1990, it is an offence to treat, keep, or dispose of controlled waste or extractive waste except in accordance with a permit (or pursuant to a permit holder's powers).

'Waste' is widely defined in Article 3(1) of the Waste Framework Directive 2008/98/EC as any substance or object which the holder discards or intends or is required to discard. However, its interpretation is complex and requires a good understanding of both European and UK case law. 'Controlled waste' is defined in s 75 of the EPA 1990 as household, industrial and commercial waste or any such waste. 'Extractive waste' is defined in Article 2 of the Mining Waste Directive 2006/21/EC as waste resulting from the prospecting, extraction, treatment and storage of mineral resources and the working of quarries.

(2) *Waste installations, waste operations and waste exemptions*

Waste installations (eg landfills and hazardous waste incineration) and waste operations (eg scrap metal and waste transfer sites) will need an environmental permit (EPR 2016, Sch 9). Other businesses may need to register a waste exemption (eg where they use or store waste below certain thresholds) (EPR 2016, Sch 3).

(3) *Duty of care*

Section 34 of the EPA 1990 imposes a general statutory duty of care regarding controlled waste. This includes preventing its escape, ensuring its transfer only to an authorised person (the fly-tipping offence) and keeping records of the transfer. Section 34(1A) of the EPA 1990 provides a statutory duty of care in relation to the management of extractive waste. It is an offence to fail to comply with these duties of care.

(4) *Electricals*

The Waste Electrical and Electronic Equipment Regulations 2013 (SI 2013/3113) impose a duty on producers, distributors and exporters of electrical and electronic equipment to reduce pollutants in and finance the collection, treatment and recovery of electrical equipment.

(5) *Recycling*

The Producer Responsibility Obligations (Packaging Waste) Regulations 2007 (SI 2007/871) place an obligation on producers to recycle and recover packaging waste. It applies to businesses that handle more than 50t of packaging waste and have a turnover of more than £2,000,000 pa. Note that the Environment Bill (discussed above) includes measures to introduce extended producer responsibility to increase producers' liability for final disposal costs.

Hazardous substances

These include corrosive, toxic and irritant substances, and biological agents as defined in the Control of Substances Hazardous to Health Regulations 2002 (SI 2002/2677).

(1) *Storage*

Holding hazardous substances above prescribed control quantities without or in contravention of a consent is an offence (Planning (Hazardous Substances) Act 1990, s 4; and Planning (Hazardous Substances) Regulations 2015 (SI 2015/627)).

Storage of larger quantities of hazardous substances also triggers the requirement to register the site as an establishment under the Control of Major Accident Hazard Regulations 2015 (COMAH) with enhanced requirements for emergency planning and controls on process safety, as well as a general duty to take all reasonable steps to prevent and limit the consequences of major accidents (reg 4).

> (2) *Exposure*
>
> The COSSH 2002 impose a general duty to control or prevent exposure to such substances at work.

8.6 CLIMATE CHANGE LAW AND ENERGY PERFORMANCE

8.6.1 Introduction

This section outlines some of the key mechanisms aimed at reducing greenhouse gas emissions. It focuses on energy efficiency schemes aimed at reducing energy usage, in particular Minimum Energy Efficiency Standards (MEES). In addition, the practical implication of the drive towards reduced-carbon buildings is addressed, for example, by way of EPCs and Green Leases, as well as through buildings regulation.

This area of law is subject to constant change.

8.6.2 United Nations Framework Convention on Climate Change (UNFCCC)

Global warming has gradually become a well-recognised and highly regulated issue internationally. The 1997 Kyoto Protocol to the United Nations Framework Convention on Climate Change (UNFCCC) set the world's first binding agreement aimed at reducing global greenhouse gas emissions. The UK was bound to reduce its emissions to 12.5% below 1990 levels by the end of 2012. The UK planned to do this using a combination of encouraging and requiring energy efficiency, and reducing emissions.

The Kyoto Protocol introduced three 'flexible' market-based mechanisms aimed at reducing emissions: the clean development mechanism (CDM), joint implementation (JI) and emissions trading. The CDM is a project-based mechanism that allows developed nations (Annex I parties) to initiate and support projects in developing nations (non-Annex I parties) that reduce greenhouse gas emissions. Joint implementation is a project-based mechanism that allows Annex I parties to initiate and support projects in another Annex I country. The most established market is the EU ETS (see **8.6.3**).

In 2012, the 18th Conference of the Parties to the UNFCCC (COP) at Doha resulted in an agreed timetable under which the Parties would adopt a universal climate agreement by 2015. At COP 21 in Paris, the parties adopted the Paris Agreement. Under the Paris Agreement, the Parties have agreed to hold global temperature rises to 'well below 2°C' above pre-industrial levels, and to 'pursue efforts' to limit temperature increases to 1.5°C above pre-industrial levels. In response to the Paris Agreement, the UK legislated to amend the Climate Change Act 2008 so as to set a binding target to reach 'net zero' emissions by 2050 – in other words, the UK has committed to ensuring that emissions in 2050 are at least 100% lower than the 1990 baseline of greenhouse gas emissions.

The Agreement sets out a number of mechanisms to achieve this, including reliance on Nationally Determined Contributions (NDCs) pledged by the parties. The NDCs set out the emissions reductions targets which each Party pledges to achieve by a specified date. The Parties submitted their first NDCs at COP26 in Glasgow. The UK committed to reducing economy-wide greenhouse gas emissions by at least 68% by 2030, compared to 1990 levels.

8.6.3 EU ETS

8.6.3.1 Overview

The EU ETS (under Council Directive 2003/87/EC ([2003] OJ L275/32) establishing a scheme for greenhouse gas emission allowance trading) is integrated with the Kyoto Protocol and is now the world's largest GHG emissions trading scheme. Under the scheme, which began in

January 2005, significant emitters of GHGs in the EU must monitor and report their emissions. The scheme covers more than 11,000 installations accounting for 45% of the EU's greenhouse gas emissions. These include energy generation activities, the production and processing of ferrous metals, mineral industries, and pulp and paper industries.

8.6.3.2 UK ETS

The UK ETS replaced the UK's participation in the EU ETS on 1 January 2021. It was established through the Greenhouse Gas Emissions Trading Scheme Order 2020 (SI 2020/1265). The UK ETS covers greenhouse gas emissions from power and heat generation, energy intensive industries and aviation.

The UK ETS operates on the 'cap and trade' principle. Participants receive free allowances, and they are also able to buy emissions allowances at auction or on the secondary market, which can be traded with other participants. The Secretary of State for Business, Energy and Industrial Strategy has issued guidance for operators participating in the UK ETS.

This legality of the creation of the UK ETS was recently challenged on the grounds that (1) the cap and auction reserve price proposed had failed to have regard to provisions of the Paris Agreement, and (2) that the UK ETS did not fulfil or serve the statutory purpose under s 44 of the Climate Change Act 2008. The challenge was refused by the High Court in June 2021 (*Elliott-Smith v Secretary of State for Business, Energy and Industrial Strategy* [2021] EWHC 1633 (Admin)).

8.6.4 Climate Change Act 2008

The Climate Change Act 2008 made the UK the first country in the world to have a legally binding, long-term framework to cut GHG emissions. The target was initially set as requiring at least an 80% reduction of GHG emissions below 1990 levels by 2050. As indicated above, that target was increased in 2019 to 100%, also known as 'net zero'.

The Act sets out a vast range of measures by which the UK Government will meet the target to 2050, including carbon-budgeting and domestic trading schemes.

In July 2022, the High Court held that the Government had breached its obligations under ss 13–14 of the Climate Change Act 2008 by failing adequately to prepare and report on proposals and policies designed to enable the carbon budgets set under the Act to be met. In March 2023, the Government published its Net Zero Growth Plan setting out the Government's overarching emissions reduction policies.

8.6.5 Energy performance, MEES and Green Leases

8.6.5.1 Introduction

A significant proportion of UK emissions (approximately 17%) are estimated to come from buildings. Emissions from heating buildings, including indirect emissions, are estimated to make up around 78% of all buildings emissions, and about 21% of all UK emissions (HM Government, *Net Zero Strategy: Build Back Greener*, October 2021).

At the EU level, the recast Energy Performance of Buildings Directive (Council Directive 2010/31/EU) aims to improve the performance of both commercial and residential buildings in the EU. The principal requirements of the Directive are as follows:

(a) Member States must set minimum energy performance requirements for buildings.
(b) New buildings and large buildings subject to major renovations must meet the minimum energy performance requirements.
(c) EPCs must be made available to prospective buyers and tenants whenever a building is constructed, sold or rented.

(d) Display Energy Certificates (DECs) must be displayed in large buildings occupied by public authorities.

(e) Boilers and air conditioning systems in buildings must be inspected on a regular basis (Articles 8 and 9).

These requirements were transposed into UK law by the Buildings Regulations 2010 (SI 2010/2214) and the Energy Performance of Buildings (England and Wales) Regulations 2012 (SI 2012/3118) (EPB Regulations 2012). These Regulations continue to have force, as amended.

8.6.5.2 Energy Performance Certificates

An EPC provides the asset rating of a building, from A to G, measuring its construction and services (by examining its insulation, boilers, radiators, glazing, etc). It also includes a recommendation report for energy efficiency improvement. An EPC must be supplied at the marketing, sale or rental of any property (EPB Regulations 2012, regs 6–7), when a building is constructed, or, in certain circumstances, when a building is refurbished (EPB Regulations 2012, reg 7A). If an EPC is not provided by a developer, the building control inspector cannot issue a completion certificate for the works. There are some exempt buildings, such as places of worship and temporary buildings used for two years or less (reg 5).

Certificates are valid for 10 years (reg 9). See **Figure 8.2** below.

Figure 8.2   Energy Performance Certificate

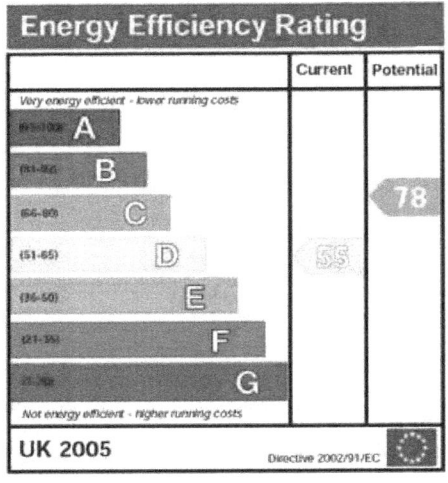
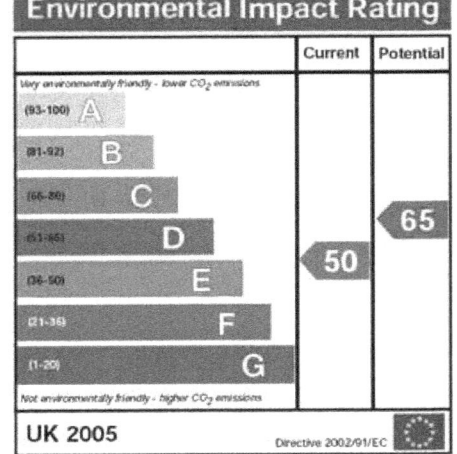

8.6.5.3 Display Energy Certificates

Buildings that are occupied by public authorities and frequently visited by the public must at all times display a valid DEC in a prominent place, clearly visible to members of the public who visit the building (EPB Regulations 2012, reg 14).

A DEC shows the *actual* energy use of the building (taken from meter readings), as well as its asset rating, and is valid for one year for buildings with a total useful floor area of more than 1000m^2. For buildings with a total useful floor area below 1000m^2 it is valid for 10 years.

8.6.5.4 Inspection of air-conditioning systems

Where a person has control over air-conditioning systems with an effective rated output of more than 12kW, Pt 4 of the EPB Regulations 2012 imposes a duty on that person to ensure that the system is inspected at least every five years by an energy assessor.

The energy assessor must provide a written report of the inspection as soon as practicable after the inspection.

8.6.5.5 Enforcement and practical effect

Failure to comply with the Regulations can result in a penalty charge notice and a fine of up to £5,000.

The Government hopes that EPCs will encourage businesses and investors to support more energy-efficient construction and usage. However, given the rise of corporate social responsibility and public scrutiny of major organisations' environmental impact, improved energy efficiency is arguably also simply good practice. Furthermore, company directors are statutorily required to promote the success of the company, and in doing so 'must have regard to the impact of the company's operations on the community and the environment' (Companies Act 2006, s 172). See LexisPSL Environment: *Directors' duties—duty to promote the success of the company and environmental considerations* and *Mandatory Environmental Reporting*, for more detail. Hence, there are ethical, financial and fiduciary motivations to be more 'green' with energy usage.

The Government has signalled its intention to consider increasing minimum performance standards for homes to ensure that all homes meet EPC Band C by 2035, and to set a minimum energy efficiency standard of EPC Band B by 2030 for privately rented commercial buildings in England and Wales (Net Zero Strategy).

8.6.5.6 MEES

MEES was introduced in March 2015 by the Energy Efficiency (Private Rented Property) (England and Wales) Regulations 2015 (SI 2015/962). It imposes a ban on landlords renting out domestic and non-domestic rented properties that fall below a specified energy rating ('E' rating) unless they make specific energy efficiency improvements or are eligible for an exemption.

Implementation has been in stages:

- since 1 April 2016, tenants of domestic private rented property have a right to request consent for energy efficiency improvement measures, which may not be unreasonably refused by the landlord where financial support is available;
- since 1 April 2018, the Regulations have applied upon the granting of a new lease to an existing or new tenant of domestic or non-domestic private rental property;
- since 1 April 2020, the Regulations have applied to all privately-rented domestic property in scope of the Regulations, including where a lease is already in place and a property is occupied by a tenant;
- since 1 April 2023, the Regulations have applied to all privately-rented non-domestic property in scope of the Regulations, including where a lease is already in place and a property is occupied by a tenant.

MEES has been considered one of the most significant pieces of legislation to affect building stock. It requires landlords to review their property portfolios to identify buildings with energy ratings of F and G.

8.6.5.7 The Future Homes Standard and Future Buildings Standard

In October 2019 the Ministry for Housing, Communities and Local Government (MHCLG) issued part 1 of a consultation on proposed changes to buildings regulations made under the Buildings Regulations 2010 applicable to new build homes. The objective of the new proposals is to reduce carbon emissions by 75–80% compared to those required by the 2013 version of Part L (Approved Document L 2013). The proposed date for compliance with the revised requirements is 2025, with a proposed interim increase to energy efficiency standards to take effect in 2020.

In early 2021, the MHCLG consulted on changes to Part L (conservation of fuel and power) and Part F (ventilation) of the Building Regulations for non-domestic buildings and dwellings, and on overheating in new residential buildings. The consultation built on the Future Homes Standard consultation, and set out proposals for a Future Buildings Standard.

In response, the Government effected changes to Part L of the Building Regulations on 15 June 2022. The new requirements set out higher performance targets and include a new emphasis on low carbon heating systems. The changes were described by the Government as being interim steps towards the Future Homes Standard and the Future Buildings Standard.

8.6.5.8 Green Leases

With the ever-increasing awareness of environmental matters, some landlords and tenants are keen to enter into leases that actively promote a reduction in the building's impact on the environment.

Both landlord and tenant will enter into obligations to achieve this. For example, the landlord may covenant to:

(a) achieve a specific energy rating throughout the term, with the tenant perhaps paying a reduced rent if that rating is not met;

(b) for multi-let buildings, separately meter the water and electricity consumption of each tenant;

(c) repair/modify buildings, plant and equipment so as to improve energy efficiency and to produce lower operating costs;

(d) instigate a green management plan; this should not be too prescriptive, and should set targets rather than set out specific obligations;

(e) ensure that all plant and equipment, particularly air-conditioning systems, operate to maximum efficiency; and

(f) obtain an annual independent audit of the building's performance level.

Similarly, the tenant may be required to:

(a) fit out or alter using recycled materials, or those that can be recycled (if practicable);

(b) make all alterations energy neutral, or provide energy savings;

(c) not partition in such a way as to make the air-conditioning system less efficient or that leads to a greater use of energy;

(d) observe and perform the landlord's green management plan; and

(e) yield up the premises with at least the same energy rating as applied at the beginning of the lease.

To facilitate the reduction of environmental impacts and help create an industry standard, the Better Buildings Partnership released a Green Lease Toolkit (updated January 2024). This contains best practice recommendations and model lease clauses.

8.6.6 Conservation covenants

The Environment Act 2021 made specific provision for the use of 'conservation covenants' by landowners. These covenants will be voluntary agreements between landowners and responsible bodies (such as private or public bodies involved in conservation) that provide for conservation.

Conservation covenant agreements must by executed as a deed, and must contain provision which is:

(a) of a qualifying kind;
(b) has a conservation purpose; and
(c) is intended by the parties to be for the public good.

Provision 'of a qualifying kind' is provision which:

(a) requires the landowner either (i) to do, or not to do, something on the land covered by the agreement, or (ii) to allow the responsible body to do something on such land; or
(b) requiring the responsible body to do something on such land.

A conservation covenant agreement will have a 'conservation purpose' if its purpose is:

(a) to conserve the natural environment of land or the natural resources of land;
(b) to conserve land as a place of archaeological, architectural, artistic, cultural or historic interest; or
(c) to conserve the setting of land with a natural environment or natural resources or which is a place of archaeological, architectural, artistic, cultural or historic interest.

Further statutory requirements for conservation covenants, and provision for their enforcement, are set out in Pt 7 of the Environment Act 2021.

On 1 February 2024, Defra published statutory guidance listing designated responsible bodies able to enter into conservation covenants in England. Currently the list includes only Natural England. Defra had also expected some local authorities to apply to be designated.

8.6.7 Law Society Guidance on Climate Change Risk and Conveyancing

In April 2023 the Law Society published Guidance on *The Impact of Climate Change on Solicitors*. The Guidance is in two parts:

Part A sets out guidance for organisations on how to manage their business in a manner which is consistent with the transition to net zero.

Part B provides guidance for solicitors on:

- how climate change physical risks and climate legal risks may be relevant to client advice;
- issues which may be relevant when considering the interplay of legal advice, climate change and solicitors' professional duties; and
- issues which may be relevant when considering the solicitor-client relationship in the context of climate change.

In the Guidance, the Law Society also stated that it would provide sector-specific guidance where its members wanted help on the expanding legal risks around climate change, elaborating on how these duties apply to their practice. Following feedback from conveyancers, the Law Society started work on a climate risk and conveyancing practice note to complement its existing practice notes on flood risk and contaminated land. In September 2024 the Law Society issued a draft practice note and announced a Consultation with members on the structure and issues covered in the note.

8.7 ASBESTOS

8.7.1 Introduction

Asbestos remains the single greatest cause of work-related deaths in the UK. According to the Health and Safety Executive (HSE), at least 3,500 people in Great Britain die each year from asbestos-related cancer as a result of past exposure.

Asbestos was used extensively as a building material in the UK from the 1950s through to the mid-1980s. It proved ideal for fireproofing and insulation, and so is likely to be found in roofing, floor tiles, around pipes (as insulation), and for wall and ceiling panels and gaskets in boilers.

Although such use is now illegal, much asbestos remains in place. It is safe to assume that any building constructed before 2000 may contain asbestos. If it is in poor condition or damaged, asbestos fibres may become airborne, which is when they pose a significant risk.

8.7.2 Control of Asbestos Regulations 2012

The Control of Asbestos Regulations 2012 (SI 2012/632) impose a duty to identify and manage asbestos in non-domestic buildings. The duty could fall on the employer, owner or occupier of premises to conduct an asbestos survey and implement an Asbestos Management Plan (AMP).

8.7.2.1 Duty to manage asbestos in non-domestic premises

In essence, reg 4 imposes an obligation on the 'dutyholder' in 'non-domestic premises' to:

(a) determine whether asbestos is present in a building, or is likely to be present (advice from the HSE is to assume that it is unless there is strong evidence to the contrary); and

(b) manage any asbestos that is or is likely to be present (this requires an AMP, and the lack of one is also an offence).

Managing asbestos could include proper containment or even removal of it, which entails even further duties.

8.7.2.2 Definition of 'dutyholder'

The 'dutyholder' is defined in reg 4(1) as:

(a) every person who has, by virtue of a contract or tenancy, an obligation of any extent in relation to the maintenance or repair of non-domestic premises or any means of access or egress to or from those premises; or

(b) in relation to any part of non-domestic premises where there is no such contract or tenancy, every person who has, to any extent, control of that part of those non-domestic premises or any means of access or egress to or from those premises.

This broad definition could encompass owners, landlords, tenants, licensees and potentially managing agents.

Where there is more than one dutyholder, the relative contributions to be made by each in complying with the reg 4 duties are determined by the 'nature and extent of the maintenance and repair obligations' owed by each dutyholder.

8.7.2.3 Enforcement

Section 33(1)(c) of the Health and Safety at Work etc Act 1974 provides that it is an offence for a person to contravene any health and safety regulations. Similar to the EPA 1990, s 37 of the Health and Safety at Work etc Act 1974 provides that where an offence is committed with the consent or connivance of, or is attributable to any neglect on the part of, any director, manager, secretary or other similar officer, then that person (as well as the organisation) can be held criminally liable. If convicted on indictment in the Crown Court, the penalty for each offence is imprisonment for no more than two years and/or an unlimited fine.

The HSE enforces asbestos regulation rigorously. In transactional work, it is imperative that enquiries are made with regard to assessments and current AMPs.

8.7.2.4 Landlord and tenant issues

In multi-let premises, the responsibility for maintenance of the common parts, services, external fabric and main structure of the building will generally lie with the landlord. The landlord will be a dutyholder, and will be required under reg 4 to arrange for asbestos surveys to be carried out and for copies of asbestos registers to be produced to each tenant.

Where a lease imposes repairing obligations on a tenant, the landlord should ensure that the tenant is aware of its obligations under reg 4 and be satisfied that the tenant has complied with those obligations.

8.8 JAPANESE KNOTWEED

8.8.1 Introduction

Japanese knotweed is the most invasive species of plant in Britain. It spreads extremely quickly, can grow 10cm a day, exists in almost any habitat and destroys native vegetation. It is now found in almost every county in the UK, particularly along rivers and railways and on brownfield sites.

8.8.2 Practical impact

The plant is an increasing problem for many developers. Japanese knotweed shoots can push through tarmac and damage pavements and building foundations. The presence of the plant on a development site can lead to significant delays and huge costs. Effective control of the plant using herbicides takes at least three years. Excavation offers rapid removal, but the costs are substantial, and the disposal at a licensed landfill site of a stand of Japanese knotweed measuring $1m^2$ will cost in the region of £27,000.

8.8.3 Liability

A developer that has Japanese knotweed on its site also faces the risk of criminal and civil liability. Under the Wildlife and Countryside Act 1981, for example, it is an offence to plant or otherwise cause the species to grow in the wild. Japanese knotweed is also classed as controlled waste under the EPA 1990, and must therefore be disposed of safely at a licensed landfill site, according to the Controlled Waste (England and Wales) Regulations 2012 (SI 2012/811).

Japanese knotweed could also give rise to civil claims for private nuisance where it causes physical damage to a neighbouring property and/or affects the use and enjoyment of land (*Waistell v Network Rail Infrastructure Ltd*; *Williams v Network Rail Infrastructure Ltd* [2018] EWCA Civ 1514) and/or where the value of the neighbouring property is diminished as a result of interference with quiet enjoyment or amenity due to physical encroachment (*Davies v Bridgend County Borough Council* [2023] EWCA Civ 80).

8.9 FLOOD RISKS

Flooding has become a major environmental risk in the past decade. Alongside global extreme weather events, the UK experienced devastating floods in 2007, 2012 and 2015. The combined damage exceeded £4 billion worth of insurance pay outs (Association of British Insurers (ABI)). The ABI agreed a Memorandum of Understanding with the Government to ensure that flood insurance remains widely affordable and available. The Flood Re scheme, introduced in Pt 4 of the Water Act 2014, replaces the ABI Statement of Principles and became operational from April 2016. It provides a not-for-profit reinsurance scheme managed by the insurance industry, for households at significant risk of flooding.

The British Insurance Brokers' Association (BIBA) has also launched a scheme which aims to help improve the availability of flood insurance for small and medium-sized enterprises (SMEs) which were excluded from the Flood Re scheme.

In response to concerns about flood risk and the availability of insurance, The Law Society issued a flood risk practice note in May 2013, which was updated in December 2014 and more recently in January 2020. The practice note states that in all conveyancing transactions, when acting for a prospective buyer, tenant or lender, solicitors should consider whether or not to mention the issue of flood risk with clients and make further investigations where appropriate.

Flooding risks are part of standard desktop studies and enquiries for sale. However, separate commercial flood reports are available, and it is likely that this area will also become more sophisticated as the risks increase.

REVIEW ACTIVITY

Below are four different scenarios, which cover many of the core environmental issues discussed above, as well as some related areas that a lawyer may need to address. The first three cover general issues and liabilities, increasing with each scenario. The last covers the Contaminated Land Regime.

(1) Operation of a dry cleaners

A client wants quick legal advice on what environmental liabilities he may face for operating a typical dry-cleaning business.

(2) Mixed use inner-city redevelopment

A developer wishes to purchase and knock down a large inner-city building (built in the 1950s), and to build hundreds of new offices and residential units. During investigations it discovers that there is a lack of complete history on the site's use, but a small petrol station was in operation on part of the land until 10 years ago. During excavation the developer finds the remnants of an old Roman wall. What environmental issues are raised on these facts alone?

(3) Sale of an aluminium and steel foundry

A PLC manufacturing giant wishes to purchase a large steel foundry, to add to its production capabilities. You know the site firsthand: it has been in use as a factory since the early 1900s and it is near a major river. What environmental issues would this raise, in addition to the typical activities and impact of a factory?

(4) Contaminated land and appropriate persons

A partnership business, Alpha, operated a large paint factory from 1970–2008. Environmental reports show there was some chemical leakage in the factory basement during this period. Company Beta, a profitable car detailer, bought the property in 2008 after Alpha said, 'Do any investigations you want – it's a pretty dirty site.' Beta began reconstruction and foundation work for a premier car garage on site, before it suffered financially in the recession. PLC Gamma acquired the land in 2012 from Beta. Gamma had received comprehensive advice from both its investment bank, Delta, and its insurers, Epsilon. Knowing there was contamination on site, Gamma got a 10% discount on the sale price.

Assuming the land is contaminated under the Contaminated Land Regime, list the potential 'appropriate persons' for a remediation notice. Consider any exclusions and the apportionment test.

Answers to this Review activity may be found in Appendix 1.

CHAPTER 9

Searches and Enquiries

9.1	Local search and enquiries	145
9.2	Planning matters	145
9.3	Drainage	146
9.4	Highways	146
9.5	Railways	146
9.6	Utilities	146
9.7	Contaminated land	147
9.8	Commons registration	147
9.9	Rights of way and access land	147
9.10	Enquiries of the seller	147
9.11	Flood searches	147
9.12	Survey and inspection	148
9.13	Investigation of title	148
	Review activity	149

A buyer of development land (or other commercial property) will make the same pre-contract searches and raise broadly similar pre-contract enquiries as a buyer of residential property. This part of the book does not intend to repeat sections of the Legal Practice Guide, **Property Law and Practice**; rather it focuses upon the particular concerns of a buyer of a development site at the pre-contract stage.

9.1 LOCAL SEARCH AND ENQUIRIES

The usual form of application for a search and enquiries should be submitted to the local authority (or the Land Registry if the local authority's data has been migrated there under the Local Land Charges Rules 2018 (SI 2018/273)) together with the fee. A plan should be attached so that the local authority can identify the land concerned. It may be necessary to search a wider area than just the land to be purchased as local searches do not reveal matters affecting neighbouring properties.

In commercial transactions, consideration ought to be given to the possibility of raising the optional enquiries which are set out in form CON29O, in addition to the usual CON29 enquiries. An additional fee is payable in respect of each optional enquiry. These enquiries are designed to cover matters which are relevant only in particular kinds of transactions.

For example, on the acquisition of a development site, the buyer's solicitor ought to consider raising the optional enquiry relating to the location of public footpaths or bridleways which may cross the development site (since consent of the local authority would be required in order to divert them), and the optional enquiry relating to the location of gas pipelines to see if any run under or near the property (since this may affect development of the land). Prudent buyers will opt for safety by paying for replies to all of the optional enquiries.

In reviewing replies to CON29 enquiries, particular attention should be given to information relating to planning matters affecting the property and access to the site over adopted highways.

9.2 PLANNING MATTERS

The developer will want to know whether planning permission currently exists in respect of all or part of the site, or whether there have been any past applications for permission which have been unsuccessful. (The fact that an application for development was recently refused will be an important consideration for a developer.) It will also need to know what type of land use is currently indicated by the local planning authority in the development plans for the area in which the site is situated. Any existing or proposed tree preservation orders must be clearly pointed out to the developer.

9.3 DRAINAGE

It will be important for the developer to establish how foul and surface water currently drains away from the property to the public sewers (ie through main drains, private drains, or watercourses) so that it can estimate whether the current drainage system will be able to cope with foul and surface drainage from the developed site, or whether new drains will have to be constructed. If the site is vacant land, there are unlikely to be any drains serving it, and therefore the developer will need to know the location of the nearest public sewer where connection of newly-constructed drains may be made. The appropriate enquiry for commercial property and development sites is CON29DW Commercial, although some water companies provide a choice of enquiries for this type of property.

9.4 HIGHWAYS

The developer will need to know that immediate access to the site can be obtained from a public highway. It will need to know about each pavement and verge lying between the title boundary of the property and the public road, because if such land is in private ownership and is not publicly adopted, it may become a ransom strip if access is needed over it.

The developer will also need to confirm that there are no new highways proposed in the vicinity of the site which would adversely affect the development. Some of this information is available from the CON29 Enquiries of the Local Authority, but the information revealed is not particularly detailed, so specific enquiries will have to be raised with the relevant highway authority.

9.5 RAILWAYS

Network Rail's website contains information about the implications of having an overground railway bordering or crossing the property. However, there is no recognised system for asking Network Rail, or the operators who use its rail infrastructure, about how the railway might affect any particular property.

It is possible to raise enquiries about the possible implications of having an underground rail network in close proximity to the property through the National Land Information Service (NLIS) or by post to the relevant authority. An underground railway search will reveal the location and ownership of the track and, in some cases, details of leases, licences and other access rights.

It is also possible to establish whether a particular property will be affected by a proposed new railway such as HS2. The replies to CON29 enquiries will indicate whether a property is subject to a compulsory purchase order and whether it is within 200m of the centre line of a proposed railway, but it is also possible to do an HS2 search: details of how to find out whether particular properties are affected are on the HS2 website.

9.6 UTILITIES

Development may be impeded, or made more expensive, if there is electricity, gas or telecommunications equipment in, on, under or over the property. Specialist searches are available for each type of utility which will reveal the route of any such services and details of any access rights, such as wayleave agreements, affecting the property. It is also possible to carry out a combined utilities search with a commercial search provider, which should be done in all cases where the property is to be developed (see *Spire Property Development LLP & Anor v Withers LLP* [2021] EWHC 2400 (Comm)).

9.7 CONTAMINATED LAND

There is a danger that a buyer of land will become liable to pay excessive clean-up costs in relation to contaminated land. See **Chapter 8** regarding contaminated land and suggested ways of reducing the risk.

9.8 COMMONS REGISTRATION

The need to raise CON29O optional enquiry 22 relating to the registration of the property in the commons register maintained by the county council will depend upon the type and location of the land being acquired, but the case of *G & K Ladenbau (UK) Ltd v Crawley and de Reya* [1978] 1 All ER 682 serves as a warning to all solicitors of the dangers of overlooking the necessity for raising such an enquiry in appropriate cases. In that case, solicitors were held to be negligent for not having carried out a commons registration search in respect of a site being acquired for a new factory development. If a rural site is being acquired, enquiry 22 should always be made. If an inner-city industrial site is being acquired for redevelopment, this enquiry might be inappropriate. However, between these two extremes there will be other cases where the buyer's solicitor is unsure as to whether or not such an enquiry is necessary, and in those cases it would therefore be prudent to raise enquiry 22.

9.9 RIGHTS OF WAY AND ACCESS LAND

If the property might be affected by rights of way, it is possible to search the local authority's definitive map and register of applications to modify the definitive map to obtain details of all footpaths, bridleways and byways, including details as to position, width and any conditions of use. Copies of the definitive map must be available for public inspection free of charge at all reasonable hours in the relevant district. Maps of 'access land' for the purposes of the Countryside and Rights of Way Act 2000 (ie land subject to public rights of access) can be viewed on the Natural England website.

9.10 ENQUIRIES OF THE SELLER

Pre-contract enquiries of the seller will be raised on one of the standard printed forms of enquiry, or on the buyer's solicitors' own word-processed form of enquiry. Additional enquiries may be raised as the buyer's solicitor considers appropriate. These may focus upon discovering further information about the planning status of the site, the location of public drains and highways, the suitability of the land for building purposes and possible past contamination of the land. Again, information regarding these matters is often discoverable from other sources, but that alone should not be a sufficient reason for the seller to refuse to provide answers.

9.11 FLOOD SEARCHES

The Government-backed Flood Re scheme, which ensures that flood cover is available for most residential properties, does not apply to commercial properties. These properties are subject to premiums based on their individual risk of flooding. A property without standard buildings insurance, including flood cover, is unlikely to be mortgageable and will therefore be difficult to sell.

The flood map on the Environment Agency's website and Land Registry's Flood Risk Indicator Online are not suitable for assessing the risk of flooding to a particular property, and the Land Registry's search does not deal with surface water flooding (which in 2007 accounted for 70% by value of property flood damage). Accordingly, many solicitors acting on the purchase of a commercial property will routinely order a flood report from a commercial provider, which will usually provide the EA floodplain data, the EA Risk of Flooding from Rivers and Sea map, and data on surface water flooding, topography, groundwater flooding, historic floods, and dam and reservoir flooding. The report may also contain practical suggestions on flood resistance and flood resilience measures.

9.12 SURVEY AND INSPECTION

Even though the land may be vacant, the developer-client should be advised to commission a survey of the land. Primarily, its surveyor will be checking on the suitability of the land for building purposes, in terms both of land stability and means of access and drainage.

It is also possible to commission a ground stability search from the British Geological Survey or the Coal Authority.

For a number of reasons, an inspection of the property must always be conducted before exchange of contracts in order to:

(a) assist in establishing ownership of, or responsibility for boundary walls, hedges and fences;

(b) discover the existence of public or private rights of way which may be evidenced by worn footpaths, stiles, or breaks in the hedgerows;

(c) spot the presence of overhead electricity power lines which would prevent or impede development. If there are power lines, the land is likely to be subject to a written wayleave agreement between the landowner and the electricity company giving the company the right to maintain its supply across the land. A copy of the agreement should be requested from the seller;

(d) discover the rights of persons in occupation of the land. Solicitors are accustomed to thinking only in terms of a contributing spouse as the type of person who has occupiers' rights. However, with a development site, it is not unknown for a solicitor to overlook the presence of several cows in the corner of a field, which is unremarkable if the seller is a farmer but could be serious if the cows are grazing by virtue of rights of common, or under an agricultural or farm business tenancy;

(e) ensure that adjoining landowners do not enjoy the benefit of easements of light or air which would impede the buyer's proposed development.

9.13 INVESTIGATION OF TITLE

Title is almost invariably deduced and investigated at the pre-contract stage of the transaction.

A thorough investigation of title is required in the same way as in the case of residential property. The developer-client will be particularly concerned to ensure that the property enjoys the benefit of all necessary easements and rights of access (both for the purpose of developing and for future occupiers of the completed development) and drainage (for foul and surface water). It will also need to be satisfied that there are no covenants restricting the proposed development or use of the land; or if there are, that they will be released, removed or modified, or that appropriate insurance will be available, and that any easements which burden the property will not prevent or restrict the proposed development or use.

An index map search is advisable even if the property is believed to be registered land, particularly where more than one registered title is involved or there is a chance that mines and minerals may be registered under a different title number. The Land Registry's MapSearch service is a quick way to check for details of the registered interests for Business e-services firms who have portal access. Where the property is agricultural land, it may be necessary to check the Land Registry's Index of relating franchises and manors for adverse third party rights (such as the right to hold a market). Another possibility is the Land Registry's commercial manorial plans and title analysis service, which combines Land Registry and Ordnance Survey data and converts hard copy plans into digital format.

REVIEW ACTIVITY

Consider the development site in Canvey Island, Essex shown in the title plan below. If you were acting for the prospective buyer of this site, what searches and enquiries would you raise?

Answers to this Review activity may be found in Appendix 1.

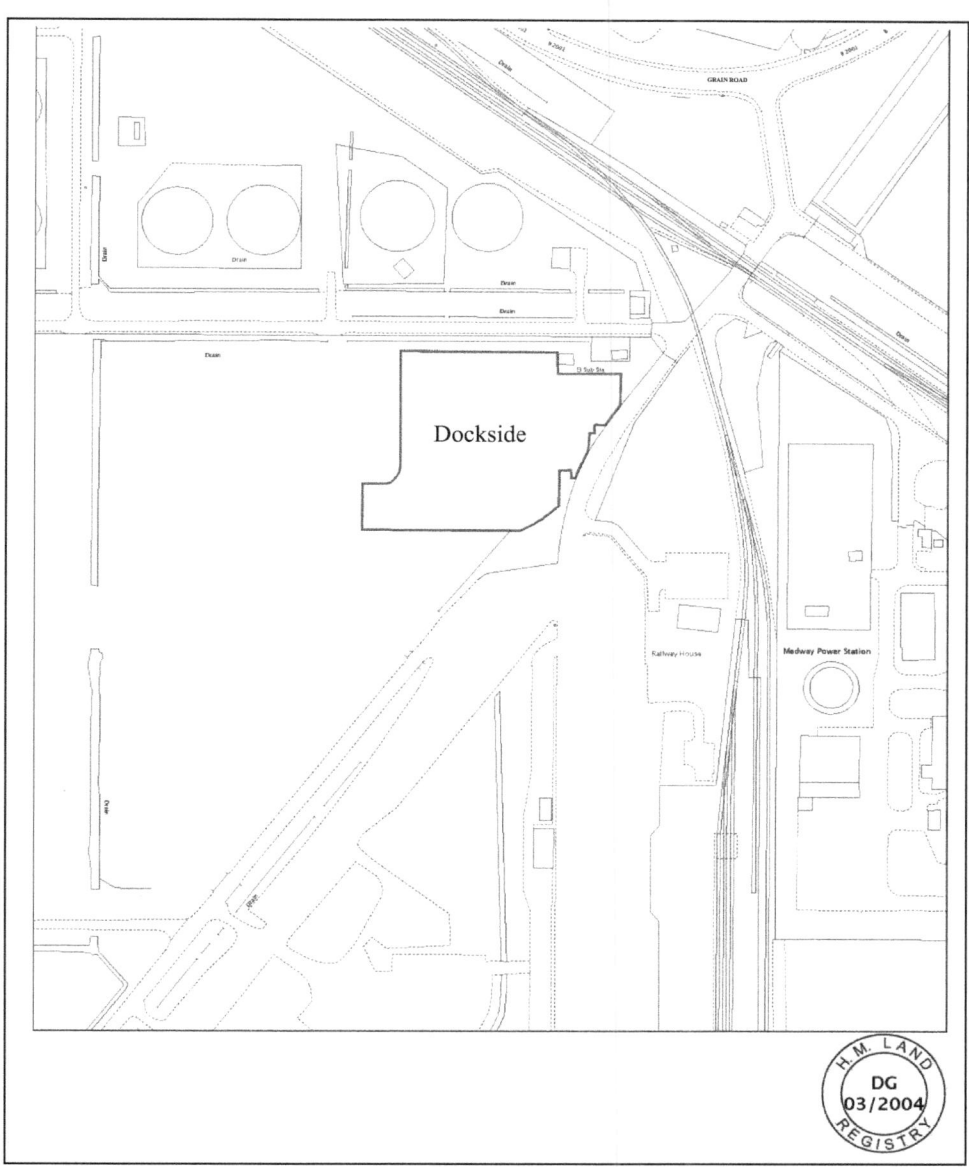

CHAPTER 10

Construction Projects

10.1	Introduction	151
10.2	Who will be involved? The design and construction team	151
10.3	Different forms of procurement	154
10.4	Duties owed to third parties	162
10.5	Protecting third parties	165
10.6	Dispute resolution	169
	Review activity	170

10.1 INTRODUCTION

Having completed the acquisition of a site that is physically capable of being developed, and which is not encumbered in a way that would impede development, and having obtained satisfactory planning permission and sufficient funds, the client will now want to obtain a building that will be completed within a satisfactory timescale, within budget and in accordance with its specified requirements.

10.2 WHO WILL BE INVOLVED? THE DESIGN AND CONSTRUCTION TEAM

10.2.1 The employer

The employer is the owner of the site who will employ various professionals to design and construct a building upon its land. For the purposes of this book, the employer is a client who has acquired a site with the aim of developing it, and who will grant leases of the completed development. This part of the book assumes that the client, whilst involved in commercial property, is not a member of the construction industry and will, therefore, need to employ other persons in connection with design and construction.

10.2.2 The building contractor

In a traditional building contract (see **10.3.2**), the building contractor is engaged by the employer to construct a building in accordance with plans and specifications prepared by the employer's architect (see **10.2.3**). The contractor (sometimes called the 'main contractor' or 'principal contractor') will enter into a building contract with the employer, although it may not necessarily carry out all, or indeed any, of the building works. Instead, the contractor may enter into sub-contracts with other builders or trade contractors who will carry out the work. These sub-contractors are likely to be specialists in particular areas of the construction industry, such as lift sub-contractors, cladding sub-contractors or mechanical and electrical sub-contractors, so that, in a large project, there may be several different sub-contractors who execute works on different parts of the development. Most traditional forms of building contract permit sub-contracting only with the prior written consent of the employer (to be given through the agency of its architect), and some building contracts require the sub-contractors to be engaged on specific terms and conditions acceptable to the employer, which may include the obligation on the sub-contractors to grant collateral warranties (see **10.5.1**) to the employer/lenders in relation to the works carried out under their sub-contracts.

There are many different standard forms of building contract used in the construction industry, and this chapter does not intend to provide a detailed analysis of the obligations of the employer and the main contractor. The basic obligations of the employer under most traditional forms of contract are to give up possession of the site to the contractor (to enable uninterrupted building works to commence), not to interfere with the execution of building works (as the contractor has an implied right to complete the works, as well as a duty to do so), to appoint an architect for the purposes of the contract (ie to supervise the execution of the works, in its role as designer of the works, and to certify when the building has been satisfactorily completed and therefore adjudged to have reached the stage of 'practical completion'), to nominate sub-contractors to carry out the works (unless the contractor is to select its own), and to pay the price payable to the contractor as and when the contract requires.

In return, the contractor agrees to complete the work set out in the contract in the form of the architect's plans and specifications. When the architect has issued a certificate of practical completion, the contractor becomes entitled to receive full payment of the contract price less an amount known as 'retention' monies, and the employer is able to resume possession of the site for the purpose of granting leases to its tenants. The retention monies are held until such time as any minor works still to be completed at practical completion, known as snagging items of work, are completed, whereupon the retention monies are released to the contractor and a 'final certificate' is issued. If the contractor does not complete the works on time, the employer will usually be able to levy liquidated damages for delay, the amounts of which the parties will have agreed at the outset of the project. Such damages must not be out of all proportion to the innocent party's legitimate interest in enforcing the counterparty's obligations under the contract, otherwise there is a danger that they will be classified as penalties which are unenforceable under English law.

Obligations as to quality and fitness of the building materials are implied under s 4 of the Supply of Goods and Services Act 1982, and s 13 of that Act implies a term that the contractor will exercise reasonable care and skill to see that the works will be of satisfactory quality and reasonably fit for their intended purpose. However, notwithstanding its implied obligations, the building contract is likely to contain an express obligation to execute the works in accordance with a standard prescribed by the contract and in accordance with the employer's requirements and performance specifications. The 'fitness for purpose' implied term referred to above is often included as an express term of the contract and is heavily negotiated between the parties. Employers sometimes seek an obligation that the contractor will carry out the works so that completed project as a whole (rather than simply the works) is fit for purpose. Conversely, contractors often seek to exclude fitness for purpose obligations altogether, spurred on by their professional indemnity insurers, by stating that such risks are uninsurable. A compromise is commonly achieved by linking the obligation of the contractor back to the wording of the Act, with a clause in the contract being inserted stating that the liability of the contractor shall be to carry out the works (rather than the completed project as a whole) so that such works are reasonably fit for their intended purpose.

It should be noted that with all forms of procurement, save for construction management (see **10.3.4.2**), there is no privity of contract between the employer and the sub-contractors since it is the main contractor who engages their services. However, the main contractor should be made liable under the terms of the main contract in respect of the acts or omissions of the sub-contractors. As noted above, in major projects, collateral warranties (see **10.5.1**) are often sought by clients from a list of principal sub-contractors, ie those whose packages of work are particularly important by size, value or the nature of their particular expertise. A client may regard any sub-contractors' warranties beyond such principal sub-contractors as an added benefit, but will likely be relying on the strength of the main contractor's covenant in the event that a defect arises in the completed works.

10.2.3 The architect

In a traditional form of contract the architect is engaged by the employer to carry out various tasks in relation to the design of the building. Broadly speaking, the architect prepares plans and specifications of the works required by the employer from which the builders will take their instructions, and it will supervise the execution of those works by the building contractor (or sub-contractors) in accordance with the plans and specifications. When the architect is satisfied that the works required by the building contract have been completed, it will issue a certificate of practical completion. As noted at **10.2.2**, this triggers the release of payments to the contractor save for retention monies, which are released only when snagging has been completed. In some instances, where, for example, there are several sections of the works comprising a building contract, the architect may issue sectional completion certificates to reflect the completion of different phases of the project.

10.2.4 The quantity surveyor/cost consultant

The quantity surveyor or cost consultant is engaged by the employer (or by the architect on behalf of the employer) to estimate the quantities of the materials to be used and to set them into bills of quantities. What the quantity surveyor or cost consultant does is to measure the amount of work and materials that will be necessary to complete construction in accordance with the architect's plans and specifications. On the basis of their bills of quantities, building contractors will be able to work out the amount of their estimated cost of construction.

10.2.5 The engineers

In large construction projects, there may be a team of consulting engineers, including a structural engineer, engaged by the employer to give advice on structural design, and mechanical, electrical, heating and ventilating engineers, who give advice to the employer on matters within their areas of competence.

The architect, quantity surveyor and team of consulting engineers, as professional people, owe the employer a duty by contract to carry out the work required of them with reasonable skill, care and diligence. The standard of care expected is the standard of the ordinary skilled man exercising and professing to have that special skill. If any one of them falls below that standard, or below any higher standard of care set by the professional appointment under which they are engaged, they will be liable in damages for breach of contract.

10.2.6 The project manager

In addition to the consultants referred to above, clients will often engage a project manager on major projects to assist with managing the contractor and professional team to achieve a successful completion of the project. The role of the project manager will be to coordinate the other team members, ensure deadlines are met and oversee the project as a whole.

10.2.7 The Principal Designer

There is also an obligation on clients involved in major construction projects in the UK to engage what is known as a 'Principal Designer' in relation to the works. The Construction (Design and Management) Regulations 2015 (SI 2015/51) (the CDM Regulations) govern the relevant obligations of the client and team members. The Principal Designer's function is to ensure that the project is carried out in accordance with applicable health and safety regulations and to prepare a health and safety file for the project. The client must also provide pre-construction information to the contractor, who is to prepare a construction phase plan for the project. There are also general duties on all team members to communicate, coordinate and cooperate effectively with one another. Breach of the CDM Regulations can lead to criminal as well as civil liability.

154 Commercial Property

10.2.8 The Building Safety Act 2022

The new Building Safety Act 2022 (BSA 2022) has recently been enacted to reform building safety legislation in the UK which was necessary well before the Grenfell Tower disaster in 2017.

Having been introduced to Parliament in July 2021, the BSA 2022 came into force on 1 April 2023 and establishes new duties for the management of fire and building safety in high-rise residential buildings (which are defined as buildings of 18m high or seven storeys or more). As of 1 October 2023, the new regime of the BSA 2022 came into law, bringing about changes to the requirements for higher-risk buildings and introducing the Building Safety Regulator as the building control authority for higher-risk buildings.

This new dutyholder regime applies to *all* construction projects, subject to limited exceptions. This means that for the majority of construction projects, a 'Principal Designer' and 'Principal Contractor' must be appointed, each carrying their own specific duties and competency requirements. Whilst labelled identically, the BSA 2022 roles are distinct from those in the CDM Regulations and involve different responsibilities and skillsets.

The primary objective of the Principal Designer role under the:

- CDM Regulations is focused on health and safety in the pre-construction phase of a project; whereas
- the secondary legislation enacted pursuant to the BSA 2022 is focused on design.

Similarly, a Principal Contractor under the:

- CDM Regulations must ensure the health and safety of those affected by the project; whereas
- the secondary legislation enacted pursuant to the BSA 2022 must take all reasonable steps to ensure compliance with Building Regulations.

Those who are designing and constructing higher-risk buildings will have formal responsibility for complying with Building Regulations, reducing risks, and ensuring that those who create Building Safety risks are responsible for managing them.

The BSA 2022 will enforce the requirements for keeping vital, up-to-date safety information about how a building has been designed, built, and managed. This 'Golden Thread of Information' will be stored digitally for the entire life of the building and will enable a user to understand a building and the steps needed to keep both the building and people safe, now and in the future.

10.3 DIFFERENT FORMS OF PROCUREMENT

10.3.1 Introduction

The way in which risks and responsibilities are allocated between the parties on a construction project is determined by the procurement process and form of construction contract used. There are various industry bodies, one of which is the Joint Contracts Tribunal (JCT), which over the years have developed their own standard-form construction documents. These contain different terms and conditions depending upon what risks the employer or the contractor will be taking in relation to the project. As these industry bodies usually represent building contractors (rather than employers), it is usually necessary for lawyers acting for the employer to amend the standard terms and conditions to redress the balance of risk in favour of the employer.

The key elements of any building contract usually centre around time (ie when the project needs to be delivered), price (ie how much the project is going to cost) and quality (ie what standard of skill and care will be required, and whether that is appropriate for the intended use of the finished project, eg a high-tech city office or tower as opposed to a low-grade warehousing facility).

The relative importance attached to each of these critical factors will often determine the procurement process adopted and the form of building contract used. Many building projects require external funders in the form of commercial lenders to finance the construction of the project. In addition, in times of economic uncertainty many projects now involve a partnering or alliancing arrangement, whereby two or more project participants combine to form a consortium which is able to share the risks and rewards inherent in any building project. Such arrangements may take the form of binding commitments to each other and be documented contractually, or alternatively reflect a more aspirational, non-binding collaboration agreement or charter. Many of the industry bodies, including the JCT, have their own standard-form agreements. Bespoke partnering arrangements are also increasingly being adopted in the public sector, with an example being the use of framework agreements by local governments for utilities or infrastructure works. Under these types of agreement, several tendering contractors all sign up to a framework agreement (usually with no guarantee of work); when an individual works contract is required to be undertaken, the government entity then selects a contractor from the framework and enters into a separate call-off contract with the successful individual contractor. This has the perceived benefit for the client of providing a pre-selected panel of quality contractors ready to commence work quickly on an individual works contract, whilst the tendering contractors have the benefit of regular workflow from a financially sound client (albeit that no work is guaranteed to be forthcoming). Partnering arrangements often measure performance by use of key performance indicators (KPIs), which can be used successfully for the benefit of the project as a whole if parties collaborate in an open manner and in the spirit of mutual trust and co-operation. However, the take-up of partnering agreements may be limited due to difficulties in being able to bring a successful claim against a party that has not met its obligations under the particular partnering arrangement.

The different forms of procurement are outlined below.

10.3.2 Traditional contract

A key feature of traditional procurement is that the design element and the construction of a project are separate. As noted at **10.2**, the building contractor is engaged to construct the project pursuant to the building contract, and the professional consultants are engaged to design the project under the terms of their professional appointments.

The typical structure of traditional procurement is set out in **Figure 10.1**.

156 Commercial Property

Figure 10.1 Structure of traditional procurement

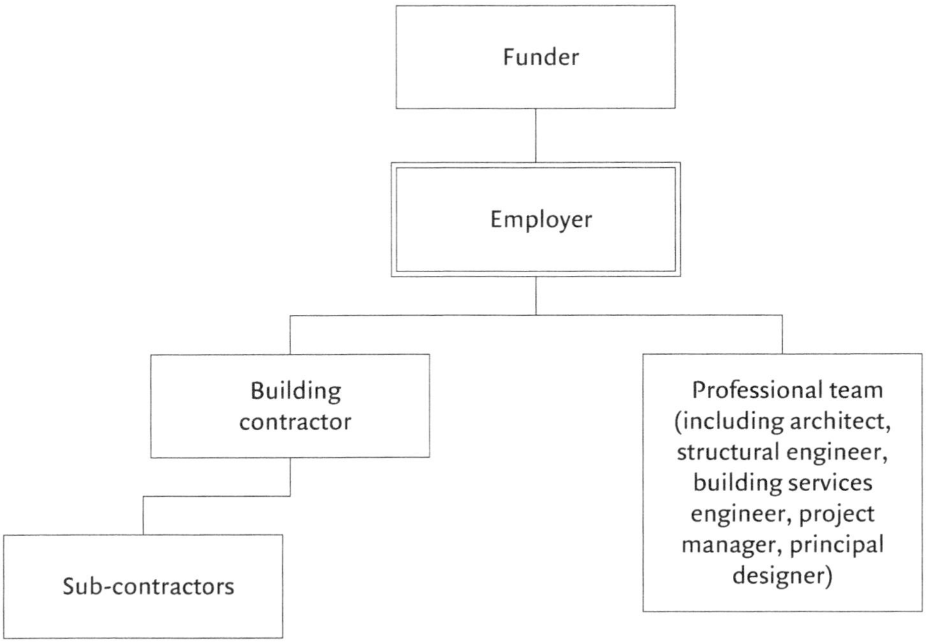

```
                    ┌──────────┐
                    │  Funder  │
                    └────┬─────┘
                         │
                    ┌────┴─────┐
                    │ Employer │
                    └────┬─────┘
              ┌──────────┴──────────┐
        ┌─────┴─────┐         ┌─────┴──────────┐
        │ Building  │         │ Professional team
        │contractor │         │ (including architect,
        └─────┬─────┘         │ structural engineer,
              │               │ building services
        ┌─────┴─────┐         │ engineer, project
        │   Sub-    │         │ manager, principal
        │contractors│         │ designer)
        └───────────┘         └────────────────┘
```

Some advantages and disadvantages of a traditional contract are listed in **Table 10.1** below.

Table 10.1 Advantages and disadvantages of a traditional contract

	Time	Money	Quality
Advantages	More certainty in the construction period, as the design is completed and the contractor therefore has to build according to the detailed plans.	Greater certainty in the fixed lump-sum contract price as the design is fully developed prior to construction.	The detailed contract documents can specify the employer's exact requirements so should lead to better quality, with the construction phase starting only after the detailed design has been completed.
Disadvantages	Longer overall, because the employer needs to complete the design before the construction phase commences. Employer-driven changes to the project during construction phase may delay the project.	Additional design fees are paid to professional consultants. Employer-driven changes to the project during construction may increase costs.	The building contractor will be responsible for the works but will not be responsible for design (unless there is a contractor designed portion), and so the employer retains both the design risk itself and the interface risk with construction. The technical documents, forming part of the building contract, need to set out precisely the requirements of the employer. This places an additional burden on the employer.

10.3.3 Design and build contract

Under a design and build building contract, the building contractor is responsible for both the design and the construction of a project. The building contractor may appoint its own design team or sub-contractors to carry out design, but the building contractor is liable to the employer for the design (as well as construction) of the project.

In major construction projects where employers often seek an effective and complete risk transfer, the employer ordinarily appoints its own professional consultants to develop initial designs. After such designs have been developed, the employer, principal members of the design team (ie the architect and engineers) and the building contractor will enter into a 'novation' agreement. This tripartite agreement transfers both rights and responsibilities from the employer to the building contractor. The building contractor is then able to instruct the consultant previously engaged by the employer to complete the detailed design for the project, and also has direct rights against the consultant in the event that such designs developed under the appointment are deficient.

The typical structure of design and build procurement is set out in **Figure 10.2**.

The University of Law would like to thank Practical Law for authorising the adaptation in this publication of figures and tables reproduced at 10.3 'Different forms of procurement', see <http://uk.practicallaw.thomsonreuters.com/0-367-5966>. For further information about Practical Law, visit <http://uk.practicallaw.thomsonreuters.com/> or call 0345 600 9355. © Thomson Reuters 2025.

Figure 10.2 Structure of design and build procurement

Pre-novation (prior to construction)

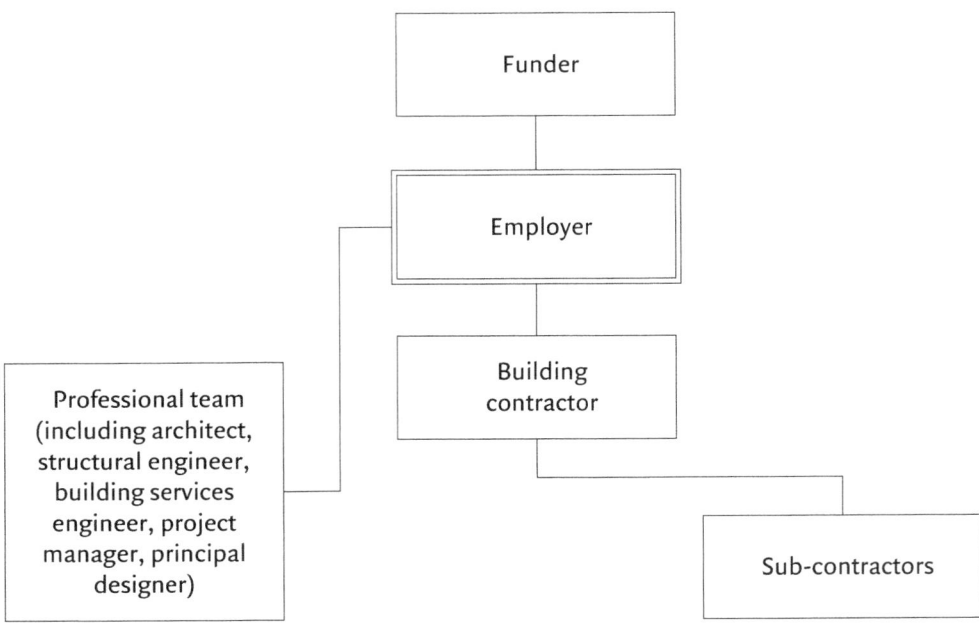

Post-novation (during construction)

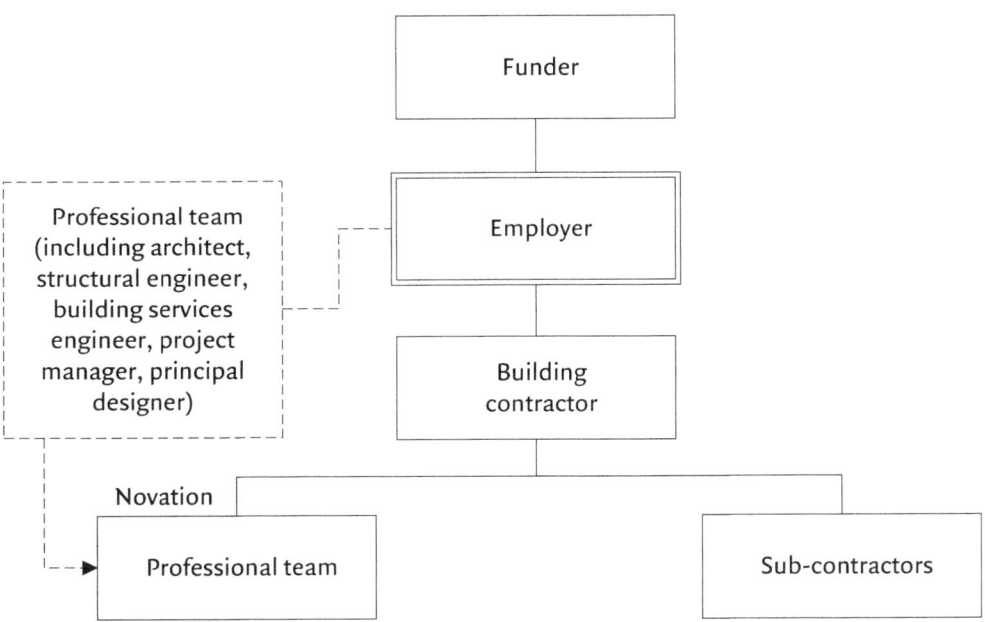

Some advantages and disadvantages of a design and build contract are listed in **Table 10.2** below.

Table 10.2   Advantages and disadvantages of a design and build contract

	Time	Money	Quality
Advantages	May be quicker than a 'traditional' contract because the employer needs to develop only outline designs.	Offers certainty by having a fixed lump-sum contract price.	The building contractor assumes a 'single point of responsibility' towards the employer rather than this being spread between the building contractor and design team.
Disadvantages	An employer who appoints and novates a team of professional consultants may take a similar total time to a traditional contract. Employer-driven changes to the project during construction phase may delay the project.	The 'single point of responsibility' assumed by the building contractor is likely to involve a price premium for the building contractor to take on this risk. Employer-driven changes to the project may significantly affect the final price paid.	Where the building contractor has single point responsibility for design and construction, there may be a temptation to drive down quality to save costs, as the building contractor's profit depends on meeting the building contract requirements at the lowest cost.

Design and build contracts are currently the most popular form of building contract, and are widely used on both simple structures and major projects.

10.3.4   Management contracting and construction management

The two forms of procurement referred to above are the most commonly used forms of procurement for building projects in the UK. However, other forms of procurement are available, one of which is called management contracting and the other of which is called construction management. These are usually adopted only by sophisticated developers on high-value projects, who are familiar with the procurement processes involved.

10.3.4.1   Management contracting

A management contractor is appointed by the employer and is similar to a professional consultant rather than a building contractor. The management contractor is responsible for managing the construction of the project.

The management contractor does not carry out the work itself, but instead appoints works contractors to carry out the work and any specialist design. The management contractor administers the works contracts. The employer looks to the management contractor to see that the work is carried out properly, but the management contractor has very limited liability to the employer for failure by the works contractors to carry out their works.

The typical structure of management contracting procurement is set out in **Figure 10.3**.

Figure 10.3 Structure of management contracting procurement

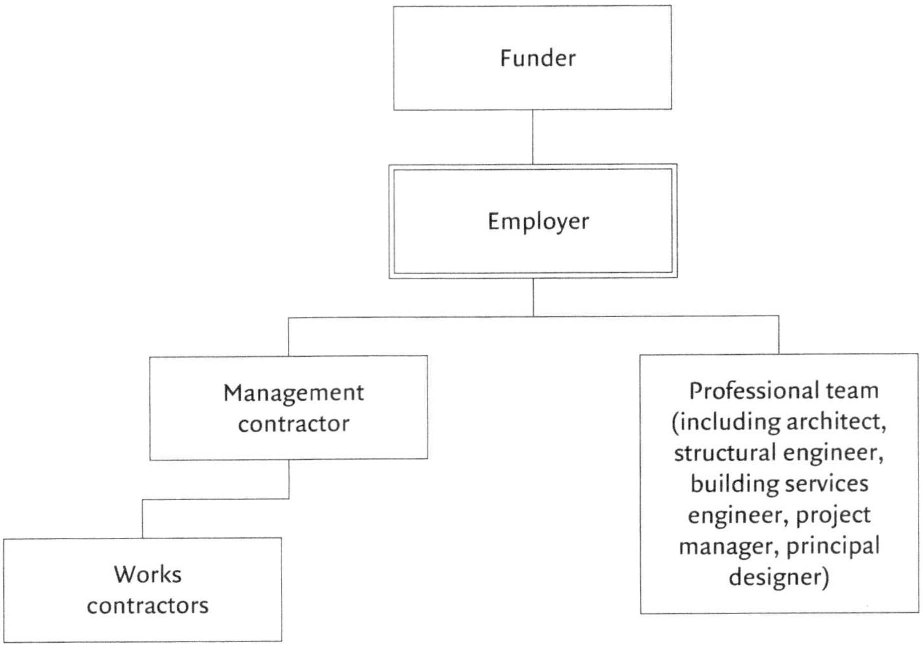

```
                    Funder
                      |
                   Employer
                   /      \
        Management         Professional team
        contractor         (including architect,
            |              structural engineer,
            |              building services
            |              engineer, project
         Works             manager, principal
       contractors         designer)
```

Some advantages and disadvantages of management contracting are listed in **Table 10.3** below.

Table 10.3 Advantages and disadvantages of management contracting

	Time	Money	Quality
Advantages	May be quick: design and construction may progress in parallel as works contractors instructed on an ad hoc basis.	Shorter construction period and more flexible arrangements may allow the project to adapt to meet employer's needs.	Management contractor and design team can work together flexibly to meet employer's requirements.
Disadvantages	No certain construction period, and could be haphazard if works contractors not managed properly. The employer may have to claim delay damages from the management contractor and many works contractors if the requirements of the works contracts and management contract are not met.	No certain construction price. Number of different works contractors involved.	Overall responsibility for quality may be diluted between the professional consultants, the management contractor and the works contractors. No single point of responsibility for design and construction.

10.3.4.2 Construction management

The employer appoints a construction manager and the professional consultants. The construction manager is responsible for managing the construction of the project. The remaining professional consultants carry out the remaining design.

Where this form of procurement differs from management contracting (see **10.3.4.1**) is that whilst the construction manager arranges for the employer to appoint specialist trade contractors and administers the trade contracts, it is the employer who actually enters into the trade contracts themselves. The trade contractors carry out construction and any specialist design directly for the employer.

The typical structure of construction management procurement is set out in **Figure 10.4** below.

Figure 10.4 Structure of construction management procurement

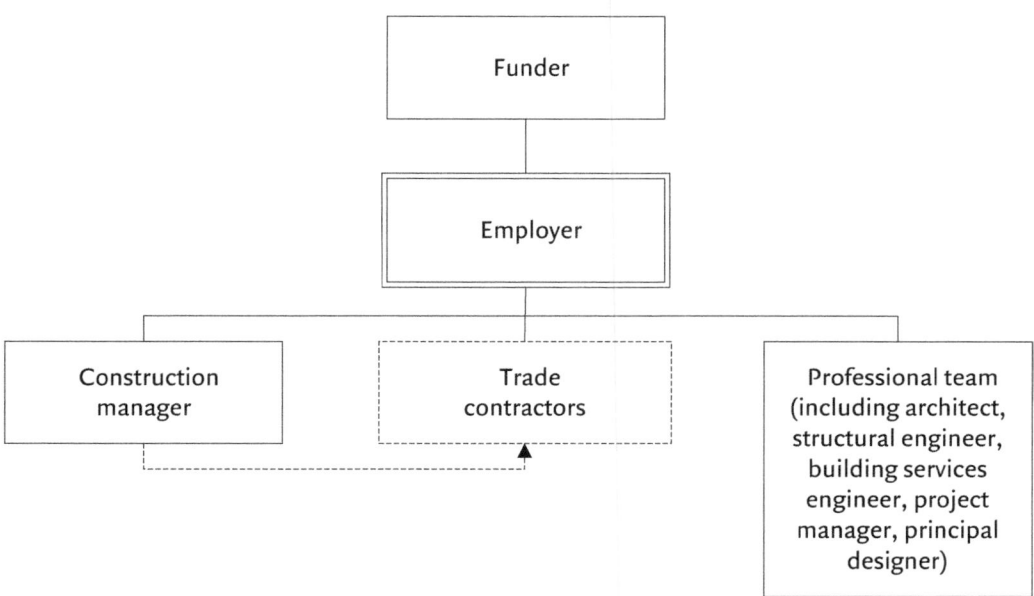

Some advantages and disadvantages of construction management are listed in **Table 10.4** below.

Table 10.4 Advantages and disadvantages of construction management

	Time	Money	Quality
Advantages	May be quick: design and construction may progress in parallel as works contractors instructed on an ad hoc basis.	Compared with management contracting, the construction manager may charge a fixed fee, rather than a percentage on the whole construction price.	Construction manager and design team can work together to meet employer's requirements. Flexible process can help meet employer's requirements.

	Time	Money	Quality
Disadvantages	No certain construction period and could be haphazard if works contractors not managed properly. The employer may have to claim delay damages from the many trade contractors if the requirements of the trade contracts and management contract are not met.	No certain construction price. Even with a construction manager, the client needs to be hands-on with the trade contractors, and this requires time, experience and resources.	Overall responsibility for quality may be diluted between professional consultants, the construction manager and the trade contractors. No single point of responsibility for design and construction.

10.3.5 Pricing mechanisms

Within the different forms of building contract, there is often flexibility as to how the price paid by the employer to the building contractor will be calculated. A 'lump-sum' contract gives the employer certainty as to what it will pay to the building contractor for the works described in the building contract, provided that the employer does not change its description of the works required to be carried out, or there are no grounds available to the building contractor to claim additional monies under the building contract.

Alternatively, certain building contracts have a guaranteed maximum price (GMP) mechanism in them for determining the price to be paid to the building contractor. This allows the employer to set a maximum price payable to the building contractor; it often includes financial incentives for the building contractor to achieve cost savings in relation to the works so that they cost less than the GMP and allow the contractor to benefit from any such cost savings.

Another way of calculating the price to be paid is found in a 'measurement' contract. Under a measurement contract, the employer pays the building contractor for expected levels of work carried out. Then, at given stages of the project or when the project is complete, the employer's professional consultants review the amount of work the building contractor has actually carried out. The building contractor or the employer makes any necessary balancing payment, if the building contractor has carried out more or less work than the parties originally expected.

There are also bespoke forms of building contract to cater for different types of contract. Major engineering contracts use their own bespoke forms of contract. Project finance transactions also have specific forms of contracts, as do projects carried out overseas, government projects and partnering or joint venture contracts. The key point to note here is that all projects place different values on the three critical objectives of time, cost and quality, and the relative importance attached to each of these factors will often determine the preferred method of procurement and the choice of contract.

10.4 DUTIES OWED TO THIRD PARTIES

10.4.1 Introduction

If the project results in the employer obtaining a completed building which turns out to be defective by reason of its design or the materials used, or by reason of the manner in which it was constructed, the employer is likely to have a claim for breach of contract against those members of the design and construction team who caused the defect. Contractual damages are assessed under the rule in *Hadley v Baxendale* (1854) 9 Exch 341, under which the claimant will be able to recover:

(a) losses arising naturally, according to the normal course of things, from the breach of contract; or

(b) such losses as may be reasonably be supposed to have been in the contemplation of the parties at the time they made the contract, as a probable result of the breach. This is likely to enable the employer to recover any costs incurred in carrying out remedial repairs, subject to the normal limitation rules under the Limitation Act 1980.

However, consider the position of a buyer from the employer who discovers a defect after completion of its purchase of the freehold; or that of a mortgagee of the freehold who discovers that the value of its security is seriously impaired because of a hidden design or construction defect; or that of a tenant of the building who enters into a lease on the basis of a full repairing covenant, which may oblige it to repair damage caused by such inherent defects. Traditionally, such third parties were unable to bring a claim for breach of contract as they did not have a contractual relationship with the employer's development team. Because of the rules of privity of contract, the practice arose of members of the development team giving a collateral warranty with such parties in order to enable them to bring a claim; as to collateral warranties, see **10.5.1**. In the absence of such a collateral warranty, and given the difficulties of a third party seeking a remedy in tort (see **10.4.3**), an alternative to collateral warranties can be found under statute (see **10.4.2**).

10.4.2 Contracts (Rights of Third Parties) Act 1999

The Contracts (Rights of Third Parties) Act 1999 came into force on 11 May 2000 and applies to contracts entered into on or after that date. It allows the parties to a contract to confer rights on third parties. A third party, such as a future tenant or mortgage lender, may enforce the contract as if it were a party to it, provided that the contract expressly provides that it may, or that it purports to confer a benefit on it. The third party must be expressly identified in the contract by name, as a member of a class or as answering a particular description, but need not be in existence when the contract is entered into.

In theory, therefore, this Act provides a mechanism whereby third parties would be able to enforce the contractual obligations of the employer's development team if, for example, the contract was stated to be for the benefit of 'all future tenants' of the building. Whilst the use of the Act has been promoted widely amongst City firms of solicitors, there has been some reluctance on the part of beneficiaries, in particulars funders, to accept it, many of whom seem to prefer the paper security of holding a document, ie in the form of a collateral warranty, rather than relying on the operation of the Act.

It still seems likely, therefore, that, for the time being at least, traditional forms of protection (eg tort or collateral warranties) will still need to be relied upon. However, the Act has great potential benefits, particularly for major projects, given the sheer number of interested third parties requiring rights. The use of the Act to grant third parties rights ought therefore to be promoted further as a way of minimising the paper trail that otherwise results in large-scale projects.

10.4.3 Liability in tort

In seeking to bring a claim in tort, the problem that the buyer, lender or tenant will encounter is that any loss they sustain as a result of faulty design, materials or workmanship is likely to be classified as pure economic loss and therefore generally irrecoverable in tort. For example, in the case of the freehold buyer, if it discovers after completion of its purchase that the foundations of the building have been laid in a negligent fashion, so that the building cannot be used without remedial works first being carried out, it can either execute the repairs itself (thereby incurring repair costs), or dispose of the defective building to someone else (probably at less than the purchase price) or simply abandon the property (thereby wasting the money paid for the building in the first place); but whichever course of action the buyer takes, the loss it incurs is purely economic, and only in limited circumstances will the courts allow the claimant to recover such loss in tort.

To establish a claim in negligence, the claimant will have to show that the defendant owed the claimant a duty of care, that the defendant breached that duty and that the claimant suffered an actionable form of damage as a result. Following a series of House of Lords decisions in the late 1980s and early 1990s, it is safe to say that liability in the tort of negligence will arise only if there is a breach of one of two categories of duty. The first duty is based upon the decision in *Donoghue v Stevenson* [1932] AC 562, where liability will arise out of a lack of care which results in reasonably foreseeable damage to persons or to property (other than to the property which causes the damage). The second duty is founded upon the case of *Hedley Byrne & Co Ltd v Heller & Partners Ltd* [1964] AC 465 and is concerned with a lack of care which causes non-physical economic loss.

10.4.3.1 Liability for physical damage

The duty of care under *Donoghue v Stevenson* [1932] AC 562 is a duty to avoid physical injury to person or property. It imposes a duty upon the manufacturer of a product (eg a builder constructing a building) to take reasonable care to avoid damage to person or property through defects in the product. However, it does not impose a duty upon the manufacturer to ensure that the product itself is free from defects. Simply because the design or construction of the building is defective does not necessarily render the person who was responsible for the defect liable in damages, even if a duty was owed and the damage was foreseeable. The case would turn upon whether the claimant suffered a type of loss recognised by the courts as legally recoverable. Pure economic loss (eg the cost of repairing the defect, and the loss of profits while repairs are carried out) is not recoverable under *Donoghue v Stevenson* principles.

In *D&F Estates Ltd v Church Commissioners for England* [1989] AC 177, the House of Lords held that liability in tort arises only where there is some physical damage to the person or to some other property, and that damage to the building itself which merely reduces its value is pure economic loss and thus irrecoverable in tort (except under *Hedley Byrne v Heller* principles – see **10.4.3.2**). In *Murphy v Brentwood District Council* [1990] 2 All ER 908, the House of Lords reaffirmed its earlier decision and stated that the idea that component parts of the same building could amount to separate species of property (the 'complex structure' theory) – so that, for example, negligently laid foundations could be said to have damaged 'other' property when they led to cracks appearing in the walls – was not correct.

To give an example of what may be recoverable, consider the position where, after completion of their purchase of the freehold, a defectively-constructed roof collapses and causes personal injury to a buyer. The buyer may be able to recover damages in respect of their personal injuries and any economic loss arising out of those injuries (eg loss of earnings), but they will not be able to recover the cost of repairing the roof itself since that loss is pure economic loss.

10.4.3.2 Liability for economic loss

Economic loss is a term which can be used to describe any monetary loss. Pure economic loss is monetary loss which is not connected to physical injury to person or property. With one or two isolated and doubtful exceptions (see, eg, *Junior Books v Veitchi* [1983] 1 AC 520), pure economic loss is recoverable in tort only where, in a special relationship of close proximity, a duty of care is owed to avoid loss arising from a negligent misstatement. In *Hedley Byrne & Co Ltd v Heller & Partners Ltd* [1964] AC 465, the House of Lords decided that, in a relationship of close proximity, where a person was seeking information from one who was possessed of certain skills, a duty was owed by the latter to exercise reasonable care if they knew, or ought to have known, that reliance was being placed upon their skill and judgement. Put simply, the duty amounts to a duty to prevent pure economic loss arising from the making of a statement or the giving of advice. In the context of a building project, many statements are made and much advice is given, but proximity of the parties and reliance are the fundamental factors.

The extent of this duty was restated and redefined by the House of Lords in *Caparo Industries plc v Dickman* [1990] 2 AC 605. It is now the case that, in order for there to be the requisite degree of proximity between the parties for the duty to arise, the defendant (ie the person who made the statement or gave the advice) must have known (both in the preparation of what was said and in the delivery) that the statement would be communicated to an identified person or group of persons in connection with a transaction of a particular type, and that the recipient would be very likely to rely upon it.

While the employer, by reason of its contractual relationship with its professional advisers (eg the architect or structural engineer), might easily establish the requisite degree of proximity and show reliance upon the advice given, its tenant, buyer or the buyer's lender is unlikely to be able to show the requisite proximity (see *Hunt & Others v Optima (Cambridge) Ltd & Others* [2014] EWCA Civ 714). In other words, the pure economic loss that a third party suffers remains irrecoverable.

As a result of this inability to recover the cost of repairing damage to the building outside a contractual relationship, various devices have been utilised by buyers, their lenders, tenants and the employer's own financiers. These are examined further at **10.5**.

10.5 PROTECTING THIRD PARTIES

10.5.1 Collateral warranties

A collateral warranty is an agreement entered into (under hand or by deed) by someone engaged in the construction or design of a building, by virtue of which that person assumes a contractual duty of care for the benefit of someone who has an interest in seeing that the building is free from defects, but who does not otherwise have a contractual relationship with the warrantor. Collateral warranties are commonly required to be given by the consultants, the main contractor and the sub-contractors to the freehold buyer of the development, its lender, the employer's financiers and possibly (if negotiated) the tenant. The employer does not need warranties from either the building contractor or the design team as it is in direct contract with such parties under the building contract and professional appointments. However, the employer may require warranties from the sub-contractors with whom it has no direct contractual relationship as additional protection behind the main contractor's warranty, or may require warranties after the consultants have been novated to the contractor.

The key advantage of having collateral warranties is that they create the certainty of a contractual relationship, as opposed to the uncertainty that exists in tort. All the claimant would need to show in order to establish a claim is that the contractual duty contained in the warranty had been breached and that damage had ensued. Losses which can be described as purely economic will also be recoverable under contractual principles where the loss suffered as a result of the breach of warranty could reasonably be said to have been in the contemplation of the parties at the time the warranty was entered into.

Many of the standard building contracts and forms of consultancy appointment also contain suggested forms of collateral warranty. However, as with the terms of such contracts themselves, it is unlikely that well-advised employer/developer clients would accept these forms of collateral warranty as they often contain unacceptable limits of liability, once again driven by the requirements of the warrantor's professional indemnity insurers. For instance, standard forms of collateral warranty have been published by the British Property Federation, the Construction Industry Council and the Joint Contracts Tribunal, and have been approved by the relevant professional bodies. Such forms of warranty will not be sufficient if acting for employer/developer clients, who will require bespoke forms of collateral warranty without extensive limitation of liability provisions. This is an area where solicitors are involved extensively in the negotiation of acceptable forms, and where the market at the time the negotiation takes place can play a large part in resolving such negotiations.

A collateral warranty will normally contain the following provisions:

(a) Confirmation that the warrantor (ie building contractor, sub-contractor or consultant) owes to the third party benefiting from the warranty a duty of care similar to that owed to the person employing them. The warrantor will already owe a duty of care to the person employing them, normally the developer, by virtue of being appointed under a contract by their employer to carry out the design or construction work. It will oblige the warrantor to use reasonable skill and care in the performance of their duties under the contract, and they will be negligent if they fail to do so.

(b) Confirmation that deleterious materials will not be used in the development. A warranty given by the architect will confirm that such materials will not be specified for use in the development, and a warranty given by the building contractor will confirm that such materials will not be used in the development. The materials that are not to be used may be listed in the warranty, cross-referenced to the list appearing in the appointment, or the warranty may exclude the use of materials that do not comply with British Standards or are known to be deleterious. Listing deleterious materials in the warranty itself has been largely replaced by a general warranty not to use deleterious materials. This is because certain materials which appeared on the lists included in warranties were found not to be deleterious, and producers of such materials were able successfully to challenge the presence of such materials on the lists and bring claims for misrepresentation. A general warranty not to use deleterious materials is therefore thought to be a safer approach to avoid claims of this nature.

(c) Confirmation that professional indemnity insurance cover will be maintained by the warrantor up to a specified amount for a specified period. The period will normally be either six years (if the warranty has been signed under hand) or 12 years (if the warranty has been entered into as a deed) from the date of issue of the certificate of practical completion in relation to the development. The beneficiary is usually entitled to request evidence that the relevant amount of professional insurance set out under the building contract/appointment is being maintained, and this can be provided in the form of a broker's certificate.

(d) Confirmation that, on giving appropriate notification to the warrantor, the person to whom the warranty is given may 'step into the shoes' of the developer and, upon paying to the warrantor any outstanding fees or sums due, may instruct the warrantor under the terms of the contract as though the person to whom the warranty is given had in fact been the warrantor's employer. This step-in right is essential for any contracting purchaser of the completed development or any funder. If the employer becomes insolvent during the development process, it will be crucial for the contracting purchaser or funder to ensure that the development is completed properly, and the best way of achieving this is to instruct the team originally appointed to carry out the development. The right of step-in is not required or appropriate for a tenant, who will enter into a lease only when the building has been completed and the risk of insolvency of the employer has passed.

(e) In the case of an architect or other person providing design material, an irrevocable, royalty-free licence to use that material in connection with the completion and subsequent maintenance of the development, with additional rights for the beneficiary to sub-licence if required. The copyright in the design material will normally remain with the designer but the person benefiting from the warranty will be able to use the material, though only to the extent that this is needed in connection with the development. This is critical, as the design material is likely to include details of how the major pieces of equipment or plant in the building operate.

(f) There will be limitations/prohibitions on the assignment of the benefit of the warranty and often commercial caps on liability requested by the warrantor, who may also wish to state specifically that it shall be entitled to rely on any rights it has under the underlying consultancy appointment in defence of any claim made by the beneficiary of the warranty. This makes it vital for solicitors acting for the beneficiary of the warranty to undertake a specific review of the underlying building contract/professional appointment at this point, to ascertain whether or not there are similar caps on liability on which the warrantor will be able to seek to rely.

It is extremely unlikely that additional warranties will be offered by the building contractor or professional team after they have been engaged, over and above those required under their terms of contract, even if an additional fee for such warranties is provided to the building contractor or professional team. It is therefore essential that the professional/building contractor is contractually committed to provide whatever warranties are required on the particular project pursuant to the building contract or professional appointment.

10.5.2 Other methods

10.5.2.1 Assignment of rights

The employer may consider attempting to satisfy the demands of its financier, buyer or tenant for protection against latent defects by assigning whatever rights the employer may have (primarily under contract law) against the contractor and the consultants. An assignment is probably appropriate only if made in favour of a financier, a buyer or a tenant of the whole of the development site. However, even where a tenant takes a lease of the whole of a development site, a landlord will be reluctant to part with its contractual rights in case the tenant's lease is forfeited or disclaimed. If collateral warranties can be provided to the interested third party instead, the landlord will be able to retain its rights against the contractor and design team.

Building contracts and contracts for the engagement of consultants may contain prohibitions on the assignment of the benefit of the contract without consent; and it seems that, following the House of Lords decision in *Linden Garden Trust Ltd v Lenesta Sludge Disposals Ltd; St Martins Property Corporation Ltd v Sir Robert McAlpine & Sons Ltd* [1993] 3 WLR 408, most prohibitions will be effective, although each clause will have to be interpreted to discover its exact meaning.

10.5.2.2 Declaring a trust of rights

Declaring a trust of rights may be considered as an alternative to an outright assignment where the employer is retaining an interest in the property and therefore does not wish to part with valuable contractual rights. In this way the employer can retain the benefit of the rights it has against the contractor and consultants, but declares that it holds them upon trust for the benefit of itself and its tenants. Again, the effectiveness of a trust has not been tested in the courts and may fall foul of the rule that the party claiming damages must have suffered a loss: in a trust arrangement the party claiming damages may have suffered no loss, for example if the employer has sold the building to a purchaser for full value (see **10.5.2.6**), and therefore damages would be irrecoverable.

10.5.2.3 Latent defects insurance

With residential properties, buyers are anxious to ensure that a newly-constructed property is covered by the National House Building Council (NHBC) Buildmark scheme, or other equivalent insurance. In the commercial field, there are no such standard schemes. However, following the Building Users Insurance against Latent Defects Report (BUILD Report), published in 1988 by the National Economic Development Office, several of the leading insurance companies in the UK have introduced latent defects insurance in respect of commercial properties. This is a concept which is very familiar on the Continent, where latent defects insurance has been used for some time. There it is known as 'decennial liability' insurance, reflecting the period of 10 years during which such an insurance policy is usually valid.

Policies will vary from company to company (and, indeed, from development to development), but the essential elements are likely to be similar across the board. Latent defects insurance commonly provides cover against damage caused by defective design or construction works for a period of 10 years after practical completion of the development (or such longer period as may be agreed with the insurer). The beneficiary of the policy is covered against the cost of making good most (but not necessarily all) damage caused by a design or construction defect (although not other risks), and the policy may cover other items of economic loss such as loss of rent, or loss of use of the building while repairs are being carried out. The policy can be taken out to cover the employer (as initial owner of the building) and its financiers. Most policies will also automatically insure subsequent owners and occupiers, which will obviously be the desired aim from the employer's point of view. The premium is likely to be substantial (perhaps 1.5% of development costs) and often prohibitive.

The advantages of such a policy are that there is no need for the claimant under the policy to establish legal liability for the damage incurred, and there ought to be easy access to funds to finance repairing costs and, possibly, to cover other economic loss. The disadvantages are that, as with other policies, the insurance may be subject to excesses (meaning that the claimant might have to fund, say, the first £50,000 of a claim), there are often significant exceptions carved out of the policy, and the insurer will invariably require some element of supervision over the execution of the works from commencement, since the risk it is taking on will be considerable. Such insurance is not something which can be obtained after the construction process is complete, and in any event, at that stage of the project risks are generally known.

10.5.2.4 Limiting repair covenants

In a landlord and tenant relationship, the tenant should consider limiting the scope of its repairing covenant. The main problem for a tenant is that the landlord is likely to insist upon the tenant entering into a lease which contains a covenant by the tenant to repair the demised premises. Provided the damage amounts to disrepair, the usual repair covenant imposed by the landlord may oblige the tenant to repair damage which is caused by a defect in the design or construction of the building. While the tenant can commission a full structural survey of the premises prior to the grant of the lease in an effort to discover defects, the very nature of a design or construction defect makes it unlikely that it will manifest itself until some time after the building has been completed and the lease granted.

It is therefore suggested that, on the grant of a lease of a relatively new building, the tenant should attempt to limit the scope of its repairing covenant by excluding (either totally, or for a limited period of, say, three or six years after the grant of the lease) liability to repair damage caused by latent defects. Not only should the tenant seek to exclude such liability from its own covenant, but it also should make sure that no vacuum is left in the repairing obligations under the lease by insisting that the landlord assumes this liability. If this is not done, there is a risk that the property may remain in disrepair. The landlord will be anxious to avoid having to bear any repair costs in respect of the building, and so the limitation of the tenant's repairing obligations is a matter to be negotiated and will depend upon the relative bargaining strengths of the parties. It is most unlikely that the tenant would succeed in its negotiations if, in the agreement for lease, the tenant had insisted upon a degree of control and supervision over the execution of the landlord's works. The landlord would probably argue that the tenant had been given every opportunity before the lease was granted to discover defects and that it should, therefore, consider taking action against its professional advisers.

On the grant of a lease of part of a building, where the tenant would not ordinarily undertake repairing responsibilities in respect of the structure and external parts but would instead be expected to contribute via the service charge to the landlord's costs incurred in maintaining those parts, the tenant would seek to ensure that it was not obliged to contribute via the service charge to the landlord's costs of repairing damage caused by design or construction defects (either throughout the term, or for a limited period). Again, while the tenant could commission a full structural survey, design defects may not be apparent at the time of the survey, or may be hidden in some other part of the building to which the surveyor was unable to gain access.

10.5.2.5 Defect liability periods

In a landlord and tenant relationship, the tenant may seek the benefit of a defect liability period. If the landlord will not agree to exclude the tenant's liability for inherent defects in the lease, the tenant ought to press for the inclusion of a clause in the agreement for lease obliging the landlord to remedy any defects which appear within a short period of time following practical completion of the building. If the landlord agrees to the inclusion of a defects liability period, it is likely to mirror a similar clause in the building contract entered into with the contractor. Quite often, building contracts provide for the contractor to remedy any defects which manifest themselves within, say, the first six or 12 months after practical completion. By including a similar clause in the agreement for lease, the landlord is indirectly passing on the benefit of the clause to the tenant, but this should not be seen as an alternative to a limiting repair covenant.

10.5.2.6 Forced enforcement of remedies

A buyer, financier or tenant may seek the inclusion of a provision whereby the employer agrees to enforce its rights as original contracting party against the contractor or the consultants in respect of defects where loss or liability to repair would otherwise fall upon the former. Difficulties have arisen in this area, in that if the employer has received full market value on a sale of the property to a buyer, or has secured the inclusion of a full repairing covenant on the grant of a lease of the property to a tenant, it cannot be said to have suffered any loss upon which a claim could be maintained.

However, the House of Lords decision in the *Linden Garden* case (see **10.5.2.1**) has shown that in a commercial contract, where it was in the contemplation of the contracting parties that legal title to the property which formed the subject matter of the contract might be transferred to a third party before a breach had occurred, the original contracting party is taken to have entered into the contract for the benefit of itself and all persons who might acquire an interest in the property before the breach occurs. What this means is that, in certain circumstances, the employer may be able to recover damages for breach of contract in respect of loss incurred by its buyer, financier or tenant. This area is not without its complications, and the full ramifications of recent developments in this area have yet to be tested in full.

10.6 DISPUTE RESOLUTION

Disputes often arise in the construction context in relation to claims by the employer or end user that the works, materials or workmanship carried out by the contractor are defective, or the contractor may bring a claim for additional time to complete the works or additional monies for doing so.

Before briefly considering the different types of dispute resolution relevant to construction contracts, whatever the contract says, in the event of a dispute, the parties are not compelled to resort to the courts for the settling of their differences. They can choose instead to attempt to settle their differences amicably. The parties are likely to consider factors including the cost and expense of bringing a claim, and the uncertain and time-consuming nature of dispute resolution in determining whether to settle disputes through the courts rather than attempting to resolve disputes in a non-adversarial manner such as through conciliation, mediation or independent private enquiry.

The main adversarial methods of dispute resolution include adjudication, arbitration and litigation, and these are examined briefly below.

10.6.1 Adjudication

There is now a statutory right to adjudication which is designed to produce a decision that is at least temporarily binding on the parties. The right to adjudication is included within Pt II of the Housing Grants, Construction and Regeneration Act 1996, as amended by the Local Democracy, Economic Development and Construction Act 2009, which provides that any party to a construction contract has the right to refer any dispute arising under the contract for adjudication under a procedure complying with the Act. In order to satisfy the Act, the contract must include certain specific provisions, an important one of which requires the adjudicator to reach a decision within 28 days, or such longer period as both parties agree. If the parties do not explicitly lay down certain minimum provisions about the right to adjudication and the process thereof, an appropriate set of procedural rules will be implied, known as the Scheme for Construction Contracts (England and Wales) Regulations 1998 (SI 1998/649), as amended by the Scheme for Construction Contracts (England and Wales) Regulations 1998 (Amendment) (England) Regulations 2011 (SI 2011/2333).

10.6.2 Arbitration

The parties may also agree that any disputes arising in relation to the contract will be resolved by arbitration. The Arbitration Act 1996 sets out the procedural and evidential matters to be adopted in relation to the settling of disputes by arbitration. In addition, there are standard arbitration rules, published by arbitral institutions such as the Institution of Civil Engineers (ICE), the International Chamber of Commerce (ICC) and the London Court of International Arbitration (LCIA). These rules are often incorporated into the arbitration agreement and contain basic provisions for commencing the arbitration, establishing the arbitral tribunal and the procedures to be adopted prior to the award. International arbitration is commonly used as a choice of dispute resolution in relation to international construction contracts.

10.6.3 Litigation

In practice, many disputes of a construction nature are resolved finally by litigation, with construction and engineering cases of any appreciable size ordinarily tried in the Technology and Construction Court, which is a specialist subdivision of the Queen's Bench Division of the High Court. The advantages of litigation include the ability to join third parties in the proceedings and the ability to deal with legal complexities. These may be outweighed by the advantages of alternative forms of dispute resolution such as arbitration or adjudication, which are often preferred as cheaper, quicker and more commercially expedient ways of resolving disputes.

REVIEW ACTIVITY

Scenario

Your client, Land UK plc (LUK), a large property developer based in the UK, intends to build a new office tower in the City of London. LUK is taking out a bank loan to fund the development from the Royal Bank of England plc (R). The new tower is set to be a landmark, iconic building in the heart of the City, and LUK would like to engage an international architect to undertake the design of the tower. There will also be a number of other consultants, including structural and building services engineers, and the client will need to comply with UK health and safety legislation. In addition, the building will contain a large auditorium for board meetings, with a specialist acoustic engineering sub-contractor appointed to undertake its design and construction. The client has entered into a pre-let agreement with a major law firm, GoodLaw and Partners (G), who will be taking space on several floors of the building, one of which it intends to sub-let to an accountancy firm, HardSums and Partners (H).

Question

Consider what form of procurement your client might use to construct the tower, including the advantages and any disadvantages of such form of procurement, together with any rights each party involved in the transaction might require in the event that a defect arises in the building after its construction.

Answers to this Review activity may be found in Appendix 1.

CHAPTER 11

An Outline of Taxation of Commercial Properties

11.1	Value added tax	173
11.2	Stamp duty land tax on leases	179
	Review activity	179

11.1 VALUE ADDED TAX

At the outset of any property transaction, it is essential to consider the impact of VAT legislation and to advise the client accordingly. The reader will already be aware of the basic principles of VAT, which dictate that VAT may be payable in respect of a supply of goods or services made in the course of a business. Whether VAT is payable depends upon a number of things, including whether the supplies in question are exempt, zero-rated or standard-rated. The reader will also be aware of the effects of such supplies, the payment and receipt of input and output tax, and the recovery of VAT incurred.

Supplies of goods and services made in relation to a property transaction may be grouped as follows:

(a) *Residential properties*
   (i) sale of a green field site – exempt (but subject to the option to tax);
   (ii) construction services – zero-rated;
   (iii) civil engineering works – zero-rated;
   (iv) professional services (eg legal and other professional fees) – standard-rated;
   (v) sale of a new house – zero-rated;
   (vi) grant of a lease of a new house (for a term exceeding 21 years) – zero-rated.

(b) *Commercial properties*
   (i) sale of a green field site – exempt (but subject to the option to tax);
   (ii) construction services – standard-rated;
   (iii) civil engineering works – standard-rated;
   (iv) professional services – standard-rated;
   (v) sale of a new freehold building or the grant of an option to purchase such a building – standard-rated;
   (vi) sale of an old freehold building – exempt (but subject to the option to tax);
   (vii) the grant of a lease (for any length of term) – exempt (but subject to the option to tax);
   (viii) the assignment of a lease – exempt (but subject to the option to tax);
   (ix) the surrender of a lease – exempt (but subject to the option to tax by the person who receives the consideration);
   (x) repair, alteration and demolition works – standard-rated.

Rules relating to work carried out on listed buildings are not considered in this book, neither are the particular problems associated with premises of mixed use.

Some of the supplies listed above are exempt supplies but are subject to what is called the 'option to tax' (also known as the 'option to waive exemption'). This is dealt with more comprehensively at **11.1.3**. What the option means is that the person who makes the supply can voluntarily convert the supply from one which is exempt, and therefore gives rise to no VAT liability, into a standard-rated supply.

The VAT consequences arising in residential and commercial developments are now considered.

11.1.1 Residential developments

In a typical new residential development, the VAT consequences will not be too complicated. If, for example, a property company, ABC Ltd, buys a green field site, the seller is making an exempt supply to ABC Ltd, which will not be subject to VAT unless the seller, being a taxable person, has elected to waive the exemption. In any event, if, as is often the case, the seller is a private individual, they are not likely to be selling the land in the course of a business, and the supply will therefore be outside the scope of VAT. Any construction services (such as work provided by builders and the provision of materials) and civil engineering works (such as the construction of the roads and sewers serving the development) supplied to ABC Ltd will be supplied at a zero-rate of VAT. It is therefore probable that the only significant VAT incurred by the property company in constructing the residential development will be in respect of professional fees paid to surveyors, solicitors, architects and selling agents for services supplied.

On completion of construction, ABC Ltd will dispose of the houses. The purchase price payable on the freehold sale of a newly-built house, or the premium (or rent) payable in respect of a lease of the house granted for a term exceeding 21 years, does not attract VAT because these supplies are zero-rated. However, when zero-rated supplies are made, while no VAT is paid for the supply, tax is deemed to be charged at a nil rate on the output (so that they are still technically regarded as taxable supplies) and therefore related input tax incurred can be recovered. What this means is that ABC Ltd will account to HM Revenue & Customs (HMRC) for output tax on supplies made (which will be nil), less input tax on related supplies received (ie the VAT paid on professional fees). This clearly leads to a deficit, which means that a refund of VAT will be due from HMRC. This process is sometimes known as 'recovering the VAT'.

A subsequent sale of a house (either freehold or leasehold) will be made by a private individual and will not, therefore, be made in the course of a business. In the event that the sale is made in the course of a business (eg by a relocation company), the supply would be exempt.

11.1.2 Commercial developments

In a typical new commercial development, the same process can be followed, with different VAT consequences. The sale of a green field site to a developer is again an exempt supply, subject to the option to tax. However, the provision of construction services and civil engineering works to a commercial developer is a standard-rated supply, which means that considerable VAT will be incurred in addition to VAT on the standard-rated supply of professional services.

Once the building has been completed, the developer may either sell the freehold, or grant a lease of it to a tenant. The sale of a 'new' or partially-completed building is a standard-rated supply. Value added tax must be charged in respect of the purchase price. In this context, a 'new' building is one that was completed within the three years preceding the sale, and 'completion' of a building takes place on the earlier of either the day upon which the certificate of practical completion was issued by the architect or the day upon which the building was completely occupied. The grant of a lease of all or part of commercial premises (whether new or old) is an exempt supply, subject to the right of the landlord to opt to tax the rents, premium and other sums payable under the lease. In both cases, whether the freehold sale or the grant of a commercial lease, the developer is able to charge VAT either because it is a standard-rated supply, or because the exemption has been waived. This means that output tax will be received to facilitate recovery of related input tax incurred.

Take, by way of example, a commercial development where the construction costs paid by the developer amount to £2 million (with VAT on a standard-rated supply of £400,000), the cost of roads and sewers amounts to £500,000 (with £100,000 VAT) and professional fees total £100,000 (with £20,000 VAT). The total input tax paid by the developer adds up to £520,000. If the developer, being a taxable person, is able to sell the 'new' freehold building for £4 million, it will have to charge VAT amounting to £800,000. This output tax can be set against related input tax incurred, resulting in only the difference (£280,000) having to be accounted for to HMRC. The developer suffers from cash-flow difficulties in that it is likely to incur the input tax some time in advance of receiving the output tax, but it is not left out-of-pocket. The same result will be achieved if, instead of selling the freehold, the developer chooses to grant a lease of the building and elects to charge VAT on the sums payable under the lease. The making of the election facilitates immediate recovery of related input tax.

11.1.3 The option to charge VAT

The election to waive exemption or, as it is more commonly called, the option to tax was introduced on 1 August 1989 in order to lessen the impact of the VAT charges on commercial developers. The purpose of the option to tax is to enable the commercial owner to convert what would otherwise be exempt supplies in respect of a particular property into supplies chargeable to VAT at the standard rate, so that the developer will be able to recover the input tax it incurred when acquiring or developing the property.

The consequence of opting to tax is that all future grants in the property by the person who opts will be subject to VAT at the standard rate.

11.1.3.1 How is the election made?

As a preliminary to opting to tax, the owner must check that it is registered for VAT or the option will be meaningless. There is no prescribed form or procedure for opting to tax, neither is there any requirement to consult with or notify anyone who might be affected by the option. However, from a practical point of view, it is advisable that a landlord notifies its tenants, since it is the tenants who will bear the VAT. The one procedural requirement that must be followed when opting to tax is that written notice of the option must be given to HMRC within 30 days.

If an exempt supply (eg the grant of a lease) has been made by the person wanting to opt to tax in respect of the relevant property in the 10 years prior to the date on which the option is to take effect, consent of HMRC will be required before the option can be made, and consent will be granted only if HMRC is satisfied that the input tax which the person will be able to recover as a consequence of their opting to tax is fair and reasonable. It is therefore advisable for a landlord intending to opt to tax to do so before it grants a lease of its property. In all other cases, consent of HMRC is not required.

11.1.3.2 Who or what is affected?

The option to tax is personal, done on a property-by-property basis and, once made, it may be revoked only within six months of the option, where there has been a lapse of six years since any relevant interest in the property has been held, or after 20 years from the date of the option. The fact that the option is personal means that while a landlord who opts to tax would have to charge VAT on the rents payable by its tenants, its tenants would not, unless they too opted to tax, have to charge VAT to their sub-tenants, and the same applies to a buyer of the landlord's interest. As an exception to the general rule, an option to tax made by a company in respect of a property will bind other companies (in respect of that property) if they are in the same VAT group of companies at the time of the option, or joined the group later when the property affected was still owned by a group company.

The fact that the option to tax is made on a property-by-property basis means that a commercial owner can pick and choose which of its properties should be voluntarily standard-rated. Once made, the option to tax affects the whole of the property, or if that person owns an interest in only part of the property, it will affect the entirety of that part. Hence, an owner cannot choose to opt to tax in respect of the ground floor and not the upper two floors if it owns the entire building. What may appear to be separate buildings, but which are linked together internally or by covered walkways, are to be treated as one building. Therefore, if a shopping precinct is owned by one landlord (as is usually the case), an option to tax by that landlord will affect all of the shops in the precinct.

11.1.3.3 Should the option to tax be made?

The reason for opting to tax is to facilitate the recovery of related input tax incurred on the acquisition or development of the property. If no related input tax has been or is likely to be incurred, there is no reason why the option to tax should be made. If considerable input tax has been or will be incurred, consideration must be given to whether or not the option to tax should be made, but the person must have regard to the effect that the option will have on the persons to whom supplies are being made.

If a developer-landlord, having incurred VAT on acquisition or development costs, wants to opt to tax and charge VAT on the rents it will receive from its tenants, and those tenants make mainly standard-rated or zero-rated supplies in the course of their businesses (eg tenants of retail food stores, solicitors or surveyors offices), the tenants would not be adversely affected by a charge to VAT on rent, since there will be output tax (actual or deemed) to offset against the input tax. The tenants will be able to recover any VAT paid and will not end up out-of-pocket.

Tenants who make only exempt supplies in the course of their businesses (eg banks, building societies, insurance companies) will be hard hit by the option to tax. The VAT that these tenants have to pay on the rent will be irrecoverable, and will have to be borne as an overhead of the business. This could have the effect of frightening off a class of tenants whom the developer might have been hoping to attract to the development, or lead to their reducing the amount of rent that they would be prepared to pay.

11.1.3.4 Drafting points

Is the option to tax on its own sufficient to render VAT payable by the person who receives the supply? It is necessary to look at two principal relationships: seller and buyer; and landlord and tenant.

Seller and buyer

If a seller sells a 'new' commercial building (whether it is the first sale, or a subsequent sale of the still 'new' building) the seller is making a standard-rated supply, and so there will be mandatory VAT on the purchase price. The basic rule is that, unless the contrary appears, the purchase price stated in the contract is deemed to include VAT. It is therefore important that the seller includes a clause in the contract obliging the buyer to pay VAT in addition to the purchase price. Failure to do so will result in the seller having to account to HMRC for the VAT out of the purchase price received, which will mean that the seller will be left with considerably less than it anticipated, and its solicitor would no doubt be liable in negligence.

If the seller sells an old commercial building (ie one that is now more than three years old) then the supply being made is an exempt supply and the position is different. If the seller opts to tax *before* exchange of contracts then it converts the supply into a standard-rated supply and the above paragraph would then be applicable. The seller would have to make an express provision in the contract obliging the buyer to pay VAT in addition to the purchase price. If the option to tax is made *after* exchanging contracts then, under s 89 of the Value Added Tax Act 1994 (VATA 1994), the option to tax would operate as a change in the rate of tax from 0% to 20% (ie from an exempt to a standard-rated supply), and accordingly the seller could add VAT to the purchase price without the need for an express clause in the contract enabling it to do so. In this case, it is important that the buyer's solicitor ensures that the contract makes it clear that the purchase price is inclusive of VAT so that no hardship is felt by the buyer if the seller chooses to opt to tax after exchange. If the contract expressly excludes s 89, or the purchase price is expressly stated to be payable inclusive of VAT, the seller will be unable to add VAT to the purchase price.

Landlord and tenant

The grant of a commercial lease (of either an old or new building) is an exempt supply, unless the landlord has opted to tax. In respect of existing leases, s 89 of the VATA 1994 again operates, so that an option to tax by the landlord after the grant of the lease effects a change in the rate of VAT from 0% to 20%. The landlord does not need the benefit of an express clause in the lease, and can simply add VAT to the rent (and other sums payable under the lease) unless there is a clause in the lease (which would not usually be the case) expressly exonerating the tenant from liability to VAT on such payments, or excluding s 89.

If the option to tax is made before the grant of the lease, so that the supply is converted to a standard-rated supply from the outset, s 89 will not operate and the rent will be deemed to be payable inclusive of VAT. It is therefore essential that the landlord's solicitor ensures that the lease contains a covenant by the tenant to pay VAT on the rent (and the other sums payable under the lease). Whenever a lease is drafted, irrespective of whether advantage can be taken of s 89, there ought to be a covenant by the tenant to pay VAT in addition to the sums payable under the lease. This avoids problems for the landlord.

11.1.4 Other areas of concern

Value added tax is a far-reaching tax in the property world that can impact on other aspects of property transactions.

11.1.4.1 Reverse premiums and rent-free periods

A reverse premium is a payment made by the landlord to a prospective tenant as an inducement to the tenant to enter the lease. Money is passing from landlord to tenant, and is the consideration for a supply being made by the tenant. This payment will be subject to VAT, and the tenant should ensure that the terms of the contract allow this to be added to the payment. The landlord will not, however, be able to recover this VAT as input tax if, when granting the lease, it is making an exempt supply. So the cost to the landlord will be increased by 20%. The landlord could recover this VAT if it opted to tax in respect of the property, but this would also mean that it would have to charge VAT on the rent. This would then be a particular problem for exempt tenants, such as banks or insurance companies, as the VAT on the rent will not be recoverable, and they may wish to try to negotiate a lower rent to compensate for this.

Rent-free periods give rise to difficult VAT problems. It appears that if the rent-free period is being given because the tenant is carrying out work to the premises that will benefit the landlord, or simply because the landlord is trying to induce the tenant to enter into the lease (as an alternative to a reverse premium), then VAT at the standard rate will be payable on the amount of rent forgone. The tenant is making a supply to the landlord (ie is positively doing something) in consideration of a rent-free period. However, if the rent-free period is given simply because the state of the market means that it is part of the bargain negotiated between landlord and tenant (eg where it is given to allow the tenant some time in which to fit out the premises for its own benefit, or arrange sub-lettings), there will be no VAT on the rent-free period, since nothing is being done in return for it.

11.1.4.2 Surrenders

When a tenant surrenders its lease to the landlord, consideration may move in either direction, either because the tenant is desperate to rid itself of the liability to pay rent and perform the covenants, or because the landlord is anxious to obtain vacant possession. By virtue of the Value Added Tax (Land) Order 1995 (SI 1995/282), the supply made in either case is an exempt supply, subject to the option to tax by the person who receives the consideration.

11.1.4.3 Transfer of a going concern (TOGC)

Transferring a business can involve the sale of assets which would normally be taxable supplies (eg a building where there is an option to tax in place). However, provided certain conditions are met, where a taxable person transfers a business *as a going concern* to a taxable person, the transfer will not be treated as a supply of goods and services and no VAT will be chargeable. This is known as TOGC relief (VATA 1994, s 49), and the sale of an investment property which is let to one or more tenants can be treated as a TOGC for these purposes.

Briefly, the conditions are that the transferee must intend to use the assets to carry on the same kind of business as the transferor and that the transferee both exercises and notifies an option to tax (and does not revoke it) on or before the date of the supply.

There are detailed rules relating to a TOGC, but these are outside the scope of this book.

11.1.4.4 VAT on costs

Sometimes, a lease will oblige the tenant to pay the landlord's legal costs incurred on the grant of the lease. Often, a lease will oblige the tenant to pay the landlord's legal costs on an application for licence to assign, or alter or change use. The position as regards VAT on those costs is complicated by the approach of HMRC, which treats the payment of the landlord's legal costs, in either case, as part of the overall consideration for the grant of the lease. Hence, the VAT position depends upon whether the landlord has opted to tax.

If the landlord's solicitor charges their client £1,000 plus VAT for legal services provided on the grant of the lease, they will issue their client with a VAT invoice requiring payment of £1,000 plus VAT of £200. The landlord, having opted to tax in respect of this property, and making use of its VAT invoice, will be able to recover the input tax (£200) from the output tax which it will receive on the rents. If the lease contains a clause obliging the tenant to pay those legal costs, the landlord will look to the tenant for a reimbursement of the outstanding £1,000. However, since HMRC treats such a payment as part of the consideration for the grant of the lease, and since the landlord has opted to tax, the tenant must pay £1,000 plus VAT, the landlord must issue the tenant with a VAT invoice, and the landlord must account to HMRC for the VAT element received. The tenant may be able to recover the VAT which it has paid, depending on the nature of its business.

If the landlord has not opted to tax, the position is different. First, it will not be able to recover the VAT charged by its solicitor, since that VAT was incurred in relation to an exempt supply. Secondly, therefore, it will require the tenant to reimburse the full amount of costs and VAT (ie, £1,200), but because this reimbursement is treated as part of the consideration for the grant of the lease, and because the supply made by the landlord is an exempt supply, no VAT invoice can be issued to the tenant (as, in fact, there is no charge to VAT being made to the tenant), and the tenant will be unable to recover any part of the reimbursement.

The same principles are adopted where, during the term, the tenant exercises a right given to it under the lease and pays the landlord's legal costs (eg on an application for licence to assign pursuant to a qualified covenant (see **20.2.2**)).

11.2 STAMP DUTY LAND TAX ON LEASES

Stamp duty land tax (SDLT) will be assessed on any premium paid and also on the rent. It must be paid within 14 days of completion of the lease.

The amount of SDLT payable on the premium is assessed in the same way as on purchases of land. The normal reduced rates of duty are available.

In relation to the rental element of leases, SDLT is payable on the 'net present value' (NPV) of the total rent payable over the term of the lease. Where the NPV of the total rent does not exceed £150,000, no duty will be payable. SDLT of 1% will be paid on the next £4,850,000 of the rent and 2% on the balance. If the term of the lease is longer than five years, the SDLT lease transactions calculator will work out the amount of SDLT due by taking the highest rent payable in the first five years. SDLT will not be chargeable on the VAT element of consideration, provided the landlord has not opted to tax by the time the lease is granted. If VAT is payable on the rent then VAT must be included in the NPV calculation.

SDLT has now become an important factor in commercial leases as the amount of duty is directly related to the length of the term, ie the longer the lease, the more duty is potentially payable. Further, if the tenant remains in possession ('holds over') after the end of a fixed term under the provisions of Pt II of the Landlord and Tenant Act 1954 (see **Chapter 31**), a further charge to duty may arise. This will be payable by the current tenant.

REVIEW ACTIVITY

1. Which one of the following statements is correct?
   VAT is a tax levied on:
   (a) Land transactions.
   (b) The gain resulting from a disposal in an interest in land.
   (c) The supply of goods or services made in the course of a business.
   (d) Fixed plant and machinery within a commercial property.

2. Which of the following statements is correct?
   Provided the supplier is registered for VAT, input tax will be paid by a business where the supply made to it is:
   (a) Standard-rated.
   (b) Zero-rated.
   (c) Exempt.
   (d) Exempt but where the supplier has exercised the option to tax.

3. Which of the following statements is correct?
   Input tax may be recovered from HMRC provided that it was incurred by a business in making supplies that are:
   (a) Standard-rated.
   (b) Zero-rated.
   (c) Exempt.
   (d) Exempt but where the supplier has exercised the option to tax.

4. Set out below are the stages in a typical commercial property *development* transaction. For each stage, state whether the supply is standard-rated, zero-rated, exempt or exempt subject to the option to tax.
   (a) Sale to the developer of a green field site for development as a retail superstore.
   (b) Payment to the building contractor for constructing the superstore.
   (c) Grant of a lease of the superstore to a retail tenant.

(d) Sale of the freehold interest in the superstore one year after construction, subject to the lease.

5. In the circumstances set out in question 4, the developer of the retail superstore can recover the input tax paid on the construction costs.

True or false?

6. Set out below are the stages in a typical commercial property *leasing* transaction. For each stage, state whether the supply is standard-rated, zero-rated, exempt or exempt subject to the option to tax.

(a) Grant of a lease to an insurance company.
(b) Payment of legal fees to the solicitors for negotiating the terms of the lease.
(c) Payment to the building contractor for fitting out the property for the tenant's business.
(d) Assignment of the lease to another tenant.

7. In the circumstances set out in question 6, the insurance company tenant will be able to recover the input tax on the legal fees, fitting-out costs and (if the landlord opts to tax) the rents payable under the lease.

True or false?

Answers to this Review activity may be found in Appendix 1.

PART II
COMMERCIAL LEASES

CHAPTER 12

LANDLORD AND TENANT LAW

12.1	Introduction	183
12.2	Lease/licence distinction	183
12.3	Security of tenure	184
12.4	Liability of the parties on the covenants in the lease	184
	Review activity	185

12.1 INTRODUCTION

Given that 55% of the UK's commercial property is rented by occupiers (PIA *Property Data Report 2023*), having comprehensive knowledge and understanding of commercial landlord and tenant law (and the ability to apply it) is essential for any commercial property lawyer. Without it, that lawyer is unable to advise a landlord or tenant client properly on the rights and obligations arising under a commercial lease. This short chapter highlights three important principles that it is crucial to grasp.

12.2 LEASE/LICENCE DISTINCTION

Many of the statutory provisions discussed in Part II of this book apply only to a lease, not to a licence. A lease is an interest in land; a licence does not confer an interest but is merely a permission to enter another's land for a stipulated purpose(s) that would otherwise be a trespass. There have been many cases on the lease/licence distinction, but the leading decision remains *Street v Mountford* [1985] 2 All ER 289. That case concerned a residential tenancy, but the principles apply equally to commercial tenancies.

The House of Lords in *Street v Mountford* held that, as a general rule, an agreement to grant *exclusive possession* for a *term* at a *rent* creates a tenancy and the court will ignore any shams or pretences aimed at misleading the court. This general rule is subject to certain exceptions, for example a lack of intention to create legal relations or allowing into occupation pending the grant of a lease.

While payment of rent is not an essential component of a lease (*Ashburn Anstalt v Arnold* [1989] Ch 1; see also the Law of Property Act (LPA) 1925, s 205(1), which refers to a term of years absolute as being with or without a rent), exclusive possession is essential. There seems to have been a greater readiness by the courts to find that exclusive possession was *not* granted in commercial property cases than in residential cases.

One factor in determining exclusive possession is the degree of control exercised over the property by the owner. For example in *Esso Petroleum Co Ltd v Fumegrange Ltd* [1994] 46 EG 199, it was held that exclusive possession of a petrol station had not been granted because the landlord had retained extensive rights to control the operation and layout of the property, going beyond usual rights of access; in *National Car Parks Ltd v Trinity Development Co (Banbury) Ltd* [2001] EWCA Civ 1686, [2001] 28 EG 144, it was held that an agreement to occupy premises as a car park was a licence not a lease, because the licensor had reserved rights to park for itself and regulated the conduct of the licensee's business.

The court will look at the intentions of the parties with regard to all admissible evidence and the agreement as a whole (as confirmed in the residential almshouse case of *Watts v Stewart*

[2016] EWCA Civ 1247 where the use of the words 'rent' and 'tenancy' in the documentation failed to counter the evidence that exclusive possession had not been given and the parties had not intended to create a lease).

In construing any agreement, the terminology used by the parties is not decisive. A lease cannot be turned into a licence simply by labelling it as such (as recently emphasised in *London College of Business Ltd v Tareem Ltd & Another* [2018] EWHC 437 (Ch)).

Conversely, *Clear Channel UK Ltd v Manchester City Council* [2005] EWCA Civ 1304 (where a right to erect advertising hoardings and display advertisements did not amount to exclusive possession of the land itself because the agreement did not sufficiently identify particular sites) suggests that it will be hard to persuade a court that an agreement amounts to a lease where substantial parties of equal bargaining strength and with the benefit of legal advice refer to that arrangement unequivocally as a licence.

12.3 SECURITY OF TENURE

A key reason to appreciate the lease/licence distinction is that a lease can entitle a business tenant to security of tenure under Pt II of the Landlord and Tenant Act (LTA) 1954, whereas a licence cannot. Where a business tenant has security of tenure, it means that:

(a) the business tenancy will automatically continue at the expiry of the contractual term on the same terms, until it is terminated in one of the ways specified in the Act; and

(b) the business tenant can apply to court for a new tenancy and the landlord may oppose that application only on certain statutory grounds (some of which involve the payment of compensation by the landlord to the tenant if the tenant's application is unsuccessful). If a new tenancy is granted, it will also benefit from security of tenure.

Whilst a licence, as mentioned above, will not attract protection of the 1954 Act, the danger of a licence where exclusive possession is given is that, despite the thrust of the decisions in the commercial cases cited above, it could later be construed as a lease and protection inadvertently obtained. Note that the parties can contract out of the 1954 Act, but certain formalities must be observed, which are considered further in **Chapter 32**.

12.4 LIABILITY OF THE PARTIES ON THE COVENANTS IN THE LEASE

As the value of a commercial property investment depends partly on the financial strength of the tenants who occupy it and their correlative ability to pay the rent, a solicitor acting for a landlord must know the rules relating to liability and enforcement. Similarly, acting for a tenant client, a solicitor must know against whom a claim may be brought for, say, non-provision of services under the landlord covenants.

If the original parties remain the same throughout the term of the lease then they remain liable to each other for their performance (under the principles of privity of contract). If the identity of the parties change during the course of the term then, on assignment, the liability of the parties and enforceability of covenants are somewhat more complex. The key to unlocking the complexity is the date of the lease.

The detailed rules relating to the enforceability of covenants are considered in **Chapter 15**. The following is intended as an outline only of the main issues involved.

12.4.1 Leases granted before 1 January 1996

12.4.1.1 Original tenant

Under the principles of privity of contract, if the original tenant assigns the lease, it will remain liable on its express covenants in the lease throughout the remaining term for any breach of covenant committed by its successors, unless the landlord agrees to the contrary. Note that a commercial lease will usually include a rent review clause (see **Chapter 19**) allowing an increase of the rent. So an original tenant could find itself pursued several years after an assignment for its successor's non-payment of rent at a level over which it had no control. It was this type of perceived unfairness that led to the then Government creating the new set of rules under the Landlord and Tenant (Covenants) Act 1995 (LT(C)A 1995).

12.4.1.2 Original landlord

In the same way, through privity of contract, the original landlord will remain liable on its express covenants to the original tenant for the whole term, even if it assigns the reversion. Accordingly, an original landlord could find itself being pursued for a breach of covenant to provide services, even though it had long ceased to have any involvement in the property.

12.4.1.3 Tenant and landlord for the time being

The doctrine of privity of estate will apply, which means that a party is only liable for breaches of covenant (which touch and concern the land) committed during its ownership of the interest under the lease. Commonly, however, any assignee of the tenant's interest would have been required to enter into direct covenants with the landlord to perform the covenants in the lease, which would have the effect of making the assignee liable on the covenants in the lease for the whole term rather than just during its ownership.

12.4.2 Leases granted on or after 1 January 1996

12.4.2.1 Tenant

The effect of the LT(C)A 1995 is that once a tenant lawfully assigns the lease, it is automatically released from the tenant covenants in the lease. Liability for pre-assignment breaches continues. This applies to the original tenant and all successive tenants; but, as succour to disgruntled landlords who lost their privity of contract rights (see **12.4.1** above), all outgoing tenants can be required to give a guarantee of their immediate assignee's performance: see **21.2.4.3**.

12.4.2.2 Landlord

The effect of the LT(C)A 1995 is that, unlike the tenant, a landlord is not automatically released when it assigns its interest but may apply to the tenant for a release (see **15.2.2**).

REVIEW ACTIVITY

NUFC Ltd (as landlord) let premises to AFC Ltd (tenant) under a lease dated 7 June 1992. AFC Ltd assigned the lease to THS Ltd in 1993. THS Ltd assigned the lease to TFA Ltd in 1997. TFA Ltd failed to pay last month's rent and NUFC Ltd wishes to recover the arrears.

1. Explain from whom NUFC Ltd can claim the arrears.
2. Explain the same position if the lease referred to above was dated 7 June 2001.

Answers to this Review activity may be found in Appendix 1.

CHAPTER 13

AGREEMENTS FOR LEASE

13.1	Introduction	187
13.2	A typical agreement	188
	Review activity	192

13.1 INTRODUCTION

In most commercial letting transactions, the parties proceed straight to the completion of the lease.

Generally, an agreement for lease will be used only where one (or both) of the parties cannot enter the lease immediately but requires the other to be bound to do so in the future. Common examples are:

(a) the landlord has commenced, or is about to commence, constructing the premises. The landlord's aim is to ensure that, when construction has been completed, the tenant will be bound to complete the lease so that the rent will become payable to the landlord to provide income to offset its building costs; or

(b) the landlord, at the request of the tenant, is carrying out substantial works of repair or refurbishment to the premises prior to the grant of the lease. The landlord may not be able to secure the funds to carry out the works without showing to the lender that the tenant is obliged to take the lease, and/or may not want to incur the expense of executing works without a commitment from the tenant to enter into a lease once the works have been carried out; or

(c) the tenant is to carry out major works to the premises prior to the grant of the lease, in which case both parties will want the security of a binding commitment to enter into a lease upon completion of the works; or

(d) third party consents are required before the lease can be granted or works can be carried out (for example, consent of a lender or a superior landlord); or

(e) the landlord is negotiating a surrender from a current tenant and wants to tie in a new tenant to the grant of a lease.

In all such cases, in order to comply with s 2 of the LP(MP)A 1989, the agreement for lease (and any subsequent variation) must be in writing, contain or incorporate all of the terms expressly agreed, and be signed by or on behalf of the parties. Accordingly, the terms of the lease should be agreed in advance and a copy of the agreed form of lease annexed to the agreement for lease, both of which will be drafted by the landlord's solicitor. For some of the examples set out above, the agreement will also stipulate the nature of the works to be carried out to the premises, the time in which they are to be carried out and the manner in which they will be executed.

As there will be a delay between exchange and completion, the tenant's solicitor should consider protecting the agreement against the possibility of the landlord selling the reversion and defeating the tenant's interest. This is achieved in unregistered land by registering a Class C(iv) land charge and in registered land by registering a notice.

13.2 A TYPICAL AGREEMENT

In considering the terms of a typical agreement we shall assume that the landlord will be obliged to construct a building, the entirety of which will be let to the tenant under the agreed form of lease. (Many of the points raised will be equally applicable, or can be adapted, to a situation where it will be the tenant who is carrying out works to the premises.)

The basic thrust of the agreement will be that the landlord, as the owner of the site, will construct (or, by engaging building contractors, cause to be constructed) premises for occupation by the tenant. Once the premises reach a stage of 'practical completion' (see **13.2.1.4**) the tenant will be obliged to enter into the form of lease attached to the agreement. Rent will then become payable under the terms of the lease, giving the developer/landlord a return on its investment.

Some of the common terms that are often the subject of negotiation are set out below.

13.2.1 Terms relating to the works

13.2.1.1 Landlord's obligations

The agreement must include a clear obligation on the landlord to carry out the works in accordance with detailed plans and specifications attached to the agreement for lease or, more commonly, in accordance with the (usually) standard form building contracts which the landlord has with its building contractors. Commonly the landlord will be obliged to ensure that the works are carried out with reasonable care and skill using good quality materials, and in accordance with all relevant statutory approvals which the landlord will be obliged to obtain (eg, planning permission, Building Regulations). The landlord must ensure that its obligations in the agreement for lease are 'back to back' with those of the builders under the building contract.

If the approvals have not been obtained prior to exchange of the agreement for lease then the agreement will be made conditional on obtaining them – see **3.2** for more detail on conditional contracts.

Often, during the course of a building project, variations are required for economic, architectural or aesthetic reasons. The landlord will be keen to have flexibility under the agreement to make such changes. The tenant, however, must be careful not to give the landlord full rein, as that could result in the tenant having to take a lease of premises radically different from those originally planned. A possible compromise is for the agreement to provide for and define 'unacceptable variations' (eg, those that substantially affect the design, layout, nature, capacity or standard of construction, or prejudice the use of the premises to be demised) and 'permitted variations' (eg, those (not being an unacceptable variation) required by the local planning authority under the terms of any planning permission for the development of the site, and any required by the landlord or required due to the unavailability of materials (provided the alterations required by the landlord or the unavailability of materials have been notified to the tenant and its consent obtained)).

13.2.1.2 Tenant's requested modifications

The tenant may want to make changes to the specification during the landlord's works. Acting for the landlord, instruction should be taken on this, but the landlord's position is often that it should be able to refuse such requests on specified grounds or to have complete discretion in refusing to incorporate them. If the tenant's ability to vary is accepted then this may have an effect on the completion date and, therefore, the date on which rent will be payable, and so provision will be required to modify these accordingly. The landlord is likely to want the tenant to have to pay for the variations, plus interest for any delay, as the landlord will have to pay the contractors to do the work.

The landlord will always have to ensure that any tenant's requested modifications can be accommodated under the building contract with the builders.

13.2.1.3 Tenant's supervision

The landlord will want complete freedom to enable its builders to progress the development of the site without any interference from the tenant, and may be able to insist upon this in negotiations. However, the tenant may have sufficient bargaining strength to demand a degree of involvement, control and supervision, for example to allow the tenant's surveyor to inspect the works as they are being carried out, in order to make comments and representations to the landlord (or its architect), to point out errors in the works and any variations not permitted by the agreement.

13.2.1.4 Practical completion

The date upon which the building is completed will trigger the commencement of the lease (and therefore liability for rent). Accordingly, the landlord is interested in achieving completion as soon as possible in order to obtain rent, whereas the tenant may have an interest in delaying completion (if, unusually, it is not especially keen to gain possession). The tenant will not want the agreement to force it to complete the lease until the premises have been fully completed to its satisfaction and are ready for immediate occupation and use. Some tenants may also not want the lease forced on them at particular times (eg, for a retail tenant between October and January). However, the landlord will not want to give the tenant any scope for delaying the transaction on the basis of only one or two imperfections.

To resolve this tension, it is often agreed that a certificate of practical completion is to be issued by the landlord's architect (as defined by the agreement). This will certify that the building has reached the stage of 'practical completion' for the purposes of the agreement and will trigger completion of the lease.

'Practical completion' usually occurs when the building works have been sufficiently completed to permit use and occupation for the intended purpose, even though there may be some minor matters outstanding (snagging works).

Issues that will concern the tenant and upon which it will need to negotiate are whether it can:

(a) have any control over who should act as the certifying architect – the tenant may prefer an independent architect rather than the architect employed by landlord;

(b) insist upon the attendance of its own representative at the final inspection of the works to make representations to the landlord's architect, or to insist on a joint inspection for the purpose of issuing the certificate;

(c) object to and delay the issue of the certificate of practical completion if, in its opinion, the works have not yet been satisfactorily completed.

13.2.1.5 Completion date for the works

The landlord is likely to seek to resist being obliged to complete the building works within a fixed time-scale as delays are commonplace in the construction industry (eg, the Crossrail project's completion in 2022 was four years longer than anticipated). However, the tenant is likely to press for the inclusion of a clause requiring the landlord to use its best (or reasonable) endeavours to ensure that the building is completed by a certain date (a long-stop date) so that it is not kept from occupation indefinitely. The landlord may be prepared to accept such a clause, provided it is not liable for delays caused by matters outside the landlord's control (see **13.2.1.6** below).

13.2.1.6 Force majeure

It is usual for the agreement to include a 'force majeure' clause to ensure that the person executing the works will not be in breach of the requirement to complete the works by a certain date if the delay is caused by matters which are outside their control, such as adverse weather conditions, strikes, lock-outs or other industrial action, civil commotion, shortages of labour or materials, and others.

13.2.1.7 Penalties for delay

The agreement will provide for the lease to be completed within a specified number of days after the issue of the certificate of practical completion.

To discourage the tenant from delaying completion, and to compensate the landlord if it does, the agreement should stipulate a 'Rent Commencement Date' from which rent will become payable under the lease, regardless of whether the tenant has completed the lease. If the tenant delays completion beyond the Rent Commencement Date, it will still be bound to pay rent to the landlord on completion of the lease calculated from the earlier Rent Commencement Date.

The Rent Commencement Date is usually stated to be the day upon which the lease is due to be completed (ie, a certain number of days after the issue of the certificate of practical completion) or, if a rent-free period is being given to the tenant, a certain number of months after the day upon which completion is due.

If the landlord fails to complete the building by any long-stop date inserted in the agreement and cannot benefit from the *force majeure* clause, the tenant might be happy simply to await completion in the knowledge that rent will not become payable until then. However, the premises are usually required by the tenant for its immediate business needs. To incentivise the landlord to complete on time, the tenant should insist upon a liquidated damages clause providing for a daily rate of damages in the event of a delay. Care must be taken to ensure that the liquidated damages clause does not amount to an unenforceable penalty.

The landlord should ensure that the building contract entered into with its building contractors runs 'back-to-back' with the agreement for lease so that it may claim liquidated damages from its contractors. The tenant may want a further provision enabling it to terminate the agreement in the event of a protracted delay.

13.2.1.8 Damage before completion of the lease

If the premises are damaged before practical completion then the certificate will not be issued until the landlord has remedied the damage. If the premises are damaged after practical completion but before actual completion of the lease, the agreement ought to stipulate that the premises remain at the landlord's risk since the tenant is not yet entitled to possession. The landlord ought to maintain insurance cover until the premises are handed over, and the agreement may make this a requirement.

13.2.1.9 Defects in the works or materials after completion

If, after completion, the tenant discovers that there are defects in the design or construction of the premises, or in the materials used, then in so far as the defects amount to disrepair (see **20.4.1.3**) the tenant will be bound to remedy them under the usual repairing covenant in the lease. A pre-completion inspection by the tenant's surveyor may discover defects that can be addressed, but often the nature of a design or construction defect is such that it rarely manifests itself until sometime after the lease has been completed. The tenant should therefore ask for some protection in the agreement (or in the lease itself) against the prospect of such liability for 'latent' or 'inherent' defects arising. There are several ways in which this may be done (see **10.5**).

13.2.2 Terms relating to the lease

13.2.2.1 Agreed form lease

Before the agreement is entered into, the final form of the lease into which the tenant will be required to enter must have been agreed between landlord and tenant. Full negotiations must have taken place regarding the terms of the lease. The agreed form of draft (a fair copy incorporating all agreed amendments) should be appended to the agreement, with an obligation in the agreement for the tenant to take a lease in that form on the date of actual completion.

If the lease is to be excluded from the security of tenure provisions of the LTA 1954 (see **12.3** and **Chapter 32**) then the whole contracting-out procedure must be completed before the tenant takes the lease or becomes contractually bound to do so. If it is not done before exchange of the agreement for lease then the agreement to exclude is void and the tenant will have protection.

13.2.2.2 Premises

The agreement will normally describe the premises by reference to the parcels clause (see **Chapter 16**) in the draft lease, which in turn may refer to plans attached to the agreement showing the exact extent of the premises. Plans will be essential where a lease of part is intended.

In some cases the landlord and tenant will have agreed that the rent payable under the lease will be a specified figure, but in other cases they may have agreed to calculate it by multiplying the measured area of the premises (either gross or net internal area in accordance with the current RICS practice) by an agreed rental value figure per sq ft.

The plans annexed to the lease will anticipate premises of a certain size, but often the build will be larger or smaller which can be problematic for the tenant and the landlord. The tenant might be committed to premises which are too small for its business, and the landlord may not get the rent it anticipated (if any, as the tenant might seek to avoid the agreement altogether); if the premises are larger than anticipated, the tenant is committed to a higher rent which forms the basis of any future rent review.

The agreement should build in protections for both parties, such as target floor areas and margins of error. If the actual floor areas exceed these then the agreement might require the tenant still to take the lease but with rent and service charge capped and the rent review assumed to be on the basis of the target floor area with margin, and not the actual size. If the actual floor area is smaller, the tenant is likely to argue for a right to terminate the agreement. A well-advised tenant should ensure that the ability to terminate in the event of under-sizing is incorporated as an express right (*Mears Ltd v Costplan Services (South East) Ltd & Others* [2019] EWCA Civ 502).

If the landlord has to accept the right to terminate then it should ensure it has remedies against the contractor or professional responsible for the under-sizing. The agreement will need to provide for the parties to measure the premises before practical completion or tenant's access (whichever is earlier), for a process to agree the measurement and for dispute resolution if agreement is not possible.

13.2.2.3 Other contractual terms

Conditions of sale

The terms of the agreement for lease ought to set out extensively the rights and obligations of the landlord and tenant, in which case there may be no need to incorporate a set of conditions of sale. However, they are usually incorporated to the extent they are applicable to the grant of a lease and are consistent with the other terms of the agreement.

Deduction of title and disclosure of incumbrances

If title is deduced to the tenant, the agreement will usually prohibit requisitions after exchange.

Non-merger

The usual conveyancing doctrine of merger applies to an agreement to grant a lease, but it is common practice to include a clause excluding the doctrine, since many of the contractual obligations are intended to continue in operation post-completion.

In so far as they do continue in operation, they may be construed as landlord or tenant covenants of the tenancy and therefore as binding upon successors in title (see the definition of 'covenant' and 'collateral agreement' in s 28(1) of the LT(C)A 1995).

REVIEW ACTIVITY

1. The landlord and the tenant have entered into an agreement for lease under which the works to be carried out by the landlord include the erection of internal brick walls. The tenant has now been told by the landlord that it intends to use breeze block and plasterboard, instead of bricks, as they will be cheaper. This will reduce the floor area for the tenant's use, and the tenant is unhappy about this proposal. Acting for the tenant, what provisions should you have asked to have included in the agreement for lease to protect your client in this scenario?

2. The landlord carries out the works specified by the agreement for lease and is seeking to have practical completion certified by the architect. Acting for the tenant, what provisions should you have asked to have included in the agreement for lease to ensure your client has some control on the issue of the certificate?

Answers to this Review activity may be found in Appendix 1.

CHAPTER 14

Lease Contents

14.1	Introduction	193
14.2	The 2020 Code for Leasing Business Premises in England and Wales	193
14.3	Model Commercial Lease	195
14.4	Drafting leases	196
14.5	Prescribed clauses leases	197
14.6	The structure of the lease	197
	Review activity	202

14.1 INTRODUCTION

A commercial property practice will have its own commercial lease precedents, which it will adapt for use in each commercial letting on which the firm is instructed to act for the landlord.

All leading commercial practices ensure that their office precedent is an 'institutional' lease, ie in a form acceptable to an institution, such as a pension fund or insurance company, as an investment. Often referred to as an FRI lease (full repairing and insuring lease), it will guarantee the landlord a 'clear rent' (ie the landlord takes the entire income without cost to itself) by imposing all the costs of repairing and insuring on the tenant and will include (where relevant) upwards only rent reviews. By granting an 'institutional' lease, any landlord should ensure its marketability on a later sale of the freehold.

Traditionally, the 'institutional' lease often has strict controls on alienation, inflexible service charge provisions and onerous provisions relating to restoration of the premises at the end of the term.

The term of the 'institutional lease' has dramatically shortened from the 25 years common in the 1980s. This reflects, particularly in the retail sector, both the desire for tenants to have greater flexibility in property arrangements and recessionary times.

14.2 THE 2020 CODE FOR LEASING BUSINESS PREMISES IN ENGLAND AND WALES

Unsurprisingly, tenants consider much of the 'institutional' lease to be insufficiently flexible to meet their increasingly fluid business requirements. Whilst not wanting to jeopardise property investment, the Government has tried to address these tenant concerns over a number of years by the introduction of a voluntary Code of Practice. Initially launched in 1995 and then again in 2002 (after consultation with representatives of the property industry), the Code tried to introduce fairness and flexibility in leasehold transactions by advocating:

(a) wherever possible, giving tenants a choice of leasing terms, where this was practicable;
(b) the relaxation of alienation provisions;
(c) that restrictions, beyond the standard 'consent not to be unreasonably withheld', should be imposed only where necessary to protect the landlord's interests, and in particular that guarantees of the incoming tenant by the outgoing tenant under a new lease should

be required only where the incoming tenant was of lower financial standing than the outgoing tenant.

There was a lacklustre response from landlords to the Code and it was found to have little impact on lease negotiations (University of Reading Report, *Monitoring the 2002 Code of Practice for Commercial Leases*, released in early 2005). In fact it was very much the norm for landlords to insist on a guarantee by outgoing tenants in all circumstances, as they had lost the benefits of privity of contract (see **12.4** and **Chapter 15**). So the Government tried again to encourage flexibility in the market, and a new version of the Code was published in March 2007 (the 2007 Code).

At the launch of the 2007 Code, the then Housing and Planning Minister, Yvette Cooper, said:

> The new code will mean all businesses get a better deal on commercial property leases ... My challenge to the industry is to make sure that it is used in all lease negotiations. We shall be keeping a close watch on the market to see that it makes a real difference ... We believe the new code should have a chance to work, but ... we have legal options if it does not succeed. Industry needs to take the lead here. We will keep an eye on the effect of the code and watch with interest to ensure that there is proper, accountable self-regulation so that legislation is not necessary.

Tough talking, but in July 2009 another report conducted by the University of Reading found a disappointing lack of awareness and use of the Code. What may have a more effective impact is the RICS Code for Leasing Business Premises 2020 ('the 2020 Code') published in February 2020 and taking effect on 1 September 2020, to replace the 2007 Code.

In substance, much of the 2020 Code mirrors the 2007 Code but, unlike the 2007 Code, it is a professional standard (reissued as one in September 2023). The importance of this designation is that all RICS members must observe its mandatory requirements and will need a 'justifiable good reason' to depart from its other best practice statements. Failure to do so will support a negligence claim against the surveyor and may lead to disciplinary action. Landlords are not themselves bound by the 2020 Code (though any in-house RICS surveyors will be), nor are landlords' solicitors or non-RICS surveyors and agents, so they are free to agree and document non-compliant leases. Surveyors who are RICS-accredited may refuse to act if their landlord clients will not comply. Whether express landlord instructions will amount to a 'justifiable good reason' to depart from the 2020 Code and be a defence to any negligence/disciplinary action remains to be seen.

The 2020 Code is structured as follows:

(a) **Part 1: Introduction**

Part 1 states, amongst other things, that the objective of the 2020 Code is to improve the quality and fairness of initial negotiations on lease terms and to promote the issue of comprehensive heads of terms that should make the legal drafting process more efficient. The 2020 Code and the heads of terms template at its Appendix A should be used as a checklist for negotiations before the grant of a new lease and at the time of any lease renewal.

(b) **Part 2: Mandatory requirements**

Part 2 states that the provisions of paras 1.1–1.4 of the 2020 Code must be complied with and that landlords or their letting agents are responsible for ensuring that heads of terms complying with those provisions are in place before the initial draft lease is circulated.

The mandatory requirements set out the spirit in which landlords should approach agreeing the lease terms (approach negotiations in a constructive and collaborative manner) and are to:

(i) advise unrepresented parties about the existence of the code and recommend that they obtain professional advice;

(ii) record the agreement in written heads of terms on a 'subject to contract' basis that summarise, as a minimum, the position on the terms of the lease set out in the code;

(iii) ensure, on a lease renewal or extension, that the heads of terms set out the position on the terms of the lease required by the code unless those terms are stated to follow the tenant's existing lease, subject to reasonable modernisation;

(iv) aim to produce in negotiations letting terms which achieve a fair balance between the parties having regard to their respective commercial interests.

(c) **Part 3: Code for leasing business premises in England and Wales 2020**

The main part of the 2020 Code includes recommended practices in relation to key lease terms, such as the extent of the premises, length of term, renewal and break rights, rent deposits, guarantees, rent and rent reviews, service charge, alienation, repairing obligations, use, alterations, insurance, management and EPCs. There are no major changes to the key terms from the 2007 Code, but the 2020 Code is less prescriptive in tone and may be slightly more landlord friendly, for example:

(i) The 2020 Code does not now refer, as the 2007 Code did, to landlords offering alternative terms for rent review if requested by the tenant – see **19.2.4.1**.

(ii) The 2020 Code is friendlier to the idea of reinstatement at the end of the term with a change in emphasis. It allows landlords to require reinstatement at the end of the term where it is reasonable to do so, whereas the 2007 Code stated that landlords should not require reinstatement unless it was reasonable to do so. See **23.5**.

(iii) The 2020 Code allows reasonable provisions restricting assignment to be included, such as where there are arrears of rent that are not the subject of legitimate dispute. See **21.3**.

(iv) The 2020 Code also allows landlords to require an AGA on assignment where reasonable, whereas the 2007 Code stated that an AGA should not be required except in certain specified circumstances where an AGA may be requested. See **21.3**.

(v) The 2020 Code states that the tenant should be notified at the outset if its 1954 Act renewal rights are to be excluded, whereas the 2007 Code referred to the circumstances in which leases should be contracted out. See **32.1.6**.

There are also new recommended practices relating to EPCs.

(d) **Part 4: Appendix A – Template heads of terms and checklist – and Appendix B – Supplemental guide**

Non-mandatory template heads of terms reflecting the 2020 Code's sections are included, along with, for those landlords or agents who want to use their own format, a checklist of mandatory terms capturing the minimum information required by the 2020 Code.

There is a supplemental guide ('the 2020 Supplemental Guide') providing helpful information to landlords and tenants, which has no regulatory implications.

The 2020 Code is set out in **Appendix 3**. In addition, a lease prepared by the Practical Law Company (PLCProperty) is set out in **Appendix 4** ('the **Appendix 4** lease') which is intended to be compliant with the 2020 Code and the RICS Professional Standard: Service Charges in Commercial Property, 1st edn (see **27.8**).

14.3 MODEL COMMERCIAL LEASE

Commissioned by the British Property Federation, the Model Commercial Lease (MCL) suite of documents was released on 10 July 2014, comprising various template commercial leases and associated documents. The MCL is intended to avoid much of the perceived unnecessary negotiation on routine lettings by representing a fair starting (and in many cases end) point. It is largely compliant with the 2007 Code. The documents are updated regularly.

As adoption of the MCL has not been universal and as it limits discussion of commonly negotiated points because it is 'fair', this book will continue to use the **Appendix 4** lease to illustrate these points.

14.4 DRAFTING LEASES

It is highly unlikely that you will have to draft a lease from scratch when acting for a landlord client as most firms have their own lease precedents and, even if they do not, there is a wealth of precedent available online and in hard-copy form. The techniques to be adopted in drafting a lease or adapting a precedent are outlined in the drafting section of **Skills for Lawyers** and are not repeated here.

When drafting a lease or adapting a precedent, bear in mind the established principles of contractual interpretation. The Supreme Court in Marks and Spencer plc v BNP Paribas Securities Services Trust Company (Jersey) Ltd [2015] UKSC 72 analysed the approach to construction of a contract and the implication of terms into a contract in the context of a break clause in a lease. The express terms of the lease must be construed first before attempting to imply terms. Accordingly, it is even more important for practitioners to focus on clarity in drafting, especially given the return to a more literal approach to contract interpretation and a more restrictive approach to implying terms, seen in the case and others.

In implying terms, the Marks and Spencer case stressed (criticising an earlier case, Attorney General of Belize and others v Belize Telecom Ltd [2009] UKPC 10) that a term should only be implied when it was really necessary to do so (ie, the contract would not work commercially without the implied term), rather than when it was simply reasonable to do so.

The Marks and Spencer case followed the approach taken in Arnold v Britton and Others [2015] UKSC 36, a case on service charges that emphasised that placing reliance on commercial common sense should not diminish the importance of the language used. So if the meaning of the language used is clear, commercial common sense could not be a relevant consideration, even if this would result in commercially detrimental consequences. This approach has been confirmed in Globe Motors Inc and others v TRW Lucas Varity Electric Steering Ltd Globe Motors, Inc and another [2016] EWCA Civ 396 and Wood v Capita Insurance Services Ltd [2017] UKSC 24.

The courts do differentiate between clauses which are simply commercially unattractive to a party (as in the Arnold case) and those clauses which are simply nonsensical or absurd (Chartbrook Ltd v Persimmon Homes [2009] UKHL 38), and this was seen in Monsolar IQ Ltd v Woden Park Ltd [2021] EWCA Civ 961 when the court allowed a clear mistake in the drafting of a rent review clause linked to RPI to be corrected as a matter of construction.

However, the court has always been generally unwilling to imply terms into a document that has been entered into after extensive negotiations between legally represented parties, and this has been illustrated in the case of Cavendish Square Holding BV v Talal El Makdessi [2015] UKSC 767 (although see the approach of the Court of Appeal in Royal Bank of Scotland plc v Jennings and Others [1997] 19 EG 152, where the rent review machinery broke down but the Court chose to supplement it to make it work).

The court will not examine the offending clause in isolation but will construe the lease as a whole, to see if some assistance can be gained from other parts of the deed, where similar words and phrases may have been used in other contexts. Ordinary and technical words of the English language will be given the meanings usually attributed to them by the layperson, unless the lease clearly directs some other meaning (eg, by use of a definitions or interpretation clause – see **14.6** below).

If, owing to a common mistake between the parties, the executed lease does not embody the common intentions of the parties, the remedy of rectification may be available. This is, however, an equitable and discretionary remedy, and there is a heavy burden upon the claimant in a claim for rectification to show the existence of a common mistake. Rectification will not be awarded so as to prejudice a bona fide purchaser of the interest of either landlord or tenant who did not have notice of the right to rectify.

If there is a discrepancy between the executed original lease (signed by the landlord) and counterpart (signed by the tenant), the former prevails over the latter, unless the original is clearly ambiguous.

14.5 PRESCRIBED CLAUSES LEASES

To facilitate registration and electronic conveyancing, the Land Registration Act 2002 empowered Land Registry to prescribe a form of lease; but following consultation, Land Registry decided against mandatory use of a prescribed form. However, the Land Registration (Amendment) (No 2) Rules 2005 (SI 2005/1982) dictate that prescribed clauses must be contained in certain leases. These leases ('prescribed clauses leases') are those that are dated on or after 19 June 2006, which are granted out of registered land and are compulsorily registrable. There are certain exceptions outside the scope of this book. Where they apply, a conveyancer's certificate or other evidence must be supplied with the application for registration.

14.5.1 Required wording

The wording required in a prescribed clauses lease must appear at the beginning of the lease, or immediately after any front cover sheet and/or front contents page. A new Sch 1A inserted into the Land Registration Rules 2005 (SI 2005/1766) sets out the required wording and gives instructions as to how the prescribed clauses must be completed. Land Registry Practice Guide 64 gives detailed guidance on use of the clauses. An example is in the **Appendix 4** lease.

14.6 THE STRUCTURE OF THE LEASE

14.6.1 Commencement, date and parties

It is customary to start the drafting of a document by describing the document according to the nature of the transaction to be effected; for example, a lease will commence with the words 'This Lease'. The date of the lease will be left blank until the date of actual completion is manually inserted on completion. The draft lease should then set out the names and addresses of each party to the lease (eg, landlord, tenant and any guarantors). You can see the layout in the **Appendix 4** lease.

14.6.2 Definitions

Every well-drafted document should contain a definitions section. If a word is to bear a specific meaning in a document, that meaning ought to be clearly defined at the start of the document. If certain phrases or words are likely to recur in the document, those phrases or words ought to be given a defined meaning at the start of the document. The use of a definitions clause in a legal document avoids needless repetition of recurring words and phrases, permitting a more concise style of drafting. If a word or phrase is to be defined in the definitions clause, the first letter of the defined term should be given a capital (upper-case) letter and every use of that word or phrase thereafter should appear in the same form.

Defined terms commonly used in commercial leases (and in the **Appendix 4** lease) are set out below.

'Insured Risks'

It is in both parties' interests to have the insured risks clearly defined as it governs (amongst other things) those risks against which the premises should be insured and liability for damage caused by an insured risk (see **25.2.4**). The risks commonly include fire, riot, malicious damage, flooding, storm and other risks commonly covered by a standard buildings insurance policy. To maintain flexibility, the landlord should retain the right to insure against other risks which it thinks are necessary. The tenant should insist on such discretion being exercised reasonably.

'Interest' (in the Appendix 4 lease defined as 'Default Interest')

If the tenant delays paying rent or any other sums due to the landlord under the lease, the landlord will want to charge the tenant interest on the unpaid sums. The rate of interest may be set out in the definitions clause. It is usually agreed at 3–5% above the base lending rate of a nominated bank. The landlord usually stipulates that if the base rate of that bank should cease to exist, the interest rate under the lease will be a reasonably equivalent rate of interest.

'Premises' (in the Appendix 4 lease defined as 'Property')

As the definition of the premises is inextricably linked to many of the tenant covenants (eg repair, alterations, etc), the definition should accurately define the premises demised by the lease with a full verbal and legal description set out either in the definitions clause (as in the **Appendix 4** lease) or in the parcels clause (see **14.6.4** and **Chapter 16**) or in one of the schedules to the lease.

'Term' (in the Appendix 4 lease defined as 'Contractual Term')

It is possible for the term commencement date to be calculated by reference to a start date before, on or after (provided not more than 21 years from the date of execution) the date the lease is executed. Note that the term may continue after the expiry date as a result of the LTA 1954 (see **12.3**), which could extend the original tenant's liability if the term is defined as including any extension, holding over or continuation of the term.

'VAT'

Value added tax may be payable on the rent and other sums due under the lease. In defining 'value added tax', it should be made clear that 'VAT' also includes any tax replacing VAT or becoming payable in addition to it, in case the fundamental principles of the tax are changed.

'Annual Rent' and 'Rents'

Careful thought should be given as to what 'Rents' is to mean and, in the light of its definition, whether it is appropriate to use the term in every reference to rent in the lease. Usually a landlord will want to reserve not just the Annual Rent (ie the basic rent), but also service charge payments, insurance premiums and VAT as rent so that the same remedies for recovery of those sums will be available (eg, forfeiture without the need to serve a s 146 notice under the LPA 1925), in which case 'Rents' should be defined to include those items. This can be seen in the **Appendix 4** lease.

It should also be made clear that 'Annual Rent' means not only the original contractual rent but also any revised rent that becomes payable by virtue of the rent review clause, and any interim rent which becomes payable under s 24A of the LTA 1954 during a statutory continuation tenancy. In this manner, it is made clear that in a case where a tenant's liability continues after assignment, the liability relates to the payment of a rent which may be increased after the date the tenant assigns its interest in the premises (see **18.1**).

The term 'Rents' is not an appropriate term in every case under the lease. For instance, in the rent review clause, it is the Annual Rent that is to be reviewed from time to time during the term, not necessarily the 'Rents' as defined. Another example is that the landlord might be prepared to allow payment of the Annual Rent to be suspended for a period of time if there is damage to the premises by an insured risk but may not wish to have suspended the payment of other sums (eg, service charge) which have been reserved as 'Rents'. A tenant may resist this given that it may not be benefiting from any services during the period of damage (see **18.5**). The **Appendix 4** lease provides for service charge payments to be suspended.

On a lease of part (of which the **Appendix 4** lease is an example), further definitions are likely to be included, for example:

'Building'

As the landlord may be entering into covenants in the lease to repair the structure and exterior of the building, it must be defined. There are likely to be other references to the 'Building' with regard to the provision of services and the grant and reservation of easements.

'Common Parts'

The tenant will be granted rights to use the 'Common Parts' of the 'Building', and their extent should be expressed clearly.

'Services/Service Charge'

The landlord will usually provide services and there will be a number of definitions included to provide for that (see the **Appendix 4** lease), although the detail of the provision of services is more often found in a schedule to the lease.

14.6.3 The interpretation clause

Certain words or phrases do not require a fixed definition for the purposes of the lease; rather, their meaning needs to be expanded or clarified to assist the reader in the interpretation and construction of the lease. Common examples of matters of interpretation are the following:

Joint and several liability (clause 66 in the **Appendix 4** lease)

The lease should make it clear that if the landlord or tenant is more than one person, the obligations placed upon those persons by the lease will be enforceable against either or all of them.

One gender to mean all genders (clause 1.9 in the **Appendix 4** lease)

Section 61 of the LPA 1925 applies in respect of all deeds executed after the 1925 Act came into force, so that any reference in a deed to the masculine will include the feminine, and vice versa. However, s 61 does not deal with the neuter (ie, 'it'), and it is therefore common to state, for the avoidance of doubt, that a reference to one gender includes all others.

References to statutes (clauses 1.20 and 1.21 in the **Appendix 4** lease)

Leases usually provide that unless a particular clause expressly provides to the contrary, a reference in the lease to a statute or to a statutory instrument is to be taken as a reference to the Act or instrument as amended, re-enacted or modified from time to time, and not restricted to the legislation as it was in force at the date of the lease. Care should be taken to ensure that this is appropriate in every case.

Expanding the meaning of words or phrases (clauses 1.11 and 1.12 in the **Appendix 4** lease)

If a tenant covenant states that the tenant is prohibited from doing a certain act, the tenant will not be in breach of covenant if that act is done by a third party. It is therefore usual to state that if the tenant is required by the lease not to do a certain act, it may not permit or suffer the act to be done by someone else either. If a tenant covenant prohibits the carrying out of a certain act without the landlord's prior consent (not to be unreasonably withheld), it is usual to stipulate that the landlord's consent may not also be unreasonably delayed.

Rather than having to repeat the wording required to deal with these matters throughout the lease, both of these points may be dealt with concisely by using an appropriate form of wording in the interpretation clause at the beginning of the lease.

14.6.4 The letting

The letting is the operative part of the lease that will create the tenant's interest, define the size of that interest, reserve rent, impose covenants, and deal with the grant and reservation of rights and easements. The clauses are usually set out in the following logical sequence.

The operative words (clause 2.1 in the **Appendix 4** lease)

Sufficient words of grant should be used to show the intention of the landlord to grant an interest in favour of the tenant. The landlord usually either 'demises' or 'lets' the premises to the tenant.

The parcels clause (clause 2.1 and Schs 1 and 2 in the **Appendix 4** lease)

A full description of the premises, including the rights to be granted to the tenant, should be contained in the parcels clause. Often, the description is removed to one of the schedules (see below) so that the parcels clause simply refers to 'the Premises' (which will be a defined term).

Exceptions and reservations (clause 2.1 and Sch 3 in the **Appendix 4** lease)

Usually, the rights to be reserved for the benefit of the landlord are referred to only briefly in this part of the lease; they are set out extensively in one of the schedules.

The habendum (clause 2.1(a) in the **Appendix 4** lease)

The habendum deals with the length of term to be vested in the tenant and its commencement date.

The reddendum (clauses 2.3, 4 and 5 in the **Appendix 4** lease)

The reddendum deals with the reservation of rent (which may be varied from time to time by a rent review clause), the dates for payment and the manner of payment (ie, whether in advance or in arrear).

The covenants

Where the covenants on the part of landlord, tenant and guarantor are set out in separate schedules, the parties expressly enter into them in the operative part of the lease. Otherwise the covenants are set out in the main body of the lease under separate clauses (see the **Appendix 4** lease).

14.6.5 The provisos

Often grouped together under the heading of 'provisos' is a wide variety of clauses that cannot easily be dealt with elsewhere in the lease, as they are in the nature neither of covenants nor easements, and do not impose obligations on any party to the lease. They are clauses that have no common thread, except that most of them are inserted into the lease for the landlord's benefit alone.

The **Appendix 4** lease has not grouped these provisos together, but many other commercial leases do. The provisos usually include the following clauses:

(a) The proviso for re-entry (ie, the forfeiture clause) (see clause 52 in the **Appendix 4** lease). This is dealt with in greater detail in **Chapter 26**.

(b) An option to determine the lease where the premises are damaged by an insured risk so that they are no longer fit for use or occupation, and where the landlord either cannot or, after a period of time, has not reinstated the premises (see **25.7**). See Sch 6 in the **Appendix 4** lease.

(c) A rent suspension clause (see Sch 6 in the **Appendix 4** lease), which provides that the rent (and, possibly, other sums payable by the tenant under the lease) should cease to be payable if the premises are rendered unusable by damage caused by an insured risk (see **25.6**).

(d) A provision that states that the landlord does not, by reason of anything contained in the lease, imply or represent that the tenant's proposed use of the premises is a permitted use under planning legislation (see clause 67.3 in the **Appendix 4** lease).

(e) A provision whereby the tenant acknowledges that it has not entered into the lease in reliance upon any statement made by or on behalf of the landlord (see clause 6.7.2 in the **Appendix 4** lease for a mutual provision to this effect). This provision seeks to prevent the tenant from pursuing a remedy against the landlord in respect of a misrepresentation, but it will be subject to s 3 of the Misrepresentation Act 1967 (as amended by s 8 of the Unfair Contract Terms Act 1977) and will have to satisfy the test of reasonableness set out in the 1977 Act.

(f) A provision regulating the method of service of notices under the lease (see clause 61 in the **Appendix 4** lease). On occasions during the lease, one party will want or need to serve a notice on the other under one of the provisions in the lease (eg, to implement a rent review clause, or to give notice of an assignment of the lease or as a preliminary step to the exercise of a right of re-entry). Whether or not a notice has been validly served will be an important issue and should, therefore, be a matter which is capable of conclusive determination. Accordingly, the lease should specify the method of service of notices, either by incorporating the provisions of s 196 of the LPA 1925 (as amended by the Recorded Delivery Service Act 1962) into the lease, or by expressly setting out the methods of service to be permitted by the lease. Section 196(3) provides that service may be effected by leaving the document at the premises, or at the person's last-known abode or place of business. Section 196(4) deems service to have been effected if the notice is sent by recorded delivery post, provided that it is not returned through the Post Office as undelivered. The importance of tenants having proper systems in place to deal with notices was emphasised in *Warborough Investments Ltd v Central Midlands Estates Ltd* [2006] PLSCS 139. In this case, a 'trigger' notice initiating a rent review (see **19.7.1**) was held validly served by the landlord when left at the customer service desk of a supermarket.

(g) Excluding compensation under the LTA 1954 (see clause 55 in the **Appendix 4** lease). The parties may agree that the tenant should not be entitled to compensation under s 37 of the LTA 1954 at the end of its lease (see **32.6.4**). If so, the lease must refer to this.

(h) Excluding the tenant's security of tenure (see clause 54 in the **Appendix 4** lease). The parties may agree that the security of tenure provisions contained in the LTA 1954, Pt II should not apply to the lease (see **32.1.6**). If that is the case, the lease should include a contracting-out provision in the provisos.

(i) Options to break (see clause 58 in the **Appendix 4** lease). If either party is to enjoy the right to terminate the lease early by the exercise of an option to break (see **17.2**), the option is usually contained in this part of the lease.

14.6.6 Schedules

Some commercial leases are drafted to have a short main body, with the detail of the lease being placed in separate schedules. This can make the lease easier to read, and from the client's point of view it may make it easier to refer to the various provisions of the lease. If this is the case then, commonly, separate schedules will deal with (amongst other matters) the premises demised, any rights granted to the tenant, any exceptions reserving rights in favour of the landlord, rent review, service charge and tenant/landlord/guarantor covenants.

(Examples of schedules dealing with service charges and guarantees may be seen in the **Appendix 4** lease.)

14.6.7 Execution

Following the main body of the lease and any schedules will be the execution clauses. The lease and its counterpart are deeds, and therefore the usual rules relating to the execution of deeds are applicable. A testimonium clause is not an essential part of a lease, but if one is included, it ought to appear immediately before the first schedule (see the wording before Schedule 1 in the **Appendix 4** lease). Attestation clauses are essential.

REVIEW ACTIVITY

Assuming all wording in parenthesis has been included, consider the **Appendix 4** lease:

1. Will the landlord be able to recover the service charge from the tenant if an explosion damages the property?

2. The landlord faxes the tenant a s 146 notice for non-payment of rent in anticipation of forfeiting the lease. Will this be a valid notice?

3. A contractor of the tenant accidentally cuts an electricity cable during some repair works to the property. The tenant argues that it is not responsible for repairing the damage as it did not cause it. What argument would you advance for the landlord?

Answers to this Review activity may be found in Appendix 1.

CHAPTER 15

THE PARTIES TO THE LEASE AND THEIR LIABILITIES

15.1	Introduction	203
15.2	The landlord	203
15.3	The tenant	205
15.4	The guarantor	209
	Review activity	213

15.1 INTRODUCTION

Following the date and commencement, the lease will set out details of the parties to the lease, namely the landlord, the tenant and any guarantor (who is also often referred to as a surety).

In respect of a corporate party, the lease should give the company's full name and either its registered office or its main administrative office, and the company's registration number. In respect of an individual party, the full name and postal address of the individual will suffice.

The purpose of this chapter is to examine the extent and duration of liability of the parties to a lease. The Landlord and Tenant (Covenants) Act 1995 (LT(C)A 1995) (which came into force on 1 January 1996) brought about considerable changes in this area. In particular, it abolished the concept of privity of contract in relation to leases which are defined as new leases for the purposes of the Act (see **15.2.2**). Accordingly, this chapter examines the law and practice both in relation to 'old leases' already in existence at the date when the Act came into force (the old regime) and in relation to those which are 'new leases' (the new regime).

15.2 THE LANDLORD

The landlord's primary purpose as a party to the lease is to grant to the tenant the leasehold interest that both parties intend, upon the terms agreed between them. These terms may require the landlord to enter into covenants with the tenant in order to ensure that the tenant peaceably enjoys occupation of the premises, and a certain quality of accommodation (see, more specifically, **Chapter 24**).

15.2.1 The old regime

15.2.1.1 The original landlord

By virtue of the principle of privity of contract, the original landlord, as an original contracting party, remains liable in respect of any covenants entered into in the lease, even after it has sold the reversion. The landlord protects itself against the possibility of being sued for a breach of covenant committed by its successor by obtaining from that successor an express indemnity covenant in the transfer of the reversion. Such a covenant is not implied at law.

If the landlord has granted a lease of an entire building, it is unlikely that it entered into many covenants with the tenant. If the landlord has granted a lease of part of a building, or of premises forming part of a larger commercial site, the landlord may have entered into covenants to provide services to the tenants. If this is the case, the landlord may have limited expressly the duration of its liability under the covenants to the time the reversion is vested in the landlord, rather than relied upon obtaining an indemnity covenant.

15.2.1.2 A successor to the reversion

The landlord's successor in title is bound during its period of ownership by all covenants imposed upon the landlord which have reference to the subject matter of the lease (see s 142(1) of the LPA 1925). At the same time, it takes the benefit of the tenant's covenants which have reference to the subject matter of the lease under s 141(1) of the LPA 1925. It will also take the benefit of any surety covenants contained in the lease, provided the lease makes it clear that a reference in the lease to the landlord includes its successors in title (P&A Swift Investments v Combined English Stores Group plc [1983] 3 WLR 313).

15.2.2 The new regime

15.2.2.1 The original landlord

When a landlord sells its reversionary interest in a new lease, there is no automatic release from its obligations. However, ss 6 and 8 of the Act provide a procedure whereby the assigning landlord can apply to the tenant to be released from its obligations under the lease. The outgoing landlord may serve a notice (in a prescribed form) on the tenant (either before or within four weeks after the assignment) requesting such release. If, within four weeks of service, the tenant objects by serving a written notice on the landlord, the landlord may apply to the county court for a declaration that it is reasonable for the covenant to be released. If the tenant does not object within that time limit, the release becomes automatic. Any release from a covenant under these provisions is regarded as occurring at the time when the assignment in question takes place. However, in the case of BHP Great Britain Petroleum Ltd v Chesterfield Properties Ltd [2001] EWCA Civ 1797, [2002] 2 WLR 672, the Court of Appeal held that the statutory release mechanism did not operate to release the landlord from those covenants which were expressed to be personal. In respect of such covenants, the original landlord would continue to be liable even after the assignment of the reversion had taken place.

Once a landlord is released under these provisions, it ceases to be entitled to the benefit of the tenant covenants in the lease as from the date of the assignment of the reversion. It would appear, however, that if the landlord does not apply for a release it will retain the benefit of the tenant covenants, even though it has sold on the reversion (see Wembley National Stadium Limited v Wembley (London) Limited [2007] EWHC 756 (Ch)).

There is an additional way for the original landlord to limit its liability following the House of Lords decision in Avonridge Property Co Ltd v Mashru [2005] UKHL 70. The House of Lords held that a provision expressly limiting the landlord's liability under the covenants to the time that the reversion was vested in it was valid. Such provisions appeal to landlords as they avoid the need to seek a release under the LT(C)A 1995. Tenants, however, should be very cautious in agreeing to such provisions when the landlord's covenants are of substantial value, eg to perform the covenants in the head-lease. If the reversion is transferred to a person unable to comply with the landlord's covenants, the tenant could be left without an effective remedy for breach of covenant.

15.2.2.2 A successor to the reversion

The landlord's successor becomes bound, as from the date of the assignment, by all of the landlord covenants in the lease (or any document collateral to it, such as an agreement for lease), except to the extent that immediately before the assignment they did not bind the assignor (eg, a covenant waived or released by the tenant). Personal covenants given by the landlord will not bind the landlord's successor (BHP Great Britain Petroleum Ltd v Chesterfield

Properties Ltd [2001] EWCA Civ 1797, [2002] 2 WLR 672). In consequence, agreements for lease will often state that building obligations imposed on a developer landlord are personal to that landlord. This prevents a successor landlord assuming liability for inherent defects in the building that have arisen during the design or construction process.

In addition, the new landlord becomes entitled to the benefit of the tenant covenants in the lease, giving the new landlord the right to enforce covenants against the tenant, even though it was not an original party to the lease.

Sections 141 and 142 of the LPA 1925 do not apply in relation to new leases, so there is no need to enquire whether the relevant landlord or tenant covenant is one which 'has reference to the subject matter of the lease'.

Surety covenants are not tenant covenants for the purposes of the Act. However, their benefit will still pass to an assignee of the reversion in accordance with *P&A Swift Investments*. This is on the basis that the assignee has acquired the legal estate, and the surety covenants touch and concern that estate. In the same manner, the benefit of a former tenant's authorised guarantee agreement (see **21.2.4.3**) will pass to the assignee.

A successor who ultimately sells on its reversion can apply to be released from its obligations in the same way as the original landlord (see **15.2.2.1**). If at that time a former landlord is still liable on the lease covenants (because it did not obtain a release from the tenant when it assigned the reversion), it can make another application to the tenant to be released. It is probably the case that a provision of the kind used in *Avonridge* (see **15.2.2.1**) would also limit the liability of a successor landlord to the period of its ownership.

15.3 THE TENANT

The person to whom the lease is granted is known as the original tenant. The person to whom the tenant later assigns its lease is known as the assignee. The original tenant will be required to enter into many covenants in the lease regulating what can be done in, on or at the premises.

15.3.1 The old regime

15.3.1.1 The original tenant – privity of contract

Prior to the LT(C)A 1995, basic principles of privity of contract dictated that the original tenant, as an original contracting party, remained liable in respect of all of the covenants in the lease for the entire duration of the term, even after it assigned the lease. If, for example, the tenant was granted a 25-year term which it assigned at the end of the fifth year to an assignee who then failed to pay rent and allowed the premises to fall into disrepair, the landlord could choose to sue the original tenant for non-payment of rent and breach of the repairing covenant. It would not matter that since the assignment the rent had been increased under the rent review clause (unless the increase was referable to a variation of the lease terms agreed between the landlord and assignee – see s 18 of the LT(C)A 1995 and the case of *Friends Provident Life Office v British Railways Board* [1995] 1 All ER 336).

The effect of privity of contract becomes increasingly significant in recessionary times. If an assignee becomes insolvent, instead of pursuing a worthless claim against the assignee, the landlord will look to the original tenant for payment of rent.

Some protection is offered by s 17 of the LT(C)A 1995. This provides that if a landlord wishes to pursue a former tenant (and/or its guarantor) for a 'fixed charge' due under the lease (such as rent or service charge), the landlord must serve notice on the former tenant (and/or its guarantor). The notice must require payment of the outstanding sum and be served within six months of the sum falling due. The former tenant or its guarantor cannot be required to pay the outstanding sum if a s 17 notice is not served. Should a former tenant or its guarantor make full payment to the landlord of a sum demanded under a s 17 notice, it may call for an 'overriding lease' of the premises. This will make it the immediate landlord of the defaulting tenant. It can then seek to forfeit the defaulting tenant's lease and re-let.

15.3.1.2 For how long is the original tenant liable?

The original tenant's liability lasts for the entire duration of the contractual term. Once it has assigned its interest in the lease, the original tenant's liability will not extend into any continuation of that term that may arise under s 24 of the LTA 1954, unless there is an express provision in the lease to the contrary (City of London Corporation v Fell [1993] 49 EG 113). Often, however, the landlord's solicitor will have defined 'the Term' in the lease to include 'the period of any holding over or any extension or continuance whether by agreement or operation of law'. The effect of this will be to extend the original tenant's liability into the continuation term. The liability relates only to the contractual rent under the lease, and not to any interim rent fixed by the court under s 24A of the LTA 1954 unless the lease states otherwise (Herbert Duncan Ltd v Cluttons [1992] 1 EGLR 101).

15.3.1.3 The original tenant's need for an indemnity

As a result of the continuing nature of the original tenant's liability under the old regime, it is essential that, on an assignment of an old lease, the original tenant obtains an indemnity from the assignee against all future breaches of covenant (whether committed by the assignee or a successor in title). An express indemnity may be taken, but this is not strictly necessary since s 77 of the LPA 1925 automatically implies into every assignment for value a covenant to indemnify the assignor against all future breaches of covenant. If the lease is registered at Land Registry, Sch 12 to the Land Registration Act 2002 (LRA 2002) implies a similar covenant for indemnity into a transfer of the lease, whether or not value is given.

From a practical point of view, it should be noted that an indemnity from an assignee (whether express or implied) is worthless if the assignee is insolvent, and this may be the very reason why the landlord is pursuing the original tenant in the first place.

Where there has been a succession of assignments, and the original tenant finds that it is unable to obtain a full indemnity against its immediate assignee, the assignee in possession may be liable at common law to indemnify the original tenant who has been sued for breach of covenant (see Moule v Garrett and Others (1872) LR 7 Exch 101), but again the indemnity may be worthless owing to the insolvency of the defaulting assignee.

15.3.1.4 The assignee – privity of estate

By virtue of the doctrine of privity of estate, an assignee under the old regime is liable in respect of all of the covenants in the lease which 'touch and concern' the demised premises, for as long as the lease remains vested in that assignee.

An assignee cannot be sued for a breach of covenant committed prior to the lease being vested in it, save to the extent that the breach in question is a continuing breach (eg, breach of a covenant to repair) which effectively becomes the assignee's breach from the date of the assignment. If, at the time of the assignment there are arrears of rent, the landlord's claim to recover the arrears would be against the assignor, not the assignee. However, from a practical point of view, the landlord is unlikely to give its consent to an assignment (assuming the lease requires its consent) unless the arrears are cleared. Further, the assignee is unlikely to take the assignment while rent is in arrear because of the risk of forfeiture of the lease on account of the outstanding breach.

Under the doctrine of privity of estate, an assignee is not liable for breaches of covenant committed after it has parted with its interest in the premises (although it may still be sued in respect of breaches committed while it was the tenant). However, if it has given a direct covenant to the landlord to observe the tenant covenants throughout the term, it can be pursued under normal contractual principles for breaches by subsequent assignees (see **15.3.1.6**).

15.3.1.5 Covenants which touch and concern

Under the old regime, an assignee is liable only in respect of those covenants which touch and concern the demised premises. These are covenants which are not in the nature of personal covenants but have direct reference to the premises in question by laying down something which is to be done or not to be done at the premises, and which affect the landlord in its normal capacity as landlord or the tenant in its normal capacity as tenant. If the purpose of the covenant is to achieve something which is collateral to the relationship of landlord and tenant then the covenant does not touch and concern.

Nearly all of the covenants in a typical commercial lease will touch and concern the demised premises. In any event, as most landlords will require a direct covenant from an incoming assignee to observe the tenant covenants in the lease, the assignee will be liable under the direct covenant regardless of whether the covenants 'touch and concern' (see **15.3.1.6**).

15.3.1.6 Direct covenants

Landlords have never liked the limited duration of an assignee's liability under the doctrine of privity of estate. In practice, therefore, it is common for the landlord to try to extend the liability of an assignee under the old regime by requiring it, as a condition of the landlord's licence to assign, to enter into a direct covenant to observe the covenants in the lease for the entire duration of the term, thereby creating privity of contract between landlord and assignee. This covenant is usually contained in the formal licence to assign (see **27.2**). The landlord will always then have a choice between original tenant and present assignee as to whom to sue for a breach of covenant committed by the latter. Where intermediate assignees have entered into direct covenants in this manner, the landlord's options are increased.

If an assignee has given a direct covenant to the landlord, the extent of its continuing liability is governed by the *City of London v Fell* case, and the definition of 'the Term' in the lease in the same way as applies to the original tenant (see **15.3.1.2**).

15.3.1.7 The assignee's need for an indemnity

The assignee from the original tenant is likely to have given an indemnity covenant to the original tenant, either expressly or impliedly (see **15.3.1.3**). It therefore needs to obtain one from its assignee. An express indemnity may be taken, but s 77 of the LPA 1925 and Sch 12 to the LRA 2002 will operate in the same way as before.

15.3.2 The new regime

As stated above, the main purpose of the LT(C)A 1995 was to abolish privity of contract in leases, and it is therefore in the area of tenant liability that the Act has had the most significant impact.

15.3.2.1 The original tenant – privity of contract release

The basic rule is that a tenant under a lease which is a new lease for the purposes of the LT(C)A 1995 is only liable for breaches of covenant committed while the lease is vested in it. Thus, on assignment of the lease, the assignor is automatically released from all the tenant covenants of the tenancy (and it ceases to be entitled to the benefit of the landlord covenants). This means that while the outgoing tenant can be sued for breaches of covenant committed at a time when the lease was vested in that tenant, it cannot be sued for any subsequent breaches.

15.3.2.2 The assignee – liability on covenants

The basic rule applies equally to assignees. As from the date of assignment, an assignee becomes bound by the tenant covenants in the lease except to the extent that immediately before the assignment they did not bind the assignor (eg, they were expressed to be personal to the original tenant); but when it assigns the lease, it is automatically released from all of the tenant covenants. In addition, under the new regime an assignee will be liable on all the tenant covenants in the lease whether or not they 'touch and concern' the land.

In the same way that the assignee becomes bound by the tenant covenants, so too does the assignee become entitled, as from the date of the assignment, to the benefit of the landlord covenants in the lease.

15.3.2.3 Excluded assignments

Assignments in breach of covenant (eg, where the tenant has not complied with a requirement in the lease to obtain its landlord's consent before assigning) or by operation of law (eg, on the death or bankruptcy of a tenant) are excluded assignments for the purposes of the LT(C)A 1995. On an excluded assignment, the assignor will not be released from the tenant covenants of the lease, and will remain liable to the landlord, jointly and severally with the assignee, until the next assignment, which is not an excluded assignment, takes place.

15.3.2.4 Authorised guarantee agreement

To counterbalance the loss to the landlord of the benefits of the old privity regime, the LT(C)A 1995 allows the landlord to require an outgoing tenant, who will be released from liability under the Act, to enter into a form of guarantee (known as an 'authorised guarantee agreement' or 'AGA') whereby the outgoing tenant guarantees the performance of the tenant covenants by the incoming tenant (see **21.2.4.3**).

15.3.2.5 Indemnity covenants?

As an assigning tenant is not liable for the breaches of covenant committed by its successor, the LT(C)A 1995 has repealed s 77 of the LPA 1925 and Sch 12 to the LRA 2002 in relation to leases granted under the new regime. However, it should be noted that an outgoing tenant may remain liable to the landlord for an assignee's breaches of covenant under the terms of an AGA, and in such circumstances an express indemnity from the assignee should be obtained.

15.3.3 Variations

Under both the old regime and the new regime, a former tenant can retain liability for a breach of covenant committed by a successor. What happens if the successor varies the terms of the lease, so that the lease terms are different (and more onerous) to those the former tenant was bound by? Should the former tenant be liable for a breach of those varied lease provisions?

Section 18 of the LT(C)A 1995 provides that regardless of whether the former tenant's liability arises under the old regime or via an AGA under the new regime, the former tenant shall not be liable to pay amounts referable to any 'relevant variation of the tenant covenants ... effected after the tenancy'. A 'relevant variation' is a variation to the lease made after 1 January 1996 which the landlord was under no obligation to agree to. This protection is also afforded to guarantors of former tenants. So, for example, if the original lease restricted the use of the premises to a clothes shop, but, after assignment, the landlord and new tenant varied the lease to allow any retail use, the former tenant (and their guarantor) would not be liable for any increase in rent on review referable to this wider use.

Whilst s 18 applies to variations made post 1 January 1996, the case of *Friends Provident Life Office v British Railways Board* [1995] 1 All ER 336 means that the position is much the same for variations made prior to that date. The court in that case held that a former tenant could not be liable for variations made between an assignee and the landlord if the variations were not envisaged by the original lease. As a result, the former tenant in that case was not liable for an increased rent effected by a deed of variation between the assignee and the landlord. The original tenant did, however, remain liable for the original rental amount agreed.

Practitioners also need to be aware that a variation to the contractual term of the lease or the extent of the premises demised, will amount to the surrender of the original lease and the re-grant of a new lease (see again *Friends Provident Life Office v British Railways Board*). This may lead the landlord to lose its ability to pursue former tenants, who will be released from liability on the re-grant of the new lease.

15.4 THE GUARANTOR

Much attention in practice is given to the financial status of the proposed tenant, and a consideration of what is called 'the strength of the tenant's covenant'. A tenant is said to give 'a good covenant' if it can be expected that the tenant will pay the rent on time throughout the term, and diligently perform its other obligations under the lease. An established, high-performing and renowned public limited company (such as one of the large retail food companies) will be regarded as giving a good covenant in the commercial letting market, whereas newly-formed public limited companies and many private companies, whose reputation, reliability and financial standing are unknown in the property market, will not be perceived as giving a good covenant. If the covenant is so bad that the landlord has reservations about the proposed tenant's ability to maintain rental payments throughout the term without financial difficulties, the landlord will consider not granting a lease to that tenant in the first place. However, in situations which fall between these two extremes, the landlord often requires a third party, known as a guarantor, to join in the lease to guarantee the tenant's obligations.

15.4.1 Practical points

The landlord's aim is to ensure that it receives the rent due under the lease on time throughout the term, either from the tenant or, if the tenant defaults, from the guarantor. Therefore, just as the landlord ought to investigate the financial status of its proposed tenant, so too it should investigate the status of the guarantor nominated by the tenant.

With private limited companies or newly-formed public limited companies (who, even with plc status, may be just as likely to be in breach as any other tenant), many landlords will ask for one or more of the company's directors to guarantee the tenant's performance of its obligations. However, the landlord should not necessarily be so blinkered in its approach, since other options may prove to be more fruitful.

Does a subsidiary company have a parent or sister company that can stand as guarantor? If the directors are not of sufficient financial standing, are the shareholders of the company in any better position to give the landlord the element of reliability it requires? Will the tenant's bank guarantee the obligation of its client?

The guarantor should be advised to seek independent advice, since there is a clear conflict of interests between tenant and guarantor. The conflict arises in that, on the one hand, the advice to be given to the tenant is that, without a guarantor, the tenant will not get a lease, while, on the other hand, the advice to give to the guarantor would be to avoid giving the guarantee. Further, in seeking to make amendments to the surety covenants in the lease on behalf of the guarantor, the solicitor may be prejudicing the negotiation of the lease terms between the landlord and their tenant-client, causing delay or disruption.

15.4.2 The extent of the guarantee

15.4.2.1 The old regime

The purpose of the guarantee is to ensure that the guarantor will pay the rent if the tenant does not, and will remedy or indemnify the landlord against any breaches of covenant committed by the tenant. Two points should be noted. First, it is usual for the landlord in drafting the lease to define 'the Tenant' to include the tenant's successors in title. This means that in guaranteeing the obligations of 'the Tenant', the guarantor has guaranteed the performance of future (and as yet unknown) assignees of the lease. Its liability would therefore extend throughout the duration of the lease (even after the original tenant had assigned the lease). Secondly, even if the guarantee was limited to a guarantee of the original tenant's obligations, an original tenant remains liable by virtue of privity of contract under the old regime to perform the covenants in the lease for its entire duration. Should, therefore, the landlord choose to sue not the assignee in possession but the original tenant, the guarantee would remain active.

Some guarantors under the old regime sought to limit the extent of their liability so that the guarantee applied only for so long as the lease remained vested in the tenant in respect of whom the guarantee was originally sought.

For guarantors who were unable to negotiate such a limitation, s 17 of the LT(C)A 1995 will offer some protection (see **15.3.1.1**).

15.4.2.2 The new regime

Abolition of the concept of privity of contract in leases applies equally to guarantors. Section 24(2) of the LT(C)A 1995 provides that where a tenant is released under the LT(C)A 1995 from the tenant covenants of the lease, the guarantor is also released. Any attempt to extend the liability of a guarantor beyond the duration of the liability of the tenant whose performance was guaranteed is likely to fall foul of the anti-avoidance provisions of s 25 of the LT(C)A 1995. This includes requiring the guarantor of an outgoing tenant directly to guarantee an incoming assignee's obligations (see *Good Harvest LLP v Centaur Services Limited* [2010] EWHC 330 (Ch)). However, s 25 would not preclude the guarantor from guaranteeing the outgoing tenant's AGA obligations and therefore indirectly guaranteeing the assignee (see *K/S Victoria Street v House of Fraser (Stores Management) Limited* [2011] EWCA Civ 904). (Both these cases are discussed further at **21.2.4.3**.)

15.4.2.3 Guarantor's liability if tenant 'holds over'

Unless there is an express provision in the lease to the contrary, the liability of the guarantor will cease upon the contractual term date and will not continue during a statutory continuation tenancy under s 24 of the LTA 1954 (see *Junction Estates Ltd v Cope* (1974) 27 P & CR 482). However, it is common practice to define the lease term to include 'the period of any holding over or any extension or continuance whether by agreement or operation of law', and to prolong the guarantor's liability by requiring it to covenant with the landlord throughout 'the term' as so defined.

15.4.3 Discharge or release

The guarantor cannot unilaterally revoke its guarantee, but in certain cases, usually where the landlord acts to the prejudice of the guarantor, the conduct of the landlord might operate as a release.

15.4.3.1 Variations

If the landlord, without obtaining the consent of the guarantor, agrees with the tenant to vary the terms of the lease (eg, by substituting more onerous repairing obligations), the variation of the lease will operate to discharge the guarantor. A guarantor cannot stand as surety and be made liable for the tenant's default in the performance of terms different from those guaranteed to be performed, unless the guarantor has agreed to the variation. However, an immaterial variation of the lease which would not prejudice the guarantor (eg, by substituting less onerous repairing obligations) is not likely to discharge the guarantor, although authority appears to suggest that it is for the guarantor to decide whether or not it would be prejudiced by the proposed variation. In *Holme v Brunskill* (1877) 3 QBD 495, a surrender of part of the premises comprised in the lease (which might not appear in any way to prejudice the guarantor, particularly if the rent is reduced as a result), agreed without the consent of the guarantor, operated to discharge the guarantee.

A surrender of the whole of the premises comprised in the lease will operate to end the liability of the guarantor as from the date of surrender, but not in respect of any breaches of covenant outstanding at that time.

Increasing the rent by exercising a rent review clause does not amount to a variation and so will not release the guarantor. This means that a guarantor may be guaranteeing the payment in future of an unknown level of rent (although see **15.3.3** for the protection given to guarantors of former tenants by s 18 of the LT(C)A 1995 and in the case of *Friends Provident Life Office v British Railways Board*).

Landlords should be aware that granting a permission to a tenant, for example to carry out works, can amount to a variation of the lease, if that permission allows for something prohibited in the original lease. So in *Topland Portfolio No 1 Ltd v Smiths New Trading Ltd* [2014] EWCA Civ 18, the landlord granted permission for the tenant to carry out substantial works to its premises by way of a Licence for Alterations. The tenant's guarantor was not a party to the Licence for Alterations and the type of work permitted by the Licence had been prohibited under the terms of the lease. The tenant subsequently went into administration and the landlord pursued the guarantor for rent arrears. Unfortunately for the landlord, since the Licence consented to something prohibited by the lease, the court considered that the Licence amounted to a variation of the lease. On that basis, as the guarantor had not been a party to the variation, it was released from its guarantee, leaving the landlord unable to recover the rent arrears.

In light of such case law, the safest course of action for landlords is to ensure any guarantor to the lease is also a party to any documentation granted supplemental to the lease.

15.4.3.2 'Giving time'

'Giving time' to the tenant may operate to discharge the guarantee. A landlord 'gives time' to a tenant if, in a binding way, it agrees to allow the tenant to pay rent late or not at all. It does not seem that a mere omission to press for payment (eg, due to an oversight, or perhaps to avoid a waiver of the right to forfeit the lease) will amount to the giving of time.

15.4.3.3 Release of co-guarantor

According to general principles of suretyship, if there is more than one guarantor, the release by the landlord of one of them operates as a release of all of them.

15.4.3.4 Death

The death of the tenant is not likely to bring an end to the guarantee, since the lease will vest in the tenant's personal representatives who, as the tenant's successors in title, will become 'the Tenant' under the lease, whose obligations are guaranteed by the guarantor. Under the new regime, such a vesting would be an excluded assignment, and so the guarantor would not be released. Further, the death of the guarantor will not necessarily bring an end to the guarantee since the guarantor's own personal representatives will remain liable under the guarantee to the extent of the deceased's assets passing through their hands. However, it is more common for the landlord to make provision for the possible death of the guarantor by obtaining a covenant from the tenant obliging it to find a suitable replacement.

15.4.3.5 Bankruptcy or liquidation

The bankruptcy or liquidation of the tenant will not operate to release the guarantor. On the bankruptcy of an individual tenant, the lease will vest in the trustee-in-bankruptcy who will become 'the Tenant' for the purposes of the lease (and such a vesting is an excluded assignment under the new regime). On the liquidation of a corporate tenant, the lease will remain vested in the company (unless the liquidator obtains an order under s 145 of the Insolvency Act 1986 (IA 1986)).

Even if the trustee or liquidator chooses to disclaim the lease, the disclaimer will not operate to end the guarantor's liability (see **33.9**).

15.4.4 Drafting points for the landlord

The landlord should ensure that the guarantor joins in the lease to give the covenants the landlord requires. A guarantee will be unenforceable if it is not in writing (see *Actionstrength Ltd v International Glass Engineering* [2003] 2 AC 541).

The two basic obligations of a guarantor are: (i) to pay the rent (and any other sums payable by the tenant under the lease) if the tenant does not pay; and (ii) to remedy, or to indemnify the landlord against loss caused by, any breaches of covenant committed by the tenant. The landlord will ensure that the guarantor is liable for the period in respect of which the tenant is liable under the lease and, possibly, under any AGA into which the tenant may enter. If the landlord wishes to extend the liability of the guarantor to cover the period of any AGA, it must ensure this is done by way of a sub-guarantee of the outgoing tenant's obligations in the AGA (see **21.2.4.3**). A direct guarantee of the incoming assignee's obligations will fall foul of the anti-avoidance provisions in s 25 of the LT(C)A 1995 (see *Good Harvest LLP v Centaur Services Limited* [2010] EWHC 330 (Ch)).

Several other provisions are usually required by the landlord:

(a) A covenant from the tenant to provide a replacement guarantor should one of several unfortunate or undesirable events happen. For instance, if the guarantor is an individual who dies, or becomes mentally incapable (ie, a receiver is appointed under s 99 of the Mental Health Act 1983) or has a petition in bankruptcy presented against them (or is affected by other proceedings under the IA 1986 which the landlord considers serious enough to warrant substitution) the landlord will require the tenant to find a replacement of equivalent financial standing. If the guarantor is a company and a winding up commences (or, as above, it is affected by other adverse insolvency proceedings), again the tenant will be required to find a reasonably acceptable replacement.

(b) A provision protecting the landlord against the tenant's trustee-in-bankruptcy or liquidator disclaiming the lease to bring the tenant's liability to an end. The effect of a disclaimer is dealt with at **33.10**. For present purposes it can be said that, whilst disclaimer does not end the liability of a guarantor, most landlords will nevertheless want the ability to require the guarantor to take a lease from the landlord in the event of disclaimer, for the full unexpired residue of the term then remaining.

(c) A provision to deal with situations which might otherwise operate to release the guarantor. As part of the guarantor's covenants, the landlord will include a declaration that a release will not be effected by the giving of time to the tenant, or by a variation in the terms of the lease (although as a concession, the landlord might accept that a variation prejudicial to the guarantor will still operate as a release unless the guarantor has consented to it). The effect of stating in the lease that the guarantor will not be released 'by any other event which, but for this provision, would operate to release the surety' is doubtful.

15.4.5 Drafting points for the guarantor

If the guarantor has accepted the principle of giving a guarantee, it should make all efforts to minimise its liability. There are several provisions a guarantor can seek to negotiate:

(a) A limit on the length of its liability. While the LT(C)A 1995 releases a guarantor to the same extent as it releases the tenant, the guarantor should try to ensure that it is not contractually bound to guarantee the tenant under any AGA (as to which, see **21.2.4.3**). This may prove difficult to negotiate if the covenant strength of the tenant is questionable.

(b) An obligation on the landlord's part to notify the guarantor of any default by the tenant. One would expect the tenant to tell its guarantor if the tenant was experiencing difficulties in meeting its obligations under the lease. However, this might not always be the case, and in order to alert the guarantor to possible claims under the guarantee and, perhaps, to enable it to put pressure on the tenant, it could seek to include a covenant by the landlord to notify the guarantor in writing whenever the tenant falls into arrears with the rent, or otherwise breaches a covenant in the lease.

(c) Participation in rent reviews. As the guarantor guarantees payment of future unascertained rents, it may try to persuade the landlord to allow it to play a part in the rent review process. This would necessitate amendments to the usual rent review clause and would not be attractive to the landlord. Further, the tenant would not be keen either to hand over the review negotiations to the guarantor, or to have it involved as a third party in the review process, and an assignee of the lease would certainly see it as an unattractive proposition.

(d) An ability to demand an assignment of the lease from the tenant where the tenant is in default under the lease. This would enable the guarantor to minimise its liability by being able to call for an assignment and then assign the lease to a more stable assignee.

15.4.6 An assignee's guarantor

The above paragraphs have concentrated on the guarantee to be provided by the original tenant on the grant of the lease. However, as a condition of granting licence to assign the lease, the landlord may require the assignee to provide a suitable guarantor in respect of its obligations. This guarantor cannot be the person or company who guaranteed the obligations of the assignor (see *Good Harvest LLP v Centaur Services Limited* [2010] EWHC 330 (Ch) and *K/S Victoria Street v House of Fraser (Stores Management) Limited* [2011] EWCA Civ 904). Under the old regime, it will be the landlord's intention to fix the new guarantor with liability for the duration of the contractual term and beyond. Under the new regime, liability should not exceed the liability of the assignee.

REVIEW ACTIVITY

1. A tenant (T) took a lease in 1994 and assigned it for value in 2000. The original contractual term has now expired but the assignee is holding over under the LTA 1954. T has now received a letter from the current landlord saying the assignee has failed to pay the last quarter's rent and demanding it from T. Is T obliged to pay?

2. A landlord (L) grants a lease in 2010 and then sells on its freehold reversionary interest. It receives a letter from the current tenant alleging that the current landlord is insolvent and has failed to pay the insurance premiums for the building. The tenant is suggesting that L is liable for the insurance premiums. Is the tenant's assertion correct?

3. Your client has just purchased the freehold of an office block subject to a recently granted lease of the whole. The tenant has told your client that it has certain contractual obligations from the previous landlord contained in an agreement for lease that pre-dates the lease. One of the obligations is to repair any damage caused to the premises by inherent defects. Your client wishes to know if it is liable to comply with these obligations.

Answers to this Review activity may be found in Appendix 1.

CHAPTER 16

THE PARCELS CLAUSE

16.1	Purpose	215
16.2	Airspace and underground	215
16.3	Fixtures	215
16.4	Rights to be granted and reserved	217
	Review activity	217

16.1 PURPOSE

The purpose of the parcels clause is accurately and unambiguously to describe the property being let to the tenant (the 'demised premises'), so that it is clear what is included and what is excluded. This is important because key provisions in the lease, such as the tenant's repairing covenant, the landlord's insurance covenant and the controls on what alterations the tenant may carry out, are given in relation to the demised premises as defined in the lease.

Where the whole of a building is being let, the parcels clause will contain the same sort of description as in the case of the sale of freehold land, for example:

> the land and building at 25 High Street, Shaftesbury, Dorset SP7 8JE, shown red on the attached plan.

In most cases, a plan will be used, although if a lease is the grant of the whole of the landlord's registered title or the boundaries are clearly identifiable on the Ordnance Survey map, it may be possible to describe the demised premises adequately in words alone. However, where a lease of part only of a building is intended, the parcels clause needs more care and attention, and a plan will be essential. This chapter deals with the description of the demised premises in a lease of a whole building; see **Chapter 27** for the issues that arise on a lease of part of a building.

16.2 AIRSPACE AND UNDERGROUND

A lease of land includes the buildings on it, the sub-soil below the land, and the airspace above it to such a height as is necessary for the ordinary use and enjoyment of the land and buildings (*Bernstein v Skyviews & General Ltd* [1978] QB 479). However, the parties may limit the extent of the parcels clause by excluding the airspace above the roof. If there is such a limitation, this will prevent the tenant from adding extra floors by extending upwards, since to do so would be a trespass. The tenant should also appreciate that problems might be caused if it had to erect scaffolding above roof height to comply with its obligation to repair the roof; that would also amount to a trespass. The tenant should therefore ensure that it has any necessary right to enter the airspace above its building to the extent necessary to comply with its obligations under the lease. Without any limitation on the airspace the tenant will be free to extend upwards subject only to obtaining any necessary planning permission and consent under the alterations covenant.

16.3 FIXTURES

The point about a fixture is that it is part of the demised premises and prima facie belongs to the landlord. If an article is not a fixture it will be a chattel. Yet despite the apparent simplicity of the matter, it is not always easy to distinguish between the two, and over the years the courts have developed a test based on the degree of annexation of the item to the land and the purpose of annexation (see, eg, *Berkley v Poulett* (1976) 242 EG 39). However, the application of this test to a given set of facts is notoriously difficult, and for the avoidance of doubt, a prospective tenant should always compile a full inventory of the fixtures which are present at the start of the lease.

16.3.1 Repair of fixtures

If an article is a fixture, it is treated as part of the demised premises and the tenant will become responsible for its repair under its obligation to repair 'the demised premises'. This can have a significant impact on the tenant, bearing in mind that many business premises include expensive fixtures such as central heating and air-conditioning plant. For this reason the tenant should always inspect the condition of the fixtures before completion of the lease. If any defects are discovered, the tenant must make sure that it does not become liable to remedy those defects under its repairing obligation. This can be achieved by getting the landlord to do any necessary repairs before the lease commences, or by agreeing the state and condition of the fixtures with the landlord and ensuring that the covenant to repair does not require any higher standard than that existing at the start of the lease.

16.3.2 Removal of fixtures

The tenant may have the right to remove fixtures at the end of the lease depending upon whether they are 'landlord's fixtures', which cannot be removed, or 'tenant's fixtures', which the tenant is entitled to remove unless the lease provides to the contrary. Tenant's fixtures are those articles:

(a) affixed by the tenant;
(b) for the purpose of its trade; and
(c) which are capable of removal without substantially damaging the building and without destroying the usefulness of the article (see *Peel Land & Property (Ports No 3) Ltd v TS Sheerness Steel Ltd* [2013] EWHC 1658 (Ch)).

The terms of the lease may require the tenant to yield up the demised premises at the end of the term together with all fixtures. Whether this excludes the tenant's right to remove tenant's fixtures depends on the form of wording used; very clear words will be required before the right is excluded. It has been held that an obligation to yield up the premises 'with all and singular the fixtures and articles belonging thereto' is sufficient to exclude the right (*Leschallas v Woolf* [1908] 1 Ch 641), and the tenant should resist such a clause. In the case of *Peel Land & Property (Ports No 3) Ltd v TS Sheerness Steel Ltd* [2014] EWCA Civ 100, a landlord successfully argued that a tenant's covenant not to make or suffer to be made any change or addition to the premises save in connection with the permitted purpose of steel making meant that a tenant could not remove a large number of pieces of equipment and plant installed by a former tenant in order to sell them. Title to a tenant's fixtures left on the premises after a tenant's lease is disclaimed vests in the landlord (*URT Group Ltd and Others v Dowers and Others* [2018] EWHC 3195 (Ch)).

Where the tenant is entitled to remove fixtures, it must make good any damage caused by their removal. As a general rule, the right exists only during the term.

The term 'landlord's fixtures' can also be problematic. In *Fivaz v Marlborough Knightsbridge Management Ltd* [2020] UKUT 138 (LC), the Upper Tribunal (Lands Chamber) held that the front door to the tenant's flat had been made part of the flat itself during construction of the flat, and therefore the tenant, who had replaced the front door, was not in breach of a covenant in the lease not to remove the landlord's fixtures from the property. However, the Upper Tribunal also noted that the decision did not mean that a front door to a flat could never be a landlord's fixture.

16.4 RIGHTS TO BE GRANTED AND RESERVED

In many cases, the demised premises will be structurally independent and directly connected to all mains services. Where this is not the case, the tenant may need to be granted rights to enable it to use the demised premises to their full extent. For example, it may need the right to enter upon the landlord's adjoining property to comply with its obligation to repair; this may be particularly important where the walls of the demised premises are flush against the boundary. The tenant may also need the right to connect into services on the landlord's adjoining property. If the landlord's title is registered, an easement expressly granted in a lease must be completed by registration or it will not be a legal easement capable of binding a successor in title to the landlord's interest in the adjoining property.

From the landlord's point of view, it may need to reserve rights such as a right to enter the demised premises to view the state and condition or to repair. The service pipes and cables for the landlord's adjoining property may pass under or through the demised premises, and the landlord will thus need to reserve rights in respect of them. From a tenant's point of view, such rights will need to be carefully negotiated so as to minimise disturbance to its business operation (see **Chapter 24** on derogation from grant and quiet enjoyment).

REVIEW ACTIVITY

1. You act for Straudley Investments Ltd, the tenant under a lease of 67–81 Mortimer Street London for a term of 99 years from 1936. The parcels clause in the lease demises:

    'ALL THAT piece or parcel of ground with the messuages and buildings erected thereon situate and being on the south side of and numbered 67, 69, 71, 73, 75, 77, 79 and 81 in Mortimer Street ...'

    The landlord has erected a fire escape and a ventilation vent on the roof of the building without your client's consent. Can your client apply to court for a mandatory injunction requiring the landlord to remove the fire escape and ventilation vent on the grounds that the landlord is trespassing on its property?

2. You act for Ms Eileen Davies who is the tenant of top-floor premises at 13 Beechcroft Avenue London. The parcels clause in the lease demises all of the first-floor flat at 13 Beechcroft Avenue, as shown on the plan annexed to the lease, and the roof and roof space thereof. Your client wishes to carry out a loft conversion. The landlord is withholding its consent on the basis that the dormer windows that would be installed as part of the conversion involve a protrusion into the airspace above the roof and would therefore constitute a trespass by the tenant. Is your client entitled to a declaration from the court that the landlord is unreasonably withholding its consent to an improvement proposed by the tenant?

Answers to this Review activity may be found in Appendix 1.

CHAPTER 17

TERM

17.1	Introduction	219
17.2	Break clauses	220
17.3	Options to renew	222
17.4	Impact of SDLT	222
	Review activity	222

17.1 INTRODUCTION

The duration of a lease for a term of years must be fixed and certain before the lease takes effect. Thus, for example, a tenancy 'until the landlord requires the land for road widening' is void for uncertainty (*Prudential Assurance Co Ltd v London Residuary Body* [1992] 2 AC 386). This principle applies to all leases, including periodic tenancies. A provision that one party is unable to determine a periodic tenancy, or for it to be determined only in certain circumstances, is inconsistent with the concept of a periodic tenancy. If termination on the happening of an uncertain event is required by either party, this can be achieved by granting a long fixed term with a break clause exercisable only on the happening of the event in question (see **17.2**).

Most business tenancies will be for a fixed term, in which case the lease must specify the date of commencement of the term and its duration (eg 'for a term of ten years from and including the 29 September 2020'). There is no need for the commencement of the term to be the same date as the date of completion of the grant of the lease. It may be more convenient for the landlord, particularly when it is granting several leases in the same block, to choose one specific date from which the term of each will run. If this is an earlier date than completion then, unless the lease provides to the contrary, the tenant's rights and obligations will arise only on completion, not the earlier date. However, for the avoidance of doubt, the lease should expressly state the precise date from which the rent is to be payable.

In specifying the date when the term of the lease commences, it is important to avoid any ambiguity. It must be clear beyond doubt when the term expires (but see **Chapter 32** for the effect of the lease being protected under Pt II of the LTA 1954). If the parties want to exclude the protection of Pt II of the LTA 1954, the term must not be defined to include any period of statutory continuation, as a lease cannot be contracted out of such protection unless it is granted for 'a term certain' (*London Borough of Newham v Thomas-Van Staden* [2008] EWCA Civ 1414). The presumption is that if the term is stated to run 'from' a particular date, the term begins on the next day. If, however, the term is expressed to begin 'on' a particular date, that day is the first day of the term. To avoid any possible argument, it is always best to use clear words such as 'beginning on', 'beginning with' or 'from and including' (see *Meadfield Properties Ltd v Secretary of State for the Environment* [1995] 03 EG 128).

In recent years, various external pressures have affected the length of the term of commercial leases. The changes brought about by stamp duty land tax (SDLT) and Government pressure (see **14.6**) resulted in shorter lease terms. For example, a 20-year lease at a rent of £250,000 per year will result in a payment of £34,031 in SDLT. Over the past few years, lease terms have fallen from the classic 25-year term of the past to less than 10 years, and even then many tenants are insisting on break clauses (see **17.2**) being included in the lease. In 2022, 50.4% of leases were for 5 years or less, 32.3% for 6–10 years, 12.7% for 11–20 years and only 4.5% for 21 years or more. 30% of new institutional leases in 2022 contained break clauses. (The figures quoted are taken from the PIA Property Data Report 2023 published by the Property Industry Alliance.) The Financial Times reported in July 2023 that average lease lengths for UK offices had dropped to two years and 10 months in the first quarter of 2023 ('UK office leases shorten and vacancies rates soar as workers stay at home' <ft.com>).

17.2 BREAK CLAUSES

17.2.1 Who may operate break clauses and when?

Either party or both parties may be given an option to determine the lease at specified times during the term, or on the happening of certain specified events. For example, the tenant may be given the option to determine a 15-year lease at the end of the fifth and tenth years, or if it is prevented from trading due to the withdrawal of any necessary statutory licences. The landlord may be given an option to determine if, at some future date, it wishes to redevelop the premises or to occupy them for its own business purposes (although if the lease is protected by Pt II of the Landlord and Tenant Act 1954, the exercise of the option may not necessarily entitle the landlord to recover possession; see **17.2.4** and **Chapter 32**).

Some options to break are expressed to be personal to the original tenant in order to prevent their being exercised by successors in title following an assignment. Indeed, a break clause can be personal and incapable of being exercised by successors in title even where no limiting words such as 'only' or 'personal' are used (see *Gemini Press Ltd v Cheryl Lindsay Parsons* [2012] EWHC 1608 (QB)). However, in *Brown & Root Technology v Sun Alliance* [1997] 18 EG 123, the court held that following the assignment of a registered lease to the tenant's parent company, the option was still exercisable by the original tenant until the assignment was completed by registration. It was only on registration of title that the legal estate vested in the assignee; until then the assignor remained the tenant and thus retained the ability to exercise the option.

17.2.2 How are break clauses exercised?

The break clause must be exercised in accordance with its terms. Thus, it must be exercised at the correct time and in the correct manner.

If there are any pre-conditions to the exercise of the break clause, they must be complied with strictly. For example, a break clause will often contain a condition that vacant possession must be given on or before the break date, and in *Riverside Park Ltd v NHS Property Services Ltd* [2016] EWHC 1313 (Ch) the tenant was deprived of the break because it had not removed the standard demountable partitions it had installed in the premises during the term of the lease. The High Court held that the partitions were chattels which substantially prevented or interfered with the landlord's right of possession. By contrast, the Court of Appeal in *Capitol Park Leeds plc v Global Radio Services Ltd* [2021] EWCA Civ 995 held that a break condition requiring vacant possession was satisfied even though the tenant left the property in a dysfunctional condition (stripped of heating, lighting and ceiling tiles); the vacant possession condition required the tenant to return the property free from people, chattels and legal interests, rather than in any particular physical state.

The RICS Code for Leasing Business Premises in England and Wales 2020 (see **14.2**) states, in Part 3 Lease negotiation best practice, that 'unless the parties have agreed stricter conditions in the heads of terms, a tenant's break should be conditional only on the tenant paying all basic rent payable on any date before the break date, giving up occupation and leaving no subtenants or other occupiers. Disputes about the state of the premises, or what has been left behind or removed, should be settled later, as at normal lease expiry.'

The tenant should be particularly wary of any provision in the lease making compliance with tenant covenants a pre-condition to the exercise of the break clause. In such a case, even a trivial, immaterial breach of covenant on the part of the tenant may prevent it from exercising the option validly (see *Avocet Industrial Estates LLP v Merol and Another* [2011] EWHC 3422 (Ch), where the tenant was deprived of the break because it had not paid negligible amounts of default interest on past arrears, and *Bairstow Eves (Securities) Ltd v Ripley* [1992] 2 EGLR 47, an analogous case concerning an option to renew that the tenant was unable to exercise because of a failure to decorate in the last year of the term despite the fact that it had decorated just before the beginning of the last year). If the landlord will not agree to the pre-condition being removed altogether, the tenant should modify it so that it requires 'substantial' or 'material' compliance (see, eg, *Bairstow Eves (Securities) Ltd v Ripley* (above) and *Fitzroy House Epworth Street (No 1) v The Financial Times Ltd* [2006] EWCA Civ 329), although this still leaves open the possibility of dispute and litigation.

Particular care should be taken by the tenant where the break right is conditional on performance of the tenant's covenants and the break date falls between rent payment days. If, as is common, the rent is payable quarterly in advance, the tenant must pay the full quarterly rent on the rent payment date before the break date, regardless of the fact that it will not be in occupation for the whole quarter (see *Marks and Spencer plc v BNP Paribas Securities Services Trust Company (Jersey) Ltd* [2015] UKSC 72). Where the break date falls between rent payment dates, the tenant should try to include in the lease an express term allowing recovery of the rent where the break right is lawfully exercised by the tenant.

Any notice requirements for the exercise of the break clause must also be complied with strictly because, unless the lease states to the contrary, time is of the essence in a break clause (*United Scientific Holdings v Burnley Borough Council* [1978] AC 904). However, if an incorrect date is specified in the break notice, the court may be prepared to declare the notice valid if it would be obvious to a reasonable recipient of the notice with knowledge of the lease that the person serving it had made a mistake so that the reasonable recipient would not have been misled (*Mannai Investment Co Ltd v Eagle Star Life Assurance Co Ltd* [1997] AC 749). Subsequent cases have shown that the courts will adopt a similar approach when dealing with other errors in break notices. However, it must always be borne in mind that each case will turn on its own facts (see, eg, the contrasting cases of *Lemmerbell Ltd v Britannia LAS Direct Ltd* [1998] 3 EGLR 67 and *Havant International Holdings Ltd v Lionsgate (H) Investments Ltd* [1999] EGCS 144).

While some degree of latitude is permitted in relation to the requirement to convey the meaning of a break notice, the requirement to serve it in the correct form or in accordance with a condition has been more strictly interpreted. For example, the doctrine in *Mannai* will not save a notice that is served in a manner different from that required by the lease. In *Hotgroup plc v Royal Bank of Scotland plc* [2010] EWHC 1193, the tenant's break was conditional on service of nine months' notice on the landlord and the landlord's managing agent; the tenant served correctly on the landlord but not on the agent. In *Claire's Accessories v Kensington High Street* [2001] PLSCS 112, the notice was held to be invalid because the landlord had served it at the tenant's premises rather than at its registered office. In *Friends Life Ltd v Siemens Hearing Instruments Ltd* [2014] EWCA Civ 382, the lease stated that the break notice must be 'expressed to be given under section 24(2) of the Landlord and Tenant Act 1954', and when the tenant served a break notice that did not refer to s 24(2), the notice was held to be invalid.

17.2.3 Effect of exercise of option on sub-tenants

The effect of the exercise of an option in a head-lease may be to terminate any sub-lease granted. This is dealt with further at **31.4**.

17.2.4 Relationship with the LTA 1954, Pt II

The landlord must be aware of the interrelationship with Pt II of the LTA 1954, and may wish to give thought to drafting the circumstances giving rise to the exercise of the option in line with the requirements of s 30(1)(f) or (g) of that Act (see **32.5**). This is desirable, because the exercise of the option may not necessarily entitle the landlord to recover possession as it must also, where necessary, comply with the provisions of the 1954 Act (see **32.2**). Further, where necessary, regard should be had to the relationship between the notice required under the break clause and the notice provisions of the 1954 Act.

17.3 OPTIONS TO RENEW

Options to renew are not often found in business leases because most tenants are protected under Pt II of the Landlord and Tenant Act 1954 and will, therefore, have a statutory right to a new tenancy which the landlord may oppose only on certain grounds (see **Chapter 32**).

17.4 IMPACT OF SDLT

Because the amount of SDLT payable will increase with the length of the lease (see **11.2**), a tenant may find it preferable to take a short lease with an option to renew, rather than a long lease with a break clause. A tenant will pay less SDLT on a five-year term with an option to renew than on a 10-year term with a right to break after five years. If the break clause is exercised, there will be no refund of SDLT paid in relation to the final five years of the term. Obviously, if a five-year lease is taken and this is renewed, extra SDLT will be then be payable, but it will be payable only if and when the lease is renewed.

REVIEW ACTIVITY

1. A lease contained an option to break the lease after 10 years. The 10-year term commenced on 24 June 1984. The tenant served a notice that purported to determine the lease on 23 June 1994. Was the notice to determine the lease valid?

2. A tenant entered into two leases, each for a term of 10 years from and including 13 January 1992. The leases were each subject to a break clause permitting the tenant to determine the lease by giving not less than six months' notice to the landlord, such notice to expire on the third anniversary of the term commencement date. What date should have been specified as the date of termination in the break notices?

3. A landlord granted a lease of a warehouse to two tenants (T1 and T2) for a term of 10 years. At the relevant time, T2 was dormant and a wholly-owned subsidiary of T1. The lease contained a break clause and the solicitors sent a break notice to the landlord, but only T1 was named as the tenant. Was the notice to determine the lease valid?

4. A lease for a term of six years granted the tenant an option to renew the term for a further six years by giving notice not more than 12 months and not less than nine months before the term date, 'if the tenant shall pay the rents hereby reserved and perform and observe all the covenants and obligations herein on the tenant's part contained until the term date, ...'. The tenant gave the requisite notice and kept the premises in a good state of repair, but in breach of covenant failed to paint and decorate in the last year of the term. Did the landlord have to grant the tenant a renewal of the lease?

Answers to this Review activity may be found in Appendix 1.

CHAPTER 18

Rent

18.1	Introduction	223
18.2	Amount	224
18.3	Time for payment	224
18.4	Other payments reserved as rent	224
18.5	Suspension of rent	224
18.6	Interest	224
18.7	VAT	225
	Review activity	225

18.1 INTRODUCTION

One of the primary purposes in granting the lease is to enable the landlord to receive income in the form of rent. However, the payment of rent by the tenant is not essential to the landlord and tenant relationship, and it is not uncommon, when property is difficult to let, for landlords to grant rent-free periods to tenants as an inducement for them to take the lease or to allow the tenant to fit out the premises.

The lease must contain a covenant by the tenant to pay the rent. In certain rare situations the tenant may have the right to deduct sums from the rent payable. For example, the tenant has the right to deduct those sums allowed by statute and, where the landlord is in breach of its repairing obligation, the tenant seemingly has an ancient right to undertake the repairs itself and deduct the expense from future payments of rent (see **29.2**). In addition, the tenant may be able to exercise a right of set-off and deduct an unliquidated sum for damages where the landlord is in breach of covenant and the tenant has thereby suffered a loss. Landlords often seek to counter the tenant's right to make deductions by stating in the covenant to pay rent that rent is to be paid 'without deduction'. However, this will not prevent a tenant from making a deduction authorised by statute, nor from exercising its right of set-off (see *Connaught Restaurants Ltd v Indoor Leisure Ltd* [1993] 46 EG 184). To exclude the tenant's right of set-off, very clear words must be used.

The covenant to pay rent is usually followed by a covenant by the tenant to pay all taxes, rates, assessments and outgoings imposed on the demised premises; this will include business rates and water rates. For the avoidance of doubt, the tenant should make it clear that this obligation does not extend to any taxes payable by the landlord arising out of the receipt of the rent or due to any dealing by the landlord with the reversion.

Unless the lease is contracted out of the security of tenure provisions in Pt II of the LTA 1954, in the definitions clause of the lease the landlord should seek to define 'Rent' as also including any 'interim rent' which may become payable under s 24A of the LTA 1954 (see **32.4**). If this were not done and a guarantor's or former tenant's liability was stated by the lease to extend into the statutory continuation (under s 24), it would remain liable only for the contractual rent during that period and not for any interim rent which the current tenant might be ordered to pay as part of any future renewal proceedings under the 1954 Act (*Herbert Duncan Ltd v Cluttons* [1992] 1 EGLR 101).

18.2 AMOUNT

The amount of rent must be certain. However, the actual amount need not be stated as long as some means are provided by which the exact amount can be ascertained. For example, the rent may be fixed at £25,000 per annum for the first five years of a 10-year lease and then at 'such revised rent as may be ascertained'. Provided the means of ascertaining the new rent are clearly stated, this is a valid method of dealing with the rent. Such rent review clauses are dealt with in **Chapter 19,** where consideration is also given to the different methods of assessing the revised rent.

18.3 TIME FOR PAYMENT

The lease should set out the following:

(a) The date from which the rent is payable and the date of the first payment. It is usual to state that the first payment, or an apportioned part of it, is payable on the date of the lease unless a rent-free period is to be given.

(b) The payment dates, otherwise, in the case of a tenancy for a fixed term of years, there is authority for the proposition that the rent will be payable yearly. It is common practice in business leases to make the rent payable on the usual quarter days, ie, 25 March, 24 June, 29 September and 25 December.

(c) Whether rent is to be payable in advance or in arrears. Unless the lease provides that the rent is to be payable in advance, which is usual, the general law provides that rent is payable in arrears.

In modern commercial leases, provision is often made for the payment of rent by way of direct debit or standing order to minimise the risk of delay.

18.4 OTHER PAYMENTS RESERVED AS RENT

It is common for leases to provide for the tenant to make other payments to the landlord, such as a service charge or reimbursement of insurance premiums paid by the landlord. Landlords will often require the lease to state that such sums are payable as additional rent. Historically, the advantage to the landlord was that if the tenant defaulted, the remedy of distress would be available (a remedy which could be used only for non-payment of rent and not for breaches of other covenants), although this is no longer a factor now that distress has been abolished and Commercial Rent Arrears Recovery enacted (see **30.1.1.3**). It is still the case that the landlord will be able to forfeit the lease for non-payment of sums defined as rent without the need to serve a notice under s 146 of the LPA 1925 (see **26.4.1**).

It is also possible for any VAT payable on the rent to be reserved as additional rent.

18.5 SUSPENSION OF RENT

In the absence of any contrary provision in the lease, the rent will continue to be payable even if the premises are damaged or destroyed and so cannot be used by the tenant. The contractual doctrine of frustration will apply to leases only in exceptional circumstances (see *National Carriers Ltd v Panalpina (Northern) Ltd* [1981] AC 675 and *Canary Wharf (BP4) T1 Ltd v European Medicines Agency* [2019] EWHC 335 (Ch)). From the tenant's point of view, therefore, it should insist on a proviso that the rent is suspended if the premises become unfit for use. If the lease contains a service charge, provision should also be made for this to be suspended as otherwise it too would continue to be payable. This issue is considered further at **23.7**.

18.6 INTEREST

Unless there is provision to the contrary, interest cannot be charged by the landlord on any late payment by the tenant of rent or other sums due under the lease (unless judgment is obtained against the tenant for such amounts). It is therefore usual for a lease to provide that interest is payable by the tenant on any late payment of money due under the lease (from the due date to the date of actual payment). If, as is usual, the rate of interest is geared to the base rate of a named bank (eg, 4% above the base rate of Barclays Bank plc), a problem may arise if that bank no longer fixes a base rate. It is therefore sensible to provide for an alternative rate should this situation arise. For the tenant's protection, this should be stated to be 'some other reasonable rate as the landlord may specify'. Without the addition of the word 'reasonable' the tenant would have no right to dispute any new rate it thought excessive.

From the landlord's point of view, it is preferable for the lease to state that the interest rate is to apply 'both before and after any judgment'.

18.7 VAT

The implications of VAT on business leases have been discussed in **Chapter 11**. The landlord should include an appropriate clause entitling it to add VAT to the rent and other payments due from the tenant, by providing that the rent and other sums are payable exclusive of VAT.

REVIEW ACTIVITY

Consider the extract from a draft commercial lease of office premises below (adapted from the lease prepared by the Practical Law Company – see **Appendix 4**) and answer the following questions:

1. Why are all the monetary payments due under the lease listed in clause 2.3?
2. Can you think of any disadvantage to the landlord of reserving all the monetary payments as additional rent?
3. In clause 3, when are the quarterly instalments of rent due, and why is it necessary to state that there must be four equal payments payable in advance?
4. The payments are to be made by banker's standing order. Can you think of any disadvantage to the landlord inherent in this method?
5. When is the first payment due?
6. What is the purpose of clause 4?

Answers to this Review activity may be found in Appendix 1.

THIS LEASE is dated [ ]

Parties

(1) ABC LIMITED incorporated and registered in England and Wales with company number [ ] whose registered office is at [address] (**Landlord**).

(2) MNO LIMITED incorporated and registered in England and Wales with company number [ ] whose registered office is at [address] (**Tenant**).

(3) XYZ LIMITED incorporated and registered in England and Wales with company number [ ] whose registered office is also at [address] (**Guarantor**).

Agreed terms

1. **Interpretation**
1.1 The definitions and rules of interpretation set out in this clause apply to this lease.

Annual Rent: rent at an initial rate of £100,000 per annum and then as revised pursuant to this lease and any interim rent determined under the 1954 Act.

Rent Commencement Date: the date which is 6 calendar months after the date of this lease.

2. **Grant**

2.1 At the request of the Guarantor, the Landlord lets with full title guarantee the Property to the Tenant for the Contractual Term.

2.2 The grant is made together with the ancillary rights set out in clause [ ], excepting and reserving to the Landlord the rights set out in clause [ ], and subject to the Third Party Rights.

2.3 The grant is made with the Tenant paying the following as rent to the Landlord:

(a) the Annual Rent and all VAT in respect of it;

(b) the Service Charge and all VAT in respect of it;

(c) the Insurance Rent;

(d) all interest payable under this lease; and

(e) all other sums due under this lease.

3. **The Annual Rent**

3.1 The Tenant shall pay the Annual Rent and any VAT in respect of it by four equal instalments in advance on or before the usual quarter days. The payments shall be made by banker's standing order or by any other method that the Landlord requires at any time by giving notice to the Tenant.

3.2 The first instalment of the Annual Rent and any VAT in respect of it shall be made on the Rent Commencement Date and shall be the proportion, calculated on a daily basis, in respect of the period from the Rent Commencement Date until the day before the next usual quarter day.

4. **No deduction, counterclaim or set-off**

The Annual Rent and all other money due under this lease are to be paid by the Tenant or any guarantor (as the case may be) without deduction, counterclaim or set-off.

CHAPTER 19

The Rent Review Clause

19.1	The need for review	227
19.2	Types of rent review clause	227
19.3	The dates for review	230
19.4	Working out the open market rent	230
19.5	The assumptions	231
19.6	The disregards	238
19.7	The mechanism for determining the rent	239
19.8	The late review	241
19.9	Recording the review	241
	Review activity	241

19.1 THE NEED FOR REVIEW

Most commercial property leases exceeding five years in length will contain provisions requiring the parties to review the annual rent payable under the lease. With such leases it is difficult to set a rent at the outset of the term that both parties are satisfied will remain appropriate throughout the life of the lease. The effects of inflation, changes in the value of the rental property market or the tenant's circumstances can be reflected in the rent at review, depending on the type of rent review used.

19.2 TYPES OF RENT REVIEW CLAUSE

There are various ways in which rent may be varied during the term.

19.2.1 Fixed increases

This type of review provides for the rent to increase to a fixed amount at the review date. For example, in a lease for a 10-year term, the rent might be set at £10,000 for the first three years of the term, £15,000 for the next three years, and £20,000 for the remainder of the term. This sort of clause would be very rare since the parties to the lease would be placing their faith in the fixed increases proving to be realistic. If the parties have not been realistic then the tenant may pay more or the landlord receive less than on comparable properties.

19.2.2 Index-linked clauses

This type of review looks to increase or decrease the rent in line with an index reflecting changes in the value of money. In practice, the index favoured by practitioners is the Retail Prices Index (RPI). This is published by the Office of National Statistics and used as the domestic measure of inflation in the UK. Although changes in the RPI do not necessarily reflect changes in the property market, they do allow rents to change in line with inflation. Such clauses are usually relatively simple to operate. They generally involve multiplying the old rent by the relevant RPI increase since the date of last review. Due to their relative simplicity, they may be considered appropriate for lower-value property or in shorter leases where the parties would still like the rent to be reviewed. They may also be used where the property is very unusual and the comparable evidence used in assessing the open market rent (OMR) is not available (see **19.2.4**).

However, a tenant who is considering accepting an RPI-linked rent review should be made aware that in periods of high inflation, the rent could increase significantly on review. A tenant's solicitor should therefore consider inserting a clause that caps the rent at a maximum amount. Alternatively, the tenant's solicitor could request a break clause, allowing it to end the lease on the review date. This would allow the tenant to walk away from the lease if the rent increased to an unaffordable level.

19.2.3 Turnover rents

A turnover rent is one which is geared to the turnover of the tenant's business, and can therefore be considered by the landlord only where turnover is generated at the premises. A turnover rent would be impractical in the case of office or warehouse property, but would be appropriate for retail premises.

There are various methods of calculating a turnover rent. Probably the most common is where the tenant pays a 'base rent' plus a 'top up rent' based on the turnover of the business. The 'base rent' is usually a percentage of OMR (typically somewhere between 70% and 80%). The 'top up rent' is typically between 7% and 15% of the tenant's trading turnover.

The main advantage of a turnover rent is that both parties have an interest in ensuring the success of the business operated from the premises. For example, the landlord of a shopping centre will have an added incentive to ensure the shopping centre attracts as many customers as possible, as this will encourage visitors to the shops within it and, it is hoped, increase their turnover. This, in turn, will lead to increased rent for the landlord.

On the downside, if the business operated from the premises fails to thrive, the landlord will share in the pain! The landlord will also need to consider whether it is happy for the turnover provisions to continue on an assignment of the lease, since the identity of the tenant in a turnover rent lease is crucial. Underletting is usually prohibited in a turnover rent lease. Thought will also need to be given to what happens if the tenant ceases to trade from the premises, either temporarily or permanently.

19.2.4 Open market rent review

An OMR review clause requires the rent to be revised in accordance with changes in the property market.

The most common form of OMR review clause will provide that at every rent review date (eg every fifth anniversary of the term) the parties should seek to agree upon a figure that equates to what is then the current OMR for a letting of the tenant's premises. The aim of the exercise is to find out how much a tenant in the open market would be prepared to pay, in terms of rent per annum, if the tenant's premises were available to let in the open market on the relevant review date. This agreement is achieved either by some form of informal negotiated process between the landlord and the tenant, or (less commonly) by the service of notices and counter-notices which specify proposals and counter-proposals as to the revised rent. If agreement cannot be reached, the clause should provide for the appointment of an independent valuer who will determine the revised rent. The valuer will be directed by the review clause to take certain matters into account in conducting their valuation, and to disregard others, and they will call upon evidence of rental valuations of other comparable leasehold interests in the locality.

There are two forms of OMR review clause that practitioners are likely to come across:

(a) the upwards only rent review; and
(b) the upwards/downwards rent review.

19.2.4.1 The upwards only rent review

In an upwards only rent review, the rent on review will be the higher of the rent currently being paid and the open market valuation. In other words, the rental level will never go down. It can either go up, if the open market revaluation is higher than the rent currently being paid, or remain static. The benefits for the landlord are obvious. It is protected against the vagaries in the property market and will never receive less annual rent than the figure agreed at the outset. It can also benefit from any increase in rental levels identified in the open market revaluation. The tenant's position is less advantageous. It will never get the benefit of a fall in rental levels but is subject to any increases in rental levels that may occur. Clearly there is a risk to the tenant that in a falling market it may end up paying far more than competitors in similar premises are paying. Its premises are said to be over-rented. Despite these risks, upward rent reviews are still demanded by institutional landlords and often accepted by tenants. Threats by the Government to legislate in this area have been met with attempts by the property industry to self-regulate.

Under the Code for Leasing Business Premises 2020 ('the 2020 Code'), RICS members will be mandatorily required to ensure that written heads of terms are prepared prior to circulation of the initial draft of the lease (see **14.2**). These mandatory heads of terms must summarise the key provisions of the letting, including the rent review frequency and basis of review. The 2020 Code also contains recommendations as to best practice in relation to the key provisions of a lease, although these are not stated to be mandatory. However, there may be legal and/or disciplinary consequences for RICS members in departing from the 2020 Code, which may lead to a finding of negligence against a surveyor. In relation to rent review, the 2020 Code provides:

> **4   Rent and rent review**
>
> 4.1   The initial rent, the frequency of payment and whether the landlord intends to charge VAT on the rent should all be clearly stated, together with details of any rent-free period or other incentive. The initial rent may be a fixed sum or expressed as a certain sum per square foot or square metre, in which case the method of measurement should be stated.
>
> 4.2   Where the landlord proposes that rent is to be subject to review, the tenant should be notified of the proposed frequency and the method or formula of review at the outset in order to obtain early professional advice as to the implications.
>
> 4.3   Rent review clauses should be clearly expressed. Definitions of market rent should not result in a 'headline rent' unless that has been expressly agreed by the parties, such as where that is agreed in return for a financial inducement. Provisions for indexed rent reviews should not contain obscure formulae designed to produce a greater increase than is proportionate to the increase in the index over the appropriate period or outside any agreed caps or collars.
>
> 4.4   Leases should allow either party to start the rent review process and should not impose time limits intended to prevent a review or set a new rent through inaction by either party.

So, the 2020 Code does not say that upward only rent reviews should not be used, but it does suggest that this should be set out in the heads of terms in order that the tenant can take advice. It also states that controversial 'headline rents' (see **19.5.8**) should only be used where 'expressly agreed by the parties' and that the tenant should be getting something in return for agreeing a headline rent (such as a financial inducement).

19.2.4.2 The upwards/downwards rent review

In an upward/downward rent review clause, the revised annual rent will be the OMR as determined in accordance with the lease. The annual rent will therefore reflect any increases or decreases in rental levels that have occurred since the start of the lease or the previous rent review. This is clearly an advantage to the tenant, but it means that the landlord cannot guarantee the amount of rent that will be generated by the lease. Sometimes, to protect itself against dramatic falls in rental levels, the landlord might provide in the lease that the rental level can never fall below a certain figure (often the initial annual rent figure).

19.3 THE DATES FOR REVIEW

19.3.1 How often should the rent be reviewed?

Most commercial property leases require the rent to be reviewed once every five years. Sometimes in a lease of less than 10 years the rent might be reviewed on a three-yearly basis.

19.3.2 The rent review dates

The tenant should ensure the dates for review are clearly set out in the lease. Usually the review dates are linked to the term commencement date (eg the fifth anniversary of the term commencement date). If this is the case, the tenant should ensure that the term commencement date does not start earlier than the date of the lease itself. Sometimes the term commencement date is backdated to enable the landlord to have all leases in a shopping centre or business park end on the same date (even though the leases have been completed on different dates). If the term commencement date has been backdated then the rent review date will be brought forward and the tenant will not enjoy the certainty of the initial rent figure for as long as it should.

Some leases specify actual dates for the rent review (eg 25 March 2020). This is probably best avoided, as it can give rise to valuation difficulties if on review the valuer is asked to value a hypothetical lease containing the same rent provisions as the actual lease (see **19.5.7**).

19.3.3 The penultimate day rent review

When specifying the rent review dates, the landlord may provide for the rent to be reviewed on the penultimate day of the term. Whilst it may seem strange to review the rent just before the lease is due to expire, there is of course the possibility of the lease continuing under the Landlord and Tenant Act 1954 (LTA 1954). By inserting a penultimate date review the landlord gives itself the possibility of obtaining an increased rent during the period of any holding over. Tenants' solicitors usually delete such penultimate day reviews, preferring instead for the parties to rely on the interim rent provisions in s 24A of the LTA 1954 (see **32.4**). These provisions can result in a more favourable review for the tenant, not least because the rent can go down on an interim rent application. This might lead one to conclude that a landlord will fight quite hard to retain a penultimate day review. However, since 2004, tenants as well as landlords have had the ability to apply for an interim rent under the 1954 Act. This now means that even if the lease contains a penultimate day review, the rent determined under it can, after one day, be replaced by the rent determined under an interim rent application made by the tenant. So in reality, the penultimate day review will now be of use to the landlord only if the tenant fails to make an interim rent application.

19.4 WORKING OUT THE OPEN MARKET RENT

As already discussed in **19.2.4**, most modern rent review provisions require the parties to agree what the OMR of the premises would be if they were being let on the rent review date. This task requires the parties to think hypothetically, since in reality the premises are not available to let as they are occupied by the tenant. So the lease will usually direct the parties to assume that a hypothetical letting of the premises is taking place on the review date and that a hypothetical market exists in which such letting can take place.

19.4.1 Defining the OMR

Different phrases are used by different clauses to define the rent to be ascertained, although in broad terms it is the OMR of the premises at the rent review date. Both landlord and tenant are usually happy to define this as the rent at which the premises 'might reasonably be expected to be let in the open market' at the relevant review date. This wording follows that in s 34 of the LTA 1954, and is therefore considered by most practitioners to be unlikely to be subject to adverse interpretation. Most tenants would want to avoid the use of the expression 'the best rent at which the premises might be let' since this might allow the valuer to consider the possibility of what is known as a special purchaser's bid. If, by chance, the market for a hypothetical letting of the premises contains a potential bidder who would be prepared to bid in excess of what would ordinarily be considered to be the market rent, the 'best' rent would be the rent which the special bidder would be prepared to pay. For example, if the premises which are the subject matter of the hypothetical letting are situated next to premises occupied by a business which is desperate to expand, the 'best' rent might be the rent which that business would be willing to pay.

19.4.2 Comparables

The parties will look at what rents similar premises in similar areas are fetching at the review date. These 'comparables' give the parties an idea of the rent that might be achieved if the premises were available to let in the market at the review date.

19.4.3 Instructions to the valuer

The parties seeking to agree the OMR, or the valuer determining it in the event of dispute, will also need instructions about what matters should be assumed about this hypothetical lease and what issues should be disregarded. For example, what happens if the tenant has carried out substantial improvements to the premises? Should those be taken into account when fixing the revised rent, or should they be ignored? What are the terms of the hypothetical lease? Are they the same as the actual lease, or are there to be differences? The instructions on these issues normally take the form of a set of 'assumptions' and 'disregards' in the lease, which are discussed in further detail in **19.5** and **19.6** below respectively.

19.5 THE ASSUMPTIONS

It is not possible to set out an exhaustive list of assumptions that can appear in a lease. It is important that the advice of a rent review surveyor is sought as to the impact on valuation of a particular set of assumptions and disregards before the lease is agreed. This is a much litigated area where significant sums can turn on the interpretation of a particular clause. The following are, however, fairly typical of the type of assumptions that will be encountered in practice.

19.5.1 The parties are to assume that the premises are available to let 'in the open market by a willing lessor to a willing lessee'

The purpose of this assumption is to create a market in which the letting can be valued. It means that the valuer must assume there are at least two hypothetical people who are prepared to enter into the hypothetical lease. The valuer must assume they are 'willing', ie neither of them is being forced to enter the arrangement or is affected by difficulties which might affect their position in open market negotiations. This wording prevents a tenant arguing, for example, that the letting market is completely dead and therefore the open market value of the premises is zero.

19.5.2 The parties are to assume that the premises are available to let 'as a whole or in parts (whichever shall produce the higher rental)'

The valuer is directed by this assumption to calculate two different rental figures. The first is the rental value if the premises are let as a whole. The second directs the valuer to calculate the cumulative rental value if the premises were to be let off in parts. It may be, for example, that small areas of space are in greater demand than larger areas, thus making smaller units (on a square foot by square foot basis) more expensive. The cumulative rental figure could, therefore, result in a higher open market valuation. Is this fair on the tenant, even though clearly to the tenant's disadvantage? In a rent review negotiation a tenant will usually accept this assumption only if the alienation provisions allow the tenant to sub-let in parts. The tenant could then, in theory, achieve any higher rental figure itself by sub-letting different parts of its demise (for example, on a floor by floor basis).

19.5.3 The parties are to assume that the premises are available to let 'with vacant possession'

If this assumption were not included, the valuer might have to take into account the fact that the tenant is still occupying the premises at the review date. The tenant could then argue that the rent a hypothetical bidder would be prepared to pay would be very low. After all, the hypothetical tenant would not be able to occupy the premises itself if the actual tenant was still in occupation. To avoid this argument, most rent review clauses of this type include an assumption that vacant possession is available for the hypothetical letting, ie it assumes that the actual tenant has moved out.

There are two issues to be aware of with such an assumption:

(a) sub-tenancies; and
(b) rent-free periods for fitting out.

19.5.3.1 Sub-tenancies

The assumption of vacant possession requires the valuer to ignore the effect on rent of any sub-tenancies in existence at the rent review date. The effect on the OMR of this will depend upon whether those sub-tenancies are high or low yielding. Lucrative sub-tenancies would undoubtedly increase the OMR if the valuer were to take them into account. The converse would be true of low yielding sub-tenancies. If either party wished to ensure that the effect on rent of sub-tenancies would be taken into account, the assumption of vacant possession would need to be amended to refer to vacant possession of only those parts of the premises not sub-let at the date of review.

19.5.3.2 Rent-free periods for fitting out

The assumption of vacant possession means that the tenant is deemed to have moved out of the premises and, as all vacating tenants would do, to have removed and taken its fixtures too. In respect of shop premises, this might mean that all of the shop fittings must be assumed to have been removed, leaving nothing but a shell behind. (Of course in reality the premises are still fully fitted out, but for hypothetical valuation purposes the tenant's fixtures are assumed to have gone.)

The tenant can argue that a hypothetical tenant bidding in the open market for these premises might demand a rent-free period in order to fit out the premises. The idea is that the rent-free period will compensate the hypothetical tenant for the cost of fitting out and the lost trade during the fit-out period. Such rent-free periods for fitting out often last between three and six months, depending on the extent of the fit-out needed.

If a rent-free period is granted at the start of the lease, it simply means the tenant will not start paying rent until the rent-free period has expired. When considering rent-free periods in the context of rent review, however, the situation is not as straightforward, as the valuer will be directed to determine an annual rental figure and will not be able to award a rent-free period.

If the valuer thinks a hypothetical tenant would have obtained a rent-free period in the market place, the valuer will need to 'spread' that rent-free period over the review period. This will reduce the amount of rent payable per annum. For example, imagine the valuer finds that the rent for the next five years should be £100,000 per annum, but that an incoming tenant would obtain a rent-free period of six months in order to fit out the premises. This is a saving to the tenant of £50,000, which the valuer will spread over the five-year review period. This would mean a £10,000 reduction per annum, ie an OMR of £90,000 rather than the £100,000 that would have been the OMR in the absence of the vacant possession assumption.

This result may not seem particularly fair on the landlord. After all, the premises will in reality be fitted out, and the actual tenant who will be paying this reviewed rent may well have had a rent-free period at the commencement of the term in order to carry out the fitting-out works. Why should the tenant in effect get another rent-free period at review (in the form of discounted rent) to compensate it for a notional fit out it does not actually need to do?

There are ways round this for the landlord when drafting the lease. It could include an assumption that the premises are fitted out (see **19.5.9**). Alternatively (or in addition), it could include an assumption that there is to be no discount or deduction made to the annual rent to represent a rent-free period for fit-out works that the hypothetical tenant would have been given (see **19.5.8**).

19.5.4 The parties are to assume that the premises are available to let 'without a fine or a premium'

This assumption is directing the valuer to assume that no capital sum is passing between the parties on the grant of the hypothetical lease. In reality, it is not uncommon for a capital sum to be given by one party to the other on the grant of the lease.

19.5.4.1 The reverse premium

A reverse premium is paid by the landlord to the tenant. The reasons for such a payment vary. It might be to induce a particularly attractive tenant to take the lease. However, it might also be that the rental level set by the landlord is higher than the market can actually support, and so to make the lease more appealing the landlord offers to pay the tenant a capital sum up front. Without such capital sum, the tenant may not be prepared to pay rent as high as the landlord wants. The landlord may prefer to keep the rent high (as it could be used as a comparable for similar units) and pay the inducement (or reverse premium).

19.5.4.2 Premiums

Sometimes, the tenant may pay a premium to the landlord for the lease in addition to an annual rent. This may be because the premises are particularly attractive to the tenant (for example, in a prime location). Or it may be because the landlord prefers to receive a capital sum up front, in return for which it will offer a lower annual rent.

19.5.4.3 The effect of premiums on rent

It can be seen from the illustrations above that the payment of a premium can distort the amount of annual rent that is paid by the tenant – increasing it where the tenant receives consideration and decreasing it where the landlord receives consideration.

To avoid such distortions on review, it is common for the rent review to assume that no 'fine or premium' (ie capital sum) is being paid for the hypothetical letting.

19.5.5 The parties are to assume that the premises are available to let 'for a term equal to the contractual term commencing on the relevant review date'

It is usual for the rent review clause to specify the length of the hypothetical lease. Often this will be the same as the original contractual term. So, in a 15-year lease with a five-year review pattern, the term of the hypothetical lease at the five-year review is 15 years, despite the fact that the actual lease has only 10 years left to run. On first glance this may appear to the disadvantage of the tenant, as it is tempting to assume that a longer hypothetical term will result in a higher OMR. This is not necessarily the case, however. In certain markets a tenant may prefer a shorter term, as it may not wish to commit itself to the premises for a long period of time. So sometimes a short-term lease can be worth more in rental terms than a longer-term lease.

Of course, at the time the lease is being negotiated it is very difficult to work out whether a shorter- or longer-term lease will command a higher rent. Whilst the advice of a rent review surveyor may be sought, this advice can only ever be speculative. For this reason the parties may agree the length of the hypothetical lease term should equal the unexpired residue of the actual lease at the date of the review. So, in our example, at the first review a 10-year term is assumed and at the second review a five-year term is assumed. This at least reflects reality.

19.5.6 The parties are to assume that the premises are available to let 'for any use falling within Class [E] of the Town and Country Planning (Use Classes) Order 1987'

It is not uncommon to find that the valuer will be directed to assume a specified hypothetical use for the premises. This is often wider than the actual permitted use within the lease, meaning in effect the valuer is ignoring the restrictions on use within the actual lease. So the landlord is 'having its cake and eating it'. On the one hand, it is able to restrict the way the tenant can actually use the premises (eg by requiring the tenant to covenant not to use the premises for anything other than offices). On the other hand, it is not penalised at review for imposing such restrictions (eg because the valuer must assume the premises can be used for any use within Class E). Such an extended hypothetical use should be strongly resisted by the tenant, since it would find itself paying on review for a freedom it did not in fact enjoy. A compromise would be to widen the user covenant within the actual lease to match the use specified in the assumption.

19.5.7 The parties are to assume that the premises are to be let 'otherwise on the terms of this lease other than as to the amount of the annual rent but including the provisions for review of the annual rent, and other than the provision in this lease for a rent-free period'

The valuer is directed to assume the hypothetical lease will be on the same terms as the actual lease, except for:

(a) any variations stipulated elsewhere in the rent review provisions. This would cover, for example, a hypothetical term that differed from the actual contractual term in the lease (see **19.5.5**);

(b) the amount of the annual rent specified in the lease. As the aim of the review exercise is to vary the amount of rent, it is clear that the rent initially reserved by the lease must not be incorporated into the hypothetical letting. But what about the rent review provisions? In the specimen wording above the valuer is directed to assume that the hypothetical lease will contain provisions for review of the annual rent. This is very important for the tenant, as most practitioners take the view that a lease without rent review provisions would be more attractive to a tenant and therefore command a higher rent. This is because the tenant would have certainty at the outset of the lease that its rent would remain the same for the duration of the term, protecting it against uplifts in rent in a rising market. So a hypothetical lease with no rent review provisions would command a higher rent than one with rent review provisions (unless the hypothetical term were less than five years, when no rent review provisions would be expected). An example of the dramatic impact this may have can be found in *National Westminster Bank plc v Arthur Young McClelland Moores & Co* [1985] 1 WLR 1123. In this case the provisions of a rent review clause were interpreted in such a way as to exclude from the hypothetical letting the rent review provisions. This alone led to the annual rent being increased from £800,000 to £1.209 million, instead of £1.003 million if the rent review clause had been incorporated. Courts today tend to shy away from interpreting a rent review clause in such a way as to exclude a provision for review from the hypothetical letting. In the absence of clear words directing the rent review clause to be disregarded, the court will give effect to the underlying purpose of the clause and will assume that the hypothetical letting contains provisions for the review of rent. However, the tenant must always check carefully that the review clause is not expressly excluded from the hypothetical letting, since the court would be bound to give effect to such clear words;

(c) any rent-free period granted in the actual lease. The tenant may have been granted a rent-free period at the outset of the lease to allow it to fit out the premises or as an inducement to enter the lease. The landlord, if it has granted such a rent-free period at the outset of the lease, will not want the hypothetical lease to have such a rent-free period. After all, the tenant will have already had the benefit of the actual rent-free period at the outset of the lease. The landlord will be concerned that the valuer will 'spread' the amount of the hypothetical rent-free period over the remaining rental period and thereby effectively discount the annual rent at review. Whilst a tenant will not normally object to the valuer ignoring any rent-free period actually granted at the outset of the lease, it will need to think more carefully about provisions that seek to ignore rent-free concessions that are being granted in the market place at the time of the rent review. The tenant must avoid ending up with a headline rent (see **19.5.8**).

19.5.8 **The parties are to assume 'the willing lessee has had the benefit of any rent-free or other concession or contribution which would be offered in the open market at the relevant review date in relation to fitting out works at the premises'**

This assumption assumes the hypothetical tenant has already had a rent-free period for fitting out purposes and will not therefore need a further rent-free concession in the form of discounted rent. It is included to counteract problems associated with an assumption that the property is available to let with vacant possession (see **19.5.3.2**). It is generally acceptable to a tenant who in reality will not need to fit out at review and who may well have had a rent-free period at the commencement of the lease.

However, the tenant must be careful with this type of assumption to ensure it is limited to rent-free periods for fitting-out purposes. Rent-free periods for fitting-out purposes are typically for a period of between three and six months. However, in practice it is not uncommon to find rent-free periods in excess of six months. These are granted by a landlord to induce the tenant to take the lease at a rental level it might otherwise not be prepared to pay. These rent-free concessions granted as inducements have a distorting effect on rent in much the same way as the payment of reverse premiums (see **19.5.4**). Take, for example, a premises with a rental of £200,000 per annum, where the tenant was granted a rent-free period of 12 months. The rental figure that will appear in the lease, and which the parties would quote if asked the annual rent, is £200,000 per annum (the 'headline rent'). However, if you take into account the 12-month rent-free period, in reality the tenant will be paying only £800,000 over a five-year period, equating to an 'effective' annual rent of £160,000.

At rent review the tenant will wish to ensure that the valuer, when looking at comparables, is not looking at 'headline' rental figures which are artificially inflated. It should therefore ensure that the lease does not assume that the willing or hypothetical tenant has received the benefit of a rent-free period (other than in respect of fitting out) which it may be the practice to give incoming tenants at the time of the review. Similar wording or provisions aiming to achieve a headline rent should be avoided. An example of such wording can be found in *Broadgate Square plc v Lehman Brothers Ltd* [1995] 1 EGLR 97, where the OMR was defined as 'the best yearly rent which would reasonably be expected to become payable after the expiry of a rent free period of such length as would be negotiated in the open market between a willing landlord and a willing tenant upon a letting of the premises'. This case was one of a number of 'headline rent' cases, suggesting that while the courts will lean against a headline rent construction, they will not be able to do so in the face of clear, unambiguous language. In the *Broadgate* case itself, the Court of Appeal determined that the OMR in the lease should be the rent payable once any rent-free period had expired (ie a headline rent). This resulted in a total rent in excess of £12 million for Nos 1 & 2 Broadgate. If the rent for the two premises had been discounted to reflect inducement rent-free periods, it would have totalled less than £9.3 million.

19.5.9 The parties are to assume that the premises 'may lawfully be used, and are fitted out and equipped so that they are ready to be used, by the willing lessee (or any potential undertenant or assignee of the willing lessee) for any purpose permitted by this lease'

This assumption is intended to ensure that no discount is made by the valuer from the annual rent to reflect the fact that an incoming tenant would ordinarily expect a rent-free period in order to carry out its fit-out works. If it is assumed the premises are fitted out then no such rent-free period is necessary.

The tenant will be concerned that an assumption that the premises are 'fitted out and equipped' may result in a rentalisation of any fitting-out works actually carried out while it has been occupying the premises. A hypothetical tenant would certainly pay more for premises that had already been fitted out and did not require further work by the tenant. Whilst a disregard of tenant's improvements might seem to deal with the tenant's concern, it is not entirely clear how this would sit with a 'fitted out' assumption. Words such as 'fitted out and equipped' should therefore be avoided by the tenant. The landlord's concerns about rent-free periods can be dealt with by including an assumption along the lines set out at **19.5.8**.

19.5.10 The parties are to assume 'the [landlord and the] tenant [have/has] fully complied with [its/their] obligations in the lease'

This is really two separate assumptions combined in one sub-clause.

19.5.10.1 Tenant's compliance

Without such an assumption, a tenant in breach of, for example, its repairing obligations could argue that the OMR of the premises should be reduced because the premises are in disrepair. After all, no hypothetical tenant will pay as much for premises in a poor state of repair as for those in full repair. This would clearly be unfair, as the tenant would be benefiting from its own wrongdoing. Most leases therefore contain this assumption; and in its absence, the courts have shown a willingness to imply it in any event (see *Family Management v Grey* (1979) 253 EG 369).

19.5.10.2 Landlord's compliance

Some leases also contain an assumption that the landlord has complied with its covenants. If the landlord were to be in breach of its obligations at the rent review date then, like a breach of the tenant's obligations, this would generally have a depressing effect on the OMR. If, for example, the landlord has failed to insure the building, a hypothetical tenant would consider the letting less attractive and be prepared to pay less rent for it. Tenants often resist this assumption. They argue that if the landlord is in breach of its covenants, it should suffer the consequences of such failure on review. The prospect of a negative impact on the rent review might well encourage the landlord to comply with its obligations. The landlord could point out that if it is in breach of its covenants, the tenant will be able to pursue other remedies for such breaches. It might consider the tenant sufficiently protected by these remedies without the need for the landlord to be penalised at review for a breach. The breach may be very minor or temporary, and it would be unfair to penalise this with a rent reduction that lasted until the next review. The extent to which this point is worth arguing between landlord and tenant really depends upon the extent of the landlord's covenants. The parties may consider compromising by accepting an assumption that the landlord's covenants have been complied with (other than in respect of material breaches).

19.5.11 The parties are to assume that 'if the premises, or any means of access to it or any service media serving the premises, has been destroyed or damaged, it has been fully restored'

The landlord needs this assumption to protect itself against a reduction in OMR arising through insured damage. If, for example, a fire causes serious damage to the premises shortly before the review date, it may well be impractical for the landlord to complete reinstatement by the review date. In the absence of this assumption, the valuer would therefore be valuing a fire-damaged building. This might result in the tenant paying a lower rent than would have otherwise been the case. Would this be a fair result? The tenant does, of course, have to suffer the consequences of damaged premises. However, this should only be temporary if the landlord is under an obligation to reinstate. Further, most leases contain a clause suspending the payment of rent during any period which the premises cannot be occupied as a result of insured damage. So, provided the rent suspension provisions are adequate, the tenant should not be prejudiced by accepting this assumption, although it might be advised to ensure it refers only to destruction or damage by insured risks.

19.5.12 The parties are to assume that 'no work has been carried out on the premises or any other part of the building that has diminished the rental value of the premises'

As a general premise, it seems fair that if the tenant has carried out works that have diminished the letting value of the premises then those works should be ignored at review. For example, if the tenant requires business-specific building works that another tenant would find unappealing, why should a landlord's rental income be prejudiced by the carrying out of those works? What, however, if the tenant is forced by statute to carry out those works? Perhaps disability discrimination legislation or fire regulations require the tenant to carry out works that reduce the lettable space, or render the premises less aesthetically pleasing. A tenant will often suggest that work it is required by statute to carry out, as opposed to work it has carried out voluntarily, should not be ignored if it has reduced the OMR of the premises.

19.5.13 The parties are to assume 'the willing lessee and its potential assignees and undertenants shall not be disadvantaged by any actual or potential election to waive exemption from VAT in relation to the premises'

If the landlord has opted to tax in respect of VAT then VAT will be payable on the annual rent under the lease. Most leases will require such VAT to be paid by the tenant. Provided the tenant itself makes taxable supplies, it will be able to recover the VAT it pays on the rent by offsetting it against the VAT it charges on its taxable supplies. If the tenant makes only exempt supplies, however, it will not be able to recover the VAT it pays on rent, which will be an additional cost to it. Tenants who make exempt supplies and are therefore unable to recover VAT include banks, building societies and insurers. These types of tenants pay 20% more rent, in real terms, than other tenants, due to their inability to recover VAT. This gives rise to the question whether such tenants, when considering renting premises, would pay less than other types of tenant to reflect the additional VAT expense that they incur. If this might be the case, should a valuer, when assessing a hypothetical letting, take into account such potential discounted bids in determining the OMR? If a premises particularly lent itself to occupation by exempt suppliers, this might result in the valuer determining a lower OMR than for premises where this was not the case. To guard against this, the landlord will often insert an assumption that the tenant will not suffer if the landlord opts to tax. It is sometimes phrased that it will be assumed that the tenant can recover any VAT charged on rents. The result is the same. Any inability to recover VAT by the actual or hypothetical tenants is ignored. The tenant should try to delete such a provision on the basis that the valuer should be directed to look at the reality of the situation, and if there would be exempt suppliers in the hypothetical market, the discounted bids that such tenants might make should be used as comparable evidence. To date, however, there has been no evidence of a 'two-tier' market (of exempt and non-exempt suppliers) with differing bid levels.

19.6 THE DISREGARDS

As with the assumptions discussed in **19.5** above, it is not possible to set out an exhaustive list of the disregards that may appear in a lease, and the advice of a rent review surveyor should always be sought before agreeing any particular form of wording. The following are examples of typical disregards that occur in leases of commercial premises.

19.6.1 The parties are to disregard 'any effect on rent of the fact that the tenant or any authorised under-tenant has been in occupation of the premises'

It is standard to disregard any effect on rent of the tenant's occupation. If this were not done, the landlord could argue at review that the actual tenant would bid more for the premises than other hypothetical tenants to save the trouble and expense of securing new premises. The tenant should ensure that the disregard extends to sub-tenants and any other type of occupier that may be permitted by the lease terms.

19.6.2 The parties are to disregard 'any goodwill attached to the premises by reason of any business carried out there by the tenant or by any authorised under-tenant or by any of their predecessors in business'

Goodwill generated by a business in the form of a regular flow of customers is a valuable asset. It therefore follows that a tenant will pay more for premises with established goodwill attached to the business than for one without. Since the goodwill will have been generated by the tenant, it seems unfair that the landlord should benefit from it at review. The tenant should ensure that the lease contains a disregard of goodwill generated by the tenant or any under-tenant (or their predecessors). While case law suggests that a valuer will imply such a disregard where occupation is disregarded (*Prudential Assurance Co Ltd v Grand Metropolitan Estate Ltd* [1993] 32 EG 74), it is good practice to do it expressly.

19.6.3 The parties are to disregard 'any effect on rent attributable to any physical improvement to the premises carried out after the date of this lease, by or at the expense of the tenant or any authorised under-tenant with all necessary consents, approvals and authorisations and not pursuant to an obligation to the landlord'

If the tenant carries out works to the premises that improve them, the premises are likely to be more valuable in the letting market. If the lease does not disregard the improvements, the valuer will take them into account when assessing the OMR. In consequence the tenant will end up paying for them twice: first, it will bear the cost of the works when they are carried out; secondly, it may end up paying more rent at review to reflect the increased letting value of the premises in consequence of the improvements. This would clearly be unfair on the tenant, and so it must ensure improvements are disregarded.

While most landlords have no objections to this in principle, differences in opinion can arise over exactly what improvements are to be disregarded. The following should be considered:

(a) *Works not carried out by the current tenant.* The tenant should ensure that improvements made by its predecessors in title or by any under-tenant are also disregarded.

(b) *Works carried out before the lease commenced.* The tenant must consider whether any works were carried out before the lease commenced. It is not uncommon for tenants to be granted access to the premises under the terms of an agreement for lease to carry out fitting-out works. If the lease disregards only works carried out after commencement of the lease (as in the specimen disregard above), such works would be rentalised at review.

(c) *Works carried out without consent.* Most disregards of improvements only ignore works carried out with 'all necessary consents, approvals and authorisations'. If this is the case, works the tenant carries out without the landlord's consent (if required under the lease) or without any other approvals that are required (such as planning permission) may be rentalised. The tenant should be mindful of the fact that many leases require the landlord's consent to be given by way of formal deed and that a less formal consent given by the landlord to the works in question may lead to arguments over whether those works fall within the scope of the disregard. The tenant's solicitor should seek to ensure that improvements are disregarded, regardless of whether all necessary consents were obtained in relation to them. This can be justified on the basis that the landlord will have other remedies available to it under the lease, if the tenant has carried out unauthorised works.

(d) *Works the tenant was obliged to carry out.* A disregard of improvements will often be drafted so as to exclude from its remit improvements that the tenant is obliged to carry out. The specimen disregard above does exactly this. This is to ensure the tenant cannot seek to disregard repair works. However, it may also catch other works the tenant carries out to comply with statute, such as works carried out to comply with disability discrimination legislation. This is because the lease will normally contain a tenant's covenant to comply with statute, and therefore the tenant has a contractual obligation to the landlord to undertake works required by statute. The tenant should be advised of this position, and if this is unacceptable the solicitor should seek an amendment to ensure that the disregard of improvements does cover works required by statute. A landlord faced with such an amendment may require the insertion of an additional assumption that the premises do comply with statutory requirements (to avoid the hypothetical premises being valued as if they are not compliant with statute).

It is also wise to check any agreements for lease or licences for alterations to ensure that permissions to carry our works are not phrased as obligations to the landlord to undertake those works. If they are, the danger is the works will be excluded from the remit of the disregard. However, the courts have indicated that in order to exclude works carried out under a licence for alteration from a disregard of improvements, they would expect very clear words to that effect in the licence itself. (See the judgment of Dillon LJ in *Historic Hotels Ltd v Cadogan Estates* [1995] 1 EGLR 117.)

19.6.4 The parties are to disregard 'any statutory restriction on rents or the right to recover them'

The above disregard requires the valuer to ignore any legislation that may be introduced by the Government restricting rent levels. Such restrictions may be introduced in times of high inflation as a counter-inflationary measure, although they have not been used since the early 1970s. The landlord is concerned that the valuer would be obliged to set a reduced OMR if such legislation were in force. This would then last until the next rent review, even though the legislation might be repealed at an earlier point. The tenant, of course, will not wish to pay a rental level higher than that of competitors whose rent levels are restricted by legislation, and it should seek to delete such a disregard. A compromise may be to agree to delay any rent review until such time as any statutory restrictions are removed. Nevertheless, the tenant will need to be aware of the risk that at the end of any such restrictions, rents could rise rapidly.

19.7 THE MECHANISM FOR DETERMINING THE RENT

The following issues should be considered:

19.7.1 Is time of the essence?

Nearly all modern leases provide that the revised rent may be agreed in writing at any time between the parties. However, some older leases provide for the rent review process to be instigated by the service of a notice setting out the landlord's proposals for the revised rent. Such initial notices are often referred to as 'trigger notices'. The amount set out in the initial notice can be as exorbitant as the landlord wishes. The lease will then provide for the tenant to serve a counter-notice within a specified time period, setting out its proposals. The existence of time periods for the serving of this counter-notice raises the question of whether time is of the essence. The parties should ensure that the lease expressly states the position. In the absence of any 'contrary indications', there is a presumption that time is not of the essence (*United Scientific Holdings Ltd v Burnley Borough Council* [1977] 2 All ER 62). However, contrary indications have been found in a number of cases (*First Property Growth Partnership v Royal & Sun Alliance Services Ltd* [2002] EWHC 305 (Ch), [2002] 22 EG 140; *Starmark Enterprises Ltd v CPL Distribution Ltd* [2001] 32 EG 89 (CS); *Central Estates Ltd v Secretary of State for the Environment* [1997] 1 EGLR 239). Care must therefore be taken if the lease is silent on the issue.

If time is of the essence, a failure to respond to the landlord's trigger notice within the time periods stipulated in the lease could mean the tenant is fixed with the rent proposed by the landlord in the trigger notice, no matter how outrageous the level. In consequence, such trigger notice provisions should be avoided, and the tenant should look for provisions that stipulate that the revised rent will be such amount as the landlord and tenant shall agree between them.

19.7.2 Appointment of a valuer

The lease must provide a mechanism by which the parties can settle the review if they are unable to reach agreement through negotiation. Most leases provide for appointment of an independent valuer to determine the rent in the absence of agreement. The tenant should ensure that such a valuer has to be agreed upon by both parties (not just appointed by the landlord). The lease should also contain a mechanism for appointing such a valuer in the absence of agreement. Most leases provide that if the parties are unable to agree upon the appointment, it shall be made by the President of the Royal Institute of Chartered Surveyors following an application by either party.

19.7.3 Capacity of the valuer

The lease should stipulate the capacity in which the valuer is to act. Are they to act as an arbitrator, or as an expert? There are considerable differences between the two.

(a) An arbitrator seeks to resolve a dispute by a quasi-judicial process, whereas an expert imposes their own expert valuation on the parties.

(b) The arbitrator is bound by the procedure under the Arbitration Act 1996, which deals with hearings, submission of evidence and the calling of witnesses. An expert is not subject to such external controls and is not bound to hear the evidence of the parties. Whilst an arbitrator decides on the basis of the evidence put before them, an expert simply uses their own skill and judgement.

(c) There is a limited right of appeal to the High Court on a point of law against an arbitrator's award, whereas an expert's decision is final and binding unless it appears that they failed to perform the task required of them.

(d) An arbitrator is immune from suit in negligence, whereas an expert is not. Using an expert tends to be quicker and cheaper and is, therefore, often provided for in lettings of conventional properties at modest rents. Where there is something unorthodox about the premises, which might make it difficult to value, or where there is a good deal of money at stake in the outcome of the review, an arbitrator is to be preferred so that a fully-argued case can be put.

The tenant should resist any provision allowing the landlord to determine the capacity of the valuer at the time of their appointment, as this may lead to a more expensive arbitration that the tenant does not consider necessary. There is usually no reason why the capacity of the valuer can not be agreed upon when the lease is being negotiated.

19.7.4 The costs of the valuer's determination

If the valuer is to act an expert, it is usual for the lease to stipulate who will pay their costs. The tenant should avoid provisions that pass the entire cost to the tenant. It should look for the costs to be shared equally.

If the valuer is to act as an arbitrator, it will be for the valuer to determine who pays their costs and expenses.

19.8 THE LATE REVIEW

The lease will contain rent review dates from which any revised rent will be payable. The lease will need to specify what is to happen if the revised rent has not been determined by the review date, as this is a common situation.

Most leases will provide that the tenant should continue to pay rent at the current level until the rent review is complete. Once the outcome of the review is known, unless the rent has remained the same, balancing payments will need to be paid. As most leases contain upward only rent review provisions (see **19.2.4.1**), this will usually involve the tenant in making up the shortfall, being the amount by which the previous rent differs from the reviewed rent for the period from the rent review date until the date of determination. Most leases provide for interest to be paid by the tenant on the shortfall. This is to compensate the landlord for the late arrival of the increase. The tenant should look out for the following:

(a) The tenant should ensure the rate of interest is not penal, as there is no reason to assume it will be the tenant's fault that the rent review has not been concluded by the rent review date.

(b) The tenant should avoid provisions that require it to pay interest on the whole of the shortfall from the rent review date. Interest should be payable only from the date each instalment of the rent fell due to be paid (which in most leases will be the usual quarter days).

(c) If the lease has an upward/downward rent review (see **19.2.4.2**), similar provisions for making balancing payments of any overpayment together with interest should apply to the landlord.

19.9 RECORDING THE REVIEW

Most leases provide that once the rent has been determined, the landlord will prepare a memorandum recording the agreement reached for signature by both parties. This memorandum is then kept with the lease. The tenant should ensure that each party bears its own costs in the preparation and completion of this memorandum.

REVIEW ACTIVITY

1. Imagine you have received a draft lease in the form set out at **Appendix 4**. The proposed Contractual Term is 15 years and the rent will be reviewed in the fifth and tenth years. The hypothetical lease term inserted into the square brackets at Sch 5, Pt 4, para 1.2 is 15 years. How will you advise a prospective tenant client on this?

2. Assume you are acting for a tenant and receive a draft lease containing the following clause:

    The amount of Annual Rent shall be reviewed on each Review Date to equal:

(a) the Annual Rent payable immediately before the relevant Review Date (or which would then be payable but for any abatement or suspension of the Annual Rent or restriction on the right to collect it); or, if greater;

(b) the open market rent agreed or determined pursuant to this clause.

Would this clause be compliant with the 2020 Code?

Answers to this Review activity may be found in Appendix 1.

CHAPTER 20

Repair

20.1	Introduction	243
20.2	Tenant's covenant to repair	244
20.3	Definition of the subject matter of the covenant	244
20.4	Extent of liability	245
20.5	Tenant's concerns and amendments	248
20.6	Enforcement of covenant by landlord	250
20.7	Covenant to yield up in repair	250
20.8	Decorating	250
20.9	Landlord's covenant to repair	251
	Review activity	251

20.1 INTRODUCTION

The commercial landlord's objective, on anything more than a short-term letting, will be to obtain a 'clear rent' (ie the landlord takes the entire income without any cost to itself) by imposing a 'full repairing' lease, so that the tenant ends up paying the cost of any repairs, regardless of who carries them out. How the landlord achieves this depends on the nature of the premises being let:

(a) *Whole of a building*

Examples of this include a warehouse or an entire office block. In this situation, the landlord will usually impose a full repairing covenant on the tenant for the entire building.

(b) *Part of a multi-occupied building*

Examples of this include one unit in a shopping mall or one floor in an office block. In this situation, the landlord will usually make the tenant responsible for internal non-structural repairs of its part of the building, whilst itself taking responsibility for the remainder of the building (the exterior, structure and common parts, eg the circulation areas of a shopping mall). The landlord will recover the costs of complying with its obligation from the various tenants of the building, usually through the service charge provisions. The particular issues associated with a lease of part of a building, including repair and service charges, are dealt with in **Chapter 27**.

In the absence of a comprehensive code of implied obligations (the nature of which is not dealt with in this book), it is imperative that the responsibility for repairs is dealt with expressly in the lease. However, even though most leases do contain express terms, there is a glut of illustrative cases on disputes over the extent of liability for repair arising out of the:

(a) meaning of 'repair';
(b) scope of the repair covenant;
(c) standard of repair required.

Please note that each of the cases turns on its own specific facts, lease clauses, premises and works of repair, and many are in the non-commercial property sector; so although guidance can be taken from them, in practice the circumstances of each particular case are crucial.

To explore the disputed areas listed above and other issues on repair, we are going to use a simplified version of clause 18 (the example clause) of the lease reproduced in **Appendix 4** ('the **Appendix 4** lease'), which is set out at **20.2** for convenience.

20.2 TENANT'S COVENANT TO REPAIR

18. Repair

18.1 The Tenant must:

(a) [subject to clause 18.2 and 18.3] keep the Property in good [and substantial] repair and condition;

(b) keep the Property clean, tidy and clear of rubbish; ...

18.2 [The Tenant's obligations under clause 18.1(a) shall not require the Tenant to put the Property into any better state of repair or condition than it was in at the date of this lease as evidenced by the Schedule of Condition [defined as 'the photographic schedule annexed to this lease at Annex [ ] and marked "Schedule of Condition"']].

18.3 The Tenant shall not be liable to repair the Property (excluding any Excluded Insurance Items forming part of the Property) [defined as glass forming part of lettable units and tenant's and other's fixtures that have become part of the Building] to the extent that any disrepair has been caused by:

(a) an Insured Risk, unless and to the extent that:

(i) the policy of insurance of the Property has been vitiated or any insurance proceeds withheld in consequence of any act or omission of the Tenant or any Authorised Person [defined as (a) undertenant or person deriving title under the Tenant; (b) workers, contractors or agents of the Tenant, undertenant or person deriving title from those in (a); or person at the Property or the Building with the actual or implied authority of the Tenant or those referred to in (a) or (b)] (except where the Tenant has paid an amount equal to any insurance money that the insurers refuse to pay in accordance with paragraph [ ] of Schedule [ ] [contains an obligation on the Tenant to pay the Landlord those monies]; or

(ii) the insurance cover in relation to that disrepair is limited as referred to in paragraph [ ] of Schedule [ ] [limitations, excesses and conditions that may be imposed by the insurers].

20.3 DEFINITION OF THE SUBJECT MATTER OF THE COVENANT

As you can note from the example clause in **20.2**, the tenant's covenant will apply to the subject matter of the lease, and so a clear definition of the subject matter will be required. In the example clause, the defined term is 'Property', but other terms are commonly used, such as 'premises' or, often in older leases, 'the demised premises' or 'the demise'.

Without a clear definition, the obvious risk (particularly on a lease of part of a building where the responsibility for repairs is to be divided between the parties) is that there may be a dispute as to who is responsible for repairing each part of the building. See **27.2**, where the definition of the subject matter of a lease of part is dealt with in more detail.

An issue that could arise in the context of defining the subject matter, particularly on a lease of a whole building, is the question of responsibility for site contamination. If the site on which the building stands is subsequently discovered to be contaminated, could the tenant be required to remove the contamination under a repairing covenant? There may be a problem for a landlord in persuading the court that a repairing covenant can be extended to the soil as well as the buildings. In the absence of judicial guidance, the matter should be dealt with expressly in the lease. The landlord could expressly include the remediation of site contamination in the tenant's repairing covenant. Where appropriate, given the nature of the premises, the tenant could exclude any possible liability by expressly excluding the sub-soil from the definition of the subject matter, and excluding remediation of contaminated land from the usual tenant's covenant in the lease to comply with all statutory obligations (for an example of a clause obliging the tenant to comply with statutory obligations see clause 31 of the **Appendix 4** lease), which, depending on the wording used, may be broad enough to extend to requirements under environmental law.

20.4 EXTENT OF LIABILITY

In examining the extent of the tenant's liability, a number of important matters arise.

20.4.1 Meaning of repair

20.4.1.1 Disrepair

Under an obligation to repair, the tenant will incur liability only if the landlord can show that the premises have 'deteriorated from some previous physical condition' (*Post Office v Aquarius Properties Ltd* [1987] 1 All ER 1055) so that they are in 'a condition worse than it was at some earlier time' (*Quick v Taff-Ely Borough Council* [1986] QB 809).

There needs to be damage to the subject matter of the covenant. In *Quick v Taff-Ely Borough Council*, a landlord covenanted to keep in repair the *structure and exterior* of a dwelling that became virtually unfit for human habitation due to condensation. However, damage was caused only to *furnishings and decoration* and not to the structure or exterior, and so the landlord was under no obligation to make good.

In *Post Office v Aquarius Properties Ltd*, the basement of a building regularly flooded due to a defect in the structure of the building that had existed since construction. Incredibly, no damage to the building (eg to the plaster on the walls, to the flooring or to electrical installations) had been caused by the flooding, and the defect itself had not worsened. As the landlord could not show damage, the tenant was not under any obligation to repair.

It is clear from other cases that if damage had been done to the building when the water entered, this would have constituted disrepair, and the tenant would have been liable for the repair (see comments on inherent defect liability at **20.4.1.3**).

20.4.1.2 To keep in repair means to put in repair

If the premises are in disrepair at the date of the lease, a covenant *to keep* in repair (as in the example clause) will require the tenant first to *put* the premises into repair (*Payne v Haine* (1847) 153 ER 1304) and then to *keep* them in repair (according to their age, character and locality) (*Proudfoot v Hart* (1890) 25 QBD 42).

The tenant may perceive this obligation to put premises into repair as onerous. See **20.5** for tenant's amendments in this respect.

20.4.1.3 Inherent defects

As with all kinds of disrepair (see **20.4.2** below), it will be a question of degree, having regard to the nature of the premises, whether what the tenant is being asked to do can properly be described as repair or, to the contrary, whether it would involve giving back to the landlord something wholly different from that which was demised (*Ravenseft Properties Ltd v Davstone (Holdings) Ltd* [1980] QB 12).

So, contrary to previous belief, a tenant can be required to repair *damage* caused by 'inherent defects' (ie defects in design or construction of the building) under a covenant to repair. Liability for damage caused by an inherent defect may require not only repair of the damage but also eradication of the defect itself, if this is the only realistic way of carrying out the repairs (*Ravenseft Properties Ltd v Davstone (Holdings) Ltd*).

If, however, the inherent defect has not caused any damage to the premises, they are not in disrepair and accordingly the tenant is not liable on its covenant (*Post Office v Aquarius Properties Ltd* [1987] 1 All ER 1055).

The possibility that they may have to put right defects in the building that have occurred through no fault of their own, and which pre-date their occupation, is deeply worrying for tenants. See **20.5** below for tenant's amendments (and **10.5.2.4** for further comment on inherent defects).

20.4.2 Scope of repair

In the example clause, the tenant is under an obligation to 'repair'. Do the works the tenant is being asked to carry out fall within that obligation, or are they more properly classified as works of renewal or improvement, for which the tenant is not responsible under a covenant to repair?

20.4.2.1 Factors to consider

Several factors to consider have evolved from the many authorities that can help in deciding the question of whether the works fall within the scope of a covenant to repair. Three particular factors are set out below, which can be approached separately or concurrently as the circumstances of the case may demand, but all are to be 'approached in the light of the nature and age of the premises, their condition when the tenant went into occupation, and the other express terms of the tenancy' (*McDougall v Easington DC* (1989) 58 P & CR 201, CA).

Whether the works go to the whole or substantially the whole of the structure, or only to a subsidiary part?

It was said in *Lurcott v Wakeley & Wheeler* [1911] 1 KB 905 that:

> Repair is restoration by renewal or replacement of subsidiary parts of the whole. Renewal, as distinguished from repair, is the reconstruction of the entirety, meaning by the entirety not necessarily the whole but substantially the whole ...

It will be a question of degree in each case whether the work to be done can properly be described as repair, involving no more than renewal or replacement of defective parts, or whether it amounts to renewal or replacement of substantially the whole. In *Lurcott v Wakeley*, the rebuilding of a defective wall of a building was held to be within the tenant's covenant to repair because it was the replacement of a defective part rather than the replacement of the whole. However, the tenant may be required to replace part after part until the whole is replaced.

Whether the effect of the works is to produce a building of a wholly different character from that which had been let?

This is commonly thought to be the overriding factor, in that the tenant cannot be required to give back something wholly different from that which it took.

In *Lister v Lane & Nesham* [1893] 2 QB 212, where the tenant was held not to be liable for the cost of rebuilding an old house built on muddy soil, which had become unsafe due to poor foundations, Lord Esher MR said:

> A covenant to repair ... is not a covenant to give a different thing from that which the tenant took when he entered into the covenant. He has to repair that thing which he took; he is not obliged to make a new and different thing ...

As indicated previously in **20.4.1.3**, it will always be a question of degree whether what the tenant is asked to do will involve simply repair or giving back to the landlord a wholly different thing from what it took (*Ravenseft Properties Ltd v Davstone (Holdings) Ltd*).

What is the cost of the works in relation to the previous value of the building, and what is their effect on the value and lifespan of the building?

In deciding whether the tenant is being asked to give back to the landlord a wholly different thing from that demised, guidance may sometimes be found by considering the proportion the cost of the disputed work bears to the value or cost of the whole premises.

It must be stressed, however, that decided cases can do no more than lay down general guidelines, and each case will turn on its own facts.

20.4.2.2 Repair v improvement/renewal/replacement

In the same way that the tenant need not renew the entire premises under a covenant to repair, a covenant to repair does not impose any obligation on the tenant to improve them. A tenant may sometimes be concerned that its landlord is trying to get it to upgrade or improve the premises under the guise of carrying out repairs.

The distinction is not always easy to make, but Lord Denning said in *Morcom v Campbell-Johnson* [1955] 3 All ER 264 that

> if the work which is done is the provision of something new for the benefit of the occupier, that is, properly speaking, an improvement; but if it is only the replacement of something already there, which has become dilapidated or worn out, then, albeit that is a replacement by its modern equivalent, it comes within the category of repairs and not improvements.

Repair (as indicated at **20.4.2.1**) can include the renewal or replacement of subordinate parts.

20.4.3 Standard of repair

20.4.3.1 Generally

The standard of repair required is determined to be such as 'having regard to the age, character and locality ... would make it [the premises] reasonably fit for the occupation of a reasonably minded tenant of the class likely to take it' (*per* Lopes LJ in *Proudfoot v Hart* (1890) 25 QBD 42). The age, character and locality by which repair is judged is that which existed at the time the lease was granted, so even if the locality now attracted a superior or inferior class of tenant, the standard required from the tenant would be neither higher nor lower than at the date of the lease (*Anstruther-Gough-Calthorpe v McOscar and Another* [1924] 1 KB 716).

It follows that:

(a) the standard required would be different for a brand new purpose-built shopping centre than for your local parade of shops (*Proudfoot v Hart*, where the standards required for Spitalfields and Grosvenor Square in London were contrasted);

(b) the premises need not be kept in perfect repair (*Proudfoot v Hart*, where Esher LJ stated that the property need not be 'put into perfect repair. It need only be put into such a state of repair as renders it fit for the occupation of a reasonably minded tenant of the class likely to take it').

In *Commercial Union Life Assurance Co v Label Ink Ltd* [2001] L & TR 29, a case that involved a leaking roof, the tenant's covenant was to keep the premises in 'good and substantial repair and condition'. The judge in this case stated that 'good and substantial does not mean pristine or even perfect repair', and that 'substantial' fell short of a requirement for perfection. It was considered that the expert evidence about the works needed to comply with the covenant was based on 'a standard of perfection: what a pristine building should look like, not what was required by a covenant to keep, what had been a pristine building, in good and substantial repair'.

20.4.3.2 Clause wording

In drafting the repairing obligation, it is possible to restrict or widen its scope from that imposed by a covenant to repair.

Additional adjectives and verbs

In the example clause, the word 'repair' is qualified by the addition of the word 'good'. Other qualifying word(s) commonly seen in practice are 'sufficient', or 'good and substantial' or 'tenantable'.

It was uncertain whether additional qualifications would strengthen (or potentially limiting words such as 'tenantable' dilute) the tenant's repair obligation. Scrutton LJ, commenting in *Anstruther-Gough-Calthorpe v McOscar and Another* [1924] 1 KB 716, suggested that they would add nothing to the word 'repair', there being no 'substantial difference in construction between "repair", which must mean "repair reasonably and properly", and "keep in good repair" or "sufficient repair" or "tenantable repair"'; but Atkin LJ held a dissenting view, stating that 'effect should be given to every word used'.

The more recent case of *Credit Suisse v Beegas Nominees Ltd* [1994] 11 EG 151 determined that it was the court's duty to give a full and proper effect to each word used. In that case, 'to keep the property in repair and good condition' was held to go beyond what is normally associated with repair.

In any event, the same words could be used in two separate leases but be given a different meaning due to the age, character and condition of the premises in question. So, to avoid being under a less or more onerous obligation than that intended, the landlord and tenant should give careful consideration to each word used.

Good condition

In *Welsh v Greenwich London Borough Council* [2000] PLSCS 149 (which involved a short-term residential lease, so a court might take a different view in a commercial context), the Court of Appeal held that a reference to keeping the premises in 'good condition' in the repairing obligation was a significant addition and would extend the obligation to defects that had not caused any damage to the structure of the premises (on the facts, damage caused by condensation). See tenant's amendments at **20.5**.

In *Pullman Foods Ltd v Welsh Ministers and another* [2020] EWHC 2521 (TCC), the tenant had appointed consultants to remove buildings from the site which then disturbed asbestos-containing materials. The yield-up covenant required the tenant to deliver up the site 'in good and substantial repair and condition to the satisfaction of the [lessor]'. The court held that the use of the word 'condition' shows that the obligation was capable of extending to doing works which went beyond strict repair. The landlord did not have unlimited discretion in deciding the appropriate standard of 'good condition' or the remediation works. It could form its own judgement as to what was needed to satisfy the appropriate standard, provided its judgement was within the range of views that could be reasonably held. In that context, removing the asbestos was reasonably required for compliance with the covenant and the tenant was liable for damages for breach of covenant.

Renew or improve

The landlord can extend the liability of the tenant by the use of clear words that make the tenant liable to renew, or improve or even rebuild the demised premises (see, eg, *Credit Suisse v Beegas Nominees Ltd* [1994] 11 EG 151, where it was held that the verbs 'amend' and 'renew' were capable of going outside the verb 'repair').

However, a landlord should always bear in mind that imposing onerous provisions could mean that it is penalised on any rent review.

20.5 TENANT'S CONCERNS AND AMENDMENTS

A tenant's broad concerns are reflected in the 2020 Code for Leasing Business Premises. Under the 2020 Code, RICS members are mandatorily required to ensure that written heads of terms are prepared prior to circulation of the initial draft of the lease (see **14.2**). These mandatory heads of terms must summarise key provisions of the letting, including the identity of the premises and repairing obligations. The 2020 Code also contains recommendations as to best practice in relation to the key provisions of a lease, although these are not stated to be mandatory. However, there may be legal and/or disciplinary consequences for RICS members in departing from the 2020 Code, which may lead to a finding of negligence against a surveyor. In relation to repair the 2020 Code provides:

> **7 Repairs**
>
> 7.1 Leases should impose tenant's repairing obligations appropriate to the length of the term, the condition of the premises and the financial terms.
>
> 7.2 If the tenant's repairing obligations are to be limited to the initial condition of the premises, a schedule of condition will normally be required and the parties should agree which party is responsible for the cost of obtaining it.
>
> 7.3 Where the premises are or will be newly built, a tenant taking on direct or indirect responsibility for repairs should be given suitable protection against inherent construction defects for an appropriate period.

From what has been said above, the tenant may be concerned to reduce its liability, and there are a number of ways in which it may seek to do so:

(a) If the premises are in disrepair at the commencement of the lease, a tenant may seek to limit its obligation to put premises into repair by reference to a schedule of condition with appropriate photographic evidence, which should be prepared by a surveyor, agreed by the parties and annexed to the lease (see optional clause 18.2 in the example clause). This should also mean that the tenant never has to give anything back to the landlord that is better than that which was given to it. See paragraph 7.2 of the 2020 Code above.

Paragraph 8 of the Supplemental Guide at Appendix B of the 2020 Code describes some of the main factors the parties should consider when agreeing a schedule of condition, including that it should be prepared at as early a stage as possible to allow ample opportunity for the parties to agree it as being an accurate record.

(b) The tenant may be alarmed at the prospect of having to repair inherent defects. For that reason, tenants of new buildings will often seek to limit their liability by excluding from their obligation liability for defects caused by design or construction faults, at least for a specified period of time. From the tenant's point of view, the landlord should covenant to repair damage caused by these defects (see **10.5.2.4**). See paragraph 7.3 of the 2020 Code above.

Paragraph 8 of the Supplemental Guide at Appendix B of the 2020 Code suggests that, when a property is newly or recently refurbished, the tenant should be given some protection in respect of construction defects that emerge within a specified initial period. This would normally be the period in which such defects, if they exist, are most likely to become apparent. There are a number of different ways in which such protection may be given, depending on the circumstances, and the parties should obtain professional advice as to what may be appropriate in individual cases. This might include warranties or defects insurance.

(c) In most leases the landlord will insure the premises against a number of stated risks. The tenant should always insist that its repairing covenant does not render it liable to repair damage caused by a risk against which the landlord has or should have insured (see clause 18.3(a) of the example clause). The landlord should not object since it should be able to claim on the insurance policy. However, the landlord will insist that the tenant remains liable if the insurance is avoided because of an act or omission of the tenant or someone at the premises with the tenant's consent (see the example clause and **25.5.1**). The tenant may also want to address the position relating to damage caused by uninsured risks (see **25.8**).

(d) The tenant may seek to dilute the wording of the covenant by excluding the various words designed to strengthen the obligation (eg, 'good', 'substantial') or to extend the obligation (eg, 'rebuild', 'reconstruct', 'replace'), or by the rejection of any obligation to keep in good 'condition' as well as repair.

(e) Although this is rarely acceptable to commercial landlords, the tenant could also try to qualify the covenant by excluding 'fair wear and tear', so excluding the normal effects of time and weather and of normal and reasonable use of the premises.

20.6 ENFORCEMENT OF COVENANT BY LANDLORD

The tenant's covenant to repair is often followed by a covenant to permit the landlord to enter the premises, usually upon reasonable notice, to ascertain their state and condition (for an example of such a clause, see clause 60 of the **Appendix 4** lease). As you can see, that well-drafted clause further includes:

(a) a provision for the landlord to serve a notice of disrepair on the tenant if it is found to be in breach of its repairing obligation;

(b) a right for the landlord, if the tenant had not commenced the works within a specified time, to enter the premises to carry out the repairs, at the tenant's expense;

(c) the expenses incurred by the landlord acting under such a power being recoverable 'as a debt'. This is an attempt to avoid the restrictions imposed by the Landlord and Tenant Act 1927 (LTA 1927) and the Leasehold Property (Repairs) Act 1938 on the recovery of damages, as opposed to a debt, for disrepair (see **30.1.2.1**).

Note that if the landlord reserves the right to enter the premises to carry out repairs in default, it will, in certain circumstances, become liable under the Defective Premises Act 1972.

The landlord may be able to forfeit the lease for breach of the tenant's covenant to repair (for an example of a clause allowing this, see clause 52.1(b) of the **Appendix 4** lease). See **Chapter 26** for more detail on the right to forfeit.

The landlord may bring a claim for damages in respect of the tenant's breach of a repairing covenant, but this may be limited by the operation of the Leasehold Property (Repairs) Act 1938 (see **30.1.2.1**).

20.7 COVENANT TO YIELD UP IN REPAIR

The tenant will often enter into a covenant to yield up the premises in repair at the end of the term (for an example of such a clause, see clause 23 of the **Appendix 4** lease). The usual form of covenant requires the tenant to yield up in the repair required under the terms of the lease and to remove any alterations made if required by the landlord. A tenant should ensure that the requirement must be reasonably made and that it is given notice in advance of the requirement (see clause 23.2 of the **Appendix 4** lease).

20.8 DECORATING

Because some doubt exists as to the amount of decoration required by a covenant to repair, the matter is best dealt with expressly in the lease (see clause 19 of the **Appendix 4** lease).

The usual form of covenant requires the tenant to decorate the premises at specified intervals during the term, and during the last year of the term.

The obligation to decorate in the last year could require the tenant to decorate in two consecutive years depending on when the lease is terminated (eg, in a 10-year lease with a decorating obligation every three years). The tenant may therefore wish to provide that the obligation to decorate in the last year shall not apply if it has decorated in the previous, say, 18 months.

The landlord may also wish to retain some control by requiring the tenant to obtain consent (not to be unreasonably withheld) before any change in the colour scheme is made. Some covenants in older leases specify the materials to be used. Unfortunately, the materials specified are sometimes inappropriate to the type of building concerned and its method of construction, so more modern covenants simply require the tenant to carry out its obligation 'in a good and workmanlike manner with good quality materials'.

On the grant of a lease of part of a building, the exterior decoration would normally be undertaken by the landlord, which would recover its expenses under the service charge.

20.9 LANDLORD'S COVENANT TO REPAIR

The only common situation in which a landlord will covenant to repair is on the grant of a lease of part of a building, where the landlord will covenant to repair the exterior, structure and the common parts, and will be able to recover its expenditure under the service charge provisions. A landlord's covenant to repair will be subject to the same rules of construction as a tenant's covenant so, for example, the landlord need not carry out works so as provide the tenant with something wholly different from that originally demised.

REVIEW ACTIVITY

1. Consider the amendments that you might make to the example clause if you were acting for a tenant on the grant of a 10-year lease of one floor of an old office building. The office premises have been left in a poor state by the previous tenant.
2. Consider the amendments that you might make to the example clause if you were acting for a tenant on the grant of a 10-year lease of a newly-constructed warehouse that was built on a brown field site.

Answers to this Review activity may be found in Appendix 1.

CHAPTER 21

ALIENATION

21.1	Dealings with the premises	253
21.2	Restrictions on alienation	255
21.3	The 2020 Code for Leasing Business Premises	259
21.4	Seeking consent from the landlord	260
21.5	Notice of assignment or sub-letting	263
21.6	Virtual assignments	264
	Review activity	264

21.1 DEALINGS WITH THE PREMISES

The term 'alienation' refers to the tenant's ability to deal with the lease. Unless the lease contains some restriction, the tenant will be free to deal with its interest in any way it wishes.

There are various ways in which a tenant may seek to deal with its premises. It may seek to divest itself of the entirety of its interest by assigning the lease. Alternatively, it might retain its own lease and create a new interest through sub-letting (otherwise known as under-letting). It might also seek to mortgage the lease or grant licences for third parties to occupy the premises, or it might seek to share possession of the premises. Complete freedom like this is unlikely to prove acceptable to the landlord for a number of reasons, and thus a fair balance between the competing concerns and aims of both parties will have to be reached. In consequence, each side must understand the concerns of the other and the type of restriction that may be appropriate for each type of potential dealing.

21.1.1 Assignment

Assignment involves the tenant transferring the whole or part of its leasehold estate to another party. From the tenant's point of view, the lease may become a burden if it is unable to assign it freely when it no longer has any use for the premises. This situation may arise, for example, where the premises have become surplus to the tenant's requirements, or because they are no longer suitable for the tenant's needs. The tenant would also be in difficulty if its business venture failed and it could no longer afford the rent. However, from the landlord's point of view, close control over assignment is essential, because without it the landlord may find its premises occupied by an unsatisfactory tenant, and the value of its reversionary interest may be reduced. The assignee will become responsible for the rent and the performance of the other covenants in the lease, and the landlord will want to ensure that it is of good financial standing. The identity and status of any potential assignee is, therefore, important to the landlord for financial reasons. Further, there may be estate management reasons why the landlord will wish to exercise some control over assignees, for example where the landlord owns the adjoining premises.

21.1.2 Sub-letting

When a tenant sub-lets, it retains its own lease and creates a new lease carved out of its term in favour of a third party. There are several situations in which a sub-letting of the premises, or part of it, may be appropriate (see **29.2**).

The landlord will want the ability to control sub-letting, because in certain circumstances the head tenancy may cease to exist and the sub-tenant will become the immediate tenant of the landlord. This could happen, for example, on the surrender of the head-lease or on the forfeiture of the head-lease followed by the sub-tenant's successful application for relief. A similar situation could arise at the end of the contractual term if the head-tenant does not apply (or is unable to apply) for a new tenancy under Pt II of the Landlord and Tenant Act 1954 (LTA 1954) but the sub-tenant does; the sub-tenant may be granted a new tenancy of its part against the head-landlord. In all these situations the landlord would want to be sure that the sub-tenant was able to pay the rent and perform the covenants, and will therefore wish to have some control over the identity and status of any proposed sub-tenant.

21.1.3 Parting with/sharing possession

Most leases contain covenants prohibiting the tenant from either parting with possession or sharing occupation of the premises. 'Parting with possession' and 'sharing occupation' are, however, two different things.

A covenant preventing the tenant from *parting with possession* of the premises prevents the tenant from doing anything that means it will no longer have legal possession of the premises. Such a covenant will prevent both assignment and sub-letting, but will go further than that. For example, it has been held to prevent parting with possession of the premises to a purchaser pending completion of an assignment (*Horsey Estate Limited v Steiger* [1899] 2 QB 79). It will not, however, prevent the tenant from allowing another person to use the premises, provided the tenant retains legal possession. It will not, therefore, prohibit a tenant from granting a licence of the premises to another, unless the licence confers exclusive possession on the licensee (see *Street v Mountford* [1985] AC 809). In practice, of course, it can be very difficult to grant a third party rights of occupation without allowing exclusive possession.

Covenants which prohibit the tenant from *sharing possession* of the premises will prevent the tenant from granting licences. Such a prohibition will prevent the tenant from sharing occupation of the premises with a group company member. It will also prevent the sort of concession arrangements frequently made by retailers, whereby another business is allowed to promote its products or services within the tenant's store. The tenant should therefore try to resist an absolute prohibition against sharing possession, unless there is no possibility of the tenant or any future tenant wishing to share with a group company or grant concessions. Most landlords will agree to a corporate tenant sharing with a group company member, provided no relationship of landlord and tenant is created, and indeed the Code for Leasing Business Premises 2020 ('the 2020 Code') (see **21.3**) recommends that leases allow this.

21.1.4 Dealings with part

Landlords often try to impose much stricter control on dealing with part only of the premises because of the estate management problems which dealings of part can create. For example, if assignment of part were permitted, there would need to be an apportionment of rents and other outgoings under the lease. It is therefore usual for rack rent leases of commercial premises to prohibit any dealings with part other than sub-letting.

When considering whether to permit sub-letting of part, the landlord will bear in mind that a sub-tenant can in certain circumstances become the immediate tenant of the head-landlord (see **21.1.2**). If a number of sub-leases have been granted, a landlord who had let a building as a whole to a single tenant could, at some future date, be faced with the estate management problems associated with having a number of different tenants, each with a lease of a different part of the building. Further, if the tenant was allowed to grant a sub-lease of part only of the premises, this could lead to the division of the premises into commercially unattractive units. If the landlord inherited tenancies of part, it might have difficulty in re-letting any part that became vacant, if that part is no longer attractive to the market.

For these reasons, landlords may attempt to prohibit sub-letting of part only of the premises, as well as other dealings with part. In considering the acceptability of any such prohibition, the tenant will need to have regard to the nature of the premises. The design of some premises does not lend itself to easy sub-division. However, other premises (eg office blocks) can often be sub-let with relative ease (say, by sub-letting one or more floors). Clearly a prohibition on sub-letting part would prevent the tenant from disposing of a surplus of space. It also reduces its ability to deal with the premises flexibly if it wishes to dispose of them as a whole. For example, if at the time the tenant comes to dispose of the premises the market is demanding smaller units, the tenant's chances of disposing of the premises will be increased if it can divide the premises up into smaller units. A tenant should therefore resist a complete prohibition on sub-letting part.

Sometimes a landlord can be persuaded to agree to sub-letting of part if the extent of the parts to be sub-let is specified (eg not less than one complete floor of the demise) and the sub-tenancy is excluded from the LTA 1954. (The latter requirement will ensure that the landlord can, if it wishes, require the sub-tenant to vacate the premises at the end of the contractual term of the sub-lease.) The tenant should be aware, however, that if a sub-lease has to be excluded from the LTA 1954, it will limit the pool of sub-tenants who would be interested in the sub-lease. The 2020 Code (see **21.3**) is rather vague on sub-lettings of part, saying that a lease 'may' allow them 'if appropriate without security of tenure'.

21.1.5 Charging or mortgaging

A tenant may wish to mortgage or charge its leasehold interest in the premises. This is usually done by way of either a fixed or a floating charge. A fixed charge may be taken where the lease has some capital value, or where the premises are critical to the success of the tenant's business. Often, however, rack rent leases of commercial premises do not have a capital value. In addition, the forfeiture provisions within the lease may make it unattractive as security. Fixed charges over commercial leasehold property are not, therefore, a common way of raising finance.

The lease may, however, be caught by a floating charge granted by a corporate tenant over all its assets and undertaking. Such floating charges are often granted by a company borrower when raising finance. They do not fix upon the assets in question unless and until certain events specified in the charge arise. These are usually events of default or insolvency.

If the tenant wants to grant either a fixed or a floating charge, it will need to check the provisions of its lease to see what is permitted. It will also need to be aware of any floating charges already in existence at the time the lease is granted, as these normally cover future assets of the company.

Most leases will contain restrictions on charging without the landlord's consent, as the landlord will be concerned that, if the tenant defaults on the mortgage, the lender may take possession of the premises or exercise its power of sale. The lender under a legal charge also has a right to relief against forfeiture in much the same way as a sub-tenant. The tenant should, however, seek a provision that allows it to grant a charge to a bank or other reputable lending institution without the landlord's consent (see the 2020 Code referred to at **21.3**).

21.2 RESTRICTIONS ON ALIENATION

For the reasons mentioned in **21.1** above, it is common for the landlord to impose restrictions on dealing. Such restrictions may be absolute or qualified.

21.2.1 Absolute covenants against dealings

An absolute covenant means that the tenant cannot carry out the specified dealing without being in breach of covenant. An example would be 'not to assign or sub-let the whole or any part of the premises'. This type of covenant would prevent an assignment of whole, an assignment of part, a sub-letting of whole and a sub-letting of part. While the landlord may be prepared to waive the covenant in a given case, the tenant will be entirely at the mercy of its landlord, who may refuse consent quite unreasonably subject only to the restrictions imposed by the Equality Act 2010. Also, if the covenant is absolute, the landlord is not obliged to give any reason for its refusal.

An absolute covenant against all dealings is unusual in business leases, except in very short-term leases or to the extent that it prohibits dealings with part of the premises (see **21.1.4**). Any wider form of absolute restriction should be resisted by the tenant; and if, exceptionally, there is such a restriction, the tenant should make sure its presence is reflected in the rent it has to pay.

21.2.2 Qualified covenants against dealings

A qualified covenant prohibits alienation by the tenant without the landlord's consent. An example would be 'not to assign or sub-let the whole or any part of the premises without the consent of the landlord'. Sometimes, the covenant will state that the landlord's consent is not to be unreasonably withheld; this is known as a fully qualified covenant. An example would be 'not to assign or sub-let the whole or any part of the premises without the consent of the landlord, such consent not to be unreasonably withheld'. However, even if these words are not expressly stated, they will be implied by s 19(1)(a) of the Landlord and Tenant Act 1927 (LTA 1927). This provides that a covenant not to assign, underlet, charge or part with possession of the premises or any part thereof without the landlord's licence or consent, is subject to a proviso that such licence or consent is not to be unreasonably withheld. In other words, a qualified covenant against dealings will be converted into a fully qualified covenant by the operation of s 19(1)(a). The section has no application to the operation of an absolute covenant, where the landlord remains free to refuse its consent quite unreasonably.

21.2.3 What is usually permitted and prohibited?

In practice the form of covenant found in a rack rent commercial property lease will contain elements of both the absolute and qualified restrictions. It will usually cover all types of potential dealing, as if a specific dealing is not referred to it will not be prohibited or restricted. So, for example, a restriction on assignment will not be broken by a sub-letting of the premises. Neither will a covenant against sub-letting prevent the tenant from granting licences. Similarly, a covenant against sub-letting 'the demised premises' will not be broken by a sub-lease of part only (*Cook v Shoesmith* [1951] 1 KB 752). If such restrictions are intended, they must be dealt with expressly.

The precise terms of the covenant will of course vary from transaction to transaction, but it is common to find that the initial draft of a lease will:

(a) prohibit absolutely dealings in relation to part only of the premises, unless the premises lend themselves to subdivision (see **21.1.4**);

(b) prohibit absolutely dealings which stop short of an assignment, sub-letting or charging of the whole, eg parting with possession or sharing occupation of the premises (see **21.1.3**);

(c) prohibit without the landlord's prior written consent assignments, charges or sub-lettings of the whole.

Such a clause will allow the tenant to assign, charge or sub-let the whole of the premises subject to obtaining the landlord's prior consent (and the landlord will not be able to unreasonably withhold its consent). This should meet the tenant's main concern of being unable to divest itself of the lease should its circumstances change. At the same time, it will allay the landlord's fears by imposing an absolute prohibition on dealings with part only of the premises. Whether or not the tenant considers the balance to be a fair one will depend on the facts of the transaction. The tenant will need to bear in mind the issues discussed in **21.1.3** and **21.1.4** when deciding whether a total prohibition on dealings with part and sharing occupation is acceptable.

The 2020 Code (see **21.3**) recommends that group company sharing is permitted, but stops short of saying that sub-lettings of part should be allowed, preferring the less prescriptive suggestion that a lease 'may allow sub-leases of part'.

21.2.4 What detailed requirements will apply to assignments?

21.2.4.1 Leases granted before 1 January 1996

Prior to the Landlord and Tenant (Covenants) Act 1995 (LT(C)A 1995), the landlord knew that the original tenant would be liable throughout the term of the lease even if it had assigned it on. Whilst this did not stop the landlord being concerned with the identity of any assignee, it meant the landlord had a safety net if such assignee failed to comply with the lease covenants. In consequence, leases granted prior to 1 January 1996 (often referred to as 'old leases') tend to have less stringent requirements relating to assignment than those granted after that date. Such leases will, however, invariably require the assignee to enter into a direct covenant with the landlord to perform the covenants in the lease. This will make the assignee liable on the covenants in the lease during the whole term, rather than just during the currency of its ownership. There may also be additional requirements, such as the assignee providing guarantors or a rent deposit, although this will vary from lease to lease.

21.2.4.2 Leases granted on or after 1 January 1996

For tenants entering into leases on or after 1 January 1996 (often referred to as 'new leases') the position changed. Such tenants are automatically released from liability under the lease once they assign it on. This is subject to two significant caveats. First, the LT(C)A 1995 specifically states that nothing in the statute prevents the tenant from entering into an authorised guarantee agreement (AGA), whereby the outgoing tenant guarantees the performance of the tenant's lease covenants by the incoming assignee (see **21.2.4.3**).

Secondly, the LT(C)A 1995 inserted s 19(1A) into the LTA 1927. Section 19(1A) operates only in relation to qualified covenants against assigning in commercial leases granted on or after 1 January 1996. The consequences of s 19(1A) are as follows:

(a) the landlord can stipulate in the lease conditions which need to be satisfied, or circumstances which must exist, before the landlord will give its consent to the assignment;

(b) if the landlord withholds its consent on the grounds that the specified circumstances do not exist, or that the specified conditions have not been satisfied, then the landlord will not be unreasonably withholding its consent;

(c) if the landlord withholds its consent on grounds other than those specified, s 19(1)(a) of the LTA 1927 will apply in the usual way (see **21.2.2** and below).

The nature and type of condition to be satisfied (or circumstances which must exist) are left to the parties to decide, but s 19(1C) of the LTA 1927 envisages their falling into two categories: those which can be factually or objectively verified; and those where the landlord has a discretion.

Factual conditions or circumstances might include a requirement that the proposed assignee is a publicly-quoted company on the London Stock Exchange or has pre-tax net profits equal to three times the rent, or a requirement that the assignor enter into an AGA (see **21.2.4.3**) or that the assignee procure guarantors.

Discretionary circumstances or conditions are those which cannot be verified objectively, and a judgement or determination will have to be made as to whether they have been satisfied. This type of condition will be valid only if either it provides for an independent third-party reference (in the event of the tenant disagreeing with the landlord's determination), or the landlord commits itself to making a reasonable determination. Typical examples of discretionary circumstances or conditions might include a provision that the proposed assignee must, in the opinion of the landlord, be of equivalent financial standing to the assignor and, should the tenant not agree, the matter is to be referred to an independent third party; or a provision that the assignee must not, in the reasonable opinion of the landlord, be in competition with other tenants in the same development.

The tenant must consider the impact of each circumstance and condition carefully before agreeing to its inclusion in the lease. For example, a blue-chip tenant who accepts a condition requiring any assignee to be of equivalent financial standing, will finds its pool of potential assignees severely restricted (effectively it will contain only other blue-chip companies). This may result in the tenant being unable to assign the lease. It will be too late for the tenant to argue at the time of an assignment that this condition is unreasonable if it has been included in the lease. It can help to remind the landlord during lease negotiations that restrictions on alienation will generally have a downward effect on rent at review, as the lease is less marketable. As a result, the trend in recent years has been away from long lists of circumstances and conditions. Indeed, it is not uncommon to find that the only precondition for assignment is the provision of an AGA. Even where this is the only condition, the tenant should consider whether it is appropriate for the provision of an AGA to be an absolute requirement in *all* circumstances. What, for example, if the tenant is assigning to someone of greater covenant strength? In such circumstances the landlord would not be disadvantaged in any way by the assignment, and so is it fair that it can require the tenant to enter into an AGA (see **21.3**)?

It should be noted that by virtue of s 19(1)(a) of the LTA 1927, the landlord can always refuse to give consent on grounds not listed in the lease, if it is reasonable to do so. So a failure to list a circumstance or condition in the lease will not prevent its being relied upon if it is a reasonable ground for refusal to the application in question.

21.2.4.3 Authorised guarantee agreements

Although the LT(C)A 1995 has abolished privity of contract in relation to leases caught by the Act, an outgoing tenant may sometimes be required to guarantee its immediate assignee's performance of the obligations contained in the lease. This is achieved by the outgoing tenant entering into an AGA with the landlord. The landlord may require an AGA from an outgoing tenant where:

(a) the lease provides that the consent of the landlord (or some other person) is required to the assignment;

(b) such consent is given subject to a condition (lawfully imposed) that the tenant is to enter into the AGA. For example, the requirement of an AGA may be one of the conditions which the parties had previously agreed had to be satisfied before the landlord was prepared to give its consent to an assignment (see **21.2.4.2**);

(c) the assignment is entered into by the tenant pursuant to that condition.

The terms of the guarantee are left to the parties, provided that the purpose of the LT(C)A 1995 is not frustrated. For typical terms, see **28.3.1** and the specimen at **Appendix 5**.

Whilst it is clear an outgoing tenant can be required to enter into an AGA, the position regarding any guarantor of the outgoing tenant has been less certain. Can the landlord validly ask the guarantor of the outgoing tenant to guarantee the obligations of the incoming tenant? In the absence of confirmation on the point from either the Act itself or case law, landlords in practice have been doing one of two things. The first is to require the outgoing tenant's guarantor to guarantee the obligations of the *assignee* in the AGA (sometimes referred to as a 'direct guarantee'). The second is to require the outgoing tenant's guarantor to guarantee the *outgoing tenant's* guarantee (sometimes referred to as a 'sub-guarantee'). Unfortunately for landlords, in the case of *Good Harvest Partnership LLP v Centaur Services Ltd* [2010] EWHC 330 (Ch), the High Court held that direct guarantees are invalid and questioned the validity of sub-guarantees (without ruling on the latter point). So any direct guarantee from an outgoing tenant's guarantor of an incoming assignee will be unenforceable. The validity of sub-guarantees, however, has been considered further in *K/S Victoria Street v House of Fraser (Stores Management) Limited* [2011] EWCA Civ 904. The Court of Appeal held that a sub-guarantee of the outgoing tenant's AGA obligations by the outgoing tenant's guarantor would be lawful, whilst upholding the decision of the High Court in *Good Harvest* regarding direct guarantees. (See also **15.4.2**.)

Where a lease contains an assignment clause requiring a direct guarantee as a condition of the landlord's consent, the requirement for a direct guarantee should be severed, leaving, in most cases, an assignment provision operating as a qualified covenant against assignment (*Tindall Cobham 1 Ltd & Others v Adda Hotels (an unlimited company) & Others* [2014] EWCA Civ 1215).

21.2.5 What detailed provisions will apply to sub-lettings?

Since there is a risk that the landlord may inherit a sub-tenant (see **21.1.2**), the lease will usually contain detailed provisions prescribing what terms any permitted sub-lease must contain. For example, the lease may contain the following:

(a) a prohibition on the sub-tenant doing any act inconsistent with the terms of the sub-lease;

(b) a requirement that the sub-tenant enter into a direct covenant with the head-landlord;

(c) a requirement that the sub-lease prohibit any further dealings other than an assignment of whole;

(d) a requirement that the sub-lease contain similar rent review provisions to the head-lease;

(e) restrictions on the level of rent that can be charged under the sub-lease.

As with assignment, the tenant should check any such requirements carefully before agreeing to them. For example, a tenant should avoid any provision requiring it to sub-let at no less than the rent currently payable under the head-lease (see paragraph 6.4 of the 2020 Code). If rents have fallen since the rent was last reviewed under the head-lease, this will make it virtually impossible to sub-let lawfully. A requirement that any sub-lease be excluded from the LTA 1954 should also be resisted, as it would limit the pool of potential sub-tenants who would be interested in the premises. If such a restriction does have to be accepted then the lease should not be prescriptive about the terms of the sub-lease (see paragraph 6.4 of the 2020 Code).

21.3 THE 2020 CODE FOR LEASING BUSINESS PREMISES

Under the 2020 Code, RICS members will be mandatorily required to ensure that written heads of terms are prepared prior to circulation of the initial draft of the lease (see **14.2**). These mandatory heads of terms must summarise the key provisions of the letting, including the tenant's rights to assign, sub-let, charge or share the premises. The 2020 Code also contains recommendations as to best practice in relation to the key provisions of a lease, although these are not stated to be mandatory. However, there may be legal and/or disciplinary consequences for RICS members in departing from the 2020 Code, which may lead to a finding of negligence against a surveyor. In relation to alienation, the 2020 Code provides:

> **6 Assigning, subletting, charging and sharing**
>
> 6.1 Leases should allow tenants to assign the whole of the premises with the landlord's consent, which is not to be unreasonably withheld or delayed. Landlords may set out circumstances in which consent can be refused, such as where there are arrears of rents, service charges or

insurance premiums that are not the subject of a legitimate dispute, or where the assignee has insufficient financial strength, but all such circumstances should be reasonable and appropriate.

6.2 Leases should also provide that, if in each case the landlord reasonably requires, the assigning tenant is to provide an authorised guarantee agreement (AGA), any existing guarantor is to guarantee that the assigning tenant complies with the AGA, and/or the assignee is to procure a new guarantor and/or rent deposit.

6.3 Leases should allow corporate tenants to share the premises with other companies while they are in the same corporate group and do not create a subletting. In appropriate cases, leases of retail units may allow the tenant to grant licences of areas for use by concessions, such as where retail brands can be given stalls in a large store.

6.4 Leases should allow tenants to sublet the whole of the premises and may allow subleases of parts, if appropriate without security of tenure, and in each case with the landlord's consent, which is not to be unreasonably withheld or delayed and at rents not less than market rent. Subleases should be required to be on terms consistent with the tenant's own lease, except that subleases which are to be excluded from statutory renewal rights and subleases of only part of the premises may be granted on different terms where appropriate. Where the tenant operates through franchisees, the tenant may require the right to sublet the unit to a franchisee on particular terms.

6.5 Leases should allow tenants to grant a bank or other reputable lending institution a charge over the lease, without the landlord's consent needing to be obtained unless the lease is to contain step-in rights for chargees if the landlord intends to take action where the tenant defaults.

6.6 Paragraphs 6.1 to 6.5 do not prevent landlords from imposing stricter provisions where justified by the particular circumstances, such as lettings of short duration or on concessionary terms, or leases of retail units where the tenant's business or brand may affect the character or value of the centre or parade or the amount of any turnover rent. Any such provisions should be on reasonable terms, for example a provision for surrender of the lease instead of assigning should apply only if the landlord is willing to pay its market value.

So the 2020 Code envisages that an AGA can be required on assignment if reasonable, rather than as an absolute requirement. Reasonable circumstances in which consent to an assignment can be refused may also be specified. These include where the assignee has insufficient financial strength and where there are arrears of rent, service charge or insurance rent, except where there is a legitimate dispute about such payments. Sub-lettings of whole should be permitted with landlord's consent, which is not to be unreasonably withheld or delayed. Mortgaging the lease to a bank or other reputable lender should not need landlord's consent and group company sharing should also be permitted. However, the 2020 Code does state that stricter alienation provisions can be imposed where 'justified by the particular circumstances' (see paragraph 6.6 of the 2020 Code). Examples of circumstances in which stricter provisions would be justified include short leases, leases on concessionary terms and retail leases where the tenant's business or brand impacts on any turnover rent payable under the lease or impacts on the value or character of the landlord's parade of shops or shopping centre.

21.4 SEEKING CONSENT FROM THE LANDLORD

Whether the landlord can refuse consent will depend upon whether the landlord has made use of s 19(1A) of the LTA 1927 or, if not, its reasonableness in the circumstances of the case. The landlord should also be mindful of its statutory obligations under the Landlord and Tenant Act 1988 (LTA 1988) (see **21.3.4**) and s 144 of the Law of Property Act 1925 (LPA 1925) (see **21.3.6**).

21.4.1 Applications for consent to assign

The landlord can lawfully withhold consent to assign if:

(a) the lease contains an absolute prohibition on assignment; or

(b) a circumstance or condition listed in the lease under s 19(1A) of the LTA 1927 has arisen (see **21.2.4.2**); or

(c) it is otherwise reasonable to do so under s 19(1)(a) of the LTA 1927 (see **21.4.3**).

21.4.2 Other applications for consent

Section 19(1A) of the LTA 1927 has no application to covenants against sub-letting, charging or mortgaging, and does not apply in relation to leases granted before 1 January 1996. In consequence, the landlord can lawfully withhold its consent to such applications if:

(a) the lease contains an absolute prohibition against the dealing in question; or

(b) it is reasonable to do so under s 19(1)(a) of the LTA 1927 (see **21.4.3**).

21.4.3 Section 19(1)(a) of the LTA 1927

Where the lease contains a qualified covenant against dealings, even if the lease says otherwise, the landlord cannot unreasonably withhold consent to an application to deal with the lease. Whether the landlord is acting reasonably in such cases has to be judged from the circumstances existing at the time of the landlord's decision.

The Court of Appeal laid down a number of guidelines on the issue of the landlord's reasonableness under s 19(1)(a) in *International Drilling Fluids Ltd v Louisville Investments (Uxbridge) Ltd* [1986] 1 All ER 321. The case concerned an application to assign, and the Court held that:

(a) the purpose of a fully qualified covenant against assignment is to protect the landlord from having its premises used or occupied in an undesirable way, or by an undesirable tenant or assignee;

(b) a landlord is not entitled to refuse its consent to an assignment on grounds which have nothing whatever to do with the relationship of landlord and tenant in regard to the subject matter of the lease;

(c) it is unnecessary for the landlord to prove that the conclusions which led it to refuse to consent were justified, if they were conclusions which might be reached by a reasonable man in the circumstances;

(d) it may be reasonable for the landlord to refuse its consent to an assignment on the ground of the purpose for which the proposed assignee intends to use the premises, even though that purpose is not forbidden by the lease;

(e) in general a landlord is bound to consider only its own relevant interests when deciding whether to refuse consent to an assignment of a lease. However, it would be unreasonable for a landlord not to consider the detriment which would be suffered by the tenant if consent were to be refused, if that detriment would be extreme and disproportionate in relation to the benefit gained by the landlord;

(f) subject to the above propositions, it is, in each case, a question of fact, depending on all the circumstances, whether the landlord's consent to an assignment is being withheld unreasonably.

The following are examples of situations where consent has been held to have been reasonably withheld:

(a) where the proposed assignee's references were unsatisfactory (*Shanley v Ward* (1913) 29 TLR 714);

(b) where there was a long-standing and extensive breach of the repairing covenant by the assignor and the landlord could not be reasonably satisfied that the assignee would be in a position to remedy the breach (*Orlando Investments v Grosvenor Estate Belgravia* [1989] 2 EGLR 74);

(c) where the assignee would be in a position to compete with the landlord's business (*Whiteminster Estates v Hodges Menswear* (1974) 232 EG 715);

(d) where the assignment would reduce the value of the landlord's reversion. However, this will not be a reasonable ground for withholding consent if the landlord has no intention of selling the reversion (*Ponderosa International Development v Pengap Securities* [1986] 1 EGLR 66 and *FW Woolworth v Charlwood Alliance Properties* [1987] 1 EGLR 53);

(e) where the proposed assignee intends to carry on a use detrimental to the premises, or a use inconsistent with the landlord's 'tenant mix' policy (see *Moss Bros Group plc v CSC Properties Ltd* [1999] EGCS 47);

(f) where the assignee would, unlike the assignor, acquire protection under Pt II of the LTA 1954 (*Re Cooper's Lease* (1968) 19 P & CR 541);

(g) where the terms of a sub-lease, when read together with a collateral agreement proposed between tenant and sub-tenant, did not mirror the terms of the lease (*Allied Dunbar Assurance v Homebase Ltd* [2002] 2 EGLR 23). In this case the lease required any sub-lease to mirror its terms, and the court held that the landlord was therefore entitled to see any collateral agreement between the tenant and sub-tenant.

The following are examples of situations where consent has been held to have been unreasonably withheld:

(a) where the landlord has refused consent in an attempt to obtain some advantage for itself. See, for example, *Bates v Donaldson* [1896] 2 QB 241 and *Re Winfrey and Chatterton's Agreement* [1921] 2 Ch 7, where the landlord's refusal to grant consent to an assignment on the grounds that he wanted possession of the premises himself was held unreasonable. See also *Norwich Union Life Insurance Society v Shopmoor Ltd* [1999] 1 WLR 531, where, on an application to sub-let the premises, the landlord refused consent because the underlease rent was to be less than the market value. This was not prohibited by the terms of the lease, but the landlord argued that it would adversely affect the reversionary value of *neighbouring* properties it owned. The landlord did not make any argument that it would affect the reversionary value of the premises, and the court held this to be a case of the landlord seeking a collateral advantage unconnected with the demised premises;

(b) where there are minor breaches of the repairing covenant (*Farr v Ginnings* (1928) 44 TLR 249);

(c) where premises had been on the market for 18 months, the rent was significant and the slight harm to the landlord would be outweighed by prejudice to the tenant (*Footwear Corporation Ltd v Amplight Properties* [1999] 1 WLR 551).

An issue which has been before the court on more than one occasion is whether the landlord would be acting unreasonably in refusing consent where it anticipated a breach of the user covenant by the assignee. In *Ashworth Frazer Ltd v Gloucester City Council* [2002] 05 EG 133, the court considered that the correct approach is to examine what the reasonable landlord would do when asked to consent in the particular circumstances. It would usually be reasonable for a landlord to withhold consent where an assignee proposed to use the premises in breach of the terms of the lease. However, there could be circumstances where the refusal of consent on this ground alone would be unreasonable (although the court did not say what these circumstances might be). In other words, each case will be looked at on its own merits in light of what a reasonable landlord would do.

Under the provisions of the Equality Act 2010, any discrimination in withholding consent for the disposal of the demised premises on grounds of race, sex or disability is generally unlawful.

21.4.4 Delays in obtaining consent

The LTA 1988 further strengthens the position of a tenant seeking consent to deal with its lease. The Act applies where the lease contains a fully qualified covenant against alienation (whether or not the proviso that the landlord's consent is not to be unreasonably withheld is express or implied by statute). It applies to assignment, sub-letting, charging and parting with possession of the premises. When the tenant has made written application for consent to such a dealing, the landlord owes a duty, within a reasonable time:

(a) to give consent, unless it is reasonable not to do so. Giving consent subject to an unreasonable condition will be a breach of this duty; and

(b) to serve on the tenant written notice of its decision whether or not to give consent (see LTA 1988, s 1(3)(b), and *Footwear Corporation Ltd v Amplight Properties Ltd* [1999] 1 WLR 551), specifying in addition:
   (i) if the consent is given subject to conditions, the conditions; or
   (ii) if the consent is withheld, the reasons for withholding it.

The burden of proving the reasonableness of any refusal or any conditions imposed is on the landlord. The sanction for breach of this statutory duty is liability in tort for damages. The LTA 1988 does not specify what is to be regarded as a reasonable time, nor when refusal of consent is to be deemed reasonable. Again, this Act has to be read in the light of s 19(1A) of the LTA 1927. The operation of the LTA 1988 and relevant case law is considered further in **Chapter 28**.

21.4.5 What if consent is refused?

If, having applied for consent to assign or sub-let, the tenant thinks its landlord is being unreasonable in its refusal to give such consent, the tenant has a number of options available. These are dealt with at **28.1**.

21.4.6 Restrictions on requiring payment for consent

In the case of a qualified covenant against dealings, s 144 of the LPA 1925 implies a proviso that no fine or similar sum of money shall be charged for giving consent to assignment, sub-letting or parting with possession, unless the lease expressly provides for this. However, this does not prevent a landlord from requiring its tenant to pay a reasonable sum for legal and other expenses incurred in connection with the grant of consent.

21.4.7 The Alienation Protocol

Applications for consent to deal with the lease can lead to disputes between the parties. In an attempt to reduce such disputes, a Protocol for Applications for Consent to Assign or Sublet (the Alienation Protocol) was published in 2015, and has been endorsed by the British Property Federation and the Royal Institute of Chartered Surveyors. The Alienation Protocol covers applications by a tenant for consent to assign or sub-let commercial premises, where the lease requires the landlord's consent. It is hoped that, by voluntarily agreeing to follow the Protocol, the parties will avoid arguments about the information and documentation forming part of the application for consent, avoid disputes about the period of time for the landlord's decision and, in the event of a dispute, be able to have the dispute resolved swiftly by an experienced tribunal, with recourse to the courts as an option of last resort only. The authors of the Alienation Protocol suggest that the alienation provisions in leases granted since the publication of the Alienation Protocol should be drafted to make express reference to the Alienation Protocol, thereby legally obliging the parties to adhere to it.

The Protocol is available at <www.propertyprotocols.co.uk>.

21.5 NOTICE OF ASSIGNMENT OR SUB-LETTING

There is no common law obligation for a tenant to give its landlord notice of any dealing with the lease, but a well-drafted lease will provide for this so that the landlord knows at any given time in whom the lease is vested and whether any sub-lease has been granted.

The clause should specify the occasions on which the covenant is to operate (eg assignment, sub-letting, mortgage). The tenant is usually required to pay a registration fee to the landlord with each notice served. When negotiating the lease the tenant should ensure such registration fee is not excessive.

In the case of assignment, it will fall to the assignee to give notice (and pay any registration fee prescribed by the lease), since it will be its interest that will be jeopardised by the breach of covenant involved in failing to give notice.

21.6 VIRTUAL ASSIGNMENTS

The usual leasehold covenants preventing assignment, etc without the landlord's consent often prove inconvenient to tenants, eg on the sale of leasehold portfolios, where time is tight and consents would have to be obtained from a multiplicity of landlords. To deal with this, a handful of large city law firms acting for tenants with a large property portfolio developed a device that became known as the 'virtual assignment'.

A virtual assignment is an arrangement under which all the economic benefits and burdens of a lease are transferred to a third party, but without any actual legal (or equitable) assignment of the lease itself or any change in the occupation of the premises (because the premises are sub-let).

The Court of Appeal case of *Clarence House Ltd v National Westminster Bank plc* [2009] EWCA Civ 1311 confirmed that such a virtual assignment is not a legal assignment and does not breach a covenant in the lease restricting assignment (unless an attempt has been made in the lease to define and restrict a 'virtual assignment'). Neither does the virtual assignment affect the landlord's remedies against the virtual assignor, who remains the legal tenant and can be pursued for any breach of covenant.

If a landlord is concerned about the possibility of a virtual assignment, it could seek to prohibit it in the lease. However, the mechanism by which a virtual assignment is effected is one that has evolved over time and may well continue to do so. It is therefore difficult to define. Further, a prohibition on it may be viewed as unduly onerous by large corporate tenants and therefore have an adverse effect on rent review.

Given that virtual assignments are rare and to date have been confined to a relatively small group of large corporate tenants, the issue of the virtual assignment is unlikely to be a cause of concern for the vast majority of landlords and tenants.

REVIEW ACTIVITY

Imagine your client has taken a lease of two upper floors of an office building in the form set out in **Appendix 4**. Read clauses 12, 13 and 14 of the lease and assume that any words in square brackets were not included in the lease (words in square brackets are optional and the draftsperson may choose to include or exclude them). Now answer the following questions:

1. Is the tenant allowed to sub-let one of the two floors it occupies in the event it no longer requires as much space?

2. On an assignment, can the landlord always insist that the outgoing tenant enters into an AGA?

3. If the tenant wishes to assign the lease, in what circumstances can the landlord withhold its consent?

Answers to this Review activity may be found in Appendix 1.

CHAPTER 22

USER

22.1	The need for a user covenant	265
22.2	The permitted use	267
22.3	The extent of the landlord's control	268
22.4	Ancillary clauses	269
22.5	Impact of competition legislation on user covenants	270
	Review activity	272

22.1 THE NEED FOR A USER COVENANT

There are several ways outside the terms of the lease in which the tenant's use of the premises may be restricted:

(a) *Planning legislation.* The tenant may not be able to carry out any building or other operations at the premises, and it will not be able to make a material change in the use of the premises without obtaining planning permission from the local planning authority. Generally, there is no implied warranty by the landlord that the tenant's use of the property is an authorised use under the planning legislation. It is, therefore, for the tenant to satisfy itself that planning permission is available for the use intended.

(b) *Covenants affecting a superior title.* There may be restrictive covenants affecting the landlord's reversionary title (or if the landlord is itself a tenant, affecting a superior title) which bind the tenant and prevent it from carrying out certain activities at the premises. Despite being restricted by statute as to the evidence of title it can call for, the tenant should always press the landlord for evidence of all superior titles.

(c) *Common law restraints.* The law of nuisance may prevent the tenant from using the premises in a such a way as to cause disturbance to a neighbour.

While these restraints operate to exert some degree of control over the tenant, they do not provide the landlord with any remedy should the tenant act in breach. A user covenant (together with several ancillary clauses) will therefore be required to give the landlord the desired level of control.

22.1.1 The landlord's concerns

There are various financial and estate management reasons why a landlord will wish to control use of the premises by the tenant:

(a) to maintain the value of the landlord's interest in the premises;
(b) to maintain the rental value of the premises;
(c) to avoid damaging the reputation of the premises by immoral or undesirable uses;
(d) to maintain the value of adjoining premises owned by the landlord;
(e) to avoid the tenant competing with other premises of the landlord in the vicinity;
(f) to maintain a good mix of different retail uses in a shopping precinct owned by the landlord.

The landlord has to be careful when drafting the user covenant to ensure that it does not restrain the tenant's use of the premises any more than is strictly necessary for the landlord's purposes, since a tight user covenant may have an adverse impact from the landlord's point of view on rental values both initially and at rent review. The wider the scope of the user covenant, the more attractive would be a letting of the premises on the open market and, therefore, the higher the rental value may be, both initially and at review. The tighter the covenant, the less attractive would be a letting of the premises on the open market (since the number of potential bidders for this letting would be restricted by the narrowness of the user covenant) and, therefore, the lower the rental value would be. The landlord is not able to argue at rent review that the valuer should assess the revised rent on the basis that the landlord might be prepared to waive a breach of the user covenant in order to permit a more profitable use (thereby increasing the rental value of the tenant's interest), nor is it allowed to vary the lease unilaterally in order to gain a benefit at review (see *Plinth Property Investments Ltd v Mott, Hay & Anderson* [1979] 1 EGLR 17 and *C&A Pension Trustees Ltd v British Vita Investments Ltd* [1984] 2 EGLR 75).

The landlord will therefore need to perform a balancing act between control of the tenant and good estate management on the one hand, and maximisation of rental values on the other. It is usually the case that if the premises are in a shopping centre or office block owned by the landlord, or the landlord owns adjoining property, the landlord will require greater control over the use. The chances of operating a successful shopping centre improve with the right mix and balance of uses. The landlord may seek valuation advice to get the right balance between control and rental income.

22.1.2 Tenant's concerns

From the tenant's point of view, a narrow user covenant ought to be avoided since, although the clause would work favourably for the tenant on rent review, its ability to dispose of the premises at some stage in the future will be hampered in that it will only be able to assign or sub-let to someone who is capable of complying with the covenant and who does not require any greater flexibility.

Additionally, the tenant must have regard to its own future use of the premises. There is a risk that the nature of the tenant's business may change to such a degree that it is taken outside the scope of the user covenant and, therefore, finds itself in breach. The tenant must ensure that sufficient flexibility is built into the covenant to permit future diversification of the tenant's business. However, it should not allow the landlord to insert a covenant that is wider than is strictly necessary for its purposes, since this may penalise the tenant at rent review by increasing the rental value of the tenant's interest. Once again a balancing act is required.

The user clause usually contains a principal covenant by the tenant governing the permitted use of the premises, followed by a range of ancillary clauses prohibiting or controlling a range of other activities.

22.1.3 The 2020 Code for Leasing Business Premises

The 2020 Code provides:

8 Change of use, alterations and fit-out

8.1 Leases should give landlords control over alterations and changes of use that are no more restrictive than are necessary to protect the value of the premises and any adjoining or neighbouring premises of the landlord, and this may differ between different types of property.

8.2 Where the landlord intends to prohibit certain changes of use or the making of certain alterations, or to require a licence from the landlord before they can take place, the tenant should be notified at the outset in order to obtain early professional advice as to the implications. This does not apply to normal provisions against changing the use outside the existing use class under planning law.

22.2 THE PERMITTED USE

There are several ways in which the permitted use can be defined in the lease. First, the landlord may be prepared to permit a wide range of uses by broadly stipulating the type of use to be permitted on the premises, for example, use as offices, or as a retail shop, or for light industrial purposes. This would give the tenant a large degree of flexibility and enable it to diversify its business operations within the broad range permitted.

Alternatively, the landlord may choose to restrict the tenant to a very narrow range of uses by defining the permitted use by reference to the nature of the business to be carried on at the premises, for example use as offices for the business of an estate agency, or as a retail shop for the sale of children's footwear, or as a factory for the manufacture of computer software. This would give the tenant no flexibility to diversify and would hamper the tenant in any efforts to assign its lease, or sub-let the premises to someone who was not in the same line of business.

As a third possibility, the landlord may adopt an approach which is mid-way between the first two by restricting the tenant's use of the premises to a class of similar uses by, for example, defining the permitted use as offices for the business of a solicitor, accountant, architect or other professional person. If the landlord intends permitting the tenant to use the premises for one of a number of similar uses, it may consider defining the use by reference to the Town and Country Planning (Use Classes) Order 1987 (SI 1987/764) (as amended).

In all cases, how strictly the user covenant operates will depend on whether it is expressed in absolute, qualified or fully qualified terms (see **22.3**).

22.2.1 Making use of the Town and Country Planning (Use Classes) Order (UCO)

It is often considered desirable that the permitted user is linked to the Use Class specified by any available planning permission. However, if this approach is to be adopted, the landlord should check carefully to ensure that there are no uses which could conceivably fall within the specified Use Class which the landlord would consider to be unattractive. For example, a planning permission may permit retail use under the relevant Use Class (class A1 prior to 1 September 2020 and class E(a) after 1 September 2020). However, there are likely to be several types of shop uses within that class which the landlord would not be prepared to tolerate at the premises. If that is the case, a more limited user should be specified in the lease (eg a retail shop for the sale of women's clothing within class E(a) of the UCO).

If the landlord is to make use of the UCO in the user covenant, it should ensure that the lease clearly states which version of the UCO it is referring to (so by referring to the UCO in existence at a particular date). Otherwise, the UCO could be amended to bring within the class of use permitted by the lease a use which the landlord considered to be undesirable, thereby converting that use into a permitted use under the lease.

22.2.2 A covenant that names the tenant

It is sometimes difficult to define the type of business to be carried on by the tenant at the premises because of its peculiar nature, and so the landlord feels inclined to restrict use of the premises to the tenant's particular business. This is a dangerous approach to adopt, and it can lead to problems for the tenant (in terms of its ability to dispose of the premises) and can give rise to complicated valuation problems at rent review (*Sterling Land Office Developments Ltd v Lloyds Bank plc* (1984) 271 EG 894 and *Post Office Counters Ltd v Harlow District Council* [1991] 2 EGLR 121).

If the user covenant restricts the use of the premises to, for example, the offices of a particular company which is named in the lease, this would effectively prevent an assignment or sub-letting by the original tenant, even if the lease otherwise anticipated alienation (*Law Land Co Ltd v Consumers Association Ltd* (1980) 255 EG 617).

If the user covenant, without specifically naming the tenant, restricts use of the premises to 'the tenant's business', problems of interpretation will arise. Does the clause refer to the original tenant, or the current tenant? Does it refer to the business being conducted at the outset or the business being conducted from time to time? The danger from the landlord's point of view is that if, as is usually the case, the lease defines 'the Tenant' to include its successors in title, such a clause is likely to be construed by the court as permitting whatever business is currently being carried on by whoever is then the tenant. In other words, the landlord will have lost control. If reference is made to 'the tenant's business as a solicitor', does that mean that only the original tenant can comply with the covenant, or can an assignee? Would sub-letting be impossible since a sub-tenant, not being a tenant under the lease, would inevitably be in breach?

In view of these complications, it is advisable to avoid the use of covenants which either name the tenant, or refer to the tenant's business without sufficient clarity.

22.2.3 A positive or negative covenant?

If the covenant is positive, it will require the tenant 'to use the premises for the purposes of [the named permitted use]'. The benefit from the landlord's point of view is that non-use (eg, because of a temporary shut-down during a recession) will amount to a breach of covenant. This will entitle the landlord to damages (but not usually specific performance or an injunction) should the landlord suffer loss (see **30.1.3**). Loss can arise where a shopping centre loses what practitioners call an 'anchor tenant'. An anchor tenant may be, say, a large supermarket, whose presence generates a flow of customers for other shops in the shopping centre. If the anchor tenant leaves, it will reduce the number of shoppers in the shopping centre, thereby affecting the profitability of other shops in the centre and resulting eventually in an adverse effect on the value of the landlord's reversion. The tenant ought to resist a positive covenant as it can make it costly to cease trading from unprofitable or unsuitable premises.

Most user covenants are negative, obliging the tenant 'not to use the premises other than for the purposes of ... [permitted purpose]', in which case a breach is committed by the tenant only if it uses the premises for a purpose not authorised by the landlord. A negative user covenant is not breached by non-use.

Neither form of covenant will be breached if the tenant uses the premises for a purpose ancillary to the permitted use. For example, use of some rooms in a shop for storage purposes where the user covenant permits the retail sale of books, magazines and periodicals would not amount to a breach.

22.3 THE EXTENT OF THE LANDLORD'S CONTROL

The principal covenant may be absolute, qualified or fully qualified.

22.3.1 Absolute covenants

An absolute covenant gives the landlord absolute control over any change in the use of the premises in that it permits the tenant to use the premises for the purpose of the permitted use and no other. The tenant will not be able to use the premises for a use falling outside the scope of the covenant without obtaining from the landlord a waiver of the tenant's breach, or getting the landlord to agree to a variation of the lease. If the permitted use is narrowly defined, the tenant should be advised to resist an absolute covenant, unless it is sure that it will not want to assign or sub-let the premises, or diversify its business. If the permitted use is sufficiently widely defined (eg, use as offices only) then an absolute covenant should not unduly concern the tenant.

22.3.2 Qualified covenants

A qualified covenant allows the tenant to alter the use of the premises from a permitted use to some other use with the landlord's prior consent, which is usually required to be given in writing. However, such a covenant gives the tenant little extra comfort than is afforded by an absolute covenant since, unlike qualified covenants relating to alienation and improvements, there is no statutorily implied proviso that the landlord's consent is not to be unreasonably withheld. This means that, despite the additional wording added to the covenant, the tenant is still at the mercy of the landlord who may decline the request for a change of use for whatever reason it chooses. The only benefit from the tenant's point of view of a qualified covenant is derived from s 19(3) of the LTA 1927 which states that, provided the change of use will not entail any structural alterations to the premises (which would not often be the case), the landlord is not allowed to demand as a condition of giving consent the payment of a lump sum or an increased rent (as to which, see *Barclays Bank plc v Daejan Investments (Grove Hall) Ltd* [1995] 18 EG 117). However, s 19(3) does allow the landlord, as a condition of giving consent, to insist upon the payment of reasonable compensation in respect of damage to or diminution in the value of the premises or any neighbouring premises belonging to the landlord (which might occur if a valuable use of the premises is abandoned), and the payment of expenses incurred in the giving of consent, such as legal and surveyor's fees. Of course, the commercial reality for many tenants is that if they want a change of use, they will often end up offering a premium for a Deed of Variation, even though it is not lawful for the landlord to require its payment.

Section 19(3) does not apply to agricultural or mining leases.

22.3.3 Fully qualified covenants

A fully qualified covenant allows the tenant to change the use of the premises from a permitted use to some other use with the prior consent (in writing) of the landlord, whose consent is not to be unreasonably withheld. Most covenants of this kind will also stipulate (either in the wording of the covenant, or in the interpretation section of the lease) that the landlord cannot unreasonably delay giving consent. Should the landlord, in the tenant's opinion, be guilty of an unreasonable refusal of consent, the tenant may, if certain of its ground, change the use of the premises without the landlord's consent. However, this course of action carries a risk, and therefore most tenants would prefer to follow the safer course of action which is to apply to the court for a declaration that the landlord is acting unreasonably, and then proceed without the landlord's consent. The question of the landlord's reasonableness is ultimately left in the hands of the court. The only potential drawbacks of such a clause for the tenant are that, without an express provision in the lease, there is no obligation on the landlord to provide the tenant with reasons for refusing consent (making it difficult for the tenant to assess whether it has a good chance of success in its application for a declaration) and there is no positive duty upon the landlord to give consent along the lines of the statutory duty imposed by the LTA 1988 in respect of alienation covenants, which means that the tenant does not have a remedy in damages if it suffers loss as a result of an unreasonable refusal.

Section 19(3) of the LTA 1927 applies equally to fully qualified covenants.

22.4 ANCILLARY CLAUSES

It is usual for the landlord to impose many other covenants upon the tenant which also impact upon user, obliging the tenant:

(a) to comply in all respects with the Planning Acts (as defined in the definitions section of the lease). It is important for the landlord to have the benefit of this covenant since enforcement action for a breach of planning control committed by the tenant could be taken against the landlord, resulting in a possible fine;

(b) not to apply for planning permission, or to carry out acts of development at the premises. This covenant may be absolute, qualified or fully qualified. The landlord will not want the tenant to have freedom to change the authorised use of the premises as this may result in an existing profitable use being lost, thereby reducing the value of the premises. Although, as owner of the reversion, the landlord may be able to raise objections at the application stage, it would prefer to be able to veto the application under the terms of the lease in the first place. It should be noted that such a covenant may restrict the tenant's ability to alter or change the use of the premises even if elsewhere in the lease such action is more freely permitted;

(c) where the landlord has consented to an application for planning permission, and development has commenced, to fully implement all permissions obtained before the end of the term in accordance with any conditions attached to the permission;

(d) not to cause a nuisance, annoyance or inconvenience to the landlord or the tenants of adjoining premises. Whether an activity amounts to a nuisance is to be determined on the basis of ordinary tortious principles. An annoyance is anything which disturbs the reasonable peace of mind of the landlord or an adjoining occupier, and is a wider concept than nuisance. The concept of inconvenience is probably wider still;

(e) not to use the premises for any immoral or illegal use (since such uses may tarnish the reputation of the building and reduce its value);

(f) not to carry out any dangerous activities, or bring any noxious or inflammable substances onto the premises. The landlord's primary purpose behind this covenant is to preserve the premises. One consequence of a breach by the tenant might be an increase in the insurance premium for the premises, and although the tenant is likely to be obliged to pay the increased premium by virtue of the insurance covenant, the landlord would not want the level of insurance premiums to rise;

(g) not to overload the premises in any way. The landlord is simply trying to preserve the premises with this covenant;

(h) not to allow anyone to sleep or reside at the premises;

(i) not to allow any licence which benefits the premises to lapse (eg, gaming licences, liquor licences). If the premises consist of a betting shop, the value of those premises will depend to a large extent on the continued existence of a betting office licence. The tenant will therefore be obliged by the landlord to maintain and, where necessary, renew the licence.

The tenant's solicitor will need to consider any and all of these ancillary clauses carefully. Without sufficient knowledge of the client's business, it is easy to miss a potential breach. For example, if your client is a retailer, might it sell fireworks at certain times of the year? Fireworks would potentially breach a restriction on the sale of inflammable items. Also, beware restrictions on the sale of alcohol. Again, if you act for a retailer, you should check whether there is any possibility of the sale of products containing alcohol. Even though it may not be the client's core business, many retailers will sell gift items at certain times of the year that include alcohol.

22.5 IMPACT OF COMPETITION LEGISLATION ON USER COVENANTS

Section 2 of the Competition Act (CA) 1998 prohibits any agreement which may affect trade within the UK and which prevents, restricts or distorts competition within the UK. Since April 2011 this prohibition has applied to land agreements (including leases) between businesses. The Act cannot be excluded and operates retrospectively but will only catch covenants which have an 'appreciable effect' on the market affected by the agreement. An agreement is exempt from the prohibition under s 9 of the CA 1998 if it either contributes to the improvement of production or distribution or promotes technical or economic progress. However, in either case, to fall within the exemption the agreement must:

- allow consumers a fair share of the resulting benefit; and
- not impose restrictions which are not indispensable to the attainment of those objectives; and
- not eliminate competition in respect of a substantial part of the products in question.

It is for the person or company claiming the benefit of the exemption to prove that the conditions of it are satisfied.

The Office of Fair Trading (OFT) has issued detailed guidance on the application of the CA 1998 to land agreements. While the OFT's competition functions have been taken over by the Competition and Markets Authority (CMA), the CMA has adopted the OFT's guidance, which therefore continues to apply. The OFT guidance suggests that, in most leases, permitted user clauses (ie those specifying permitted uses) and restricted user clauses (those specifying uses that are not permitted) would be unlikely to restrict competition. This would include clauses restricting the lines of business that could be carried out by a tenant in order to achieve a good 'retail mix' and ensure the attractiveness of a shopping centre. However, a covenant by a landlord not to permit another business of the same type as the tenant to open in its shopping centre or restricting use where the landlord is active in a related market does have the potential to restrict competition and therefore be prohibited.

To date, there has been only one UK case that has considered the interaction of the CA 1998 Act with leasehold user covenants. The claimant in *Martin Retail Group Ltd v Crawley Borough Council* (CC (Central London), 24 December 2013) operated a newsagents from a parade of shops and on expiry of its lease sought a renewal lease with an extended user provision allowing for the sale of alcohol and convenience goods. The parade of shops already included a small supermarket selling such items and so the landlord objected to the proposed user and suggested a clause which specifically prohibited the sale of such items.

This dispute was referred to the County Court as a preliminary issue to the tenant's application for renewal of its lease under the Landlord and Tenant Act 1954. The court did not need to determine the issue of whether the user clause would be restrictive of competition, as the landlord conceded that this was the case. The judge did, however, comment that this concession was rightly made as the clause would restrict the sale of convenience goods on the parade. Interestingly, the relevant market was identified as within a relatively short walking distance from the parade. The issue for the court to determine, therefore, was whether the clause satisfied the conditions for exemption. The court was not satisfied that, as a matter of fact, the distribution of goods was improved or economic progress promoted through the existence of a number of different retailers, rather than via a supermarket or number of similar retailers, as the landlord had argued. On the evidence, it was not accepted that the community would benefit from the proposed restrictions, nor had the landlord proved the indispensability of them. The proposed user clause clearly provided a means of eliminating competition in convenience goods on the parade, contravening s 2 of the CA 1998. The court was not satisfied that the agreement fell within the s 9 exemption.

This case may cause some alarm for landlords who routinely impose restricted user covenants on tenants. However, it must be remembered that no argument was actually held on the issue of whether the user clause contravened s 2, as this was conceded by the landlord. In addition, the failure to persuade the court that the provision ought to fall within the s 9 exemptions, seems primarily to have resulted from the paucity of evidence presented by the landlord. Finally, a key factor in the court's decision seems to have been the determination that the relevant market was within a short walking distance from the parade and the absence of other nearby convenience stores.

REVIEW ACTIVITY

1. Look at the following lease extract:

   Clause 1 – definitions and interpretation

   Permitted Use:

   use as offices within Use Class E(g) of the Town and Country Planning (Use Classes) Order 1987 (as it applied in England at the date this lease was granted).

   24.1 User

   The Tenant must not use the Property for any purpose other than the Permitted Use

   Which of the following statements is correct?

   The user covenant contains:

   (a) an absolute covenant;

   (b) a qualified covenant;

   (c) a fully qualified covenant.

2. Imagine that a client wishes to change the use of its property. It has been advised by a planning consultant that its change of use is material and will not be covered by the General Permitted Development Order 2015. In addition to considering the Permitted Use definition under the lease, if the lease were in the form attached at **Appendix 4**, what other clause would be relevant and what does it require?

Answers to this Review activity may be found in Appendix 1.

CHAPTER 23

ALTERATIONS

23.1	Introduction	273
23.2	Lease controls	274
23.3	Restrictions outside the lease	277
23.4	Compensation for improvements	278
23.5	The 2020 Code for Leasing Business Premises	278
23.6	The Alterations Protocol	279
	Review activity	279

23.1 INTRODUCTION

A tenant will often wish to be able to make alterations to the premises, either immediately at the start of the lease (eg, fitting-out works at shop premises to enable it to start trading, or to erect partitioning in an open-plan office) or during the term of the lease to suit its changing business needs. A tenant will be concerned that the proposed restrictions in the lease are flexible enough to allow it to carry out its plans, that they will not affect assignability and that it will not suffer at rent review if the provisions are too flexible.

A landlord, however, usually wants to restrict the tenant's ability to make alterations for a number of reasons:

(a) to maintain the rental and capital value of the premises by preserving the character, reputation, appearance and physical integrity of the premises;

(b) to ensure that at the end of the lease the tenant gives back premises which are substantially the same as those demised to the tenant at the beginning;

(c) to ensure the landlord does not inadvertently become responsible for any breach by the tenant of the external restrictions which impact on alterations (see **23.3**).

The extent to which the landlord will want to restrict the tenant's ability will depend on the following:

(a) *The nature of the premises*

For example, in a letting of a large warehouse, or factory or other industrial premises, the landlord may require absolute control only over alterations affecting the structure and exterior of the premises, leaving the tenant free to do more or less as it pleases on the inside, as the landlord will know that the state of the interior will not affect its rental or capital interest. However, in a shopping parade, in order to maintain the general appearance of the parade and the quality of the development, and therefore its rental and capital value, the landlord may feel that it wants to have a very tight control over all alterations, inside and out.

In office leases, where the initial design of the building is open-plan, the landlord often allows the tenant to erect internal partitioning walls without having to obtain the landlord's prior consent, as long as the tenant notifies the landlord and agrees to remove them at the end of the term if the landlord so requires.

(b) *The length of the proposed term*

In a short-term letting (three years or less) the landlord is likely to want tight control over the tenant's ability to make alterations, in which case an absolute prohibition against all alterations may be appropriate.

However, in a longer-term letting (10 years or more), where the tenant may need to adapt the premises during the term to suit its changing business needs, or may anticipate the possibility of assigning the lease to an assignee who may wish to make alterations, the landlord will usually be prepared to allow the tenant a greater degree of freedom. Severe restrictions on a longer-term letting would give the landlord problems at the outset in securing a letting of the premises, and later on at rent review where the restrictive alterations covenant may be taken into account to reduce the rental value of the premises.

(c) *The type of alterations*

The landlord may allow the tenant unrestricted freedom to carry out non-structural alterations or additions, for example the partitioning in an open-plan office mentioned above, which do not affect the rental or capital value of the landlord's interest.

In most cases the landlord will impose an absolute covenant against structural alterations, for the simple reason that the structure, being such a fundamental part of the building, should not be tampered with by the tenant.

23.2 LEASE CONTROLS

23.2.1 Alterations clause

As with other covenants, the covenant against alterations may be absolute (completely prohibited), qualified (prohibited unless the landlord consents) or fully qualified (prohibited unless the landlord consents, such consent not to be withheld unreasonably). The alterations clause may be a mixture, so that some alterations are completely prohibited, some are prohibited unless consent is obtained and some may be carried out without consent.

For example, a typical lease of office premises might contain the following alterations clause:

12.1 The Tenant shall not make any alteration to the Property except those expressly permitted by this clause.

12.2 The Tenant shall not make any internal non-structural alterations without the prior written consent of the Landlord.

12.3 The Tenant may erect internal demountable partitioning without the consent of the Landlord provided that the Tenant makes good any damage to the Property caused and within one month of completion of the alterations the Tenant provides the Landlord with a copy of 'as built' drawings.

In all cases, the landlord must first consider the type of premises involved, and the length of term proposed.

23.2.1.1 Absolute covenants

Subject to certain exceptions mentioned below, if the lease contains an absolute covenant against the making of any alterations or a particular type of alteration (for example in clause 12.1 of the typical office lease, set out at **23.2.1**, structural alterations are absolutely prohibited), the landlord will have total control over the tenant. The tenant can always ask the landlord for permission to make the prohibited alteration, but the landlord can simply refuse. If the landlord did agree then this could be by way of a one-off waiver of the proposed breach of covenant, or by a permanent variation of the lease (by deed of variation). However, if the landlord did choose to consent to works which are otherwise prohibited under the lease, this may put it in breach of any obligations in other leases to enforce tenant covenants (*Duval v 11-13 Randolph Crescent Ltd* [2020] UKSC 18).

There are statutory exceptions to the landlord's absolute control. For example, the tenant can obtain a court order to enable it to carry out works required by some statutory bodies (eg a fire authority ordering the tenant to install a fire escape). In addition, the tenant of business premises can (although rarely does) use the provisions of the LTA 1927 (see **23.4**) to enable it to carry out works in the face of an absolute covenant.

The tenant should be advised to argue against an absolute covenant except, perhaps, where the covenant relates only to structural or external alterations (in which case the tenant may agree that it is reasonable that it should not be allowed to tamper with the structural parts of the building), or where the letting is for a short term and the tenant is confident that it will not need to alter the premises in the future to accommodate changes in its business, and that it will not need or want to assign the lease during the term. However, the longer the term, the more the tenant should ensure that it has sufficient flexibility to alter the premises.

23.2.1.2 Qualified covenants

A qualified covenant against alterations prohibits alterations to the premises by the tenant without the landlord's prior consent (which is usually required to be given in writing). An example of this is clause 12.2 of the typical office lease set out at **23.2.1**.

Other than in mining and agricultural leases, s 19(2) of the LTA 1927 implies into a qualified covenant against making *improvements* a proviso that the landlord's consent is not to be withheld unreasonably. Improvements are works carried out that increase the value or usefulness of the premises seen through the tenant's eyes (*Lambert v FW Woolworth & Co Ltd (No 2)* [1938] 2 All ER 664). There will therefore be few occasions where the landlord can argue that s 19(2) would not apply.

23.2.1.3 Fully qualified covenants

As said in **23.2.1.2** above, s 19(2) of the LTA 1927 converts a qualified covenant against alterations into a fully qualified covenant in so far as the alterations are *improvements*. To avoid any argument that the tenant's works are not improvements, most tenants will insist on converting a qualified covenant into a fully qualified covenant expressly by adding to the qualified covenant drafted by the landlord the words 'such consent not to be unreasonably withheld or delayed'.

23.2.1.4 Landlord's consent

Where landlord's consent is required, it will usually be given by deed in a document known as a licence for alterations or licence for works. The licence is usually negotiated between the landlord's solicitors and tenant's solicitors, and once agreed it will be produced in original and counterpart (or in duplicate) for signature by the landlord and the tenant.

The licence will often impose conditions on how the works are to be carried out to protect the landlord in respect of its concerns set out in **23.1** above, and these must be reasonable in all the circumstances. Common conditions are that the tenant must comply with statute in carrying out the works, obtain all necessary consents, carry out the works in a good and workmanlike manner, using good quality materials, comply with approved plans and specifications, and reinstate the premises to their previous condition at the end of the term. See **23.2.2** below.

Where s 19(2) of the LTA 1927 applies, or where there is a fully qualified covenant in the lease, consent from the landlord cannot be withheld unreasonably. The tenant must have supplied the landlord with all the information necessary for the landlord to reach an informed decision (*Kalford Ltd v Peterborough City Council* [2001] EGCS 42). If that has been done, then a landlord will be acting reasonably in refusing consent only where its reasons follow the general principles laid down in *International Drilling Fluids Ltd v Louisville Investments (Uxbridge) Ltd* [1986] Ch 513 (see **Chapter 21**) (as identified by the Court of Appeal in *Iqbal v Thakrar* [2004] All ER

(D) 304). This effectively means that the refusal must have something to do with the relationship of landlord and tenant and must not involve the landlord in simply seeking a collateral advantage outside the landlord and tenant relationship.

Section 19(2) allows the landlord to be compensated for damage to or reduction in the value of the premises or adjoining premises owned by the landlord, and to have its properly incurred legal and other (eg surveyor's fees) expenses met. It is therefore not reasonable for the landlord to refuse consent simply because the works will reduce the value of the reversionary interest.

Where the tenant thinks that the landlord is unreasonably withholding consent, the tenant could seek a declaration from the court that the landlord is acting unreasonably (coupled with an application for a declaration that the tenant can proceed with the alterations without any further need to seek the landlord's consent), or, with more risk, it could proceed with the works without consent and then use the landlord's alleged unreasonable withholding of consent as a defence to any claim for breach of covenant brought by the landlord.

The tenant is not, however, entitled to damages in respect of an unreasonable refusal of consent.

The landlord must be careful to ensure that any guarantor of the tenant is a party to the consent documentation where the permission may relate to a variation of the lease (eg, to allow the tenant to carry out works not permitted under the lease – see **15.4.3.1**).

23.2.2 Other lease clauses

The landlord is likely to include many other covenants in the lease that will affect the tenant's ability to carry out alterations to the premises. For example:

(a) *Reinstatement*

Section 19(2) of the LTA 1927 enables the landlord to impose a reinstatement obligation on the tenant in the case of an improvement that does not add to the value of the premises, where it is reasonable to do so.

The lease, however, usually contains an express reinstatement provision in any event for all alterations and additions (if requested by the landlord), so that it is less likely to be viewed as an unreasonable condition in giving consent. The tenant is likely to want to qualify an absolute obligation to reinstate by requiring that any such request be reasonable.

By obliging the tenant to reinstate the premises at the end of the term, the landlord may be able to avoid paying compensation to the tenant for improvements (see **23.4**) as, if the improvements have been removed, there is nothing to which the compensation requirement can attach.

(b) *Access to inspect*

The lease may contain an express right to inspect a tenant's works to ensure that it is carrying them out properly. This should avoid any argument that a condition to that effect in the licence for alterations is an unreasonable one.

(c) *Waste*

The doctrine of waste may operate to prevent the tenant from altering the premises. Waste is any act that changes the nature of the premises, and can be voluntary, permissive, ameliorating or equitable. If required, reference should be made to textbooks on land law for a more detailed consideration of the doctrine of waste. It is common to find a prohibition on waste (save to the extent that it might otherwise be permitted in the lease) in the alterations covenant.

(d) *Electrical supply and installations*

Many landlords impose a covenant on the tenant not to tamper with the electrical supply or installations, especially in a lease of part of a building.

(e) *Planning applications*

The landlord will want to control the tenant's ability to make applications for planning permission with an absolute, qualified or fully qualified covenant.

(f) *Signs and advertisements*

The landlord will usually require a qualified covenant by the tenant not to display any signs or advertisements at the premises, to guard against a proliferation of signs or advertising hoardings giving the premises an unsightly appearance that might reduce the value of the landlord's interest in the building. The landlord may require control over the size or type of sign or advertisement.

(g) *Decoration*

The decorating covenant may control the manner in which the tenant may alter the premises, since it is likely to dictate that the tenant is not to change the colour of the premises (either inside or outside, or both) without the landlord's prior consent.

(h) *No nuisance*

There will usually be a covenant imposed on the tenant not to do anything that would causes a nuisance or an annoyance to other tenants or owners or occupiers of adjoining properties, which may act as a control on how the tenant is able to carry out any works (eg, noise, times).

(i) *Rent review*

See **Chapter 19** for the treatment of alterations and improvements at rent review.

If the tenant secures an alterations covenant that is too flexible, in that it gives the tenant extensive freedom to alter and improve the premises as it sees fit, the rental value of the letting may be increased at review as a result. On the other hand, if the landlord secures a very restrictive covenant, it may be penalised at review.

23.3 RESTRICTIONS OUTSIDE THE LEASE

As with user covenants, there are external restraints, outside the scope of the lease, that may prevent the tenant from altering the premises, or which may at least regulate the way in which they are carried out. For example:

(a) *Planning legislation*

Any alterations falling within the definition of 'development' within s 55 of the TCPA 1990 will require planning permission.

(b) *Building Control*

Works to be carried out by the tenant may have to comply with the Building Control regime.

(c) *Covenants affecting a superior title.*

The tenant's proposed works may be prohibited by the terms of a covenant affecting the landlord's reversion (which may either be the freehold title, or a leasehold title if the landlord is itself a tenant) or may require the consent of the current beneficiary of the covenant.

(d) *The common law*

The tenant will have to ensure that any works it carries out at the premises do not give rise to a cause of action in the tort of nuisance. The tenant will also have to ensure that it will not, in executing its works, infringe an easement benefiting an adjoining property (eg, a right to light or air over the tenant's premises).

(e) *Fire legislation*

The tenant will have to bear in mind any requirements of the fire authority in regard to fire safety.

278   Commercial Property

(f) *Environmental legislation*

If the tenant's works are more than just minor works, the tenant must have regard to environmental legislation regarding noise and other kinds of pollution.

(g) *Equality Act 2010*

Where reasonable, a landlord may have to waive or modify an absolute prohibition on alterations to allow the tenant to carry out 'reasonable adjustments' so that a disabled person is not put at a substantial disadvantage in the building under the Equality Act 2010. Such alterations, however, would still be subject to the landlord's consent which may be reasonably withheld, which will depend on the circumstances in question.

The landlord may 'have to carry out' reasonable adjustments in respect of any common parts. It is likely to want to pass on any costs incurred to its tenants through the service charge. The landlord will need to ensure that the service charge provision allows for this.

On rent review the tenant will be concerned to ensure that any works it carries out to comply with statute, including those pursuant to the 2010 Act, are disregarded (see **19.6.3**).

23.4 COMPENSATION FOR IMPROVEMENTS

Under Pt I of the LTA 1927 (as amended by Pt III of the LTA 1954), the tenant may claim compensation for improvements that at the end of the term 'add to the letting value of the holding'. The concept is fair, in that the tenant will be returning to the landlord an asset that has increased in value as a result of the tenant's expenditure.

In addition, the LTA 1927 provides a mechanism whereby the tenant may obtain permission for improvements it would like to carry out to the premises even in the face of an absolute covenant.

In order to be entitled to compensation on quitting, the tenant must have obtained prior authorisation from the landlord to make the improvements by using a statutory procedure, and it must claim within the statutory time limits. It does not matter that the covenant in the lease is absolute or is qualified and the landlord has reasonable grounds to withhold consent.

The amount of compensation payable to the tenant is a sum deemed to be either the additional value of the premises directly resulting from the improvements, or the reasonable cost (as at the date of termination of the tenancy) of carrying out the improvement.

Although the parties cannot contract out of the provisions relating to compensation for improvements, it is a procedure that is rarely relevant in practice given that most leases will contain a requirement to reinstate.

23.5 THE 2020 CODE FOR LEASING BUSINESS PREMISES

The 2020 Code provides:

8   Change of use, alterations and fit-out

8.1   Leases should give landlords control over alterations and changes of use that are no more restrictive than are necessary to protect the value of the premises and any adjoining or neighbouring premises of the landlord, and this may differ between different types of property.

8.2   Where the landlord intends to prohibit certain changes of use or the making of certain alterations, or to require a licence from the landlord before they can take place, the tenant should be notified at the outset in order to obtain early professional advice as to the implications. This does not apply to normal provisions against changing the use outside the existing use class under planning law.

8.3   In a lease of an entire building, a landlord should not normally prohibit, or require its consent to be obtained for, internal non-structural alterations that do not adversely affect the character, value, structural stability, statutory compliance or energy efficiency performance of the building, but landlords will require the tenant to carry out such works properly and without causing damage or nuisance and to give written details to the landlord.

8.4 In a lease of a unit in a multi-let building, a landlord may require that its consent for internal non-structural alterations is to be obtained and that such consent is not to be unreasonably withheld or delayed, and may prohibit any alterations that adversely affect the character, value, structural stability, statutory compliance or energy efficiency performance of the building or its building services.

8.5 Except where the heads of terms state that there will be a reinstatement specification or an obligation on tenants to remove alterations, a lease should allow the tenant to leave alterations in place unless it is reasonable for the landlord to require their removal.

8.6 The tenant should be notified at the earliest practicable time if the landlord intends to impose any obligations for an initial fit-out that might involve material cost or to restrict how the tenant can fit-out or use the premises. The heads of terms and the lease should set out any agreed minimum requirements and any capital contributions.

See also para 9 of the Supplemental Guide in Appendix B of the 2020 Code.

23.6 THE ALTERATIONS PROTOCOL

A group of barristers and solicitors have published a Protocol for Applications for Consent to Carry Out Alterations (the Alterations Protocol). By following the Alterations Protocol it is intended that the landlord and tenant:

(a) will avoid arguments as to the information and documentation that should form part of any application for consent to alterations;

(b) will avoid disputes as to the period of time within which the landlord should give its decision in response to an application for consent;

(c) will, in case of disputes as to any matter arising, be able to have such disputes decided swiftly by an experienced tribunal, with recourse to the courts being an option of last resort only.

The Protocol is available at <www.propertyprotocols.co.uk>, and para 14 of the Supplemental Guide at Appendix B of the 2020 Code refers to 'information on the process to be followed for the approval of alterations' as being found in the Alterations Protocol.

REVIEW ACTIVITY

1. You are acting for a landlord of a multi-let office block. You have received a letter from a tenant's solicitor stating that the tenant wishes to carry out works. The tenant has a lease of the first floor of the office block (with six years left to run). The lease is in the form set out in **Appendix 4** (assume all bracketed wording in clause 20 has been incorporated). The proposed works are:

    (a) to fix an aerial to the exterior of the Building (ie the office block);

    (b) to erect internal partitioning; and

    (c) to drill holes in an internal structural wall of the Property (ie that part of the Building demised to the tenant and defined in the lease) in order to hang the modern art collection of the tenant.

    Advise the landlord whether the tenant is entitled to carry out the proposed works.

2. Consider the lease in the form set out in **Appendix 4** (assume all bracketed wording has been incorporated) and advise how it is compliant with the 2020 Code.

Answers to this Review activity may be found in Appendix 1.

CHAPTER 24

THE LANDLORD'S COVENANT FOR QUIET ENJOYMENT

24.1	Nature of the covenant	281
24.2	Negotiating the covenant	281
24.3	Acts constituting a breach	282
	Review activity	283

24.1 NATURE OF THE COVENANT

The landlord is under an *implied* obligation to give the tenant 'quiet enjoyment' of the premises. This means that the landlord must ensure that there is no interference with the tenant's use and enjoyment of the premises. However, most leases will contain an *express* covenant for quiet enjoyment by the landlord. The inclusion of an express covenant makes the obligation clearer to the parties (who may not know about the implied covenant) and helps to establish the status of the arrangement as a lease rather than a licence. It also gives each party the opportunity to modify the implied covenant in its favour.

24.2 NEGOTIATING THE COVENANT

Consider this example of an express covenant:

> The Landlord covenants with the Tenant that, so long as the Tenant pays the rents reserved by and complies with its obligations in this lease, the Tenant shall have quiet enjoyment of the Property without any interruption by the Landlord or any person claiming under the Landlord except as otherwise permitted by this lease.

The tenant will want to extend the protection of the covenant by making the following amendments:

> The Landlord covenants with the Tenant that~~, so long as the Tenant pays the rents reserved by and complies with its obligations in this lease~~, the Tenant shall have quiet enjoyment of the Property without any interruption by the Landlord or any person claiming under the Landlord <u>or by any person with title paramount</u> except as otherwise permitted by this lease.

The tenant will argue that there are more appropriate ways to deal with breaches of the tenant's covenants in the lease (including forfeiture) than disturbing the tenant's quiet enjoyment, particularly where there is a dispute as to whether a breach has actually taken place. The tenant will also want to extend the protection offered by the covenant to include the acts of those with a superior title.

The landlord will want to resist these amendments. It is reasonable to expect the tenant to comply with its covenants and it would be dangerous to take on liability for a superior landlord over which it has no control. Even if the inserted words do not appear, the landlord should check the definition of 'landlord' in the lease to see that it does not include superior landlords.

The landlord may also prefer not to take on liability for the actions of those claiming under it:

The Landlord covenants with the Tenant that, so long as the Tenant pays the rents reserved by and complies with its obligations in this lease, the Tenant shall have quiet enjoyment of the Property without any interruption by the Landlord ~~or any person claiming under the Landlord~~ except as otherwise permitted by this lease.

The tenant will argue that the landlord should take responsibility for its employees, agents and tenants as it has some control over them. Moreover, the covenant only extends to the *lawful* acts of those claiming under the landlord since, if they are *unlawful* (eg trespass), the tenant will have its own remedies against the person committing the act. This means that there is no breach of the covenant in the event of an interruption by an adjoining tenant which is unauthorised by the landlord.

24.3 ACTS CONSTITUTING A BREACH

The covenant will provide the tenant with a remedy in the case of unlawful eviction or where there is substantial interference with the tenant's use or enjoyment of the demised premises. A landlord will not usually be liable for activities carried out outside the demised premises (*Stonecrest Marble Ltd v Shepherds Bush Housing Association Ltd* [2021] EWHC 2621 (Ch)), but this is a question of fact in each case and the following situations have given rise to a breach:

(a) Where the landlord erected scaffolding on the pavement in front of a shop which blocked the access to the shop (*Owen v Gadd* [1956] 2 QB 99). This illustrates that it is not necessary for there to be any physical intrusion into the demised premises provided that there is physical interference with the enjoyment of the premises.

(b) Where the demised premises were flooded due to the landlord's failure to repair a culvert on his adjoining land (*Booth v Thomas* [1926] Ch 397).

(c) Where the landlord carried out work to the building in a manner which caused prolonged and substantial interference to the tenant by reason of 'dust, noise, dirt ... deterioration of common parts ... general inconvenience ... and water penetration' (see *Mira v Aylmer Square Investments Ltd* [1990] 1 EGLR 45). If the landlord is under an obligation to repair the premises, it must take all reasonable precautions to prevent disturbance (*Goldmile Properties Ltd v Lechouritis* [2003] EWCA Civ 49, [2003] 15 EG 143).

(d) Where the landlord carried out rebuilding work to the floors above the tenant's ground floor art gallery, making excessive amounts of noise and wrapping the gallery in scaffolding so that it looked closed (see *Timothy Taylor Ltd v Mayfair House Corporation and another* [2016] EWHC 1075 (Ch)).

It used to be thought that the word 'quiet' in the covenant did not refer to the absence of noise and that some direct and physical interference was required before the landlord incurred liability under it. However, in the case of *Southwark London Borough Council v Mills and Others; Baxter v Camden London Borough Council* [1999] 3 WLR 939, the House of Lords held that no such limitation exists. The fact that the tenant was complaining of noise from adjoining premises in the block due to poor sound insulation did not in itself preclude a claim for breach of the covenant for quiet enjoyment. However, it was also held that the covenant applies only to the subject matter of the lease at the date of the grant. If, at that date, the premises already suffer from poor soundproofing qualities, the covenant is one not to interfere with the tenant's use or enjoyment of premises with that feature.

A landlord will not be liable for breach of the covenant for quiet enjoyment where the nuisance to the tenant is caused by another tenant and the landlord has not expressly or impliedly authorised the actions that are causing the nuisance (see *Fouladi v Darout Ltd and others* [2018] EWHC 3501 (Ch)).

The covenant for quiet enjoyment is closely linked with the landlord's implied obligation not to derogate from its grant. This requires a landlord not to do anything which substantially interferes with the use of the demised premises for the purpose for which they were let. (See **30.2.2.2**.)

REVIEW ACTIVITY

1. You act for a tenant under a lease containing an express covenant for quiet enjoyment. The landlord wants to enter the premises and carry out an environmental investigation that involves drilling boreholes and taking samples from under the ground. The landlord says that it is entitled to do this as the lease contains a right for the landlord to enter for the purpose of making a survey. Your client has refused the landlord entry to drill boreholes and take samples. If the landlord does so, will your client have a remedy for breach of the covenant of quiet enjoyment?

2. You act for a landlord who has recently carried out repairs to the outside of the building pursuant to its repairing covenant under the lease. Although your client took all *reasonable* steps to minimise the disruption and loss of profit caused to the tenant's restaurant business, the tenant is suing for damages for breach of the express covenant of quiet enjoyment because your client did not take all *possible* steps to minimise disruption and loss of profit. Will the tenant have a remedy for breach of the covenant of quiet enjoyment?

Answers to this Review activity may be found in Appendix 1.

CHAPTER 25

INSURANCE

25.1	Introduction	285
25.2	The obligation to insure	286
25.3	The obligation to pay for the insurance	288
25.4	Compliance with the terms of the insurance	289
25.5	The obligation to reinstate	289
25.6	Rent suspension	291
25.7	Termination	292
25.8	Damage by uninsured risks	293
25.9	Additional provisions	294
25.10	Insurance by the tenant	294
	Review activity	294

25.1 INTRODUCTION

There is no implied obligation on either party to insure the premises demised by the lease. However, it is very important to both parties and their lenders that their respective interests are fully protected, and it is therefore essential for the lease to make express provision for insurance.

There are a number of important issues which will need to be addressed by the draftsman. These include not only imposing an obligation to insure, but also specifying what will happen if damage does occur: Who will reinstate? Will the tenant continue to pay rent? Should the lease be terminated? As with any lease negotiation, there will be some areas that prove contentious between the parties. This chapter highlights some of those areas and identifies issues of which the parties should be particularly aware. The Code for Leasing Business Premises 2020 ('the 2020 Code') also contains recommendations as to how some of these difficult issues should be dealt with. It provides as follows:

> **9 Insurance and damage**
>
> 9.1 Where the landlord will insure the property, leases should provide that the policy will be on normal market terms, that full terrorism cover will be provided if it is available at reasonable rates of premium, and that the landlord will insure with reputable insurers and provide details of the insurance to the tenant on reasonable request.
>
> 9.2 Leases should state that rent suspension will apply if the premises or any landlord's areas or services serving them are damaged by an insured risk or, other than where due to an act or default of the tenant, an uninsured risk. If the lease limits the period in which rent is to be suspended, either party should be allowed to terminate the lease if reinstatement of significant damage is not completed within that period.
>
> 9.3 Leases should state that if the whole or a substantial part of the premises or any landlord's areas or services serving them are so damaged by an uninsured risk as not to be capable of normal use by the tenant, either party should be allowed to terminate the lease unless the landlord agrees to rebuild at its own cost.
>
> 9.4 Landlords should pass on to tenants the benefit of discounted premiums and should disclose to tenants whether the landlord benefits from insurance commissions.

Unless specifically drafted to be compliant with the 2020 Code, many leases will not contain such obligations, and the tenant will have to amend the lease if it wishes the landlord to be bound by such obligations. For an example of a lease that complies with the 2020 Code, see **Appendix 4** to this book.

Under the 2020 Code, RICS members will be mandatorily required to ensure that written heads of terms are prepared prior to circulation of the initial draft of the lease (see **14.2**). These mandatory heads of terms must summarise the key provisions of the letting, including the tenant's liability to pay insurance premiums.

The Code's recommendations as to best practice in relation to the key insurance provisions (and other key provisions) of a lease are not stated to be mandatory, but there may be legal and/or disciplinary consequences for RICS members in departing from them.

25.2 THE OBLIGATION TO INSURE

25.2.1 Who is to insure?

In a lease of commercial premises, it is common practice for the landlord to take out the insurance cover. On a lease of part of a building (eg one unit in a shopping centre, or a suite of offices in a block) it is more appropriate for the landlord to arrange insurance for the whole building, including any car parks, pedestrian areas, etc, as in this way only one policy is needed. Further, all the common parts of the building will be covered under the same policy and there is no danger of any parts of the building being left uninsured. On the grant of a lease of the whole of a building, either party could be made to insure, but the landlord will usually wish to assume the responsibility rather than face the risk of the tenant failing to comply with its covenant to insure. While the landlord would be able to sue the tenant for breach of covenant, the tenant may have insufficient funds to satisfy the judgment.

If the landlord takes out the insurance before completion of the lease, the tenant should ask to see a copy of the policy so that it can satisfy itself as to the amount and terms of cover. As the tenant has a continuing interest in the insurance of the premises, it should also impose an obligation on the landlord in the lease to produce evidence of the terms of the policy and of payment of the premiums, at any time during the term of the lease.

25.2.2 What is to be insured?

On the grant of a lease of the whole of a building, it is quite clear that the insurance and reinstatement obligations will need to apply to the whole of that building.

On the grant of a lease of part, the insurance and reinstatement obligations should also apply to the whole of the building of which the premises form part. The building will often provide access or contain services essential to useful occupation of the premises. Even if it does not, most tenants would consider it undesirable to occupy premises in a damaged building, even if their premises were undamaged.

In the case of either a lease of whole or a lease of part, if the building is on an estate or business park owned by the landlord, the tenant should check that the insurance and reinstatement obligations apply to any other essential common parts. It would clearly be unacceptable to the tenant if, for example, the building it occupied were reinstated but the estate roads needed to access that building were not.

25.2.3 In whose name?

Where the landlord is to insure, the tenant should consider amending the lease to require the insurance to be effected in the joint names of the landlord and tenant. This will be to the tenant's advantage because the insurance company will not allow the policy to lapse unless both parties have been given notice. It will also ensure that the proceeds of the policy will be paid out to both parties jointly, and thus give the tenant some control over how they are spent.

Another advantage to the tenant is that insurance in joint names may prevent subrogation. This is the right of the insurer to step into the shoes of the insured and pursue any claims that the insured has against third parties to recover the loss. This means that, where the tenant is not named on the policy, if the landlord had a cause of action against the tenant arising out of some default on the tenant's part which caused the damage, the insurers would be able to pursue that claim. If, however, the insurance is in the joint names of the landlord and tenant, subrogation may not be possible, depending on the intentions of the parties (see the judgment of Rix LJ in *Tyco Fire & Integrated Solutions (UK) Ltd v Rolls Royce Motor Cars Ltd* [2008] EWCA Civ 286).

However, even in those cases where the insurance is in the landlord's name alone, the tenant may still be able to prevent subrogation occurring where it can be shown that the insurance has been taken out for the mutual benefit of both parties (eg see *Mark Rowlands Ltd v Berni Inns Ltd* [1986] 1 QB 211, where the tenant agreed to reimburse the landlord the premiums paid; see also *Lambert v Keymood Ltd* [1997] 43 EG 131).

Whether the landlord agrees to the insurance being in joint names depends to a large extent on the nature of the tenant's interest in the premises. If the tenant occupies only part of the property that is insured, the landlord should not agree to the insurance being in joint names. It would be impractical to have more than one tenant named as a joint insured, and in any event, the landlord will be reluctant to share control of the insurance monies with a tenant who does not occupy the whole of the insured property. Institutional landlords will often have block insurance policies under which their whole portfolio of properties is insured. In those circumstances joint insurance will not be possible.

If, however, the tenant occupies the whole of the insured property and it is not insured under a block policy, in theory there is nothing to stop the insurance being in joint names. However, the landlord will be conscious of the fact that it has the more valuable interest in the premises and that it has the obligation to reinstate. It may therefore still be reluctant to agree to joint insurance.

If the landlord objects to insurance in joint names, the tenant should ensure that the lease provides that its interest will be 'noted' on the landlord's policy. This will mean the tenant will be notified of any claim or of any event that might invalidate the insurance. It might also be possible for the landlord to obtain a non-subrogation clause for the benefit of the tenant in the insurance policy.

25.2.4 Risks and losses covered

The lease should contain a comprehensive definition of the risks against which the insured party is to insure. A definition of 'insured risks' will typically include fire, lightning, explosion, impact, storm, tempest, flood, overflowing and bursting of water tanks or pipes, riot, civil commotion and many other risks commonly included in a buildings insurance policy. To give the landlord flexibility, at the end of the definition there should be a 'sweeping-up' provision along the lines of 'and such other risks as the landlord may from time to time reasonably consider to be necessary'.

It is important that the tenant carefully checks the definition of insured risks. If a risk is not insured against, the cost of any damage caused by it will usually be borne by the tenant, either under the repairing obligation or through the service charge provisions. The tenant must therefore make sure that the definition of insured risks includes all risks normally covered by a comprehensive buildings insurance policy. It should look out for any provisions allowing the landlord to vary the list of insured risks or be relieved from the obligation to insure against them.

25.2.4.1 Terrorism

Consideration also needs to be given to the issue of insurance cover against terrorist acts. The 2020 Code stipulates that terrorism cover should be provided 'if it is available at reasonable rates of premium'. However, such cover is no longer provided automatically by all insurers of commercial properties following a series of terrorist incidents in London in the early 1990s linked to the troubles in Northern Ireland. Cover can still be obtained, however, through a Government-backed scheme called Pool Re. This was set up in 1993 in response to the withdrawal of terrorist cover by the insurance industry.

The landlord and the tenant must therefore decide whether they think cover against terrorism is necessary. This will depend on the location of the property and the nature of the occupier and its business. It will also, of course, depend on the cost of obtaining such insurance. If it is required, it should be referred to in the list of insured risks. If it is not specified, an obligation to insure against 'explosion' may be sufficient to cover it (as it was in *Qdime Ltd v various leaseholders at Bath Building (Swindon)* [2014] UKUT 0261 (LC)), but this is uncertain. If there is no requirement to insure against terrorism, any damage caused in consequence of it would then be an uninsured loss. Both parties to the lease need to be aware of who is responsible for such uninsured loss (see **25.8**).

25.2.4.2 Flood

Certain properties are at a greater risk of flooding than others, and there has recently been a significant increase in extreme flood events in the UK. Concern exists that those properties in areas with a high flood risk may become either uninsurable for flood damage or insurable only at great cost (see **9.8**).

If the tenant occupies premises at high risk of flood, it should therefore be advised to consider the risk that insurance premiums (which it will normally pay for via the insurance rent) may become very high at some point during the lease term. If the risk is such that, at some point, insurance for flooding cannot be obtained at all, any damage caused as a result of flooding would constitute uninsured loss (see **25.8**). As with terrorism, the parties must be advised as to how such uninsured loss is dealt with.

25.2.4.3 Loss of rent

Most leases will also allow the landlord to insure against loss of rent for a specified period, usually three or five years. The landlord will wish to carry such insurance, as in most leases the tenant's obligation to pay rent will be suspended if the premises cannot be occupied due to damage caused by insured risks (see **25.6**).

25.2.5 The sum insured

The tenant should ensure the landlord is obliged to insure the premises for their full reinstatement value. This will mean the landlord will have adequate funds to replace the building should it be totally destroyed. Care must be taken to ensure that site-clearance costs, professional fees, and fees for any necessary planning applications and any VAT are also covered. As to the actual amount of cover, specialist advice will be needed and the insuring party should consult experienced insurance brokers. The tenant, if it has obtained a covenant from the landlord to insure for the full reinstatement value, will have a claim for breach of covenant if the policy proceeds are inadequate due to the landlord underinsuring. A successful claim would mean the landlord would have to make up any shortfall from its own resources.

25.3 THE OBLIGATION TO PAY FOR THE INSURANCE

Where the landlord has insured the premises, there will be a covenant in the lease requiring the tenant to reimburse the cost of insurance to the landlord. This sum is likely to be reserved as rent in order to give the landlord better remedies for recovery. If the premises are part of a larger building which the landlord has insured, recovery can either be through the service charge provisions or, alternatively, there may be a separate covenant by the tenant to reimburse an apportioned part of the premium. The tenant must ensure that the apportionment of the premium between the tenants is fair, particularly if the business of some of the tenants involves hazardous activities which lead to an increase in the premium.

It should be noted that a covenant by the tenant to reimburse premiums that the landlord 'shall from time to time properly expend' does not impose an obligation on the landlord to shop around for a reasonable level of premium (see *Havenridge Ltd v Boston Dyers Ltd* [1994] 49 EG 111).

In addition to reimbursement of the buildings insurance, the landlord will usually also require the tenant to reimburse it for the cost of insuring against loss of rent. This will protect the landlord if the rent payments by the tenant are suspended (see **25.6**).

25.4 COMPLIANCE WITH THE TERMS OF THE INSURANCE

Anyone who has ever read an insurance policy will know there are usually various requirements that need to be complied with for the insurance to be effective. Most leases will require that the tenant complies with these requirements. This is another reason for the tenant to ensure that the lease requires the landlord to supply a copy of the insurance policy. Further, the lease will often provide that the tenant must not invalidate the policy. A failure to comply with, for example, a requirement to service a security alarm, may lead to a policy being invalidated in the event of theft from the premises. In these circumstances, the tenant would then be left to bear the loss.

Being entitled to sight of the policy obviously means that the tenant has the information to enable it to comply with its requirements. However, what if the tenant is unhappy with the requirements or terms of the policy? In an ideal world, the tenant would ensure that the lease stipulated that the terms of the insurance policy were subject to its approval. This qualification may be possible where the tenant is a tenant of whole. However, a landlord will resist such a provision where the tenant occupies part only, as seeking approval of more than one tenant to the terms of a policy becomes administratively cumbersome, if not impractical, in the event of disagreement between the tenants. Nonetheless, even a tenant of part should seek to ensure that it is obliged to comply only with the reasonable requirements of the insurer of which it has received written notice. It should also ensure that the landlord is obliged to place the insurance with a reputable and substantial insurer. This will minimise the risk of unusual terms and conditions. The 2020 Code does provide that the landlord should 'insure with reputable insurers' (see **25.1**).

The tenant should also be wary of any excess payable under the insurance policy. The terms of the lease may require the tenant to bear the cost of such excess. This could be quite an onerous liability if the landlord accepts a large excess in return for a lower premium. The tenant should resist such a requirement, or restrict it to reasonable excesses of the kind usually imposed by insurers.

If the tenant sells combustible or flammable goods (eg lighter fuel, fireworks), it should be aware of any restriction on the storage of such items in the lease and insurance policy, and qualify such provisions accordingly.

25.5 THE OBLIGATION TO REINSTATE

If the premises are damaged or destroyed, the lease should contain provisions dealing with who will be liable for their repair and reinstatement.

25.5.1 Will the tenant's repairing covenant apply?

Since the tenant will be paying for the insurance taken out by the landlord, it should ensure that it is not obliged to repair the premises if they are damaged by one of the insured risks. It is common practice to exclude from the tenant's repairing covenant liability for damage caused by an insured risk. However, this exclusion will not usually apply if the insurance policy has been invalidated, or the insurance proceeds are not fully paid out by reason of the act or omission of the tenant (or some other person who was at the premises with the tenant's authority). The landlord may also attempt to stipulate that the exclusion will not apply to damage caused by insured risks for which it has not been able to obtain insurance on reasonable terms. The tenant should be wary of this exclusion as it passes the responsibility for uninsured losses to the tenant (see **25.8**).

25.5.2 Who will reinstate?

If the insurance is in the joint names of landlord and tenant, the proceeds of the policy will be paid to both of the insureds, who have equal control over the application of the proceeds and therefore the reinstatement of the premises. However, where the policy is in the sole name of the landlord, unless the lease provides to the contrary, there is no obligation on the landlord to use the proceeds of the policy to reinstate the premises. In those cases where the tenant is under an obligation to pay the cost of the insurance, it has been held that the landlord may be presumed to have insured on behalf of the tenant as well as itself, and thus the tenant can require the proceeds to be laid out on reinstatement (*Mumford Hotels Ltd v Wheler and Another* [1964] Ch 117).

Nonetheless, in any event, it is good practice for the lease to contain an express obligation on the party obliged to insure, to apply the proceeds of insurance in reinstating the premises. This will usually be the landlord. The landlord should make it clear that any insurance money in respect of loss of rent is not to be applied in the reinstatement of the premises, as this is to compensate it for the loss of the tenant's rent when the rent suspension clause is operating (see **25.6**).

From the tenant's point of view, it should pay particular attention to the wording of the covenant, which is often an obligation just to lay out the insurance monies received in respect of damage to the premises in their reinstatement. There are two potential issues with this. First, such an obligation does not deal with the situation where the insurance proceeds are insufficient to cover the entire cost of reinstatement. Although the landlord might be in breach of covenant for underinsuring the premises, the tenant should nevertheless press for a covenant by the landlord to make up the difference. The second potential issue with a simple obligation to lay out the insurance monies in reinstating the premises is that it does not deal with the situation where the landlord delays (or indeed fails altogether) to make a claim on the insurance. The tenant should insert an obligation to make such a claim promptly.

An alternative way around both of these issues is to impose on the landlord an absolute covenant to reinstate (unconnected to and regardless of any insurance pay out). Where this latter form of covenant is chosen, the landlord should qualify the absolute nature of its obligation to reinstate by providing that it is not liable in the event that the policy is invalidated, or where the proceeds are irrecoverable by reason of the act or omission of the tenant (or anyone at the premises with the tenant's consent). If the landlord accepts an obligation to make up any shortfall in the proceeds of the insurance then, again, this obligation should exclude any shortfall arising from the act or omission of the tenant (or anyone at the premises with the tenant's consent).

In any event, the landlord would not want to be liable to reinstate the premises for so long as circumstances beyond the landlord's control contrive to prevent it from doing so (eg strikes, lock-outs, shortages of materials, a failure to obtain planning).

The tenant should look out for any provision allowing the landlord to vary the premises on reinstatement. Whilst it is useful for the landlord to have flexibility to reflect changes in building practices, the tenant does not want reinstated premises that are unsuitable for its needs. Any such provision should therefore be amended to require the landlord, as a minimum, to provide premises that are of a similar size and no less suitable for the tenant than the original premises. The tenant should also consider requesting a landlord's covenant to provide collateral warranties (see **10.5.1**) in the event the premises require a complete rebuild.

25.6 RENT SUSPENSION

25.6.1 What is rent suspension?

Unless the lease is frustrated, rent continues to be payable by the tenant where the premises are damaged, even if the damage is extensive. It is therefore common to include a provision in the lease that if the premises are damaged by an insured risk, and become unfit for occupation or use by the tenant, the rent (or a fair proportion of it, depending on the extent of the damage) should cease to be payable. This is often referred to by practitioners as 'rent suspension' or 'rent cesser'. The landlord does not usually lose out by including such a provision, as it will usually insure against loss of rent when it takes out buildings insurance (see **25.2.4**).

25.6.2 When will rent suspension apply?

A tenant of part of a building should ensure that the rent suspension provisions apply if any part of the building is damaged so as to render the premises unusable. For example, a tenant would not want to pay rent for undamaged premises on the fifth floor of the building if all the staircases and lifts leading to the premises were unusable. A tenant of the whole of a building should give consideration as to whether it has any essential services or rights running over any other land of the landlord. If it does, the rent should be suspended in the event that such essential services are damaged or destroyed, Provided the landlord owns and controls the land over which such services or rights run, it will not usually object to such a provision.

The lease will usually provide for suspension of rent only if the damage results from an insured risk, so that the tenant will remain liable for rent where the premises become unusable as a result of damage by uninsured risks. Again, it is therefore important that the tenant examines the defined list of insured risks to ensure that they are adequate. Otherwise, it will not benefit from rent suspension where it was expecting to, and may also be left with an unexpected repair bill (see **25.8**).

Thought will need to be given as to whether rent will be suspended when damage arises as a result of a risk that the landlord has been unable to insure against, such as terrorism. The 2020 Code envisages that rent will be suspended where such uninsured loss arises (see **25.1**). However, the landlord may be reluctant to accept this given that it is unlikely to receive loss of rent insurance where damage is caused by an uninsured risk (see **25.8**).

The landlord will want to qualify the rent suspension further by stipulating that rent continues to be payable where the landlord's insurance policy has been invalidated by the act or omission of the tenant (or someone at the premises with the tenant's consent). Without this qualification, the landlord would not receive rent or loss of rent insurance proceeds.

25.6.3 How long will rent suspension last?

The suspension will continue for such period as is specified in the lease. It is usual for the rent to become payable as soon as the premises have been reinstated and are again fit for use and occupation, for the purpose permitted by the lease. It should be noted that there is a subtle difference between premises being fit for occupation *and* use, and the premises being fit for occupation *or* use. The tenant should ensure that the premises have to be fit for occupation *and* use, as premises can sometimes be occupied without being usable for the purposes of the tenant's business.

The lease will often specify a maximum period of rent suspension. This is usually the period for which the landlord has loss of rent insurance, and is therefore normally either three or five years. The problem for the tenant is that the rent suspension will end on the expiry of this three- or five-year period, even if the premises have not been fully reinstated. One way of dealing with this is to insist that there be no time limit on the rent suspension. Practitioners sometimes refer to this as an 'unlimited rent cesser'. The other method is to insert in the lease an option for the tenant to end the lease if the premises have not been reinstated by the end of the rent suspension period (see **25.7**).

25.6.4 Will other payments be suspended?

The tenant should also press for a similar suspension in respect of other payments under the lease, such as the service charge and insurance rent. If the premises are damaged and the tenant is unable to occupy them, it will not be able to take advantage of the services provided by the landlord. In addition, it will probably have to relocate while the premises are reinstated, and will have to pay service charge and insurance rent for the alternative premises.

The landlord may try to argue against suspension of these additional sums. If damage is occasioned to the tenant's premises alone, this is not likely to reduce significantly the level of services provided to the rest of the tenants. The landlord may therefore argue that it is not prepared to suffer any reduction in the amount of service charge income. It will also have to continue to insure the premises, even while the tenant is not in occupation.

One way forward may be for the landlord to insure against loss of service charge in the same way as it insures against loss of rent. Some policies do cover loss of service charge as well as loss of rent. This may extend to insurance rent, depending on the wording of the policy. Much will depend on the bargaining strength of the tenant and the landlord's willingness to be dictated to on the terms of its insurance policy. Institutional landlords in particular will resist the suspension of these sums if their loss is not insured, as they generally require FRI (full repairing and insuring) leases with clear rents. A tenant who has business interruption insurance cover may be able to recover the increased costs arising from operating alternative premises, depending on the wording of its policy.

25.7 TERMINATION

Although the doctrine of frustration is capable of applying to leases (*National Carriers Ltd v Panalpina (Northern) Ltd* [1981] AC 675), it will do so only in exceptional circumstances (*Canary Wharf (BP4) T1 Ltd v European Medicines Agency* [2019] EWHC 335 (Ch)). Accordingly, unless the doctrine applies, the lease will continue notwithstanding any accidental damage to the premises, and the loss will fall on the party obliged to repair. As a result, the lease will need to specify the circumstances (if any) in which the lease can be terminated following damage or destruction.

25.7.1 By the tenant

If the premises are damaged or destroyed by an insured risk so as to be unfit for occupation or use, the tenant will be faced with the possibility of relocating its business during the reinstatement period. Ideally, in such circumstances, the tenant would be able to end the lease of the damaged premises, leaving it free to take up a lease of new premises on a permanent basis. To do this the tenant would need a break clause in the lease of the damaged premises operable in these circumstances.

If the landlord agreed to this, however, it would be left with no tenant and potentially no loss of rent insurance (because once the lease is gone, no rent is contractually payable on it). For these reasons the landlord will usually require the tenant to reoccupy the premises once they have been reinstated. The problem for the tenant is it does not know how long such reinstatement might take.

Most landlords will not accept an obligation to reinstate within any particular timescale, as there are too many factors that may cause delay. Planning permission may prove difficult to obtain, there maybe historic contamination that has to be dealt with of which the parties were unaware when the site was originally developed, or there may be delays in the building programme caused by weather or shortage of materials or labour. Rather than have complex clauses in the lease to deal with these possibilities, the parties often agree that the landlord will reinstate the premises as soon as reasonably practicable. This creates a lack of certainty for the tenant, who does not know how long it will be left operating out of temporary premises.

On possible solution is for the tenant to have an option to end the lease in the event that the premises have not been reinstated within a particular time period. This time period is usually identical to the loss of rent insurance period. The option to end the lease then deals with two possible problems – the lack of a time-specific reinstatement obligation and a limited rent suspension. This solution is recommended by the 2020 Code.

25.7.2 By the landlord

For the reasons explored above, the landlord will not usually want the lease to be terminated where damage or destruction by an insured risk occurs. However, if reinstatement proves impossible (eg because planning permission cannot be obtained), the landlord will need the ability to end the lease and its reinstatement obligations. The landlord will usually insert into the lease a provision allowing it to terminate the lease in these circumstances.

The landlord should always bear in mind that the tenancy may be protected by Part II of the LTA 1954, and consequently the lease would need to be terminated in accordance with the provisions of that Act (see **Chapter 32**).

25.7.3 Who retains the insurance monies?

If reinstatement is not possible (or the parties do not desire it), in the absence of an express provision in the lease it is unclear to whom the insurance proceeds will belong, and it will be left to the court to ascertain the intention of the parties by looking at the lease as a whole.

For this reason the lease will often provide that following termination in the circumstances discussed above, the landlord will retain the insurance monies. The tenant may consider this unfair – after all, it is usually the tenant who will have reimbursed the landlord for the insurance premium. The tenant should try to insert a provision that the insurance monies will be shared between the landlord and tenant according to the values of their respective interests in the premises. The tenant would need to be aware that this may result in its receiving nothing, as a lease where an open market rent is paid on a quarterly basis often has no capital value. The landlord may also resist the amendment using this argument. Further, if reinstatement still remains a possibility, payment of a portion of the insurance monies to the tenant will leave the landlord with a reduced fund from which to reinstate.

25.8 DAMAGE BY UNINSURED RISKS

Historically, the risk of damage caused by an uninsured risk has been carried by the tenant. The landlord would not be obliged to reinstate the property, there would be no rent suspension and the terms of the tenant's repairing covenant would probably be wide enough to require it to carry out the necessary remedial work.

However, in recent years tenants have become more aware of the potential financial consequences of accepting such provisions. Should, for example, terrorism cover become unavailable for a particular type of property, a tenant who accepted the responsibility for uninsured losses would find itself in an unenviable position if its premises were destroyed by a terrorist act. Despite the fact that it might have a short-term lease with little time left to run, it could be left paying the cost of rebuilding the premises while continuing to pay rent on it.

Lawyers for both landlords and tenants now tend to be more attuned to the issue of uninsured losses. The problem is, of course, that the risk has to be borne by one party or the other for such losses, despite no one being at fault for the loss having arisen.

Given that it is the landlord who has the long-term capital interest in the premises, the view might be taken that the landlord is the more appropriate party to bear the risk of such losses. The 2020 Code provides that if the premises (or areas serving them) are damaged by an uninsured risk so as not to be capable of normal use, either party should be allowed to terminate the lease unless the landlord agrees to rebuild at its own cost.

25.9 ADDITIONAL PROVISIONS

Certain other covenants on the part of the tenant are commonly included in relation to the insurance of the premises:

(a) to pay any increased or additional premiums that become payable by reason of the tenant's activities at the premises;

(b) to pay the cost of annual valuations for insurance purposes (which the tenant should specify must be reasonable and proper);

(c) to insure and reinstate any plate glass at the premises. Some retail tenants prefer to pay the cost of plate glass replacement themselves rather than insure against it. If this is the case, a requirement in the lease to insure plate glass will need to be amended so that it does not apply to the tenant in question.

25.10 INSURANCE BY THE TENANT

If, exceptionally, the tenant covenants to insure the premises, the landlord must make sure that its interest as landlord is fully protected. The landlord will have concerns similar to those expressed above on behalf of the tenant, and so will wish to ensure:

(a) that insurance is taken out in the joint names of the landlord and tenant, with insurers to be approved by the landlord;

(b) that the insurance is taken out on terms to be approved by the landlord (eg as to the basis of cover, the risks insured, the amount and any excesses);

(c) that in the event of damage or destruction, the tenant covenants to reinstate the premises.

There will not usually be a rent suspension clause if the tenant assumes the insuring obligation.

REVIEW ACTIVITY

Imagine your client has taken a lease of two upper floors of an office building in the form set out in **Appendix 4**. The ground-floor reception area of the Building is seriously damaged by a flood. There is an excess on the landlord's insurance policy of £5,000. Read Sch 6 of the lease at **Appendix 4** and answer the following questions:

1. Will your client be obliged to pay rent and other sums whilst the reception area is repaired?

2. Who will have to bear the cost of the excess?

3. What will happen if the reception area has not been reinstated after three years?

Answers to this Review activity may be found in Appendix 1.

CHAPTER 26

Forfeiture

26.1	Introduction	295
26.2	Express reservation of the right	295
26.3	Waiver of the right to forfeit	296
26.4	Strict procedural rules and relief against forfeiture	296
26.5	Additional rules in special cases	300
26.6	Position of sub-tenants and mortgagees on forfeiture	302
26.7	The 2020 Code for Leasing Business Premises	302
26.8	Reform	302
	Review activity	302

26.1 INTRODUCTION

Forfeiture is the right of the landlord to retake possession of the premises and so prematurely end the lease on the happening of certain specified events. Forfeiture is primarily a remedy rather than a method of termination (for which see **Chapter 30**), albeit that the result of a successful forfeiture will be the termination of the lease.

The landlord should think carefully before it proceeds to forfeit the lease. In a rising market the landlord should have no difficulty in subsequently re-letting the premises, possibly at a higher rent. However, in a falling market, re-letting the premises may not be so easy and the landlord may be left with an empty property on its hands for a long time, leading to a loss of income and a potential detrimental effect on any adjoining property of the landlord (eg, other shops in a parade or shopping mall).

The right is enforced in one of two ways: by court order or peaceable re-entry. Landlords are sometimes reluctant to adopt peaceable re-entry because it is an offence to use or threaten violence (Criminal Law Act 1977, s 6) to achieve re-entry where the landlord knew that there was someone on the premises opposed to the entry.

The right to forfeit is restricted in a number of ways which are discussed below.

26.2 EXPRESS RESERVATION OF THE RIGHT

The right to forfeit is not automatic; it only exists where the lease expressly includes such a right (or where, rarely, the lease is made conditional upon the performance of the tenant's covenants or where the tenant denies the landlord's title).

The right is typically expressed as a proviso and is sometimes referred to as a 'right of re-entry'. The events commonly specified as giving rise to the right can be seen in clause 52 of the **Appendix 4** lease (briefly non-payment of rent, breach of other covenant or condition, events of insolvency).

The landlord's intention is to give itself as many opportunities as possible to forfeit the lease where the tenant is in financial difficulty. You can see from clause 52 of the **Appendix 4** lease that, in some insolvency proceedings, the landlord gives itself two attempts at forfeiting the tenant's lease (eg, once on the presentation of the petition in bankruptcy and once on the making of the bankruptcy order – see definition of Insolvency Event (i)) in case the landlord inadvertently waives its right to forfeit on the first occasion (see below).

A tenant should resist the inclusion of some of the less serious events (eg, the mere presentation of the petition) or those insolvency events that are designed to cure insolvency (eg, administration proceedings, voluntary arrangements, liquidations for the purpose of restructuring). Further, if the tenant's lease has sufficient capital value to provide security for a loan (though this may be unlikely), the tenant should try to restrict the landlord's right to forfeit in those circumstances.

26.3 WAIVER OF THE RIGHT TO FORFEIT

Once a landlord knows of the breach (or existence of the specified event) giving rise to a right to forfeit, if it does something to recognise the continued existence of the lease, it will be deemed to have waived the right to forfeit (albeit without prejudice to its ability to pursue its other remedies).

Knowledge of the breach can be actual or imputed where the premises are managed by an agent.

Waiver can be express or implied. It is judged objectively, without regard to motive or intention. The most common way a landlord acknowledges the continued existence of the lease is by accepting or demanding rent falling due after the right to forfeit has arisen. That will amount to waiver notwithstanding a clerical error by the landlord's agent (*Central Estates (Belgravia) Ltd v Woolgar (No 2)* [1972] 1 WLR 1048), receipt of rent paid under a standing order or that the rent is demanded or received 'without prejudice to the landlord's right to forfeit' (*Segal Securities Ltd v Thoseby* [1963] 1 QB 887). However, the banking of a cheque covering both payment to avoid a bankruptcy order and payment to discharge arrears of rent and then returning the sum to discharge the arrears did not amount to waiver (*Osibanjo v Seahive Investments Ltd* [2008] EWCA Civ 1282). In *Faiz v Burnley Borough Council* [2021] EWCA Civ 55, the Court held that once a landlord has knowledge of a breach of covenant which entitles it to forfeit the lease, it will be found to have waived the right to forfeit if it demands rent which became payable after the breach of covenant even if the rent became payable before the landlord had knowledge of the breach.

Other examples of conduct that have been held to amount to waiver are: suing on provisions in the lease, serving notices under the lease provisions, granting licences to assign/sublet and exercising Commercial Rent Arrears Recovery (see **30.1.1.3**).

Waiver of the right to forfeit operates only in respect of past breaches of covenant. Where the landlord waives it in respect of a 'once and for all' breach (eg, breach of a covenant against sub-letting, against alterations or payment of rent for a particular rent period), the right to forfeit is lost for ever. If, however, the breach is of a continuing nature (eg, breach of a repairing covenant or user covenant), the right to forfeit, though waived on one occasion, will arise again, as the property continues to be in disrepair or used for an unauthorised purpose.

26.4 STRICT PROCEDURAL RULES AND RELIEF AGAINST FORFEITURE

Even if the landlord has a right to forfeit, it must exercise it; the lease does not end automatically on the happening of the particular event specified in the forfeiture clause. The right must be exercised in accordance with strict procedural rules, which are different for non-payment of rent than breach of any other covenant. Even where the strict procedural rules have been complied with, there is yet one further limitation on forfeiture in that the tenant may obtain relief from forfeiture.

26.4.1 Forfeiture for non-payment of rent

26.4.1.1 Procedural rules

The landlord is required to make a formal demand for the rent, but this requirement is usually negated in the lease by providing for forfeiture if the tenant is, for example, 21 days or more in arrears 'whether the rent is formally demanded or not'. The forfeiture clause in the lease should be checked to confirm the position (see the **Appendix 4** lease).

There is also no need for a formal demand if at least half a year's rent is in arrears and the goods available on the premises for recovery are insufficient to cover the arrears (Common Law Procedure Act 1852, s 210 (High Court) and County Courts Act 1984, s 139(1) (County Court)).

If the rent falls into arrears, the landlord may proceed to forfeit either by court proceedings or by peaceable re-entry. See **Figure 26.1** below for a summary of the process.

Figure 26.1 Forfeiture by landlord for breach of tenant's covenant in lease: payment of rent

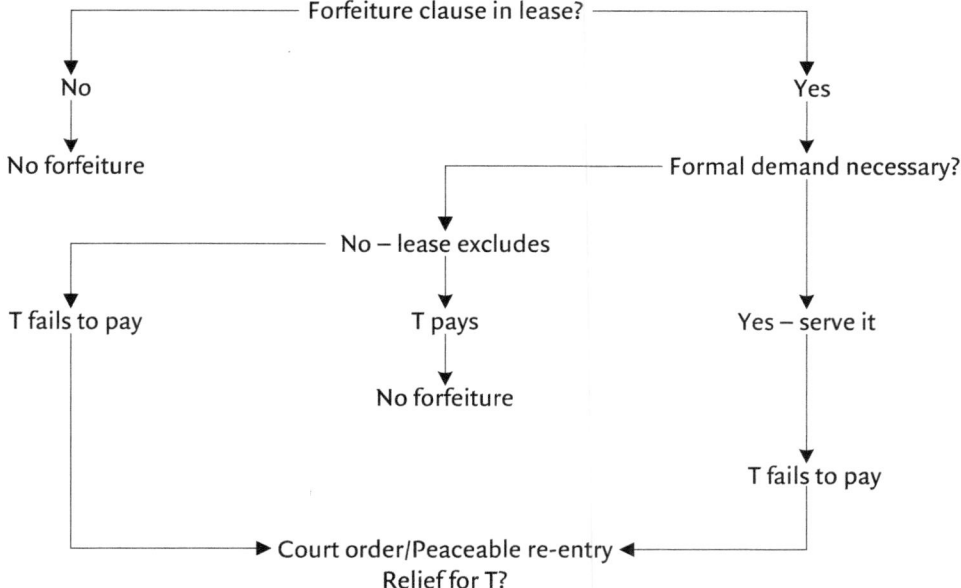

26.4.1.2 Relief from forfeiture for non-payment of rent

As **Figure 26.1** indicates, the tenant can apply to court for relief from forfeiture, which, if granted, will mean that the tenant continues to hold under the existing lease.

Where the landlord is proceeding by way of court action, relief will generally be granted if the tenant pays the arrears and costs of the action. In certain cases, the tenant may also apply for relief within six months from the landlord's recovery of possession, although the rules differ between the High Court and county court.

Where the landlord is proceeding by way of peaceable re-entry, the tenant may still apply to the court for relief. Again, the tenant will have to pay the arrears and costs. If applying for relief in the County Court, the tenant must do so within six months of re-entry by the landlord. If applying for relief in the High Court, the court has the power to grant relief under its inherent equitable jurisdiction and the tenant must make its application with 'reasonable promptitude'.

The case of *Keshwala and another v Bhalsod* [2021] EWCA Civ 492 confirms that the court's discretion to grant relief is to be exercised under ordinary equitable principles and, while the court is likely to adopt a similar time limit of six months, there is no legal principle that an application made within the six-month window will be deemed to have been made with reasonable promptitude. A tenant that wishes to get back into the premises must act promptly and communicate well with the landlord, advising the landlord of its intention to apply for relief and of any reasons why it may need to delay doing so.

A few days delay is unlikely to be fatal and, in exceptional circumstances, the court may be prepared to grant relief well outside this six-month period, as illustrated in the case of *Pineport v Grangeglen* [2016] EWHC 1318 (Ch). In that case, a tenant's long lease granted for a premium had been forfeited by peaceable re-entry for non-payment of rent. The court considered whether an application delayed for 14 months had been made with 'reasonable promptitude', and concluded that it had been, albeit recognising that 14 months was 'near to the breaking point for the concept's elasticity'. However, in *Gibson v Lakeside Developments Ltd* [2018] EWCA Civ 2874, obiter remarks expressed 'considerable doubts' as to whether *Pineport* was decided correctly. In *Gibson*, a long residential lease had been forfeited when the flat was unoccupied and a new long lease granted to a third party. The tenant applied for relief nearly 18 months after re-entry and brought a claim for unjust enrichment. The application for relief was abandoned, but the judge considered it would have been too late for the County Court to have granted relief given the six-month statutory relief period and that the position would have been the same under the equitable jurisdiction of the High Court.

At a subsequent hearing of *Pineport* ([2016] EWHC 2170 (Ch)), the court considered the extent to which a tenant can be required to pay the landlord's costs for relief from forfeiture as a condition of the grant of relief. The High Court decided that only the costs of the forfeiture itself can be required to be paid as a condition of relief. Costs of the application for relief from forfeiture are to be determined in accordance with the CPR.

26.4.2 Forfeiture for breach of other covenants

26.4.2.1 Procedural rules

Before a landlord is able to forfeit for a breach of covenant, other than for the payment of rent, the landlord must serve a notice on the tenant under s 146 of the LPA 1925, which must:

(a) specify the breach

(b) require it to be remedied within a reasonable time, if it is capable of being remedied

The right of re-entry must have arisen before service of the s 146 notice (*Toms v Ruberry* [2017] EWHC 2970 (QB)).

If the breach is remediable, the notice must require its remedy; otherwise the notice will be invalid.

Whether a breach is remediable is a question of fact in each case. The distinction is not always easy to make, but the modern courts seem to have arrived at a test of whether the breach causes irreparable harm (described as the 'mischief' in *Savva v Hussein* (1997) 73 P & CR 150) to the landlord, rather than whether the breach itself is capable of remedy. Only if the harm suffered by the landlord cannot be put right by the tenant remedying the breach and paying compensation to the landlord will a breach be considered irremediable (*Expert Clothing Service & Sales Ltd v Hillgate House Ltd* [1986] Ch 340).

The majority of breaches should be capable of remedy, and a practical rather than technical approach must be taken to the question whether a breach is remediable or not (*Akici v LR Butlin Ltd* [2006] 1 WLR 201).

The following breaches (amongst others) have been held to be *incapable* of remedy:

(a) breach of an assignment covenant (*Scala House & District Property Co Ltd v Forbes* [1974] QB 575; *Expert Clothing Service & Sales Ltd v Hillgate House Ltd* [1986] Ch 340; *Savva v Hussein* (1997) 73 P & CR 150; *Akici v LR Butlin Ltd* [2006] 1 WLR 201);

(b) breach of a sub-letting covenant (*Scala House*);

(c) breach of a covenant against immoral or illegal user (because of the stigma that would attach to the premises, for example, if used as a brothel (*Rugby School (Governors) v Tannahill* [1935] 1 KB 87)) consisting of direct use by the tenant. If the use is not direct then it is remediable so long as the tenant acts promptly on discovering the relevant use by the sub-tenant (*Glass v Kencakes Ltd* [1966] 1 QB 611; *Patel, Patel v K & J Restaurants Ltd, MP Catering Ltd* [2010] ECWA Civ 1211);

(d) breach of a covenant against trading without appropriate licences (*Bickerton's Aerodromes v Young* (1958) 108 LJ 217);

(e) bankruptcy or liquidation of a tenant (*Civil Service Co-operative Society v McGrigor's Trustee* [1923] 2 Ch 347).

The following breaches (amongst others) have been held to be *capable* of remedy:

(a) breach of a covenant against parting or sharing with possession, at least where it falls short of creating or transferring a legal interest (*Akici*);

(b) breach of a covenant to reconstruct premises by a stated date – remedied by the tenant carrying out the work within a reasonable time (*Expert Clothing*);

(c) breach of a covenant against making alterations and erecting signs – remedied by their removal (*Savva*).

If the landlord is in any doubt about whether a particular breach can be remedied, the notice should require the tenant to remedy the breach 'if it is capable of remedy'.

What is a 'reasonable' period for compliance is a question of fact in each case (*Hopley v Tarvin Parish Council* (1910) 54 JP 209). *Albany Holdings Ltd v Crown Estate Commissioners* [2003] EWHC 1480 held that a period of one month would normally be sufficient. However, where the work to remedy a breach would take longer than one month to carry out, a longer period may be necessary.

(c) require the tenant to pay compensation for the breach, if the landlord so requires

If this is lacking, the notice is not, however, invalidated (*Lock v Pearce* [1893] 2 Ch 271).

If the tenant does not comply with the requirements of a valid s 146 notice, the landlord may proceed to forfeit the lease by court proceedings or peaceable re-entry. See **Figure 26.2** for a summary of the process.

Figure 26.2 Forfeiture by landlord for breach of tenant's covenant in lease

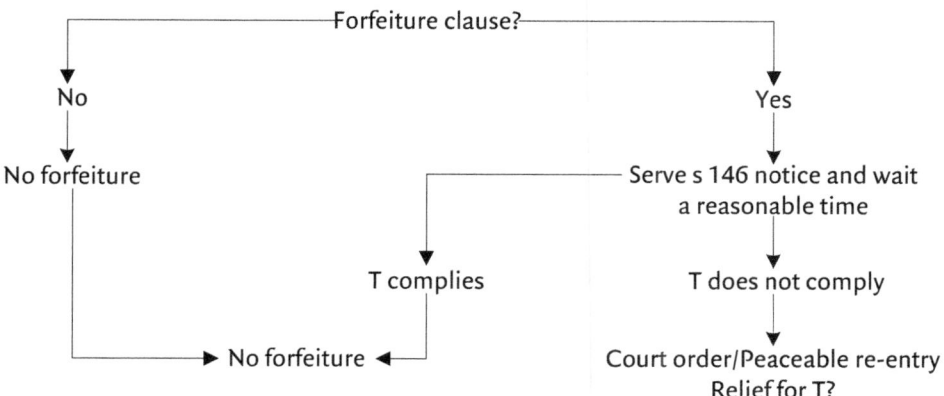

26.4.2.2 Relief from forfeiture for breach of covenant (other than non-payment of rent)

As **Figure 26.2** indicates, the tenant may be able to seek relief from forfeiture in respect of which the courts have a statutory discretion (LPA 1925, s 146(2)). If the landlord takes court proceedings, the tenant may seek relief at any time before the landlord actually re-enters the premises; no relief can be granted afterwards. However, if the landlord re-enters peaceably, the tenant can seek relief even after the landlord has re-entered, though the court will take into account all the circumstances, including any delay by the tenant in seeking relief (*Billson v Residential Apartments Ltd* [1992] 1 AC 494).

In deciding whether or not to grant relief, each case will turn on its own facts, and the courts have refused to lay down any rigid rules on the exercise of their discretion (*Hyman v Rose* [1912] AC 623). The courts tend to lean in favour of granting relief, and the principles upon which the statutory discretion is exercised are equitable.

The case of *Magnic Ltd v Ul-Hassan & Another* [2015] EWCA Civ 224 usefully considered the factors a court might take into account when exercising its discretion to grant relief from forfeiture, as did the case of *Freifield v West Kensington Court Limited* [2015] EWCA Civ 806.

As said, in the absence of any fixed rules, the court will have regard to the purpose of the reservation of the right to forfeit (to provide the landlord with some security for the performance of the tenant's covenants), the conduct of the parties (eg deliberate breach by the tenant, the landlord having renovated or re-let the property), the nature and seriousness of the breach, the value of the property and the extent of damage caused by the breach, the loss that the tenant will suffer if relief is not granted, any windfall to the landlord and all other relevant circumstances. In *Freifield*, where the tenant had deliberately breached a covenant against subletting, the court still leaned against forfeiture as it considered that the sanction was too severe, the windfall to the landlord (the investment value being estimated at some £2 million) was too disproportionate and the tenant had cured the breach.

Relief is usually granted where the breach has been remedied and is unlikely to re-occur and where to grant it would not damage the landlord's interests. Clearly, the landlord should not be able to forfeit for any trivial breaches or breaches of minor covenants that would not damage the landlord's interests.

Where a breach is irremediable then the court is less likely to grant relief. In the context of immoral user causing a stigma to the premises, it is likely that relief would be refused, but there are cases where relief has been granted (eg, in *Patel* where, given the nature of the surrounding area, there would be no stigma attached to the premises and possession would result in a substantial windfall to the landlord).

In the context of breach of covenant to assign or sub-let, the courts may grant relief (*Scala House*) unless the assignment or sub-letting resulted in the assignee or sub-tenant acquiring statutory protection that the tenant would not have had (*Leeward Securties v Lilyheath* (1983) 17 HLR 35).

If relief is granted, it will be granted on such terms as the court thinks fit (LPA 1925, s 146(2)), such as compensation or an injunction to restrain further breach.

26.5 ADDITIONAL RULES IN SPECIAL CASES

26.5.1 Breach of a tenant's repairing covenant

If a lease was originally granted for a term of seven years or more and has at least three years unexpired, the provisions of the Leasehold Property (Repairs) Act 1938 (LP(R)A 1938) apply. These provide that when a landlord serves a notice under s 146 of the LPA 1925 prior to forfeiture, it must include a statement of the tenant's right to serve a counter-notice within 28 days. If the tenant does so, the landlord may proceed with its claim (ie forfeiture) only if it receives the leave of the court. See **Figure 26.3** below. Leave will be granted only in the specified circumstances set out in s 1(5) of the LP(R)A 1938 (eg that the value of the reversion has been substantially diminished) (see **30.1.2.1**).

Figure 26.3 Forfeiture by landlord for breach of tenant's covenant in lease: repair covenant

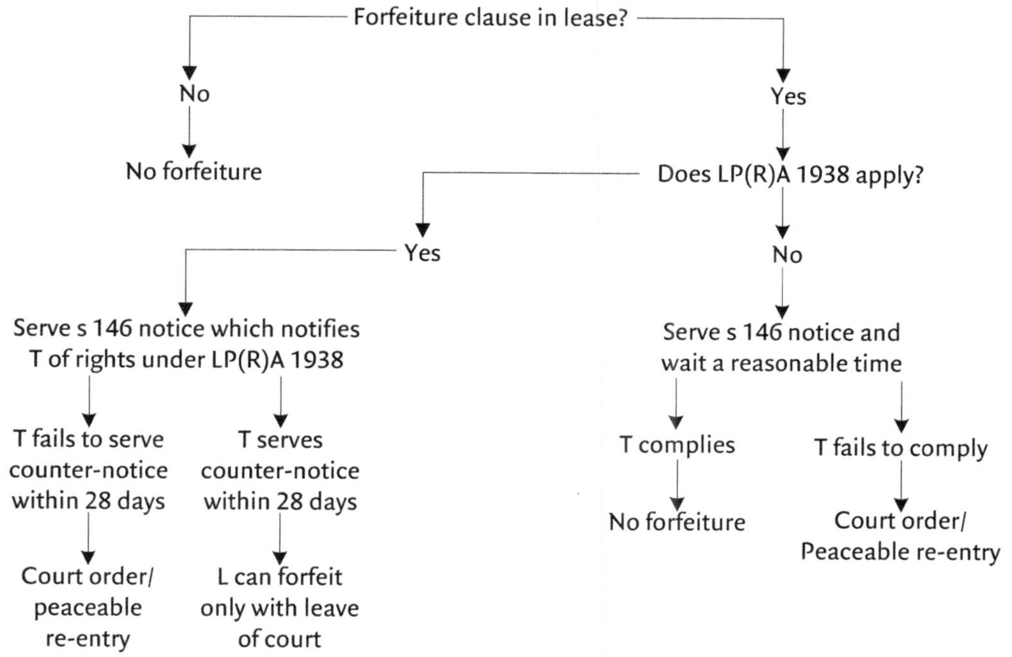

```
                    Forfeiture clause in lease?
                   /                            \
                  No                            Yes
                  |                              |
             No forfeiture              Does LP(R)A 1938 apply?
                                         /                    \
                                       Yes                     No
                                        |                       |
                     Serve s 146 notice which notifies    Serve s 146 notice and
                     T of rights under LP(R)A 1938        wait a reasonable time
                         /              \                     /            \
                  T fails to serve    T serves         T complies      T fails to comply
                  counter-notice      counter-notice        |                |
                  within 28 days      within 28 days   No forfeiture    Court order/
                         |                 |                            Peaceable re-entry
                  Court order/      L can forfeit
                  peaceable         only with leave
                  re-entry          of court
```

26.5.2 Internal decorative repairs

Where the s 146 notice relates to internal decorative repairs, the tenant has a special right to apply to the court for relief under s 147 of the LPA 1925. This is separate from the general right to apply for relief under s 146. If the court is satisfied that the notice is unreasonable (having regard to all the circumstances of the case, including the length of the unexpired term), it may wholly or partially relieve the tenant from liability. The court has no power to award relief under s 147 if (inter alia) the notice relates to repairs required under an express covenant to put the property in a decorative state of repair that has never been performed, or if it relates to any matter necessary or proper to keep the property in a sanitary condition, or for the maintenance or preservation of the structure, or to any covenant to yield up the premises in a specified state of repair at the end of the term.

26.5.3 Tenant's bankruptcy or liquidation

A lease will usually give the landlord the right to forfeit upon the tenant's bankruptcy (or liquidation) or having the lease taken in execution. If the landlord wishes to forfeit, it needs only serve a s 146 notice, and the tenant may only apply for relief during the first year following the bankruptcy or taking in execution. However, there is an important exception to this rule. If, during that first year, the trustee or liquidator sells the lease, the s 146 protection lasts indefinitely. Without such an exception, it would be difficult for the trustee or liquidator to find a buyer for the lease because of the risk of forfeiture taking place after the expiration of the first year without the service of a s 146 notice and with no right to seek relief.

For further detail on the impact of insolvency events on the landlord's right to forfeit, see **33.7.2**.

26.5.4 Particular premises

Section 146(9) provides that there is no need for the landlord to serve a s 146 notice, and the tenant has no right to apply for relief, if the lease is of agricultural land, mines or minerals, a public house, a furnished house or any premises where the personal qualifications of the tenant are important for the preservation of the nature or character of the premises or on the ground of neighbourhood to the landlord (see *Hockley Engineering Ltd v V & P Midlands Ltd* [1993] 1 EGLR 76 for meaning) or anyone holding under it.

26.6 POSITION OF SUB-TENANTS AND MORTGAGEES ON FORFEITURE

If the head-lease is forfeited, this will automatically end any sub-lease. This is unfair to sub-tenants, who stand to lose their interest through no fault of their own. Under s 146(4), a sub-tenant can apply to the court for relief and the court may make an order vesting, for the whole term of the head-lease or any less term (but not longer than that remaining under the sub-lease), the property comprised in the head-lease or any part of it in the sub-tenant, and otherwise on terms it thinks fit in its absolute discretion. The court has absolute discretion as to whether to refuse or grant relief and considers the same factors as those when the tenant applies and other additional factors (eg, whether the sub-tenant will enjoy security of tenure when its sub-lease expires or is in breach of the sub-lease). The court can impose any conditions as to payment of rent, costs, expenses, damages, compensation, giving security or otherwise as the court in the circumstances of each case may think fit.

Lenders (whether by sub-demise or legal charge) are classed as sub-tenants for the purposes of s 146(4) and can apply for relief from forfeiture of the lease, but only if arrears and costs are paid within six months of the landlord's re-entry (see *United Dominion Trust Ltd v Shellpoint Trustees* [1993] EGCS 57).

26.7 THE 2020 CODE FOR LEASING BUSINESS PREMISES

The 2020 Code provides:

> 10   Landlords should handle defaults promptly and deal with tenants and any guarantors in an open constructive way

See the **Appendix 4** lease, which complies with the 2020 Code.

Under the 2020 Code (see **14.2**), forfeiture does not need to be addressed in the mandatory heads, and the non-mandatory recommendations as to best practice do not refer to forfeiture.

Paragraph 14 of the Supplemental Guide at Appendix B of the 2020 Code sets out the need for the parties to try to stay on good terms, the availability of remedies on tenant breach and advises landlords to note that if they forfeit the lease they will resume responsibility for the property and its outgoings.

It also refers to the procedure necessary to forfeit and the right of the tenant to apply for relief and counsels that the parties should each seek professional advice if circumstances arise where forfeiture is being contemplated.

26.8 REFORM

The Law Commission published a recommendation in October 2006 that the current law be abolished and replaced by an entirely new statutory scheme, on the basis that it considered the law of forfeiture to be overly complex and could lead to injustice. In March 2019, the Housing, Communities and Local Government Select Committee recommended that the Government implement the Law Commission's recommendations. In response, the Government asked the Law Commission to update its report. In August 2021, the Law Commission provided the Department for Levelling Up, Housing and Communities with possible options and updates to the Law Commission's work (their recommendations remain the same as in 2006) which are being considered.

REVIEW ACTIVITY

Mercurial Ltd ('the landlord') owns two-storey office premises in a somewhat run-down area of east London. Two years ago, the landlord granted a lease of the ground floor to Tiempo Trading Ltd ('Tiempo') and a lease of the first floor to Grantham solicitors ('Grantham'). Both leases were for a term of 10 years and were granted in the form of the **Appendix 4** lease.

Six months ago, the landlord consented to a sub-letting of the ground floor by Tiempo to Escorta Ltd. Recently, following a complaint by Grantham, the landlord discovered that the sub-tenant is using the ground floor premises as a brothel.

The landlord has also just checked its bank account to discover that Grantham has not paid the quarter's rent which was due four weeks ago.

Explain to the landlord whether it can forfeit the lease of the ground floor and/or the lease of the first floor, and in each case the procedure that must be followed. In addition, explain whether the tenant can apply for relief against forfeiture and on what conditions relief might be granted.

Answers to this Review activity may be found in Appendix 1.

CHAPTER 27

LEASE OF PART

27.1	Introduction	305
27.2	Defining the demised premises	305
27.3	Rights granted and reserved	306
27.4	Repairs	306
27.5	Service charges	307
27.6	Sinking and reserve funds	312
27.7	Insurance	312
27.8	RICS Professional Statement: Service Charges	312
	Review activity	313

27.1 INTRODUCTION

The purpose of this chapter is not to deal with every single issue of relevance on the lease of part of a building; some can be dealt with only in the context of particular clauses. The reader will therefore find references to leases of part elsewhere in this book. However, there are some important issues which can be dealt with separately, and by drawing these together in this chapter, particularly the service charge provisions, the reader will become aware of the special considerations which apply whenever a lease of part of a building is contemplated.

It should be noted that this chapter deals with leases of part of commercial properties. Leases of multi-occupied residential buildings are subject to various statutory provisions, particularly in relation to the provision of services and service charge. These statutory provisions are outside the scope of this book, and a specialist text should be consulted when dealing with multi-occupied residential buildings.

27.2 DEFINING THE DEMISED PREMISES

It is important that the lease fully and accurately identifies the boundaries of the property to be let. This is particularly important bearing in mind that the tenant's liability to repair is often co-extensive with the demise; if it has to repair the 'demised premises', it must be clear where they start and finish. The following are some of the matters which will need consideration:

(a) *Walls.* It must be clear which walls fall within the demise and which outside. The demise often excludes the structural walls and outer half of the internal non-structural walls dividing the demised premises from the other parts of the building. The plaster finishes of such walls are often within the demise.

(b) *Floors, ceilings and roofs.* These often fall outside of the demise. However, floor and ceiling finishes and coverings, false ceilings and floor screeds are often within the demise.

(c) *Windows.* In a lease of part, windows in the exterior walls normally fall outside the demise.

(d) *Conducting media (such as pipes and cables) and plant (such as air conditioning units and boilers).* Those that exclusively serve the premises are usually demised to the tenant. Those that serve the premises and other parts of the building are normally excluded from the demise.

Practitioners often refer to leases of part that deal with the demise as described above as 'internal only' demises.

27.3 RIGHTS GRANTED AND RESERVED

As far as easements are concerned, the tenant will usually need to be granted rights over the parts of the building retained by the landlord or let to other tenants. The following are some of the rights that will need considering:

(a) rights over staircases, lifts, landing areas and corridors;
(b) rights over estate roads and footpaths and rights to use shared car parks;
(c) rights over shared facilities such as bin stores, sign boards and toilets;
(d) rights to use shared conducting media;
(e) rights of access onto retained parts of the building to carry out repairs to the premises.

The landlord will need to be satisfied that such rights do not unduly restrict its use of the remainder of the building. The case of *B&Q plc v Liverpool and Lancashire Properties Ltd* [2000] EGCS 101 illustrated the way in which rights granted to tenants may hinder the landlord's future development proposals. In that case the tenant successfully applied for an injunction against the landlord, preventing the latter from constructing a 3,500 square foot extension to one of the units on its retail park. The extension would have reduced the area of a service yard used by B&Q. B&Q had been granted rights over the service yard in its lease, and although the yard could still be used if the extension went ahead, the fact that it was rendered 'materially less convenient' than before was sufficient for the tenant to succeed.

The landlord will, of course, wish to reserve certain rights over the property being let. These will often include rights of access to carry out repairs and to run services through the service media on the demise. More contentiously, they may also include rights to re-route accesses and service media, to erect scaffolding and to extend or alter other parts of the landlord's estate. The tenant will need to consider the possible impact on its business before unconditionally accepting such reservations. If possible, the tenant's solicitor should obtain a qualification to such reservations that no interference is caused to the tenant's use and occupation of the premises or the rights granted to it.

27.4 REPAIRS

It is usual, in a large multi-occupied building, to make the tenant responsible for repair of the internal non-structural parts of the demised premises and the landlord responsible for repair of the remainder of the building. This can be achieved by creating an 'internal only demise' (see **27.2**) which the tenant covenants to repair. The landlord then covenants to repair all other parts of the landlord's property excluding the demised premises (and sometimes the internal parts of other lettable units). These retained areas for which the landlord assumes responsibility are often referred to as the common parts. Any expense incurred by the landlord in complying with its obligations for the common parts will usually be recoverable under the service charge provisions (see **27.5**).

For the repairing obligations to work effectively, great care must be exercised in drafting the definitions of the demised premises and the common parts (see **27.2**). If the tenant has taken an internal only demise, it must ensure the definitions and obligations work to oblige the landlord to repair all other parts of the building and estate. This would include the structural parts of the building, such as the roof, main load bearing walls and foundations. It may also include entrances, staircases, corridors and lifts, together with shared conducting media, and external areas (including any landscaped areas, forecourts, roadways and fences). The landlord may resist accepting responsibility for other units capable of being let, as the tenants of such units would be responsible for their repairs.

In considering repairing obligations, practitioners must also appreciate the precise meaning of certain words and phrases which have been judicially defined in a plethora of case law. Thus, for example, 'structural repairs', 'main walls', 'external walls' and 'exterior' have all been judicially considered; reference should be made to one of the standard works on landlord and tenant law for a more detailed analysis of such technicalities.

27.5 SERVICE CHARGES

As discussed at **27.4**, in a lease of part, the landlord will often be responsible for the repair of all parts of the building and estate other than the internal only demises let to the tenants. There may also be other services provided by the landlord (see **27.5.1**). The landlord will want to recover the costs of providing these services from the tenants. It could charge a higher inclusive rent to cover its anticipated costs, but the landlord then runs the risk of inflation or unexpected outgoings making its estimate incorrect. The inclusive rent method is unpopular with institutional landlords and lenders who prefer a 'clear lease', where the rent will always represent the landlord's clear income from the property and the landlord is reimbursed for the expenditure on the provision of services by means of a service charge which fluctuates annually according to the actual costs incurred.

From the landlord's point of view, it is necessary to decide whether the service charge should be reserved as additional rent. The advantages of reserving it as rent have already been considered (see **18.4**).

27.5.1 Services to be provided

Tenants need pay for the provision only of those services specified in the lease. There is no presumption that a landlord should receive full recovery of its maintenance and repair costs from a tenant (see *Campbell v Daejan Properties Ltd* [2012] EWCA Civ 1503). If there is no provision for the tenant to pay for a particular cost, the landlord cannot recover its expenditure. Therefore, when drafting the service charge provisions, the landlord's solicitor will aim to include all the expenditure the landlord may lay out on the building. The tenant's solicitor will need to check that each item of expenditure listed in the lease is reasonable and appropriate. Tenants' solicitors will often seek express provisions in the lease that only expenditure reasonably and properly incurred by the landlord is recoverable.

This can be a very contentious area for the parties. Whilst both parties wish to have a well-serviced building, the tenant will want this at the lowest possible cost to it. It will not wish to pay for services it perceives as unnecessary or disproportionately expensive when compared to benefit.

Some common items of expenditure and the issues that can arise in relation to them are set out below.

27.5.1.1 Repairs and decoration

The landlord will want to recover all its expenses in performing its repairing obligation. Leases will often allow the recovery of expenses for inspecting, cleaning, maintaining, repairing and decorating the common parts and any other parts of the building for which the landlord is responsible. Usually the lease will also allow for the recovery of similar expenditure in relation to plant and equipment, service media and landlord's fittings. This will often include potentially expensive items of plant, such as air conditioning, security and heating systems and fire alarms.

Whether the landlord can go beyond 'repair', and rebuild or carry out improvements, is a question of construction of the relevant clause, but the tenant must be aware of the danger of having to contribute to work which would be outside a simple covenant to 'repair', for example the replacement of defective wooden window frames with modern double-glazed units. A tenant that accepts that it will pay the landlord's costs in 'renewing' or 'replacing' items for which the landlord is responsible, risks the landlord deciding to upgrade the property at the tenant's cost. If such an upgrade were to be carried out towards the end of the lease term, the tenant would bear the cost without experiencing the benefit of the works. It is therefore wise for the tenant's solicitor to specify that the costs of renewal and replacement are only recoverable where the item in question is beyond economic repair.

Another concern of the tenant is that the clause may require its contribution to expenditure incurred by the landlord in remedying inherent defects in the building, for example those caused by a design defect or through the use of defective materials. The tenant should seek to expressly exclude such costs.

The landlord should pay particular attention to the wording of the service charge provision. In *Northways Flats Management Co v Wimpey Pension Trustees* [1992] 31 EG 65, the clause required the landlord, before carrying out the work, to submit details and estimates to the tenants. The court held that this was a precondition to the recovery of the service charge and, since it had not been complied with, the landlord was unable to recover its expenditure.

27.5.1.2 Heating, air conditioning, etc

The landlord will wish to recover its costs in supplying heating, lighting, air conditioning and hot and cold water to the common parts of the building and possibly the demised premises as well. This will include the costs of maintaining the plant, equipment and service media associated with such services. Sometimes, the landlord will restrict the provision of heating, air conditioning and lighting to certain times. The tenant must ensure it is happy with such restrictions. The landlord should also ensure that it is not liable to the tenant for any temporary interruption in supply due to a breakdown.

As a separate matter, a landlord of a multi-let building who supplies heat, hot water or cooling through a communal system may be bound by heat regulations which require the landlord to issue bills in accordance with certain standards and install meters, heat cost allocators and thermostatic radiator valves.

27.5.1.3 Staff

The landlord will wish to recover its costs in employing staff in connection with the management of the building such as receptionists, maintenance staff, caretakers and security personnel. This will include the cost of any equipment or uniform provided to such staff, together with their wages, taxes, national insurance contributions and any other benefits they receive. The clause should also extend to any staff employed by the managing agents for the purpose of providing services at the building. From the tenant's point of view, it should guard against having to pay the full-time wages of staff who are not wholly engaged in providing the services. The tenant should also consider whether such staff are necessary and appropriate.

27.5.1.4 Managing agents

Most modern leases allow the landlord to recover the cost of employing managing agents to manage the building and services. A company owned by the landlord can be employed as managing agent provided such an arrangement is not a sham (*Skilleter v Charles* [1992] 13 EG 113). If the landlord performs its own management services, the service charge will usually enable it to recover its reasonable costs for this. In the absence of an express provision, it is unlikely such management costs can be recovered.

The tenant must make sure that the amount of fees recoverable is reasonable and may want some restriction placed on them in the lease. There is clearly a danger, where the landlord performs the management services itself, that the tenant is overcharged. The tenant will not want the landlord to profit out of the service charge. The tenant should also seek to ensure it does not pay the costs of the managing agent in performing additional duties such as rent collection. Attempts by the landlord to charge a notional rent for premises within the building used in connection with the management of the building should also be resisted.

27.5.1.5 Other common items of expenditure

Other common items of expenditure include:

(a) refuse removal;
(b) maintenance of signage and sign boards;
(c) window cleaning and cleaning of common parts;
(d) fire prevention equipment;
(e) insurance (although sometimes this is dealt with outside the service charge provisions);
(f) security equipment (such as CCTV);
(g) maintenance of car parks and landscaped areas;
(h) costs in complying with statute and insurers' requirements;
(i) borrowing costs to fund major expenditure;
(j) outgoings payable by the landlord;
(k) advertising and promotion costs, in the case of a shopping centre;
(l) legal and other professional fees (in particular those incurred in the preparation and auditing of the service charge certificate and accounts (see **27.5.4.3**)).

Each of these items can be contentious. The landlord may, for example, be keen to have the landscaped areas regularly replanted, but a tenant with a unit that does not adjoin such areas may not wish to pay for such a service. The tenant's solicitor will need to check each item of expenditure listed as recoverable is appropriate. The tenant's solicitor may wish to specify that such expenditure is only recoverable if reasonably and properly incurred for the benefit of the tenant. Obviously, any such qualifications the landlord accepts bring with them the risk that the tenant will argue certain expenditure is irrecoverable.

27.5.1.6 'Sweeper' clause

No matter how comprehensive the landlord thinks it has been in compiling the list of services to be provided, it is advisable to include a 'sweeper' clause to take account of any new services to be provided over the lifetime of the lease. However, careful drafting of such a clause is required as the courts construe them restrictively (see *Mullaney v Maybourne Grange (Croydon) Ltd* [1986] 1 EGLR 70). From the tenant's point of view, it should guard against the clause being drafted too widely. The sweeper should only allow the landlord to provide services not contemplated when the lease was granted; it should not be used to cover something left out in error. The draft lease should require the landlord to act reasonably and in accordance with the principles of good estate management before being able to recover expenditure under the sweeper clause. The tenant's solicitor may require the sweeper clause to specify that any service provided under it be of some benefit to the tenant.

27.5.2 Landlord's covenant to perform the services

The services to be provided often fall into two categories: essential services which the landlord should be obliged to provide (eg, heating and lighting the common parts and repairing and maintaining the structure) and other non-essential services which it has discretion to provide. From the tenant's point of view, it must make sure that, in return for paying the service charge, the landlord covenants to provide the essential services. Without such an express provision, it is by no means certain that one would be implied, leaving the tenant with no remedy if the services were not provided (see, however, *Barnes v City of London Real Property Co* [1918] 2 Ch 18).

The tenant would also be ill-advised to leave non-essential services within the absolute discretion of the landlord. Whilst, for example, maintenance of adjacent landscaped areas may not be 'essential', if poorly maintained the tenant may find that its trade is detrimentally affected. It is wise, therefore, for the tenant to provide that the landlord's discretion must be exercised reasonably and in the interests of the tenants of the building.

From the landlord's point of view, it may wish to restrict the covenant so that the landlord is liable to use only 'reasonable endeavours' or 'best endeavours' to provide the services, rather than be under an absolute obligation to do so. In any event, the covenant should be limited so that the landlord is not liable to the tenant for failure to provide the services due to circumstances outside its control, such as industrial action. The tenant's solicitor will need to advise the client that if it accepts such qualifications, there may be circumstances in which the tenant has no remedy against the landlord for a failure to supply the services.

Turning to the standard of the services, the tenant's solicitor should seek an express provision that the services be provided in an efficient and economical manner and to a reasonable standard, rather than a standard the landlord considers adequate. The Supply of Goods and Services Act 1982 provides that, where a service is provided in the course of a business, there is an implied term that the supplier will carry out the service with reasonable care and skill, but it is obviously better for the tenant to deal with the matter expressly. As a general rule, the obligation to provide the services is independent of the obligation to pay for them. Therefore, in the event of non-payment by the tenant, the landlord cannot withdraw services (and in any event it is unlikely that the landlord could withdraw services from one tenant alone). Tenants should be wary of any clause that links provision of the services to payment of the service charge. In the event of a legitimate dispute over the service charge, the ability of the landlord to withdraw services from the tenant may well compel the tenant to pay the disputed sum.

27.5.3 The tenant's contribution: basis of apportionment

In addition to setting out the items which can be charged to the tenant, the clause must deal with how the total cost is to be apportioned between the tenants in the building. It can be difficult to decide on an appropriate basis of apportionment. In many buildings, not all occupiers will benefit from the services to the same extent. For example, a tenant on the ground floor of a shopping centre will not benefit from the provision of lifts and escalators to upper floors.

The following are some commonly used methods of apportionment:

(a) *According to floor area.* This can be a relatively simple method, depending on the nature of the building, but some method of measurement will have to be agreed.

(b) *According to anticipated use of services.* This can be difficult to assess and depends on the nature of each tenant's business and its location within the building.

(c) *As a fixed percentage.* This provides certainty for both parties but is inflexible. Further, the landlord must make provision for any future enlargement of the building which would necessitate a recalculation of the percentages.

In older leases, the service charge may be apportioned by reference to rateable value. This can be arbitrary since rateable values can vary for reasons which bear no relationship to the amount of services consumed, such as value and location. It is therefore no longer recommended by the RICS as an appropriate method for calculating service charge apportionments.

Each method has its own advantages and disadvantages, and reference should be made to one of the standard works on the drafting of business leases for further consideration of the matter. Whatever method is adopted, the tenant will want to ensure that it does not become liable for any un-let units or units occupied by the landlord for its own purposes; the landlord should be required to pay the service charge for these. The tenant's solicitor should also ensure that if special service charge concessions have been given to individual occupiers, the tenant is not left to make up the shortfall via its own service charge contribution. Again, this should be borne by the landlord.

27.5.4 Payment of the charge

27.5.4.1 Advance payments

Typical service charge provisions stipulate that the service charge is to be paid by the tenant periodically in advance (usually on rent days). Advance payment is necessary because otherwise the landlord would have to fund the provision of work and services out of its own resources and recoup its expenditure from the tenants later. The amount of the advance payment may give rise to disputes between the parties unless the tenant can be sure such amount is not excessive. There are different ways of calculating the service charge, for example it may be based on the previous year's actual expenditure or on an estimate of the likely expenditure in the current year. If the latter method is adopted, the tenant should insist on the amount payable being certified by, for example, the landlord's surveyor, and that the payment is to be made only upon receipt of such a certificate (see **27.5.4.3**).

The tenant may wish to consider a requirement that the landlord is to pay the advance payments into a separate account to be held on trust in order to avoid the problems which may arise if the landlord becomes insolvent. All interest earned should be credited to the service charge account.

27.5.4.2 Final payments and adjustments

At the end of the year, the service charge provisions will, typically, require the landlord to prepare annual accounts showing its actual expenditure in the year (see **27.5.4.3**). Where advance payments have been made, an adjustment will be necessary to correct any over- or underpayment. In the case of underpayment, the tenant will be required to pay this amount within a specified time. If there is an overpayment, the lease may provide for its refund to the tenant or, more usually, it will be credited to the following year's payments. The tenant's solicitor should consider requiring the landlord to notify it of any significant variation between budgeted and actual expenditure, as soon as the landlord becomes aware of such a variation.

27.5.4.3 Certification of amounts due

At the end of the service charge year, most leases will provide for the tenant to be provided with two items. The first is a service charge statement or certificate. This usually provides a summary of service costs and sets out the calculation of the service charge. The second item is the service charge accounts on which the statement is based.

Most tenants will want some reassurance that the service charge statement and accounts are accurate. In consequence, many leases will set out requirements for such statements and accounts.

As far as the service charge statement goes, it is common to find a requirement that this be 'certified' as a true and accurate record of the landlord's expenditure incurred in accordance with the lease. The lease will need to specify who can carry out such certification. This should be an appropriately qualified accountant or surveyor. Some leases allow such a person to be an employee of the landlord, although the tenant may not find this acceptable. The tenant should be aware, however, that if the lease provides for the certification to be done by an independent third party, the charges payable by that third party will normally be paid by the tenant via the service charge.

Turning to the service charge accounts, some leases require that the service charge accounts be 'audited'. This will require an external review of the accounts by a registered auditor, which can be a costly and time-consuming process. It has the benefit of additional reassurance to the tenant, but this will need to be weighed against the additional cost which is likely to be passed back to the tenant via the service charge. An alternative (and generally less costly) option is to have the accounts examined by an independent accountant, who should check that the correct figures have been extracted from the accounting records maintained by the manager and that entries in the accounting records are supported by receipts. Although cheaper, there will still be a cost involved in this and the parties should consider whether the expenditure involved justifies the cost.

The landlord will be keen to avoid challenges by the tenant to the service charge certificate. If the certificate is said to be 'final and conclusive as to the facts stated', its finality is likely to be upheld by the courts. If the lease makes the expert's certificate conclusive on matters of law, for example as to the construction of the lease, there are conflicting views on its validity. It may be that it will be upheld if the expert is given the exclusive right to determine the issue and the lease is clear on the party's intention to exclude the jurisdiction of the courts (see *National Grid Co plc v M25 Group Ltd* [1999] 08 EG 169 and *Morgan Sindall v Sawston Farms (Cambs) Ltd* [1999] 1 EGLR 90). From the tenant's perspective, statements that the certificate is final and binding should be avoided as this may leave the tenant without any way of challenging its service charge. One option may be to make provision for disputes about the service charge to be dealt with by alternative dispute resolution (ADR). This can provide a quicker and more cost effective way of dealing with disputes than court action.

27.6 SINKING AND RESERVE FUNDS

The object of sinking and reserve funds is to make funds available when needed for major items of irregular expenditure. A sinking fund is a fund established for replacing major items such as boilers and lifts which may only be necessary once or twice during the lifetime of the building. A reserve fund is established to pay for recurring items of expenditure such as external decoration which may need attending to, not annually, but perhaps every four or five years. The estimated cost of such decoration will be collected over each five-year period so that tenants are not faced with a large bill every five years.

The advantage of such funds is that money is available to carry out these major works when needed without any dramatic fluctuations in the service charge payable from one year to another. However, the creation of such a fund needs careful thought, and many difficult questions will need to be addressed at the drafting stage. Who is to own the fund? Is it to be held absolutely or on trust? What is to happen to the fund when the landlord sells the reversion? What will be the position upon termination of the lease? (See *Secretary of State for the Environment v Possfund (North West) Ltd* [1997] 39 EG 179.) Further, there may be considerable tax disadvantages. Such matters are beyond the scope of this book, but the parties will need specialist advice on them.

27.7 INSURANCE

On a lease of part of a building in multi-occupation, the landlord will usually insure the whole building and recover the premium from the tenants under the service charge provisions or in a separate insurance clause. Insurance is dealt with in **Chapter 25**.

27.8 RICS PROFESSIONAL STATEMENT: SERVICE CHARGES

Unfortunately, disputes over service charges in commercial properties are commonplace. Tenants regularly complain that they have been charged for services or items that should not have been charged at all, that they are bearing too high a percentage of the costs relative to other tenants and/or that, in relation to properly incurred expenditure, they have been charged an uncompetitive price. Because of such problems, RICS has published a professional statement entitled 'Service Charges in Commercial Property (1st edition)'. This includes certain mandatory obligations that RICS members and regulated firms engaged in property management must comply with. These mandatory provisions are contained in section 2 of the statement and include, for example, obligations to:

- recover expenditure in accordance with the terms of the lease;
- recover no more than 100% of the proper and actual costs of the provision or supply of the services;
- ensure that service charge budgets, including appropriate explanatory commentary, are issued annually to all tenants;
- ensure that an approved set of service charge accounts showing a true and accurate record of the actual expenditure constituting the service charge are provided annually to all tenants;
- ensure that service charge monies (including reserve and sinking funds) are held in a discrete (or virtual) bank account and that a proper amount of interest is credited to that service charge account.

Section 3 of the statement contains core principles that underpin the mandatory obligations, and section 4 contains detailed advice on best practice to support these core principles.

The existence of the statement gives those negotiating and approving leases on behalf of tenants strong grounds for resisting any service charge terms not complying with the statement. A tenant's solicitor negotiating a new or renewal lease should therefore consult the statement to ensure that the draft lease contains the type of best practice service charge provisions the statement advocates. The City of London Law Society has drawn up service charge lease provisions that have been specifically designed to comply with the principles and provisions of the statement. These can be accessed from the City of London Law Society website.

A tenant with an existing lease, who feels that the service charge of their premises is inappropriately administered, should consult the professional statement to see if the property manager is following best practice. Whilst the RICS confirms that the professional statement cannot override the lease, there may be legal and/or disciplinary consequences for members in departing from professional statements, which may lead to a finding of negligence against a surveyor.

At the time of writing, RICS is consulting on proposed changes to the professional statement on Service Charges. The consultation closes on 29 October 2024 and the RICS website should be consulted for the latest position.

REVIEW ACTIVITY

Read Sch 7 of the **Appendix 4** lease. Answer the following questions and identify the relevant lease clauses that support your answer:

1. Will the tenant have to pay for upgrades to the plant in the building that it does not consider necessary?
2. Will the landlord be able to recover its expenditure from the tenant if it decides to provide a new service to the building not envisaged when the lease was granted?
3. What can the tenant do if it is unhappy with the level of expenditure shown in the service charge certificate and certified accounts?

Answers to this Review activity may be found in Appendix 1.

CHAPTER 28

Selling the Lease

28.1	Applications for consent to assign	315
28.2	The landlord's licence	317
28.3	Authorised guarantee agreements	318
	Review activity	319

28.1 APPLICATIONS FOR CONSENT TO ASSIGN

28.1.1 The lease provisions

It will nearly always be the case that the lease will restrict the tenant's right to assign the lease. There may be an absolute covenant against assignment, in which case the tenant is absolutely prohibited from assigning the lease. The landlord may (or may not) agree to waive the breach in a particular case but the tenant will be entirely at the mercy of the landlord. An assignment in breach of an absolute covenant will be effective, but the lease will be liable to forfeiture by the landlord because of the breach of covenant. More commonly, there will be a qualified covenant, ie, not to assign without the landlord's prior written consent. In the case of a qualified covenant against assignment, s 19(1)(a) of the LTA 1927 implies a proviso that, notwithstanding any contrary provision, the landlord's licence or consent is not to be unreasonably withheld. The reasonableness of the landlord's refusal of consent has been dealt with earlier in this book (see **21.3**), and it will be recalled that if the parties have specified for the purposes of s 19(1A) of the LTA 1927 conditions to be satisfied, or circumstances to exist, before consent is to be given, a refusal of consent on the grounds that they are not satisfied, or they do not exist, is not an unreasonable withholding of consent.

28.1.2 The consequences of failing to obtain consent

Assuming the alienation covenant is qualified, the first step is for the tenant to make written application to the landlord for consent to assign. If the landlord consents, the tenant can proceed with the assignment. If the landlord unreasonably refuses consent, the tenant can proceed to assign and will not be deemed in breach of covenant. The danger for the tenant is in knowing whether the landlord's refusal is unreasonable or not, because if the landlord's refusal turns out to have been reasonable, the landlord will have the right to forfeit the lease. Further, for the purposes of the LT(C)A 1995, the assignment will be an excluded assignment, meaning that the assignor will not be released from the tenant covenants in the lease. Alternatively, the tenant may pursue the safer course of action by seeking a court declaration that the landlord is acting unreasonably in withholding consent, but this may prove costly and time-consuming. A further problem, prior to the passing of the LTA 1988, was that the tenant could not, in the absence of an express covenant by the landlord, obtain damages if the landlord withheld consent unreasonably.

28.1.3 The landlord's statutory obligations

As discussed at **28.1.1**, by virtue of s 19(1)(a) of the LTA 1927, the landlord is under an obligation not to unreasonably withhold consent in relation to a qualified covenant against alienation. Additionally, s 1 of the LTA 1988 (which only applies to qualified covenants) provides that where the tenant has made written application to assign, the landlord owes a duty, within a reasonable time:

(a) to give consent, unless it is reasonable not to do so. Giving consent subject to an unreasonable condition will be a breach of this duty; and

(b) to serve on the tenant written notice of its decision whether or not to give consent, specifying in addition:

    (i) if the consent is given subject to conditions, the conditions; or

    (ii) if the consent is withheld, the reasons for withholding it.

Usually the landlord will wish to see a bank reference, audited accounts (eg, for the last three years) and, if appropriate, trade references for the proposed assignee, and these should accompany the tenant's application. If the landlord needs any further information to enable it to process the application, it should request this from the tenant.

28.1.3.1 To respond within a 'reasonable time'

The LTA 1988 does not define what amounts to a reasonable time and each case will turn on its own facts. However, in *Go West Ltd v Spigarolo* [2003] EWCA Civ 17, [2003] 07 EG 136, the judge commented:

> I find it hard to imagine that a period of ... almost four months could ever be acceptable, save perhaps in the most unusual and complex situations ... it may be that the reasonable time ... will sometimes have to be measured in weeks rather than days; but, even in complicated cases, it should be measured in weeks rather than months.

In *Blockbuster Entertainment Ltd v Barnsdale Properties Ltd* [2003] EWHC 2912, a landlord who was asked for consent on 28 May and gave it on 15 July was held to have unreasonably delayed in giving that consent. Similarly, in *Mount Eden Land Ltd v Folia Ltd* [2003] EWHC 1815, the judge, while emphasising that each case turned on its own facts, thought that a period of four to five weeks was 'generous'. At the other end of the scale, in *E.ON UK plc v Gilesports Ltd* [2012] EWHC 2172 (Ch), the court considered 11 working days too short a period.

It should be noted that the landlord will not be under an obligation to respond at all if the tenant has failed to make its application in accordance with the provisions of the lease. So, in *E.ON UK plc v Gilesports Ltd* (above), the court held that service of the tenant's application by e-mail did not trigger the landlord's statutory duty to consider the application. The lease did not provide for service of applications or notices by e-mail, and the fact the landlord had actually received the e-mail application was considered irrelevant.

28.1.3.2 Not to withhold consent unreasonably

As to whether the landlord is unreasonably withholding its consent, this is left to the general law (see **21.3.3**). The burden of proving the reasonableness of any refusal or any conditions imposed is on the landlord, and the sanction for breach of the statutory duty is liability in tort for damages. As a result of the Act, landlords must give careful consideration to the financial consequences of having delayed or refused consent unreasonably, and they should set up efficient procedures to ensure that each application for consent is dealt with expeditiously and in accordance with the Act.

In considering whether or not to give consent, the landlord does not owe earlier tenants a duty of care to ensure that the assignee is of sufficient financial standing. If the assignee turns out to be unsatisfactory, the landlord will still be able to serve a default notice on those former tenants who may still be liable to the landlord (according to whether it is an 'old' or 'new' lease for the purposes of the LT(C)A 1995) (*Norwich Union Life Insurance Society v Low Profile Fashions Ltd* (1992) 21 EG 104). In such a situation, the earlier tenants may then be able to secure an overriding lease under the provisions of the LT(C)A 1995 (see **30.1.4**).

The landlord's solicitor, on receiving the tenant's application to assign, will often seek an undertaking from the tenant's solicitor to pay the landlord's legal and other costs of dealing with the application and preparing the licence (plus VAT). This is acceptable, provided the costs for which the undertaking is required are reasonable (see *Dong Bang Minerva (UK) Ltd v Davina Ltd* [1996] 31 EG 87). Care should be taken in drafting the undertaking to make it clear whether the obligation to pay the landlord's costs applies in the event of the licence not being granted; this may be a requirement of the lease in any case.

28.1.4 Superior landlord's consent

If may be that the landlord is itself a tenant and the applicant for consent is the sub-tenant. If this is the case and the head-lease requires the head-landlord's consent to the assignment, the LTA 1988 imposes the following:

(a) a duty on the immediate landlord to pass on a copy of the application to the head-landlord within a reasonable time.

(b) a similar duty to that contained in s 1 on the head-landlord towards the sub-tenant.

28.1.5 Avoiding disputes

Applications for consent to assign often give rise to disputes between landlord and tenant. In an attempt to reduce such disputes, a group of barristers and solicitors have written a Protocol for Applications for Consent to Assign or Sublet, freely available under the Property Protocols website (<www.propertyprotocols.co.uk>). The initial intention of the authors is that parties agree to adopt the steps set out in the Protocol at the outset of any application for consent. The stated aim is to improve communication between the parties and establish a timetable for exchange of relevant information. The authors' ultimate wish is that the Protocol is referred to in the alienation provisions within leases. See **21.3.7**.

28.2 THE LANDLORD'S LICENCE

If the landlord is prepared to give its consent to the assignment, a licence to assign will usually be prepared by the landlord's solicitor in which the landlord will formally grant its consent. The landlord and its advisers must take care to ensure that correspondence entered into prior to completion of the licence does not amount to consent for the purposes of the lease. In several cases that have come before the court, correspondence from the landlord or its advisers indicating the landlord's agreement to the proposed assignment has been held to amount to consent. This has been so even where the correspondence has been marked 'subject to contract' or 'subject to licence' (see *Next plc v National Farmers Union Mutual Insurance Co Ltd* [1997] EGCS 181), or where the consent has been described as 'in principle' and subject to completion of a formal licence (see *Aubergine Enterprises Ltd v Lakewood International Ltd* [2002] EWCA Civ 177). The landlord will, however, be protected if the lease requires that consent be given by deed.

If the tenant and assignee are to enter into covenants in the licence then all three (ie, landlord, tenant and assignee) will be parties to the licence, which will be in the form of a deed. Often the licence will be prepared in triplicate, so that on completion each party receives a signed and dated part. The licence will include various covenants and conditions such as:

(a) A direct covenant by the assignee to the landlord to observe and perform the covenants in the lease. If the lease to be assigned is a 'new lease' for the purposes of the LT(C)A 1995, this covenant should be limited to the period the assignee is actually the tenant (see **15.3.2.2**). However, in an old lease, a covenant by the assignee to observe and perform the covenants in the lease for the entire duration of the term would be permitted and is usual (see **15.3.1.4**).

(b) A covenant by the tenant:

(i) to pay the landlord's costs and expenses in dealing with the tenant's application;

(ii) not to allow the assignee to take up possession until the assignment has been completed.

(c) That the licence extends only to the transaction specifically authorised.

(d) That the licence is not to act as a waiver of any breach committed by the tenant prior to the date of the licence.

(e) That the licence shall cease to be valid unless the assignment is completed within, say, two months. This is because, although the proposed assignee is now acceptable to the landlord, the assignment might otherwise be delayed to a time when the assignee is of a poorer financial standing.

(f) In a new lease, the landlord will probably require the assignor to enter into an AGA (see **21.2.4.3**). As to the lawfulness of such a requirement, see **28.3**.

28.3 AUTHORISED GUARANTEE AGREEMENTS

It is currently standard practice for a landlord to insist on an outgoing tenant entering into an AGA on an assignment of a new lease, guaranteeing that the assignee will perform the covenants in the lease. This is often a requirement set out in the lease in accordance with s 19(1A) of the LTA 1927, in which case it must be complied with. If it is not set out in the lease, it would be lawful to require an AGA provided that this was reasonable in the circumstances.

As noted (at **21.3**), the Code for Leasing Business Premises 2020 recommends that an AGA should be provided where the landlord reasonably requires it (as opposed to being an automatic requirement on an assignment). Assignors should therefore cite the 2020 Code to landlords insisting on an AGA, but may well find that most landlords will not be sympathetic and will still insist on the guarantee.

As to the position of the guarantor of an outgoing tenant requested to enter an AGA, see **21.2.4.3**.

28.3.1 Content of an authorised guarantee agreement

A specimen AGA is set out in **Appendix 5**. It will typically contain covenants by the assignor:

(a) guaranteeing that the assignee will perform the tenant's covenants in the lease;
(b) promising to perform such covenants if the assignee does not;
(c) promising to take a new lease if the liability of the assignee is disclaimed on insolvency (see **33.9**).

It should be ensured that the assignor's liability does not extend beyond that of the assignee; and it should be provided that on the assignee being released from liability under the LT(C)A 1995 (see **15.3.2**), so is the assignor.

28.3.2 LTA 1954 considerations

If the AGA does contain a provision that the outgoing tenant will take a new lease in the event of a disclaimer ((c) in **28.3.1** above) then the provisions of the LTA 1954 need to be considered. If the original lease is contracted out of the LTA 1954, it is likely the landlord will want any new lease granted to the outgoing tenant following disclaimer to be similarly contracted out. However, to contract out after 1 June 2004, the landlord is required to serve notice (in the prescribed form) prior to the tenant becoming bound to take the lease. As it is the AGA that obliges the tenant to take a new lease, it is suggested that the notice should be served prior to the AGA being entered into (see **32.1.6**).

REVIEW ACTIVITY

1. In what circumstances would clauses 6.2.4 and 6.3 of the specimen AGA at **Appendix 5** be included?

2. You act for a client that wishes to assign its lease. It is in the form of the lease at **Appendix 4**. The client informs you the landlord has provided a letter of consent to the proposed assignment. On this basis, the client instructs you to complete the assignment. You see the landlord's letter which is signed and does confirm the landlord's consent to the assignment. It is, however, headed 'subject to licence'. What should you advise the client about the letter of consent?

Answers to this Review activity may be found in Appendix 1.

CHAPTER 29

Sub-leases

29.1	The nature of a sub-lease	321
29.2	Reasons for sub-letting	321
29.3	Consent to the sub-letting	322
29.4	Liability to the head-landlord	323
29.5	Drafting the sub-lease	323
	Review activity	326

29.1 THE NATURE OF A SUB-LEASE

A sub-lease (like any other lease) is an estate in land. It is called a sub-lease (or sometimes an underlease) as it is carved out of and derives from another leasehold estate (often referred to as the head-lease). The sub-lease must be for a shorter term than the head-lease from which it is granted (although in practice it is often shorter by only a couple of days) or the transaction will amount to an assignment.

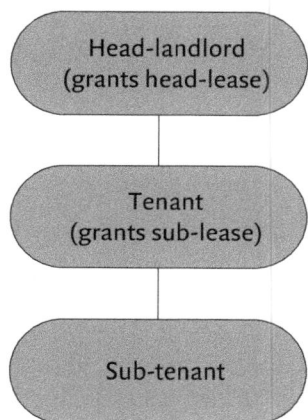

29.2 REASONS FOR SUB-LETTING

There are many reasons why a tenant may want to grant a sub-lease of all or part of the premises demised by the head-lease. It may be that the tenant finds that it has surplus accommodation which is not required for the purpose of its business; therefore, instead of leaving that part vacant (thereby wasting money), the tenant may try and cut its losses by finding a sub-tenant. Indeed, the tenant may well seek to create space for a sub-letting in the knowledge that the current market would lead to the sub-tenant paying a rent per square foot in excess of what the tenant is paying to the head-landlord, thereby enabling the tenant to make a profit.

On other occasions, the tenant may be sub-letting the premises as an alternative to assigning the lease. There are several reasons for this. It may be because the head-landlord is more willing to grant consent to sub-letting than to assignment, as its direct relationship with the tenant remains. Alternatively, if the tenant has any concerns about the covenant strength of the sub-tenant, it may wish to retain control of the premises by sub-letting rather than assigning. If the tenant assigns and the assignee defaults, the tenant would have to claim an overriding lease to regain control of the premises (see **30.1.4**). The tenant may also anticipate a need to reoccupy the premises at some point in the future. By granting a fixed-term sub-lease excluded from the Landlord and Tenant Act 1954 (LTA 1954), the tenant can then reoccupy the premises for the balance of the head-lease reversionary term. Finally, when rents are falling, the tenant may find it difficult to assign: it may not find a tenant willing to take on the lease when lower rents are being offered on similar premises currently being let. In that case, it may be that the only alternative for the tenant is to sub-let at a rent lower than that of the head-lease and cover the shortfall itself. There can be difficulties in doing this if the head-lease controls the sub-lease rental level (see **29.5.2**).

29.3 CONSENT TO THE SUB-LETTING

29.3.1 Restrictions on sub-letting

Where the tenant proposes to grant a sub-lease of all or part of the premises, it must have regard to the terms of its own lease, and in particular to the terms of the alienation covenant which is likely to control or regulate sub-letting. The prospective sub-tenant must also ensure any restrictions in the head-lease are complied with. If they are not, then the head-lease is at risk of forfeiture (see **Chapter 26**). If the head-lease is forfeited, then any sub-lease granted from it will fall too.

There are two main reasons why a head-landlord will wish to control sub-letting, even though, on the face of it, its relationship with the head-tenant remains unchanged. First, it is possible the head-landlord may end up with the sub-tenant as its direct tenant. This can occur if the head-lease is forfeited and the sub-tenant (whose sub-lease would also come to an end on forfeiture of the head-lease) successfully applies for relief from forfeiture. It can also occur if the head-lease is surrendered or disclaimed or, at the end of the sub-lease term, if the sub-tenant applies for a new lease under the LTA 1954 but the head-tenant does not. Secondly, whilst legally the head-tenant will remain liable to perform the head-lease covenants, regardless of the sub-letting, in reality the performance of many of the head-lease covenants will be undertaken by the sub-tenant.

As a result, most leases of commercial property will strictly regulate sub-lettings. Indeed, it is quite common for head-leases to bar sub-leases of part altogether. This is because of the estate management difficulties faced by a landlord with a building occupied by different tenants. Usually, at the very least, the head-lease will require the tenant to obtain the consent of the head-landlord before granting any sub-lease (whether of whole or part). Often, the head-lease will also be prescriptive about the terms of the sub-letting and require the terms of the sub-lease to match (or be at least as onerous as) the head-lease. It should be noted, however, that s 19(1)(a) of the LTA 1927 and s 1 of the LTA 1988 apply to qualified covenants against sub-letting. In consequence, where required, consent cannot be unreasonably withheld or delayed.

29.3.2 Licences to sub-let

Most head-landlords will require formal consent to the sub-letting to be given in the form of a licence to sub-let. This is a tripartite document entered in to by the head-landlord, tenant and sub-tenant.

The usual condition of granting consent is that the sub-tenant is to enter into a direct covenant with the head-landlord to perform the covenants in both the sub-lease and the head-lease. The latter covenant usually excludes the head-lease covenants to pay rent and only applies in so far as the head-lease covenants relate to the sub-let premises. Ordinarily, there is no privity of contract or estate between a head-landlord and a sub-tenant, but the direct covenant creates a contractual relationship. This enables the head-landlord to sue the sub-tenant for any breaches of either the head-lease (other than for non-payment of rent) or the sub-lease.

29.4 LIABILITY TO THE HEAD-LANDLORD

Ordinarily, there is neither privity of contract nor privity of estate between a head-landlord and a sub-tenant and, therefore, the head-landlord is unable to sue a sub-tenant in respect of any breaches of the terms of the head-lease. There are, however, three methods by which the head-landlord may acquire such a right to sue.

29.4.1 Under the common law

A sub-tenant may be bound by those restrictive covenants in the head-lease of which it had notice when it took its sub-lease. As the sub-tenant is entitled to call for production of the head-lease on the grant of its sub-lease (LPA 1925, s 44), the sub-tenant will be deemed to have notice of the contents of the head-lease even if it does not insist on its right to inspect it. This will not, however, assist the head-landlord with the enforcement of positive covenants.

29.4.2 By a direct covenant

As discussed at **29.3.2**, it is common practice for a direct covenant with the head-landlord to be given in the licence to sub-let. This covenant will make the sub-tenant liable to the head-landlord in contract. However, a new direct covenant will need to be obtained on each and every assignment of the sub-lease from the proposed assignee.

29.4.3 Use of the Contracts (Rights of Third Parties) Act 1999

As an alternative to requiring the sub-tenant to enter into a direct covenant with the head-landlord, use could be made of the Contracts (Rights of Third Parties) Act 1999. Under the provisions of this Act, a non-contracting third party (such as the head-landlord) has the right to enforce a contract term if the contract expressly provides that it may or, subject to contrary intention, if the term purports to confer a benefit on that party. In the context of sub-leases, the tenant's covenants in the sub-lease could be expressed to be for the benefit of both the landlord and head-landlord. This would enable the head-landlord to sue the sub-tenant for any breach of the sub-lease, despite not being a party to the sub-lease. An advantage of this method is that, as each of the sub-tenant's covenants would be a 'tenant's covenant' for the purpose of the Landlord and Tenant (Covenants) Act 1995, they would automatically bind any assignee of the sub-tenant. In consequence, the head-landlord could, on assignment of the sub-lease, sue the sub-tenant's assignee without the need to take a direct covenant from the assignee. Despite this advantage, practitioners still tend to pursue a direct covenant (from both the original sub-tenant and any assignee) as it is a tried and tested method.

29.5 DRAFTING THE SUB-LEASE

In drafting the sub-lease, the tenant should bear in mind the following matters.

29.5.1 The term

The tenant should ensure that the term of the sub-lease is at least one day shorter than the unexpired residue of its head-lease term, since a sub-lease for the whole residue of the head-lease term will take effect as an assignment of that term. Not only will this be contrary to the tenant's intention, it will also probably breach the alienation covenant in the head-lease, as the landlord will have given its consent to a sub-letting, but not an assignment. In *Allied Dunbar Pension Services Ltd v Baker* [2001] All ER (D) 46, the High Court refused to grant rectification to a tenant who had granted a sub-lease for a term due to expire on the same day as the term of the head-lease. The court considered it plain that the parties had intended the sub-lease to expire on the same day as the head-lease. It was irrelevant that the tenant had not realised that by making the expiry dates of the sub-lease and head-lease coincide, it was effectively assigning its interest.

In taking up possession, the sub-tenant will be in occupation for the purpose of a business and may, therefore, enjoy security of tenure under Pt II of the LTA 1954 (see **Chapter 32**). The tenant may want to consider excluding the sub-letting from the protection of the Act so that it can be sure to resume occupation at the end of the sub-lease. Indeed, it may be a requirement of the alienation covenant in the head-lease that any sub-leases are to be contracted out of the LTA 1954, so that if the tenant's interest is terminated in circumstances which result in the sub-tenant becoming the immediate tenant of the head-landlord, the head-landlord will be guaranteed possession at the end of the sub-lease.

29.5.2 The rent

The tenant will want to ensure that the rent to be paid by the sub-tenant is as high as the market will currently allow, and if the sub-lease is to be granted for anything longer than a short term, the tenant will want to review the rent from time to time. Careful attention must again be paid to the alienation covenant in the head-lease which might dictate the terms upon which any sub-lettings are to be granted.

In the past, it was common for the head-landlord to include several requirements in the head-lease:

(a) that any sub-letting by the tenant be granted at a rent equal to the greater of the rent payable under the head-lease and the full open market rent for the premises;

(b) that any sub-letting be granted without the payment of a premium; and

(c) that any sub-letting contain provisions for the review of rent (in an upwards direction only) which match the head-lease review provisions in terms of frequency, timing and basis of review.

The reason head-landlords sought to impose such conditions was that, at some future date, the head-lease might determine (eg by reason of surrender), leaving the sub-tenant as the head-landlord's immediate tenant upon the terms of the sub-lease. However, if the tenant, at the grant of its head-lease, had agreed to the restrictions described in (a) and (b) above, it could find it difficult to arrange a sub-letting, particularly at times when rents were depressed and potential sub-tenants would only pay a rent lower than the head-lease rent. One popular way around this was for the tenant to enter into a side letter or collateral agreement with the proposed sub-tenant in which the tenant agreed to reimburse the sub-tenant the difference between the head-lease rent and the current market rent. However, the case of *Allied Dunbar Assurance plc v Homebase Ltd* [2002] EWCA Civ 666, [2002] 27 EG 144 ruled that this was not a valid way of avoiding restrictions in the head-lease preventing sub-letting below the head-lease rent. The result of this was to render sub-leases containing such restrictions inalienable in times of falling rents. Whilst clearly problematic for the tenant, this also caused problems for the head-landlord. First, a lease that cannot in reality be disposed of will not be valued highly when it comes to rent review. Secondly, the practical effect of an inalienable lease may be the insolvency or financial difficulty of the tenant, leading to non-payment of rent. In consequence, many institutional head-landlords no longer require sub-lettings to be at the higher of the head-lease rent or open market rent. Note that the 2020 Code stipulates that if sub-letting is allowed, the rent should be not less than the market rent as at the time of sub-letting.

If the sub-tenant is prepared to pay the same rent as that payable under the head-lease, it should be wary of an obligation in the sub-lease which simply requires it to pay the rents payable from time to time under the head-lease. Such a provision would give the sub-tenant no input into any negotiations for the review of rent during the term, and is likely to give little incentive to the tenant to argue with any vigour against the head-landlord at review, since it knows that whatever figure is agreed, it will be paid by the sub-tenant.

If the head-landlord has opted to tax for VAT purposes, so that VAT is payable by the tenant, the option in no way affects the sub-lease rents. It would, therefore, be wise for the tenant to opt to tax in respect of these premises so that VAT can be charged to the sub-tenant, although careful consideration must always be given to the effect of opting to tax.

29.5.3 The covenants

In drafting the sub-lease, the tenant will attempt to mirror the provisions of the head-lease. The tenant should be careful not to allow the sub-tenant scope to do anything at the premises which is forbidden under the provisions of the head-lease.

Particular attention should be paid to:

(a) *Alienation.* It is unlikely that the head-lease will allow any further sub-letting of the premises. Care should, therefore, be taken to impose appropriate restrictions in the sub-lease. There ought to be an absolute covenant against sub-letting (or sharing or parting with possession of the premises), with a qualified covenant against assigning the sub-lease.

(b) *Repair.* The same repairing obligation as affects the tenant (or an even tighter one) ought to be imposed upon the sub-tenant. In interpreting a repair covenant, regard is to be had to the age, character and locality of the premises at the time the lease was granted. If there has been a considerable lapse of time between the grant of the head-lease and the grant of the sub-lease, different standards of repair might be required by the respective repair covenants, leading to a possible residual repair liability on the part of the tenant. The sub-tenant's obligation will be to repair 'the premises'. The tenant must make sure that 'the premises' are defined in the sub-lease to include all of the premises demised by the head-lease or, if a sub-letting of part is contemplated, that the division of responsibility is clearly stated.

(c) *Insurance.* In all probability, the head-landlord will be insuring the premises, with the tenant reimbursing the premium. The sub-lease should, therefore, provide that the sub-tenant reimburses the premiums paid by the tenant (or a proportionate part if a sub-lease of part is contemplated).

(d) *Decoration.* The tenant should ensure that the sub-lease obliges the sub-tenant to decorate the premises as frequently as, at the times and in the manner required by the head-lease.

29.5.4 Rights of access

The tenant may resist attempts to extend the usual covenant in the sub-lease for quiet enjoyment to cover liability for the acts and omissions of someone with a title paramount (eg, the head-landlord). If the tenant did so, it would be in breach of the covenant if the head-landlord disturbed the sub-tenant's occupation by exercising a right of entry contained in the head-lease. However, in any case, to avoid a possible dispute, the tenant should ensure that, in reserving rights of entry onto and access over the sub-let premises, those rights are reserved for the benefit of the tenant and head-landlord.

29.5.5 Covenant to observe head-lease

Despite imposing broadly similar covenants in the sub-lease to those contained in the head-lease, the tenant will also want to include a sweeping-up provision obliging the sub-tenant to perform all of the covenants in the head-lease (other than those relating to the payments of rent) in so far as they affect the sub-let premises, and to indemnify the tenant against liability for breach. The sub-tenant might prefer, however, to enter into a negative obligation not to cause a breach of the head-lease covenants. Either way, the result will be that the sub-tenant's solicitor will need to conduct a careful review of the head-lease terms in addition to those of the sub-lease. Care must be taken on a sub-lease of part to ensure that a correct division of liability is made between tenant and sub-tenant in respect of the head-lease covenants.

29.5.6 Other drafting points

When drafting and negotiating the sub-lease, the following additional points may be borne in mind:

(a) Where there is to be a direct covenant in the licence to sub-let, it is important for the sub-tenant to remember that it will not work both ways, and so the sub-tenant does not have any means of enforcing a breach of covenant by the head-landlord. The sub-tenant should consider insisting upon a covenant by the tenant in the sub-lease obliging the tenant to enforce a breach of covenant by the head-landlord as and when required by the sub-tenant. The sub-tenant is likely to concede that it should bear the cost of any such action.

(b) The usual covenant for quiet enjoyment will not impose liability on the tenant in respect of the acts or omissions of the head-landlord. The sub-tenant may consider extending the usual covenant. See, however, **29.5.4**.

(c) The sub-tenant should ask the tenant to covenant with it to pass on to it any notices received from the head-landlord (eg LPA 1925, s 146 notices).

(d) The sub-tenant should explore the possibility of having its interest noted on the head-landlord's insurance policy. It should ask for details of the policy and ensure that provision is made to enable the policy to be produced to it from time to time. The provision referred to at (a) above should enable the sub-tenant to force the tenant to require the head-landlord to reinstate the premises if they are damaged by an insured risk.

REVIEW ACTIVITY

1. Imagine that several years ago your client entered into a lease in the form set out at **Appendix 4**. No wording in square brackets was included. The annual rent was £100,000. Your client now wishes to sub-let the whole of the premises and has found a prospective sub-tenant. The sub-tenant is only prepared to take a sub-letting at an annual rent of £80,000. Is this permissible under the terms of the lease?

2. Would the client referred to in Question 1 be entitled to grant a sub-lease protected by Part II of the LTA 1954?

3. What is the purpose of clause 14.2(f) of the **Appendix 4** lease?

Answers to this Review activity may be found in Appendix 1.

CHAPTER 30

REMEDIES FOR BREACH OF COVENANT

30.1	Landlord's remedies	327
30.2	Tenant's remedies	333

30.1 LANDLORD'S REMEDIES

Before the landlord takes any steps against a defaulting tenant, it should first consider whether any other party is also liable. For example, are there any sureties or guarantors, is the original tenant under a continuing liability, or did any of the previous assignees give the landlord a direct covenant on assignment upon which they may still be liable? The ability of the landlord to proceed against some of these other parties is affected by the Landlord and Tenant (Covenants) Act 1995 (LT(C)A 1995) and these issues have been dealt with earlier in the book.

Before proceeding against a former tenant or its guarantor for a 'fixed charge', that is:

(a) rent; or
(b) service charge; or
(c) any liquidated sum payable under the lease; or
(d) interest on such sums,

the LT(C)A 1995, s 17 requires the landlord to serve a notice of the claim (usually referred to as a 'Default Notice') upon the former tenant or its guarantor, as the case may be, within six months of the current tenant's default (there is no requirement to serve a notice also on a former tenant before serving a notice on that tenant's guarantor (*Cheverell Estates Ltd v Harris* [1998] 02 EG 127)). Failure to serve a valid notice will mean that the landlord is unable to recover that sum from the former tenant or guarantor concerned. This requirement applies to all leases and not just those granted after the commencement of the LT(C)A 1995.

The Court of Appeal, in *Scottish & Newcastle plc v Raguz* [2007] EWCA Civ 150, had held that a s 17 notice had to be served by a landlord where a rent review date had passed without the new rent having been assessed, whether or not there were actually any arrears outstanding. The House of Lords ([2008] UKHL 65) reversed that decision. Should the delayed fixing of the new rent result in an increased amount being payable (which would be backdated to the review date), this would normally be due as a lump sum on the date specified in the lease. The landlord would then have six months from that date to serve a s 17 notice should it not be paid by the current tenant.

Where the landlord does proceed against a former tenant or its guarantor, that person may be able to regain some control over the property by calling for an overriding lease (see **30.1.4**).

In addition to considering whether there are other parties that it can pursue, the landlord should check whether it has another fund from which to meet the sums that are due, for example a rent deposit. If so, then it should first check that the contractual terms of that deposit permit deduction of the relevant amount and that the necessary preconditions (perhaps due notice) have been satisfied.

30.1.1 For non-payment of rent

Only six years' arrears of rent are recoverable, whether by claim or Commercial Rent Arrears Recovery (Limitation Act 1980).

30.1.1.1 By claim

If the tenant, or one of the parties mentioned above, is liable for the rent, the landlord may pursue its normal remedies for recovery through the High Court or county court. As to the choice of court and type of proceedings, see the Legal Practice Guide, *Civil Litigation*.

30.1.1.2 Bankruptcy and winding up

If the sum owed to it exceeds £750 (in the case of a company) or £5,000 (in the case of an individual), the landlord can consider starting insolvency proceedings against the tenant, in the hope that this will bring pressure to bear and the tenant will pay the debt rather than face insolvency. This approach has risks, though. If the tenant does not pay and the insolvency proceeds, the landlord may rank as only one of the unsecured (ordinary) creditors. These creditors may not receive payment in full.

If the landlord wants to start insolvency proceedings (bankruptcy for an individual tenant, liquidation for a corporate tenant), it will first have to serve a statutory demand for payment of the debt. More details of insolvency processes are given in **Chapter 33**.

30.1.1.3 Commercial Rent Arrears Recovery

Part 3 of the Tribunals, Courts and Enforcement Act 2007 (TCEA 2007) contains provisions which replace the ancient common law remedy of distress with a more limited, court-based system called Commercial Rent Arrears Recovery (CRAR). CRAR allows a landlord of commercial property (where the tenancy is in writing) to instruct an enforcement agent to take control of the tenant's goods and sell them to recover the amount of the rent arrears. Rent, for these purposes, means the pure income rent plus any VAT and does not include sums in respect of services, repairs or insurance, even if such sums are reserved as rent in the lease.

The procedure for CRAR is set out in Sch 12 to the TCEA 2007. Under CRAR, the landlord has to serve an enforcement notice on the tenant before seizing the goods. The minimum period of notice is currently at least seven clear days, unless a court orders a shorter period in circumstances where it thinks that the tenant will use the notice period to dispose of the goods. The landlord then needs to authorise (in writing) an enforcement agent to carry out CRAR on its behalf. The enforcement agent (an individual holding a certificate issued by a judge) may then take control of and sell the chattels in order to recover the rent arrears.

Under s 77 of the TCEA 2007, the tenant must be in arrears of rent before the enforcement notice is served, the amount of the rent arrears must be certain or capable of being calculated with certainty, and the net unpaid rent (ie the rent less interest, VAT or any sums owing to the tenant) must be equal to or exceed an amount prescribed in regulations, currently an amount equal to seven days' rent. These requirements must be met at the time the enforcement notice is given and when the enforcement agent takes control of the goods. If they are not, then CRAR cannot be exercised. The sale of goods cannot take place until at least seven clear days have passed since the goods were removed, unless delay would cause the goods to be unsaleable, or their value would be extinguished or substantially reduced. The tenant must be given at least seven clear days notice of the date, time and place of the sale, and the sale must be by public auction unless a court orders otherwise. If the CRAR provisions are breached, the tenant can bring a claim against the enforcement agent or the landlord, and the court can either return the goods to the tenant or award damages for loss suffered by the tenant because of the breach.

30.1.1.4 Collecting the rent from a sub-tenant

If the premises have been sub-let, the superior landlord can serve notice on the sub-tenant under s 81 of the TCEA 2007, requiring the sub-tenant to pay its rent to the superior landlord until the arrears are paid off. The sub-tenant should pay the rent to the superior landlord after the expiry of 14 clear days from the date when the notice was served on it.

30.1.1.5 Forfeiture

Forfeiture for non-payment of rent is dealt with at **26.4.1**.

Landlords should bear in mind that exercising CRAR may constitute a waiver of the right to forfeit (see *Thirunavukkrasu v Brar* [2018] EWHC 2461 (Ch)).

30.1.1.6 Covid-19 arrangements

As part of its response to the Covid-19 pandemic, the Government legislated to ringfence rent debt accrued during the pandemic by businesses affected by enforced closures and set out a process of binding arbitration to be undertaken between landlords and tenants (see the Commercial Rent (Coronavirus) Act 2022). The commercial tenant protection measures only apply to ringfenced arrears. This means that landlords are able to evict tenants for the non-payment of rent prior to March 2020 and after the end of restrictions for their sector and those who were not affected by business closures during this period.

The Government also imposed a moratorium on forfeiture of commercial leases for non-payment of rent until 25 March 2022 and increased the minimum amount of unpaid rent that must be outstanding before the remedy of CRAR could be exercised. Until 25 March 2022, the minimum amount was 554 days' rent.

30.1.2 Breach of tenant's repairing covenant

From a practical point of view, and as a first step, the landlord, exercising its right of entry in the lease, should enter onto the demised premises with its surveyor to draw up a schedule of dilapidations. This should be served on the tenant with a demand that the tenant comply with its repairing obligation. If the tenant remains in breach of its obligation to repair the demised premises, the landlord has various remedies available to it.

30.1.2.1 Claim for damages

The measure of damages

The landlord may bring a claim for damages against the tenant either during the term or after its expiry. Section 18 of the LTA 1927 limits the maximum amount recoverable in all cases by providing that the damages cannot exceed the amount by which the value of the reversion has been diminished by the breach. It follows that the cost of repairs will be irrecoverable to the extent that it exceeds this statutory ceiling.

Where proceedings are commenced during the term of the lease, the reduction in the value of the reversion will be influenced by the length of the unexpired residue of the term. The longer this is, the less the reduction should be.

In proceedings commenced at or after the end of the lease, the court may be prepared, at least as a starting point, to accept the cost of repairs as evidence of the measure of damages, subject to the ceiling imposed by s 18 (see *Smiley v Townshend* [1950] 2 KB 311). For examples of how this has been applied, see *Ultraworth Ltd v General Accident Fire and Life Assurance Corporation* [2000] 2 EGLR 115 (a case where the diminution in the value of the reversion was unaffected by the tenant's breach of the repairing obligation) and *Ravensgate Estates Ltd v Horizon Housing Group Ltd* [2007] All ER (D) 294 (where the landlord was planning to redevelop, so the full cost of repairs was not awarded). The correct approach is set out in *Van Dal Footwear v Ryman Ltd* [2009] EWCA Civ 1478.

If a sub-tenant is in breach of a repairing covenant in the sub-lease, the measure of damages is the reduction in value of the intermediate landlord's reversion. If the sub-tenant knows of the terms of the superior tenancy, the intermediate landlord's liability to the superior landlord will be relevant in assessing these damages.

Section 18 of the 1927 Act further provides that no damages are recoverable for failure to put or leave the premises in repair at the termination of the lease, if the premises are to be pulled down shortly after termination or if intended structural alterations would render the repairs valueless. To benefit from this provision the tenant must show that the landlord had a firm intention (to pull down or alter) at the end of the lease.

It is important to appreciate that s 18 applies only to claims for damages by the landlord and has no application where the sum owed by the tenant is in the nature of a debt. If, therefore, the tenant covenants to spend £x per year on repairs, but fails to do so, the landlord may recover the deficiency as a debt without regard to the statutory ceiling in s 18. This is the reason behind the clause in many leases, which permits the landlord to enter and carry out repair work that the tenant has failed to do (the *Jervis v Harris* clause, discussed in more detail at **30.1.2.2**).

The need for leave to sue

If the lease was granted for seven years or more and still has at least three years left to run, the Leasehold Property (Repairs) Act 1938 lays down a special procedure which the landlord must follow before being able to sue for damages (or forfeit the lease) for breach of the tenant's repairing covenant. Where the Act applies, it requires the landlord to serve a notice on the tenant under s 146 of the LPA 1925. Apart from the normal requirements of such a notice (see **26.4.2.1**), it must in addition contain a statement informing the tenant of its right to serve a counter-notice within 28 days claiming the benefit of the Act. If such a counter-notice is served, the landlord cannot proceed further without leave of the court, which will not be given unless the landlord proves (and not just shows an arguable case):

(a) that the immediate remedying of the breach is required for preventing substantial diminution, or for complying with any Act or by-law, or for protecting the interests of occupiers other than the tenant, or for the avoidance of much heavier repair costs in the future; or

(b) that there are special circumstances which render it just and equitable that leave be given.

Even if the landlord makes out one of the grounds, the court still has a discretion to refuse leave, but this should be exercised only where the court is clearly convinced that it would be wrong to allow the landlord to continue. The court may, in granting or refusing leave, impose such conditions on the landlord or tenant as it thinks fit. The relevant date for determining whether the grounds are established is the date of the hearing; see *Landmaster Properties Ltd v Thackeray Property Services* [2003] 35 EG 83.

The Act does not apply to breach of a tenant's covenant to put premises into repair when the tenant takes possession or within a reasonable time thereafter.

30.1.2.2 Self-help

If the tenant is in breach of its repairing obligations, can the landlord enter the demised premises, carry out the necessary works and recover the cost from the tenant? In the absence of a statutory right or an express provision in the lease, the landlord has no general right to enter the demised premises even where the tenant is in breach of its obligations. Indeed, the tenant may be able to obtain an injunction to restrain the landlord's trespass. For that reason most leases will contain an express right for the landlord to enter the demised premises and carry out any necessary repairs at the tenant's expense, in default of the tenant complying with a notice to repair. In the case of *Jervis v Harris* [1996] Ch 195, the court accepted the landlord's argument that his claim against the tenant to recover this expenditure was in the nature of a debt claim rather than one for damages. Thus, the landlord was able to evade the statutory restrictions in the 1927 and 1938 Acts, mentioned above.

Enforcing a *Jervis v Harris* clause (either to do the works or to recover all the money expended) can be very tricky. For example, the tenant may refuse the landlord entry to the building. The landlord will have to seek an injunction to compel the tenant to give access, and *Creska Ltd v Hammersmith and Fulham London Borough Council (No 2)* (1999) 78 P & CR D46 shows that the court may refuse such an injunction (in that case the circumstances were most unusual – the proposed repair works were of no benefit to the tenant, there was a long unexpired residue of the lease, and the tenant was willing to deposit monies in an escrow account to do the repairs at the end of the lease). Alternatively, the tenant may argue that the works being done do not qualify as repairs (but something more extensive, lying outside the ambit of the clause) or have been done at too great a cost.

30.1.2.3 Specific performance

In *Rainbow Estates Ltd v Tokenhold Ltd* [1999] Ch 64, the court held that, in principle, there is no reason why the equitable remedy of specific performance should not be available to enforce compliance by a tenant with its repairing obligation. However, other remedies are likely to be more appropriate, and the court stressed that specific performance will be awarded only in exceptional circumstances. In this case there was no alternative remedy for the landlord – unusually, the lease contained no forfeiture clause, nor a provision allowing the landlord to enter and carry out the repairs itself.

30.1.2.4 Forfeiture

The landlord may be able to forfeit the lease for breach of the tenant's covenant to repair; forfeiture is dealt with in **Chapter 26**.

30.1.3 Breaches of other covenants by the tenant: an outline

30.1.3.1 Damages

Damages for breach of covenant are assessed on a contractual basis, the aim being to put the landlord in the same position as if the covenant had been performed. The general principle is that the landlord may recover as damages all loss which may be fairly and reasonably considered as arising in the natural course of things from the breach, or such as may be reasonably supposed to have been in the contemplation of both parties, at the time of entering into the lease, as the probable result of that breach (*Hadley v Baxendale* (1854) 9 Exch 341). In the majority of cases the damages will be equal to the diminution in the value of the reversion.

The breach of some particular covenants will now be considered.

Covenant to insure

The landlord usually assumes responsibility for insurance. If, however, the tenant has covenanted to insure, there will be a breach of covenant if the premises are uninsured or underinsured at any time during the term. If the premises are damaged during the period of default, the measure of damages will be the cost of rebuilding (*Burt v British Transport Commission* (1955) 166 EG 4).

Covenant against dealings

There is little authority on the measure of damages obtainable by a landlord where, for example, the tenant has assigned the lease without consent. However, the landlord will probably be entitled to compensation for the fact that its new tenant is less financially sound than the assignor and the value of its reversion is thus reduced.

User covenant

Damages may be awarded for breach by the tenant of a positive covenant to keep the premises open. For example, if the anchor tenant, in breach of covenant, closes its shop premises in a shopping centre, it may have such an adverse effect on the profitability of the other shops in the centre that the landlord may be forced to offer rental concessions to the other tenants. The landlord should be compensated for this loss by an award of damages; but there may be difficult problems in quantifying the amount of the damages. If the landlord can prove that its financial loss arises wholly from the tenant's breach, there should be no difficulty for the landlord. However, it may be the case that the centre was already in decline long before the tenant ceased trading, so that the defaulting tenant's breach merely contributed to the already falling profitability of the centre (see, generally, *Transworld Land Co Ltd v J Sainsbury plc* [1990] 2 EGLR 255).

In *SHB Realisations Ltd v Cribbs Mall Nominee (1) Ltd* [2019] 3 WLUK 588, an insolvent tenant of a 125 year premium lease who could not remedy the breach of the keep open covenant or comply with it in the future was granted relief from forfeiture, but only on condition that the tenant completed an assignment of the lease within three months.

30.1.3.2 Injunction

In certain circumstances, the landlord may be able to obtain an injunction against the tenant. An injunction is an equitable remedy and thus at the discretion of the court, which may award damages instead. In an appropriate case the landlord may be able to obtain an interim injunction pending the full hearing. There are two types of injunction:

(a) *Injunctions prohibiting a breach of covenant.* The landlord may consider the use of such an injunction to prevent, for example:
 (i) an assignment in breach of covenant;
 (ii) the carrying out of unauthorised alterations;
 (iii) an unauthorised use.

(b) *Mandatory injunctions.* These injunctions compel the tenant to do something to ensure the performance of a covenant. The court is cautious in its grant of mandatory injunctions.

Standard works on landlord and tenant law contain a more detailed consideration of the subject of injunctions.

30.1.3.3 Specific performance

Like the injunction, this is an equitable remedy and is therefore discretionary. The House of Lords confirmed that specific performance is not available against a tenant who is in breach of its 'keep open' covenant (*Co-operative Insurance Society Ltd v Argyll Stores (Holdings) Ltd* [1997] 23 EG 137).

30.1.3.4 Forfeiture

Often the landlord's most effective remedy will be to commence (or threaten to commence) forfeiture proceedings against the tenant with a view to ending the lease. This remedy is dealt with in **Chapter 26**.

30.1.4 Right of former tenant or its guarantor to an overriding lease

If a former tenant, or guarantor, is served with a notice by the landlord requiring payment of a fixed charge (see **30.1**), the LT(C)A 1995 allows it to call for an overriding lease within 12 months of payment. For example, L granted a lease to T in 1980. The lease is now owned by A which fell into arrears with its rent. L served notice on T requiring T to pay this sum. T duly made full payment and now claims an overriding lease from L. This will be a head-lease 'slotted in' above the lease of the defaulting tenant. The lease of the defaulting tenant moves one step down the reversionary line and becomes a sub-lease. Thus, T will become the immediate landlord of A and in the event of continued default by A can decide what action to take against A, eg forfeiture of the occupational lease (sub-lease). Under the overriding lease, T now has some control over the premises for which it is being held liable. The same situation would arise in leases granted on or after 1 January 1996 where the former tenant had been required under an authorised guarantee agreement to guarantee the performance of its immediate assignee, and that assignee is now in default (see **21.2.4.3**).

The terms of the overriding lease will be on the terms of the defaulting tenant's lease (with consequential adjustments to add a small reversionary period).

Before deciding to call for an overriding lease, a former tenant (or guarantor) should be made aware that it may become liable for landlord's covenants (eg repairing obligations).

30.2 TENANT'S REMEDIES

30.2.1 Breach of an express covenant

In general, a breach by the landlord of one of its covenants in the lease will entitle the tenant to bring a claim for damages. The measure of damages will usually be the difference between the value of the tenant's interest in the premises with the covenant performed and the value with the covenant broken. In certain circumstances, the tenant may seek a more appropriate remedy, such as specific performance or an injunction.

Particular attention should be paid to the landlord's repairing covenant.

30.2.1.1 Breach of landlord's repairing covenant

Unless the lease is of part of a building, it is unusual for the landlord to enter into a covenant to repair. In *Stonecrest Marble Ltd v Shepherds Bush Housing Association Ltd* [2021] EWHC 2621 (Ch), the High Court held that the landlord was not liable to the tenant, under either the express quiet enjoyment covenant in the lease or in tort, to repair damage caused to the property by water ingress caused by debris blocking a gutter in the landlord's retained premises. Even where the landlord has assumed the responsibility for repairs, it will generally be liable only if it has notice of disrepair. If the landlord fails to carry out the repairs for which it is liable, the tenant has various remedies available to it. These include the following.

Claim for damages

The tenant's normal remedy will be to bring a claim against its landlord for damages for breach of covenant. Section 18 of the LTA 1927, which restricts a landlord's claim for damages (see **30.1.2.1**), is not relevant to a tenant's claim. Here, damages will be assessed by comparing the value of the premises to the tenant at the date of assessment with their value if the landlord had complied with its obligation. The tenant will also be entitled to damages for consequential loss such as damage caused to the tenant's goods. If the disrepair was such that the tenant was forced to move into temporary accommodation, the cost of this should also be recoverable, provided the tenant had acted reasonably to mitigate its loss.

Self-help

Subject to notifying the landlord and giving it a reasonable opportunity to perform its covenant, the tenant is entitled to carry out the repair itself and deduct the reasonable cost of so doing from future payments of rent (*Lee-Parker v Izzet* [1971] 1 WLR 1688). If the landlord sues the tenant for non-payment of rent, the tenant will have a defence (see **18.1**).

Specific performance

The tenant, unlike the landlord, may be able to obtain an order of specific performance. The granting of the order is entirely at the discretion of the court, and being an equitable remedy it will not be granted if damages are an adequate remedy. Further, there must be a clear breach of covenant and must be no doubt over what is required to be done to remedy the breach. In *Blue Manchester Ltd v North West Ground Rents Ltd* [2019] EWHC 142 (TCC), the tenant succeeded in its claim for specific performance, and the landlord was required to replace defective glazing units in an exterior facade of the Beetham Tower in Manchester.

Appointment of receiver

In the tenant's claim against the landlord for breach of covenant, the tenant may seek the appointment of a receiver to collect the rents and manage the property in accordance with the terms of the lease (including the performance of the landlord's covenants). The court has this power whenever it appears just and convenient to make such an appointment (Senior Courts Act 1981, s 37). The power has been exercised not only where the landlord had abandoned the property, but also where it has failed to carry out urgently needed repairs in accordance with its covenant (see *Daiches v Bluelake Investments Ltd* [1985] 2 EGLR 67).

The tenant must nominate a suitably qualified person to act as receiver, for example a surveyor; and before agreeing to act, the potential appointee should ensure that the assets of which they will have control will be sufficient to meet their fees, or that they obtain an indemnity in respect of them from the applicant.

A receiver may also be appointed where the landlord collects a service charge from the tenants but fails to provide the services it has promised.

30.2.2 Breach of an implied covenant

30.2.2.1 Covenant for quiet enjoyment

Most leases will contain an express covenant by the landlord for quiet enjoyment (see **Chapter 24**). In the absence of an express covenant, one will be implied arising out of the relationship of landlord and tenant. The implied covenant extends only to interruption of or interference with the tenant's enjoyment of the demised premises by the landlord or any person lawfully claiming under it; it does not extend to acts done by anyone with a title superior to that of the landlord. Express covenants are often similarly restricted, in which case the only significant difference between the express and the implied covenant is that under an express covenant the landlord will remain liable throughout the term granted (unless, under a 'new lease', the landlord is released on assignment under the LT(C)A 1995), whereas under an implied covenant the landlord's liability operates only during the currency of its ownership of the reversion.

The covenant will provide the tenant with a remedy in the case of unlawful eviction, or where there is any substantial interference with the tenant's use and enjoyment of the premises either by the landlord or by the lawful (rightful) acts of anyone claiming under it. The acts likely to amount to a breach of the covenant are discussed at **24.2**. The normal remedy will be damages, assessed on a contractual basis, to compensate the tenant for the loss resulting from the breach.

30.2.2.2 Derogation from grant

A landlord is under an implied obligation not to derogate from its grant. This covenant complements the covenant for quiet enjoyment, and sometimes the two overlap. The landlord will be in breach of its obligation if it does anything which substantially interferes with the use of the demised premises for the purpose for which they were let. Having given something with one hand, the landlord cannot take away its enjoyment with the other (see *Rees v Windsor-Clive* [2020] EWCA Civ 816 where the principle of derogation from grant was considered in the context of the landlord's rights of entry under a lease).

The principle is often used to prevent the landlord from using its retained land in a way which frustrates the purpose of the lease. Thus, it has been held to be a derogation from grant for a landlord to grant a lease for the purpose of storing explosives and then to use its retained land in such a way as to render the storage of explosives on the demised premises illegal (*Harmer v Jumbil (Nigeria) Tin Areas Ltd* [1921] 1 Ch 200; see also *Petra Investments Ltd v Jeffrey Rogers plc* [2000] 3 EGLR 120, a case concerning the landlord's ability to alter the original concept of a shopping centre, and *Platt v London Underground* [2001] 20 EG 227, where the landlord closed off the entry to the station and reduced footfall past the unit). Similarly, if the landlord uses machinery on its retained land which by reason of vibration affects the stability of the demised premises, there will be a breach of the implied covenant. However, there will be no derogation from grant where the landlord's use of the adjoining land merely makes the user of the demised premises less attractive, for example by letting the adjoining premises to a business competitor of the tenant (*Port v Griffith* [1938] 1 All ER 295 and *Romulus Trading Co Ltd v Comet Properties Ltd* [1996] 2 EGLR 70; but see also *Oceanic Village Ltd v Shirayama Shokusan Co Ltd* [2001] All ER (D) 62 (Feb), in which the High Court was prepared, exceptionally, to find the landlord in breach of the obligation in such circumstances).

Until the decision in *Chartered Trust plc v Davies* [1997] 49 EG 135, it was generally believed that it was insufficient to amount to derogation from grant for a landlord to stand back while tenant A, in breach of covenant, committed acts of nuisance against tenant B thus driving tenant B out of business. Just because the landlord failed to take action against tenant A to prevent the nuisance did not, so it was thought, amount to a repudiation of B's lease. However, the Court of Appeal held that inaction by the landlord in these circumstances may amount to derogation from grant. The implications of this decision will be felt most where, as in the instant case, the landlord has retained management control of a shopping centre and is responsible for the common parts. If, in breach of covenant, one of the tenants does something in the common parts which adversely affects another tenant, the landlord will have to consider acting to enforce the lease obligations or else run the risk of being found to have derogated from grant (see also *Nynehead Developments Ltd v RH Fibreboard Containers Ltd and Others* [1999] 9 EG 174).

CHAPTER 31

METHODS OF TERMINATION

31.1	Introduction	337
31.2	Expiry	337
31.3	Notice to quit	337
31.4	Operation of break clause	338
31.5	Surrender	338
31.6	Merger	339
	Review activity	339

31.1 INTRODUCTION

There are a number of ways at common law in which a lease may be ended. Before looking at these in detail, it is important to appreciate that if the tenant enjoys the protection of the security of tenure provisions under Pt II of the LTA 1954, the lease may be ended only in one of the ways specified by that Act (for which see **Chapter 32**).

In addition, forfeiture is a way in which a lease may come to an end, and this is considered in detail in **Chapter 26**.

The methods of termination to be considered here are:

(a) expiry (effluxion of time);
(b) notice to quit;
(c) operation of break clause;
(d) surrender;
(e) merger.

31.2 EXPIRY

A fixed-term tenancy will terminate automatically at the end of that term; there is no need for either party to take any steps at all. If the tenant remains in possession beyond the expiry date with the landlord's consent, it holds over as a tenant at will (ie, on terms that either party may end the tenancy at any time). A tenant at will may become an implied periodic tenant by the payment and acceptance of rent.

31.3 NOTICE TO QUIT

A periodic tenancy will not end by effluxion of time but may be determined by service of a notice to quit by either party. There are many technical rules surrounding the drafting and service of such notices, and reference should be made to one of the standard works on landlord and tenant law for a consideration of these. What follows is only intended as a reminder of some of the more important rules.

In the absence of contrary agreement, the minimum length of notice required is as follows:

(a) yearly tenancy: half a year's notice (or two quarters if the tenancy expires on a quarter day);
(b) monthly tenancy: one month's notice;
(c) weekly tenancy: one week's notice.

Not only must the length of notice be correct, it must also expire at the end of a completed period of the tenancy. In the case of a yearly tenancy, this means that the notice must expire on the anniversary of the commencement of the tenancy or on the day before the anniversary. For example, with a yearly tenancy beginning on 1 January in one year, the notice should expire on 1 January or 31 December in any subsequent year. A similar rule applies to other periodic tenancies.

At common law no particular form of notice is required, but it must be unambiguous and, for the avoidance of doubt, in writing.

As a general rule, unless the lease provides to the contrary, a notice to quit must relate to all of the land in the lease and not just part.

31.4 OPERATION OF BREAK CLAUSE

A fixed-term tenancy may contain a provision, known as a break clause, for the tenancy to be terminated by either landlord or tenant before it has run its full term. An example of a break clause is at clause 58 of the **Appendix 4** lease, which includes common conditions that must be met to exercise the break successfully.

Conditional break rights and the formalities required to break a lease are dealt with further at **17.2**.

If a head-lease is terminated by the exercise of a break right, any sub-lease that has been created will also end. If the underlease term would have expired after the break date, the sub-tenant may have a claim against the tenant for derogation from grant (*Barrett v Morgan* [2000] 2 AC 264). However, if the sub-tenant is protected under Pt II of the LTA 1954, it would have the right to apply for a renewal lease.

31.5 SURRENDER

Surrender occurs where a tenant yields up its lease to its immediate landlord who accepts the surrender. It is a consensual arrangement. The lease is said to merge in the landlord's reversion and is extinguished.

Surrender can be express or by operation of law. An express surrender of a lease exceeding three years must be made by deed (LPA 1925, s 52). Surrender by operation of law occurs where the parties act in an unequivocal way that is inconsistent with the continuance of the lease (emphasised in the case of *Padwick Properties Ltd v Punj Lloyd* [2016] 502 (Ch) – see below. There are many examples of conduct where a surrender by operation of law *has been inferred*, including:

(a) the parties agree a new lease, to commence during the currency of the existing lease;

(b) the tenant gives up possession and returns the key to the landlord, and the landlord accepts this as surrender (but if the key is merely left with the landlord, this in itself will not amount to surrender unless the landlord accepts it as surrender, for example by re-letting the premises (see *Arundel Corporation v The Financial Training Co Ltd* [2000] 3 All ER 456)).

Examples of conduct where a surrender by operation of law *has not been inferred* include:

(a) where a third party occupant is negotiating a lease (*QFS Scaffolding Limited v Sable and Another* [2010] EWCA Civ 682);

(b) the landlord failing to demand rent and service charge when it knew the tenant no longer wanted the lease (*Belcourt Estates Ltd v Adesina* [2005] EWCA Civ 208);

(c) the tenant vacating and returning the key, which the landlord accepted, after which the landlord changed the locks, installed additional security and marketed the property, all the while making it clear that it did not accept a surrender (*Padwick*).

In *Artworld Financial Corporation v Safaryan* [2009] 23 EG 94, it was held a surrender had occurred due to the cumulative effect of the landlord's conduct, even though the landlord's individual acts (accepting the keys from the tenant, redecorating, allowing occupation by a third party related to the landlord) might not have supported that effect.

A provision in a lease protected under Pt II of the LTA 1954 that requires the tenant to offer to surrender the lease before seeking consent to assign is void under s 38 of the LTA 1954 unless the parties can and do follow the procedure for contracting out (*Allnatt London Properties Ltd v Newton* [1984] 1 All ER 423, and see **32.1.5**). This is a complex area and outside the scope of this book.

A surrender will release the tenant from any future liability under the lease, but not in respect of past breaches. A well-advised tenant should therefore seek a release from all breaches.

The surrender of a head-lease will not terminate any sub-lease (*Mellor v Watkins* (1874) LR 9 QBD 400). The sub-tenant will become the immediate tenant of the head-landlord on the terms of the sub-lease (LPA 1925, s 139). Sometimes, a head-tenant will agree to surrender its head-lease with a view to taking a new fixed term from its landlord; this may happen where the head-lease is coming to the end of its fixed term. In this situation, any new head-lease granted following the surrender will be subject to the sub-lease (LPA 1925, s 150).

If the landlord's title is charged, the terms of the charge may require the mortgagee's consent. A surrender without that consent will usually be ineffective. In *Cooperative Bank PLC v Hayes Freehold Limited (In Liquidation)* [2017] EWHC 1820 (Ch), the High Court refused to imply a condition precedent into a deed of surrender that such consent had been obtained.

31.6 MERGER

Merger occurs where a tenant acquires its immediate landlord's reversion, or a third party acquires both the lease and the immediate reversion. In such a case the lease will end. However, merger will take place only where the person acquiring both the lease and immediate reversion holds both estates in the same capacity and intends merger to take place.

As with surrender, merger of a lease will not affect the position of any sub-tenant (LPA 1925, s 139).

REVIEW ACTIVITY

Complete the grid below by placing a cross in the relevant column.

	Sub-lease survives	Sub-lease does not survive
Surrender		
Merger		
Break exercised		
Forfeiture		

Answers to this Review activity may be found in Appendix 1.

CHAPTER 32

The Landlord and Tenant Act 1954, Part II

32.1	Introductory matters	341
32.2	Termination under the Act	347
32.3	The application to court	351
32.4	Interim rents	352
32.5	Grounds of opposition	353
32.6	Compensation for failure to obtain a new tenancy	358
32.7	The renewal lease	359
32.8	The order for the new lease	361
32.9	Procedural flowchart – s 25 notice	362
32.10	Future developments	362
	Review activity	363

32.1 INTRODUCTORY MATTERS

32.1.1 The protection of the Act

The principal Act conferring security of tenure on business tenants and regulating the manner in which business tenancies can be terminated is the LTA 1954 (statutory references in this chapter are to this Act, unless otherwise stated). The protection given to tenants covered by Pt II of the Act is twofold. First, a business tenancy will not come to an end at the expiration of a fixed term, nor can a periodic tenancy be terminated by the landlord serving an ordinary notice to quit. Instead, notwithstanding the ending of the contractual term, the tenancy will be automatically continued under s 24 until such time as it is terminated in one of the ways specified in the Act. Secondly, upon the expiration of a business tenancy in accordance with the Act, business tenants normally have a statutory right to apply to court for a new tenancy and the landlord may only oppose that application on certain statutory grounds. Any new tenancy granted will also enjoy the protection of the Act.

Selected extracts from the Act are set out in **Appendix 6**.

32.1.2 The application of the Act

Section 23(1) provides that

> this ... Act applies to any tenancy where the property comprised in the tenancy is or includes premises which are occupied by the tenant and are so occupied for the purposes of a business carried on by him or for those and other purposes.

This involves a number of elements.

32.1.2.1 There must be a 'tenancy'

Tenancy includes an agreement for a lease and an underlease (even an unauthorised one). However, licences are not protected. The lease/licence distinction is further considered at **11.4**. In view of the danger for landlords in inadvertently creating a protected tenancy, the use of licences as a means of avoiding the Act needs very careful consideration. Certain tenancies are specifically excluded from the protection of the Act and these are dealt with at **32.1.3**.

32.1.2.2 The premises must be occupied by the tenant

Occupation need not be by the tenant personally. It has been held that occupation may be sufficient where it is conducted through the medium of a manager or agent provided that such representative occupation is genuine and not a sham arrangement. Similarly, s 23(1A) and (1B) provides that the Act will apply where an individual is the tenant but the premises are then occupied by a company in which the tenant has a controlling interest. 'Controlling interest' is defined by s 46(2). There are also special rules as to occupation in ss 41, 41A and 46 where a tenancy is held on trust, vested in partners as trustees, or held by one member of a group of companies but occupied by another member of the same group.

Occupation need not be continuous provided that the 'thread of continuity' of business user is not broken (*Hancock & Willis v GMS Syndicate Ltd* (1982) 265 EG 473 and *Flairline Properties Ltd v Hassan* [1997] 1 EGLR 138). In *Pointon York Group plc v Poulton* [2006] EWCA Civ 1001, it was held that parking a car in a car parking space during normal business hours could amount to occupation for the purposes of the LTA 1954.

Problems may arise where a business tenant sub-lets part of the property to a business sub-tenant. In such a situation, they cannot both qualify for protection in respect of the sub-let part; there can be no dual occupation for the purposes of the Act. In normal circumstances, it will be the sub-tenant who enjoys the protection of the Act, although in an exceptional case the head-tenant may reserve sufficiently extensive rights over the sub-let part that it remains the occupier (see *Graysim Holdings Ltd v P&O Property Holdings Ltd* [1995] 3 WLR 854). The case of *Pointon York Group plc v Poulton* [2006] EWCA Civ 1001 shows the problems landlords can face due to the rule that any sub-lease must of necessity be shorter than the head-lease out of which it is granted. In this case, the head-tenant moved back into occupation in the short period between the end of the sub-lease and the later ending of the head-lease and was thus enabled to claim the protection of the Act. It is arguable that a landlord cannot serve a s 25 notice at a time when the tenant is not in business occupation, and so in situations like the *Poulton* case the landlord would not be able to serve the s 25 notice until the tenant actually took up occupation. Since the landlord must give at least six months' notice (see **32.2.1.1**), this would seriously delay the landlord's ability to obtain possession or grant a renewal lease at an increased rent.

32.1.2.3 The premises must be occupied for the purposes of a business carried on by the tenant

'Business' is widely defined in s 23 to include a 'trade, profession or employment and includes any activity carried on by a body of persons, whether corporate or unincorporate'. Where the business is carried on by an individual, it must amount to a trade, profession or employment; but where it is carried on by a body of persons (corporate or unincorporate) 'any activity' may suffice. Thus, it has been held that the organising of a tennis club and the activities of the governors in running a hospital, both amounted to a business use (*Addiscombe Garden Estates v Crabbe* [1958] 1 QB 513 and *Hills (Patents) Ltd v University College Hospital Board of Governors* [1956] 1 QB 90). This does not mean, however, that the Act will apply whenever the tenant is a body of persons; the 'activity' must be correlative to the conceptions involved in the words 'trade, profession or employment'.

Two problem areas may arise with this requirement.

(a) The demised premises will sometimes be used for two purposes, only one of which is a business user. For example, the letting may consist of a shop on the ground floor with living accommodation above. Does the Act still apply? In cases of mixed user the Act will apply provided the business activity is a significant purpose of the occupation and not merely incidental to the occupation of the premises as a residence (*Cheryl Investments Ltd v Saldhana* [1978] 1 WLR 1329 and *Gurton v Parrot* [1991] 1 EGLR 98). In the example mentioned, the Act is likely to apply. If, however, a residential tenant occasionally brought work home with them, this would not result in their tenancy being protected under the Act. Moreover, a residential lease of a house where there is a degree of home business use will not have security of tenure under the Act. A home business is defined as 'a business of a kind which might reasonably be carried on at home' (s 43ZA).

(b) The business user may be in breach of a covenant of the lease. How does that affect the tenant's rights? If the lease merely forbids a specific business use (eg, not to use the shop as a newsagents), or any use except the business use specified (eg, not to use the premises for any purpose other than as a newsagents), a business use in breach of such a provision will not deprive the tenant of the protection of the Act. However, s 24(3) does exclude from protection any tenancy where the use of the premises for business purposes is in breach of a general prohibition preventing all business use (eg, not to carry on any business, trade, profession or employment) although if the landlord had consented to or acquiesced in the breach, the Act would still apply. The Act will not apply, even where the landlord has agreed to or acquiesced in it, where the business use is solely for the purposes of a home business.

32.1.3 Exclusions from the Act

Apart from those tenancies which fail to satisfy the requirements of s 23, there are other tenancies which are not protected by the Act. These include:

(a) Tenancies at will. In *Javad v Aqil* [1991] 1 WLR 1007, a prospective tenant who was allowed into possession while negotiations proceeded for the grant of a new business lease was held, on the facts, to be a tenant at will, and thus excluded from protection. A similar decision was reached in *London Baggage Co (Charing Cross) Ltd v Railtrack plc* [2000] EGCS 57, where a tenant holding over after the expiry of its lease, pending the negotiation of a new lease, was held to be a tenant at will. (See also *Barclays Wealth Trustees (Jersey) Ltd v Erimus Housing Ltd* [2014] EWCA Civ 303, where it was held that the inference of a tenancy at will, rather than a periodic tenancy, is even stronger where a periodic tenancy would have security of tenure but the intended new lease is to be contracted out.)

(b) Tenancies of agricultural holdings: these have their own form of protection under the Agricultural Holdings Act 1986.

(c) A farm business tenancy.

(d) Mining leases.

(e) Service tenancies. These are tenancies granted to the holder of an office, appointment or employment from the landlord and which continue only so long as the tenant holds such office, etc. For the exclusion to apply the tenancy must be in writing and express the purpose for which it was granted.

(f) Fixed-term tenancies not exceeding six months. These tenancies are excluded unless the tenancy contains provisions for renewing the term or extending it beyond six months, or the tenant (including any predecessor in the same business) has already been in occupation for a period exceeding 12 months (see *Cricket Ltd v Shaftesbury plc* [1999] 3 All ER 283).

(g) 'Contracted out' tenancies (see **32.1.5**).

32.1.4 Two important definitions

32.1.4.1 The competent landlord

It is between the tenant and the competent landlord that the procedure under the Act must be conducted. It is important, therefore, that the tenant identifies its competent landlord and deals with that landlord. Where a freeholder grants a lease, there is no cause for concern as the tenant's competent landlord can be no other than the freeholder. However, where the tenant is a sub-tenant, the statutory definition of competent landlord means that the sub-tenant's immediate landlord may not be its competent landlord. Using s 44 of the Act, the sub-tenant must look up the chain of superior tenancies for the first person who either owns the freehold or who has a superior tenancy which will not come to an end within 14 months. The following examples may assist:

As the first example involves a sub-letting of the whole of the premises, T will not be in occupation, and will not, therefore, enjoy the protection of the Act. This means that the head-lease will come to an end on its contractual expiry date, with the result that as soon as the head-lease has entered the last 14 months of its contractual term, ST's competent landlord will be the freeholder. However, in the second example, because it is a sub-letting of part only, then provided T occupies the remaining part for business purposes, the head-lease will be protected. Therefore, it will not expire by effluxion of time. So even if the head-lease has entered the last 14 months of its contractual term, the sub-tenant's competent landlord will still be T (unless, eg, the freeholder has served an appropriate notice terminating the head-lease within 14 months, see **32.2.1**).

It is therefore very important for sub-tenants to identify their competent landlord, and this can be done by serving a notice on their immediate landlord under s 40 of the Act seeking information about the landlord's interest. A s 40 notice should always be served by a sub-tenant before taking any other steps under the Act. The prescribed form is set out in **Appendix 2**.

32.1.4.2 The 'holding'

The definition of the holding is important because the tenant's right to a new lease normally extends to only that part of the premises known as the 'holding'. Further, many of the landlord's grounds of opposition refer to the holding. This term is defined in s 23(3) of the Act as being the property comprised in the current tenancy excluding any part which is not occupied by the tenant or a person employed by the tenant for the purposes of the tenant's business. In practice, in the majority of cases, it is correct to describe the holding as comprising all the premises originally let except those parts which the tenant is currently sub-letting.

32.1.5 Contracting out – before 1 June 2004

As a general rule, s 38(1) forbids any contracting out of the Act. This means that any agreement purporting to exclude or modify the tenant's security of tenure is void. However, under s 38(4) of the Act the court was empowered to make an order excluding the security of tenure provisions, provided certain conditions were satisfied:

(a) The proposed letting must have been for a term of years certain.
(b) There must have been a joint application to court by both parties.
(c) The lease entered into must have been substantially the same as the draft lease attached to the court order (*Receiver for Metropolitan Police District v Palacegate Properties Ltd* [2001] 2 Ch 131).

Further, and most importantly, the court's approval must have been obtained before the tenancy was granted (*Essexcrest Ltd v Evenlex Ltd* [1988] 1 EGLR 69).

These provisions were changed with regard to leases entered into on or after 1 June 2004. However, the old rules will still be relevant in the case of a dispute between the parties to a contracted-out lease granted before this date if the tenant were to claim that the contracting-out procedures were not correctly followed and that the lease does have security of tenure. Equally, any potential purchaser of the landlord's reversion to a contracted-out lease will need to check carefully that the correct procedures were followed in order to avoid as far as possible any such claim by a tenant.

32.1.6 Contracting out – on or after 1 June 2004

The rules no longer require a court order, but still require the proposed letting to be for a term of years certain. Instead the landlord must serve a notice on the tenant in the prescribed form and the tenant (or someone duly authorised by the tenant) must sign a declaration that it has received the notice and accepts the consequences of the agreement to contract out. If the notice is served within the 14 days prior to the grant of the tenancy, the tenant must make a statutory declaration as to this before an independent solicitor. The prescribed form of notice contains a 'health warning' advising the tenant that it is giving up the right to security of tenure and advising it to seek advice not only from a solicitor or surveyor but also from its accountant. The 'instrument creating the tenancy', ie, normally the lease, must then contain reference to the exclusion agreement, the notice and the declaration. The prescribed form of notice is set out below:

> **IMPORTANT NOTICE**
>
> **You are being offered a lease without security of tenure. Do not commit yourself to the lease unless you have read this message carefully and have discussed it with a professional adviser.**
>
> Business tenants normally have security of tenure – the right to stay in their business premises when the lease ends.
>
> **If you commit yourself to the lease you will be giving up these important legal rights.**
>
> - You will have **no right** to stay in the premises when the lease ends.
> - Unless the landlord chooses to offer you another lease, you will need to leave the premises.
> - You will be unable to claim compensation for the loss of your business premises, unless the lease specifically gives you this right.
> - If the landlord offers you another lease, you will have no right to ask the court to fix the rent.
>
> It is therefore important to get professional advice – from a qualified surveyor, lawyer or accountant – before agreeing to give up these rights.
>
> If you want to ensure that you can stay in the same business premises when the lease ends, you should consult your adviser about another form of lease that does not exclude the protection of the Landlord and Tenant Act 1954.
>
> If you receive this notice at least 14 days before committing yourself to the lease, you will need to sign a simple declaration that you have received this notice and have accepted its consequences, before signing the lease.
>
> **But if you do not receive at least 14 days' notice, you will need to sign a 'statutory' declaration. To do so, you will need to visit an independent solicitor (or someone else empowered to administer oaths).**
>
> Unless there is a special reason for committing yourself to the lease sooner, you may want to ask the landlord to let you have at least 14 days to consider whether you wish to give up your statutory rights. If you then decided to go ahead with the agreement to exclude the protection of the Landlord and Tenant Act 1954, you would only need to make a simple declaration, and so you would not need to make a separate visit to an independent solicitor.

The Government anticipated that the 14-day 'ordinary' notice would be the one most used. However, in practice, the statutory declaration procedure is the one most used. This is largely because solicitors are reluctant to serve the notice until the form of the lease has been finalised – and once it has been finalised, parties do not want to have to wait 14 days before the tenant can take up occupation and start paying rent.

The reason for the reluctance stems from a lack of clarity in the new procedure. Under the old law, it had been held (see **32.1.5**) that the lease entered into must be in substantially the same form as the one approved by the court for contracting out. It was not made clear under the new provisions whether a similar rule might apply. What if the contracting-out notice was signed and then the terms of the lease were substantially renegotiated. Would that original notice still be valid? In order to avoid any possible problems, it is usual practice for the notice not to be signed until the terms of the lease have been substantially agreed.

Another problem to bear in mind with the procedure is the position of any guarantors. It is not unusual in a guarantee agreement to find a covenant by the guarantor that it will enter into a new lease of the premises if the tenant should become insolvent and the liquidator should then disclaim the lease. If it is intended that such lease is also to be contracted out of the Act, notice must be served on and signed by the guarantor before it is legally obliged to take that lease, ie before it signs the guarantee agreement, not before the lease itself is granted. Similar principles must be applied where an outgoing tenant is entering into an AGA (see **20.2.4.3**). It is likely that this will require the tenant to take a new lease on disclaimer.

32.1.7 Continuation tenancies

A business tenancy protected by the Act will not come to an end on the expiry of the contractual term. Instead, s 24 continues the tenancy on exactly the same terms (except those relating to termination) and at exactly the same rent until it is terminated in accordance with the Act. However, the landlord may be able to obtain an increased rent by asking the court to fix an interim rent under s 24A (see **32.4**).

If the tenant ceases occupation of the premises on or before the contractual termination date then one of the qualifying conditions for the Act to apply is no longer fulfilled (see **32.1.2**). In these circumstances a fixed-term tenancy will come to an end by effluxion of time and no continuation tenancy will arise (see s 27(1A), confirming the decision in *Esselte AB v Pearl Assurance plc* [1997] 1 WLR 891; see also *Surrey County Council v Single Horse Properties Ltd* [2002] EWCA Civ 367, [2002] 1 WLR 2106). In this situation the tenant will not incur any further liability for rent (the tenant may also choose to serve a s 27 notice in these circumstances, see **32.2**).

32.2 TERMINATION UNDER THE ACT

A tenancy protected under the Act will not end automatically at the expiration of a lease for a fixed term, nor, if it is a periodic tenancy, can it be ended by an ordinary notice to quit given by the landlord. Instead, such a tenancy can only be terminated in one of the ways prescribed by the Act:

(a) By the service of a landlord's statutory notice (a 's 25 notice').

(b) By the tenant's request in statutory form (a 's 26 request').

(c) Forfeiture (or forfeiture of a superior tenancy).

(d) Surrender. To be valid the surrender must take immediate effect.

(e) For a periodic tenancy, by the tenant giving the landlord a notice to quit, unless this was given before the tenant has been in occupation for a period of one month.

(f) Where the lease is for a fixed term, by written notice under s 27 of the Act. Where there is at least three months before the contractual expiry date, the tenant can serve a notice under s 27(1), terminating the tenancy on or after the contractual expiry date. As noted above, s 27(1A), confirming the case of *Esselte AB v Pearl Assurance plc* [1997] 1 WLR 891, provides that if a tenant ceases to occupy the premises for business purposes on or before the contractual expiry date, the lease will come to an end by effluxion of time and a s 27 notice is not needed. However, *Esselte* (and s 27(1A)) must now be read in the light of subsequent cases (*Bacchiocci v Academic Agency Ltd* [1998] 1 WLR 1313 and *Sight and Sound Education Ltd v Books etc Ltd* [1999] 43 EG 61) which have created uncertainty over the period of absence required before it can be established that the tenant has ceased occupation for the purposes of the Act. In light of these cases it may be safer for a tenant to proceed by service of a s 27 notice (see also *Arundel Corporation v The Financial Training Co Ltd* [2000] 3 All ER 456 which, again, emphasises the desirability of a s 27 notice). Where the tenancy is already continuing, or where there is less than three months left to the contractual expiry date, the tenant can serve a notice under s 27(2) giving the landlord not less than three months' notice of the date of termination.

It is the first two of the above methods, the s 25 notice and s 26 request, which are the usual methods of terminating a protected business tenancy.

32.2.1 Section 25 notices

32.2.1.1 Form

If such a notice is to be effective, it must be in the prescribed form and be given to the tenant by the competent landlord not less than six months, nor more than 12 months, before the date of termination specified in it. The prescribed forms are contained in the Landlord and Tenant Act 1954, Part II (Notices) (England and Wales) Regulations 2004 (SI 2004/1005), although a form 'substantially to the like effect' can be used instead. Two slightly different forms are prescribed: one for use where the landlord does not oppose the grant of a new tenancy; and one for use where it does. The forms are set out in **Appendix 2**.

A tenant will often seek to attack the validity of its landlord's notice on the ground that it is not in the correct form. The task of the court in these circumstances is to ascertain whether the notice served is substantially the same as the prescribed form. In doing this, any omission from the notice of matters irrelevant to the tenant's rights or obligations may not affect the validity of the notice. However, if the court decides that the notice is not the same as, or substantially to the same effect as, the prescribed form, it is irrelevant that the recipient did not suffer any prejudice: the notice will be invalid (*Sabella Ltd v Montgomery* [1998] 09 EG 153).

In *Smith v Draper* [1990] 2 EGLR 69, it was held that a landlord who had served what turned out to be an invalid notice, could withdraw it and serve a second valid notice.

32.2.1.2 Content

The notice must comply with the following requirements:

(a) The notice must state the date upon which the landlord wants the tenancy to end. The specified termination date must not be earlier than the date on which the tenancy could have been terminated at common law, and, as mentioned above, the notice must be given not less than six months, nor more than 12 months, before this specified termination date.

For a periodic tenancy or a fixed term with a break clause, the specified termination date cannot be earlier than the date upon which the landlord could have ended the tenancy with an ordinary common law notice. If there is a break clause, it would appear that a separate contractual notice is unnecessary provided the s 25 notice states a date for termination no earlier than the date the break clause would operate (*Scholl Manufacturing Ltd v Clifton (Slim-Line) Ltd* [1967] Ch 41). If the tenancy is for a fixed term without a break clause, the specified termination date cannot be earlier than the last day of the contractual term. If, however, the contractual tenancy has already expired and the tenancy is being continued under the Act, the s 25 notice need only comply with the six–12-month rule mentioned above.

(b) The notice must state whether or not the landlord will oppose an application to court by the tenant for the grant of a new tenancy and, if so, on which statutory ground(s). The tenant has the right to apply to court for a new tenancy but the landlord can oppose that application on one or more of the seven grounds of opposition set out in s 30 of the Act (see **32.5**). If this is the landlord's intention, it must state in the s 25 notice the ground(s) upon which it intends to rely. As there is no provision in the Act allowing the landlord to amend its notice, the choice of ground(s) is a matter which must be given very careful consideration.

It will not be in every case that the landlord states a ground of opposition. Often the landlord will be quite happy with the tenant's presence and is seeking to end the current tenancy simply with a view to negotiating a new tenancy upon different terms, for example, at an increased rent. In this type of situation the landlord should consult a valuer and obtain expert advice before proceeding further. Where the landlord is not opposing the grant of a new tenancy, the landlord's notice must set out its proposals for the new tenancy, including the property to be comprised in it (ie, all or part of the property contained in the existing tenancy), the rent to be payable and the other terms proposed.

(c) The notice must relate to the whole of the premises contained in the lease. A s 25 notice cannot relate to part only of the demised premises (*Southport Old Links Ltd v Naylor* [1985] 1 EGLR 66 and see also *M&P Enterprises (London) Ltd v Norfolk Square Hotels Ltd* [1994] 1 EGLR 129).

(d) The notice must be given and signed by, or on behalf of, the landlord. If there are joint landlords, all their names must be given (*Pearson v Alyo* [1990] 1 EGLR 114).

32.2.2 Section 26 requests

Rather than wait for the landlord to serve a s 25 notice, the tenant can sometimes take the initiative and request a new tenancy from its landlord under s 26 of the Act. However, the tenant must remember that the sooner there is a new tenancy, the sooner the new rent will be payable, which may be higher than the rent payable under the old tenancy. Nevertheless, there are situations where the service of a request by the tenant has tactical advantages for it.

Not all tenants can request a new tenancy. A request cannot be served if the landlord has already served a s 25 notice. Further, a request is only possible where the tenant's current lease was granted for a term of years exceeding one year (or during its continuance under s 24). This will exclude both periodic tenants and those with fixed terms of one year or less; although these tenants still enjoy security of tenure.

32.2.2.1 Form

To be valid, the request must be in the prescribed form as laid down in the Landlord and Tenant Act 1954, Part II (Notices) (England and Wales) Regulations 2004 (SI 2004/1005) and served on the competent landlord. As with the s 25 notice, a form 'substantially to the like effect' can be used instead. The prescribed form is set out in **Appendix 2**.

32.2.2.2 Content

The request must comply with the following requirements:

(a) It must state the date on which the new tenancy is to begin. The current tenancy will terminate on that date. This date must not be more than 12 months nor less than six months after the making of the request, and cannot be earlier than the date on which the tenancy would have expired by effluxion of time or been brought to an end by notice to quit given by the tenant.

(b) It must give the tenant's proposals as to:
  (i) the property to be comprised in the new tenancy, which must be either the whole or part of the property comprised in the current tenancy;
  (ii) the proposed new rent (this issue requires the advice of a valuer);
  (iii) the other terms of the tenancy (eg, as to duration).

(c) The request must be signed by or on behalf of all the tenants.

A landlord who is unwilling to grant a new tenancy must, within two months of receipt of the request, give notice to the tenant that it will oppose any application to court for a new lease stating on which statutory ground(s) of opposition it intends to rely. This is effected by means of a landlord's counter-notice (see **32.2.3**).

As with a s 25 notice, the landlord must choose its ground(s) of opposition with care because it will be confined to those stated in its counter-notice.

350 Commercial Property

If the tenant serves a valid s 26 request and then fails to apply to court for a new tenancy within time (see **32.3**), it will not be allowed to withdraw it and serve a new one with a view to complying with the time limit the second time since the effect of the s 26 request was to fix the date of termination of the tenancy (*Stile Hall Properties Ltd v Gooch* [1979] 3 All ER 848).

32.2.2.3 Reasons for making a request

Usually a tenant is best advised not to make a request because it is not always in a tenant's interest to bring its current tenancy to an end. However, there are some situations in which it might be advisable. For example:

(a) If the rent payable under the current tenancy is more than that presently achievable in the open market. In a falling market like this the landlord is unlikely to serve a s 25 notice, as it is in its interests to let the existing tenancy continue under the Act. Therefore, the tenant should give careful consideration to ending the current tenancy and obtaining a new one at a reduced rent.

(b) If, as is more often the case, the current rent is less than the present market rent, it is in the tenant's interest to prolong the tenancy for as long as possible. In this case the tenant may be able to make what is sometimes called a pre-emptive strike. Say the lease is contractually due to expire on 30 September. In the previous March the landlord is considering serving a s 25 notice with a view to bringing the tenancy to an end on 30 September and negotiating a new tenancy at an increased rent. If the tenant knows or suspects the landlord's plans, it can, before the landlord has acted, serve a request specifying sometime in the following March as the date for the new tenancy. The tenant has thus achieved an extra six months at the old rent.

(c) If the tenant has plans to improve the premises, it may prefer the certainty of a new fixed term as opposed to the uncertainty of a statutory continuation.

(d) If the tenant has plans to sell the lease, a buyer would prefer the security of a new fixed term rather than the uncertainty of a statutory continuation.

32.2.3 Counter-notices

32.2.3.1 The tenant's counter-notice

Under the procedure applicable prior to 1 June 2004 both landlord and tenant had to serve a counter-notice following receipt of a s 26 request or a s 25 notice respectively. However, the requirement for a tenant to serve a counter-notice on receipt of a s 25 notice has now been abolished. The requirement for a landlord to serve a counter-notice remains, however.

32.2.3.2 The landlord's counter-notice

The service of a s 26 request by the tenant will require a counter-notice by the landlord if it wishes to oppose the tenant's application to court for a new tenancy. This must state any ground(s) of opposition that the landlord intends to rely on to oppose the tenant's application (see **32.5**). If the landlord fails to serve a counter-notice within two months of receipt of the tenant's request, it will lose its right to raise any ground of opposition to the tenant's application to court for a new tenancy although it will be allowed to raise issues relating to the terms of the new tenancy.

A landlord who has served a counter-notice stating that it will not oppose the tenant's application for a new tenancy will be bound by that decision. Similarly, the landlord cannot later amend its stated grounds of opposition.

There is no prescribed form of counter-notice but it should be unequivocal and in writing.

32.2.4 Service of notices and requests

Notices and requests given under the Act require service. Section 23(1) of the LTA 1927 provides for personal service or by leaving the notice at the last known place of abode (which includes the place of business of the person to be served; *Price v West London Investment Building Society* [1964] 2 All ER 318), or by sending it through the post by registered or (as now applies) recorded delivery. Service on a company may be effected at its registered office (s 1139 of the Companies Act 2006). The effect of complying with one of the methods of service laid down in the LTA 1927 is that there is a presumption of service so that it does not matter that the recorded delivery letter may not have been received by the intended recipient because it went astray in the post. Other methods of service may be effective (eg, the ordinary post) if in fact the notice is received by the person to whom it has been given. But the risk is that the letter may be lost in the post, in which case, notice will not have been given. The question also arises as to the date on which the notice is treated as having been served. In *Railtrack plc v Gojra* [1998] 08 EG 158, it was held that if the registered or recorded delivery method is used (both being methods laid down in the LTA 1927), the notice (or request) is served on the date on which it is posted. This decision was confirmed by the Court of Appeal in *CA Webber Transport Ltd v Railtrack plc* [2004] 1 WLR 320. When, however, notice is sent through the ordinary post, it is served on the date it would have been delivered in the ordinary course of post.

32.3 THE APPLICATION TO COURT

32.3.1 The need for an application

It will become apparent after service of a s 25 notice or counter-notice to a s 26 request, whether or not the landlord is willing to grant a new tenancy. Where a s 25 notice has been served, the contents will have told the tenant whether or not the landlord intends to oppose its application. If the tenant initiated the termination procedure with a s 26 request, the landlord will have responded with a counter-notice if it is not prepared to grant a new tenancy.

Either the landlord or the tenant may apply to the court (although, of course, one cannot make an application if the other has already done so). It will usually be the tenant who will apply to the court. Even if the landlord has stated that it is prepared to grant a new tenancy, the tenant will lose its entitlement unless an application is made to the court within the prescribed time limits (see **32.3.2**), or the parties have entered into a legally-binding contract for a new lease. Where the landlord is opposing the grant, there is obviously little possibility of such an agreement and so an application must be made.

The landlord will normally only apply to the court where it is opposing the grant and wants an order determining the tenancy on one of the s 30 grounds to be made as quickly as possible. It could wait for the tenant to apply for a new tenancy, but making its own application would mean the matter could be brought before the court as soon as possible. A tenant who fears it will lose in court may delay making its own application for as long as possible in order to gain an extra few weeks or months in the premises. The landlord can only make such application if it has served a s 25 notice opposing renewal or served a counter-notice to a tenant's s 26 notice to that effect.

Where a landlord is not opposing the grant, it can again apply to the court for the grant of that new lease, again in order to have the matter determined as soon as possible. Otherwise, a tenant may delay its own application for as long as possible in order to enjoy the benefit of the more favourable terms of the old lease for as long as possible.

Unless the parties have already entered into a binding lease, the tenant must always apply to court at the appropriate time otherwise it will lose the right to a new tenancy.

32.3.2 The application

Applications may be commenced in either the High Court or, as is more usual, in the county court.

The application must be made within the 'statutory period'. This is defined in s 29A(2) to mean a period ending, where the landlord served a s 25 notice, on the date specified in its notice; and, where the tenant made a s 26 request, a period ending immediately before the date specified in its request.

However, where the tenant has made a s 26 request, the court cannot entertain an application which is made before the end of the period of two months beginning with the date of the making of the request, unless the application is made after the landlord has served its counter-notice.

32.3.3 Agreements extending time limits

By s 29B the parties can by written agreement extend the time limit for applications and they may do so any number of times. The only provisos are that the first agreement to extend must be made prior to the end of the statutory period and any subsequent agreement must be made before the expiry of the period of extension agreed in the previous agreement.

Following the tenant's application to court it is advisable to protect the application by registration of a pending land action under the Land Charges Act 1972. This will make the tenant's application binding on a buyer of the reversion. Where the landlord's title is registered, the application may be an overriding interest under the Land Registration Act 2002, Sch 3, but it would nevertheless be prudent to register a unilateral notice against the reversionary title.

32.4 INTERIM RENTS

32.4.1 The need for an interim rent

Where the tenant validly applies to court for a new tenancy, its current tenancy does not terminate on the date specified in the s 25 notice or s 26 request. Instead, the Act provides that the current tenancy will be continued until three months after the proceedings are concluded. If the tenancy were to continue at the old rent, there would be an incentive for tenants to delay proceedings as much as possible, because the longer the current tenancy lasts, the longer the old rent (which was usually below current market rents) remains payable. This is unfair to landlords, particularly in those cases where, due to the effects of inflation, there is a substantial difference between the old contractual rent and the rent achievable in the open market. So, under s 29A of the Act, the court may, on the application of either party, determine an 'interim rent' to be substituted for the old contractual rent until such time as the current tenancy ceases.

The interim rent will be payable from the earliest date for the termination of the existing tenancy that could have been specified in the s 25 notice or s 26 request that was served to bring the tenancy to an end. So a tenant who serves a s 26 request but states a commencement date for the new tenancy 12 months after service when the contractual termination date is only six months away (and so it could have served six months' notice) will find that the interim rent will be payable from that earlier date. Either landlord or tenant can apply for an interim rent. Normally, it will be the landlord who will apply as the interim rent is likely to be higher than the existing rent which may have been fixed several years previously. However, in times on falling property values, it might be advantageous for the tenant to apply if the current market rent will be below that being paid under the lease.

32.4.2 Amount

The interim rent will normally be the same as the rent payable under the new tenancy, ie, an open market rent assessed as set out at **32.7.3**. However, this will not be the case where there is a significant movement in the market (upwards or downwards) in the intervening period or where the terms of the new tenancy are so different from the terms of the old one to make a substantial difference in the rent. (Bear in mind here that normally the new lease will be on very similar terms to the old lease; see **32.7.4**.) Nor will this be the case where the landlord opposes the grant of a new tenancy. In both cases, the following provisions apply:

(a) Section 24A requires the court to assess the interim rent on the basis of a yearly tenancy, while the rent payable under the new lease is usually assessed on the basis of a term of years. Market rents under yearly tenancies are usually less than under fixed terms, since the latter guarantee tenants a more substantial period of occupation.

(b) The court is obliged to have regard to the rent payable under the current tenancy. This is so that the court can exercise a discretion to 'cushion' the tenant from too harsh a blow in moving from the old out-of-date contractual rent to the new rent (see *English Exporters (London) Ltd v Eldonwall Ltd* [1973] Ch 415). However, a 'cushion' does not have to be provided in every case. The court has a discretion which it may use to specify the full market rent, especially in those cases where the tenant has already benefited from a low contractual rent for a long time (see, eg, *Department of the Environment v Allied Freehold Property Trust Ltd* [1992] 45 EG 156).

32.4.3 Avoiding s 24A

While the introduction of interim rents has been a step in the right direction for landlords, many still feel that the application of the 'cushion' can produce unfairness. Accordingly, the landlord may wish to avoid s 24A altogether by including a penultimate day rent review in the lease. This would revise the contractual rent just before the contractual term expired. In such a case the harshness of changing from the old rent to the new rent would be suffered during the contractual term without the imposition of any 'cushion'. Tenants, on the other hand, will wish to resist such a clause.

Another way of avoiding s 24A would be for the landlord, at the lease-drafting stage, to make it clear that the contractual rent review provisions are to continue to apply notwithstanding the ending of the contractual term. Careful drafting would be required to achieve this but the case of *Willison v Cheverell Estates Ltd* [1996] 26 EG 133 indicates that this is another possibility for the landlord.

32.5 GROUNDS OF OPPOSITION

When the landlord serves its s 25 notice or counter-notice in response to the tenant's s 26 request, it must, if it is intending to oppose the grant of a new tenancy, set out one or more of the seven grounds of opposition in s 30 of the Act. The landlord can rely only on the stated ground(s); no later amendment is allowed.

If the landlord has stated a ground of opposition and the tenant's application proceeds to a hearing, a 'split trial' will usually be ordered with the question of opposition being dealt with first as a preliminary issue. Only if the ground is not made out will the terms of the new tenancy be dealt with.

The statutory grounds of opposition are all contained in s 30(1) of the Act and, as will be seen, some of the grounds ((a), (b), (c) and (e)) confer a discretion on the court whether or not to order a new tenancy even if the ground is made out.

32.5.1 Ground (a): tenant's failure to repair

The landlord can oppose the tenant's application for a new tenancy on the ground of the tenant's failure to repair the holding. To succeed, the landlord will have to show that the tenant was under an obligation to repair or maintain the holding and that the tenant is in breach of that obligation. Problems can arise where the repairing obligation is divided between the landlord and tenant, for example, where the landlord is responsible for the exterior and the tenant for the interior of the premises. In such cases, an inspection will be necessary to determine the party in breach. The ground only applies to failure to repair the holding, and not to the disrepair of another part of the demised premises not forming part of the tenant's holding (eg, where the tenant has sub-let part and it is that part which is in disrepair).

This is one of the discretionary grounds and the landlord is only likely to succeed if the tenant's breaches are both serious and unremedied at the date of the hearing.

As an alternative, the landlord may be able to commence forfeiture proceedings to terminate the tenancy, this being one of the permitted methods of termination under the Act. This remedy may be available throughout the term and while the tenant may apply for relief, this will usually only be granted if the tenant rectifies the breach.

32.5.2 Ground (b): persistent delay in paying rent

The requirement of 'persistent delay' suggests that the tenant must have fallen into arrears on more than one occasion. However, the rent need not be substantially in arrears nor need the arrears last a long time. Indeed, there need not be any arrears at the date of the hearing; the court will look at the whole history of payment (see *Hazel v Akhtar* [2002] EWCA Civ 1883, [2002] 07 EG 124). Again, this is one of the discretionary grounds and the court is entitled to take into account the likelihood of future arrears arising should a new tenancy be ordered. The tenant should, therefore, consider offering to provide a surety for any new lease ordered.

32.5.3 Ground (c): substantial breaches of other obligations

Discretionary ground (c) requires other substantial breaches by the tenant of its obligations in the lease, or some other reason connected with the tenant's use or management of the holding. Ground (c) is rarely encountered in practice. Any breach of an obligation may be relied upon by the landlord (eg, breach of the user covenant) but the breach must be substantial and this will be a question of fact and degree. In *Youssefi v Mussellwhite* [2014] EWCA Civ 885, the Court of Appeal found that the tenant's failure to allow access to the property and its failure to open a business were substantial breaches of the lease.

The ground also extends to reasons connected with the tenant's use or management of the holding and this has been held to include carrying on a use in breach of planning control (see *Fowles v Heathrow Airport Ltd* [2008] EWCA Civ 1270). In *Horne & Meredith Properties v Cox, Billingsley* [2014] EWCA Civ 423, a tenant was denied a new tenancy because his conduct in bringing litigation against the landlord for alleged obstructions to a right of way granted by the lease had 'grossly exceeded any reasonable balance' and he was 'a legal menace'.

32.5.4 Ground (d): alternative accommodation

The landlord must have offered and be willing to provide or secure alternative accommodation for the tenant. The accommodation must be offered on reasonable terms having regard to the terms of the current tenancy and all other relevant circumstances. Further, the accommodation must be suitable for the tenant's requirements (including the requirement to preserve goodwill), bearing in mind the nature and type of its business and the location and size of its existing premises. It seems that offering the tenant part only of its existing premises may qualify as alternative accommodation.

This ground, unlike the three previously mentioned, is not discretionary. If the landlord proves the requirements of the ground, the court must refuse the tenant's application.

32.5.5 Ground (e): current tenancy created by sub-letting of part only of property in a superior tenancy

Ground (e) is the least used ground because the necessary requirements are seldom fulfilled. It only applies where the current tenancy was created by a sub-letting of part of the property in a superior tenancy, and the sub-tenant's competent landlord is the landlord under the superior tenancy. The competent landlord will succeed if it can show that the combined rents from the sub-divided parts of a building are substantially less than the rent to be obtained on a single letting of the whole building, and that it requires possession to let or dispose of the whole.

This is the last of the discretionary grounds.

32.5.6 Ground (f): demolition or reconstruction

Ground (f) is the most frequently used ground. The landlord must show that on termination of the tenancy:

(a) it has a firm intention;

(b) to demolish or reconstruct the premises in the holding (or a substantial part of them), or to carry out substantial work of construction on the holding (or part of it); and

(c) that it could not reasonably do so without obtaining possession of the holding.

Each of these elements is considered in turn.

32.5.6.1 The landlord's intention

The landlord must prove a firm and settled intention to carry out relevant work. It has been said that the project must have 'moved out of the zone of contemplation ... into the valley of decision' (per Asquith LJ in *Cunliffe v Goodman* [1950] 2 KB 237, approved in *Betty's Cafes Ltd v Phillips Furnishing Stores Ltd* [1959] AC 20). In the case of *S Frances Ltd v The Cavendish Hotel (London) Ltd* [2018] UKSC 62, the Court concluded that the landlord's intention to carry out only such works as were necessary to get the tenant out under ground (f) would not be sufficient to satisfy ground (f). Not only must the landlord have made a genuine decision to carry out relevant work, it must also show that it is practicable for it to carry out that intention. This will be a question of fact in each case but the landlord's position will be strengthened if it has:

(a) obtained (or shown a reasonable prospect of obtaining) planning permission and building regulation approval (if necessary);

(b) instructed professional advisers;

(c) prepared the necessary drawings and contracts;

(d) obtained quotations and secured finance; and

(e) obtained the consent of any superior landlord (if necessary).

Where the landlord is a company, intention is normally evidenced by a resolution of the board of directors. Similarly, local authority landlords should pass an appropriate resolution and have it recorded in their minutes.

The landlord's intention must be established at the date of the hearing (*Betty's Cafes Ltd v Phillips Furnishing Stores Ltd*, above). It is thus irrelevant that the s 25 notice (or s 26 counter-notice) was served by the landlord's predecessor who did not have the necessary intention. See also *Zarvos v Pradhan* [2003] 2 P & CR 9 where a landlord failed at the hearing because the judge was not satisfied that it would be able to finance the project. The landlord appealed and by the time of the appeal has received assurances from its bank that finance would be available. The Court of Appeal refused to allow the landlord to adduce this evidence at the appeal as this would be unfair to the tenant.

If the court is not satisfied that the landlord's intention is sufficiently firm and settled at the date of the hearing, a new tenancy will be ordered. In such cases, however, the court, in settling the terms of the new tenancy, may take into account the landlord's future intentions, and limit the duration of the new tenancy so as not to impede development later when the landlord is able to fully establish intention and the ability to carry it out (see **32.7.2**).

32.5.6.2 The nature of the works

The landlord must prove an intention to do one of six things:

(a) Demolish the premises comprised in the holding (see *Coppin v Bruce-Smith* [1998] EGCS 45).

(b) Reconstruct the premises comprised in the holding. For the works to qualify as works of reconstruction it has been held that they must entail rebuilding and involve a substantial interference with the structure of the building but need not necessarily be confined to the outside or loadbearing walls (*Romulus Trading Co Ltd v Henry Smith's Charity Trustees* [1990] 2 EGLR 75).

(c) Demolish a substantial part of the premises comprised in the holding.

(d) Reconstruct a substantial part of the premises comprised in the holding.

(e) Carry out substantial work of construction on the holding. It has been held that such works must directly affect the structure of the building and must go beyond what could be more properly classified as works of refurbishment or improvement (*Barth v Pritchard* [1990] 1 EGLR 109).

(f) Carry out substantial work of construction on part of the holding.

32.5.6.3 The need to obtain possession

The landlord must show that it could not reasonably execute the relevant work without obtaining possession of the holding. This means the landlord must show that it needs 'legal' (not just 'physical') possession of the holding. It has to show that it is necessary to put an end to the tenant's interest, and this may not always be the case. Accordingly, if the lease contains a right of entry for the landlord which is sufficiently wide to enable it to carry out the relevant work, its ground of opposition will fail. In such a situation, the tenant will be able to argue that the work can be carried out under the terms of the lease and there is thus no need to end it.

Even if the lease does not include a right of entry, the landlord may still fail in its opposition if the tenant is able to rely on s 31A of the Act. This provides that the court shall not find ground (f) to be established if the tenant will either:

(a) agree to a new lease which includes access and other rights for the landlord, which enable the landlord to reasonably carry out the relevant work without obtaining possession and without substantially interfering with the use of the holding for the tenant's business; or

(b) accept a new lease of an economically separable part of the holding with, if necessary, access rights for the landlord.

32.5.7 Ground (g): landlord's intention to occupy the holding

Ground (g) is another frequently used ground. The landlord must prove that on the termination of the current tenancy it intends to occupy the holding for the purposes, or partly for the purposes, of a business to be carried on by it, or as its residence. There are a number of elements to this ground which will be considered in turn.

32.5.7.1 The landlord's intention

As with ground (f), the landlord's intention must be firm and settled, and many of the matters discussed at **32.5.6** will be equally relevant here. Therefore, not only must the landlord be able to show a genuine intention to occupy the holding, it must also show that it has a reasonable prospect of being able to do so. It is, therefore, necessary for the court to take into account, for example, whether planning permission would be required to use the premises for the landlord's business and, if so, whether it would be likely to be granted. In some cases, the court has accepted as evidence of intention to occupy, an undertaking to do so given by the landlord. Such an undertaking is not conclusive but it is a relevant consideration when the court is determining the issue (see, eg, *London Hilton Jewellers Ltd v Hilton International Hotels Ltd* [1990] 1 EGLR 112 and also *McDonald's Restaurants Ltd v Shirayama Shokusan Company Ltd* [2024] EWHC 1133 (Ch) where the landlord was held liable to compensate its former tenant under s 37A of the Landlord and Tenant Act 1954 because it had obtained an order terminating the lease by a misrepresentation to the court as to the nature of the business it intended to operate at the premises). As with ground (f), the landlord's intention must be shown to exist at the date of the hearing.

The court will not assess the viability of the landlord's proposed business venture provided its intention to occupy is genuine. Thus, the court has held the ground to be established even where they thought the landlord's business plans to be ill thought out and likely to fail; its intention was nevertheless genuine. See, for example, *Dolgellau Golf Club v Hett* [1998] 2 EGLR 75, CA, but also the contrasting case of *Zarvos v Pradhan* [2003] EWCA Civ 208, where possession was refused as the landlord could not establish a reasonable prospect of being able to raise finance.

32.5.7.2 The purpose of occupation

Occupation must be for the purpose of the landlord's business or as its residence. The landlord need not intend to occupy all the holding immediately, provided that within a reasonable time of termination it intends to occupy a substantial part of the holding for one of these purposes.

The wording of this ground refers to a business to be carried on by the landlord. However, the landlord need not physically occupy the premises and it will be sufficient if occupation is through a manager or agent provided that the arrangement is genuine. Further, the ground is still available where the landlord intends to carry on the business in partnership with others. Where the landlord has a controlling interest in a company, any business to be carried on by the company, is treated as a business carried on by the landlord. The landlord has a controlling interest for this purpose, either if it beneficially holds more than half of the company's equity share capital, or if it is a member and able, without consent, to appoint or remove at least half of the directors (s 30(3)). Where the landlord is a company in a group of companies, it may rely on ground (g) where another member of the group is to occupy the premises (s 42). If the landlord is a trustee, it may be able to rely on an intention to occupy by a beneficiary (s 41).

32.5.7.3 The five-year rule

The most important limitation on the availability of this ground of opposition is the 'five-year rule' in s 30(2) of the Act. A landlord cannot rely on ground (g) if its interest was purchased or created within five years before the end of the current tenancy, ie, the termination date specified in the s 25 notice or s 26 request. However, the restriction only applies if, throughout those five years, the premises have been subject to a tenancy or series of tenancies within the protection of the Act.

The idea behind the provision is to stop a landlord buying a reversion within five years of the end of the lease, and then using this ground to obtain possession for itself at the end of the term. Thus, a landlord will not be able to rely on this ground if it purchased the premises subject to the tenancy within the last five years. However, the restriction does not apply where a landlord buys premises with vacant possession, grants a lease, and then seeks to end the lease within five years relying on this ground.

The wording of the provision refers to the landlord's interest being 'purchased' and this is used in its popular sense of buying for money (*Bolton (HL) Engineering Co Ltd v Graham & Sons Ltd* [1957] 1 QB 159). Thus, it will not cover a freeholder who has accepted the surrender of a head-lease without payment, and then seeks to use this ground against the sub-tenant.

Finally, a landlord who is unable to rely on ground (g) because of this restriction, may be able to rely on ground (f) if it intends to demolish or reconstruct the premises. This remains so even if the landlord then intends to use the reconstructed premises for its own occupation.

32.6 COMPENSATION FOR FAILURE TO OBTAIN A NEW TENANCY

On termination, a tenant may be entitled to compensation for any improvements it has made. Additionally, if the tenant is forced to leave the premises it may lose the goodwill which it has built up and it will be faced with all the costs of relocation. This is particularly unfair to those tenants that are forced to leave the premises through no fault of their own, ie, if the landlord establishes one of the grounds of opposition (e), (f) or (g). In certain circumstances, therefore, the tenant may be entitled to compensation for failing to obtain a new tenancy where the landlord establishes one of these 'no fault' grounds.

32.6.1 Availability

Compensation is only available on quitting the premises in one of the following situations:

(a) Where the landlord serves a s 25 notice or counter-notice to a s 26 request stating one or more of the grounds of opposition (e), (f) or (g) but no others, and the tenant either:
   (i) does not apply to court for a new tenancy or does so but withdraws its application; or
   (ii) does apply to court for a new tenancy, but its application is refused because the landlord is able to establish its stated ground.

(b) Where the landlord serves a s 25 notice or counter-notice to a s 26 request specifying one or more of the grounds (e), (f) or (g) and others; the tenant applies to court for a new tenancy but the court refuses to grant a new tenancy solely on one or more of the grounds (e), (f) or (g). Here the tenant must apply to court for a new tenancy and ask the court to certify that a new tenancy was not ordered solely because one of these three 'no fault' grounds has been made out.

32.6.2 Amount

The amount of compensation is the rateable value of the holding multiplied by the 'appropriate multiplier' which is a figure prescribed from time to time by the Secretary of State, and is currently 1. In some cases, the tenant will be entitled to double compensation.

32.6.3 Double compensation

Sometimes the appropriate multiplier is doubled. This happens when the tenant or its predecessors in the same business have been in occupation for at least 14 years prior to the termination of the current tenancy. These provisions are summarised in the illustration below.

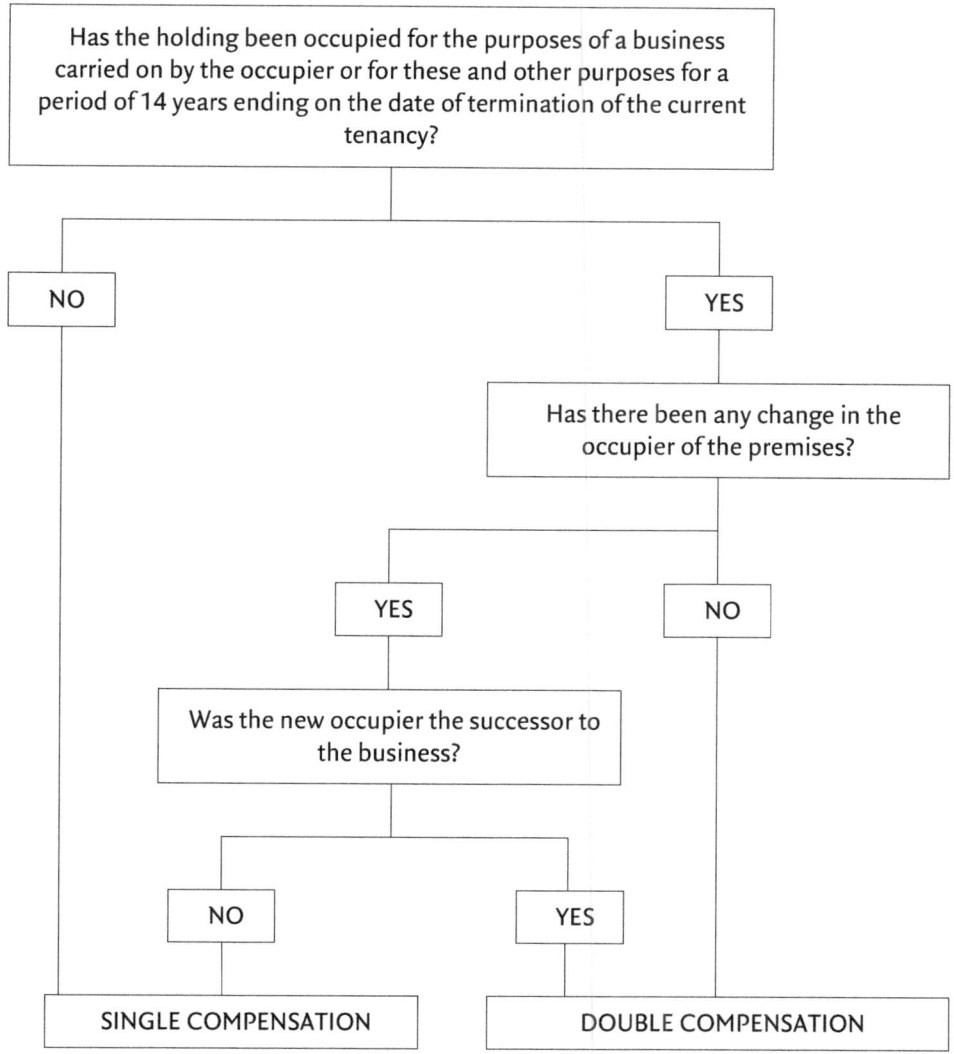

32.6.4 Contracting out

In some situations the tenant's right to compensation can be excluded by agreement between the parties. This agreement is often in the lease itself. However, s 38(2) of the Act provides that where the tenant or its predecessors in the same business have been in occupation for five years or more prior to the date of quitting, any agreement to exclude or reduce the tenant's right to compensation is void.

32.7 THE RENEWAL LEASE

If the tenant follows all the correct procedures and properly applies to court for a new tenancy, the court will make an order for a new lease in two situations:

(a) if the landlord fails to make out its s 30 ground of opposition; or
(b) if the landlord did not oppose the tenant's application for a new tenancy.

The terms of this new lease are usually settled by agreement between the parties and it is only in default of such agreement that the court will be called upon to decide the terms. In either event, any new lease will also enjoy the protection of the Act.

The court has jurisdiction over the premises, duration, rent and the other terms.

32.7.1 The premises

The tenant is entitled to a new tenancy of the holding only as at the date of the order. This term was defined in **32.1.4.4**, and excludes any part of the premises which have been sub-let. However, the landlord (but not the tenant), has the right to insist that any new tenancy to be granted shall be a new tenancy of the whole of the demised premises including those parts sub-let.

The court may grant a new lease of less than the holding under s 31A, where the landlord establishes ground (f), the redevelopment ground, but the tenant takes a new lease of an 'economically separable part' of the holding (see **32.5.6**).

The new lease may also include appurtenant rights enjoyed by the tenant under the current tenancy.

32.7.2 The duration

The length of any new lease ordered by the court will be such as is reasonable in all the circumstances but cannot exceed 15 years (often it is much less than this). In deciding this issue the court has a very wide discretion and will take into account matters such as:

(a) the length of the current tenancy;
(b) the length requested by the tenant;
(c) the hardship caused to either party;
(d) current open market practice;
(e) the landlord's future proposals.

It may be that the landlord was unable to rely on ground (f) because it could not prove that its intention to demolish or reconstruct was sufficiently firm and settled at the date of the hearing (see **32.5.6**). If, however, the court is satisfied that the landlord will be able to do so in the near future, it may order a short tenancy so as not to impede development later. Similarly, if the premises are shown to be ripe for development, the new lease may be granted subject to a break clause (*National Car Parks Ltd v The Paternoster Consortium Ltd* [1990] 15 EG 53). In the same way, where the landlord has narrowly missed being able to rely on ground (g) because of the five-year rule, the court may be prepared to grant a short tenancy.

32.7.3 The rent

The amount of rent to be paid is the greatest source of disagreement between the parties and specialist valuation advice will be essential. If the question of rent comes before the courts, they will assess an open market rent having regard to the other terms of the tenancy. However, in assessing the rent the court is obliged to disregard certain factors which may otherwise work to the detriment of the tenant, ie:

(a) Any effect on rent of the fact that the tenant or its predecessors have been in occupation. The classic landlord's argument would be that the tenant, being a sitting tenant, would pay more in the open market for these premises simply to avoid relocation. This would inflate an open market rent and is thus to be disregarded.

(b) Any goodwill attached to the holding due to the carrying on of the tenant's business. The tenant should not have to pay a rent assessed partly on the basis of goodwill it generated.

(c) Any effect on the rent of improvements voluntarily made by the tenant (certain conditions must also be satisfied).

(d) Where the holding comprises licensed premises, any addition in value due to the tenant's licence.

Where the premises are in disrepair due to the tenant's failure to perform its repairing obligation, conflicting views have been expressed on whether the court should disregard this in setting the rent of the new tenancy. One view is that the premises should be valued in their actual condition. This will probably produce a lower rent but the landlord may be able to sue the tenant for breach of its repairing obligation.

The other view is that the premises should be valued on the basis that the tenant has complied with its obligation, thus preventing the tenant benefiting from its own breach. This view is supported by cases such as *Crown Estate Commissioners v Town Investments Ltd* [1992] 08 EG 111.

In *Fawke v Viscount Chelsea* [1980] QB 441, the premises were in disrepair because the landlord was in breach of his repairing obligation. The court decided that the premises should be valued in their actual condition and, therefore, fixed a new rent which was below open market value but which increased once the landlord had complied with his obligation.

Under s 34(3), the court has power to insert a rent review clause in the new lease whether or not the previous lease contained such a provision. The frequency and type of review is at the discretion of the court which may be persuaded by the tenant to make provision for downward revisions as well as upward (see *Forbuoys plc v Newport Borough Council* [1994] 24 EG 156).

As to the effect of the LT(C)A 1995, see **32.7.4**.

Finally, the court does have power to require the tenant to provide guarantors.

32.7.4 Other terms

It will only fall to the court to decide other terms in the absence of agreement between the parties. In fixing the other terms the court must have regard to the terms of the current tenancy and all other relevant circumstances. For that reason, the terms will be much the same as before. The leading case in this area is *O'May v City of London Real Property Co Ltd* [1983] AC 726 which held that if one of the parties seeks a change in the terms, it is for that party to justify the change. Further, the change must be fair and reasonable and 'take into account, amongst other things, the comparatively weak negotiating position of a sitting tenant requiring renewal, particularly in conditions of scarcity' (per Lord Hailsham in *O'May*). Therefore, the tenant should be on its guard against any attempt by the landlord to introduce more onerous obligations into the new lease (eg, a more restrictive user covenant). In the *O'May* case the landlord was, in effect, trying to transfer the responsibility for the repair and maintenance of office premises to the tenant. This would have increased the value of the reversion by more than £1 million but the House of Lords held that the landlord was not entitled to do this.

Notwithstanding the effect of the *O'May* case, variations may be made in the renewal lease to reflect the changes introduced by the LT(C)A 1995. The renewal lease will, of course, be subject to the provisions of that Act. This will often mean that under the current lease (granted before 1 January 1996) the original tenant was liable for the entire duration of the term through privity of contract; whereas for the renewal lease, privity of contract will not apply. This change is one of the circumstances to which the court must have regard in fixing the rent and other terms of the new lease. For example, the landlord may wish to alter the terms of the alienation covenant to balance the effect of the loss of privity of contract (see *Wallis Fashion Group Ltd v General Accident Life Assurance Ltd* [2000] EGCS 45; and **21.2.4.2**). (See also *WH Smith Retail Holdings Ltd v Commerz Real Investmentgesellshaft mbH* (unreported, 25 March 2021) – a county court case where a pandemic rent suspension clause was included in a renewal lease – and *Poundland Ltd v Toplain Ltd* (unreported, 7 April 2021), where the county court refused the inclusion of a use prevention pandemic clause in a renewal lease which would have reduced the rent payable during a lockdown.)

32.8 THE ORDER FOR THE NEW LEASE

Any new lease ordered by the court will not commence until three months after the proceedings are 'finally disposed of'. This is when the time for appeal has elapsed, and for appeals to the Court of Appeal the time limit is four weeks from the date of the order. The tenant continues to occupy under its old tenancy during this period. Either party may appeal.

If the court makes an order for a new tenancy upon terms which the tenant finds unacceptable (eg, as to rent), the tenant may apply for revocation of the order within 14 days. In such a case, the existing tenancy will continue for such period as the parties agree or the court determines as necessary to enable the landlord to re-let the premises.

32.9 PROCEDURAL FLOWCHART – s 25 NOTICE

The flowchart below shows the stages and time limits following service of a landlord's s 25 notice opposing the grant of a new tenancy.

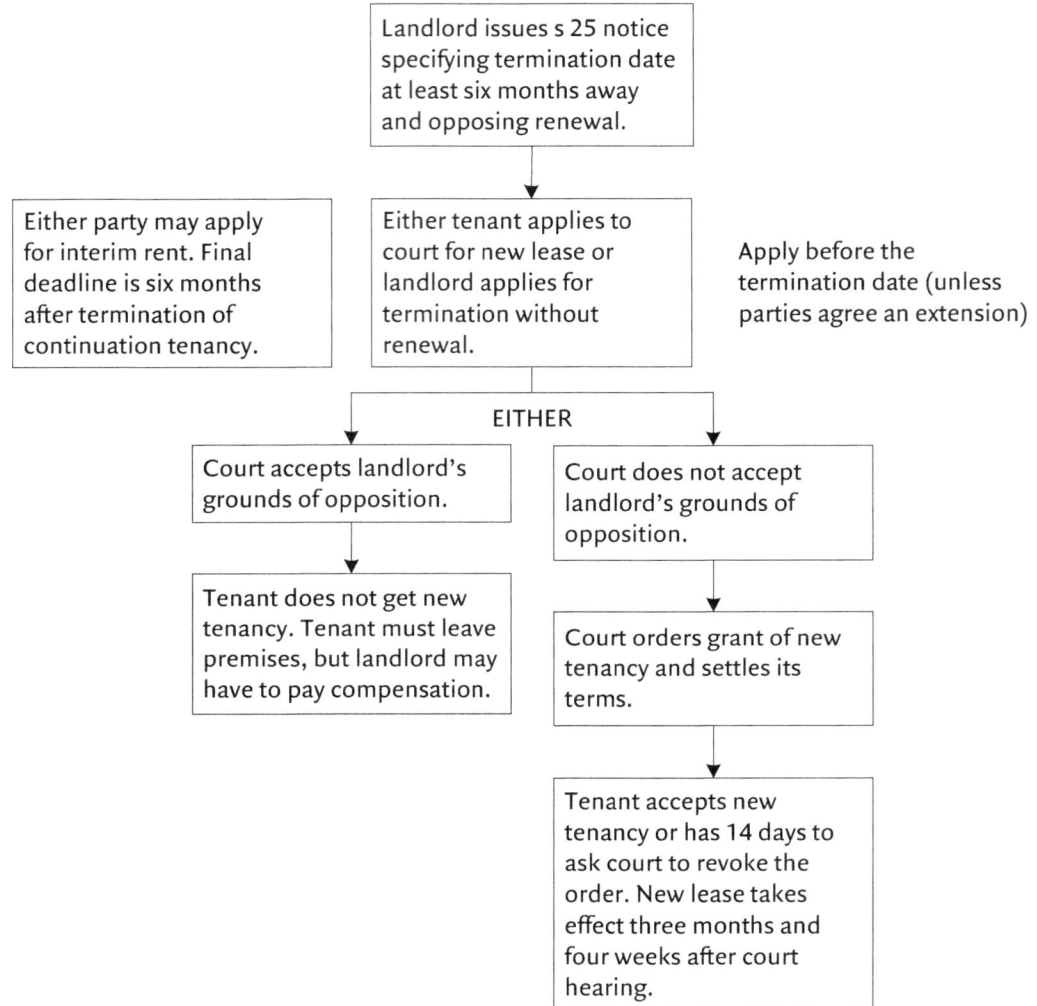

32.10 FUTURE DEVELOPMENTS

The Law Commission of England and Wales is reviewing the right to renew business tenancies set out in Pt II of the Landlord and Tenant Act 1954. Its stated aims are:

> to conduct a wide review of Part 2 of the Landlord and Tenant Act 1954 with a view to modernising commercial leasehold legislation, with an emphasis on:
>
> • creating a legal framework that is widely used rather than opted out of, without limiting the rights of parties to reach their own agreements, by making sure legislation is clear, easy to use, and beneficial to landlords and tenants;

- supporting the efficient use of space in high streets and town centres, now and in future, by making sure current legislation is fit for today's commercial market, taking into account other legislative frameworks and wider government priorities, such as the 'net zero' and 'levelling up' agendas; and
- fostering a productive and beneficial commercial leasing relationship between landlords and tenants.

As at 1 September 2024, the project is at the Pre-consultation stage.

REVIEW ACTIVITY

1. When does the Act apply?
2. What are the consequences of the Act applying?
3. How can a landlord let premises without giving a business occupier security of tenure?
4. How can a secure tenant that wants to leave its business premises at the end of the contractual term bring its tenancy to an end?
5. How can a secure tenant that wants to stay in its business premises after the expiry of the contractual term request a new lease?
6. How can a secure sub-tenant of business premises identify its competent landlord for the purposes of the Act?
7. How can a landlord obtain vacant possession of premises occupied by a secure tenant?
8. How can a landlord ensure that a secure tenant that wants to stay in the premises enters into a new lease, rather than continuing the old one?

Answers to this Review activity may be found in Appendix 1.

PART III
PROPERTY AND INSOLVENCY

CHAPTER 33

Insolvency and its Effect on Commercial Property

33.1	Why insolvency matters	367
33.2	Measures to reduce the perceived risk of insolvency	370
33.3	Always establish the type of insolvency regime	370
33.4	Identify the type of contract	372
33.5	The different types of insolvency regime	373
33.6	Setting aside transactions which have already been completed	380
33.7	The effect of a tenant becoming insolvent	382
33.8	Requiring the insolvency official to pay rent	389
33.9	Requiring the insolvency official to observe the lease covenants	390
33.10	Disclaimer and its effects	391

Note: 'The insolvency official'

Each of the insolvency regimes listed throughout this chapter is implemented by a different insolvency professional as described in **33.3.2** below. For convenience, in this chapter, all of these persons are called 'insolvency officials'.

In addition, for ease of reference, the two parties to the relevant property transaction are referred to as party 'X' and party 'Y' throughout this chapter.

33.1 WHY INSOLVENCY MATTERS

If one party (X) to an existing contract becomes insolvent, this will cause the other party (Y) significant problems. X is likely to breach its obligations and may pull out of the contract altogether. Completed transactions to which X is a party may be reversed by the court. Y's normal remedies for breach will be restricted, in practice, either as to what Y can do, or how quickly it can act. All this may put Y in breach of its own obligations to others. For example, an insolvent tenant's failure to pay rent will reduce the landlord's income stream, which may mean it defaults on its mortgage payments. Similarly, in a chain of related sales, if one buyer becomes insolvent and fails to complete, buyers higher up the chain may well not have sufficient funds to complete their own purchases. This is why, before entering into the contract, Y should always check X's financial track record and resources (by, amongst other things, taking references, establishing its credit rating and looking at its accounts). There is also no substitute for personal knowledge of X's position being considered.

Also, when X becomes insolvent, it usually loses the ability to deal with its assets. Even if it retains legal ownership, any purported disposition by X (without the involvement of its insolvency official or the court) may well be void. This is why Y should always check that a party with whom it proposes to enter into a contract is not insolvent. Ways to ascertain any potential insolvency status are discussed at **33.3.1** below. If entering into a contract with an insolvency official, Y will usually find that the contractual terms will need to be modified.

The Insolvency Act 1986 (referred to subsequently in this chapter as the 'IA 1986') (as amended) is the primary source of insolvency legislation. The Insolvency (England and Wales)

Rules 2016 (IR 2016) are also very relevant, and they apply (for the purposes of this book) to the vast majority of insolvency situations that have occurred since 6 April 2017.

Corporate Insolvency and Governance Act 2020

It is appropriate at this point to introduce the insolvency remedies that were created by the Corporate Insolvency and Governance Act 2020 ('CIGA'), although, for the purposes of this chapter, only an overview is required.

This Act received Royal Assent in June 2020, and the immediate background to it was clearly the Covid-19 pandemic, and it was, in the main, born out of that hugely challenging situation.

The IA 1986 had created new practices and procedures that are now very familiar to us, such as administration, corporate and individual voluntary arrangements and statutory demands. CIGA created two new corporate insolvency rescue procedures, as well as bringing into force other temporary and permanent insolvency reforms. The temporary provisions have now ceased to be operative as the country has emerged from the pandemic.

The overarching objective of CIGA was to create structures that would provide businesses with the flexibility and breathing space they needed to continue trading and avoid insolvency during that period of economic uncertainty and beyond. It runs to almost 250 pages and consists of 50 substantive sections and 14 Schedules. Many amendments to existing legislation are included, alongside completely novel provisions.

There were five main insolvency-related measures (as stated above, some were permanent and some temporary) included in this new Act, together with some miscellaneous company reporting and filing changes. Some of the company rescue proposals had already been announced by the Government and were in development before Covid-19, through the 2018 Consultation on Insolvency and Corporate Governance. This was part of the (then) Government's focus on delivering a strong business environment in the UK. It sought views on ways to improve the insolvency rescue framework and also to reduce the risk of company failures occurring through poor governance or stewardship. Some of the measures in the new Act arise directly out of the Government response to that 2018 consultation, although other ones, notably around the areas of greater potential consequences, both financial and otherwise, for directors, have not yet been implemented through CIGA, and currently there are no active proposals to further legislate.

In summary, the relevant provisions of CIGA for the property practitioner are as follows:

(1) *Company moratorium*

The Act gives struggling businesses a formal breathing space to pursue a rescue plan. It creates a moratorium during which no legal action can be taken against a company without leave of the court. The decision to introduce the moratorium in 2020 was in order to ensure that companies that were struggling as a direct result of the pandemic were given the opportunity to survive. However, this is a permanent measure from the Act, albeit supplemented with some special temporary provisions. This procedure is not to be confused with the references to the moratorium in either a company voluntary arrangement, administration or liquidation which are considered later in this chapter. CIGA has now been in force for several years, but this procedure has not been greatly used by company directors, and no part of it has been tested in the courts. However, it could be significant in the commercial property field as it will prevent landlords (amongst others) taking or continuing with any action whatsoever, unless leave of the court is obtained, once the moratorium commences.

(2) *Restructuring plan*

The provisions here are to enable viable companies struggling with debt obligations to restructure under a new procedure. They allow courts to sanction a plan that binds creditors to a restructuring plan if it is fair, equitable and in the interests of creditors. Creditors vote on the plan, but the court can impose it on dissenting creditors. It is similar to, but distinctive from, the existing Scheme of Arrangement which is laid out in the Companies Act 2006.

In the case of *Re Virgin Active Holdings Ltd & Ors* [2021] EWHC 1246 (Ch), the High Court sanctioned Virgin Active restructuring plans despite objections from landlords and a lack of support for the plans from most classes of creditor.

The decision added to earlier case law which had supported the use of this new and flexible restructuring tool. This was a significant test of the new 'cross-class cram down' mechanism; the court rejected objections from landlords and exercised its discretion to sanction the Virgin Active restructuring plans. It was the first use of restructuring plans to restructure landlord liabilities and has potentially laid down a marker for their wider use going forwards.

It is also worth mentioning that landlords and tenants should be aware of the impact of any proposals for restructuring on rent arrears claims. In the case of *Riverside CREM 3 Ltd v Virgin Active Health Clubs Ltd* [2021] EWHC 746 (Ch), the High Court stayed the landlord's rent arrears claim, because the tenant had proposed a restructuring plan under Part 26A of the Companies Act 2006 *after* the landlord's claim had been issued.

The court ordered a stay as the interests of the wider class of creditors trumped the private interests of the landlord. In this case, it was clear that a majority of more than 75% of the tenant's secured creditors would vote in favour of the restructuring plan. If the landlord had obtained and enforced judgment, it would have received substantially more than the other landlords in its class under the restructuring plan. One of the more recent restructuring plans that was sanctioned by the courts concerned the Italian restaurant chain Prezzo, and in the decision HMRC was crammed down; see *Re Prezzo Investco Ltd* [2023] EWHC 1679 (Ch). Several more restructuring plans have been considered by the courts in 2024, and, in the main, applications by companies for these plans have been successful.

It remains to be seen if the restructuring plan procedure features more going forward in commercial property matters where tenants are seeking rent renegotiations, particularly given the ongoing battle between commercial landlords and commercial tenants over the proper use of the CVA procedure (see **33.5.1.1** below).

It is also worthwhile considering here one further case that arose out of the Virgin Active restructuring plan, and that is *Oceanfill Ltd v Nuffield Health Wellbeing Ltd, Cannons Group Ltd* [2022] EWHC 2178 (Ch). In that case, the claimant owned the freehold of a gym which was let to Nuffield Health Wellbeing Ltd in 1998 for a term of 25 years. In 2000 the Lease was assigned to Virgin Active Ltd, the current sitting tenant. Nuffield assigned the lease by way of a licence to assign, for which a guarantee was provided by Nuffield for Virgin Active's performance under the lease. A further guarantee was provided by Cannons Group Ltd for Nuffield's performance of the terms of the licence to assign. Having lost money through the approved restructuring plan for Virgin Active, Oceanfill issued proceedings against both Nuffield and Cannons Group pursuant to guarantee obligations.

Despite the defences put forward by both defendants, the court determined that the Virgin Active restructuring plan did not rewrite the lease and did not erase the liability for rent from the lease but released the current tenant (and the tenant only) from the liabilities. Consequently, the judge concluded that the plan had not affected the rights and liabilities of third parties to the lease, and that therefore Nuffield and Cannons were both liable.

(3) *'Ipso facto'* (termination) clauses

When a company enters an insolvency or restructuring procedure, key suppliers will often either stop or threaten to stop supplying the company. The supply contract may well give them the right to do this, but doing so could materially jeopardise any attempt to rescue the business. The Act ensures that suppliers will not be able to hinder a rescue in this way. There are safeguards to ensure that continued supplies are paid for, but there are protective mechanisms for suppliers if the requirement to supply causes hardship to their business.

(4) *Statutory demands and winding-up petitions*

The Act also brought in some temporary provisions which have certainly affected commercial landlords, in that it was made much harder to commence winding-up proceedings against a company from March 2020. However, for all practical purposes, these temporary provisions have now been removed and the law in this area has reverted to the position that existed pre-pandemic. The relevant law here is considered at **33.5.5.1** below.

33.2 MEASURES TO REDUCE THE PERCEIVED RISK OF INSOLVENCY

If X's financial strength is in doubt, Y may still be willing to contract with X if additional financial reassurance is provided. If X subsequently becomes insolvent, Y should then have meaningful ways to ensure performance of the contract (or at very least, payment of damages for breach) without becoming embroiled in the insolvency process. These could include:

(a) requiring another person (with a better financial track record) to enter into the contract at the outset, either as joint covenantor with X or as guarantor for X. This could include requiring the existing tenant (who wishes to assign to X) to act as guarantor by way of an authorised guarantee agreement (AGA);

(b) requiring X to obtain a bank bond or guarantee. Here the bank agrees to perform the obligations, or pay damages, if X is in breach. Usually, the bank's liability is capped at a specified amount;

(c) where the contract is the grant of a new lease, or the assignment of an existing lease to X, requiring X to deposit cash in a rent deposit, held either by a neutral party or (more likely) by the landlord;

(d) drafting the contract to include a right for Y to rescind if X becomes insolvent or is likely to do so. At least Y is then free to do a different deal with someone else. A forfeiture clause in a lease, which is triggered by an insolvency event, is very similar to this. For more details on forfeiture, see **Chapter 26**;

(e) keeping a close eye on X's financial and trading performance, so that Y picks up very quickly any signs of impending insolvency. This might include watching for press announcements of the loss of a major contract, reacting quickly to late payments of rent by the tenant or investigating the background to a request from an occupation tenant to pay rent monthly rather than quarterly.

If X becomes insolvent, Y should always check whether it can take advantage of any of these measures (as they may be quicker or more productive than pursuing X for performance or damages).

33.3 ALWAYS ESTABLISH THE TYPE OF INSOLVENCY REGIME

When Y first becomes aware of X's insolvency or likely insolvency, it is critical to establish precisely which type of insolvency regime is involved. Y's range of remedies will vary considerably from one regime to another, and the terminology can be misleading. For example, being told 'the receivers have gone in' might refer to a Law of Property Act Receiver under the Law of Property Act 1925 (a 'LPA receiver'), an Administrative Receiver or the Official Receiver, acting either as liquidator or as trustee in bankruptcy. The range of insolvency regimes is set out in **Table 33.1** below, and a more detailed explanation of the types of regime and their consequences is given in the appropriate part of **33.5**.

Table 33.1 The alternative insolvency regimes

Where X is an individual	Where X is a company
Law of Property Act Receiver (an LPA receiver, or sometimes called a fixed charge receiver)	Law of Property Act Receiver (an LPA receiver, or sometimes called a fixed charge receiver)
Individual Voluntary Arrangement (IVA)	Company Voluntary Arrangement (CVA)
Debt Relief Orders (DROs) – but these are not really prevalent in the commercial property arena	Administrative Receivership
–	Administration
Bankruptcy (either on X's own application or that of a creditor)	Liquidation • compulsory • voluntary (triggered by creditors) • voluntary (triggered by members) (Liquidation is also known as winding up)

(Note also the references above to the moratorium and restructuring plan procedures created by the Corporate Insolvency and Governance Act 2020, as they are now part of the insolvency landscape going forward.)

33.3.1 How to check which insolvency regime applies

Y can check which insolvency regime applies by following these guidelines:

(a) *Voluntary arrangements (CVA or IVA).* Once a CVA has been agreed, it should be registered at Companies House and thus be discoverable by a company search. An IVA that has been agreed should be registered on the Insolvency Service Register, and this can be searched on-line. Also, the supervisor of the voluntary arrangement (corporate or personal) must give notice to all X's known creditors, so Y (if it is X's landlord) may find out that way. An interim order (for an IVA) can be discovered only by asking the relevant court, and even then, the information may not always be supplied.

(b) *Appointment of a receiver where X is a company.* This will be registered at Companies House (regardless of whether this is a LPA receiver, or an administrative receiver). All business correspondence has to state that a receiver has been appointed, and an administrative receiver also has to notify all known creditors promptly after their appointment.

The appointment of either receiver cannot be noted on the title to any registered property belonging to X that is affected by the receivership, but this will not matter, as the debenture or charge under which the receiver is appointed will have been noted on the title already. However, the receiver may wish to ensure that any notices served by the Land Registry will reach them. They may therefore wish to register their own address as an additional address for service.

(c) *Administration order.* Once made, this should show up as an entry in the Companies House file, but to find out about any recent administration application or order that has not yet been registered at Companies House, Y should telephone the Central Registry of Winding Up Petitions and also enquire of the county court for the area where X's registered office is situated. A notice of the administrator's appointment may be entered on the register of title of any property that is affected by the administration, but the absence of such a notice is not conclusive as no application for this entry may have been made.

(d) *Voluntary liquidation.* The winding-up resolution must be registered at Companies House within 15 days, so will be revealed by a company search. A notice of the liquidator's appointment may be entered on the registers of title of any property that is affected by the liquidation, but the absence of such a notice is not conclusive as no application for this entry may have been made.

(e) *Compulsory liquidation.* The winding-up order will be registered at Companies House 'forthwith', so will be revealed by a company search. To be sure that there are no more recent applications or orders for compulsory liquidation, Y should telephone the Central Registry of Winding Up Petitions (which covers petitions for compulsory liquidation, whether submitted in the High Court or the county court). A notice of the liquidator's appointment may be entered on the register of title of any property that is affected by the liquidation, but the absence of such a notice is not conclusive as no application for this may have been made.

(f) *Bankruptcy.* The Register of bankruptcy orders can be searched on-line at the Insolvency Service. Bankruptcy petitions are recorded at the debtor's county court hearing centre, the Royal Courts of Justice or the Central London County Court (sometimes at more than one of these). These registers can be inspected in person. Both bankruptcy petitions and orders are ultimately also recorded at the Land Charges Department as a pending action (PA) when the petition is issued and as a writ and order (WO) when a bankruptcy order is made (and can be searched using Form K16). Details may also have been entered on the register of title for X's properties as the court is required to notify the Land Registry when a bankruptcy petition is issued.

It is worth noting here that there is also the Debt Relief Order regime that exists for those owing low levels of money (£50,000 or less) and having limited assets. It is not considered any further here as it will not really be applicable to many property insolvency cases. In May 2021, a new 'breathing space' regime was introduced for personal insolvency to protect debtors for a 60-day period from enforcement action whilst their financial options were considered. A useful document providing guidance for creditors on this scheme can be found at <www.gov.uk/government/publications/debt-respite-scheme-breathing-space-guidance/debt-respite-scheme-breathing-space-guidance-for-creditors>.

33.3.2 The insolvency official

As stated at the outset of this chapter, each of the insolvency regimes listed at **33.3.1** is implemented by a different person and the designations are different. For example, they are called the supervisor (initially the nominee) of a company or individual voluntary arrangement; an LPA receiver; an administrative receiver; an administrator; a liquidator, or a trustee in bankruptcy respectively for the appropriate regimes. As stated, for convenience, in this chapter, all of these individuals are called the 'insolvency official' or 'insolvency officials' unless there is a specific need to specify the actual designation for a particular purpose.

33.4 IDENTIFY THE TYPE OF CONTRACT

It is equally important to know what type of contract exists between X and Y, as this can also affect the remedies available to Y when X becomes insolvent. For example, it may be:

(a) an existing lease;
(b) an agreement for lease (lease not yet granted);
(c) a recently completed transfer;
(d) an exchanged contract for sale which has yet to complete;
(e) an existing freehold restrictive covenant;
(f) a pure contract, with no property interest at all – such as a contractual licence to occupy;
(g) a new sale contract or lease into which the insolvency official is proposing to enter with Y as part of the process of realising X's assets.

33.5 THE DIFFERENT TYPES OF INSOLVENCY REGIME

33.5.1 Voluntary arrangements (CVAs and IVAs)

Voluntary arrangements can arise under ss 1 to 7 of the IA 1986 (for companies) or ss 252 to 263 of the IA 1986 (for individuals). They are a statutory compromise agreement between X (who is insolvent) and the majority of the creditors. Where X is a company, the arrangement is known as a Company Voluntary Arrangement (CVA), and where X is an individual, it is known as an Individual Voluntary Arrangement (IVA).

The aims of a voluntary arrangement, whether corporate or personal, are for the unsecured creditors to agree to proposals that secure them better payments than would be the case under a formal insolvency distribution, but which reduce the overall burden on X by giving it longer to pay its debts or by reducing the amount it has to pay. A voluntary arrangement can compromise both existing and future debts (such as rent that will become due under a lease). Indeed, there has been much focus in recent times on the use of CVAs, in particular in the retail sector, and the consequences for landlords in these situations, as analysed below. A voluntary arrangement rarely lasts for more than five years. The distribution of assets in accordance with the agreed arrangement is undertaken by a licensed insolvency practitioner (indeed once the arrangement has been approved, they are called 'the supervisor').

A voluntary arrangement cannot include proposals which would adversely affect the rights of secured creditors or preferential debtors, unless they consent. Interestingly, a voluntary arrangement can, potentially, propose changes to third-party liabilities (usually the release from liability of guarantors or former tenants who have given an AGA). Such proposals have, however, been challenged successfully on grounds of unfair prejudice (see **33.5.1.1**) in several cases.

The advantage of a CVA/IVA is that it avoids the more formal insolvency regime. This is particularly important where X as an individual would be initially prohibited, for example by the rules of their professional organisation, from practising (a solicitor has this prohibition), or would have to give up their other directorships, if they were declared bankrupt. It may also be less expensive than the alternative insolvency regimes and can be more flexible.

33.5.1.1 Approval of the voluntary arrangement

A voluntary arrangement requires the consent of 75% or more in value (not number) of the creditors who attend the initial meeting to discuss the proposals. There is also a requirement that more than 50% of the votes in favour must be from independent creditors who are not associates (IR 2016, r 15.34). Creditors who oppose the arrangement can challenge its terms on grounds that they cause unfair prejudice or that there has been a material irregularity in the arrangement. They must do so quickly (within 28 days). The IA 1986 does not define unfair prejudice, but case law has upheld claims by landlords that a CVA should be revised on this ground. See *Prudential Assurance Company Ltd & Others v PRG Powerhouse Ltd & Others* [2007] EWHC 1002 and *Mourant & Co Trustees Ltd v Sixty UK Ltd (in administration)* [2010] EWHC 1890, where the CVA proposed stripping some landlords of their rights to pursue the guarantor of the leases for rent arrears. In both *Powerhouse* and *Mourant*, the original terms of the CVA were held to offer the landlord inadequate compensation for being deprived of its rights against the guarantors. A similar decision was reached in the more recent case of *Re Mizen Design/Build Ltd (in company voluntary arrangement)* [2023] EWHC 127 (Ch).

A further challenge to a company voluntary arrangement on various grounds of unfair prejudice was heard in *Discovery (Northampton) Ltd and others v Debenhams Retail Ltd and others* [2019] EWHC 2441 (Ch). In essence, for the property practitioner, it confirmed that future rent can be compromised under a CVA and, further, the fact that future rent is reduced under the CVA does not inevitably render a CVA unfair as the court will consider it in the round.

However, that case made it clear, very much to the benefit of landlords, that a CVA cannot vary or remove a right of re-entry.

The CVA battleground between commercial landlords and commercial tenants has certainly developed from 2021 onwards. The case of *Lazari Properties 2 Ltd & Ors v New Look Retailers Ltd & Ors* [2021] EWHC 1209 (Ch) considered in detail the issues of jurisdiction, unfair prejudice and material irregularity in a CVA. The decision was decided against the landlords on all three grounds, and many think this is a major setback for them in their ongoing battle to challenge and supress the use of CVAs as a restructuring tool. It suggests that the use of CVAs as a rescue mechanism is far from over.

Although permission to appeal the decision to the Court of Appeal was granted, the case settled on confidential terms shortly before that hearing and so the law as set out in the first instance decision remains operative. Following the first instance decision in the *New Look* case, a similar defeat for landlords followed in *Young v Nero Holdings Ltd* [2021] EWHC 2600 (Ch).

33.5.1.2 Moratorium

There is no moratorium to prevent Y seeking to enforce its remedies during the period leading up to formal approval of a CVA, unlike in an insolvency rescue out of administration.

There are, however, complex moratorium arrangements in an IVA (IA 1986, ss 252 and 254). More details are given in **Flowchart 1** at **33.7.2**. In essence, the moratorium is one of the fundamental differences between a CVA and an IVA. In an IVA, it is a fundamental tool to protect the insolvent debtor from ongoing risk of creditor action and one that debtors avail themselves of in the vast majority of situations. It is termed obtaining an interim order prior to seeking an approval by creditors of the IVA and gives that valuable protection for debtors.

It is indeed important to realise that the moratorium provisions apply only up to the point that the IVA is approved. After that, X may dispose of property solely in accordance with the terms of the approved voluntary arrangement.

The use of this moratorium procedure is also not to be confused with the moratorium procedure introduced by the Corporate Insolvency and Governance Act 2020 referred to earlier in the chapter. That is a completely standalone procedure. Similarly, references later in this chapter to a moratorium in administration and liquidation are purely in relation to those procedures.

33.5.2 Receivership

As stated earlier, this is something of a loose term, and lawyers should really be clearer in their usage of it and specifically distinguish between the two types of receivership, namely a Law of Property Act (LPA) Receiver and an Administrative Receiver. Receivership occurs where a person is appointed (by the holder of a mortgage or charge) to realise the charged assets (either taking income from them or selling them) in order to secure repayment of the debt due from the borrower. Thus, receivership is only available to lenders who hold security. In a property context, the most likely receiver to be encountered will be an LPA receiver, with an administrative receiver being less frequently encountered now. The rules that govern what such a receiver can do (and thus how these operate to affect other parties such as Y) differ significantly from those applicable to other types of insolvency official (administrators, liquidators or trustees in bankruptcy).

Table 33.2 below indicates how these two types of receiver differ.

Table 33.2 The differences between an LPA receiver and an administrative receiver

Law of Property Act Receiver (also called a fixed charge receiver) – the LPA receiver	Administrative Receiver
Can be appointed if X is an individual or a company.	Can be appointed only if X is a company
Appointed by a lender with a fixed charge over the property as security. It is unusual for a rack rent lease to be used as security (since it often has no capital value), so an LPA receiver is more likely to be appointed in respect of freehold land or long leases granted for a premium.	Appointed by a lender who has a floating charge over the whole or substantially the whole of X's undertaking and - that floating charge was executed on or before 15 September 2003; or - that floating charge was executed after that date but falls into one of the limited categories that continue to qualify for administrative receivership (such as capital market arrangements; public-private partnerships and other project loans).
Appointed either under the terms of the mortgage, or under the default power in s 101 of the Law of Property Act 1925, in circumstances where the mortgagee's power of sale has arisen.	Appointed under the terms of the floating charge, as expanded by s 28 of the IA 1986 and following.
Receiver acts only in relation to the charged asset (the particular property).	Receiver acts in relation to the class of assets covered by the floating charge.
Need not be a licensed insolvency practitioner.	Must be a licensed insolvency practitioner.
The LPA receiver can always collect the income of the property. Usually, the mortgage document expands these powers to include sale and letting of the property. The aim is for the LPA receiver to realise enough from the asset to allow repayment of the debt, though they must use reasonable endeavours to secure the market value of the asset. The LPA receiver is not interested in maximising the amount that other classes of creditor will recover.	The administrative receiver's powers depend on the mortgage, but these are expanded by statutory powers of sale, granting and surrendering leases, and carrying on X's business (because the floating charge is over all of X's undertaking). The aim is for the administrative receiver to realise enough from the assets to allow repayment of the debt, though they must use reasonable endeavours to secure the market value of the asset. The administrative receiver is not interested in maximising the amount that other classes of creditor will recover.

Law of Property Act Receiver (also called a fixed charge receiver) – the LPA receiver	Administrative Receiver
Legal title to the assets remains in X	
The LPA receiver *cannot* • disclaim the charged property (whether onerous or not); • ignore any obligations that bind the charged property, eg restrictive covenants, leases or easements. The LPA receiver must observe these, negotiate to escape from them or modify them, or run the risk that X is sued for breach. The LPA receiver has no personal liability to observe these obligations.	The administrative receiver *cannot* • disclaim any assets (whether they are onerous or not); • ignore any obligations that bind the property asset, eg restrictive covenants, leases or easements. The administrative receiver must observe these, negotiate to escape from them or modify them, or run the risk that X is sued for breach. The administrative receiver has no personal liability to observe these obligations.
The LPA/administrative receiver acts as agent of X (IA 1986, s 44)	
If the LPA/administrative receiver enters into a new contract, they will be personally liable on that contract (unless the terms of the contract state otherwise, as they usually will).	
The appointment of an LPA/administrative receiver does not impose a moratorium on actions against X by other creditors or contracting parties. Thus, Y can seek to enforce any contract that it has with X.	

33.5.3 Bankruptcy

Bankruptcy is applicable only to an insolvent individual (X). A licensed insolvency practitioner (either the Official Receiver, who is an employee of The Insolvency Service, or one selected by the creditors) is appointed to act as the trustee in bankruptcy, to collect in the realisable assets belonging to X, convert them to cash and distribute this to the creditors in accordance with the statutory order of payment. Once this process is complete, X is released from any of the debts X incurred up to the date of bankruptcy if they have not been fully settled in the bankruptcy.

A bankruptcy order is made by the court following presentation of a bankruptcy petition by a creditor or, following an application by X to the Adjudicator at the Insolvency Service, by the Adjudicator themselves. The adjudication process is a relatively recent procedure which commenced in April 2016 to replace the former procedure of a debtor making an application to court to become bankrupt. The Adjudicator is also an employee of The Insolvency Service. This procedure is an 'online' one commenced by the debtor themselves. The procedure for a creditor to make someone bankrupt is quite detailed, but, in essence, an application can be made by an unsecured creditor of X who is owed £5,000 or more and can demonstrate that X cannot pay this debt or has no reasonable prospect of doing so.

33.5.3.1 Effect of bankruptcy

Once the trustee in bankruptcy is appointed, X's assets vest in the trustee in bankruptcy automatically. Where this includes leasehold property, this automatic assignment does not need the consent of the landlord. It is an 'excluded assignment' for the purposes of the Landlord and Tenant (Covenants) Act (LT(C)A) 1995.

Once the assets have vested in the trustee in bankruptcy, X loses the ability to dispose of them, so Y should not enter into new contracts with X in relation to X's property. Y should deal only with the trustee in bankruptcy. However, there is limited protection, in the case of registered land, under s 86 of the Land Registration Act 2002, where Y, in good faith, buys the property from X for value without knowing there has been a bankruptcy petition or order and without these having been registered (as a notice or restriction) against the title to the property (see *Pick v Chief Land Registrar* [2011] EWHC 206).

33.5.3.2 Powers of trustee in bankruptcy

The trustee in bankruptcy has a wide range of powers (detailed in the IA 1986), enabling them to manage the assets and eventually sell them. The trustee in bankruptcy must observe any existing restrictions and covenants that affect existing properties vested in them in this way (eg registered restrictive covenants affecting the property). This includes paying rent on existing leases (see **33.8.2.3**). However, the trustee in bankruptcy is not obliged to implement any outstanding contracts (such as sale or purchase contracts), though they may choose to do so if this is consistent with the proper realisation of X's assets. If the trustee considers the properties or contracts to be onerous, the trustee can disclaim them (in the same way as a liquidator, but not other insolvency officials, can). For more details about disclaimer and its effect, see **33.10**.

33.5.3.3 Restrictions placed on the bankrupt

During the bankruptcy process, there are restrictions both on what X can do and on the action the creditors may take against X to recover sums due to them or secure performance of obligations. These restrictions include the following:

(a) Between presentation of the bankruptcy petition and the vesting of the property in the trustee in bankruptcy, any purported disposition of that property by X is void (IA 1986, s 284(1)) unless it is:

   (i) made with the court's permission or subsequent ratification; or

   (ii) a disposition of registered land to a purchaser acting in good faith, for value and without notice of the presentation of the petition (see **33.5.3.1**).

(b) Between presentation of the bankruptcy petition and making the bankruptcy order the court can, if asked, stay any action or legal process brought against X or its property (IA 1986, s 285(1)).

(c) Once the bankruptcy order has been made, unsecured creditors, caught by bankruptcy, may not enforce a remedy against X or its property, or bring any action or legal proceedings against X, unless they have the leave of the court to do so (IA 1986, s 285(3)). Secured creditors are not affected by this restriction (IA 1986, s 285(4)).

33.5.4 Administration

Administration is applicable only to an insolvent company (X). It is intended to provide an opportunity to rescue X from insolvency (perhaps selling it as a going concern). If this is impossible, the administration will focus instead on realising X's assets in a manner that produces a better result for the creditors as a whole than they would achieve in a liquidation. The final option is for the administrator to obtain the objective of realising property in order to make a distribution to one or more secured or preferential creditors. (See IA 1986, Sch B1, para 3(1), as amended.)

33.5.4.1 Appointment of the administrator

The administrator may be appointed by the court (on the request either of the company itself, the directors of the company or of one or more creditors of the company) or directly (without court involvement) by resolution of X in general meeting, or by resolution of its directors or by the holder of a qualifying floating charge (dated on or after 15 September 2003) over the whole or substantially the whole of X's assets.

It is important to note that there are restrictions on the ability of the company or its directors to appoint an administrator without court involvement. However, the holder of a qualifying floating charge always has the ability to appoint an administrator without asking permission of the court. The administrator must always be a licensed insolvency practitioner.

33.5.4.2 Powers and duties of the administrator

The administrator has powers and duties as set out in the IA 1986. These are designed to equip the administrator to manage X's business and property, with a view to rescuing X from insolvency or at least achieving one of the objectives set out in **33.5.4** above. To achieve this objective, the administrator will put forward proposals as to which assets should be sold and which retained; which debts should be compromised and at what level; which contracts (to which X is a party) will be performed by X and which the administrator proposes should be terminated, and whether and how X should continue to trade. The administrator is an officer of the court, so must act fairly. In essence, their duty is to manage the business effectively through the administration period for the overall benefit of creditors.

An administrator cannot disclaim any property of X, neither can they simply repudiate contracts into which X has entered. The administrator must negotiate their termination or allow X to be in breach of them and let the other party pursue what remedies it may have for that breach.

The administrator acts as X's agent and has no personal liability on the contracts into which X has already entered, or new ones into which it enters during the course of the administration, which will always be made clear in the terms of any contract that is negotiated. X's property does not vest in the administrator, so if the administrator wishes to dispose of properties, the administrator does so in X's name. Once X is in administration, the directors lose their ability to determine the disposal of the properties.

Administration usually lasts for no more than one year, although there are options to extend this period. If the company is still insolvent at that point, the administration will generally change either to a CVA or to a creditors' voluntary or compulsory liquidation. It should be remembered that the insolvency procedures set out in this chapter are not mutually exclusive, and it is possible for the same company to, at various times, enter into a CVA, administration or liquidation. Indeed, that is what happened in the well-publicised corporate failures of British Home Stores (BHS) and Debenhams.

33.5.4.3 Moratorium

Whilst X is in administration, a statutory moratorium applies (IA 1986, Sch B1, para 43). This prevents both forfeiture by peaceable re-entry and any 'legal process' against X without the consent of the administrator or the court. Such consent was given in *Lazari GP Ltd v Jervis* [2012] EWHC 1466, when a landlord of one the properties previously used by Game Retail (UK) Ltd successfully applied to forfeit the lease rather than assign it to the buyer of the business. The moratorium also restricts X's creditors from seeking specific performance by X of its contracts with them (perhaps a contract to purchase land); suing for damages in lieu of performance; or seeking repayment of debts owed to them by X (such as a landlord trying to recover rent arrears). Similarly, those creditors cannot issue a petition to put X into liquidation, and the restriction on legal process means that a tenant will need consent before it can apply for a new lease under Pt II of the LTA 1954 where its landlord is in administration (*Somerfield Stores Ltd v Spring (Sutton Coldfield) Ltd* [2009] EWHC 2384). While consent will sometimes be given, the delay and uncertainty mean that the moratorium can be very frustrating for creditors.

For completeness, it should be mentioned that the statutory moratorium can be triggered by the filing at court of a Notice of Intention to appoint an Administrator, which lasts for 14 days, and service of that notice on all known creditors. This procedure has been analysed in a number of cases due to the possibility of abuse, for example, see the case of *JCAM Commercial*

Real Estate Property XV Ltd v Davis Haulage Ltd [2017] EWCA Civ 267. In practical terms, the courts have sought to cut down the service of multiple Notices of Intention to appoint an Administrator, and so most Insolvency Practitioners will now advise that a maximum of two only should be served, creating a moratorium of 28 days, before making the decision whether or not to enter into administration.

33.5.5 Liquidation

Liquidation is also applicable only to companies (not individuals). They are usually (but not always) insolvent (see **33.5.5.1**). Where X is insolvent but cannot be rescued, liquidation is appropriate. All X's assets must be realised (that is converted into cash) for distribution to its creditors (or shareholders if there is a surplus). In such circumstances, the unsecured creditors may receive very little towards the debt or damages for a breach of contract caused to them by X.

33.5.5.1 Types of liquidation

There are two types of voluntary liquidation, creditors' (CVL) and members' (MVL). Both are voluntary in the sense that the directors and members of the company initiate the process, rather than a creditor, but only the MVL is truly voluntary, in that the members and directors control the process from start to finish. It is important to remember that the members and directors of a company may not be the same persons. In small private companies, they may be of course. Directors undertake the day-to-day management of the company, and this would include managing situations when financial issues (positive and negative) raise their head. Hence, it is often appropriate to talk of directors initiating formal insolvency processes, but the members also have their part to play at the outset as the owners of the company.

A CVL is initiated by the directors of the company and is then taken forward by the creditors of the company. However, whilst the CVL procedure is voluntary (in that the directors are not being forced to recommend liquidation), it is usually the result either of outside creditor pressure or of professional advice to the directors that the company is insolvent. Directors are usually unwilling to put the company into liquidation, as they always think that better times are around the corner. However, the threat of potential actions against them for misfeasance or fraudulent or wrongful trading usually concentrates their minds. No court order is needed to confirm a voluntary liquidation. The way a company commences the CVL process changed quite substantially with the coming into force of the IR 2016, and, in simple terms, it became potentially a speedier and quicker process for a company to enter into liquidation.

Alternatively, compulsory liquidation occurs where the court makes an order following presentation of a winding-up petition against X because it cannot pay its debts. Such a petition is often lodged by a creditor. A statutory demand would often proceed a compulsory winding-up petition. As stated earlier, it was much more difficult to obtain a winding-up order during the pandemic because of a series of temporary provisions that had been brought in via the Corporate Insolvency and Governance Act 2020 and related statutory instruments. However, these temporary provisions have now ceased to have effect and so we are back to the pre-Covid-19 position in terms of compulsory liquidation practice and procedure. This means that a debt as low as £750 could found a winding up petition. This is to be contrasted with the issue of bankruptcy proceedings when a debt of £5,000 or more is required.

However, one limited exception remained for commercial landlords to prevent them pursuing winding-up proceedings because of the passing of the Commercial Rent (Coronavirus) Act 2022 which received Royal Assent on 24 March 2022. This Act ringfenced outstanding unpaid rent for business tenancies built up whilst businesses were closed during lockdown. An agreement was to be sought between the parties and, if unsuccessful, there would be a legally binding arbitration process. The arbitration is delivered by private arbitrators in accordance with guidelines set out in the legislation. This arbitration had to be commenced by 24

September 2022 and in default the landlord's remedies revive, to include compulsory liquidation proceedings. Although it is possible that some existing arbitrations are continuing into 2023/24, the reality is that this provision is not really seen in practice now.

33.5.5.2 Powers and duties of the liquidator

The liquidator deals with realisation of X's assets and distribution of the proceeds, but X's assets do not vest in the liquidator. The liquidator must be a licensed insolvency practitioner. They have wide-ranging powers and duties as set out in the IA 1986, but may need approval for some actions, depending on whether the liquidation is voluntary or compulsory.

Unlike other insolvency officials, a liquidator (and a trustee in bankruptcy) has the ability to disclaim any property or other assets belonging to X that are considered to be onerous. Section 178(3)(a) of the IA 1986 allows the liquidator to disclaim an unprofitable contract. A contract is not unprofitable just because it is financially disadvantageous. The liquidator has to balance the benefit to the creditors from complying with the contract against the liability the contract imposes on the company. Contracts that impose obligations on X, either to do things or to pay money, would generally be onerous. This would include contracts in which X agrees to take a new lease or purchase property, or existing leases where X is the tenant. It might also include a sale agreement where X is the seller (perhaps where the sale price is rather low). Disclaimer terminates X's rights and obligations under the contract and is possible regardless of whether there is a termination clause in the contract. It is very rare for freehold property to be considered onerous, as it usually has a positive value. However, if the obligations associated with its ownership are extensive and costly, it could be disclaimed as onerous. For more on disclaimer, see **33.10**.

33.5.5.3 Moratorium

Unlike administration, no moratorium applies in a voluntary liquidation. Thus creditors, and other parties (such as Y) to contracts into which X entered (but of which it is now in breach) can take enforcement action, unless the liquidator obtains a court order (under s 112 of the IA 1986) to prevent this. However, practically, Y has to consider what would be the benefit of acting in this way, as the enforcement is unlikely to be wholly successful due to the nature of the insolvency of X. For the property professional, forfeiture is a principal remedy, and in a CVL this can be undertaken even after that process has started. However, the liquidator can still apply for relief from forfeiture as was demonstrated in the case of *SHB Realisations Ltd v Cribbs Mall Nominee (1) Ltd* [2019] 3 WLUK 588.

In a compulsory liquidation, once the winding-up order is made by the court, Y cannot take any action or proceedings against X or its property without the consent of the court. Also, from the earlier point when the winding-up petition is presented, any purported disposition by X of its property is void, unless made with the court's permission or it receives subsequent ratification.

33.6 SETTING ASIDE TRANSACTIONS WHICH HAVE ALREADY BEEN COMPLETED

Perhaps one of the interesting implications of insolvency is that certain kinds of insolvency official (liquidators, administrators and trustees in bankruptcy) can ask the court to set aside completed transactions (potentially resulting in the return of the property or an award of damages against Y as the current owner). This power is designed to prevent some creditors taking unfair advantage to the detriment of the remainder.

The two most important categories of completed transaction that can be set aside are transactions at an undervalue and preferences. **Table 33.3** shows the essential features of both. There are other rules that operate in different circumstances to set aside dealings with insolvent companies (eg the 'anti-deprivation' principle), but these are not discussed further here.

Table 33.3 Transactions at an undervalue and preferences

Transactions at an undervalue	Preferences
IA 1986, s 238 (insolvent companies). IA 1986 s 339 (insolvent individuals).	IA 1986, s 239 (insolvent companies). IA 1986 s 340 (insolvent individuals).
X was a party to a completed transaction (either direct with Y, or with a predecessor in title of Y).	Y is one of X's creditors or a guarantor of X's debts.
X (or someone at X's direction) received substantially less than the value of the property disposed of in the transaction (perhaps it was a gift, or only nominal consideration was paid).	X does something that has the effect of putting Y in a better position than it would have been if X were subject to a formal insolvency process (gave a 'preference' to Y direct or to someone else with Y's agreement and benefiting Y as a result)
X's intention in entering into the undervalue transaction is irrelevant.	X must do this with the *desire* to produce the effect of putting Y in a better position. Where Y is connected to X in some way, this desire is presumed to exist.
X subsequently goes into administration or liquidation (companies) or becomes bankrupt (individuals). Other forms of insolvency process cannot take advantage of this process.	
The completed transaction took place within: • the 2-year period leading up to the start of the administration or liquidation (where X is a company). • the 5-year period leading up to the bankruptcy (where X is an individual).	The preference was given within: • the 2-year period leading up to the start of the administration, liquidation or bankruptcy, where Y is connected to X; or • the 6 months leading up to that point, where Y is not connected to X.
At the time of the transaction, or immediately after and in consequence of the transaction, X is in practice insolvent (ie cannot pay its debts, even if it is not yet subject to any formal insolvency process). Where X is an individual, this requirement does not apply in the 2 years immediately before the bankruptcy – it applies only during the earlier part of the 5-year period	At the time of the giving the preference, or immediately after and in consequence of giving it, X is in practice insolvent (ie cannot pay its debts, even if it is not yet subject to any formal insolvency process).
Where X is a company, the transaction, even if at an undervalue and completed during the 2-year period, will not be at risk of being reversed if X can show that it entered into the transaction in good faith, for the purposes of carrying on its business, and at the time of the transaction there were reasonable grounds for believing that the transaction would benefit the company. There is no equivalent escape clause if X is an individual.	No equivalent.

Transactions at an undervalue	Preferences
The administrator, liquidator and the trustee in bankruptcy (as appropriate) can ask the court to set the transaction aside. The court can make such order as it sees fit, including ordering the return of the property or payment of damages. However, it can refuse to make the order, even if the criteria to do so are satisfied (eg *Claridge* [2011] EWHC 2047 (Ch), a bankruptcy case).	
If Y was the other party to the undervalue transaction with X, Y cannot argue (as a defence to any such court order) that it did not know: • X was insolvent or in danger of becoming so; or • the value Y was giving was significantly less than market value.	If Y was the party given the preference, it cannot argue (as a defence to any such court order) that it did not know: • X was insolvent or in danger of becoming so; or • X had the desire to give Y a preference.
If Y is not the other party to the undervalue transaction/preference but is a successor in title to the party that was, then Y may be protected from any such court order to return the property or pay damages (IA 1986, ss 241/342). Protection is available where Y: • acted in good faith when it entered into its own transaction; and • gave value for its own transaction. Y will be presumed *not* to act in good faith if, at the time of its own transaction, either: • Y was connected to the party to whom X transferred at an undervalue or to whom X gave the preference; or • Y had notice of both the previous undervalue transaction/preference *and* the fact that X had since entered into administration, liquidation or bankruptcy. If Y can prove otherwise, then the protection will once more apply. If Y gave no value for its own transaction, then it cannot benefit from this protection.	

This is why, when investigating title, if there is evidence of an undervalue transaction it is necessary to carry out either a company search or a land charges (bankruptcy) search against the company or individual that was the 'donor' under that transaction (X), to see if they subsequently went into administration, liquidation or became bankrupt.

Finally, it is worth noting that there is another section in the IA 1986, s 423, which can also be used to set aside or challenge transactions that have been carried out to the detriment of creditors. This section is often linked with transactions at an undervalue claims, although the requisite criteria are different. There have been two interesting recent decisions on this section which assist practitioners in understanding the legal position; see *Investment Bank PSC v El-Husseini and others* [2023] EWCA Civ 555 and *Henderson & Jones Ltd v Ross and others* [2023] EWHC 1276 (Ch).

33.7 THE EFFECT OF A TENANT BECOMING INSOLVENT

33.7.1 The range of remedies available to a landlord

Where an insolvent tenant (X) fails to pay its rent or perform its obligations, the landlord may want to pursue all or any of the following remedies:

(a) sue for unpaid rent (proceedings);
(b) exercise Commercial Rent Arrears Recovery (CRAR) rights – see **30.1.1.3**;
(c) divert to itself the rent due from a sub-tenant to X (under s 81 of the Tribunals, Courts and Enforcement Act (TCEA) 2007) (a 's 81 TCEA notice');
(d) sue for specific performance (proceedings);
(e) sue for damages for breach of covenant (proceedings);

(f) forfeit the lease on grounds either of insolvency or breach (for more details see **Chapter 26**);

(g) start insolvency proceedings (perhaps a petition for bankruptcy or compulsory liquidation) in order to bring pressure to bear;

(h) force a trustee in bankruptcy or liquidator, acting for X, to decide whether to disclaim the lease or not, so that (if they do disclaim) at least Y is free to re-let.

(i) persuade the insolvency official to surrender the lease

In some cases, the insolvency official may be personally liable to pay the rent, or the rent may qualify as an expense of the insolvency (see **33.8** and **33.10.5**). This gives the landlord an extra remedy.

As indicated in **33.2**, the landlord should also consider whether it has meaningful remedies against third parties (for example, guarantors, or through a rent deposit or a performance bond from a bank). Bear in mind, if X is subject to a voluntary arrangement, the obligations of those third parties may have sought to have been amended in the agreement that creditors are being asked to support (see the discussion on this area in **33.5.1.1**).

33.7.2 The restrictions on exercise of these various remedies

To illustrate how the various principles outlined in **33.5** impact on the landlord's remedies against the tenant, see **Flowcharts 1 to 5** below. It is important to consult the correct flowchart for the insolvency regime that affects X. Note that CRAR and s 81 TCEA notices can only be used where there is a written lease of commercial property.

Flowchart 1 Where an individual tenant (X) is subject to an IVA

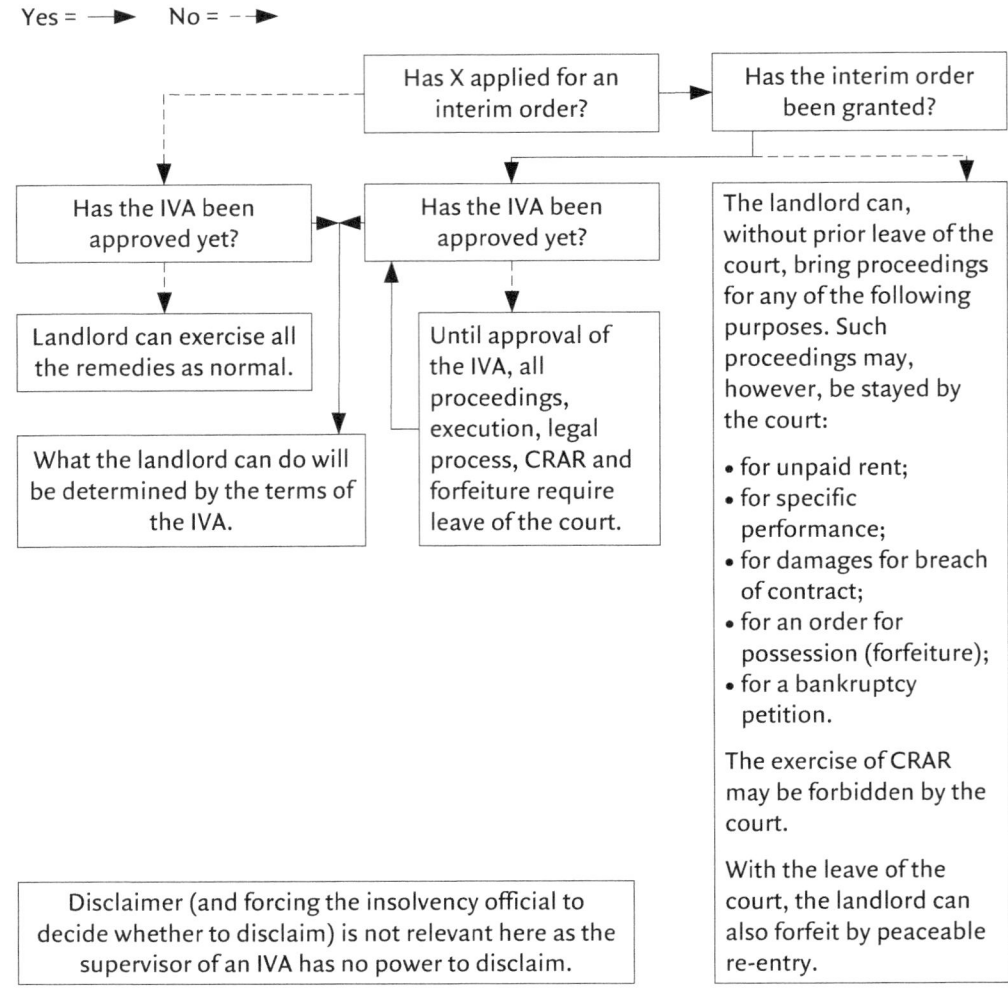

Insolvency and its Effect on Commercial Property 385

Flowchart 2 Where an individual tenant (X) is bankrupt

Yes = ⟶   No = --▶

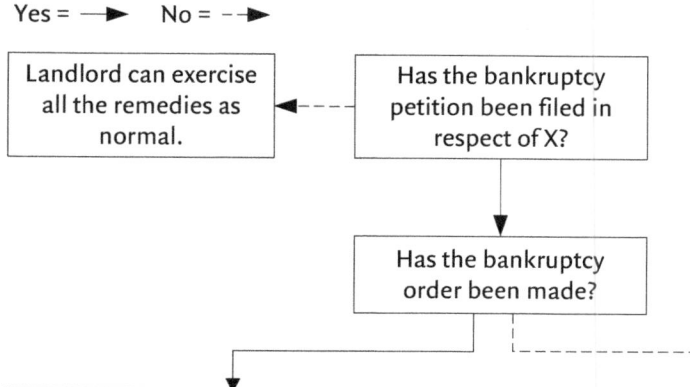

With leave of the court, the landlord can bring any of the following proceedings:

- for unpaid rent;
- for specific performance;
- for damages for breach of contract;
- CRAR for a maximum of six months' rent.

The court may refuse leave where the landlord is seeking a remedy for a debt provable in the bankruptcy (IA 1986, s 285(3)).

The landlord can do the following without leave of the court:

- serve a s 81 TCEA notice;
- forfeit by peaceable re-entry;
- seek a court order for possession (forfeiture) (*Christina Sharples v Places for People Homes Ltd* [2011] EWCA Civ 513).

However, the court may stay proceedings for possession (IA 1986, s 285(1)).

The landlord can serve notice on the trustee in bankruptcy requiring confirmation of whether it plans to disclaim the lease (IA 1986, s 316).

The landlord can bring any of the following proceedings (but they may be stayed by the court (IA 1986, s 285(1))):

- for unpaid rent;
- for specific performance;
- for damages for breach of contract;
- for forfeiture.

The landlord can do the following without leave of the court:

- serve a s 81 TCEA notice.

The landlord cannot yet serve notice on the trustee requiring confirmation of whether it plans to disclaim the lease, because the trustee is not yet appointed.

386 Commercial Property

Flowchart 3 Where a corporate tenant (X) is in administration

Yes = ⟶   No = --▶

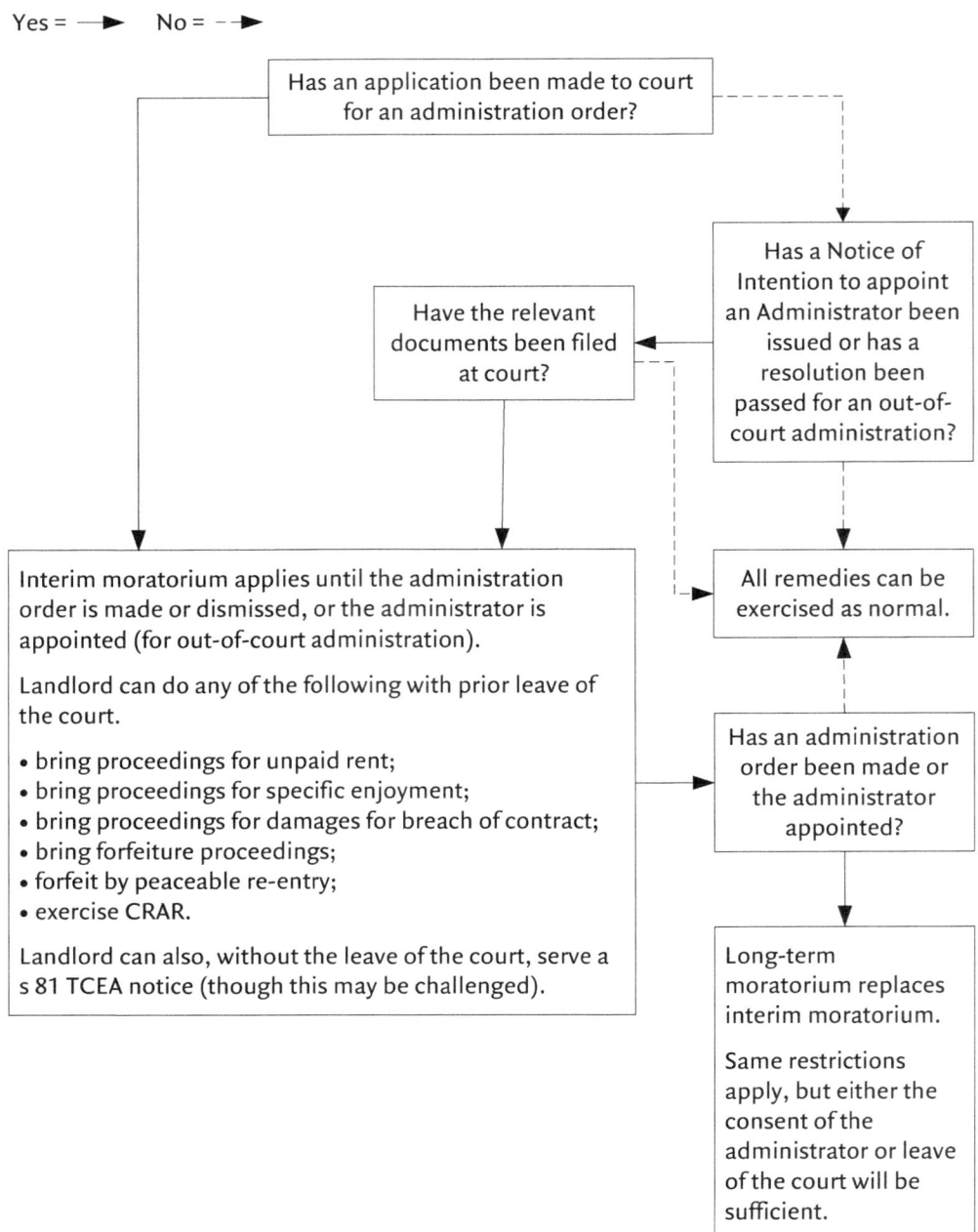

Flowchart 4 Where a corporate tenant (X) is in voluntary liquidation

Yes = ⟶   No = --▶

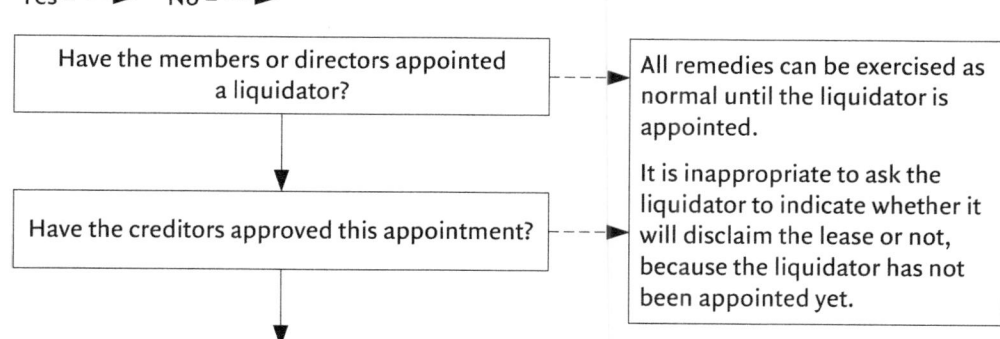

```
┌──────────────────────────────────┐        ┌─────────────────────────────────────┐
│ Have the members or directors    │ ---▶   │ All remedies can be exercised as    │
│ appointed a liquidator?          │        │ normal until the liquidator is      │
└──────────────┬───────────────────┘        │ appointed.                          │
               │                            │                                     │
               ▼                            │ It is inappropriate to ask the      │
┌──────────────────────────────────┐        │ liquidator to indicate whether it   │
│ Have the creditors approved this │ ---▶   │ will disclaim the lease or not,     │
│ appointment?                     │        │ because the liquidator has not      │
└──────────────┬───────────────────┘        │ been appointed yet.                 │
               │                            └─────────────────────────────────────┘
               ▼
```

Liquidator has been appointed.

There is no moratorium.

Landlord can make use of the following procedures without leave of the court or the liquidator. However, if it does so, the liquidator can ask the court to stay the proceedings:

- proceedings for unpaid rent;
- proceedings for specific enjoyment;
- proceedings for damages for breach of contract;
- forfeiture proceedings or forfeiture by peaceable re-entry;
- exercise CRAR.

Landlord can take the following action without leave of the court or the liquidator, and the liquidator *cannot* apply for a stay or otherwise stop such action:

- serve notice requiring the liquidator to decide whether it will disclaim the lease or not (IA 1986, s 178).

At the time of writing it is not clear whether a s 81 TCEA notice requires court permission.

Flowchart 5 Where a corporate tenant (X) is in compulsory liquidation

Yes = →   No = --→

- Has a petition been presented to court for compulsory liquidation?
  - No → All remedies except CRAR can be exercised as normal.
  - Yes ↓
- Has a winding-up order been made?
  - No → All remedies except CRAR can be exercised as normal, but most can be stayed by the court (on the application of the company or a creditor) (IA 1986, s 126).

    CRAR proceedings are void, but once the winding up order has been made, the landlord can seek the leave of the court to exercise CRAR.

    It is inappropriate to ask about the liquidator's intention to disclaim the lease, because the liquidator has not yet been appointed.
  - Yes ↓
- Liquidator has been appointed.

  Landlord can use the following procedures only with prior leave of the court or the liquidator (IA 1986, s 130):
  - proceedings for unpaid rent;
  - proceedings for specific enjoyment;
  - proceedings for damages for breach of contract;
  - forfeiture proceedings;
  - exercise CRAR.

  Landlord can take the following action without leave of the court or the liquidator, and the liquidator *cannot* apply for a stay or otherwise stop such action:
  - forfeit by peaceable re-entry (this may be challenged);
  - serve notice requiring the liquidator to decide whether it will disclaim the lease or not (IA 1986, s 178 and IR 2016, r 19.9).

  At the time of writing it is not clear whether a s 81 TCEA notice requires court permission.

33.7.3 Recovering the premises – forfeiture and its drawbacks

The forfeiture clause in most leases includes insolvency events as a trigger for possible forfeiture. These usually include the appointment of an administrator, a liquidator or a trustee in bankruptcy, but can extend to voluntary arrangements or the appointment of a receiver, or even if a tenant seeks a restructuring plan or, going further, if the insolvency definition of 'cannot pay their debts as and when they fall due' in the IA 1986 is triggered generally. Usually, the preliminary steps in those insolvency processes (such as lodging a petition for winding up, rather than just the making of the winding-up order) are enough to give the landlord the right to forfeit. It is important to check the exact wording of the clause, however, to ensure it covers the situation that has occurred.

Where the landlord can insist that a third party or other source pays the rent and performs the covenants (perhaps there is a guarantor or a rent deposit available), it may prefer to keep the lease alive, for once it has been forfeited these remedies will generally cease with it. One exception may be if the guarantee states that the guarantor will take a replacement lease if the original is forfeited. The landlord may also be reluctant to forfeit if it will be difficult to find a replacement tenant quickly, or if the cost of the necessary incentives to achieve a re-letting will be prohibitive. Finally, the landlord may be reluctant to forfeit if the bill for rates whilst the property stands empty is unaffordable.

If the landlord decides to forfeit on an insolvency ground, it must serve a notice on the tenant under s 146 of the LPA 1925. However, the insolvency ground is irremediable, so the tenant need not be given a reasonable time to remedy the breach. The greatest source of delay in forfeiture is likely to be the need for consent from the court or the insolvency official to allow forfeiture (either by proceedings or by peaceable re-entry). Consult **Flowcharts 1 to 5** for further details of what consent is required and when. The main case to consider whether such consent should be given for forfeiture proceedings is Re Atlantic Computer Systems plc [1990] EWCA Civ 20.

Even if forfeiture is permitted and achieved, X or its insolvency official can apply for relief from forfeiture. The court has a wide discretion to permit this and can set terms for doing so (eg requiring X to pay off the arrears or remedy the breach of covenant). This was seen in the case of SHB Realisations Ltd v Cribbs Mall Nominee (1) Ltd [2019] 3 WLUK 588 mentioned in **33.5.5.3** above.

For more details on forfeiture, see **Chapter 26**.

33.8 REQUIRING THE INSOLVENCY OFFICIAL TO PAY RENT

33.8.1 Rent arrears for the period leading up to the insolvency event

These must be claimed for by the landlord in the insolvency.

33.8.2 Rent/service charge arising after the start of the insolvency

Whether these are payable in full depends on the type of insolvency.

33.8.2.1 Voluntary arrangements

The terms of the CVA/IVA will determine whether X is liable for the ongoing rent in full or in part, or not at all. The supervisor of the CVA/IVA is not liable personally to pay these sums.

33.8.2.2 Receiver

The tenant company remains liable for the rent and service charge, and the receiver may choose to require the tenant company to pay those sums, or it may not. The receiver is not personally liable to pay these sums (even if it chooses to direct the tenant company to pay them). Moreover, the receiver can collect in sub-lease rents and account for these to the mortgagee even if the main lease rent is not being paid.

If the ongoing rent is not paid, the tenant company will be in breach and the landlord will have its normal remedies, which may include forfeiture, diverting any sub-lease rents under s 81 of the TCEA 2007 or commencing more formal insolvency proceedings (such as bankruptcy or liquidation). The unpaid rent will usually rank as an unsecured claim in such an insolvency. For more details on remedies, see **33.7.1** and **Chapter 30**.

33.8.2.3 Bankruptcy

The lease becomes vested in the trustee in bankruptcy, who will be personally liable on the covenants in the lease. The trustee should therefore pay the rent and other sums that fall due whilst the lease is vested in the trustee. Generally, the trustee will try to bring their liability for rent and other payments to an end by assigning, surrendering or disclaiming the lease.

If the trustee disclaims the lease (see **33.10** below), the landlord cannot sue the trustee for rent arrears accruing for the period prior to the disclaimer. Instead, the landlord will have to submit a claim in the bankruptcy for that sum, as an unsecured creditor, and may well recover only part of the debt. It is possible (but not yet established by case law) that where the trustee has been using the let premises for the purpose of realising the assets (perhaps continuing to trade X's business from them pending sale of that business as a going concern), the landlord's claim for rent arrears (for the period from the making of the bankruptcy order to the date of disclaimer) might be treated as an expense of the bankruptcy and therefore more likely to be paid in full. A landlord should certainly raise that argument to maximise recovery possibilities.

33.8.2.4 Administrator or liquidator

Rent and other sums need not be paid by an administrator or a liquidator as they are not personally responsible for the contracts into which X has entered. However, if they choose to occupy the property (or part of it) for the purposes of the administration or winding up, then they may be liable to pay both rent and service charge that fall due during that period (as an expense of the administration or liquidation). What qualifies as use for such purposes was considered in *Sunberry Properties Limited v Innovate Logistics Ltd (in administration)* [2008] EWCA Civ 1261. If the rent and service charge qualify as expenses of the administration or liquidation, they will be settled as a priority debt in the insolvency (ahead of the remuneration of the insolvency official) and, therefore, should be paid in full.

There have been many cases on which rent and service charges must be paid and for what periods, but the law was clarified, with the previous leading cases (*Leisure Norwich (II) Ltd v Luminar Lava Ignite Ltd & Others* [2012] EWHC 951 (Ch) and *Goldacre (Offices) Ltd v Nortel Networks (UK) Ltd (in administration)* [2009] EWHC 3389 (Ch)) being overruled by the case of *Pillar Denton Ltd and Others v Jervis and Others* [2014] EWCA Civ 180 (24 February 2014). This case related to the administration of the Game group of companies.

The Court of Appeal held that an administrator (or a liquidator) must make payments at the rate of the rent for the duration of any period during which they retained possession of the premises for the benefit of the administration, and that the rent would be treated as accruing from day to day. The period of beneficial possession was to be determined as a question of fact.

This is a welcome simplification of the previous law and can best be described as an administrator or liquidator now having to pay for the usage of premises regardless of the day the insolvency formally commenced.

33.9 REQUIRING THE INSOLVENCY OFFICIAL TO OBSERVE THE LEASE COVENANTS

The insolvency official acting for an insolvent corporate tenant is not personally liable to perform the other covenants in the lease (for example, to carry out repairs, make good dilapidations at the end of the lease, or observe the user covenant). The insolvency official is merely the agent of the tenant for the lease (which continues to exist). By contrast, a trustee in bankruptcy acting for an insolvent individual tenant is personally liable to perform the lease covenants. This is an important distinction to remember.

Where the tenant remains liable to observe the lease covenants and fails to do so, the landlord will have its normal remedies, subject to any relevant restrictions on their exercise. For more details of those restrictions, see **33.7.2** and the related flowcharts.

33.9.1 Voluntary arrangements (CVA or IVA)

The tenant is still bound to perform the covenants in the lease (though the extent of the obligation to perform them may be varied by the CVA or IVA terms). The supervisor (see **33.5.1**) is not personally liable.

33.9.2 Receiver

The tenant company remains liable as tenant under the lease. The receiver can control whether the tenant will discharge its obligations under the lease. The receiver is not personally liable.

33.9.3 Administrator

The tenant company remains liable as tenant under the lease. The administrator will not be personally liable, although they will control whether the tenant discharges its obligations under the lease. If the administrator has chosen to continue to occupy and trade from the property for the purposes of the administration, then they will have a powerful incentive to observe the lease covenants, in order to avoid the risk of the landlord applying for leave to forfeit the lease. It is possible (by analogy with the previously mentioned *Pillar Denton* case – see **33.8.2.4**) that any debts due to the landlord from the tenant, arising as a result of its failure to comply with the lease covenants during the period of occupation for the purposes of administration, may qualify as a priority debt, as being an expense of the administration.

33.9.4 Liquidator

The tenant company remains liable as tenant under the lease. The liquidator will not be personally liable. If the liquidator has continued to trade from the premises (rather than disclaiming the lease or leaving the premises empty) or wishes to sell the lease (because it has some capital value) then the liquidator will have an incentive to observe the lease covenants, in order to avoid the risk of the landlord applying for leave to forfeit the lease. It is very unclear whether debts arising due to failure to observe the covenants of the lease during such period would be recoverable as a priority debt in the liquidation, as an expense of the liquidation.

33.9.5 Trustee in bankruptcy

The lease vests in the trustee in bankruptcy, who is therefore bound to observe all its provisions, unless the trustee chooses to disclaim (see **33.10**). The trustee can claim (from the bankrupt's estate) reimbursement for any costs incurred in complying with the lease. The tenant will also remain bound (as the statutory assignment to the trustee in bankruptcy does not release the tenant from liability under the LT(C)A 1995).

33.10 DISCLAIMER AND ITS EFFECTS

33.10.1 Who can disclaim?

Only trustees in bankruptcy (IA 1986, s 315) and liquidators (IA 1986, s 178) can disclaim property.

33.10.2 What is disclaimer?

The insolvency official, by notice filed in court, renounces future involvement by X in the contract, or future ownership by X of the property (as appropriate). Copies of that notice have to be served on the other people who may be interested in the disclaimed property, or who will remain under an obligation in relation to it despite the disclaimer. This gives them the chance to decide whether they want to apply for an order vesting the disclaimed property in them. For more on vesting orders see **33.10.7**.

Where X is a tenant, and the insolvency official wishes to bring liability under the lease to an end, it may prefer to do so by methods other than disclaimer. It may be possible to terminate the lease by notice to quit (a periodic tenancy), or by exercising a break right. The landlord may be willing to take a surrender of the lease (particularly if there are sub-leases, as this will be a more reliable way for the landlord to take over those sub-leases). Alternatively, the insolvency official may choose to do nothing, fail to pay the rent or observe the provisions of the lease, and hope that the landlord takes the initiative and chooses to forfeit the lease. This could be a risky strategy, however.

33.10.3 What can be disclaimed?

Any property that the insolvency official considers to be onerous can be disclaimed. Onerous property is defined (IA 1986, s 178(3)) as property which is either unsaleable or not readily saleable, or which might give rise to a liability to pay money or perform any onerous act. This will include:

1. Leasehold property

(a) a lease where X is the tenant (because a tenant has a range of obligations that involve paying money or doing things);

(b) a lease where X is the landlord, if the obligations the landlord must discharge (perhaps carrying out repairs) may cost more than it can recover from the tenants. This is rarely done where X is the freeholder, as well as the landlord, because disclaimer of the lease requires disclaimer of the underlying freehold interest too, and this usually has some value.

2. Sale contracts

(c) a sale contract or agreement for lease where X is the buyer/tenant, if that contract is unprofitable (see **33.5.5.2**);

(d) a sale contract or agreement for lease where X is the seller/landlord, and the contract is unprofitable (perhaps because it imposes on X obligations beyond the mere transfer of the property for the agreed price – for example to carry out extensive repair works).

In each case, disclaimer of the contract must be accompanied by disclaimer of the property to which it relates (so, in the case of a sale contract where X is the seller, the freehold or leasehold property it covers). This is unlikely where the freehold property has value.

3. Freehold property

Freehold property is rarely encumbered with such extensive obligations that it will be onerous, so disclaimer of freehold property is very unusual.

33.10.4 Is consent needed for disclaimer?

In most cases consent is not needed to disclaim (there are a few situations where a trustee in bankruptcy will need the consent of the court to disclaim, but these are beyond the scope of this book).

33.10.5 When can the onerous property be disclaimed?

The insolvency official can disclaim whenever they wish, as long as they do so before the insolvent party is discharged from bankruptcy (where X is an individual) or finally dissolved (where X is a company).

If the insolvency official delays, the other party to the contract is left in limbo, not knowing whether the contract will be observed. That other party can force the pace, by serving on the insolvency official a notice to elect whether or not to disclaim (IA 1986, s 316(1) or s 178(5)). The insolvency official then has 28 days to serve notice of disclaimer. If no notice is served in time:

(a) the trustee in bankruptcy is deemed to have adopted the contract and will be personally liable to perform it;

(b) the liquidator is still not personally liable to perform the contract, but (at least in the case of a lease) may be taken to have retained the premises for the benefit of the liquidation, in which case rent and other payments due under the lease will rank as expenses of the liquidation and be payable as a priority debt (*ABC Coupler and Engineering Co Ltd (No 3)* [1970] 1 All ER 650).

33.10.6 Effect of disclaimer

33.10.6.1 On the insolvent party (X) and the insolvency official

The disclaimer releases X from its obligations (and rights) under the contract from the date of the disclaimer. It also releases the insolvency official from any such liability.

33.10.6.2 On the other party to the contract

The other party to the disclaimed contract will be left with a claim in the insolvency for the damages or losses it suffers as a result of the contract not being performed by X. In some circumstances it may be able to secure performance by a third party and will not, therefore, suffer any loss (see **33.10.6.3**).

Where it is a lease that is disclaimed, the landlord will be entitled to retake possession. However, it should not do so if it wishes to require a third party to take on the responsibility for the lease (see **33.10.6.3**).

33.10.6.3 On third parties

Disclaimer does not (unless this is necessary in order to release X from its obligations) affect the liabilities and rights of any third party (IA 1986, s 178(4)). For example, if X has agreed, jointly with Z, to purchase a property from Y, X's insolvency official can disclaim the purchase contract, but Y may still seek specific performance against Z. This comes up most often in the context of a lease where there is a guarantor for X, or possibly previous tenants who are still liable to perform the lease (either as original tenant under a pre-1996 lease, or under an AGA for a more recent lease). All will remain liable to the landlord under the guarantee arrangements, despite the disclaimer, unless the terms of the guarantee state that it terminates on disclaimer (*Hindcastle v Barbara Attenborough Associates* [1997] AC 70 and *Doleman v Shaw* [2009] EWCA Civ 283).

In such circumstances, the landlord can, despite disclaimer, still sue the guarantor or former tenant for the rent or performance of the lease covenants. If (as is usual) the guarantee clause provides for this, the landlord can, alternatively, require the guarantor or former tenant to take up a replacement lease.

The landlord must be careful not to retake possession of the premises following disclaimer, if it wishes to be able to pursue such remedies against third parties. If the landlord does retake possession, this will be treated rather as if it had successfully forfeited the lease, which brings the lease to an end, and with it the liability of the guarantors and former tenants (see *Hindcastle*, above, and *Active Estates Ltd v Parness* [2002] EWHC 893).

33.10.6.4 On sub-tenancies

Sub-tenants are a special variety of third party where a lease is disclaimed, and the rules are very complex. In simple terms, disclaimer of the head-lease brings to an end the obligations that X had as landlord of the sub-leases and the sub-tenants' rights against and obligations to X. However, it does not:

(a) terminate the sub-tenants' interests in the property (so disclaimer differs from forfeiture in this respect);

(b) substitute the superior landlord as landlord of the sub-leases (as would occur if X's lease had been surrendered).

There is privity neither of contract nor estate between the superior landlord and the sub-tenant. In effect, the disclaimed head-lease is treated as still being in existence, unless and until the superior landlord chooses to forfeit it (for default in rent payments or performance of other conditions). If that forfeiture is successful, then the sub-lease will be forfeit too (assuming the sub-tenant does not obtain relief from forfeiture). Until that point, the sub-tenant has a continued right to possession (not under the sub-lease but under a *sui generis* set of rights).

This means that if the sub-tenant continues, in practice, to pay the rent and observe the covenants of the disclaimed head-lease, the superior landlord may have no grounds for forfeiture. If the sub-tenant pays more rent (under the head-lease) than it was obliged to do under the sub-lease, it can claim in the insolvency for the difference.

33.10.7 Vesting orders

Where a third party (perhaps a guarantor, former tenant or sub-tenant) ends up paying the rent under X's disclaimed lease, it may want to apply for a vesting order. Likewise, a mortgagee of X's disclaimed property may want to apply for a vesting order. If successful, the lease or property will be transferred to the third party. This gives that party control over the property, and thus the ability to ensure performance of relevant covenants and to sell or assign the property, in order to bring their liability to a close.

The court has discretion over whether to make a vesting order and on what terms. Generally, it will require the person in whom the property is vested to be subject to the same obligations (in relation to that property) as X was before the disclaimer. If more than one person applies for a vesting order, the court applies an established pecking order in deciding who should succeed (sub-tenants come higher up this order than guarantors, former tenants or the landlord). If the landlord applies for a vesting order (so as to be sure that the lease is under its control), the court will give people higher up the pecking order (such as sub-tenants) the chance to take the vesting order instead. If they do not take up this opportunity reasonably quickly, they will lose the right to apply for a vesting order at a later date.

If the vesting order is granted, ownership of the lease or other property transfers automatically. There is no need for a conveyance, an assignment or a transfer.

A party seeking a vesting order must apply for it within three months of becoming aware of or being notified of the disclaimer. This period can be extended by the court on an application being made.

APPENDIX 1

Review Activity Answers

Chapter 1

1. The three main types of commercial property are offices, retail and industrial.
2. Renting avoids the need to find or borrow the purchase money at the outset and means that capital is not tied up in the building.
3. Investors hope to make an income by letting the property to tenants and a capital gain as the property rises in value.
4. Developers hope to make a profit by selling the completed development for more than it cost to purchase and develop the original site.
5. An investor may join with another investor to spread the financial risk and/or make it easier to obtain funding for the development. It may join with a developer to gain specialist expertise in areas such as project management, planning, environmental remediation and construction. It may join with a prospective buyer of the completed development to give the buyer some input into design and construction, and thereby strengthen the buyer's commitment to the purchase.
6. Contractual joint ventures and joint venture partnerships (all three types) are 'tax transparent' and pay no tax in their own right. Tax is paid only once the profits and gains have reached the joint venture parties. An SPV, being a separate legal entity, pays tax in its own right, and tax is charged again when the SPV dividends are paid to the joint venture parties, hence the term 'double taxation'.
7. Both an SPV and an LLP, as legal entities separate from the joint venture parties, offer the participants limited liability for losses incurred in the development. A limited partnership offers limited liability for the limited partners, although the liability of the general partner will be unlimited. Traditional partnerships and contractual joint ventures have unlimited liability, and a traditional partner is also liable for the defaults of its partners.
8. Which joint venture structure is most efficient in terms of SDLT depends on the stage of the development. At the outset, a contractual joint venture is the more efficient, as the necessary transfer of the property into the joint venture partnership or SPV gives rise to a charge to SDLT. On the eventual sale of the developed property, an SPV offers the possibility of selling the shares with 0.5% stamp duty instead of the property with consideration exceeding £250,000 being charged at 5% SDLT.

Chapter 2

There are potential risks to Western if the issues raised are not addressed prior to the release of the loan. The issues raised are best dealt with in the loan agreement in conditions precedent. Conditions precedent must be satisfied prior to the release of the loan and, accordingly, unless Western is satisfied with the position, the loan will not proceed.

(a) *Subsidence*

Unit 3 may be suffering from subsidence. If so, the building may require significant and expensive remedial works, which are not included in the development budget. Ross may need to borrow further monies from Western. This may impact on the loan-to-value ratio, and Ross may struggle to meet the interest obligations under an increased loan. Any remedial works may delay the development which may affect the period of the loan. If the development is delayed, the institutional investor may no longer be interested in buying the property and Ross would need to find another buyer for the completed development. This may delay the repayment of the loan.

Condition precedent – Western is in receipt of a satisfactory structural engineer's report in respect of Unit 3 confirming that the movement to the property is long-established settlement and there is no subsidence.

(b) *Right of way*

If the dispute with the owner of Unit 4 cannot be resolved, the extension cannot be built. Resolving the dispute may require litigation, which would be expensive and time-consuming. This drain on Ross's resources and management time may affect Ross's ability to pay the capital and interest due under the loan. The alternative would be to proceed without the extension, but the project may be viable only with the extension. The institutional investor may no longer be interested in purchasing Unit 3 if it cannot be extended.

Condition precedent – The dispute relating to the right of way with the owner of Unit 4 is resolved to Western's satisfaction.

(c) *Flooding*

The recent flooding may make it difficult to insure Unit 3 against the risk of flooding. If this risk is not covered, Ross may find it difficult to let the property. Tenants may be unwilling to accept the risk that they may be faced with expensive remedial works and clean-up costs if the flooding recurs, unless the lease provides that the landlord will be responsible for uninsured risks. The institutional investor would object to any such term in the lease, as it would expect there to be no circumstances in which it would be required to make any expenditure. If the property cannot be let/sold, this will affect Ross's ability to repay the loan.

Condition precedent – Western is satisfied with details of the fully comprehensive insurance policy, which includes the risk of flooding, and which will be put in place on completion of the acquisition of Unit 3.

Chapter 3

1. A call option combined with a non-returnable fee and/or overage.

    Both a put option and a right of pre-emption would give all the decision-making power to the seller, who would presumably trigger the relevant provisions immediately as there is an alternative buyer already in the wings. ABC must offer the seller an immediate incentive not to sell to the rival developer whilst not committing itself to buy the land. The incentive could take the form of a non-returnable fee and/or the offer of an overage payment if and when the barn conversion takes place. Either (or both) of these could be incorporated into a conditional contract or a call option. However, although it would be possible to draft a contract conditional upon the obtaining of funding on acceptable terms, it would be very difficult to agree a test of acceptability. A call option would avoid these drafting difficulties and is obviously preferable for ABC as there would be no commitment to buy. It should be borne in mind, however, that the seller is likely to demand a high option fee/overage payment for the grant of a call option, to reflect the fact that it is passing up the chance to sell to the rival developer with no certainty that ABC will ever buy the land.

2. A right of pre-emption.

    A call option would not serve any useful purpose as the housing association might never be in a position to exercise it, and in the meantime MBC will be prevented from selling to anyone else. Similarly, the housing association is presumably not in a position to enter into a put option; and even if it does, it may not be able to comply with the obligation to complete if and when MBC exercises the put option. It will be difficult to draft a contract conditional upon the housing association getting sufficient funding to allow it to proceed, as the sources and amount of its funding will be variable from year to year. A right of pre-emption might be suitable here as it does not commit the housing association to a purchase it may not be able to afford but gives MBC a way of imposing a timetable on the decision-making process.

Chapter 4

1. The statement is incorrect. The basis on which LPAs are required to make decisions on whether to grant planning permission (and on what terms) is set out in s 38(6) of the Act. In simple terms, decisions should be made in line with the terms of the development plan unless material considerations indicate to the contrary. (See **4.1.3**.)

2. The statement is incorrect.

    First, permitted development rights under the GPDO amount to the grant of planning permission in any event (albeit that such permission is granted 'automatically' by the order rather than as a result of an express application). Secondly, the conversion of a building into more than one dwelling house is a material change of use and so will require planning permission. (See **4.2.2.1**.)

3. Provided there is no condition preventing this within any planning permission allowing the current use, change of use from one A1 (or E) shop use to another A1 (or E) shop use would not amount to development. (See **4.2.2.1** and **4.2.2.2**.)

4. An Article 4 Direction removes permitted development rights given under the GPDO (to the extent stated in the relevant Direction). This will mean that an individual will have to make an express application for planning permission should it wish to carry out an activity amounting to development that is the subject of such a Direction. (See **4.2.3.3**.)

5. When seeking to rely on the permitted development rights granted by the GPDO it should be remembered that the rights are not unqualified. (See **4.2.3.2**.)

6. The statement is not correct. An outline planning permission will typically require that approval of reserved matters be obtained within three years of the grant of the permission. Implementation must take place within two years of approval of the last of such reserved matters. In this way, an outline planning permission potentially has a life span of up to five years before implementation. (See **4.3.1** and **4.3.4.3**.) But this is merely the default position. The LPA can specify whatever time limits it chooses, within reason.

7. In the case of a full planning permission, implementation of the permission must usually be commenced within three years of grant. The meaning of 'commenced' is set out in s 56 of the Act and includes such steps as digging a trench for foundations and any work of demolition in connection with the development. The erection of the building does not have to be completed within the three year period. (See **4.3.4.3** and **4.3.4.5**.)

8. An appeal against an adverse planning decision by an LPA is a total rehearing of the matter and so an Inspector must put himself in the position he would be in if he were the LPA making the decision in the first instance. This is different to many appeals (such as from the High Court to the Court of Appeal) where the appeal is made on a point of law and points of evidence cannot generally be considered. (See **4.4.1**.)

9. In most cases, the time limit is six months from the date of the LPA's notice of decision or its failure to determine. (See **4.5**.)

10. The danger for the farmer is that if he appeals against the decision, it is possible that an Inspector would refuse the application altogether (see Question 8) and so the farmer would be worse off than is the case currently.

    A way round this is for the farmer to submit a fresh application for planning permission under s 73 of the Act in order to discharge the offending condition. If refused, he can appeal against the refusal in respect of that application. This will leave the original planning permission intact. (See **4.4.3.1**.)

Chapter 5

1. It is not possible to require the payment of money as a condition attached to planning permission. Such a requirement could be imposed by way of a planning obligation. (See **4.3.3** and **5.1**.) The LPA may alternatively wish to fund such work through CIL, if this kind of infrastructure is specified in its infrastructure list. The LPA may alternatively consider accepting provision of certain infrastructure as a payment in kind towards a CIL payment (see **5.6.1.8**).

2. Planning obligations can require the payment of money. The general land law principle that only the burden of restrictive covenants can bind successors in title does not apply to planning obligations. The burden of both positive and restrictive covenants contained in a planning obligation can be enforced against successors in title. (See **5.2**.) The LPA may also consider using CIL contributions to cover such work, but must consider the interaction of CIL and planning obligations (see **5.7**).

3. The Government's policy on planning conditions and obligations is set out in the NPPF and PPG (see **5.3**). Planning conditions should only be used where they are necessary, relevant to planning and to the development to be permitted, enforceable, precise and reasonable in all other respects. If there is already a need for the roundabout, a requirement to contribute towards it would not necessarily be directly relevant to the development to be permitted, so may be considered an unreasonable requirement. As a contribution under a condition, it would also offend the prohibition against payments. However, contributions towards infrastructure improvements may also be made by way of a highways agreement or a CIL payment, depending on what types of infrastructure the LPA decide to fund through CIL (although it is up to the LPA to choose what to spend CIL on and the roundabout would not be set out as the reason for charging CIL, which would depend on the existence of a charging schedule and other matters set out in this chapter). The LPA may alternatively accept provision of certain infrastructure as a payment in kind towards a CIL payment.

4. The LPA will generally insist on all parties with an interest in the relevant land entering into a planning obligation (see **5.2.4**). In light of this, the current freehold owner of the land in question will need to be made a party to the planning obligation. (See **5.2**.)

5. The owner of the land will be keen to ensure that it does not take on any unnecessary liability. It would, in particular, be keen to ensure there was no obligation to pay until the development linked to the planning obligation has been commenced. It would also wish to have its liability limited to its period of ownership. (See **5.8**.)

Chapter 6

1. First, it does not follow from the question that there is a breach of planning control at all. The works could have been permitted by an existing express planning permission or under permitted development rights under the GPDO. Even if there is a breach of planning control, it is not an offence in itself to be in breach. It is only if the LPA takes enforcement action that this can occur (such as failing to comply with a planning contravention notice or an enforcement notice). (See **Chapter 4** generally and **6.1**.)

2. The LPA does not have an automatic right to issue an enforcement notice. There must be an apparent breach of planning control and the service of the notice must be expedient having regard to the provisions of the development plan and other material considerations. (See **6.7.2**.)

3. Once served with a planning contravention notice, it is an offence not to reply to it within 21 days without reasonable excuse (See **6.5.2**.)

4. Enforcement action must be taken within four years in the case of building and other operational development (and change of use to a dwelling house). Once this time limit has passed, the LPA is unable to take enforcement action. On the facts of Question 4, therefore, the extension would be immune from being the subject of enforcement action.

5. A Certificate of Lawful Use or Development could be obtained in the circumstances envisaged in Question 4. This would act as proof that the development is lawful. (See **6.3**.)

6. There are various information gathering tools available to an LPA in respect of possible breaches of planning control. In particular, LPAs have a right of entry to ascertain whether there has been a breach of planning control and a planning contravention notice could be served requiring information about the use to which a relevant property is being put. (See **6.4** and **6.5**.)

7. The LPA could serve a breach of condition notice (given the nature of the breach in question). It could also consider serving an enforcement notice (and associated stop notice: see Question 8). One major advantage of the service of a breach of condition notice is that, unlike an enforcement notice, it cannot be appealed against. There are defences to being prosecuted for being in contravention of a breach of condition notice, but they are more limited than the grounds of appeal in respect of the service of an enforcement notice. Further, if an enforcement notice is appealed, its effect is suspended until the appeal has been heard. (See **6.6** and **6.7**.)

    The LPA could always choose not to enforce at all. (See **6.1**.)

8. A stop notice cannot be served in isolation and instead depends upon an enforcement notice having first been issued. A stop notice cannot be served once the enforcement notice has taken effect. (See **6.8.2**.)

9. Notice of appeal against the service of an enforcement notice must be given to the DLUHC before the date on which the relevant enforcement notice takes effect. (See **6.10.2**.)

10. There are seven grounds of appeal. (See **6.10.1**.)

    On the facts, ground (c) (no breach of planning control) might be relevant. The firm's use of the property could be within use class A2 in any event and so there would be no breach of planning control at all. (See **4.2.2.2**.)

    If the firm's use of the property does amount to a breach of development control, ground (a) (planning permission should be granted) might be relevant. The facts indicate that under the plan-led principle which governs when planning permission should be granted, the use stands a good chance of being granted. (See **4.1.3.1**.)

    Ground (g) might also be relevant as six weeks is a very short time limit within which to cease to operate.

    Note that other grounds might also be relevant would but the above are particularly relevant from the facts.

Chapter 7

1. For a blight notice, the property has a reasonable existing use value, but due to the threat of compulsory purchase the property is 'blighted', in that it is impossible or difficult to sell. To serve a blight notice, the land must be within a 'specified description' and the claimant must have a 'qualifying interest'. The claimant serves the blight notice over the whole unit on the 'appropriate authority'. That authority can then accept the notice and acquire the land or issue a counter-notice giving reasons for refusal. The claimant on receipt of the counter-notice can refer the matter the Upper Tribunal (Lands Chamber). The authority must give reasons in the counter-notice as to why it does not accept the blight notice. If the blight notice is accepted, compensation will be based on the same principles as if the land had been compulsory purchased. (See **7.2.2**.)

The essence of a purchase notice is that planning permission has been refused for development or is subject to conditions, and the refusal of permission or the planning conditions leaves the land virtually useless in its existing state. The essential question is that the land must have become incapable of reasonably beneficial use in its existing state. A restrictive interpretation regarding the meaning of the phrase 'incapable of reasonably beneficial use' has been favoured by the courts. If the purchase notice is accepted by the authority or on appeal to the relevant Minister, it is a deemed compulsory purchase. (See **7.2.3**.)

2. The legal basis of compensation will be in accordance with the principles in Horn v Sunderland Corporation [1941] 2 KB 26, which states that the claimant's true loss is to be compensated – no more, no less. This means that a claimant has a choice of claiming the value of the property, including full development potential, or the property's existing use value only plus disturbance. (See **7.4**)

3. In assessing the market value of the property with full development potential, s 5, rule 2 of the Land Compensation Act 1961 states that the market value assessment is the value if sold in the open market by a willing seller (see **7.4.1**). This will include such factors as:
   - existing use value;
   - marriage and ransom values;
   - disregards, such as any increases or decreases due to the scheme unless a private developer could do the work (see **7.4.1(c)**);
   - development potential. There must be two elements: first, market demand for the development and, secondly, planning permission. The following planning permissions can be taken into account for assessment:
     – existing planning permission,
     – acquiring authority's planning permission,
     – development under the current development plan,
     – hope value (to be assessed as loss of a chance if the chance of obtaining the permission is below 50% – see **7.4.2(e)**),
     – development allowed pursuant to a certificate under s 17 of the Land Compensation Act 1961 (see **7.4.2(f)**);
   - additional payments: whichever part of the Horn v Sunderland Corporation method is chosen, the claimant can also claim a basic loss payment and an occupier's loss payment (see **7.6.6**).

4. Where some land has been compulsory purchased, the claimant is in a more advantageous position than if no land has been acquired. The full depreciation in market value of the land remaining is claimable regardless of the reason for the depreciation. The market value of the land acquired is assessed under normal principles (see **Question 2** above). (See **7.5**.)

   Where no land is taken from the claimant, rights to compensation are very limited. The claimant must be able to prove that the depreciation has been caused by tortious factors such as noise and smell. Mere proximity or loss of privacy is not enough. The claim can be made under the very restrictive McCarthy rules that only allow for compensation for when the works are being built and, under Pt 1 of the Land Compensation Act 1973, for when the works are being used. (See **7.5**.)

5. Disturbance is not related to the market value of the property. It includes loss of goodwill, loss of existing profits, moving costs, adaptation of new premises and legal costs relating to the new premises. According to the rule in Horn v Sunderland Corporation, a claimant's true loss is either the value of the property including full development potential, or existing use value only plus disturbance. (See **7.6**.)

   To claim a disturbance payment, the claimant must be in occupation of the property, the loss must not be too remote and must fairly and reasonably relate to the acquisition. A deduction will be made if the claimant receives value for money, such as moving into a new building with better facilities.

Generally, a payment for goodwill is only available if the business occupier moves into another premises to continue the business. However, if the occupier is over 60 and undertakes to retire, he can receive a goodwill payment under s 46 of the Land Compensation Act 1973. (See **7.6.5**.)

As well as disturbance payments, there are a number of additional payments that can be claimed, regardless of which *Horn v Sunderland* head is claimed. In particular, these include the basic and occupier's loss payment and the home loss payment. (See **7.6.6**.)

6. Scenario (a)

    Sometimes a claimant might have other land in the vicinity which appreciates due to the works, as opposed to depreciates. For example, the land retained might now benefit from a key access route to the highway which causes that land to appreciate. As the claimant is only entitled to his true loss then any increase in value of retained land is 'set off' against the compensation payable for the land taken. (See **7.4.1(d)**.)

Scenario (b)

   Hope value applies to a situation where the land is likely to gain planning permission sometime in the future. Consideration of the planning background, the emergence of new development plans and comparable land in the vicinity may give some idea of future planning permission. Thus Orchard Tailors Ltd may be able to claim for the prospects of later residential development. Where the chance of obtaining the planning permission is less than 50%, compensation is assessed according to the 'loss of a chance' principle, not the 'all or nothing' balance of probabilities. (See **7.4.2(e)**.)

   If the claimant is carrying on a business in breach of planning control or doing anything illegal on the land, any increase in the value of the property caused by the breach or illegality is disregarded (Land Compensation Act 1961, s 5, rule 4). Thus any increase in the value of the property caused by the breach of planning law in selling hot food will be disregarded. (See **7.4.1(c)**.)

Scenario (c)

   Generally, payment will be made on completion of the vesting of the legal title in the acquiring authority (expropriation). However s 52 of the Land Compensation Act 1973 permits an advanced payment of compensation to be made if the authority takes possession before compensation is paid. The authority undertakes this by means of the notice of entry procedure. The amount is 90% of the agreed compensation or 90% of the acquiring authority's estimate if compensation has not been agreed. Interest is payable on the full amount of compensation agreed until the entire payment is made. (See **7.4.1**.)

Chapter 8

Scenario 1

As always, you would need to ascertain the size of the operation and its environment. In particular, what equipment or chemicals does it use, and are there other shops or even residences nearby? However, a 'typical' dry-cleaner may need to consider:

- use of harsh chemicals – hazardous substances regulation applies;
- smell and noise – potential nuisance claims from neighbours;
- emissions and waste – environmental permit or exemption may be required.

Scenario 2

You would need to consider the following:

- Building constructed in 1950s – asbestos removal probably required.
- Petrol station previously on site – contaminated land regime/planning condition for assessment and remediation of, say, any leaks from underground storage tanks.
- Roman wall on site – protection of archaeological sites; special building consent and preservation requirements.
- Limited information on previous use – transactional risk management (enquiries and warranties from seller) and possibly insurance needed for contingent risks.
- Mixed use commercial/residential planned – requirement to provide affordable housing under planning regime.

Scenario 3

This would raise the following environmental issues:

- Buildings on site since 1900 – asbestos management plan required.
- Long site history of industrial use and a nearby river – contaminated land and water pollution liability.
- Industrial chemicals and solvents used – hazardous substances and potentially any *Rylands v Fletcher* claim.
- Produces substantial waste – waste management regulations.
- Strong burning smells and smoke – nuisance and statutory nuisance issues.
- Heavy industry activity – requires environmental permit(s).
- Depending on activity use – caught by the ETS, so needs requisite greenhouse gas permit and allowances (could trade on the carbon market).
- Purchase from another plc – transactional risk management, complex indemnities and agreement on liabilities.

Scenario 4

Each party – Alpha, Beta, Gamma, Delta, Epsilon – could constitute a Class A appropriate person, as each caused or knowingly permitted the significant contaminants. Failing that, Gamma could be a Class B person, as the present owner or occupier.

However, for the Group A persons, Alpha may be excluded as it sold the property with information to Beta (Test 3), mostly by allowing it to undertake extensive investigations. Alpha may also be excluded under Test 6, if the only reason there is a significant contaminant linkage is because Beta introduced pathways or receptors with its construction work.

Beta, though, may also be excluded, as it effectively paid for the remediation when it sold the property at a discount to Gamma, reflecting the cost of the contamination (Test 2). It is likely that Test 3 would also exclude Beta.

Delta and Epsilon may have known of the contaminants during their due diligence, but will likely both be excluded for committing only lending and insuring activities for Gamma (Test 1).

Gamma is unlikely to be able to use an exclusion, either as a Class A or Class B appropriate person.

If, however, none of Alpha, Beta or Gamma is excluded, the enforcing authority should consult the Guidance on apportionment of liability. Between Alpha (allowing the entry of the substance) and Beta (permitting its continuation), it is arguable that Beta's liability should diminish as it arguably had less means and opportunity (it went bust) to deal with the contamination. Likewise, between Beta and Gamma (both knowing permitters), it is possible that Gamma may not receive a substantially reduced apportionment, as it is likely to have more means as a PLC.

Appendix 1 – Review Activity Answers   403

Chapter 9

1. Usual searches:
   (a) A search of the local land charges register on form LLC1.
   (b) Enquiries of the local authority on form CON29, paying particular attention to the replies to enquiries 1 (planning consents and refusals), 2 (are the access roads maintainable at public expense and/or subject to rights of way) and 3.13 (notices in relation to the remediation of contaminated land).
   (c) Optional enquiries of the local authority on form CON29O, all enquiries to be raised except those relating to parks and countryside, houses in multiple occupation, food safety notices and hedgerow notices.
   (d) Water and drainage enquiries.
   (e) Enquiries of the seller, paying particular attention as to by what right access is gained to the site and whether any maintenance contributions are required.
   (f) Chancel repairs liability search.
   (g) Survey (ground conditions only as site has no buildings).
2. Additional searches:
   (a) Inspection of the property.
   (b) Full environmental survey as the land is clearly in an industrial area.
   (c) Flooding report. Apart from the risk of surface water flooding, the name suggests proximity to river or coastal water.
   (d) Highways search, particularly as it is clear that parts of the site do not immediately abut the road.
   (e) Public index map search, to try to find out who owns the land between the site and the access road.
   (f) Note that a coal mining search is not indicated as Canvey Island is not listed in the *Coal Authority Gazette for England and Wales* as a place where a mining search is required.

Chapter 10

There is no simple right or wrong answer in these circumstances. However, suggested points you should consider are as follows:

- In considering the most appropriate form of procurement, you ought to consider the type of building and nature of the project, ie 'landmark', 'iconic' and the relevant importance of each of the different factors of time/cost/quality. The facts suggest that design is going to be an important consideration as 'an international architect' is being engaged.

- You should also consider the pros and cons of different forms of procurement, eg traditional, design and build, and even construction management. While the importance of design is usually associated with using traditional procurement, you could also consider the possibility of design and build with novation, which would allow the client to employ the architect and control the conceptual design for the building, prior to the architect (and other consultants) being novated to the contractor, to ensure single point responsibility for the client.

- You should also set out the consultancy appointments to be entered into, which should include the Principal Designer under both the CDM Regulations and the BSA 2022 (as the building must comply with health and safety legislation). In addition, a project manager is almost certainly required for a large development of this nature.

- You should set out details of those parties requiring collateral warranties/third party rights, ie the client (if design and build), R, G and H. Details of the warrantors providing the collateral warranties/third party rights, ie the different consultants and key sub-contractors (especially the specialist acoustic engineering sub-contractor) should also be set out. Note that warranties/third party rights may be given to G in respect of each floor it is letting (to enable G to assign the benefit of that warranty to H whilst retaining warranties for its other floors), rather than for the whole of its letting.

- Other forms of protection in the event of a defect arising may also be considered, eg defects liability insurance.

Chapter 11

1. (c)

    Value added tax is charged on any supply of goods or services made in the United Kingdom where it is a taxable supply made by a taxable person in the course or furtherance of a business carried on by him.

    In general terms, SDLT is levied on land transactions, CGT on the gain resulting from a disposal of an interest in land, and capital allowances are a form of tax relief that a buyer of commercial property may be entitled to claim on any fixed plant and machinery.

2. (a) and (d)

    Input tax is not paid when the supply is zero-rated or exempt.

3. (a), (b) and (d)

    In order to recover input tax, the business must make 'taxable' supplies, ie supplies that are standard or zero-rated, or where the option to tax has been exercised. A zero-rated supply is a taxable supply, albeit with VAT chargeable at the zero rate.

    When it makes a taxable supply, the business will charge output tax from which it will deduct input tax paid by it, so that it pays only the balance to HMRC.

4. The sale of the green field site to the developer and the grant of the retail lease are both exempt, subject to the option to tax. The payment to the building contractor and the freehold sale of the superstore (being a 'new' building) are both standard-rated.

5. True. The input tax can be recovered if the developer makes a taxable supply by opting to tax the rent due under the retail lease. Alternatively, the developer will be making a taxable supply when it sells the 'new' freehold superstore.

6. The grant and assignment of the lease are both exempt subject to the option to tax, the legal fees and fitting out costs are both standard-rated.

7. False. The insurance company tenant will *not* be able to recover the input tax as it makes only exempt supplies in the course of its business. The irrecoverable VAT will have to be borne as an overhead of the business.

Chapter 12

1. This is an 'old' lease granted prior to 1 January 1996. NUFC Ltd can claim against AFC Ltd, who remains liable to pay the rent throughout the entire term. NUFC Ltd can also claim the arrears from TFA Ltd, who is liable for breaches during its occupation. NUFC Ltd cannot claim the arrears from THS Ltd unless, on the assignment to TFA Ltd, THS Ltd was required to give a direct covenant to NUFC Ltd to perform the covenants in the lease.

2. This is a 'new' lease granted after 1 January 1996. NUFC Ltd can claim against TFA Ltd. NUFC Ltd can also claim against THS Ltd, but only if THS Ltd guaranteed the performance of TFA Ltd as its immediate assignee.

Chapter 13

1. The tenant's solicitor should have asked to have included a provision dealing with 'unacceptable variations' and 'acceptable variations'. 'Unacceptable variation' should have included any variation which would reduce the capacity of the demise or standard of the works. Sometimes the parties will agree a percentage of leeway in capacity (usually not more than 10% difference either way), with a provision for joint measurement of the premises before practical completion is certified. The tenant's solicitor should also have asked to have included a right to supervise the works so that the tenant or its surveyors could point out any 'unacceptable variations'. The tenant's solicitor should have argued for an express right to terminate the agreement if the floor area was less than any agreed tolerances (*Mears*).

2. The tenant's solicitor should have asked to have included provisions relating to:
   (a) a pre-completion inspection by the tenant's representative to identify major defects and snagging works;
   (b) the attendance of the tenant's representative at the final inspection of the works to make representations to the landlord's architect or to carry out a joint inspection for the purpose of issuing the certificate;
   (c) the tenant's ability to object to and delay the issue of the certificate of practical completion if in its opinion the works have not yet been satisfactorily completed.

   Note that the tenant may also have a remedy against the architect for improper issue of the certificate (see **10.4**).

Chapter 14

1. Yes. Under para 4 of Sch 6, if the building (defined as including the property) is damaged by an insured risk (defined as including explosion) then payment of the annual rent and service charge or a fair proportion of them depending on the nature and extent of the damage shall be suspended for a specified time.
2. Yes. Under clause 61.1(c) a notice given pursuant to the lease may be sent by fax.
3. Clause 1.11 states that an obligation on the tenant not to do something includes an obligation not to agree to or suffer that thing to be done and an obligation to use best endeavours to prevent that being done by another person.

Chapter 15

1. T is the original tenant of an 'old lease' governed by the old regime. T therefore remains liable throughout the term of the lease, even if it has assigned it on. T is consequently obliged to pay the rent if the definition of 'the Term' in the lease includes the period of any holding over. If it does not then T's liability ended on the expiry of the contractual term. If T is obliged to pay, T may be able to recover the sum from the assignee if it has an indemnity from the assignee. Under the old regime, an indemnity is implied into every assignment for value. Of course, if the assignee is in financial difficulty, it may not be worthwhile T's pursuing the assignee.

2. The lease is a 'new lease' governed by the new regime. L would not have been automatically released from the landlord's covenants when the reversion was sold on. There are two ways in which it may escape liability. First, if L served a notice on the tenant requesting a release before or within four weeks of the sale, and the tenant did not object to the request, L will have been released. Secondly, if no notice was served, L will need to check the drafting of the lease. If the covenants were expressed to be binding only while the reversion was vested in L then it will have no liability. If L had not served a notice requesting a release and the lease does not limit L's liability for the landlord's covenants, L will be liable. On the assumption that L obtained an indemnity

covenant from the buyer on the sale of L's reversionary interest, L may have a claim against the buyer. However, if the current tenant's assertion of insolvency is correct, the buyer is unlikely to be worth pursuing.

3. As the lease will be a new lease, all 'landlord covenants' will transmit automatically. This includes covenants not only in the lease but also in any 'collateral agreement'. Section 28 of the LT(C)A 1995 defines 'collateral agreement' to include agreements made before the date of the tenancy. Unless, therefore, the obligations in the agreement for lease are expressed to be personal to the previous landlord, they will constitute 'landlord covenants' and will bind your client.

Chapter 16

1. Yes, a demise of a whole building will prima facie include the roof and airspace above the building, even if this is not expressly mentioned in the demise. These are the facts of *Straudley Investments Ltd v Barpress Ltd* [1987] 1 EGLR 69. Counsel for the landlord argued that the upper surface of the roof and the airspace above the roof were not part of the premises demised to the tenant. However, the Court of Appeal held that the terms of the lease were 'crystal clear' that the roof did pass under the demise, and granted the tenant the mandatory injunction it sought.

2. Yes. These are the facts of *Davies v Yadegar* [1990] 1 EGLR 71. Counsel for the landlord sought to draw a distinction between a unitary building (where the demise would have included the airspace above the roof) and a building divided into flats (where it would not). The Court of Appeal rejected that distinction and said that the demise includes the airspace above the roof. Therefore, there was no trespass and the tenant was entitled to the declaration.

    The position would have been different if the flats had been divided horizontally and the landlord had retained the roof and roof space (see **Chapter 27** for the considerations which apply to a lease of part).

Chapter 17

1. Yes. These are the facts of *Meadfield Properties Ltd v Secretary of State for the Environment* [1995] 03 EG 128. The landlord argued that the term of 10 years started immediately after midnight on 24 June 1984, so that the lease could only be determined on 24 June 1994. However, it was held that a term stated to start on a certain date will start at the beginning of that day rather than at the end. Consequently, the term started on 24 June 1984 and terminated at the last moment of 23 June 1994, so the tenant's notice to determine the lease on 23 June 1994 was valid.

2. 13 January 1995. In fact, the tenant in the case of *Mannai Investment Co Ltd v Eagle Star Life Assurance Co Ltd* [1997] AC 749 specified 12 January 1995, but the House of Lords held that the notices were valid because it would have been obvious to the landlord, as a reasonable recipient with knowledge of the lease's terms and date of the third anniversary, that the tenant wanted to determine the leases on the third anniversary date but had made an immaterial error in wrongly describing the date as '12' rather than '13'.

3. No. These are the facts of *Prudential Assurance Co Ltd v Exel UK Ltd* [2009] EWHC 1350 (Ch), and the court held that the notice was invalid as it would not unambiguously have been understood to be an effective notice by a reasonable recipient. Because it was known that T2 was a tenant under the lease, there would have been real doubt as to whether the notice had been served on T2's behalf. Indeed, there was some evidence that the omission of T2 from the notice was not accidental.

4. No. These are the facts of *Bairstow Eves (Securities) Ltd v Ripley* [1992] 2 EGLR 47. The tenant argued that the condition precedent should be regarded as satisfied unless at the

term date there were breaches for which substantial damages would be recoverable. The judge at first instance agreed with the tenant, but the Court of Appeal rejected the tenant's argument and agreed with the landlord that the condition precedent – requiring performance and observance of the tenant's covenants until the term date – was not satisfied.

Chapter 18

1. All the monetary payments due under the lease have been reserved as rent under clause 2.3 because it makes it easier for the landlord in terms of the remedies it can exercise if the tenant fails to pay. First, under current law the landlord can exercise the remedy of distress for non-payment of rent (when the remedy of distress is replaced by CRAR (see **30.1**) this will no longer be the case). Also, no s 146 notice needs to be served on the tenant in relation to a failure to pay rent.

2. Where a sum is reserved as rent, a notice under s 17 of the LT(C)A 1995 must be served on any former tenant or guarantor of a former tenant before the landlord can recover rent from that person. The s 17 notice has to be served within six months of the default. Section 17 applies to service charge and other fixed charges anyway, but if acting for the landlord, it may be worth considering not reserving as rent 'all other sums due under this lease' which are not easily ascertainable.

3. The quarterly instalments are due on the usual quarter days which are 25 March, 24 June, 29 September and 25 December. These dates, originally linked to religious festivals, have been the traditional dates for rent payment going back many centuries. It is necessary to state that the payments must be equal because the quarters are not of equal length. It is necessary to state that the payments are in advance because if the lease is silent, the payments are due in arrears.

4. If the rent is paid automatically, there is a danger that a landlord who is aware of a breach of covenant will accept rent from a defaulting tenant and thereby waive the right to forfeit in respect of that breach (see **31.5.1**).

5. The first payment is not due until the Rent Commencement Date, which is six months after the grant of the lease. Thus the tenant has a six-month rent-free period. It may have been given this to allow time for fitting out the premises ready for occupation and/or as an effective discount on the rent to encourage it to take the lease.

6. The purpose of clause 4 is to stop the tenant making deductions from the rent when, for example, it is owed money by the landlord or feels it should not have to pay the amount demanded. For the landlord, the lease is an investment product, and it is important that the rent is 'clear', ie as fixed and certain as possible.

Chapter 19

1. If the lease is completed in the form set out at **Appendix 4**, then on review the valuer will assume the hypothetical lease term is 15 years. In reality, by the second review date, only five years of the lease will be left. The effect of this on the open market rent will depend on whether longer or shorter terms are favoured in the market at the date of review. It is therefore sensible to seek the advice of a rent review surveyor on the length of the hypothetical lease term before agreeing the draft lease. However, this advice will be speculative, since the surveyor cannot judge with any certainty what length of lease will be most valuable in the market at the date of review. In consequence, the rent review surveyor may advise having a hypothetical term that equals the unexpired residue of the term. This at least reflects the reality of the situation at the date of review and is therefore fair to both parties.

2. In the form received, the rent will be reviewed on an upwards only basis. The 2020 Code does not prohibit upwards only rent reviews. It suggests, however, that the heads of

terms (that record the terms the parties have agreed when the initial deal was struck) should be clear that this will be the basis of review. This allows the tenant to seek legal advice on the implications of an upwards only rent review at an early stage.

Chapter 20

1. If the premises are in disrepair at the beginning of the lease, a tenant may be concerned not to be obliged to repair the premises to a higher standard, so would include the provision for a schedule of condition (see **20.5**).

    A tenant might resist the inclusion of the words 'good' and 'condition', as potentially imposing a more onerous obligation on the tenant (see **20.4**).

2. The tenant may be alarmed by the prospect of having to repair inherent defects, and so an exclusion of liability for defects caused by design or construction faults should be included, at least for a specified period (see **10.5.2.4**).

    A tenant might resist the inclusion of the words 'good' and 'condition', as potentially imposing a more onerous obligation on the tenant (see **20.4**).

    A tenant might seek to exclude liability for historic contamination (see **20.3**).

Chapter 21

1. No, the tenant cannot sub-let only one floor. Clause 12(a) prohibits dealings with part unless permitted by clauses 13 to 16. Clause 14 deals with sub-lettings and you were told to assume that the lease did not contain wording in square brackets. Clause 14 would, therefore, only permit underletting of whole.

2. No, the landlord cannot always insist on the outgoing tenant entering into an AGA. Clause 13.2 provides that the landlord can only impose the conditions set out in clause 13.2(a) to (d) (which include the provision of an AGA) if reasonably required.

3. Under clause 13.3 the landlord can withhold its consent if, in the reasonable opinion of the landlord, the incoming tenant is not of sufficient financial strength. The landlord can also withhold its consent where annual rent, insurance rent or service charge are outstanding. Under clause 13.4 the landlord reserves the right to refuse consent in any other circumstances where it is reasonable to do so.

Chapter 22

1. The user covenant is contained in clause 24.1. It states that the tenant shall not use the property for any purpose other than the Permitted Use. 'Permitted Use' is defined at clause 1.1 as offices within Class E(g). This is therefore an absolute covenant – there is no mechanism provided in the lease for the use to be changed.

2. Clause 31.3(a) states that the tenant shall not apply for planning permission for the property without the landlord's consent. The proposed change of use will require planning permission, as it constitutes a material change of use and is not permitted by the GPDO. Consent is not to be unreasonably withheld if the change of use is permitted under the lease.

    So, an application will need to be made to the landlord for consent to make the planning application. Whether or not the landlord will need to act reasonably will depend on whether the proposed use is permitted under the user provisions. If it is, the landlord must act reasonably in considering the tenant's request to apply for planning permission. If it is not, the landlord can refuse consent to the tenant's request to apply for planning. If the tenant successfully obtains landlord's consent and planning permission, it will still need landlord's consent to implementing the planning permission (clause 31.3(b)).

Chapter 23

1. The approach to be taken would be to analyse and categorise the nature of the works, and then read and apply the relevant lease clause to the facts:
    (a) Affixing the aerial to the exterior of the building would involve external structural works. The tenant is not entitled to carry out these works as they are works outside the demised premises (clause 1.1 definition of 'Property').
    (b) The erection of internal partitioning is likely to be non-structural work (although any plans or specifications would need to be checked to ensure this). As non-structural alterations, under clause 20.3, the tenant would be able to carry out the works without the consent of the landlord, provided that before carrying them out the tenant provides details to the insurers and provides a specified number of plans and specifications within a specified time scale. The tenant must also make good any damage caused.
    (c) This is a structural alteration. Under clause 20.4, subject to there being no impact on the EPC rating, the tenant may carry out minor alterations that consist of making minor perforations in any boundary of the demised premises or in the structural elements of the building that are at the demised premises provided the alterations are reasonably required in connection with works permitted under clause 20, they do not adversely impact on the structural integrity of the building and the tenant obtains the landlord's consent (not to be unreasonably withheld or delayed). Further details would be required to determine whether the hanging of the art collection fell within clause 20.4.

2. The 2020 Code's recommendations are that in a lease of part of a building, a landlord may require its consent for internal non-structural alterations (such consent not to be unreasonably withheld or delayed) and may prohibit any alterations that adversely affect the character, value, structural stability, statutory compliance or energy efficiency performance of the building or its building services. It recommends that, except where heads of terms state that there will be a reinstatement specification or obligation on tenants to remove alterations, a lease should allow the tenant to leave alterations in place unless it is reasonable for the landlord to require their removal.

    Clause 20 allows the tenant to make internal alterations with landlord's consent not to be unreasonably withheld or delayed.

    Clause 23 provides for two options on reinstatement: (a) the tenant must reinstate if the landlord reasonably requires it and gives notice, or (b) the tenant must reinstate except if the landlord gives notice to the tenant not to.

    The first option is 2020 Code compliant but there is a risk to the landlord that it forgets to serve the notice and is left with fixtures and alterations it does not want. The second option is not strictly compliant but is likely to be the preferred option for the landlord.

Chapter 24

1. Yes. These are the facts of *Heronslea (Mill Hill) Ltd v Kwik-Fit Properties Ltd* [2009] EWHC 295. In that case it was held that the landlord was not permitted to enter the premises to carry out a 'survey' that involved drilling boreholes and taking samples because the proper interpretation of 'survey' under the lease meant a survey of, not under, the premises.

2. No. These are the facts of *Goldmile Properties Ltd v Lechouritis* [2003] EWCA Civ 49, in which it was held that the landlord's obligation to repair co-existed with the tenant's right to quiet enjoyment, so the landlord should take all reasonable precautions, not all possible precautions, before causing a disturbance by carrying out repairs. Moreover, the repair covenant was for the benefit of both parties, and it would have been apparent to both parties when they agreed to the lease that the tenant's enjoyment of the

premises might occasionally be less quiet by reason of the landlord having to carry out necessary repairs.

Chapter 25

1. Paragraph 4 of Sch 6 is a rent suspension clause. One of the circumstances in which it applies is if any 'Building Damage' occurs. This is defined as damage that makes the Property inaccessible or unfit for occupation. So the tenant needs to show that the Property cannot be accessed or cannot be used in consequence of the damage to the reception area. If it can show this then the Annual Rent and service charge will be suspended. The rent suspension will end once the Property is reusable or after three years (whichever event occurs first). Insurance Rent and other outgoings will continue to be payable by the tenant.

2. Paragraph 1.3 of Sch 6 states that the landlord's obligation to insure is subject to any excess imposed by the landlord's insurer. Paragraph 3.1(b) of Sch 6 states that the tenant will pay (on demand) either a fair proportion of any excess or an agreed percentage of the excess. Which of these options applies will have been agreed at the time the lease was negotiated. If the parties agreed the fair proportion option then the landlord and tenant will have to agree between them what 'fair proportion' of the £5,000 the tenant should pay.

3. If the reception area has not been reinstated after three years, the tenant can determine the lease with immediate effect under para 8.1 of Sch 6. If it does not, the rent suspension clause at para 4 will cease to operate and the tenant will have to pay Annual Rent again. As flood falls within the definition of Insured Risks in clause 1.1, the landlord should, if it was available, have obtained insurance against it in accordance with para 1.1 of Sch 6. The landlord should then, subject to obtaining any required planning permission, have repaired the damage (para 5 of Sch 6). The tenant may therefore have a claim for damages against the landlord for breach of para 5.

Chapter 26

Lease of ground floor – Tiempo

There is likely to be a breach of clause 24.3 of the lease, which entitles the landlord to exercise its right to forfeit in clause 52(1)(b).

As this is a breach (other than non-payment of rent), the landlord must serve a s 146 notice to give the tenant an opportunity to rectify the breach. The notice must specify the breach, requiring the breach to be remedied (if it is capable of being so) within a reasonable time and requiring the tenant to pay compensation (if the landlord so requires).

The breach is of a covenant against illegal user, which would generally be classed as an irremediable breach and so the landlord would not need to require it to be remedied in the notice. However, the breach is not by the tenant's direct use, so it is remediable so long as the tenant acts promptly on discovering the sub-tenant's use (*Glass v Kencakes Ltd* [1966] 1 QB 611; *Patel, Patel v K & J Restaurants Ltd, MP Catering Ltd* [2010] ECWA Civ 1211).

If there is any doubt as to whether it is remediable or not then the landlord should require it to be remedied 'if it is capable of being remedied'.

The landlord must give the tenant a reasonable time to remedy the breach and may then proceed to forfeit by peaceable re-entry or court proceedings. Successful forfeiture will bring both the lease and the sub-lease to an end.

The tenant (and sub-tenant) can apply for relief against forfeiture which may be granted where the breach has been remedied and is unlikely to re-occur and where to grant it would not damage the landlord's interests.

Where a breach is irremediable then the court is less likely to grant relief. If the illegal use causes a stigma to the premises, it is likely that relief would be refused, but if there is no stigma because of the area (on the facts it is run down but this may be countered by the fact there is a firm of solicitors in the area) then relief may be granted (eg in *Patel*).

Lease of first floor – Grantham

Grantham has breached clause 4 (payment of annual rent) on the relevant payment dates in the lease (the quarter days). Clause 52.1(a) entitles the landlord to forfeit the lease if the rent is in arrears for 21 days. On the facts the tenant has been in arrears for four weeks. The landlord need not serve a formal demand as this has been negated in clause 52.1(a). There is no need to serve a s 146 notice as the breach is of a covenant to pay rent.

The landlord is therefore entitled to forfeit the lease by peaceable re-entry or court proceedings. Successful forfeiture will bring the lease to an end. However, Grantham will be entitled to apply for relief against forfeiture. It is likely that relief would be granted if Grantham pays the arrears and the court is satisfied that the breach is unlikely to re-occur.

Chapter 27

1. Paragraph 2 of Part 4 of Sch 7 obliges the tenant to pay the service charge. Paragraph 11.10 of Part 4 of Sch 7 specifies that the landlord shall not charge any of the excluded service costs as part of the service charge. 'Excluded service costs' is defined in clause 1.1 as the costs set out in Part 3 of Sch 7. By virtue of para 1.8 of Part 3, the landlord will not be able to recover the cost of replacing the plant unless:
    (a) replacement is appropriate because the fabric, plant, equipment or materials are beyond economic repair at reasonable cost or beyond efficient or economic operation;
    (b) the cost of replacement is relatively low when compared to the greater cost anticipated if replacement is postponed materially; or
    (c) replacement is required by statute or the insurers of the Building.
2. Paragraph 2 of Part 4 of Sch 7 obliges the tenant to pay the service charge. 'Service charge' is defined in clause 1.1 as a proportion (to be determined in accordance with Part 4 of Sch 7) of the 'Service Costs'. The 'Service Costs' are defined in Part 2 of Sch 7 and include the costs of providing the 'Services'. The 'Services' are defined in Part 1 of Sch 7, and para 1.26 is a sweeper clause. The landlord can therefore recover the cost of providing a new service via the service charge if it is for the benefit of the tenants and occupiers of the building. However, the landlord must have acted reasonably and in accordance with the principles of good estate management in deciding to provide it.
3. Under para 8 of Part 4 of Sch 7, the tenant is also allowed a period of 4 months in which to raise enquiries in respect of the service charge statement. The landlord is obliged to respond promptly and efficiently to any such enquires and allow the tenant to see any relevant paperwork and documentation it requests. Further, under para 8.2, if the tenant requests, the landlord must agree to an independent audit of the service costs, although the tenant would bear the cost of such an audit. Paragraph 13 of Part 4 of Sch 7 provides for any dispute on service charge issues to be referred for third party determination under clause 63 of the Lease.

Chapter 28

1. These clauses should be included if the original lease under which the AGA is required is excluded from the LTA 1954. If the original lease is disclaimed following the insolvency of the assignee, the landlord has the right under clause 6.1 of the AGA to require the outgoing tenant to take a new lease. For the new lease to be excluded from the LTA 1954, the relevant notice must have been served prior to the tenant being committed to the new lease. This will be prior to the AGA being entered into. Clause 6.2.4 reflects an intention to exclude any new lease, and clause 6.3 recites the fact that the correct procedure has been followed. Of course, for these clauses to be effective, the correct procedure must in fact have been followed – see **32.1.6**.

2. Clause 13.1 states that the tenant must not assign the lease without the consent of the landlord. Whilst the case of *Next plc v National Farmers Union Mutual Insurance Co Ltd* [1997] EGCS 181 indicates that consent can be given effectively without a formal licence (and even if correspondence is marked 'subject to licence'), this is subject to the terms of the lease. Clause 62.1 of the lease stipulates that consent under the lease must be given by deed unless the circumstances in paragraphs (a) and (b) apply. So in this case, unless the landlord's letter expressly waives the requirement for a deed, a Licence to Assign in the form of a deed will be required.

Chapter 29

1. Clause 12 of the lease provides that the tenant shall not sub-let the property except in accordance with clause 14. Clause 14.1 allows sub-letting with the consent of the landlord and in accordance with the remainder of clause 14). Clause 14.3(b) provides that any sub-letting shall be at the open market rent of the premises at the date the property is sub-let. If, therefore, £80,000 is the current market rent payable for the premises then this would be permissible, subject to the landlord's consent and compliance with the remainder of clause 14.

2. Yes. Whilst clauses 14.2(d) and 14.3(a) provide for sub-leases to be excluded from the protection of the LTA 1954, this wording is in square brackets. Wording in square brackets is optional and the parties must decide at the time the lease is negotiated whether it should be included. The facts of question 1 tell you to assume the wording in square brackets was not included and therefore this requirement would not apply.

3. Clause 14.2(f) requires that any sub-letting contains a covenant by the sub-tenant to observe the tenant's covenants in the sub-lease. This should allow the head-landlord to sue the sub-tenant for a breach of its covenants in the sub-lease, even though there is no privity of contract or estate between the head-landlord and sub-tenant.

Chapter 31

	Sub-lease survives	Sub-lease does not survive
Surrender	X	
Merger	X	
Break exercised		X
Forfeiture		X

Chapter 32

1. The Act applies when there is a **t**enancy of premises **o**ccupied for **b**usiness purposes which has not been **e**xcluded from the protection of the Act. Many lawyers use 'TOBE' to help them remember this.

2. When the Act applies, the tenancy will not come to end on the contractual expiry date but will automatically continue until terminated in one of the ways permitted by the Act. Moreover, the tenant is entitled to apply to court for a new tenancy and the landlord may oppose this only on certain limited grounds.

3. A landlord can let premises without giving a business occupier security of tenure by the following means:
    - a tenancy at will (these are specifically excluded from the protection of the Act);
    - a licence rather than a lease (a licence is not a tenancy for the purposes of the Act);
    - a fixed-term tenancy not exceeding six months (these are specifically excluded from the protection of the Act);
    - a fixed-term tenancy of any length, but contracted out of the protection of the Act by following the prescribed procedure.

4. A secure tenant who wants to leave its business premises at the end of the contractual term can bring its tenancy to an end by moving out before the contractual expiry date (so it is no longer in occupation) or by serving a s 27(1) notice on the landlord not less than three months before the contractual expiry date.

5. A secure tenant who wants to stay in its business premises after the expiry of the contractual term can request a new lease by serving a s 26 request on its competent landlord and applying to court within the statutory period (which must be before the date specified in its request). If the competent landlord has already served a s 25 notice, the tenant can still request a new lease by making an application to court before the date specified in the s 25 notice.

6. A secure sub-tenant of business premises can identify its competent landlord for the purposes of the Act by serving a s 40 notice on its immediate landlord to see whether that landlord's tenancy has at least 14 months to run.

7. A landlord can obtain vacant possession of premises occupied by a secure tenant by:
    - serving a s 25 notice stating one or more of the statutory grounds for opposition and succeeding in proving at least one of those grounds at the subsequent court hearing;
    - giving counter-notice to the tenant's s 26 request stating that the landlord wishes to oppose the tenant's application to court for a new tenancy on one or more of the statutory grounds and succeeding in proving at least one of those grounds at the subsequent court hearing;
    - accepting a surrender of the lease, if the tenant is willing (or can be incentivised) to surrender;
    - forfeiting the lease, provided that the tenant is in default of its obligations under the lease and does not obtain relief from forfeiture.

8. A landlord can ensure that a secure tenant which wants to stay in the premises enters into a new lease, rather than continuing the old one, by serving a s 25 notice on the tenant stating that the landlord does not wish to oppose the tenant's application to court for a new tenancy and applying to court for the grant of a new lease. The landlord may also want to consider making an application to court for interim rent.

APPENDIX 2

Prescribed forms of notice under the Landlord and Tenant Act 1954

Form 1
LANDLORD'S NOTICE ENDING A BUSINESS TENANCY WITH PROPOSALS FOR A NEW ONE

Section 25 of the Landlord and Tenant Act 1954

IMPORTANT NOTE FOR THE LANDLORD: If you are willing to grant a new tenancy, complete this form and send it to the tenant. If you wish to oppose the grant of a new tenancy, use form 2 in Schedule 2 to the Landlord and Tenant Act 1954, Part 2 (Notices) Regulations 2004 or, where the tenant may be entitled to acquire the freehold or an extended lease, form 7 in that Schedule, instead of this form.

To: (*insert name and address of tenant*)

From: (*insert name and address of landlord*)

    1. This notice applies to the following property: (*insert address or description of property*).

    2. I am giving you notice under section 25 of the Landlord and Tenant Act 1954 to end your tenancy on (*insert date*).

    3. I am not opposed to granting you a new tenancy. You will find my proposals for the new tenancy, which we can discuss, in the Schedule to this notice.

    4. If we cannot agree on all the terms of a new tenancy, either you or I may ask the court to order the grant of a new tenancy and settle the terms on which we cannot agree.

    5. If you wish to ask the court for a new tenancy you must do so by the date in paragraph 2, unless we agree in writing to a later date and do so before the date in paragraph 2.

    6. Please send all correspondence about this notice to:

Name:

Address:

Signed: Date:

*[Landlord] *[On behalf of the landlord] *[Mortgagee] *[On behalf of the mortgagee]

*(*delete if inapplicable*)

SCHEDULE

LANDLORD'S PROPOSALS FOR A NEW TENANCY

(*attach or insert proposed terms of the new tenancy*)

IMPORTANT NOTE FOR THE TENANT

This Notice is intended to bring your tenancy to an end. If you want to continue to occupy your property after the date specified in paragraph 2 you must act quickly. If you are in any doubt about the action that you should take, get advice immediately from a solicitor or a surveyor.

The landlord is prepared to offer you a new tenancy and has set out proposed terms in the Schedule to this notice. You are not bound to accept these terms. They are merely suggestions as a basis for negotiation. In the event of disagreement, ultimately the court would settle the terms of the new tenancy.

It would be wise to seek professional advice before agreeing to accept the landlord's terms or putting forward your own proposals.

NOTES

The sections mentioned below are sections of the Landlord and Tenant Act 1954, as amended, (most recently by the **Regulatory Reform** (Business Tenancies) (England and Wales) Order 2003).

Ending of tenancy and grant of new tenancy

This notice is intended to bring your tenancy to an end on the date given in paragraph 2. Section 25 contains rules about the date that the landlord can put in that paragraph.

However, your landlord is prepared to offer you a new tenancy and has set out proposals for it in the Schedule to this notice (section 25(8)). You are not obliged to accept these proposals and may put forward your own.

If you and your landlord are unable to agree terms either one of you may apply to the court. You may not apply to the court if your landlord has already done so (section 24(2A)). If you wish to apply to the court you must do so by the date given in paragraph 2 of this notice, unless you and your landlord have agreed in writing to extend the deadline (sections 29A and 29B).

The court will settle the rent and other terms of the new tenancy or those on which you and your landlord cannot agree (sections 34 and 35). If you apply to the court your tenancy will continue after the date shown in paragraph 2 of this notice while your application is being considered (section 24).

If you are in any doubt about what action you should take, get advice immediately from a solicitor or a surveyor.

Negotiating a new tenancy

Most tenancies are renewed by negotiation. You and your landlord may agree in writing to extend the deadline for making an application to the court while negotiations continue. Either you or your landlord can ask the court to fix the rent that you will have to pay while the tenancy continues (sections 24A to 24D).

You may only stay in the property after the date in paragraph 2 (or if we have agreed in writing to a later date, that date), if by then you or the landlord has asked the court to order the grant of a new tenancy.

If you do try to agree a new tenancy with your landlord remember:

- that your present tenancy will not continue after the date in paragraph 2 of this notice without the agreement in writing mentioned above, unless you have applied to the court or your landlord has done so, and
- that you will lose your right to apply to the court once the deadline in paragraph 2 of this notice has passed, unless there is a written agreement extending the deadline.

Validity of this notice

The landlord who has given you this notice may not be the landlord to whom you pay your rent (sections 44 and 67). This does not necessarily mean that the notice is invalid.

If you have any doubts about whether this notice is valid, get advice immediately from a solicitor or a surveyor.

Form 2
LANDLORD'S NOTICE ENDING A BUSINESS TENANCY AND REASONS FOR REFUSING A NEW ONE

Section 25 of the Landlord and Tenant Act 1954

IMPORTANT NOTE FOR THE LANDLORD: If you wish to oppose the grant of a new tenancy on any of the grounds in section 30(1) of the Landlord and Tenant Act 1954, complete this form and send it to the tenant. If the tenant may be entitled to acquire the freehold or an extended lease, use form 7 in Schedule 2 to the Landlord and Tenant Act 1954, Part 2 (Notices) Regulations 2004 instead of this form.

To: (*insert name and address of tenant*)

From: (*insert name and address of landlord*)

1. This notice relates to the following property: (*insert address or description of property*)

2. I am giving you notice under section 25 of the Landlord and Tenant Act 1954 to end your tenancy on (*insert date*).

3. I am opposed to the grant of a new tenancy.

4. You may ask the court to order the grant of a new tenancy. If you do, I will oppose your application on the ground(s) mentioned in paragraph(s)* of section 30(1) of that Act. I draw your attention to the Table in the Notes below, which sets out all the grounds of opposition.

*(*insert letter(s) of the paragraph(s) relied on*)

5. If you wish to ask the court for a new tenancy you must do so before the date in paragraph 2 unless, before that date, we agree in writing to a later date.

6. I can ask the court to order the ending of your tenancy without granting you a new tenancy. I may have to pay you compensation if I have relied only on one or more of the grounds mentioned in paragraphs (e), (f) and (g) of section 30(1). If I ask the court to end your tenancy, you can challenge my application.

7. Please send all correspondence about this notice to:

Name:

Address:

Signed: Date:

*[Landlord] *[On behalf of the landlord] *[Mortgagee] *[On behalf of the mortgagee]

(*delete if inapplicable)

IMPORTANT NOTE FOR THE TENANT

This notice is intended to bring your tenancy to an end on the date specified in paragraph 2.

Your landlord is not prepared to offer you a new tenancy. You will not get a new tenancy unless you successfully challenge in court the grounds on which your landlord opposes the grant of a new tenancy.

If you want to continue to occupy your property you must act quickly. The notes below should help you to decide what action you now need to take. If you want to challenge your landlord's refusal to renew your tenancy, get advice immediately from a solicitor or a surveyor.

NOTES

The sections mentioned below are sections of the Landlord and Tenant Act 1954, as amended, (most recently by the **Regulatory Reform** (Business Tenancies) (England and Wales) Order 2003).

Ending of your tenancy

This notice is intended to bring your tenancy to an end on the date given in paragraph 2. Section 25 contains rules about the date that the landlord can put in that paragraph.

Your landlord is not prepared to offer you a new tenancy. If you want a new tenancy you will need to apply to the court for a new tenancy and successfully challenge the landlord's grounds for opposition (see the section below headed 'Landlord's opposition to new tenancy'). If you wish to apply to the court you must do so before the date given in paragraph 2 of this notice, unless you and your landlord have agreed in writing, before that date, to extend the deadline (sections 29A and 29B).

If you apply to the court your tenancy will continue after the date given in paragraph 2 of this notice while your application is being considered (section 24). You may not apply to the court if your landlord has already done so (section 24(2A) and (2B)).

You may only stay in the property after the date given in paragraph 2 (or such later date as you and the landlord may have agreed in writing) if before that date you have asked the court to order the grant of a new tenancy or the landlord has asked the court to order the ending of your tenancy without granting you a new one.

If you are in any doubt about what action you should take, get advice immediately from a solicitor or a surveyor.

Landlord's opposition to new tenancy

If you apply to the court for a new tenancy, the landlord can only oppose your application on one or more of the grounds set out in section 30(1). If you match the letter(s) specified in paragraph 4 of this notice with those in the first column in the Table below, you can see from the second column the ground(s) on which the landlord relies.

Paragraph of section 30(1)	Grounds
(a)	Where under the current tenancy the tenant has any obligations as respects the repair and maintenance of the holding, that the tenant ought not to be granted a new tenancy in view of the state of repair of the holding, being a state resulting from the tenant's failure to comply with the said obligations.
(b)	That the tenant ought not to be granted a new tenancy in view of his persistent delay in paying rent which has become due.

Paragraph of section 30(1)	Grounds
(c)	That the tenant ought not to be granted a new tenancy in view of other substantial breaches by him of his obligations under the current tenancy, or for any other reason connected with the tenant's use or management of the holding.
(d)	That the landlord has offered and is willing to provide or secure the provision of alternative accommodation for the tenant, that the terms on which the alternative accommodation is available are reasonable having regard to the terms of the current tenancy and to all other relevant circumstances, and that the accommodation and the time at which it will be available are suitable for the tenant's requirements (including the requirement to preserve goodwill) having regard to the nature and class of his business and to the situation and extent of, and facilities afforded by, the holding.
(e)	Where the current tenancy was created by the sub-letting of part only of the property comprised in a superior tenancy and the landlord is the owner of an interest in reversion expectant on the termination of that superior tenancy, that the aggregate of the rents reasonably obtainable on separate lettings of the holding and the remainder of that property would be substantially less than the rent reasonably obtainable on a letting of that property as a whole, that on the termination of the current tenancy the landlord requires possession of the holding for the purposes of letting or otherwise disposing of the said property as a whole, and that in view thereof the tenant ought not to be granted a new tenancy.
(f)	That on the termination of the current tenancy the landlord intends to demolish or reconstruct the premises comprised in the holding or a substantial part of those premises or to carry out substantial work of construction on the holding or part thereof and that he could not reasonably do so without obtaining possession of the holding.
(g)	On the termination of the current tenancy the landlord intends to occupy the holding for the purposes, or partly for the purposes, of a business to be carried on by him therein, or as his residence.

In this Table 'the holding' means the property that is the subject of the tenancy.

In ground (e), 'the landlord is the owner an interest in reversion expectant on the termination of that superior tenancy' means that the landlord has an interest in the property that will entitle him or her, when your immediate landlord's tenancy comes to an end, to exercise certain rights and obligations in relation to the property that are currently exercisable by your immediate landlord.

If the landlord relies on ground (f), the court can sometimes still grant a new tenancy if certain conditions set out in section 31A are met.

If the landlord relies on ground (g), please note that 'the landlord' may have an extended meaning. Where a landlord has a controlling interest in a company then either the landlord or the company can rely on ground (g). Where the landlord is a company and a person has a controlling interest in that company then either of them can rely on ground (g) (section 30(1A) and (1B)). A person has a 'controlling interest' in a company if, had he been a company, the other company would have been its subsidiary (section 46(2)).

The landlord must normally have been the landlord for at least five years before he or she can rely on ground (g).

Compensation

If you cannot get a new tenancy solely because one or more of grounds (e), (f) and (g) applies, you may be entitled to compensation under section 37. If your landlord has opposed your application on any of the other grounds as well as (e), (f) or (g) you can only get compensation if the court's refusal to grant a new tenancy is based solely on one or more of grounds (e), (f) and (g). In other words, you cannot get compensation under section 37 if the court has refused your tenancy on *other* grounds, even if one or more of grounds (e), (f) and (g) also applies.

If your landlord is an authority possessing compulsory purchase powers (such as a local authority) you may be entitled to a disturbance payment under Part 3 of the Land Compensation Act 1973.

Validity of this notice

The landlord who has given you this notice may not be the landlord to whom you pay your rent (sections 44 and 67). This does not necessarily mean that the notice is invalid.

If you have any doubts about whether this notice is valid, get advice immediately from a solicitor or a surveyor.

Form 3

TENANT'S REQUEST FOR A NEW BUSINESS TENANCY

Section 26 of the Landlord and Tenant Act 1954

To (*insert name and address of landlord*):

From (*insert name and address of tenant*):

1. This notice relates to the following property: (*insert address or description of property*).

2. I am giving you notice under section 26 of the Landlord and Tenant Act 1954 that I request a new tenancy beginning on (*insert date*).

3. You will find my proposals for the new tenancy, which we can discuss, in the Schedule to this notice.

4. If we cannot agree on all the terms of a new tenancy, either you or I may ask the court to order the grant of a new tenancy and settle the terms on which we cannot agree.

5. If you wish to ask the court to order the grant of a new tenancy you must do so by the date in paragraph 2, unless we agree in writing to a later date and do so before the date in paragraph 2.

6. You may oppose my request for a new tenancy only on one or more of the grounds set out in section 30(1) of the Landlord and Tenant Act 1954. You must tell me what your grounds are within two months of receiving this notice. If you miss this deadline you will not be able to oppose renewal of my tenancy and you will have to grant me a new tenancy.

7. Please send all correspondence about this notice to:

Name:

Address:

Signed: Date:

*[Tenant] *[On behalf of the tenant] (*delete whichever is inapplicable*)

SCHEDULE

TENANT'S PROPOSALS FOR A NEW TENANCY

(*attach or insert proposed terms of the new tenancy*)

IMPORTANT NOTE FOR THE LANDLORD

This notice requests a new tenancy of your property or part of it. If you want to oppose this request you must act quickly.

Read the notice and all the Notes carefully. It would be wise to seek professional advice.

NOTES

The sections mentioned below are sections of the Landlord and Tenant Act 1954, as amended, (most recently by the **Regulatory Reform** (Business Tenancies) (England and Wales) Order 2003).

Tenant's request for a new tenancy

This request by your tenant for a new tenancy brings his or her current tenancy to an end on the day before the date mentioned in paragraph 2 of this notice. Section 26 contains rules about the date that the tenant can put in paragraph 2 of this notice.

Your tenant can apply to the court under section 24 for a new tenancy. You may apply for a new tenancy yourself, under the same section, but not if your tenant has already served an application. Once an application has been made to the court, your tenant's current tenancy will continue after the date mentioned in paragraph 2 while the application is being considered by the court. Either you or your tenant can ask the court to fix the rent which your tenant will have to pay whilst the tenancy continues (sections 24A to 24D). The court will settle any terms of a new tenancy on which you and your tenant disagree (sections 34 and 35).

Time limit for opposing your tenant's request

If you do not want to grant a new tenancy, you have two months from the making of your tenant's request in which to notify him or her that you will oppose any application made to the court for a new tenancy. You do not need a special form to do this, but the notice must be in writing and it must state on which of the grounds set out in section 30(1) you will oppose the application. If you do not use the same wording of the ground (or grounds), as set out below, your notice may be ineffective.

If there has been any delay in your seeing this notice, you may need to act very quickly. If you are in any doubt about what action you should take, get advice immediately from a solicitor or a surveyor.

Grounds for opposing tenant's application

If you wish to oppose the renewal of the tenancy, you can do so by opposing your tenant's application to the court, or by making your own application to the court for termination without renewal. However, you can only oppose your tenant's application, or apply for termination without renewal, on one or more of the grounds set out in section 30(1). These grounds are set out below. You will only be able to rely on the ground(s) of opposition that you have mentioned in your written notice to your tenant.

In this Table 'the holding' means the property that is the subject of the tenancy.

Paragraph of section 30(1)	Grounds
(a)	Where under the current tenancy the tenant has any obligations as respects the repair and maintenance of the holding, that the tenant ought not to be granted a new tenancy in view of the state of repair of the holding, being a state resulting from the tenant's failure to comply with the said obligations.
(b)	That the tenant ought not to be granted a new tenancy in view of his persistent delay in paying rent which has become due.
(c)	That the tenant ought not to be granted a new tenancy in view of other substantial breaches by him of his obligations under the current tenancy, or for any other reason connected with the tenant's use or management of the holding.
(d)	That the landlord has offered and is willing to provide or secure the provision of alternative accommodation for the tenant, that the terms on which the alternative accommodation is available are reasonable having regard to the terms of the current tenancy and to all other relevant circumstances, and that the accommodation and the time at which it will be available are suitable for the tenant's requirements (including the requirement to preserve goodwill) having regard to the nature and class of his business and to the situation and extent of, and facilities afforded by, the holding.
(e)	Where the current tenancy was created by the sub-letting of part only of the property comprised in a superior tenancy and the landlord is the owner of an interest in reversion expectant on the termination of that superior tenancy, that the aggregate of the rents reasonably obtainable on separate lettings of the holding and the remainder of that property would be substantially less than the rent reasonably obtainable on a letting of that property as a whole, that on the termination of the current tenancy the landlord requires possession of the holding for the purposes of letting or otherwise disposing of the said property as a whole, and that in view thereof the tenant ought not to be granted a new tenancy.
(f)	That on the termination of the current tenancy the landlord intends to demolish or reconstruct the premises comprised in the holding or a substantial part of those premises or to carry out substantial work of construction on the holding or part thereof and that he could not reasonably do so without obtaining possession of the holding.
(g)	On the termination of the current tenancy the landlord intends to occupy the holding for the purposes, or partly for the purposes, of a business to be carried on by him therein, or as his residence.

Compensation

If your tenant cannot get a new tenancy solely because one or more of grounds (e), (f) and (g) applies, he or she is entitled to compensation under section 37. If you have opposed your tenant's application on any of the other grounds mentioned in section 30(1), as well as on one or more of grounds (e), (f) and (g), your tenant can only get compensation if the court's refusal to grant a new tenancy is based solely on ground (e), (f) or (g). In other words, your tenant cannot get compensation under section 37 if the court has refused the tenancy on other grounds, even if one or more of grounds (e), (f) and (g) also applies.

If you are an authority possessing compulsory purchase powers (such as a local authority), your tenant may be entitled to a disturbance payment under Part 3 of the Land Compensation Act 1973.

Negotiating a new tenancy

Most tenancies are renewed by negotiation and your tenant has set out proposals for the new tenancy in paragraph 3 of this notice. You are not obliged to accept these proposals and may put forward your own. You and your tenant may agree in writing to extend the deadline for making an application to the court while negotiations continue. Your tenant may not apply to the court for a new tenancy until two months have passed from the date of the making of the request contained in this notice, unless you have already given notice opposing your tenant's request as mentioned in paragraph 6 of this notice (section 29A(3)).

If you try to agree a new tenancy with your tenant, remember:

- that one of you will need to apply to the court before the date in paragraph 2 of this notice, unless you both agree to extend the period for making an application.
- that any such agreement must be in writing and must be made before the date in paragraph 2 (sections 29A and 29B).

Validity of this notice

The tenant who has given you this notice may not be the person from whom you receive rent (sections 44 and 67). This does not necessarily mean that the notice is invalid.

If you have any doubts about whether this notice is valid, get advice immediately from a solicitor or a surveyor.

Form 4

LANDLORD'S REQUEST FOR INFORMATION ABOUT OCCUPATION AND SUB-TENANCIES

Section 40(1) of the Landlord and Tenant Act 1954

To: (*insert name and address of tenant*)

From: (*insert name and address of landlord*)

1. This notice relates to the following premises: (*insert address or description of premises*)

2. I give you notice under section 40(1) of the Landlord and Tenant Act 1954 that I require you to provide information—

   (a) by answering questions (1) to (3) in the Table below;
   (b) if you answer 'yes' to question (2), by giving me the name and address of the person or persons concerned;
   (c) if you answer 'yes' to question (3), by also answering questions (4) to (10) in the Table below;
   (d) if you answer 'no' to question (8), by giving me the name and address of the sub-tenant; and
   (e) if you answer 'yes' to question (10), by giving me details of the notice or request.

TABLE

(1)	Do you occupy the premises or any part of them wholly or partly for the purposes of a business that is carried on by you?
(2)	To the best of your knowledge and belief, does any other person own an interest in reversion in any part of the premises?
(3)	Does your tenancy have effect subject to any sub-tenancy on which your tenancy is immediately expectant?
(4)	What premises are comprised in the sub-tenancy?
(5)	For what term does it have effect or, if it is terminable by notice, by what notice can it be terminated?
(6)	What is the rent payable under it?
(7)	Who is the sub-tenant?
(8)	To the best of your knowledge and belief, is the sub-tenant in occupation of the premises or of part of the premises comprised in the sub-tenancy?
(9)	Is an agreement in force excluding, in relation to the sub-tenancy, the provisions of sections 24 to 28 of the Landlord and Tenant Act 1954?
(10)	Has a notice been given under section 25 or 26(6) of that Act, or has a request been made under section 26 of that Act, in relation to the sub-tenancy?

3. You must give the information concerned in writing and within the period of one month beginning with the date of service of this notice.

4. Please send all correspondence about this notice to:

Name:

Address:

Signed: Date:

*[Landlord] *[on behalf of the landlord] *delete whichever is inapplicable

IMPORTANT NOTE FOR THE TENANT

This notice contains some words and phrases that you may not understand. The Notes below should help you, but it would be wise to seek professional advice, for example, from a solicitor or surveyor, before responding to this notice.

Once you have provided the information required by this notice, you must correct it if you realise that it is not, or is no longer, correct. This obligation lasts for six months from the date of service of this notice, but an exception is explained in the next paragraph. If you need to correct information already given, you must do so within one month of becoming aware that the information is incorrect.

The obligation will cease if, after transferring your tenancy, you notify the landlord of the transfer and of the name and address of the person to whom your tenancy has been transferred.

If you fail to comply with the requirements of this notice, or the obligation mentioned above, you may face civil proceedings for breach of the statutory duty that arises under section 40 of the Landlord and Tenant Act 1954. In any such proceedings a court may order you to comply with that duty and may make an award of damages.

NOTES

The sections mentioned below are sections of the Landlord and Tenant Act 1954, as amended, (most recently by the **Regulatory Reform** (Business Tenancies) (England and Wales) Order 2003).

Purpose of this notice

Your landlord (or, if he or she is a tenant, possibly your landlord's landlord) has sent you this notice in order to obtain information about your occupation and that of any sub-tenants. This information may be relevant to the taking of steps to end or renew your business tenancy.

Time limit for replying

You must provide the relevant information within one month of the date of service of this notice (section 40(1), (2) and (5)).

Information required

You do not have to give your answers on this form; you may use a separate sheet for this purpose. The notice requires you to provide, in writing, information in the form of answers to questions (1) to (3) in the Table above and, if you answer 'yes' to question (3), also to provide information in the form of answers to questions (4) to (10) in that Table. Depending on your answer to question (2) and, if applicable in your case, questions (8) and (10), you must also provide the information referred to in paragraph 2(b), (d) and (e) of this notice. Question (2) refers to a person who owns an interest in reversion. You should answer 'yes' to this question if you know or believe that there is a person who receives, or is entitled to receive, rent in respect of any part of the premises (other than the landlord who served this notice).

When you answer questions about sub-tenants, please bear in mind that, for these purposes, a sub-tenant includes a person retaining possession of premises by virtue of the Rent (Agriculture) Act 1976 or the Rent Act 1977 after the coming to an end of a sub-tenancy, and 'sub-tenancy' includes a right so to retain possession (section 40(8)).

You should keep a copy of your answers and of any other information provided in response to questions (2), (8) or (10) above.

If, once you have given this information, you realise that it is not, or is no longer, correct, you must give the correct information within one month of becoming aware that the previous information is incorrect. Subject to the next paragraph, your duty to correct any information that you have already given continues for six months after you receive this notice (section 40(5)). You should give the correct information to the landlord who gave you this notice unless you receive notice of the transfer of his or her interest, and of the name and address of the person to whom that interest has been transferred. In that case, the correct information must be given to that person.

If you transfer your tenancy within the period of six months referred to above, your duty to correct information already given will cease if you notify the landlord of the transfer and of the name and address of the person to whom your tenancy has been transferred.

If you do not provide the information requested, or fail to correct information that you have provided earlier, after realising that it is not, or is no longer, correct, proceedings may be taken against you and you may have to pay damages (section 40B).

If you are in any doubt about the information that you should give, get immediate advice from a solicitor or a surveyor.

Validity of this notice

The landlord who has given you this notice may not be the landlord to whom you pay your rent (sections 44 and 67). This does not necessarily mean that the notice is invalid.

If you have any doubts about whether this notice is valid, get advice immediately

Form 5

TENANT'S REQUEST FOR INFORMATION FROM LANDLORD OR LANDLORD'S MORTGAGEE ABOUT LANDLORD'S INTEREST

Section 40(3) of the Landlord and Tenant Act 1954

To: (insert name and address of reversioner or reversioner's mortgagee in possession [see the first note below])

From: (insert name and address of tenant)

1. This notice relates to the following premises: (insert address or description of premises)

2. In accordance with section 40(3) of the Landlord and Tenant Act 1954 I require you—

    (a) to state in writing whether you are the owner of the fee simple in respect of the premises or any part of them or the mortgagee in possession of such an owner,

    (b) if you answer 'no' to (a), to state in writing, to the best of your knowledge and belief—

     (i) the name and address of the person who is your or, as the case may be, your mortgagor's immediate landlord in respect of the premises or of the part in respect of which you are not, or your mortgagor is not, the owner in fee simple;

     (ii) for what term your or your mortgagor's tenancy has effect and what is the earliest date (if any) at which that tenancy is terminable by notice to quit given by the landlord; and

     (iii) whether a notice has been given under section 25 or 26(6) of the Landlord and Tenant Act 1954, or a request has been made under section 26 of that Act, in relation to the tenancy and, if so, details of the notice or request;

    (c) to state in writing, to the best of your knowledge and belief, the name and address of any other person who owns an interest in reversion in any part of the premises;

    (d) if you are a reversioner, to state in writing whether there is a mortgagee in possession of your interest in the premises; and

    (e) if you answer 'yes' to (d), to state in writing, to the best of your knowledge and belief, the name and address of the mortgagee in possession.

3. You must give the information concerned within the period of one month beginning with the date of service of this notice.

4. Please send all correspondence about this notice to:

Name:

Address:

Signed: Date:

*[Tenant] *[on behalf of the tenant] (*delete whichever is inapplicable)

IMPORTANT NOTE FOR LANDLORD OR LANDLORD'S MORTGAGEE

This notice contains some words and phrases that you may not understand. The Notes below should help you, but it would be wise to seek professional advice, for example, from a solicitor or surveyor, before responding to this notice.

Once you have provided the information required by this notice, you must correct it if you realise that it is not, or is no longer, correct. This obligation lasts for six months from the date of service of this notice, but an exception is explained in the next paragraph. If you need to correct information already given, you must do so within one month of becoming aware that the information is incorrect.

The obligation will cease if, after transferring your interest, you notify the tenant of the transfer and of the name and address of the person to whom your interest has been transferred.

If you fail to comply with the requirements of this notice, or the obligation mentioned above, you may face civil proceedings for breach of the statutory duty that arises under section 40 of the Landlord and Tenant Act 1954. In any such proceedings a court may order you to comply with that duty and may make an award of damages.

NOTES

The sections mentioned below are sections of the Landlord and Tenant Act 1954, as amended, (most recently by the Regulatory Reform (Business Tenancies) (England and Wales) Order 2003).

Terms used in this notice

The following terms, which are used in paragraph 2 of this notice, are defined in section 40(8):

> 'mortgagee in possession' includes a receiver appointed by the mortgagee or by the court who is in receipt of the rents and profits;
>
> 'reversioner' means any person having an interest in the premises, being an interest in reversion expectant (whether immediately or not) on the tenancy; and
>
> 'reversioner's mortgagee in possession' means any person being a mortgagee in possession in respect of such an interest.

Section 40(8) requires the reference in paragraph 2(b) of this notice to your mortgagor to be read in the light of the definition of 'mortgagee in possession'.

A mortgagee (mortgage lender) will be 'in possession' if the mortgagor (the person who owes money to the mortgage lender) has failed to comply with the terms of the mortgage. The mortgagee may then be entitled to receive rent that would normally have been paid to the mortgagor.

The term 'the owner of the fee simple' means the freehold owner.

The term 'reversioner' includes the freehold owner and any intermediate landlord as well as the immediate landlord of the tenant who served this notice.

Purpose of this notice and information required

This notice requires you to provide, in writing, the information requested in paragraph 2(a) and (c) of the notice and, if applicable in your case, in paragraph 2(b), (d) and (e). You do not need to use a special form for this purpose.

If, once you have given this information, you realise that it is not, or is no longer, correct, you must give the correct information within one month of becoming aware that the previous information is incorrect. Subject to the last paragraph in this section of these Notes, your duty to correct any information that you have already given continues for six months after you receive this notice (section 40(5)).

You should give the correct information to the tenant who gave you this notice unless you receive notice of the transfer of his or her interest, and of the name and address of the person to whom that interest has been transferred. In that case, the correct information must be given to that person.

If you do not provide the information requested, or fail to correct information that you have provided earlier, after realising that it is not, or is no longer, correct, proceedings may be taken against you and you may have to pay damages (section 40B).

If you are in any doubt as to the information that you should give, get advice immediately from a solicitor or a surveyor.

If you transfer your interest within the period of six months referred to above, your duty to correct information already given will cease if you notify the tenant of that transfer and of the name and address of the person to whom your interest has been transferred.

Time limit for replying

You must provide the relevant information within one month of the date of service of this notice (section 40(3), (4) and (5)).

Validity of this notice

The tenant who has given you this notice may not be the person from whom you receive rent (sections 44 and 67). This does not necessarily mean that the notice is invalid.

If you have any doubts about the validity of the notice, get advice immediately from a solicitor or a surveyor.

APPENDIX 3

Code for Leasing Business Premises, England and Wales 2020

Part 1 Introduction

This RICS professional statement is the result of pan-industry discussion between representatives of landlords, tenants and other trade bodies.

The objective is to improve the quality and fairness of negotiations on lease terms and to promote the issue of comprehensive heads of terms that should make the legal drafting process more efficient. The statement and code do not prescribe the outcome, but seek to make it fair and balanced by identifying the terms that are usually important and encouraging both parties to obtain advice from property professionals. This enables negotiations to proceed properly so that each party can make an informed decision about whether to proceed on the terms that they negotiate.

The lease code and the accompanying template heads of terms and checklist should be used as a reminder for negotiations before the grant of a new lease and at the time of any lease renewal. They should assist RICS members in ensuring that landlords, tenants and guarantors who they are advising have a clear understanding of the commitments that they are entering into.

The professional statement applies to lettings of premises in England and Wales to tenants who will carry on trade, professional or other business activities in them, but it does not apply to agricultural lettings, to premises that will only be used for housing plant and equipment (such as electricity transformers or telecoms) or advertising media (such as hoardings), to premises that are intended to be wholly sublet by the tenant, or to premises being let for a period of not more than six months.

RICS standards and regulatory requirements

You must comply with the **RICS Rules of Conduct for Firms**, the **RICS Rules of Conduct for Members** and the five RICS ethical principles, which say that you must:

- Act with integrity.
- Always provide a high standard of service.
- Act in a way that promotes trust in the profession.
- Treat others with respect.
- Take responsibility.

You must also comply with any related RICS professional statement – global and UK.

For ease of reference these include the current editions of:

- **RICS property measurement**, RICS professional statement.
- **UK commercial real estate agency**, RICS professional statement.
- **Conflicts of interest**, RICS professional statement.
- **Conflicts of interest – UK commercial property market investment agency**, RICS professional statement.
- **Service charges in commercial property**, RICS professional statement.

Further information can be found on the **RICS website**.

Effective date

This professional statement is effective from 1 September 2020.

Part 2 Mandatory requirements

1 Negotiations and heads of terms

1.1 Negotiations over the lease must be approached in a constructive and collaborative manner.

1.2 A party that is not represented by an RICS member or other property professional must be advised by the other party or its agents about the existence of this code and its supplemental guide and must be recommended to obtain professional advice.

1.3 The agreement as to the terms of the lease on a vacant possession letting must be recorded in written heads of terms, stating that it is 'subject to contract' and summarising, as a minimum, the position on each of the following aspects:

- the identity and extent of the premises (and requiring the landlord to arrange the provision of a Land Registry-compliant plan if the lease is registerable)
- any special rights to be granted, such as parking or telecom/data access
- the length of term and whether the Landlord and Tenant Act 1954 will apply or be excluded
- any options for renewal or break rights
- any requirements for a guarantor and/or rent deposit
- the amount of rent, frequency of payment and whether exclusive of business rates
- whether the landlord intends to charge VAT on the rent
- any rent-free period or other incentive
- any rent reviews including frequency and basis of review
- liability to pay service charge and/or insurance premiums
- rights to assign, sublet, charge or share the premises
- repairing obligations
- the initial permitted use and whether any changes of use will be allowed
- rights to make alterations and any particular reinstatement obligations
- any initial alterations or fit-out (if known) and
- any conditions of the letting, such as subject to surveys, board approvals or planning permission.

1.4 At a lease renewal or extension, the heads of terms must comply with the above except for any terms that are stated to follow the tenant's existing lease subject to reasonable modernisation.

1.5 Negotiations should aim to produce letting terms that achieve a fair balance between the parties having regard to their respective commercial interests.

The landlord, or its letting agent where relevant, will be responsible for ensuring that heads of terms complying with those provisions are in place before the initial draft lease is circulated.

The remaining provisions of the lease code indicate good practice. They include not only matters to be covered by the parties and their agents in the negotiations leading to the heads of terms but also matters to be considered by the parties and their legal advisers in the preparation and negotiation of the lease itself.

Part 3 Lease negotiation best practice

1 The premises

1.1 The identity and extent of the premises being let should be clearly defined, including which elements of the structure or fabric are included.

1.2 A lease plan should be supplied by the landlord for attaching to the lease if that is necessary or desirable for identifying the premises and in all cases where the duration of the lease will exceed seven years, where it should comply with the requirements for registration of the lease at the Land Registry.

1.3 The tenant should be granted all rights necessary for the intended use of the premises. This includes clear arrangements for any special rights such as parking or for electronic communication connections including, where necessary, the right to require the landlord to grant wayleaves for data cabling.

2 Length of term, renewal rights and break rights

2.1 The length of term should be clearly specified and any date when it is intended to start.

2.2 Where the landlord proposes that statutory rights of renewal under the Landlord and Tenant Act 1954 are to be excluded, the tenant should be notified at the outset in order to obtain early professional advice as to the implications.

2.3 Any break rights or options for renewal for either party should be clearly specified, including the dates (or range of dates) when a party can end the lease, the length of prior notice to be given and any pre-conditions for the break being effective.

2.4 Unless the parties have agreed stricter conditions in the heads of terms, a tenant's break should be conditional only on the tenant paying all basic rent payable on any date before the break date, giving up occupation and leaving no subtenants or other occupiers. Disputes about the state of the premises, or what has been left behind or removed, should be settled later, as at normal lease expiry.

2.5 Leases should require landlords to repay any rent, service charge or insurance paid by the tenant for any period after a break takes effect. Repayment of service charges may be deferred until the service charge accounts are finalised.

3 Rent deposits and guarantees

3.1 Details of any rent deposit should include the amount (including where required any sum to cover VAT), the time it will be held, whether it will be security for only the rent or all the tenant's obligations under the lease and the circumstances in which the deposit will be returned to the tenant with any accrued interest.

3.2 Rent deposit agreements should provide that landlords will hold rent deposit funds in bank accounts designated for holding only rent deposits and that any bank interest will accrue for the tenant.

3.3 Details of any guarantee should include whether it will cover only the rent or all the tenant's obligations under the lease, the amount of any cap on the guarantor's liability and the circumstances (if any) in which the guarantee will be released.

3.4 Landlords and managing agents should refer to the current edition of *Client money handling*, RICS professional statement for further information on the steps that should be taken when handling deposit funds.

4 Rent and rent review

4.1 The initial rent, the frequency of payment and whether the landlord intends to charge VAT on the rent should all be clearly stated, together with details of any rent-free period or other incentive. The initial rent may be a fixed sum or expressed as a certain sum per square foot or square metre, in which case the method of measurement should be stated.

4.2 Where the landlord proposes that rent is to be subject to review, the tenant should be notified of the proposed frequency and the method or formula of review at the outset in order to obtain early professional advice as to the implications.

4.3 Rent review clauses should be clearly expressed. Definitions of market rent should not result in a 'headline rent' unless that has been expressly agreed by the parties, such as where that is agreed in return for a financial inducement. Provisions for indexed rent reviews should not contain obscure formulae designed to produce a greater increase than is proportionate to the increase in the index over the appropriate period or outside any agreed caps or collars.

4.4 Leases should allow either party to start the rent review process and should not impose time limits intended to prevent a review or set a new rent through inaction by either party.

5 Service charges, insurance costs and other outgoings

5.1 The landlord should indicate the range of main services, if any, and provide proper estimates of service charges and insurance payments. The landlord should also disclose the types of other outgoings (such as business rates) that the tenant will incur under the lease. Landlords should disclose known irregular events that would have a significant impact on the amount of future service charges.

5.2 The parties should have regard to the current edition of **Service charges in commercial property**, RICS professional statement and, so far as practicable in the circumstances, service charge provisions in leases should be drafted in conformity with the core principles and mandatory provisions of that professional statement.

6 Assigning, subletting, charging and sharing

6.1 Leases should allow tenants to assign the whole of the premises with the landlord's consent, which is not to be unreasonably withheld or delayed. Landlords may set out circumstances in which consent can be refused, such as where there are arrears of rents, service charges or insurance premiums that are not the subject of a legitimate dispute, or where the assignee has insufficient financial strength, but all such circumstances should be reasonable and appropriate.

6.2 Leases should also provide that, if in each case the landlord reasonably requires, the assigning tenant is to provide an authorised guarantee agreement (AGA), any existing guarantor is to guarantee that the assigning tenant complies with the AGA, and/or the assignee is to procure a new guarantor and/or rent deposit.

6.3 Leases should allow corporate tenants to share the premises with other companies while they are in the same corporate group and do not create a subletting. In appropriate cases, leases of retail units may allow the tenant to grant licences of areas for use by concessions, such as where retail brands can be given stalls in a large store.

6.4 Leases should allow tenants to sublet the whole of the premises and may allow subleases of parts, if appropriate without security of tenure, and in each case with the landlord's consent, which is not to be unreasonably withheld or delayed and at rents not less than market rent. Subleases should be required to be on terms consistent with the tenant's own lease, except that subleases which are to be excluded from statutory renewal rights and subleases of only part of the premises may be granted on different terms where appropriate. Where the tenant operates through franchisees, the tenant may require the right to sublet the unit to a franchisee on particular terms.

6.5 Leases should allow tenants to grant a bank or other reputable lending institution a charge over the lease, without the landlord's consent needing to be obtained unless the lease is to contain step-in rights for chargees if the landlord intends to take action where the tenant defaults.

6.6 Paragraphs 6.1 to 6.5 do not prevent landlords from imposing stricter provisions where justified by the particular circumstances, such as lettings of short duration or on concessionary terms, or leases of retail units where the tenant's business or brand may affect the character or value of the centre or parade or the amount of any turnover rent. Any such provisions should be on reasonable terms, for example a provision for surrender of the lease instead of assigning should apply only if the landlord is willing to pay its market value.

7 Repairs

7.1 Leases should contain tenant's repairing obligations appropriate to the length of the term, the condition of the premises and the financial terms.

7.2 If the tenant's repairing obligations are to be limited to the initial condition of the premises, a schedule of condition will normally be required and the parties should agree which party is responsible for the cost of obtaining it.

7.3 Where the premises are or will be newly built, a tenant taking on direct or indirect responsibility for repairs should be given suitable protection against inherent construction defects for an appropriate period.

8 Change of use, alterations and fit-out

8.1 Leases should give landlords control over alterations and changes of use that are no more restrictive than are necessary to protect the value of the premises and any adjoining or neighbouring premises of the landlord, and this may differ between different types of property.

8.2 Where the landlord intends to prohibit certain changes of use or the making of certain alterations, or to require a licence from the landlord before they can take place, the tenant should be notified at the outset in order to obtain early professional advice as to the implications. This does not apply to normal provisions against changing the use outside the existing use class under planning law.

8.3 In a lease of an entire building, a landlord should not normally prohibit, or require its consent to be obtained for, internal non-structural alterations that do not adversely affect the character, value, structural stability, statutory compliance or energy efficiency performance of the building, but landlords will require the tenant to carry out such works properly and without causing damage or nuisance and to give written details to the landlord.

8.4 In a lease of a unit in a multi-let building, a landlord may require that its consent for internal non-structural alterations is to be obtained and that such consent is not to be unreasonably withheld or delayed, and may prohibit any alterations that adversely affect the character, value, structural stability, statutory compliance or energy efficiency performance of the building or its building services.

8.5 Except where the heads of terms state that there will be a reinstatement specification or an obligation on tenants to remove alterations, a lease should allow the tenant to leave alterations in place unless it is reasonable for the landlord to require their removal.

8.6 The tenant should be notified at the earliest practicable time if the landlord intends to impose any obligations for an initial fit-out that might involve material cost or to restrict how the tenant can fit-out or use the premises. The heads of terms and the lease should set out any agreed minimum requirements and any capital contributions.

9 Insurance and damage

9.1 Where the landlord will insure the property, leases should provide that the policy will be on normal market terms, that full terrorism cover will be provided if it is available at reasonable rates of premium, and that the landlord will insure with reputable insurers and provide details of the insurance to the tenant on reasonable request.

9.2 Leases should state that rent suspension will apply if the premises or any landlord's areas or services serving them are damaged by an insured risk or, other than where due to an act or default of the tenant, an uninsured risk. If the lease limits the period in which rent is to be suspended, either party should be allowed to terminate the lease if reinstatement of significant damage is not completed within that period.

9.3 Leases should state that if the whole or a substantial part of the premises or any landlord's areas or services serving them are so damaged by an uninsured risk as not to be capable of normal use by the tenant, either party should be allowed to terminate the lease unless the landlord agrees to rebuild at its own cost.

9.4 Landlords should pass on to tenants the benefit of discounted premiums and should disclose to tenants whether the landlord benefits from insurance commissions.

10 Management and operational performance

10.1 Leases of parts of multi-let buildings should contain provisions, appropriate to the characteristics of the building, that encourage cooperation between the parties to improve operational efficiencies in the building and to share available data.

10.2 Consideration should be given to including in the lease other 'green' provisions, see examples in the Better Building Partnership's Green Lease Toolkit.

11 Energy Performance Certificates (EPCs)

11.1 Leases should state which party is responsible for obtaining any EPC that may be needed during the lease term.

11.2 Landlords should be required to act reasonably if they reserve the right to choose which EPC assessor the tenant may use.

12 Landlord's title

12.1 Where the landlord's title (freehold or leasehold) is subject to enforceable covenants that prevent the landlord from complying with any provision of this Code, the landlord should act in conformity with those covenants but if challenged should explain the position to the tenant.

12.2 The landlord should be responsible for obtaining any consent for the grant of the lease required from a superior landlord, mortgagee or other third party.

Informatives

This code is supplemented by:

- template heads of terms and checklist (appendix A)
- supplemental guide for the parties, containing useful additional information (appendix B).

Appendix A Template heads of terms and checklist

This template should be read in conjunction with Parts 1 to 3 of this document.

This template heads of terms mirrors the sections of the lease code. These items are also listed in the checklist that follows the template heads of terms, which can be used as an alternative. The checklist is likely to be a useful tool when a landlord or their agent wishes to use their own form of heads of terms document, and the checklist should then be used to ensure that at the very least the minimum information required by the lease code is being captured.

The items marked with an asterisk (*) must be included within the heads of terms in order to comply with paragraph 1.3 of this professional statement's mandatory requirements.

A1 Template heads of terms

1 Initial information

1.1 Type of lease

Head lease ☐ sublease ☐

1.2 Landlord

Name of landlord: .... Registered no.: ....

Registered office: ....

Correspondence address: ....

Contact name: ....

email: ....

Telephone: ....

Mobile: ....

1.3 Tenant

Name of tenant: .... Registered no.: ....

Registered office: ....

Correspondence address: ....

Contact name: ....

email: ....

Telephone: ....

Mobile: ....

2 Premises and rights

2.1 Description of the premises *

Detailed description, measured area and Land Registry-compliant plan attached if available:

....

....

2.2 Rights *

Detailed description of any special rights being granted:

....

....

3 Length of term, renewal rights and break rights

3.1 Lease length and start date *

...... years and ...... months commencing on ....

3.2 Landlord and Tenant Act 1954 protection *

Lease to benefit from the protection of the 1954 Act: Yes ☐ No ☐

3.3 **Options to renew**

    (a) Any option to renew: Yes ☐ No ☐

    (b) Notice period for exercising ...... months

    (c) New term to be ...... years

    (d) New rent to be ....

    (e) Details of any other terms ....

3.4 **Break rights ***

    (a) Any break rights: Yes ☐ No ☐

    (b) Notice period for exercising ...... months

    (c) Single break date on .... or at any time after ....

    (d) Break operable by: landlord ☐ tenant ☐ both ☐

    (e) Details of any break clause payments or pre-conditions: ....

    ....

4 Rent deposits and guarantees

4.1 **Rent deposits ***

    (a) Rent deposit required: Yes ☐ No ☐

    (b) If yes, amount of rent deposit: £ ....

    (c) Period of time the deposit will be held: ....

    (d) Deposit held as security for: rent ☐ all obligations ☐

    (e) Details of circumstances in which the deposit will be returned: ....

    ....

4.2 **Guarantors ***

    (a) Guarantor required: Yes ☐ No ☐

    (b) If yes, identity of guarantor ....

    (c) Guarantor providing security for: rent ☐ all obligations ☐

    (d) Guarantor's liability capped: Yes ☐ No ☐

    (e) If yes, amount of cap: £............

    (f) Details of circumstances in which the guarantor will be released: ....

    ....

5 Rent and rent review

5.1 **Rent ***

    (a) If fixed amount: £ .... per annum exclusive of VAT

    (b) If based on area: £ .... per [sq ft] [sq m] [GIA] [NIA] [IPMS1] [IPMS2] [IPMS3A] [IPMS3B], per annum exclusive of VAT

    (c) Payment dates: monthly ☐ quarterly ☐

5.2 **VAT ***

    Will VAT be charged on the rent and other lease payments: Yes ☐ No ☐

5.3 **Rent-free period (and other incentives) ***

    (a) Rent-free period: Yes ☐ No ☐

    (b) If yes, length of rent-free period ...... months

    (c) Details of any other incentives: ....

    ....

5.4 **Rent reviews** *

    (a)   The lease includes rent review provisions: Yes ☐ No ☐

    (b)   Basis of review: ....

    (c)   Reviews every ...... years

6 Assigning, subletting, charging and sharing

6.1 **Requirements before alienation can take place** *

	Prohibited	Consent not to be unreasonably withheld	Permitted without consent
Assignment of whole	☐	☐	☐
Sublease whole	☐	☐	☐
Sublease part	☐	☐	☐
Sub-sublease	☐	☐	☐
Concession	☐	☐	☐
Group sharing	☐	☐	☐
Charging	☐	☐	☐

7 Services and service charge

7.1 **Is a service charge payable?** *

    (a)   Service charge payable: Yes ☐ No ☐

    (b)   Proportion ......% and estimate or actual annual charge £ ....

    (c)   Any special or unusual provisions: ....

            ....

8 Repairs

8.1 **Repairing responsibilities** *

    (a)   Tenant repairs: whole building ☐ interior only ☐ interior, windows and doors ☐

    (b)   Landlord repairs structure and common parts ☐

8.2 **Schedule of condition/hand back specification**

    (a)   Schedule of condition to be completed: Yes ☐ No ☐

    (b)   Responsibility for cost of preparing this: landlord ☐ tenant ☐

    (c)   Tenant to hand back the property to a pre-stated specification: Yes ☐ No ☐

9 Use and alterations

9.1 **Permitted use** *

    (a)   Permitted use: ....

    (b)   Limitations on changing use: ....

9.2 **Landlord's initial works** *

    (a)   Landlord to undertake works: Yes ☐ No ☐

    (b)   If yes, brief description of works: ....

            ....

    (c)   Long stop date by which works must be done: ....

    (d)   Specification agreed: Yes ☐ No ☐

    (e)   If no, to be provided by: landlord ☐ tenant ☐

    (f)   Tenant to make contribution: Yes ☐ No ☐

    (g)   If yes, amount or formula: ....

9.3 **Tenant's initial works** *

    (a) Tenant to undertake works: Yes ☐ No ☐

    (b) If yes, brief description of works: ....

....

    (c) Long stop date by which works must be done: ....

    (d) Specification agreed: Yes ☐ No ☐

    (e) If no, to be provided by: landlord ☐ tenant ☐

    (f) Landlord to make contribution: Yes ☐ No ☐

    (g) If yes, amount or formula : ....

9.4 **Alterations** *

    (a) Landlord's control over alterations:

	Prohibited	Consent not to be unreasonably withheld	Permitted without consent
External structural	☐	☐	☐
External non-structural	☐	☐	☐
Internal structural	☐	☐	☐
Internal non-structural	☐	☐	☐

    (b) Tenant to hand back the property to a pre-stated specification: Yes ☐ No ☐

    (c) Tenant to remove all alterations at lease end: Yes ☐ No ☐

    (d) Tenant to remove alterations at lease end if the landlord reasonably requires: Yes ☐ No ☐

10 Insurance

10.1 Liability for insurance costs

    (a) Landlord to insure the property: Yes ☐ No ☐

    (b) Premium to be recovered from tenant: Yes ☐ No ☐

    (b) Terrorism to be an insured risk: Yes ☐ No ☐

    (c) Mutual break clause for insured damage: Yes ☐ No ☐

    (d) Mutual break clause for uninsured damage: Yes ☐ No ☐

11 Other issues

11.1 Rates and utilities

    (a) Responsibility for paying business rates: landlord ☐ tenant ☐

11.2 Legal costs

(a) Each party to pay own legal costs including costs of approval for tenant's fit-out.

11.3 Conditions

Completion of the lease conditional on:

    (a) Board approvals ☐

    (b) Planning or other local authority consents ☐

    (c) References ☐

    (d) Superior landlord's consent ☐

    (e) Survey/schedule of condition ☐

    (f) Other ☐ please specify: ....

12 Contact details

12.1 Landlord's solicitor

Name of solicitor's practice: ....

Address: ....

Contact name: ....

email: ....

Telephone: ....

Mobile: ....

12.2 Tenant's solicitor

Name of solicitor's practice: ....

Address: ....

Contact name: ....

email: ....

Telephone: ....

Mobile: ....

12.3 Landlord's agent

Name of agent's practice: ....

Address: ....

Contact name: ....

email: ....

Telephone: ....

Mobile: ....

12.4 Tenant's agent

Name of agent's practice: ....

Address: ....

Contact name: ....

email: ....

Telephone: ....

Mobile: ....

No contract

These heads of terms are subject to contract.

A2 Checklist

As a minimum, written heads of terms should answer the following questions:

- ☐ What is the extent of the premises?
- ☐ Will a Land Registry-compliant plan be obtained by the landlord?
- ☐ Are any special rights being granted under the lease?
- ☐ What is the duration of the lease?
- ☐ When does the lease start?
- ☐ Will the lease be protected by the 1954 Act?
- ☐ Are there any options to renew or break rights?

- ☐ Will a rent deposit be required?
- ☐ Will a guarantor be required?
- ☐ How much is the annual rent?
- ☐ Is that rent exclusive of business rates?
- ☐ On which dates will the rent be payable?
- ☐ Will VAT be charged on the rent and other lease payments?
- ☐ Is there a rent-free period or any other incentives?
- ☐ What are the rent review dates and the basis for the reviews?
- ☐ Can the tenant assign, sublet, charge or share occupation?
- ☐ Will a service charge and/or insurance premiums be payable?
- ☐ Who has responsibility for repairing the premises?
- ☐ What is the initial permitted use of the premises and will any changes of use be allowed?
- ☐ What rights does the tenant have to make alterations to the premises?
- ☐ What initial works/fit out will the landlord be completing and when?
- ☐ What initial works/fit out will the tenant be completing and when?
- ☐ Is the letting subject to survey, board approval, planning or other conditions?

© RICS 2020

APPENDIX 4

Lease of part: office (complies with Lease Code 2020)

> The University of Law would like to thank Practical Law for authorising the use in this publication of the following document: Lease of part: office (complies with Lease Code 2020) (http://uk.practicallaw.thomsonreuters.com). For further information about Practical Law, visit http://uk.practicallaw.thomsonreuters.com/ or call 0345 600 9355. © Thomson Reuters 2025.

DATED

[UNDER] LEASE

relating to

[DESCRIPTION OF PROPERTY]

between

[LANDLORD]

and

[TENANT]

and

[GUARANTOR]

Contents

CLAUSE

1. Interpretation
2. Grant
3. Tenant covenants
4. Payment of Annual Rent
5. Payment method
6. No set-off
7. Interest
8. Rates and Taxes
9. Utilities
10. Common items
11. Costs
12. Prohibition of dealings
13. Assignments
14. Underletting
15. Sharing Occupation
16. Charging
17. Notification and registration of dealings
18. Repair
19. Decoration
20. Alterations
21. Signs
22. Window cleaning
23. Returning the Property to the Landlord
24. Use
25. [Use of Parking Space[s]
26. Regulations
27. [Loading and deliveries
28. Exercise of the Rights
29. Allow entry

30. Keyholders and emergency contact details
31. Compliance with laws
32. Energy Performance Certificates
33. Third Party Rights
34. [Superior Lease
35. [Registration of this lease
36. [Closure of registered title and] [Removal OR removal] of entries in relation to this lease and easements granted by this lease
37. Encroachments and preservation of rights
38. [Replacement guarantor
39. Procure guarantor consent
40. Indemnity
41. Landlord covenants
42. Quiet enjoyment
43. [Superior Lease obligations
44. Landlord's obligation to apportion Utility Costs
45. [Variation in extent of Building
46. Designation of alternative areas, routes and facilities
47. [Relocation of Tenant's Plant Area, Tenant's Plant and Tenant's Plant Service Media
48. Exercise of right of entry
49. Scaffolding
50. Landlord to enter wayleave
51. [Guarantor covenants
52. Re-entry and forfeiture
53. Section 62 of the LPA 1925, implied rights and existing appurtenant rights
54. [Exclusion of sections 24 to 28 of the LTA 1954
55. [Compensation on vacating
56. No restriction on Landlord's use
57. Limitation of liability
58. [[Landlord's OR Tenant's OR Mutual] option to break
59. [Variation of Tenant's Proportion
60. Breach of repair and maintenance obligation
61. Notices
62. Consents and approvals
63. Expert determination
64. [Disputes under the Superior Lease
65. VAT
66. Joint and several liability
67. Entire agreement
68. Contracts (Rights of Third Parties) Act 1999
69. Governing Law
70. Jurisdiction

SCHEDULE
Schedule 1 Property
Schedule 2 Rights
Schedule 3 Reservations
Schedule 4 Third Party Rights
Schedule 5 [Rent review
Part 1 Definitions
Part 2 Assumptions
Part 3 Disregards
Part 4 Hypothetical Lease
Part 5 Review of the Annual Rent
1. Review
2. Determination by the Expert
3. Late review of Annual Rent
4. Time not of the essence

	5.	Guarantor
Schedule 6		Insurance
	1.	Landlord's obligation to insure
	2.	Landlord to provide insurance details
	3.	Tenant's obligations
	4.	Rent suspension
	5.	Landlord's obligation to reinstate following damage or destruction by an Insured Risk
	6.	[Termination if reinstatement impossible or impractical following Building Damage by an Insured Risk
	7.	[Building Damage by an Uninsured Risk
	8.	Termination if reinstatement not complete by expiry of rent suspension
	9.	Consequences of termination
	10.	Landlord not obliged to reinstate other Lettable Units
	11.	[Tenant Damage
Schedule 7		Service Charge
Part 1		Services
Part 2		Service Costs
Part 3		Excluded Service Costs
Part 4		Service Charge administration and obligations
	1.	Provision of Services
	2.	Tenant's obligation to pay the Service Charge
	3.	Apportionments in Current Service Charge Year and Final Service Charge Year
	4.	Estimated Service Charge calculation
	5.	Tenant's obligation to pay the Estimated Service Charge
	6.	Unexpected Service Costs
	7.	Service Charge Statement
	8.	Tenant's inspection and audit
	9.	Balancing payments of Service Charge
	10.	Alternative annual accounting period
	11.	Landlord's general rights and obligations
	12.	Tenant's general obligations
	13.	Disputes
Part 5		[Service Charge Cap
	1.	Definitions
	2.	Service Charge Cap
	3.	Changes to the Index
Schedule 8		Guarantee and indemnity
	1.	Guarantee and indemnity
	2.	Guarantor's liability
	3.	Variations and supplemental documents
	4.	Guarantor to take a new lease or make payment
	5.	[Rent at the date of forfeiture or disclaimer
	6.	Payments in gross and restrictions on the Guarantor
	7.	Other securities

ANNEX

LR1. Date of lease

[DATE]

LR2. Title number(s)

LR2.1 Landlord's title number(s)

[INSERT TITLE NUMBER(S) OR LEAVE BLANK IF NONE]

LR2.2 Other title numbers

[TITLE NUMBER(S)] OR [None]

LR3. Parties to this lease

Landlord

[[COMPANY] NAME]

[[REGISTERED OFFICE] ADDRESS]
[COMPANY REGISTERED NUMBER]
Tenant
[[COMPANY] NAME]
[[REGISTERED OFFICE] ADDRESS]
[COMPANY REGISTERED NUMBER]
Other parties
[[None
OR
[[COMPANY] NAME]
[[REGISTERED OFFICE] ADDRESS]
[COMPANY REGISTERED NUMBER]
Guarantor]

LR4. **Property**

In the case of a conflict between this clause and the remainder of this lease then, for the purposes of registration, this clause shall prevail.

See the definition of "Property" in Clause 1.1 and Schedule 1 of this lease.

The Property is let without the benefit of any existing easements or other rights which are appurtenant to the whole or any part of the Building [except those set out in paragraph 2 of Schedule 2].

LR5. **Prescribed statements etc.**

LR5.1 Statements prescribed under rules 179 (dispositions in favour of a charity), 180 (dispositions by a charity) or 196 (leases under the Leasehold Reform, Housing and Urban Development Act 1993) of the Land Registration Rules 2003.

None.

LR5.2 This lease is made under, or by reference to, provisions of:

None.

LR6. **Term for which the Property is leased**

The term specified in the definition of "Contractual Term" in Clause 1.1 of this lease.

LR7. **Premium**

None.

LR8. **Prohibitions or restrictions on disposing of this lease**

This lease contains a provision that prohibits or restricts dispositions.

LR9. **Rights of acquisition etc.**

LR9.1 Tenant's contractual rights to renew this lease, to acquire the reversion or another lease of the Property, or to acquire an interest in other land

None.

LR9.2 Tenant's covenant to (or offer to) surrender this lease

None.

LR9.3 Landlord's contractual rights to acquire this lease

None.

LR10. **Restrictive covenants given in this lease by the Landlord in respect of land other than the Property**

None.

LR11. **Easements**

LR11.1 Easements granted by this lease for the benefit of the Property

The easements set out in paragraph 1 of Schedule 2 to this lease are granted by this lease for the benefit of the Property.

LR11.2 Easements granted or reserved by this lease over the Property for the benefit of other property

The easements set out in paragraph 1 of Schedule 3 to this lease are granted or reserved over the Property for the benefit of other property.

LR12. **Estate rentcharge burdening the Property**

None.

LR13. **Application for standard form of restriction**

[The Parties to this lease apply to enter the following standard form of restriction [against the title of the Property] [against title number [NUMBER]]]

OR

[None].

LR14. **Declaration of trust where there is more than one person comprising the Tenant**

[OMIT ALL INAPPLICABLE STATEMENTS]

[The Tenant is more than one person. They are to hold the Property on trust for themselves as joint tenants.]

[The Tenant is more than one person. They are to hold the Property on trust for themselves as tenants in common in equal shares.]

[The Tenant is more than one person. They are to hold the Property on trust [COMPLETE AS NECESSARY].]

This lease is dated [DATE]

PARTIES

(1) [FULL COMPANY NAME] incorporated and registered in England and Wales with company number [NUMBER] whose registered office is at [REGISTERED OFFICE ADDRESS] OR [INDIVIDUAL NAME] of [INDIVIDUAL ADDRESS] (**Landlord**)

(2) [FULL COMPANY NAME] incorporated and registered in England and Wales with company number [NUMBER] whose registered office is at [REGISTERED OFFICE ADDRESS] OR [INDIVIDUAL NAME] of [INDIVIDUAL ADDRESS] (**Tenant**)

(3) [[FULL COMPANY NAME] incorporated and registered in England and Wales with company number [NUMBER] whose registered office is at [REGISTERED OFFICE ADDRESS] OR [INDIVIDUAL NAME] of [INDIVIDUAL ADDRESS] (**Guarantor**)]

BACKGROUND

(A) The Landlord is [the freehold owner of the Building **OR** entitled to possession of the Building under the Superior Lease].

(B) The Property forms part of the Building.

(C) [The residue of the term of the Previous Lease is vested in the Tenant.]

(D) The Landlord has agreed to grant [a lease **OR** an underlease] of the Property to the Tenant on the terms set out in this lease.

(E) [The Guarantor has agreed to guarantee the Tenant's obligations under this lease.]

AGREED TERMS

1. Interpretation

The following definitions and rules of interpretation apply in this lease.

1.1 Definitions:

Annual Rent: [rent at [an initial OR a] rate of £[AMOUNT] per annum [and then as revised under Schedule 5] [and any interim rent determined under the LTA 1954]

OR

rent at a rate of:

(a) £[AMOUNT] per annum for the period from and including the Rent Commencement Date to and including [DATE]; [and]

(b) [£[AMOUNT] per annum for the period from and including [DATE] to and including [DATE]; [and]]

(c) £[AMOUNT] per annum for the period from and including [DATE];

[and then as revised under Schedule 5] [and any interim rent determined under the LTA 1954].]

Authorised Person: any:

(a) undertenant or person deriving title under the Tenant;

(b) workers, contractors or agents of the Tenant or of any person referred to in paragraph (a) of this definition; or

(c) person at the Property or the Building with the actual or implied authority of the Tenant or any person referred to in paragraph (a) or paragraph (b) of this definition.

[**Break Date:** [[DATE(S)] **OR** A date which is at least [NUMBER] [weeks **OR** months] after service of the Break Notice].]

[**Break Notice:** written notice to terminate this lease specifying the [relevant] Break Date and served in accordance with clause 58.1.]

Building: shall:

(a) be the land and buildings known as [BUILDING DESCRIPTION] [registered under title number[s] [TITLE NUMBER[S]]] and shown edged [COLOUR] on the Building Plan[.**OR** ;]

[(b) include any adjoining or neighbouring land and buildings that the Landlord from time to time designates as being part of the Building and any alteration, addition or improvement made from time to time to any land or building forming part of the Building at any time; and

(c) exclude any land and buildings that the Landlord from time to time designates as not being part of the Building.]

Building Damage: damage to or destruction of the Building (excluding the Excluded Insurance Items) that makes the Property wholly or partially unfit for occupation and use or inaccessible.

Building Plan: the plan annexed to this lease at ANNEX C and marked "Building Plan".

[Building Services Hours: the hours of [TIME] to [TIME] on Mondays to Fridays (inclusive) [, **OR** and] [the hours of [TIME] to [TIME] on Saturdays] [and the hours of [TIME] to [TIME] on Sundays] (except bank and public holidays) or such alternative hours as the Landlord (acting reasonably) may stipulate from time to time as the usual hours for the provision of the Services.]

[Car Park: the car park shown [coloured **OR** edged **OR** hatched] [COLOUR] on the Building Plan or such alternative area designated from time to time by the Landlord in accordance with paragraph 1.6(a) of Schedule 3.]

CDM Regulations: the Construction (Design and Management) Regulations 2015 (SI 2015/51).

Common Parts: subject to paragraph 1.6 of Schedule 3, the parts of the Building (excluding the Lettable Units and the Management Areas) that are provided from time to time by the Landlord for common use by the tenants and occupiers of the Building and their employees, agents, licensees and visitors.

Contractual Term: a term of years from and including [the date of this lease **OR** [DATE]] to and including [DATE].

Current Service Charge Year: the Service Charge Year current at the date of this lease.

Data Service Media: Service Media for the transmission of data to and from the Property.

Data Service Media Works: works to install, repair and maintain Data Service Media [(excluding Tenant's Plant Service Media)] to and from the Property through other parts of the Building.

Default Interest Rate: [4]% per annum above the Interest Rate.

Energy Assessor: an individual who is a member of an accreditation scheme approved by the Secretary of State in accordance with regulation 22 of the EPC Regulations.

Energy Performance Certificate: a certificate as defined in regulation 2(1) of the EPC Regulations.

EPC Regulations: Energy Performance of Buildings (England and Wales) Regulations 2012 (SI 2012/3118).

Estimated Service Charge: [subject to paragraph 2 of Part 5 of Schedule 7,]a sum assessed by the Landlord or its agents as being a fair and reasonable estimate of the Service Charge for a Service Charge Year.

Excluded Insurance Items: any:

(a) glass forming part of the Lettable Units; and

(b) tenant's fixtures that are installed by or for the tenant, any undertenant or occupier of any Lettable Unit and that form part of the Building.

Excluded Service Costs: the costs set out in Part 3 of Schedule 7.

Expert: an independent surveyor:

(a) who is a Member or Fellow of the Royal Institution of Chartered Surveyors;

(b) with [at least ten years' post-qualification experience including] relevant experience in the subject matter of the dispute; and

(c) appointed in accordance with clause 63.

Extended Hours: the hours of [TIME] to [TIME] on Mondays to Fridays (inclusive) [, **OR** and] [the hours of [TIME] to [TIME] on Saturdays] [and the hours of [TIME] to [TIME] on Sundays] (except bank and public holidays).]

Final Service Charge Year: the Service Charge Year during which the Termination Date occurs.

Group Company: a company within the same group of companies as the Tenant within the meaning of section 42(1) of the LTA 1954.

Insolvency Event: subject to clause 1.16 any one or more of the following:

(a) the taking of any step in connection with any voluntary arrangement or any other compromise or arrangement for the benefit of any creditors of the Tenant or any guarantor;

(b) the making of an application for an administration order or the making of an administration order in relation to the Tenant or any guarantor;

(c) the giving of any notice of intention to appoint an administrator, or the filing at court of the prescribed documents in connection with the appointment of an administrator, or the appointment of an administrator, in any case in relation to the Tenant or any guarantor;

(d) the appointment of a receiver or manager or an administrative receiver in relation to any property or income of the Tenant or any guarantor;

(e) the commencement of a voluntary winding-up in respect of the Tenant or any guarantor, except a winding-up for the purpose of amalgamation or reconstruction of a solvent company in respect of which a statutory declaration of solvency has been filed with the Registrar of Companies;

(f) the making of a petition for a winding-up order or a winding-up order in respect of the Tenant or any guarantor;

(g) the striking-off of the Tenant or any guarantor from the Register of Companies or the making of an application for the Tenant or any guarantor to be struck-off;

(h) the Tenant or any guarantor otherwise ceasing to exist (but excluding where the Tenant or any guarantor dies);

(i) the making of an application for a bankruptcy order, the presentation of a petition for a bankruptcy order or the making of a bankruptcy order against the Tenant or any guarantor; or

(j) [the making of an application to court for, or obtaining, a moratorium under Part A1 of the Insolvency Act 1986 in relation to the Tenant or any guarantor[. **OR** ; or]]

(k) [the levying of any execution or other such process on or against, or taking control or possession of, the whole or any part of the Tenant's assets.]

Insurance Rent: the aggregate in each year of:

(a) [a fair proportion **OR** the Tenant's Proportion] of the gross cost of any premiums that the Landlord expends (after any discount, but before any commission, is allowed or paid to the Landlord) and any fees and other expenses that the Landlord reasonably incurs in insuring the Building (excluding the Excluded Insurance Items) against the Insured Risks for the Reinstatement Cost in accordance with this lease;

(b) [a fair proportion **OR** the Tenant's Proportion] of the gross cost of the premium that the Landlord expends in effecting public liability insurance in relation to the Common Parts in accordance with this lease (after any discount, but before any commission, is allowed or paid to the Landlord);

(c) the gross cost of the premium (after any discount, but before any commission, is allowed or paid to the Landlord) for insurance for loss of Annual Rent from the Property for [three] years; and

(d) any IPT and any VAT (except to the extent that the Landlord obtains credit for such VAT as input tax or otherwise recovers it) payable on any sum set out in paragraphs (a) to (c) of this definition.

Insured Risks: (except to the extent any of the following are Uninsured Risks) fire, explosion, lightning, earthquake, tempest, storm, flood, bursting and overflowing of water tanks, apparatus or pipes, damage to underground water, oil or gas pipes or electricity wires or cables, impact by aircraft and aerial devices and articles dropped from them, impact by vehicles, terrorism, subsidence, ground slip, heave, riot, civil commotion, strikes, labour or political disturbances, malicious damage, and any other risks against which the Landlord decides to insure against from time to time and **Insured Risk** means any one of the Insured Risks.

Interest Rate: the base rate from time to time of [NAME OF BANK] or, if that base rate stops being used or published, a comparable commercial rate specified by the Landlord (acting reasonably).

IPT: Insurance Premium Tax chargeable under the Finance Act 1994 or any similar replacement or additional tax.

[Landlord's Neighbouring Property: the [freehold **OR** leasehold] property known as [DESCRIPTION OR ADDRESS OF THE LANDLORD'S NEIGHBOURING PROPERTY] [registered at HM Land Registry with title number[s] [TITLE NUMBER[S] IF REGISTERED]] [shown edged [COLOUR] on the Building Plan].]

Lettable Unit: any part of the Building which from time to time is, or is intended to be, let or occupied but excluding any Management Areas.

[Loading and Delivery Hours: the hours of [TIME] to [TIME] on Mondays to Fridays (inclusive) [, **OR** and] [the hours of [TIME] to [TIME] on Saturdays] [and the hours of [TIME] to [TIME] on Sundays] (except bank and public holidays) or such alternative hours as the Landlord (acting reasonably) may stipulate from time to time.]

LPA 1925: Law of Property Act 1925.

LTA 1927: Landlord and Tenant Act 1927.

LTA 1954: Landlord and Tenant Act 1954.

LTCA 1995: Landlord and Tenant (Covenants) Act 1995.

Management Area: any part of the Building retained by the Landlord for use by the Landlord or any other person (excluding providers of Utilities) in connection with the management of the Building and provision of the Services including any management office, storage area and plant room.

Management Fee: the costs specified in paragraph 1.2(a) of Part 2 Schedule 7.

[Management Fee Cap: [AMOUNT OF CAP].]

[Offices: the offices that form part of the Property and which are described in Schedule 1.]

[Parking Space[s]: any parking space[s] within the Car Park that the Tenant uses in exercise of the Right granted at Paragraph 1.4 of Schedule 2.]

Permitted Hours: the hours of [TIME] to [TIME] on Mondays to Fridays (inclusive) [, **OR** and] [the hours of [TIME] to [TIME] on Saturdays] [and the hours of [TIME] to [TIME] on Sundays] (except bank and public holidays) or such alternative hours as the Landlord (acting reasonably) may stipulate from time to time.

[Permitted Part: [that part of the Property shown [coloured **OR** edged **OR** hatched] [COLOUR] on the Property Plan **OR** the whole of any part of the Property situated on any one floor of the Building [[or on any two adjoining floors of the Building **OR** or on up to [NUMBER] adjoining floors of the Building]].]

[Permitted Storage Area Use: for the storage of goods and materials in connection with the Permitted Use of the Offices.]

Permitted Use: [[for the Offices only,] use as offices within Use Class [E(g) **OR** E(c)] of the Town and Country Planning (Use Classes) Order 1987 (as it applied in England at the date this lease was granted).

OR

[for the Offices only,] use as offices within Use Class [B1 **OR** A2] of the Town and Country Planning (Use Classes) Order 1987 (as it applied in Wales at the date this lease was granted).]

President: the president for the time being of the Royal Institution of Chartered Surveyors or a person acting on their behalf.

[Previous Lease: a lease of the Property dated [DATE] made between (1) [LANDLORD] [and] (2) [TENANT] [and (3) [GUARANTOR]] including any deed, licence, consent, approval or other instrument supplemental or collateral to it.]

[Previous Lease Alterations: any alterations undertaken by or for any tenant, undertenant or occupier during or in anticipation of the Previous Lease.]

Property: the property described in Schedule 1.

Property Plan: the plan annexed to this lease at ANNEX A and marked "Property Plan".

Rates and Taxes: all present and future rates, taxes and other impositions and outgoings payable in respect of the Property, its use and any works carried out there (or a fair proportion of the total cost of those rates, taxes, impositions and outgoings if any are payable in respect of the Property together with any other property) but excluding any taxes:

(a) payable by the Landlord in connection with any dealing with or disposition of the reversion to this lease [or the Landlord's interest in the Superior Lease]; [or]

(b) [payable by the Superior Landlord in connection with any dealing with, or disposition of, the reversion to the Superior Lease; or]

(c) (except VAT) payable by the Landlord by reason of the receipt of any of the Rents due under this lease [or by the Superior Landlord by reason of the receipt of any of the rents due under the Superior Lease].

Recommendation Report: a report as defined in regulation 4 of the EPC Regulations.

Reinstatement Cost: the full cost of reinstatement of the Building (excluding the Excluded Insurance Items) taking into account inflation of building costs and including any costs of demolition, site clearance, site protection, shoring up, professionals' and statutory fees and incidental expenses and any other work to the Building that may be required by law and any VAT on all such costs, fees and expenses.

[Relocation Notice: a notice given or to be given (as the case may be) by the Landlord under clause 47.1.]

[Relocation Works: the works to be carried out by the Tenant to relocate the Tenant's Plant Area, Tenant's Plant and Tenant's Plant Service Media to the alternative locations or routes designated in a Relocation Notice.]

Rents: the rents set out in clause 2.2.

Rent Commencement Date: [subject to paragraph 4.3 of Schedule 6,][[DATE] **OR** the date of this lease].

Rent Payment Dates: [25 March, 24 June, 29 September and 25 December **OR** the [first] day of every month **OR** [ALTERNATIVE RENT PAYMENT DATES]].

Reservations: the rights excepted and reserved in paragraph 1 of Schedule 3.

Retained Parts: all parts of the Building including (but not limited to) all of:

(a)   the structural parts of the Building;
(b)   the Service Media;
(c)   the Common Parts; and
(d)   the Management Areas;

but excluding the Lettable Units.

RICS Statement: the RICS professional statement known as "Service Charges in Commercial Property (first edition, September 2018)".

Rights: the rights granted in paragraph 1 of Schedule 2.

[Schedule of Condition: the photographic schedule annexed to this lease at ANNEX D and marked "Schedule of Condition".]

Services: the services set out in Part 1 of Schedule 7.

[Service Accesses and Facilities: the goods lifts and service accessways and corridors shown [coloured **OR** edged **OR** hatched] [COLOUR] on the Building Plan or such alternative areas or facilities designated from time to time by the Landlord in accordance with paragraph 1.6(a) of Schedule 3.]

[Service Area: the service area shown [coloured **OR** edged **OR** hatched] [COLOUR] on the Building Plan or such alternative area designated from time to time by the Landlord in accordance with paragraph 1.6(a) of Schedule 3.]

Service Charge: [subject to paragraph 2 of Part 5 of Schedule 7,]such proportion of the Service Costs as is allocated to the Property in accordance with paragraph 11.2 of Part 4 of Schedule 7.

Service Charge Account: any account set up and maintained by the Landlord or its agents into which the service charge payments by the occupiers of the Building are paid.

Service Charge Statement: a statement that sets out the Service Costs and Service Charge for a Service Charge Year and is certified by or on behalf of the Landlord.

Service Charge Year: subject to paragraph 10.2(a) of Part 4 of Schedule 7, the annual accounting period ending on [DATE] in each year or such alternative annual accounting period as the Landlord may from time to time stipulate and notify to the Tenant in accordance with paragraph 10.1 of Part 4 of Schedule 7.

Service Costs: the costs set out in Part 2 of Schedule 7.

Service Costs Budget: a budget that sets out the estimated Service Costs for a Service Charge Year.

Service Media: all media for the supply or removal of Utilities and all structures, machinery and equipment ancillary to those media.

[Service Road: the service road shown [coloured **OR** hatched] [COLOUR] on the Building Plan or such alternative service road designated from time to time by the Landlord in accordance with paragraph 1.6(a) of Schedule 3.]

Signs: signs, fascia, placards, boards, posters and advertisements.

Site Management Staff: those persons directly employed by the Landlord or its agents to deliver or administer delivery of the Services (whether employed full or part time and whether based at the Building or not).

[Storage Area: the storage area described in Schedule 1.]

Storage Area Plan: the plan annexed to this lease at ANNNEX B and marked "Storage Area Plan".]

[Superior Landlord: the landlord for the time being of the Superior Lease.]

[Superior Landlord's Covenants: the obligations in the Superior Lease to be observed by the Superior Landlord.]

[Superior Lease: the lease dated [DATE] and made between (1) [LANDLORD] [and] (2) [TENANT] [and (3) [GUARANTOR]] including any deed, licence, consent, approval or other instrument supplemental or collateral to it.]

[Tenant Damage: damage or destruction caused by an act or omission of the Tenant or any Authorised Person.]

[Tenant's Plant: any [air-conditioning plant][, **OR** and] [wireless network equipment][, **OR** and] [television aerials] [, **OR** and] [satellite dishes] [[and other] plant and equipment] reasonably required by the Tenant in connection with the Tenant's use of the [Property **OR** Offices] for the Permitted Use [but not exceeding [NUMBER] metres in height] and installed or to be installed (as the case may be) in the Tenant's Plant Area.]

[**Tenant's Plant Area:** that part of the roof of the Building shown [coloured **OR** edged **OR** hatched] [COLOUR] on the Tenant's Plant Area Plan or such other area on the roof of the Building designated from time to time by the Landlord in accordance with clause 47.]

[**Tenant's Plant Area Plan:** the plan annexed to this lease at ANNEX E and marked "Tenant's Plant Area Plan".]

[**Tenant's Plant Service Media:** the Service Media connecting the Tenant's Plant to the Property installed or to be installed (as the case may be) at the Building in accordance with the Landlord's consent given in accordance with clause 20.8 or along such alternative route or routes designated from time to time by the Landlord in accordance with clause 47.]

[**Tenant's Plant Works:** works to install, repair and maintain the Tenant's Plant and the Tenant's Plant Service Media but excluding any Relocation Works.]

[**Tenant's Proportion:** subject to cllause 59, [PERCENTAGE]%.]

Term: the Contractual Term [and any statutory continuation of this lease].

Termination Date: the date on which this lease determines (however it determines).

Third Party Rights: the matters set out in Schedule 4.

Transaction: is:

(a) any dealing with this lease or the devolution or transmission of or parting with possession of any interest in it;

(b) the creation of any underlease or other interest out of this lease or out of any interest or underlease derived from it and any dealing, devolution or transmission of or parting with possession of any such interest or underlease; or

(c) the making of any other arrangement for the occupation of the Property.

Uninsured Risks: any of the risks specified in the definition of Insured Risks where such risks are not insured against at the date of the relevant damage or destruction because of an exclusion imposed by the insurers or insurance for such risks was not available in the London insurance market on reasonable terms acceptable to the Landlord at the time the insurance policy was entered into and **Uninsured Risk** means any one of the Uninsured Risks.

Utilities: electricity, gas, water, sewage, air-conditioning, heating, energy, telecommunications, data and all other services and utilities.

Utility Costs: all costs in connection with the supply or removal of Utilities to or from the Property (or a fair proportion of the total cost if any of those costs are payable in respect of the Property together with any other property).

VAT: value added tax [or any equivalent tax] chargeable in the UK.

[**Written Replies:** [subject to clause 1.22,] are any:

(a) written replies that [DETAILS OF ORIGINAL LANDLORD'S LEGAL ADVISERS] has given before the date of [this lease **OR** [DETAILS OF AGREEMENT FOR LEASE]] to any written enquiries raised by [DETAILS OF ORIGINAL TENANT'S LEGAL ADVISERS]; or

(b) written replies to written enquiries given before the date of [this lease **OR** [DETAILS OF AGREEMENT FOR LEASE]] by [DETAILS OF ORIGINAL LANDLORD'S LEGAL ADVISERS].]

1.2 A reference to this **lease**, except a reference to the date of this lease or to the grant of this lease, is a reference to this deed and any deed, licence, consent, approval or other instrument supplemental or collateral to it.

1.3 The Schedules form part of this lease and shall have effect as if set out in full in the body of this lease. Any reference to **this lease** includes the Schedules.

1.4 Unless the context otherwise requires, references to clauses, Schedules and Annexes are to the clauses, Schedules and Annexes of this lease and references to paragraphs are to paragraphs of the relevant Schedule.

1.5 Clause, Schedule and paragraph headings shall not affect the interpretation of this lease.

1.6 A reference to:

(a) the **Landlord** includes a reference to the person entitled to the immediate reversion to this lease;

(b) the **Tenant** includes a reference to its successors in title and assigns; [and]

(c) [the **Superior Landlord** includes a reference to the person entitled to the immediate reversion to the Superior Lease; and]

(d) a **guarantor** [is a reference to any guarantor **OR** includes a reference to the Guarantor and to any other guarantor] of the tenant covenants of this lease including a guarantor who has entered into an authorised guarantee agreement.

1.7 [Subject to clause 64, in **OR** In] relation to any payment, a reference to a **fair proportion** is to a fair proportion of the total amount payable, determined conclusively (except as to questions of law) by the Landlord.

1.8 A **person** includes a natural person, corporate or unincorporated body (whether or not having separate legal personality).

1.9 Unless the context otherwise requires, a reference to one gender shall include a reference to the other genders.

1.10 The expressions **authorised guarantee agreement**, **landlord covenant** and **tenant covenant** each has the meaning given to it by the LTCA 1995.

1.11 Any obligation on the Tenant not to do something includes an obligation not to allow that thing to be done and an obligation to use best endeavours to prevent that thing being done by another person.

1.12 References to:
   (a) the consent of the Landlord are to the consent of the Landlord given in accordance with clause 62.1;
   (b) the approval of the Landlord are to the approval of the Landlord given in accordance with clause 62.3; and
   (c) any consent or approval required from the Landlord shall be construed as also including a requirement to obtain the consent or approval of:
       (i) [the Superior Landlord; and]
       (ii) any mortgagee of the Landlord [or of the Superior Landlord];
       where such consent or approval is required under the terms of [the Superior Lease or] the mortgage. Except that nothing in this lease shall be construed as imposing on [the Superior Landlord or] any mortgagee any obligation (or indicating that such an obligation is imposed on [the Superior Landlord or] any mortgagee by the terms of [the Superior Lease or] the mortgage) not unreasonably to refuse any such consent.

1.13 Unless the context otherwise requires, references to the **Building**, the **Common Parts**, [the **Landlord's Neighbouring Property**,] a **Lettable Unit**, the **Management Areas**, the **Property** and the **Retained Parts** are to the whole and any part of them or it.

1.14 [For the purposes of each of the following:
   (a) the easements set out in paragraph 1 of Schedule 2 that burden the Building (excluding the Property);
   (b) the easements set out in paragraph 1 of Schedule 3 that benefit the Building (excluding the Property);
   (c) the registration of the easements referred to in clause 1.14(a) and 1.14(b) and at HM Land Registry;
   (d) LR4; and
   (e) clause 53.2;
   the Building shall only include the land and buildings specified at paragraph (a) of the definition of the Building and no other land or buildings.]

1.15 Unless the context otherwise requires, any words following the terms **including, include, in particular, for example** or any similar expression shall be construed as illustrative and shall not limit the sense of the words, description, definition, phrase or term preceding those terms.

1.16 For the purposes of the definition of **Insolvency Event**:
   (a) where any of the paragraphs in that definition apply in relation to:
       (i) a partnership or limited partnership (as defined in the Partnership Act 1890 and the Limited Partnerships Act 1907 respectively), that paragraph shall apply subject to the modifications referred to in the Insolvent Partnerships Order 1994 (SI 1994/2421) (as amended); and
       (ii) a limited liability partnership (as defined in the Limited Liability Partnerships Act 2000), that paragraph shall apply subject to the modifications referred to in the Limited Liability Partnerships Regulations 2001 (SI 2001/1090) (as amended); and
   (b) **Insolvency Event** includes any analogous proceedings or events that may be taken pursuant to the legislation of another jurisdiction in relation to a tenant or guarantor incorporated or domiciled in such relevant jurisdiction.

1.17 [Except in relation to clause 1.22, a reference **OR** a reference] to **writing** or **written** [includes fax but not email **OR** excludes fax and email].

1.18 Unless the context otherwise requires, words in the singular shall include the plural and in the plural shall include the singular.

1.19 A **working day** is any day which is not a Saturday, a Sunday, a bank holiday or a public holiday in [England **OR** Wales].

1.20 Unless expressly provided otherwise in this lease, a reference to legislation or a legislative provision is a reference to it as amended, extended or re-enacted from time to time.

1.21 Unless expressly provided otherwise in this lease, a reference to legislation or a legislative provision shall include all subordinate legislation made from time to time under that legislation or legislative provision.

1.22 [For the purposes of the definition of **Written Replies, written replies** and **written enquiries** include:

(a) any pre-contract enquiries and any replies to pre-contract enquiries that are requested or given by reference to the [STANDARD FORM OF ENQUIRIES USED, INCLUDING EDITION] [and include enquiries or replies so requested or given by email]; and

(b) the following pre-contract enquiries and replies that were sent or received by email: [EMAILS].]

1.23 If any provision or part-provision of this lease is or becomes invalid, illegal or unenforceable, it shall be deemed deleted, but that shall not affect the validity and enforceability of the rest of this lease.

2. Grant

2.1 [At the request of the Guarantor, the **OR** The] Landlord lets the Property to the Tenant:

(a) for the Contractual Term;
(b) with [full **OR** limited] title guarantee;
(c) together with the Rights;
(d) excepting and reserving the Reservations; and
(e) subject to the Third Party Rights.

2.2 The grant in clause 2.1 is made with the Tenant paying as rent to the Landlord:

(a) the Annual Rent;
(b) the Insurance Rent;
(c) the sums payable by way of Service Charge pursuant to Schedule 7;
(d) all interest payable under this lease; [and]
(e) [all other sums payable under this lease; and]
(f) all VAT chargeable on the other rents set out in this clause 2.2.

3. Tenant covenants

The Tenant covenants with the Landlord to observe and perform the tenant covenants of this lease during the Term or (if earlier) until the Tenant is released from the tenant covenants of this lease by virtue of the LTCA 1995.

4. Payment of Annual Rent

The Tenant must pay the Annual Rent by [four **OR** twelve **OR** [OTHER]] equal instalments in advance on or before the Rent Payment Dates except that:

(a) the Tenant must pay the first instalment of Annual Rent on the Rent Commencement Date; and

(b) that first instalment of Annual Rent shall be [the proportion of the Annual Rent calculated on a daily basis **OR** £[AMOUNT]] for the period from and including the Rent Commencement Date to and including the day before the next Rent Payment Date after the Rent Commencement Date.

5. Payment method

The Tenant must pay the Annual Rent and all other sums payable under this lease by:

(a) electronic means from an account held in the name of the Tenant to the account notified from time to time to the Tenant by the Landlord; or

(b) any other method that the Landlord reasonably requires from time to time and notifies to the Tenant.

6. No set-off

The Tenant must pay the Annual Rent and all other sums payable under this lease in full without any set-off, counterclaim, deduction or withholding (other than any deduction or withholding of tax as required by law).

7. Interest

7.1 If any of the Annual Rent or any other sum payable by the Tenant under this lease has not been paid [by **OR** within [five] working days of] its due date (whether it has been formally demanded or not), the Tenant must pay to the Landlord interest on that amount at the Default Interest Rate (both before and after any judgment). Such interest shall accrue on that amount on a daily basis for the period beginning on and including its due date to and including the date of payment.

7.2 If the Landlord does not demand or accept any of the Annual Rent or any other sum due from, or tendered by, the Tenant under this lease because the Landlord reasonably believes that the Tenant is in breach of any of the tenant covenants of this lease, then, when that amount is accepted by the Landlord, the Tenant must pay to the Landlord interest on that amount at the Interest Rate. Such interest shall accrue on that amount on a daily basis for the period beginning on and including its due date to and including the date it is accepted by the Landlord.

8. Rates and Taxes

8.1 The Tenant must pay all Rates and Taxes.

8.2 The Tenant must not make any proposal to alter the rateable value of the Property (or that value as it appears on any draft rating list) without the approval of the Landlord.

8.3 [If, after the Termination Date, the Landlord loses rating relief (or any similar relief or exemption) because it has been allowed to the Tenant, the Tenant must pay the Landlord an amount equal to the relief or exemption that the Landlord has lost.]

9. Utilities

9.1 The Tenant must pay promptly all Utility Costs including any reasonable administrative charge made by the Landlord for calculating such costs, where they are not billed by the relevant utility supplier directly to the Tenant.

9.2 The Tenant must comply with all laws and with any recommendations of the relevant utility suppliers relating to the supply and removal of Utilities to or from the Property.

10. Common items

Except to the extent that such costs are included within the Service Costs, the Tenant must pay to the Landlord on demand [a fair proportion **OR** the Tenant's Proportion] of all costs payable by the Landlord for the maintenance, repair, lighting, cleaning and renewal of all Service Media, structures and other items not on or in the Building but used or capable of being used by the Building in common with other land.

11. Costs

The Tenant must pay on demand and on a full indemnity basis the costs and expenses of the Landlord [and those of the Superior Landlord] including any solicitors' or other professionals' costs and expenses (whether incurred before or after the Termination Date) in connection with, or in contemplation of, any of the following:

(a) the enforcement of the tenant covenants of this lease;

(b) serving any notice or taking any proceedings in connection with this lease under section 146 or 147 of the LPA 1925 (notwithstanding that forfeiture is avoided otherwise than by relief granted by the court);

(c) serving any notice in connection with this lease under section 17 of the LTCA 1995;

(d) the preparation and service of a schedule of dilapidations in connection with this lease [provided that that schedule is served on or before the date which is [six] months from and including the Termination Date]; or

(e) any consent or approval applied for under:

    (i) this lease, whether or not it is granted (unless the consent or approval is unreasonably withheld by the Landlord)[. **OR** ; or]

    (ii) [the Superior Lease where the consent of the Superior Landlord is required under this lease (whether or not it is granted).]

12. Prohibition of dealings

Except as expressly permitted by clause 13, clause 14, clause 15 and clause 16, the Tenant must not:

(a) assign, underlet, charge, part with or share possession or occupation of the whole or part of either this lease or the Property; [or]

(b) [assign, part with or share any of the benefits or burdens of this lease, or in any interest derived from it, whether by a virtual assignment or other similar arrangement; or]

(c) hold the lease on trust for any person (except pending registration of a dealing permitted by this lease at HM Land Registry or by reason only of joint legal ownership).

13. Assignments

13.1 The Tenant may assign the whole of this lease with the consent of the Landlord (such consent not to be unreasonably withheld).

13.2 The Landlord and the Tenant agree that, for the purposes of section 19(1A) of the LTA 1927, the Landlord may give its consent to an assignment subject to all or any of the following conditions (provided that, in the case of each condition, it is reasonably required by the Landlord):

(a) a condition that the assignor enters into an authorised guarantee agreement in favour of the Landlord which:

(i) is in respect of all the tenant covenants of this lease;
(ii) is in respect of the period beginning with the date the assignee becomes bound by those covenants and ending on the date when the assignee is released from those covenants by virtue of section 5 of the LTCA 1995;
(iii) imposes principal debtor liability on the assignor;
(iv) requires (in the event of a disclaimer of this lease) the assignor to enter into a new tenancy for a term equal to the unexpired residue of the Contractual Term; and
(v) is otherwise in a form reasonably required by the Landlord;

(b) a condition that any guarantor of the assignor (other than a guarantor under an authorised guarantee agreement) enters into a guarantee in favour of the Landlord in a form reasonably required by the Landlord guaranteeing that the assignor will comply with the terms of the authorised guarantee agreement;

(c) a condition that a person of standing acceptable to the Landlord (acting reasonably) enters into a guarantee and indemnity of the tenant covenants of this lease in favour of the Landlord in the form set out in Schedule 8 (but with such amendments and additions as the Landlord may reasonably require); or

(d) a condition that the assignee enters into a rent deposit deed with the Landlord in a form reasonably required by the Landlord and for an initial deposit of [six] months' Annual Rent (as at the date of assignment) plus a sum equivalent to VAT on that Annual Rent.

13.3 The Landlord and the Tenant agree that, for the purposes of section 19(1A) of the LTA 1927, the Landlord may refuse its consent to an assignment if any of the following circumstances exist (provided that, in the case of each circumstance that does exist, it is reasonable and appropriate to do so):

(a) any of the Annual Rent, Service Charge or Insurance Rent is outstanding (provided that such outstanding sum is not the subject of a legitimate dispute with the Landlord); or

(b) the assignee is not of sufficient financial strength to enable it to comply with the Tenant's covenants and conditions in this lease.

13.4 Nothing in this clause shall prevent the Landlord from giving consent subject to any other reasonable condition nor from refusing consent to an assignment in any other circumstance where it is reasonable to do so.

14. Underletting

14.1 The Tenant may underlet the whole of the Property [or [a **OR** the] Permitted Part] in accordance with this clause 14 and with the consent of the Landlord (such consent not to be unreasonably withheld) [provided that the Tenant may not underlet more than [NUMBER] Permitted Parts at any one time].

14.2 The Tenant must not underlet the whole of the Property [or [a **OR** the] Permitted Part]:

(a) together with any property, or any right over property, that is not included within this lease;
(b) at a fine or premium or reverse premium;
(c) allowing any rent-free period to the undertenant that exceeds the period that is then usual in the open market for such a letting;
(d) [unless [, in the case of an underlease of [a **OR** the] Permitted Part,] the underlease has first been validly excluded from the provisions of the LTA 1954 (where it is a lease that might otherwise acquire security of tenure under Part II of the LTA 1954);]
(e) for a term that will expire by effluxion of time later than [three] days before the Contractual Term expires by effluxion of time;
(f) unless the undertenant has first entered into a direct covenant in favour of the Landlord [and the Superior Landlord] to observe and perform the tenant covenants in the underlease and any document that is collateral or supplemental to it; and
(g) unless [(if reasonably required by the Landlord)] a person of standing acceptable to the Landlord (acting reasonably) enters into a guarantee and indemnity of the tenant covenants of the underlease in favour of the Landlord in the form set out in Schedule 8 (but with such amendments and additions as the Landlord may reasonably require).

14.3 Any underletting by the Tenant must include:

(a) [an agreement between the Tenant and the undertenant that the provisions of sections 24 to 28 of the LTA 1954 are excluded from applying to the tenancy created by the underlease (where the underlease was required to be contracted out under clause 14.2(d);]
(b) the reservation of a rent which is not less than the open market rental value of the Property [(or, if the underletting is of [a **OR** the] Permitted Part only, the open market rental value of that Permitted Part)]

at the date on which the Landlord grants consent to the underletting and which is payable at the same times as the Annual Rent under this lease (but this shall not prevent an underlease providing for a rent-free period of a length permitted by clause 14.2(c));

(c) [[provisions for the review of rent at the same dates and on the same basis as the review of the Annual Rent in this lease [unless the term of the underlease is five years or less] **OR** provisions for the review of rent every [five years] from the date of the commencement of the underlease term];]

(d) a covenant by the undertenant not to:
  (i) [(except on the same terms as this lease (but made applicable to the undertenant and the underlease))] assign or charge the whole or any part of the underlease;
  (ii) [(except on the same terms as this lease (but made applicable to the undertenant and the underlease))] part with, share possession or share occupation of the whole or any part of the underlet property;
  (iii) underlet the whole or part only of the underlet property;
  (iv) [assign, part with or share any of the benefits or burdens of the underlease, or any interest derived from it, whether by a virtual assignment or other similar arrangement;]
  (v) hold the underlease on trust for any person (except pending registration of a dealing permitted by the underlease at HM Land Registry or by reason only of joint legal ownership); and
  (vi) (if the underlease permits the undertenant to assign the underlease) assign the underlease without first procuring a direct covenant in favour of the Landlord [and the Superior Landlord] to observe and perform the covenants in the underlease and any document that is collateral or supplemental to it;

(e) a covenant by the undertenant to comply with the terms of this lease [(but, in relation to an underlease of [a **OR** the] Permitted Part, only insofar as they relate to the [relevant] Permitted Part and rights granted to the undertenant)] except the covenant to pay the Annual Rent [provided that the obligation in this clause 14.3(e) shall not apply to any underlease which has been validly excluded from the provisions of the LTA 1954 (or which would otherwise not acquire security of tenure under Part II of the LTA 1954)]; [and]

(f) [[provisions that allow the Tenant (as the landlord of the underlease) to terminate the underlease no later than [the [first] Break Date **OR** the earliest date on which this lease may be terminated pursuant to clause 58]; [and]]

(g) provisions requiring the consent or approval of the Landlord to be obtained in respect of any matter for which the consent or approval of the Landlord is required under this lease [and of the Superior Landlord in accordance with the terms of the Superior Lease][. **OR** ; and]

(h) [in the case of an underletting of [a **OR** the] Permitted Part, appropriate tenant covenants requiring the undertenant to pay an appropriate proportion of:
  (i) the amounts payable by way of Insurance Rent under this lease;
  (ii) the amounts payable by way of Service Charge under this lease; and
  (iii) the costs of repair, maintenance, decoration, renewal, lighting and cleaning of, and any other service, amenity or facility provided to, any land, buildings, service media, structures and other items that do not form part of the underlet property but that are used or capable of being used by the underlet property in common with other parts of the Property.]

14.4 Any underletting by the Tenant must otherwise be:
  (a) by deed;
  (b) consistent with the terms of this lease [(but, in the case of an underlease of [a **OR** the] Permitted Part, only insofar as they relate to the Permitted Part being underlet)] [except that any underlease which has been validly excluded from the provisions of the LTA 1954 (or which would otherwise not acquire security of tenure under Part II of the LTA 1954) may be granted on different terms to those in this lease]; and
  (c) in a form approved by the Landlord (such approval not to be unreasonably withheld).

14.5 In relation to any underlease granted by the Tenant, the Tenant must:
  (a) not vary the terms of the underlease nor accept a surrender of the underlease without the consent of the Landlord (such consent not to be unreasonably withheld);
  (b) enforce the tenant covenants in the underlease and not waive any of them nor allow any reduction in the rent payable under the underlease; and
  (c) ensure that in relation to any rent review the revised rent is not agreed without the approval of the Landlord (such approval not to be unreasonably withheld).

15. **Sharing Occupation**

    The Tenant may share occupation of the Property with a Group Company for as long as that company remains a Group Company and provided that no relationship of landlord and tenant is established by that arrangement.

16. **Charging**

    The Tenant may charge the whole of this lease to a bank or other reputable lending institution without the consent of the Landlord.

17. **Notification and registration of dealings**

17.1 Within [one month] of any Transaction, the Tenant must:

   (a) give the Landlord notice of the Transaction;

   (b) deliver [a certified copy **OR** [two] certified copies] of any document effecting or evidencing the Transaction to the Landlord (including [a certified copy **OR** [two] certified copies] of any notice served under, or any declaration or statutory declaration made in accordance with, section 38A of the LTA 1954 as part of such Transaction); and

   (c) pay the Landlord a registration fee of [£50] (plus VAT) [together with any charges payable to the Superior Landlord in accordance with the terms of the Superior Lease].

17.2 In respect of every Transaction that is registrable at HM Land Registry, the Tenant must:

   (a) apply to register a Transaction promptly following completion of that Transaction;

   (b) respond promptly and properly to any requisitions raised by HM Land Registry in connection with an application to register a Transaction; and

   (c) send the Landlord official copies of its title (and where applicable of the undertenant's title) within [one month] of completion of the registration.

   For the purpose of clause 17.2, any obligation on the Tenant to do something includes an obligation to procure that the thing is done.

17.3 If requested by the Landlord, the Tenant must promptly supply the Landlord with full details of the occupiers of the Property and the terms on which they occupy it.

18. **Repair**

18.1 The Tenant must:

   (a) subject to [clause 18.2 and clause 18.3, keep the Property[, **OR** and] the Data Service Media [, the Tenant's Plant and the Tenant's Plant Service Media] in good [and substantial] repair and condition [which shall include having regard to the nature and condition of the Property at the date on which the Previous Lease was granted];

   (b) [ensure that any Service Media forming part of the Property[, **OR** and] the Data Service Media [, the Tenant's Plant and the Tenant's Plant Service Media] is kept in good working order;]

   (c) keep the Property clean, tidy and clear of rubbish; and

   (d) replace as soon as possible with glass of similar appearance and of similar or better quality any glass forming part of the Property that becomes cracked or broken.

18.2 [The Tenant's obligations under clause 18.1(a) shall not require the Tenant to put the Property into any better state of repair or condition than it was in at the date of this lease as evidenced by the Schedule of Condition.]

18.3 The Tenant shall not be liable to repair the Property (excluding any Excluded Insurance Items forming part of the Property) to the extent that any disrepair has been caused by:

   (a) an Insured Risk unless and to the extent that:

      (i) the policy of insurance of the Property has been vitiated or any insurance proceeds withheld in consequence of any act or omission of the Tenant or any Authorised Person (except where the Tenant has paid an amount equal to any insurance money that the insurers refuse to pay in accordance with paragraph 3.2(f) of Schedule 6); or

      (ii) the insurance cover in relation to that disrepair is limited as referred to in paragraph 1.3 of Schedule 6 [. **OR** ; or]

   (b) [Building Damage by an Uninsured Risk unless such Building Damage is Tenant Damage.]

19. **Decoration**

19.1 The Tenant must:

   (a) decorate the [Property **OR** Offices] as often as is reasonably necessary and also in the last three months before the Termination Date;

(b) carry out all decoration (including all appropriate preparatory work) in a good and proper manner using good quality materials that are appropriate to the [Property **OR** Offices] and the Permitted Use; and

(c) carry out the decoration required in the last three months before the Termination Date to the reasonable satisfaction of the Landlord and using materials, designs and colours approved by the Landlord (acting reasonably).

19.2 [Within the three months before the Termination Date, the Tenant must replace the floor coverings at the [Property **OR** Offices] with new floor coverings of good quality and appropriate to the [Property **OR** Offices] and the Permitted Use.]

20. Alterations

20.1 Except as permitted by this clause 20, the Tenant must not make any:

(a) alteration or addition to the Property; or

(b) opening in any boundary of the Property.

20.2 Any alterations permitted by this clause are subject to clause 20.10.

20.3 The Tenant may make internal non-structural alterations to the Property with the consent of the Landlord (such consent not to be unreasonably withheld or delayed).

20.4 [The Tenant may install or remove non-structural demountable partitioning at the Property without the consent of the Landlord provided that the Tenant must:

(a) not carry out any such works until it has:

(i) provided details of the works to the insurers of the Property; and

(ii) at least [NUMBER] working days before commencing the works, given the Landlord [NUMBER] copies of the plans and specification for the works; and

(b) make good any damage to the Building caused by the carrying out of those work.]

20.5 The Tenant may carry out minor alterations that consist of making minor perforations in any boundary of the Property or in the structural elements of the Building that are at the Property provided that:

(a) those alterations are reasonably required in connection with any works permitted under this clause 20;

(b) those alterations do not adversely impact on the structural integrity of the Building; and

(c) the Tenant obtains the consent of the Landlord (such consent not to be unreasonably withheld or delayed).

20.6 With the consent of the Landlord (such consent not to be unreasonably withheld or delayed), the Tenant may:

(a) install any Service Media at the Property; or

(b) alter the route of any Service Media at the Property.

20.7 The Tenant may carry out Data Service Media Works with the consent of the Landlord (such consent not to be unreasonably withheld or delayed).

20.8 [The Tenant may carry out Tenant's Plant Works with the consent of the Landlord (such consent not to be unreasonably withheld or delayed).]

20.9 [Following receipt of a Relocation Notice, the Tenant must carry out and complete the relevant Relocation Works in accordance with the terms of that Relocation Notice.]

20.10 The Tenant must not carry out any alteration to the Property[, **OR** or] the Data Service Media [or the Tenant's Plant and Tenant's Plant Service Media] which would [, or may reasonably be expected to,] have an adverse effect on the asset rating in any Energy Performance Certificate for the Property or the Building.

21. Signs

The Tenant must not attach any Signs inside the Property that are visible from the Common Parts or outside the Building.

22. Window cleaning

As often as reasonably necessary, the Tenant must clean the internal surfaces of any:

(a) windows; and

(b) other glass;

at the Property (whether or not such windows and other glass form part of the Property).

23. Returning the Property to the Landlord

The Tenant must return the Property to the Landlord on the Termination Date with vacant possession and in the repair and condition required by this lease.

23.2 [If the Landlord reasonably so requires and gives the Tenant notice no later than [two] months before the Termination Date, then **OR** Subject to clause 23.3], the Tenant must by the Termination Date:

(a) remove:
  (i) any tenant's fixtures from the Property;
  (ii) any alterations to the Property undertaken by or for any tenant, undertenant or occupier during or in anticipation of this lease[, OR and] any Data Service Media[[, OR and] any Previous Lease Alterations] [and any Tenant's Plant and Tenant's Plant Service Media]; and
  (iii) any Signs erected by the Tenant at the Building; and
(b) make good any damage caused to the Building by the removal of those items and alterations.

23.3 [If the Landlord gives notice to the Tenant no later than [two] months before the Termination Date specifying which of the tenant's fixtures, alterations and other matters set out in clause 23.2(a)(i) and clause 23.2(a)(ii) shall not be removed pursuant to clause 23.2, the Tenant must not remove the specified tenant's fixtures, alterations or other matters pursuant to that clause.]

23.4 On or before the Termination Date, the Tenant must remove from the Property all chattels belonging to or used by it.

23.5 The Tenant:
(a) irrevocably appoints the Landlord to be the Tenant's agent to store or dispose of any chattels or items fixed to the Building by the Tenant and left by the Tenant for more than ten working days after the Termination Date; and
(b) must indemnify the Landlord in respect of any claim made by a third party in relation to that storage or disposal.

The Landlord shall not be liable to the Tenant by reason of that storage or disposal.

24. Use

24.1 The Tenant must not use the [Property OR Offices] for any purpose other than the Permitted Use [and the Storage Area for any purpose other than the Permitted Storage Area Use].

24.2 The Tenant must:
(a) not use the Property outside the [Permitted Hours [without the approval of the Landlord] OR Extended Hours];
(b) observe all [reasonable and proper] regulations that the Landlord makes relating to any use of the Property outside the Permitted Hours if such use is permitted by the Landlord; and
(c) if the Tenant uses the Property outside the Permitted Hours, pay to the Landlord on demand all costs [reasonably and properly] incurred by the Landlord in connection with that use (including (but not limited to) the whole of the cost of any Services provided by the Landlord attributable to that use).

24.3 The Tenant must not:
(a) use the Property for any illegal purposes nor for any purpose or in a manner that would cause loss, damage, injury, nuisance or inconvenience to the Landlord[, the Superior Landlord], the other tenants or occupiers of the Building or any property that neighbours the Building;
(b) use the Property as a betting shop or an amusement arcade or otherwise for the purposes of gaming or gambling;
(c) hold any auction at the Property;
(d) allow any noise, music, flashing lights, fumes or smells to emanate from the Property so as to cause a nuisance or annoyance to any other tenants or occupiers of the Building or any property that neighbours the Building;
(e) overload any part of the Building nor overload or block any Service Media at or serving the Property;
(f) store, sell or display any offensive, dangerous, illegal, explosive or highly flammable items at the Property;
(g) [(except as permitted by the Rights and clause 20.8)] place or keep any items on any external part of the Property or on the Common Parts;
(h) (except as permitted by the Rights and clause 20.6) interfere with any Service Media in the Building;
(i) keep any pets or any other animal, bird, fish, reptile or insect at the Property (except guide dogs or other animals used as aids provided they are not kept at the Property overnight or left unattended); or
(j) allow any person to sleep at or reside on the Property.

25. [Use of Parking Space[s]

25.1 The Tenant must not:
(a) use any Parking Space for any purpose except to park one roadworthy validly taxed and insured private vehicle belonging to the Tenant or its employees in accordance with paragraph 1.4 of Schedule 2;
(b) obstruct any of the entrances to or exits from the Car Park or any other parking spaces in the Car Park;

(c) store on or in any Parking Space any petrol, oil or other inflammable material (except that inside the fuel tank and engine of any vehicle parked on any Parking Space); or

(d) maintain, repair (except for minor mechanical repairs in cases of breakdown or other emergency) or refill the petrol tank of any vehicle parked on any Parking Space.

25.2 [The Tenant must:

(a) ensure that all security barriers or gates at the entrances to and exits from the Car Park are operated correctly and closed after use[. **OR** ; and]

(b) [return to the Landlord any keys or control cards to any security barriers or gates to the Car Park on the Termination Date.]]

26. Regulations

The Tenant must observe all [reasonable and proper] regulations made by the Landlord from time to time in accordance with the principles of good estate management and notified to the Tenant relating to the use of the Building[, the Landlord's Neighbouring Property] and any other neighbouring or adjoining property [provided that:

(a) such regulations do not materially interfere with the Tenant's use of the [Property **OR** Offices] for the Permitted Use [and te Storage Area for the Permitted Storage Area Use] and the Tenant's exercise of the Rights; and

(b) if there is any conflict between such regulations and the terms of this lease, the terms of this lease shall prevail].

27. [Loading and deliveries

The Tenant must:

(a) not use any other part of the Building in connection with the loading and delivery of goods and materials to the Property except the Service Area, Service Road and Service Accesses and Facilities in accordance with the rights granted under 1.7 of Schedule 2;

(b) only load or unload vehicles in the Service Area;

(c) when exercising its rights under paragraph 1.7 of Schedule 2, comply with:

  (i) any regulations made by the Landlord under in relation to the Service Area, Service Accesses and Facilities and Service Road; and

  (ii) the requirements and regulations of the local highway authority in relation to the Service Area and Service Road; and

(d) not obstruct the Service Area, Service Road and Service Accesses and Facilities.]

28. Exercise of the Rights

28.1 The Tenant must exercise the Rights:

(a) only in connection with the Tenant's use of the [Property **OR** Offices] for the Permitted Use [and the Storage Area for the Permitted Storage Area Use];

(b) in accordance with any regulations made by the Landlord under clause 26; and

(c) in compliance with all laws relating to the Tenant's use of the Building [, the Landlord's Neighbouring Property] and any other neighbouring or adjoining property pursuant to the Rights.

28.2 In exercising any right of entry on to any of the Common Parts or any Lettable Unit pursuant to paragraphe 1.13 of Schedule 2, the Tenant must:

(a) except in case of emergency, give reasonable notice of its intention to exercise that right to the Landlord and any occupiers of the relevant Lettable Unit;

(b) where reasonably required by the Landlord or the occupier of the relevant Lettable Unit, exercise that right only if accompanied by a representative of the Landlord, the tenant or the occupier of the relevant Lettable Unit;

(c) cause as little damage as possible to the Common Parts and any other Lettable Unit and to any property belonging to or used by the Landlord or the tenants or occupiers of any other Lettable Unit;

(d) cause as little inconvenience as reasonably possible to the Landlord and the tenants and occupiers of the other Lettable Units; and

(e) promptly make good any damage caused by reason of the Tenant exercising that right.

29. Allow entry

29.1 Subject to clause 29.2, the Tenant must allow all those entitled to exercise any right to enter the Property to enter the Property:

(a) except in the case of an emergency (when no notice shall be required), after having given reasonable notice (which need not be in writing) to the Tenant;

(b) at any reasonable time (whether or not during usual business hours); and
(c) with their workers, contractors, agents and professional advisers.

29.2 The Tenant must allow any person authorised by the terms of a Third Party Right to enter the Property in accordance with that Third Party Right.

30. Keyholders and emergency contact details

The Tenant must provide to the Landlord in writing the names, addresses[, email addresses] and telephone numbers of at least [two] people who each:

(a) hold a full set of keys for the Property;
(b) hold all the access codes for the Tenant's security systems (if any) at the Property; and
(c) may be contacted in case of emergency at any time outside the Tenant's usual business hours.

31. Compliance with laws

31.1 The Tenant must comply with all laws relating to:
(a) the Property and the occupation and use of the Property by the Tenant;
(b) the use or operation of all Service Media[, the Tenant's Plant, the Tenant's Plant Service Media] and any other machinery and equipment at or serving the Property whether or not used or operated;
(c) any works carried out at the Property[, any Tenant's Plant Works and any Relocation Works]; and
(d) all materials kept at or disposed of from the Property.

31.2 Within [five] working days of receipt of any notice or other communication affecting the Property, the Data Service Media [, the Tenant's Plant or Tenant's Plant Service Media] or the Building (and whether or not served pursuant to any law) the Tenant must:
(a) send a copy of the relevant document to the Landlord; and
(b) to the extent that it relates to the Property, the Data Service Media[, the Tenant's Plant or Tenant's Plant Service Media], take all steps necessary to comply with the notice or other communication and take any other action in connection with it as the Landlord may require.

31.3 The Tenant must not:
(a) apply for any planning permission for the Property without the Landlord's consent (such consent not to be unreasonably withheld where the application relates to works permitted or required under this lease); or
(b) implement any planning permission for the Property without the Landlord's consent (such consent not to be unreasonably withheld).

31.4 Unless the Landlord otherwise notifies the Tenant, before the Termination Date the Tenant must carry out and complete any works stipulated to be carried out to the Property (whether before or after the Termination Date) as a condition of any planning permission for the Property that is implemented before the Termination Date by the Tenant, any undertenant or any other occupier of the Property.

31.5 The Tenant must:
(a) comply with its obligations under the CDM Regulations;
(b) maintain the health and safety file for the Property in accordance with the CDM Regulations;
(c) give that health and safety file to the Landlord at the Termination Date;
(d) procure, and give to the Landlord at the Termination Date, irrevocable, non-exclusive, non-terminable, royalty-free licence(s) for the Landlord to copy and make full use of that health and safety file for any purpose relating to the Building. Those licence(s) must carry the right to grant sub-licences and be transferable to third parties without the consent of the grantor; and
(e) supply all information to the Landlord that the Landlord reasonably requires from time to time to comply with the Landlord's obligations under the CDM Regulations.

31.6 As soon as the Tenant becomes aware of any defect in the Property, the Tenant must give the Landlord notice of it.

31.7 The Tenant must indemnify the Landlord against any liability under the Defective Premises Act 1972 in relation to the Property by reason of any failure of the Tenant to comply with any of the tenant covenants in this lease.

31.8 The Tenant must keep:
(a) the Property equipped with all fire prevention, detection and fighting machinery and equipment and fire alarms which are required under all relevant laws or required by the insurers of the Property [or recommended by them] or reasonably required by the Landlord; and
(b) that machinery, equipment and alarms properly maintained and available for inspection.

32. Energy Performance Certificates

32.1 The Tenant must:

(a) co-operate with the Landlord so far as is reasonably necessary to allow the Landlord to obtain an Energy Performance Certificate and Recommendation Report for the Property or the Building [including providing the Landlord with copies of any plans or other information held by the Tenant that would assist in obtaining an Energy Performance Certificate and Recommendation Report]; and

(b) allow such access to any Energy Assessor appointed by the Landlord as is reasonably necessary to inspect the Property for the purposes of preparing an Energy Performance Certificate and Recommendation Report for the Property or the Building.

32.2 The Tenant must not commission an Energy Performance Certificate for the Property unless required to do so by the EPC Regulations.

32.3 Where the Tenant is required by the EPC Regulations to commission an Energy Performance Certificate for the Property, the Tenant must at the request of the Landlord either:

(a) commission an Energy Performance Certificate from an Energy Assessor approved by the Landlord (acting reasonably); or

(b) pay the reasonable costs of the Landlord of commissioning an Energy Performance Certificate for the Property.

32.4 The Tenant must deliver to the Landlord a copy of any Energy Performance Certificate and Recommendation Report for the Property that is obtained or commissioned by the Tenant or any other occupier of the Property.

33. Third Party Rights

33.1 The Tenant must:

(a) comply with the obligations on the Landlord relating to the Third Party Rights to the extent that those obligations relate to the Property; and

(b) not do anything that may interfere with any Third Party Right.

33.2 The Rights are granted subject to the Third Party Rights to the extent that the Third Party Rights affect the parts of the Building over which the Rights are granted.

34. [Superior Lease

The Tenant must observe and perform the tenant covenants in the Superior Lease (to the extent that they relate to the Property and the Rights) except that this obligation shall not apply to the covenants to pay the rents reserved by the Superior Lease [and the Tenant shall not be required to put the Property into any better state of repair or condition than required by clause 18.2].

35. [Registration of this lease

35.1 The Tenant must:

(a) apply to register this lease at HM Land Registry promptly [and in any event within [one month]] following the grant of this lease;

(b) ensure that any requisitions raised by HM Land Registry in connection with its application to register this lease at HM Land Registry are responded to promptly and properly; and

(c) send the Landlord [and the Superior Landlord] official copies of its title within [one month] of completion of the registration.

35.2 [The Tenant must not:

(a) apply to HM Land Registry to designate this lease as an exempt information document for the purposes of the Land Registration Rules 2003;

(b) object to an application by the Landlord to HM Land Registry to designate this lease as such an exempt information document; or

(c) apply for an official copy of any exempt information document version of this lease.]]

36. [Closure of registered title and] [Removal OR removal] of entries in relation to this lease and easements granted by this lease

36.1 The Tenant must make an application to HM Land Registry to [close the registered title of this lease and] remove from the Landlord's title any entries relating to this lease and any easements granted by this lease promptly [(and in any event within [one month])] following the Termination Date.

36.2 The Tenant must:

(a) ensure that any requisitions raised by HM Land Registry in connection with its application to HM Land Registry pursuant to clause 36.1 are responded to promptly and properly; and

(b) keep the Landlord informed of the progress and completion of that application.

37. **Encroachments and preservation of rights**

37.1 The Tenant must not permit any encroachment over the Property or permit any easements or other rights to be acquired over the Property.

37.2 If any encroachment over the Property is made or attempted or any action is taken by which an easement or other right may be acquired over the Property, the Tenant must:

(a) immediately inform the Landlord and give the Landlord notice of that encroachment or action; and

(b) at the request and cost of the Landlord, adopt such measures as may be reasonably required or deemed proper for preventing any such encroachment or the acquisition of any such easement or other right.

37.3 The Tenant must preserve all rights of light and other easements enjoyed by the Property.

37.4 The Tenant must not prejudice the acquisition of any right of light or other easement for the benefit of the Property by obstructing any window or opening or giving any acknowledgement that the right is enjoyed with the consent of any third party or by any other act or default of the Tenant.

37.5 If any person takes or threatens to take any action to obstruct or interfere with any easement or other right enjoyed by the Property or any such easement in the course of acquisition, the Tenant must:

(a) immediately inform the Landlord and give the Landlord notice of that action; and

(b) at the request and cost of the Landlord, adopt such measures as may be reasonably required or deemed proper for preventing or securing the removal of the obstruction or the interference.

38. **[Replacement guarantor**

38.1 Subject to clause 38.2, if:

(a) an Insolvency Event occurs in relation to a guarantor; or

(b) any guarantor (being an individual) dies or becomes incapable of managing their affairs;

the Tenant must, if the Landlord so requests, procure that a person of standing acceptable to the Landlord (acting reasonably), within [NUMBER] working days of that request enters into a replacement or additional guarantee and indemnity of the tenant covenants of this lease in the same form as that entered into by that guarantor.

38.2 clause 38.1 shall not apply in the case of a person who is a guarantor by reason of having entered into an authorised guarantee agreement.]

39. **Procure guarantor consent**

For so long as any guarantor remains liable to the Landlord, the Tenant must, if the Landlord so requests, procure that that guarantor does all or any of the following:

(a) joins in any consent or approval required under this lease; and

(b) consents to any variation of the tenant covenants of this lease.

40. **Indemnity**

The Tenant must keep the Landlord indemnified against all liabilities, expenses, costs (including, but not limited to, any solicitors' or other professionals' costs and expenses), claims, damages and losses (including, but not limited to, any diminution in the value of the Landlord's interest in the Building and loss of amenity of the Building) suffered or incurred by the Landlord arising out of or in connection with:

(a) any breach of any tenant covenants in this lease;

(b) any use or occupation of the Property or the carrying out of any works permitted or required to be carried out under this lease; or

(c) any act or omission of the Tenant or any Authorised Person.

41. **Landlord covenants**

The Landlord covenants with the Tenant to observe and perform the landlord

covenants of this lease during the Term.

42. **Quiet enjoyment**

The Landlord covenants with the Tenant that the Tenant shall have quiet enjoyment of the Property without any interruption by the Landlord or any person claiming under

the Landlord except as otherwise permitted by this lease.

43. **[Superior Lease obligations**

43.1 The Landlord must pay the rents reserved by the Superior Lease and perform the tenant covenants in the Superior Lease so far as the Tenant is not liable for such performance under the terms of this lease.

43.2 [At the request and cost (on a full indemnity basis) of the Tenant, the **OR** The] Landlord must use [all] reasonable endeavours to procure that the Superior Landlord complies with the Superior Landlord's

Covenants while the Superior Lease subsists [and, if reasonable, the Landlord may require that the Tenant pay it reasonable security in advance in respect of anticipated costs for enforcing such compliance].]

44. **Landlord's obligation to apportion Utility Costs**

    Where any of the costs referred to in clause 9.1 are billed to the Tenant by the Landlord, rather than directly by the relevant utility supplier, the Landlord must:

    (a) apportion those costs fairly, based on the Tenant's actual usage of that supply; and

    (b) with any demand by the Landlord for payment of those costs referred to in clause 9.1, supply a written explanation of how those costs are calculated.

45. **[Variation in extent of Building**

    If the Landlord varies the extent of the Building, that variation must not:

    (a) materially adversely impact on:

        (i) the Tenant's use and occupation of the Property; or

        (ii) the rights and facilities granted to the Tenant under this lease; or

    (b) materially increase the Service Charge payable by the Tenant.]

46. **Designation of alternative areas, routes and facilities**

    46.1 The Landlord must:

    (a) when exercising any right under paragraph 1.6 of Schedule 3, give the Tenant [reasonable **OR** at least [NUMBER] [hours' **OR** working days']] notice (except in case of emergency when no notice shall be required);

    (b) when exercising its right under paragraph 1.6a) of Schedule 3, use reasonable endeavours to designate alternative routes, areas or facilities that are not materially less convenient for the Tenant; and

    (c) (except in case of emergency) when exercising its right under paragraph 1.6(b) of Schedule 3;

        (i) use reasonable endeavours to provide alternative routes, areas or facilities that are not materially less convenient for the Tenant; and

        (ii) ensure that access to the relevant Common Parts is prevented or restricted for as short a period as is reasonably practicable.

    46.2 [When exercising the right under paragraph 1.7 of Schedule 3, the Landlord must act reasonably and in the interests of good estate management.]

47. **[Relocation of Tenant's Plant Area, Tenant's Plant and Tenant's Plant Service Media**

    47.1 Subject to [clause 47.2 and] clause 47.3, the Landlord may from time to time during the Term give notice to the Tenant:

    (a) designating all or any of the following:

        (i) an alternative part of the roof of the Building as the location of the Tenant's Plant Area;

        (ii) alternative locations for the Tenant's Plant within the Tenant's Plant Area; and

        (iii) an alternative route or routes for any of the Tenant's Plant Service Media; and

    (b) specifying:

        (i) the Landlord's reasonable requirements as to the method and manner in which the Tenant must carry out the Relocation Works; and

        (ii) a reasonable period of not less than [NUMBER] [weeks **OR** months] from the Tenant's receipt of the Relocation Notice during which the Tenant must carry out and complete the Relocation Works (except in case of emergency where the Landlord may specify that the Tenant must carry out and complete the Relocation Works immediately).

    47.2 [Except in case of emergency, the Landlord may only serve a Relocation Notice if the relocation of the Tenant's Plant Area, Tenant's Plant and Tenant's Plant Service Media to the alternative location(s) or routes specified in the Relocation Notice is reasonably required to enable the Landlord to:

    (a) carry out works for redevelopment, repair, inspection, maintenance, reinstatement or renewal of any part of the Building;

    (b) comply with all laws;

    (c) improve the arrangement of plant, equipment or other items on the roof of the Building; or

    (d) accommodate the reasonable requirements of any other tenant or occupier of the Building.]

    47.3 The Landlord must use reasonable endeavours to ensure that the alternative location(s) and routes specified in the Relocation Notice are not materially less convenient for the Tenant.

    47.4 The Landlord must pay the reasonable and proper costs and expenses incurred by the Tenant in connection with the carrying out of any Relocation Works on a full indemnity basis (including any irrecoverable VAT) within [NUMBER] working days of demand.]

48. **Exercise of right of entry**

   In exercising any right of entry on to the Property pursuant to paragraph 1.2 of Schedule 2, the Landlord must:

   (a) except in case of emergency, give reasonable notice of its intention to exercise that right to the Tenant;

   (b) where reasonably required by the Tenant, exercise that right only if accompanied by a representative of the Tenant;

   (c) cause as little damage as possible to the Property and to any property belonging to or used by the Tenant;

   (d) cause as little inconvenience as reasonably possible to the Tenant; and

   (e) promptly make good any physical damage caused to the Property by reason of the Landlord exercising that right.

49. **Scaffolding**

   In relation to any scaffolding erected pursuant to 1.5 of Schedule 3, the Landlord must:

   (a) ensure that the scaffolding causes the least amount of obstruction to the entrance to the Property and the Building as is reasonably practicable;

   (b) remove the scaffolding as soon as reasonably practicable;

   (c) following removal of the scaffolding, make good any damage to the exterior of the Property caused by the scaffolding; and

   (d) if the scaffolding obstructs any Signs erected by the Tenant in accordance with this lease, allow the Tenant to display on the exterior of the scaffolding one sign of a size and design and in a location approved by the Landlord (such approval not to be unreasonably withheld or delayed).

50. **Landlord to enter wayleave**

   50.1 Subject to clause 50.2, at the request of the Tenant, the Landlord must enter into any wayleave with an operator to whom a direction applies under section 106(3) of the Communications Act 2003 that is required to enable the Tenant to connect any Data Service Media to that operator's electronic communications network (as defined by section 32 of the Communications Act 2003) pursuant to the Rights.

   50.2 The Landlord's obligation in clause 50.1 is subject to the Tenant:

   (a) obtaining the Landlord's prior approval (not to be unreasonably withheld or delayed) to the route of such Data Service Media and to the form and terms of the wayleave; and

   (b) paying the Landlord's reasonable and proper costs in connection with such approval and entering into such wayleave on a full indemnity basis (including any irrecoverable VAT).

51. **[Guarantor covenants**

   The Guarantor covenants with the Landlord on the terms set out in Schedule 8.]

52. **Re-entry and forfeiture**

   52.1 The Landlord may re-enter the Property (or any part of the Property in the name of the whole) at any time after any of the following occurs:

   (a) the whole or any part of the Rents is unpaid 21 days after becoming payable (whether it has been formally demanded or not);

   (b) any breach of any condition of, or tenant covenant in, this lease; or

   (c) an Insolvency Event.

   52.2 If the Landlord re-enters the Property (or any part of the Property in the name of the whole) pursuant to this clause, this lease shall immediately end but without prejudice to any right or remedy of the Landlord in respect of any breach of covenant by the Tenant or any guarantor.

53. **Section 62 of the LPA 1925, implied rights and existing appurtenant rights**

   53.1 The grant of this lease does not create by implication any easements or other rights for the benefit of the Property or the Tenant and the operation of section 62 of the LPA 1925 is excluded.

   53.2 The Property is let without the benefit of any existing easements or other rights which are appurtenant to the whole or any part of the Building [except those set out in paragraph 2 of Schedule 2.

54. **[Exclusion of sections 24 to 28 of the LTA 1954**

   54.1 [The parties:

   (a) confirm that:

   (i) the Landlord served a notice on the Tenant, as required by section 38A(3)(a) of the LTA 1954, applying to the tenancy created by this lease, [not less than 14 days] before [this lease **OR** [DETAILS OF AGREEMENT FOR LEASE]] was entered into;

(ii) [the Tenant OR [DECLARANT'S NAME] who was duly authorised by the Tenant to do so] made a [statutory] declaration dated [DATE] in accordance with the requirements of section 38A(3)(b) of the LTA 1954; [and]

(iii) [there is no agreement for lease to which this lease gives effect; and]

(b) agree that the provisions of sections 24 to 28 of the LTA 1954 are excluded in relation to the tenancy created by this lease.]

54.2 [The parties confirm that:

(a) the Landlord served a notice on the Guarantor, as required by section 38A(3)(a) of the LTA 1954, applying to the tenancy to be entered into by the Guarantor pursuant to 4.1 of Scheddule 8, [not less than 14 days] before [this lease OR [DETAILS OF AGREEMENT FOR LEASE]] was entered into; and

(b) [the Guarantor OR [DECLARANT'S NAME], who was duly authorised by the Guarantor to do so,] made a [statutory] declaration dated [DATE] in accordance with the requirements of section 38A(3)(b) of the LTA 1954.]]

55. [Compensation on vacating

Any right of the Tenant (or anyone deriving title under the Tenant) to claim compensation from the Landlord on leaving the Property under the LTA 1954 is excluded (except to the extent that the legislation prevents that right being excluded).]

56. No restriction on Landlord's use

Nothing in this lease shall impose or be deemed to impose any restriction on the use by the Landlord of the Building (excluding the Property)[, the Landlord's Neighbouring Property] or any other neighbouring or adjoining property.

57. Limitation of liability

The Landlord shall not be liable to the Tenant for any failure of the Landlord to perform any landlord covenant in this lease unless the Landlord knows it has failed to perform the covenant (or reasonably should know this) and has not remedied that failure within a reasonable time.

58. [[Landlord's OR Tenant's OR Mutual] option to break

58.1 [[The Landlord OR The Tenant OR Either the Landlord or the Tenant] may terminate this lease by serving a Break Notice on the [Tenant OR Landlord OR other party] at least [NUMBER] [weeks OR months] before the [relevant] Break Date.

OR

[The Landlord OR The Tenant OR Either the Landlord or the Tenant] may terminate this lease by serving a Break Notice on the [Tenant OR Landlord OR other party] at any time [on or after [EARLIEST DATE FOR SERVICE OF THE BREAK NOTICE]].]

58.2 [A Break Notice served by the Tenant shall be of no effect if at the Break Date stated in the Break Notice:

(a) the Tenant has not paid by way of cleared funds any part of the Annual Rent (plus any VAT) which was due to have been paid;

(b) the Tenant or any other occupier remains in occupation of any part of the Property; or

(c) there are any continuing underleases of the Property.]

58.3 [Subject to clause 58.2, following OR Following] service of a Break Notice this lease shall terminate on the [relevant] Break Date.

58.4 Termination of this lease on [the OR a] Break Date shall not affect any other right or remedy that either party may have in relation to any earlier breach of this lease.

58.5 If this lease terminates in accordance with clause 58.3, then, within [ten] working days of the [relevant] Break Date, the Landlord must refund to the Tenant the proportion (calculated on a daily basis) of any Annual Rent (together with any VAT paid in respect of it) and any Insurance Rent (together with any VAT paid in respect of it) paid in advance by the Tenant for the period from but excluding the [relevant] Break Date up to but excluding the next Rent Payment Date.

59. [Variation of Tenant's Proportion

If the Landlord increases or decreases the extent of the Building at any time during the Term, then:

(a) the percentage specified as the Tenant's Proportion must be varied to reflect that increase or decrease. That varied percentage shall be agreed between the Landlord and Tenant at any time or may, in the absence of such agreement, be referred at any time by either party for determination by the Expert in accordance with clause 63;

(b) as soon as practicable after that varied percentage has been agreed or determined, a memorandum recording that varied percentage as the Tenant's Proportion must be signed by or on behalf of the Landlord, the Tenant and any guarantor. The parties must bear their own costs in connection with the memorandum; and

(c) the varied percentage as agreed or determined shall apply as the Tenant's Proportion from a date notified by the Landlord to the Tenant provided that that date must not be earlier than the date of the agreement or determination of the varied percentage.]

60. Breach of repair and maintenance obligation

60.1 The Landlord may enter the Property to inspect its condition and state of repair and give the Tenant a notice of any breach of any of the tenant covenants in this lease relating to the condition or repair of the Property.

60.2 Following the service of a notice pursuant to clause 60.1 the Landlord may enter the Property and carry out the required works if the Tenant:

(a) has not begun any works required to remedy any breach specified in that notice within two months of the notice or, if works are required as a matter of emergency, immediately; or

(b) is not carrying out the required works with all due speed.

60.3 The costs incurred by the Landlord in carrying out any works pursuant to clause 60.2 (and any professional fees and any VAT in respect of those costs) shall be a debt due from the Tenant to the Landlord and payable on demand.

60.4 Any action taken by the Landlord pursuant to this clause 60 shall be without prejudice to the Landlord's other rights (including those under clause 52).

61. Notices

61.1 Except where this lease specifically states that a notice need not be in writing, any notice given under or in connection with this lease shall be in writing and given:

(a) by hand:
  (i) if the party is a company incorporated in the United Kingdom, at that party's registered office address;
  (ii) if the party is a company not incorporated in the United Kingdom, at that party's principal place of business in the United Kingdom; or
  (iii) in any other case, at that party's last known place of abode or business in the United Kingdom; [or]

(b) by pre-paid first-class post or other next working day delivery service:
  (i) if the party is a company incorporated in the United Kingdom, at that party's registered office address;
  (ii) if the party is a company not incorporated in the United Kingdom, at that party's principal place of business in the United Kingdom; or
  (iii) in any other case, at that party's last known place of abode or business in the United Kingdom[. **OR** ; or]

(c) [by fax to the party's main fax number.]

61.2 If a notice complies with the criteria in clause 61.1, whether or not this lease requires that notice to be in writing, it shall be deemed to have been received if:

(a) delivered by hand, at the time the notice is left at the proper address; [or]

(b) sent by pre-paid first-class post or other next working day delivery service, on the [second] working day after posting[. **OR** ; or]

(c) [sent by fax, at [9.00 am] on the next working day after transmission.]

61.3 This clause does not apply to the service of any proceedings or other documents in any legal action or, where applicable, any arbitration or other method of dispute resolution.

62. Consents and approvals

62.1 Where the consent of the Landlord is required under this lease, a consent shall only be valid if it is given by deed unless:

(a) it is given in writing and signed by the Landlord or a person duly authorised on its behalf; and

(b) it expressly states that the Landlord waives the requirement for a deed in that particular case.

62.2 If a waiver is given pursuant to clause 62.1, it shall not affect the requirement for a deed for any other consent.

62.3 Where the approval of the Landlord is required under this lease, an approval shall only be valid if it is in writing and signed by or on behalf of the Landlord unless:

(a) the approval is being given in a case of emergency; or

(b) this lease expressly states that the approval need not be in writing.

62.4 If the Landlord gives a consent or approval under this lease, the giving of that consent or approval shall not:
 (a) imply that any consent or approval required from a third party has been obtained; or
 (b) obviate the need to obtain any consent or approval from a third party.

62.5 Where the Tenant requires the consent or approval of [the Superior Landlord or] any mortgagee to any act or omission under this lease, then (subject to clause 1.12) at the cost of the Tenant the Landlord must use [all] reasonable endeavours to obtain that consent or approval.

62.6 Where:
 (a) the consent of [the Superior Landlord or] a mortgagee is required under this lease, a consent shall only be valid if it would be valid as a consent given under the terms of the [Superior Lease or] mortgage; or
 (b) the approval of [the Superior Landlord or] a mortgagee is required under this lease, an approval shall only be valid if it would be valid as an approval given under the terms of the [Superior Lease or] mortgage.

63. Expert determination

This clause 63 applies in relation to any matter referred to an Expert for determination pursuant to:
 (a) [clause 59[. **OR**; [or]]]
 (b) [paragraph 2.1 of Part 5 of schedule 5[. **OR** ; [or]]]
 (c) [paragraph 13 of Part 4 of schedule 7[. **OR** ; [or]]
 (d) [paragraph 3.4 of Part 5 of schedule 7.]

63.2 The Landlord and Tenant shall agree on the appointment of an Expert and shall agree with the Expert the terms of their appointment.

63.3 If the Landlord and Tenant are unable to agree on an Expert or the terms of their appointment within [NUMBER] working days of either party serving details of a suggested expert on the other, either party shall then be entitled to request the President to appoint an Expert and agree with the Expert the terms of appointment.

63.4 The Expert shall be required to prepare a written decision including reasons and give notice (including a copy) of the decision to the parties within a maximum of [NUMBER] working days of the matter being referred to the Expert.

63.5 If the Expert dies or becomes unwilling or incapable of acting, or does not deliver the decision within the time required by this clause, then:
 (a) either party may apply to the President to discharge the Expert and to appoint a replacement Expert with the required expertise; and
 (b) this clause 63 shall apply to the new Expert as if they were the first Expert appointed.

63.6 The parties are entitled to make submissions to the Expert [including oral submissions] and must provide (or procure that others provide) the Expert with such assistance and documents as the Expert reasonably requires for the purpose of reaching a decision.

63.7 [To the extent not provided for by this cllause 63, the Expert may in their reasonable discretion determine such other procedures to assist with the conduct of the determination as they consider just or appropriate [including (to the extent considered necessary) instructing professional advisers to assist them in reaching their determination].

63.8 The Expert shall act as an expert and not as an arbitrator. The Expert shall determine the matter referred to the Expert under this lease. The Expert may award interest as part of their decision. The Expert's written decision on the matters referred to them shall be final and binding on the parties in the absence of manifest error or fraud.

63.9 The Landlord and Tenant must bear their own costs in relation to the reference to the Expert.

63.10 The Landlord and Tenant must bear the Expert's fees and any costs properly incurred by them in arriving at their determination (including any fees and costs of any advisers appointed by the Expert) equally or in such other proportions as the Expert shall direct.

63.11 [If either the Landlord or the Tenant does not pay its part of the Expert's fees and expenses within [ten] working days of demand by the Expert, then:
 (a) the other party may pay instead; and
 (b) the amount so paid shall be a debt of the party that should have paid and shall be due and payable on demand to the party that made the payment pursuant to clause 63.11(a).]

63.12 The Landlord and Tenant must act reasonably and co-operate to give effect to the provisions of this clause and otherwise do nothing to hinder or prevent the Expert from reaching their determination.]

64. [Disputes under the Superior Lease

Notwithstanding the other terms of this lease, if any dispute, issue, question or matter arising out of or under or relating to the Superior Lease also affects or relates to the provisions of this lease, the determination of that dispute, issue, question or matter pursuant to the provisions of the Superior Lease shall be binding on the Tenant as well as the Landlord for the purposes both of the Superior Lease and this lease [provided that this provision shall not apply to the provisions for the review of Annual Rent payable under this lease].]

65. VAT

65.1 All sums payable by either party under or in connection with this lease are exclusive of any VAT that may be chargeable.

65.2 A party to this lease must pay VAT in respect of all taxable supplies made to that party in connection with this lease on the due date for making any payment or, if earlier, the date on which that supply is made for VAT purposes.

65.3 Every obligation on either party, under or in connection with this lease, to pay any sum by way of a refund or indemnity, includes an obligation to pay an amount equal to any VAT incurred on that sum by the receiving party (except to the extent that the receiving party obtains credit for such VAT).

65.4 [The Tenant warrants that it does not intend or expect that the Property will become exempt land (within paragraph 12 of Schedule 10 to the Value Added Tax Act 1994) and that the purposes for which the Property are or are to be used will not affect the application or effect of any option to tax made by the Landlord in respect of the Property.]

66. Joint and several liability

Where a party comprises more than one person, those persons shall be jointly and severally liable for the obligations and liabilities of that party arising under this lease. The party to whom those obligations and liabilities are owed may take action against, or release or compromise the liability of, or grant time or other indulgence to, any one of those persons without affecting the liability of any other of them.

67. Entire agreement

67.1 This lease [and the documents annexed to it] constitute[s] the whole agreement between the parties and supersede[s] all previous discussions, correspondence, negotiations, arrangements, understandings and agreements between them relating to [its OR their] subject matter.

67.2 Each party acknowledges that in entering into this lease [and any documents annexed to it] it does not rely on[, and shall have no remedies in respect of,] any representation or warranty (whether made innocently or negligently) [other than those contained in any Written Replies].

67.3 Nothing in this lease constitutes or shall constitute a representation or warranty that the Property may lawfully be used for any purpose allowed by this lease.

67.4 [Nothing in this clause shall limit or exclude any liability for fraud.]

68. Contracts (Rights of Third Parties) Act 1999

This lease does not give rise to any rights under the Contracts (Rights of Third Parties) Act 1999 to enforce any term of this lease.

69. Governing Law

This lease and any dispute or claim (including non-contractual disputes or claims) arising out of or in connection with it or its subject matter or formation shall be governed by and construed in accordance with the law of England and Wales.

70. Jurisdiction

[Subject to clause 63, each OR Each] party irrevocably agrees that the courts of England and Wales shall have [exclusive OR non-exclusive] jurisdiction to settle any dispute or claim (including non-contractual disputes or claims) arising out of or in connection with this lease or its subject matter or formation.

This document has been executed as a deed and is delivered and takes effect on the date stated at the beginning of it.

Schedule 1   Property

1. The premises [comprising the offices] situated on [part of] the [NUMBER OR NUMBERS] floor[s] of the Building and shown edged red on the Property Plan [and the storage area [known as [STORAGE AREA

NUMBER OR ADDRESS]] situated on the [NUMBER] floor of the Building and shown edged red on the Storage Area Plan]:

1.1 Including [in respect of each of the floors on which those premises are situated]:
- (a) the whole of any non-structural walls and columns wholly within those premises;
- (b) one-half severed vertically of any interior non-structural walls and columns separating those premises from any adjoining Lettable Unit;
- (c) the interior plaster and other interior surface finishes on the:
  - (i) exterior non-structural walls and columns bounding those premises;
  - (ii) interior non-structural walls and columns separating those premises from any adjoining Retained Parts; and
  - (iii) structural walls and columns within or bounding those premises;
- (d) the interior plaster and other interior surface finishes on the ceilings within those premises;
- (e) the floor screed and other interior surface finishes on the floors within those premises;
- (f) the doors, door frames and fittings within all the walls within and bounding those premises;
- (g) the windows, window frames and fittings within all the walls within and bounding those premises (except the exterior walls);
- (h) all Service Media and any other media, plant, machinery and equipment within and exclusively serving those premises;
- (i) all landlord's fixtures and fittings within those premises; and
- (j) all additions and improvements to those premises.

1.2 Excluding [in respect of each of the floors on which those premises are situated]:
- (a) subject to paragraph 1.1(c), paragraph 1.1(f) and paragraph 1.1(g) of this Schedule, the whole of the:
  - (i) exterior non-structural walls and columns bounding those premises;
  - (ii) interior non-structural walls and columns separating those premises from any adjoining Retained Parts; and
  - (iii) structural walls and columns within or bounding those premises;
- (b) the windows, window frames and fittings within the exterior walls bounding those premises;
- (c) subject to paragraph 1.1(d) and paragraph 1.1(e) of this Schedule, the floors and ceilings within those premises;
- (d) all Service Media and any other media, plant, machinery and equipment within but not exclusively serving those premises; and
- (e) all structural parts of the Building (except any set out in paragraph 1.1 of this Schedule).

Schedule 2 Rights

1.1 In common with the Landlord and any other person authorised by the Landlord, the Landlord grants to the Tenant the following easements (for the benefit of the Property) and the following other rights:

1.1 The right to support and protection for the Property from the other parts of the Building to the extent that those parts of the Building provide support and protection to the Property at the date of this lease.

1.2 The right to use:
- (a) [the external areas of the Common Parts shown [coloured **OR** edged **OR** hatched] [COLOUR] on the Building Plan or such other external areas designated from time to time by the Landlord in accordance with paragraph 1.6(a) of Schedule 3 for the purposes of [vehicular or] pedestrian [(in accordance with any Landlord's designation under paragraph 1.7 of Schedule 3)] access to and egress from the interior of the Building and those external parts of the Building over which the Tenant is granted rights in this Schedule; and]
- (b) the lifts, [escalators,] hallways, corridors, stairways and landings of the Common Parts shown [coloured **OR** edged **OR** hatched] [COLOUR] on the Building Plan or such other internal areas designated from time to time by the Landlord in accordance with paragraph 1.6(a) of Schedule 3 for the purpose of pedestrian access to and egress from the Property and those internal parts of the Building over which the Tenant is granted rights in this Schedule.

1.3 [The right during the [Permitted Hours **OR** Extended Hours] to use the toilet facilities within the Common Parts on the [NUMBER OR NUMBERS] floor[s] of the Building shown [coloured **OR** edged **OR** hatched] [COLOUR] on the Building Plan or such other toilet facilities designated from time to time by the Landlord in accordance with paragraph 1.6(a) of Schedule 3.]

1.4 [Subject to there being sufficient available parking spaces within the Car Park, the right to park during the [Permitted Hours **OR** Extended Hours] no more than [NUMBER] private car[s] belonging to the Tenant and its employees in any of the parking spaces within the Car Park.]

1.5 [Subject to there being sufficient available cycle racks, the right to park bicycles belonging to the Tenant and its employees during the [Permitted Hours **OR** Extended Hours] in the cycle racks in the area [coloured **OR** edged **OR** hatched] [COLOUR] on the Building Plan or such alternative area designated from time to time by the Landlord in accordance with paragraph 1.6(a) of Schedule 3.]

1.6 [The right to deposit refuse during the [Permitted Hours **OR** Extended Hours] in [NUMBER] refuse bins situated in the area [coloured **OR** edged **OR** hatched] [COLOUR] on the Building Plan or such alternative area designated from time to time by the Landlord in accordance with paragraph 1.6(a) of Schedule 3.]

1.7 [The right [during the Loading and Delivery Hours only] to use:
   (a) the Service Area (with or without vehicles or trolleys) for loading and unloading goods and materials;
   (b) the Service Road (with vehicles only) for access to and egress from the Service Area in connection with the loading and unloading of goods and materials permitted under paragraph 1.7(a) of this Schedule; and
   (c) the Service Accesses and Facilities (on foot only and with or without trolleys) for access to and egress from the Service Area and the Property in connection with the loading and unloading of goods and materials permitted under paragraph 1.7(a) of this Schedule.]

1.8 [The right to use for the purpose of emergency egress on foot from the Property the emergency and fire escape routes shown [coloured **OR** edged **OR** hatched] [COLOUR] on the Building Plan or such other emergency and fire escape routes designated from time to time by the Landlord in accordance with paragraph 1.6(a) of Schedule 3.]

1.9 [The right to install, retain, inspect, repair and maintain the Tenant's Plant and the Tenant's Plant Service Media. Provided that, where the Tenant requires the consent of the Landlord to carry out works in relation to the Tenant's Plant and the Tenant's Plant Service Media, the Tenant may only exercise this right:
   (a) when that consent has been granted; and
   (b) in accordance with the terms of that consent.]

1.10 The right to install, retain, inspect, repair and maintain Data Service Media [(excluding Tenant's Plant Service Media)] in such positions at the Building as are designated from time to time by the Landlord in accordance with paragraph 1.6(a) of Schedule 3. Provided that, where the Tenant requires the consent of the Landlord to carry out works in relation to such Data Service Media, the Tenant may only exercise this right:
   (a) when that consent has been granted; and
   (b) in accordance with the terms of that consent.

1.11 The right to use and to connect into any Service Media at the Building that belong to the Landlord and serve (but do not form part of) the Property which are in existence at the date of this lease or are installed or constructed during the Term. Provided that the Landlord may, at its discretion and at any time, re-route or replace any Service Media at the Building pursuant to paragraph 1.3(c) of Schedule 3 and this right shall then apply in relation to the Service Media as re-routed or replaced.

1.12 [The right to display the trading name and logo of the Tenant (and any authorised undertenant) on a sign or noticeboard provided by the Landlord in the entrance hall of the Building and in the Common Parts at the entrance[s] to the [Offices **OR** Property] in each case in a form and manner approved by the Landlord (such approval not to be not be unreasonably withheld or delayed).]

1.13 Subject to the Tenant complying with clause 28.2, the right to enter the Common Parts or any other Lettable Unit so far as is reasonably necessary to carry out any works to the Property or any works relating to the Data Service Media [, Tenant's Plant or Tenant's Plant Service Media] required or permitted by this lease.

1.14 [[OTHER RIGHTS].]

2. [For the purposes of clause 53.2, the Property is let with the benefit of the following easements or other appurtenant rights:

2.1 [DESCRIPTION OF EACH EASEMENT OR OTHER APPURTENANT RIGHT THAT IS TO BE INCLUDED IN THE GRANT OF THIS LEASE] [which [is **OR** are] referred to in the property register of [TITLE NUMBER[S]] **OR** which benefit[s] [TITLE NUMBER[S]]] at the date of this lease **OR** which benefit[s] [DESCRIPTION OF UNREGISTERED REVERSION] at the date of this lease].]

Schedule 3 Reservations

1. Subject to paragraph 2 and paragraph 3 of this Schedule, the Landlord excepts and reserves from this lease the following easements (for the benefit of the Building (excluding the Property) [and the Landlord's Neighbouring Property]) and the following other rights:

1.1 Rights of light, air, support and protection to the extent those rights are capable of being enjoyed at any time during the Term.

1.2 Subject to the Landlord complying with clause 48, the right to enter the Property:
   (a) to repair, maintain, install, construct, re-route or replace any Service Media or structure relating to any of the Reservations;
   (b) to carry out any works to any other part of the Building; and
   (c) for any other purpose mentioned in or connected with:
       (i) this lease;
       (ii) [the Superior Lease and the Superior Landlord's interest in the Building;]
       (iii) the Reservations; or
       (iv) the Landlord's interest in the Building [, **OR** or] [the Landlord's Neighbouring Property] [or] [any neighbouring or adjoining property in which the Landlord acquires an interest during the Term].

1.3 The right to:
   (a) use and connect into Service Media at, but not forming part of, the Property which are in existence at the date of this lease or which are installed or constructed during the Term;
   (b) install and construct Service Media at the Property to serve any other part of the Building [, **OR** or] [the Landlord's Neighbouring Property] [or] [any neighbouring or adjoining property in which the Landlord acquires an interest during the Term]; and
   (c) re-route and replace any Service Media referred to in this paragraph.

1.4 At any time during the Term, the full and free right to build, rebuild, alter or develop the Building [, **OR** or] [the Landlord's Neighbouring Property] [or] [any neighbouring or adjoining property in which the Landlord acquires an interest during the Term] as the Landlord may think fit.

1.5 Subject to the Landlord complying with clause 49, the right to erect scaffolding at the Property and attach it to any part of the Property in connection with any of the Reservations.

1.6 Subject to the Landlord complying with clause 46.1, the right from time to time to:
   (a) designate alternative areas, routes or facilities over which the Rights may be exercised [except for the Rights in relation to the Tenant's Plant Area, the Tenant's Plant, and Tenant's Plant Service Media which the Landlord may relocate from time to time in accordance with clause 47]; or
   (b) prevent or restrict access to any of the Common Parts if reasonably required to enable works to be carried out to any part of the Building [or the Landlord's Neighbouring Property] or in case of emergency.

1.7 [Subject to the Landlord complying with clause 46.2, the right from time to time to designate which of the Common Parts may be used by the Tenant on foot only, by vehicles only or both on foot and by vehicles and this shall include the right to specify which type, size and weight of vehicles are permitted to use any of those Common Parts designated by the Landlord for use by vehicles.]

1.8 [[OTHER RESERVATIONS].]

2. The Reservations:

2.1 Are excepted and reserved notwithstanding that the exercise of any of the Reservations or the works carried out pursuant to them result in a reduction in the flow of light or air to the Property or the Common Parts or loss of amenity for the Property or the Common Parts [provided that they do not materially adversely affect the use and enjoyment of the [Property **OR** Offices] for the Permitted Use] [and the Storage Area for the Permitted Storage Area Use].

2.2 May be exercised by:
   (a) the Landlord;
   (b) [the Superior Landlord;]
   (c) anyone else who is or becomes entitled to exercise them; and
   (d) anyone authorised by the Landlord [or the Superior Landlord].

2.3 [Are excepted and reserved to the extent possible for the benefit of any neighbouring or adjoining property in which the Landlord acquires an interest during the Term.]

3. No party exercising any of the Reservations, nor its workers, contractors, agents and professional advisers, shall be liable to the Tenant or to any undertenant or other occupier of or person at the Property for any loss, damage, injury, nuisance or inconvenience arising by reason of its exercising any of the Reservations except for:

3.1 Physical damage to the Property.

3.2 Any loss, damage, injury, nuisance or inconvenience in relation to which the law prevents the Landlord from excluding liability.

Schedule 4   Third Party Rights

1. All easements and other rights, covenants and restrictions affecting the Building and any land over which the Rights are granted [including those [set out or referred to in the register entries of [[TITLE NUMBER[S]] as at the date of this lease **OR** [DETAILS OF HOW THE RIGHTS ARE SET OUT OR REFERRED TO IN THE UNREGISTERED TITLE]]].

2. [[OTHER THIRD PARTY RIGHTS].]

Schedule 5   [Rent review

Part 1 Definitions

1. **Definitions**

   The following definitions apply in this Schedule 5.

   Assumptions: the assumptions set out in Part 2 of this Schedule 5.

   Disregards: the disregards set out in Part 3 of this Schedule 5.

   Hypothetical Lease: the lease described in Part 4 of this Schedule 5.

   [Maximum Rent: [[PERCENTAGE]% of the Annual Rent payable immediately before the [relevant] Review Date (or which would then be payable but for any abatement, suspension, concession or reduction of the Annual Rent or restriction on the right to collect it) **OR** £[AGREED AMOUNT]].]

   [Minimum Rent: [[PERCENTAGE]% of the Annual Rent payable immediately before the [relevant] Review Date (or which would then be payable but for any abatement, suspension, concession or reduction of the Annual Rent or restriction on the right to collect it) **OR** £[AGREED AMOUNT]].]

   Open Market Rent: the best annual rent (exclusive of VAT) at which the Property could reasonably be expected to be let:

   (a) in the open market;
   (b) at the [relevant] Review Date; and
   (C) applying the Assumptions and Disregards.

   Review Date[s]: [DATE] [and [DATE]].

   Shortfall Payment Date: the date [which is [ten] working days from and including the date] that the revised Annual Rent is agreed or determined.

Part 2 Assumptions

1. The matters to be assumed are:

1.1 The Property is available to let in the open market:

   (a) on the terms of the Hypothetical Lease;
   (b) by a willing landlord to a willing tenant;
   (c) with vacant possession; and
   (d) without a fine or a premium.

1.2 The willing tenant has had the benefit of any rent-free or other concession or contribution which would be offered in the open market at the [relevant] Review Date in relation to fitting-out works at the Property.

1.3 The Property may lawfully be used, and is in a physical state to enable it to be lawfully used, by the willing tenant (or any potential undertenant or assignee of the willing tenant) for any use permitted by this lease.

1.4 The Tenant and the Landlord [(except where the Landlord is in material and persistent breach)] have fully complied with their obligations in this lease.

1.5 If the Property or any means of access to it or any Service Media serving the Property has been destroyed or damaged, it has been fully restored.

1.6 No work has been carried out on the Property [(including any Previous Lease Alterations)] that has diminished its rental value [other than work carried out in compliance with clause 31].

1.7 Any fixtures, fittings, machinery or equipment supplied to the Property by the Landlord that have been removed by or at the request of the Tenant, or any undertenant or their respective predecessors in title (otherwise than to comply with any law) remain at the Property.

1.8 [The willing tenant and its potential assignees and undertenants shall not be disadvantaged by any actual or potential exercise of an option to tax under Part 1 of Schedule 10 to the Value Added Tax Act 1994 in relation to the Property.]

1.9 [[ANY ADDITIONAL ASSUMPTIONS SPECIFIC TO THE LETTING].]

Part 3 Disregards

1. The matters to be disregarded are:

1.1 Any effect on rent of the fact that the Tenant or any authorised undertenant has been in occupation of the Property.

1.2 Any goodwill attached to the Property by reason of any business carried out there by the Tenant or by any authorised undertenant or by any of their predecessors in business.

1.3 Any effect on rent attributable to any physical improvement to the Property carried out before or after the date of this lease (including any physical improvement to any Service Media servicing the Property), by or at the expense of the Tenant or any authorised undertenant with all necessary consents, approvals and authorisations and not pursuant to an obligation to the Landlord (other than an obligation to comply with any law).

1.4 Any effect on the rent attributable to any Data Service Media Works carried out by or at the expense of the Tenant or any authorised undertenant before or after the date of this lease.

1.5 [Any effect on the rent attributable to any Tenant Plant Works carried out by or at the expense of the Tenant or any authorised undertenant before or after the date of this lease.]

1.6 [Any effect on the rent attributable to any Previous Lease Alterations.]

1.7 Any effect on rent of any obligation on the Tenant [to fit-out the Property or] to reinstate the Property to the condition or design it was in before any alterations or improvements were carried out.

1.8 [Any effect on rent of the installation of a mezzanine floor in the Property.]

1.9 Any statutory restriction on rents or the right to recover them.

1.10 [[ANY ADDITIONAL DISREGARDS SPECIFIC TO THE LETTING].]

Part 4 Hypothetical Lease

1. A lease:

1.1 Of the whole of the Property.

1.2 [For a term equal to the unexpired residue of the Contractual Term at the [relevant] Review Date or a term of [MINIMUM LENGTH OF HYPOTHETICAL TERM] years commencing on the [relevant] Review Date, if longer **OR** For a term of [LENGTH OF HYPOTHETICAL TERM] years commencing on the [relevant] Review Date].

1.3 [[With rent review dates every [NUMBER] years from the [relevant] Review Date **OR** With a rent review date on [DATE[S]].]

1.4 [With the right for the [willing tenant **OR** willing landlord **OR** parties] to terminate the lease in accordance with clause 58 [but assuming the Break Date[s] in clause 58 [is **OR** are] on [or at any time after] [[DATE[S]] **OR** the [day preceding] [every **OR** the] [ORDINAL NUMBER] anniversary of the [relevant] Review Date].]

1.5 Otherwise on the terms of this lease (other than the amount of the Annual Rent[, **OR** and] [paragraph 1.2 of Part 5 of Schedule 5][, **OR** and] [the Break Date[s]][, **OR** and] [the Review Date[s]][, **OR** and] [ANY OTHER PROVISIONS OF THE LEASE TO BE DISREGARDED] [and the provision in this lease for a rent-free period]).

Part 5 Review of the Annual Rent

1. **Review**

1.1 The Annual Rent shall be reviewed on [the **OR** each] Review Date to equal:
   (a) the amount agreed between the Landlord and Tenant at any time (whether or not that amount is the Open Market Rent); or
   (b) in the absence of such agreement, the greater of:
      (i) the Annual Rent payable immediately before the [relevant] Review Date (or which would then be payable but for any abatement, suspension, concession or reduction of the Annual Rent or restriction on the right to collect it); and
      (ii) [subject to paragraph 1.2 of this Part of this Schedule,] the Open Market Rent agreed or determined pursuant to this Schedule 5.

1.2 [If, at the [relevant] Review Date, the Open Market Rent is:
   (a) less than the Minimum Rent, the Open Market Rent will be deemed to be the Minimum Rent; or
   (b) more than the Maximum Rent, the Open Market Rent will be deemed to be the Maximum Rent.]
1.3 The Landlord and Tenant may agree the revised Annual Rent at any time before it is determined by the Expert.
1.4 [The Landlord must not agree the revised Annual Rent without the consent of the Superior Landlord.]
1.5 As soon as practicable after the amount of the revised Annual Rent has been agreed or determined, a memorandum recording the amount shall be signed by or on behalf of the Landlord, the Tenant and the guarantor. The parties shall each bear their own costs in connection with the memorandum.

2. Determination by the Expert

2.1 If the Landlord and Tenant have not agreed the revised Annual Rent by the date three months before the [relevant] Review Date, then either party may at any time refer the revised Annual Rent for determination by the Expert in accordance with clause 63. The Expert can be appointed in accordance with the terms of this lease irrespective of whether the Landlord and Tenant have tried to first reach an agreement on the revised Annual Rent.

3. Late review of Annual Rent

3.1 If the revised Annual Rent has not been agreed or determined on or before the [relevant] Review Date, the Tenant must:
   (a) continue to pay the Annual Rent at the rate payable immediately before that Review Date; and
   (b) on [or before] the Shortfall Payment Date, pay:
      (i) the shortfall (if any) between the amount of Annual Rent that the Tenant has paid for the period from and including that Review Date and the amount of Annual Rent for that period that would have been payable had the revised Annual Rent been agreed or determined on or before that Review Date; and
      (ii) interest at the Interest Rate on that shortfall. That interest shall be calculated on a daily basis by reference to the Rent Payment Dates on which parts of the shortfall would have been payable if the revised Annual Rent had been agreed or determined on or before that Review Date and the Shortfall Payment Date [(or, if the Tenant pays the shortfall earlier than the Shortfall Payment Date, the date of that payment)].

4. Time not of the essence

4.1 Time is not of the essence for the purposes of this Schedule 5.

5. Guarantor

If at any time there is a guarantor, the guarantor shall not have any right to participate in the review of the Annual Rent but will be bound by the revised Annual Rent.]

Schedule 6 Insurance

1. Landlord's obligation to insure

1.1 Subject to paragraph 1.2 and paragraph 1.3 of this Schedule, the Landlord must insure (and keep insured):
   (a) the Building with reputable insurers on normal market terms against loss or damage by the Insured Risks for the Reinstatement Cost;
   (b) against public liability of the Landlord in relation to the Common Parts in such amount and on such terms as the Landlord shall reasonably consider appropriate; and
   (c) loss of Annual Rent from the Property for [three] years.
1.2 The Landlord shall not be obliged to insure:
   (a) the Excluded Insurance Items or repair any damage to or destruction of the Excluded Insurance Items. References to the Property and the Building in this Schedule 6 shall exclude the Excluded Insurance Items;
   (b) any alterations to the Property that form part of the Property unless:
      (i) those alterations are permitted or required under this lease;
      (ii) those alterations have been completed in accordance with this lease and (where applicable) in accordance with the terms of any consent or approval given under this lease; and
      (iii) the Tenant has notified the Landlord of the amount for which those alterations should be insured and provided evidence of that amount that is satisfactory to the Landlord (acting reasonably); or

(c) the Building when the insurance is vitiated by any act or omission of the Tenant or any Authorised Person.

1.3 The Landlord's obligation to insure is subject to any limitations, excesses and conditions that may be imposed by the insurers.

2. Landlord to provide insurance details

2.1 In relation to any insurance effected by the Landlord under this Schedule 6, the Landlord must:
   (a) at the reasonable request of the Tenant supply the Tenant with:
      (i) full details of the insurance policy;
      (ii) evidence of payment of the current year's premiums; and
      (iii) details of any commission paid to the Landlord by the Landlord's insurer;
   (b) procure that the Tenant is informed of any change in the scope, level or terms of cover [as soon as reasonably practicable after **OR** within five working days of] the Landlord or its agents becoming aware of the change[. **OR** ; and]
   (c) [use [all] reasonable endeavours to procure that the Landlord's insurer:
      (i) waives its rights of subrogation against the Tenant and any lawful undertenants or occupiers of the Property;
      (ii) includes in the insurance policy a non-invalidation provision in respect of any act or default of the Tenant; and
      (iii) permits the interest of the Tenant to be noted on the policy of insurance either specifically or by way of a general noting of tenants' interests under the conditions of the insurance policy.]

3. Tenant's obligations

3.1 The Tenant must pay to the Landlord on demand:
   (a) the Insurance Rent;
   (b) [a fair proportion **OR** the Tenant's Proportion] of any amount that is deducted or disallowed by the insurers pursuant to any excess provision in the insurance policy; and
   (c) [a fair proportion **OR** the Tenant's Proportion] of any costs that the Landlord incurs in obtaining a valuation of the Building for insurance purposes [provided that the Tenant shall not be obliged to contribute towards the costs of any such valuations carried out more frequently than once every [two] years].

3.2 The Tenant must:
   (a) immediately inform the Landlord if any matter occurs in relation to the Tenant or the Property that any insurer or underwriter may treat as material in deciding whether or on what terms to insure or to continue to insure the Building and must also give the Landlord notice of that matter;
   (b) not do or omit to do anything as a result of which:
      (i) any insurance policy for the Building may become void or voidable or otherwise prejudiced;
      (ii) the payment of any policy money may be withheld; or
      (iii) any increased or additional insurance premium may become payable (unless the Tenant has previously notified the Landlord and has paid any increased or additional premium (including any IPT due on that amount));
   (c) comply at all times with the requirements and recommendations of the insurers relating to the Property and the use by the Tenant of any other part of the Building [where written details of those requirements or recommendations have first been given to the Tenant];
   (d) give the Landlord immediate notice of the occurrence of:
      (i) any damage or loss relating to the Property arising from an Insured Risk [or an Uninsured Risk]; or
      (ii) any other event that might affect any insurance policy relating to the Property;
   (e) except for the Excluded Insurance Items forming part of the Property, not effect any buildings insurance of the Property but, if the Tenant becomes entitled to the benefit of any buildings insurance proceeds in respect of the Property, pay those proceeds or cause them to be paid to the Landlord;
   (f) pay the Landlord an amount equal to any insurance money that the insurers of the Building refuse to pay in relation to the Building by reason of any act or omission of the Tenant or any Authorised Person; and
   (g) insure (and keep insured) against public liability of the Tenant in relation to the Property in such amount as the Landlord shall reasonably consider appropriate and, at the request of the Landlord, supply the Landlord with:
      (i) full details of that insurance policy; and

(ii) evidence of payment of the current year's premiums.

4. **Rent suspension**

4.1 Subject to paragraph 4.2 [and paragraph 4.3] of this Schedule, if any Building Damage by an Insured Risk [or an Uninsured Risk] occurs, payment of the Annual Rent and Service Charge (or a fair proportion of the Annual Rent and Service Charge according to the nature and extent of that Building Damage) shall be suspended until the earlier of:

(a) the date on which the Building has been reinstated so as to make the Property fit for occupation and use and accessible; and

(b) the date which is [three] years from and including the date on which that Building Damage occurred.

4.2 The Annual Rent and Service Charge shall not be suspended under paragraph 4.1 of this Schedule if the Building Damage is caused by:

(a) an Insured Risk and:
  (i) the policy of insurance in relation to the Building has been vitiated in whole or in part as a result of any act or omission of the Tenant or any Authorised Person; and
  (ii) the Tenant has not complied with paragraph 3.2(f) of this Schedule[. **OR** ; or]

(b) [an Uninsured Risk and the Building Damage was Tenant Damage.]

4.3 [If payment of the Annual Rent would be suspended under paragraph 4.1 of this Schedule but the rent suspension period would have commenced before the Rent Commencement Date, the following shall apply:

(a) the "Original Rent Commencement Date" shall be the date specified in the definition of Rent Commencement Date in clause 1.1;

(b) the "Suspension Period" shall be the period for which the Annual Rent would have been suspended under paragraph 4.1 of this Schedule had the Annual Rent been payable from the date on which this lease was granted;

(c) the "Rent Resumption Date" shall be the day after the last day of the Suspension Period;

(d) X shall be:
  (i) the number of days from and including the date on which the Suspension Period commences to and including the earlier of the last day of the Suspension Period and the day before the Original Rent Commencement Date; or
  (ii) if only a proportion of the Annual Rent due would have been suspended during the Suspension Period, an equivalent proportion of the number of days calculated under paragraph 4.3(d)(i) of this Schedule (rounding up to the nearest whole day);

(e) if the Rent Resumption Date is on or before the Original Rent Commencement Date, then the Rent Commencement Date shall instead be the day which is X days after the Original Rent Commencement Date; and

(f) if the Rent Resumption Date is after the Original Rent Commencement Date, then the Rent Commencement Date shall instead be the day which is X days after the Rent Resumption Date.]

5. **Landlord's obligation to reinstate following damage or destruction by an Insured Risk**

5.1 Following any damage to or destruction of the Building by an Insured Risk, the Landlord must:

(a) use reasonable endeavours to obtain all necessary planning and other consents to enable the Landlord to reinstate the relevant parts of the Building; and

(b) reinstate the relevant parts of the Building except that the Landlord shall not be obliged to:
  (i) reinstate unless all necessary planning and other consents are obtained;
  (ii) reinstate unless the Tenant has paid the sums due under paragraph 3.1(b) and paragraph 3.2(f) of this Schedule;
  (iii) provide accommodation or facilities identical in layout or design so long as accommodation reasonably equivalent to that previously at the Property and its access, services and amenities is provided; or
  (iv) reinstate after a notice to terminate has been served pursuant to this Schedule 6.

5.2 If the Landlord is obliged to reinstate the relevant parts of the Building pursuant to paragraph 5.2(b) of this Schedule, the Landlord must:

(a) use all insurance money received (other than for loss of rent) and all sums received under paragraph 3.1(b) and paragraph 3.2(f) of this Schedule for the purposes of that reinstatement; and

(b) make up any shortfall out of its own funds

6. **[Termination if reinstatement impossible or impractical following Building Damage by an Insured Risk**

6.1 Following Building Damage by an Insured Risk, if the Landlord (acting reasonably) considers that it is impossible or impractical to reinstate the relevant parts of the Building, the Landlord may terminate this lease by giving notice to the Tenant within [six months] from and including the date on which that Building Damage occurred.]

7. **[Building Damage by an Uninsured Risk**

7.1 If the Annual Rent and the Service Charge (or a fair proportion of the Annual Rent and Service Charge) are suspended under paragraph 4.1 of this Schedule due to Building Damage by an Uninsured Risk, then, within [12] months from and including the date on which that Building Damage occurred, the Landlord must either:

    (a) terminate this lease by giving notice to the Tenant; or
    (b) notify the Tenant that it intends to reinstate the relevant parts of the Building at its own cost.

7.2 If the Landlord notifies the Tenant under paragraph 7.1(b) that it intends to reinstate the relevant parts of the Building, then the Landlord must use:

    (a) reasonable endeavours to obtain all necessary planning and other consents to enable the Landlord to reinstate the relevant parts of the Building; and
    (b) its own monies to reinstate the relevant parts of the Building but the Landlord shall not be obliged to:
        (i) reinstate unless all necessary planning and other consents are obtained;
        (ii) provide accommodation or facilities identical in layout or design so long as accommodation reasonably equivalent to that previously at the Property and its access, services and amenities is provided; or
        (iii) reinstate after a notice to terminate has been served pursuant to this Schedule 6.

7.3 If paragraph 7.1 applies but the Landlord has not served a notice under either paragraph 7.1(a) or paragraph 7.1(b) by the date which is [12] months from and including the date on which the relevant Building Damage occurred, the Tenant may at any time thereafter terminate this lease by giving notice to the Landlord provided that such notice is served before the Property is made fit for occupation and use and accessible.]

8. **Termination if reinstatement not complete by expiry of rent suspension**

If Building Damage by an Insured Risk [or by an Uninsured Risk (where the Landlord elected to reinstate under paragraph 7.1(b) of this Schedule)] occurs and the relevant parts of the Building have not been reinstated so as to make the Property fit for occupation and use and accessible by the date which is [three] years after the date on which that Building Damage occurred, either party may at any time thereafter terminate this lease by giving notice to the other provided that:

    (a) such notice is served before the relevant parts of the Building have been reinstated so as to make the Property fit for occupation and use and accessible; and
    (b) where the Tenant serves the notice, the failure to reinstate so that the Property is fit for occupation and use is not caused by a breach of the Tenant's obligations under clause 18 or this Schedule 6.

9. **Consequences of termination**

If either party gives a notice to terminate this lease in accordance with this Schedule 6:

    (a) this lease shall terminate with immediate effect from the date of the notice;
    (b) none of the parties shall have any further rights or obligations under this lease except for the rights of any party in respect of any earlier breach of this lease; and
    (c) any proceeds of the insurance for the Building shall belong to the Landlord.

10. **Landlord not obliged to reinstate other Lettable Units**

Nothing in this Schedule 6 shall oblige the Landlord to reinstate any Lettable Unit (except the Property).

11. **[Tenant Damage**

11.1 In this paragraph, the term **Uninsured Tenant Damage** shall mean any damage to or destruction of the Building by an Uninsured Risk that is caused by Tenant Damage provided that that damage or destruction does not solely affect the Property.

11.2 If any Uninsured Tenant Damage occurs, the Landlord shall not be obliged to reinstate the Building but, notwithstanding the provisions of clause 18 and clause 60, (in its absolute discretion) the Landlord may give the Tenant a notice that it intends to reinstate the Building.

11.3 If the Landlord serves a notice pursuant to paragraph 11.2 of this Schedule, the Landlord shall not be obliged to:

    (a) reinstate unless all necessary planning and other consents are obtained; or
    (b) provide accommodation or facilities identical in layout or design so long as accommodation reasonably equivalent to that previously at the Building is provided.

11.4 Following the service of a notice pursuant to paragraph 11.2 of this Schedule, the Landlord may enter the Property and carry out the works required to reinstate the Property.

11.5 The Tenant must pay on demand all costs [reasonably and properly] incurred by the Landlord in reinstating any Uninsured Tenant Damage pursuant to this paragraph 11 of this Schedule (including, but not limited to, any professional fees and any VAT in respect of those costs) and any such payment shall be a debt due from the Tenant to the Landlord.

11.6 Any action taken by the Landlord pursuant to this paragraph 11 of this Schedule shall be without prejudice to the Landlord's other rights (including those under clause52).]

Schedule 7 Service Charge

Part 1 Services

1. The Services are:

1.1 Cleaning, maintaining, decorating and repairing the Retained Parts [and remedying any inherent defect in the Retained Parts] and cleaning the windows and other glass forming part of the Lettable Units provided that the Landlord's obligation in respect of cleaning the windows and other glass at the Lettable Units is limited to cleaning the external surfaces only of such windows and other glass.

1.2 Lighting the Common Parts [and the Lettable Units] and cleaning, maintaining, repairing and replacing lighting machinery and equipment on the Common Parts [and the Lettable Units].

1.3 Providing heating to the internal areas of the Common Parts [and the Lettable Units] during such periods of the year as the Landlord reasonably considers appropriate and cleaning, maintaining, repairing and replacing the heating machinery and equipment serving those areas.

1.4 [Providing air conditioning for the internal areas of the Common Parts [and the Lettable Units] and cleaning, maintaining, repairing and replacing air-conditioning equipment serving those areas.]

1.5 [Supplying hot and cold water to the Lettable Units.]

1.6 Storing, compacting, recycling and disposing of refuse from the Building and cleaning, maintaining, repairing and replacing refuse bins on the Common Parts.

1.7 Cleaning, maintaining, repairing and replacing signage for the Common Parts.

1.8 Cleaning, maintaining, repairing, operating and replacing security machinery and equipment (including closed-circuit television) on the Common Parts.

1.9 Cleaning, maintaining, repairing, operating and replacing fire prevention, detection and fighting machinery and equipment and fire alarms on the Common Parts.

1.10 Keeping the lifts on the Common Parts in reasonable working order and cleaning, maintaining, repairing and replacing the lifts and lift machinery and equipment.

1.11 [Keeping the escalators on the Common Parts in reasonable working order and cleaning, maintaining, repairing and replacing the escalators and escalator machinery and equipment.]

1.12 Providing, maintaining, repairing, replacing and operating wireless, phone, data transmission and other telecommunications systems and equipment in or on the Common Parts.

1.13 Cleaning, maintaining, repairing and replacing any signs or noticeboards in or on the Common Parts showing the names and logos of the tenants and other occupiers at the Building.

1.14 Maintaining the landscaped, ornamental, decorative and grassed areas and items in the Common Parts.

1.15 Cleaning, maintaining, repairing and replacing the floor coverings on the internal areas of the Common Parts.

1.16 Cleaning, maintaining, repairing and replacing the furniture and fittings on the Common Parts.

1.17 Cleaning, maintaining, repairing and replacing the furniture, fittings and equipment in the lavatories, washrooms, kitchens and utility areas on the Common Parts and providing hot and cold water, soap, paper, towels and other supplies for them.

1.8 Providing [security,] [reception,] cleaning and maintenance staff for the Common Parts.

1.19 Providing, maintaining, repairing, replacing and operating any loudspeakers, music and/or public-address systems at the Building.

1.20 [Controlling and regulating vehicular traffic using [the Car Park][,] [Service Areas][,] [Service Road] [and] any roadways or accessways forming part of the Building.]

1.21 [Gritting and clearing snow from [the Car Park][,] [Service Areas][,] [Service Road] [and] any roadways or accessways forming part of the Building.]

1.22 Controlling pests and vermin in or on the Common Parts.

1.23 Providing and maintaining any seasonal display, decoration or attraction on the Common Parts.

1.24 Effecting the following insurances in such amount and on such terms as the Landlord (acting reasonably) shall consider appropriate:

   (a) engineering insurances in respect of any plant and machinery at the Common Parts [and the Lettable Units]; and

   (b) employer's liability insurance against all liability of the Landlord to third parties arising out of or in connection with any matter involving or relating to the Building.

1.25 [[ANY OTHER SPECIFIC SERVICES REQUIRED].]

1.26 Any other service, amenity or facility that the Landlord may in its reasonable discretion (acting in accordance with the principles of good estate management) provide for the benefit of the tenants and occupiers of the Building.

Part 2 Service Costs

1. Subject to paragraph 11.10 of Part 4 of this Schedule, the Service Costs are the total of:

1.1 All of the reasonable and properly incurred costs of:

   (a) providing the Services;

   (b) providing the Services in respect of any of the Retained Parts as the Landlord may in its reasonable discretion consider appropriate for the purposes of good estate management;

   (c) the supply and removal of Utilities to and from the Retained Parts;

   (d) reading any meters at the Building;

   (e) complying with the recommendations and requirements of the insurers of the Building (insofar as those recommendations and requirements relate to the Retained Parts);

   (f) complying with all laws relating to the Retained Parts, their use and any works carried out to them, relating to the use of all Service Media, machinery and equipment at or serving the Retained Parts and relating to any materials kept at or disposed of from the Retained Parts;

   (g) complying with the Third Party Rights insofar as they relate to the Retained Parts;

   (h) taking any steps (including proceedings) that the Landlord considers necessary to prevent or remove any encroachment over the Retained Parts or to prevent the acquisition of any right over the Retained Parts (or Building as a whole) or to remove any obstruction to the flow of light or air to the Retained Parts (or the Building as a whole); and

   (i) borrowing to fund major expenditure on any Service which is infrequent or of an unusual nature.

1.2 The total of the reasonable and properly incurred costs, fees and disbursements of:

   (a) any managing agent or person employed by the Landlord, or by the managing agents, or otherwise retained by the Landlord to act on the Landlord's behalf (or, where no such person is employed or retained, the Landlord itself) in relation to the carrying out and provision of the Services, calculation of the Service Costs and the administration of the Service Charge (excluding Site Management Staff) [provided that the aggregate of such fees shall not exceed the Management Fee Cap];

   (b) the accountants employed by the Landlord in relation to the preparation, auditing, certification and review of the Service Charge accounts; and

   (c) a procurement specialist who is employed or retained to achieve greater value for money and cost effectiveness in relation to the Service Costs.

1.3 Subject to paragraph 11.11 of Part 4 of this Schedule, all of the reasonable and properly incurred costs in relation to the Site Management Staff as follows:

   (a) salaries (and all appropriate benefits);

   (b) employers' costs (including, but not limited to, national insurance contributions and tax, costs of compliance with statutory requirements, pension, welfare and insurance contributions) and any associated administrative costs;

   (c) training;

   (d) uniforms; and

   (e) all equipment and supplies needed for the proper performance of their duties.

1.4 All rates, taxes and impositions payable in respect of the Retained Parts, their use and any works carried out on them (other than any taxes payable by the Landlord in connection with any dealing with or disposition of its reversionary interest in the Building).

1.5 The reasonable and proper administrative cost of complying with any of the Landlord's obligations contained in Part 4 of this Schedule (except as specified in paragraph 11.17 of Part 4 of this Schedule).

1.6 All costs incurred or contributed by the Landlord in respect of the [construction,] repair, maintenance or renewal of any road, pathway or other accessway which serves, but does not form part of, the Building.

1.7 [Subject to a fair and reasonable credit (or contribution) being made to the Service Charge Account or Service Charge by the Landlord, any fair and reasonable costs incurred in maintaining or allocating any of the Services for the benefit of any facilities at the Building.]

1.8 Any VAT payable in respect of any of the items mentioned above except to the extent that the Landlord obtains credit for such VAT.

1.9 [[OTHER SERVICE COSTS].]

Part 3 Excluded Service Costs

1. The Excluded Service Costs are any costs which relate to or arise from:

1.1 Matters between the Landlord and an occupier in the Building including (but not limited to) costs relating to or arising from:
   (a) enforcement of covenants to pay rent and other monies payable under the occupier's lease or licence;
   (b) the letting or licensing of any Lettable Unit;
   (c) any consents required under the relevant lease or licence, including, but not limited to, consents to assign, underlet, alterations, change of use and extended hours of use;
   (d) the provision of any Service to any Lettable Unit beyond the [Building Services Hours **OR** Permitted Hours] or beyond the usual times during which the Services are provided; and
   (e) rent reviews.

1.2 Negligence of the Landlord or of any person referred to in paragraph 1.2 of Part 2 of this Schedule.

1.3 Any Lettable Unit which is not let or occupied.

1.4 Any shortfall in the costs of providing any of the Services to a Lettable Unit for which the Landlord has agreed a special concession.

1.5 The maintenance or operation of or the provision of any service or support to:
   (a) any premises within the Building used by the Landlord solely for its own purposes (except where such use is wholly or partly in connection with the management of the Building itself, in which case the whole or a fair and reasonable part, as the case may be, of such costs shall be a Service Cost); and
   (b) any cost centre within the Building that generates income for the Landlord (except where such income is (at least in part) credited to the Service Charge Account, in which case the whole or a fair and reasonable proportion of such costs shall be a Service Cost).

1.6 The initial provision of any items that are reasonably to be considered part of the original design and construction of the fabric, plant or equipment of the Building [or any accessway serving the Building] together with the initial setting up that is reasonably to be considered part of the original development of the Building.

1.7 Any future redevelopment of the Building.

1.8 The replacement of any item of the fabric, plant, equipment or materials necessary for the operation of the Building, except where analysis of the reasonable options and alternatives determines that:
   (a) replacement is appropriate because the fabric, plant, equipment or materials are beyond economic repair at reasonable cost or beyond efficient or economic operation;
   (b) the cost of replacement is relatively low when compared to the greater cost anticipated if replacement is postponed materially; or
   (c) replacement is required by statute or the insurers of the Building.

1.9 The improvement of any item (where the cost exceeds the costs of normal maintenance, repair or replacement) except where the expenditure can be justified following the analysis of reasonable options and alternatives and having regard to a cost benefit analysis over the term of the leases in the Building.

1.10 Any Services provided by reason of damage to or destruction of the Retained Parts by an Insured Risk [or an Uninsured Risk].

1.11 Any costs incurred in relation to any dealing with the Landlord's interest in the Building.

1.12 Any asset management services provided to the Landlord by its managing agent.

1.13 [Costs, fees and disbursements of any person referred to in paragraph 1.2(a) of Part 2 of this Schedule which are in excess of the Management Fee Cap.]

1.14 [[OTHER EXCLUDED SERVICE COSTS].]

Part 4 Service Charge administration and obligations

1. **Provision of Services**

1.1 Subject to the other provisions of this paragraph 1 and paragraph 11.4 of this Part of this Schedule, the Landlord:

    (a) must provide the Services [set out in paragraph 1.1 to [paragraph 1.12 **OR** [OTHER PARAGRAPH NUMBER]] (inclusive) of Part 1 of this Schedule][. **OR** ; and]

    (b) [may (but shall not be obliged to) provide any of the other Services set out in Part 1 of this Schedule.]

1.2 [The Landlord may (in its absolute discretion) add to, extend, vary, withdraw or withhold any of the Services [provided that in doing so the Landlord must act reasonably and in the interests of good estate management].]

1.3 The Landlord shall not be obliged to:

    (a) [carry out any works where the need for those works has arisen by reason of any damage or destruction by an Uninsured Risk (unless the Landlord has elected to carry out such works under paragraph 7.1 of Schedule 6); [or]]

    (b) [provide any of the Services outside the [Building Services Hours **OR** Permitted Hours]; or]

    (c) replace or renew any part of the Building or any item or system within the Building unless it is beyond economic repair.

1.4 The Landlord shall not be liable for any interruption in, or disruption to, the provision of any of the Services for any reason that is outside the reasonable control of the Landlord [provided that the Landlord must use reasonable endeavours to restore the provision of the relevant Service as soon as reasonably practicable].

2. **Tenant's obligation to pay the Service Charge**

2.1 Subject to paragraph 3 of this Part of this Schedule, the Tenant must pay to the Landlord the Service Charge for each Service Charge Year by way of:

    (a) on account payments of the Estimated Service Charge in accordance with paragraph 5 of this Part of this Schedule;

    (b) any payment payable under paragraph 6 of this Part of this Schedule; and

    (c) any payment payable under paragraph 9.1(a) of this Part of this Schedule.

3. **Apportionments in Current Service Charge Year and Final Service Charge Year**

3.1 For the Current Service Charge Year:

    (a) the Tenant shall only be obliged to pay to the Landlord apportioned amounts of the Estimated Service Charge and Service Charge for that Service Charge Year; and

    (b) those apportioned amounts shall be calculated on a daily basis for the period from and including [the date of this lease **OR** [DATE]] to and including the last day of the Current Service Charge Year.

3.2 For the Final Service Charge Year:

    (a) the Tenant shall only be obliged to pay to the Landlord an apportioned amount of the Service Charge for that Service Charge Year; and

    (b) that apportioned amount shall be calculated on a daily basis for the period from and including the first day of the Final Service Charge Year to and including the Termination Date.

4. **Estimated Service Charge calculation**

4.1 At least one month before the start of each Service Charge Year, the Landlord must prepare and send to the Tenant:

    (a) a Service Costs Budget for that Service Charge Year (in such form to enable the Tenant to compare it with the previous Service Charge Statement) [including details of the Management Fee Cap], together with appropriate explanatory commentary;

    (b) a statement of the Estimated Service Charge for that Service Charge Year; and

    (c) an apportionment matrix that shows the basis of calculation and the apportionment of Service Costs across the Building.

4.2 The Landlord shall, so far as reasonably practicable, endeavour to ensure that the form and content of the information provided pursuant to paragraph 4.1 of this Part of this Schedule reflects the principles contained in the RICS Statement.

5. **Tenant's obligation to pay the Estimated Service Charge**

5.1 Subject to paragraph 5.2 of this Part of this Schedule, the Tenant must pay to the Landlord:

    (a) for the Current Service Charge Year, the apportioned amount of the Estimated Service Charge calculated in accordance with paragraph 3.1 of this Part of this Schedule by equal instalments in advance on the date of this lease and each of the subsequent Rent Payment Dates during the Current Service Charge Year; and

(b) for each subsequent Service Charge Year, the Estimated Service Charge for that Service Charge Year by equal instalments in advance on each of the Rent Payment Dates during that Service Charge Year.

5.2 Following receipt by the Tenant of a revised statement of the Estimated Service Charge pursuant to paragraph 10.2(c) of this Part of this Schedule, then, for the Service Charge Year to which that revised statement relates:

(a) the amount specified in that revised statement for the purposes of paragraph 10.2(c)(i) of this Part of this Schedule shall apply in substitution for the Estimated Service Charge previously payable by the Tenant for that Service Charge Year; and

(b) the Tenant must pay to the Landlord the amount specified in that revised statement for the purposes of paragraph 10.2(c)(ii) of this Part of this Schedule by equal instalments in advance on each of the remaining Rent Payment Dates during that Service Charge Year.

6. **Unexpected Service Costs**

6.1 If the Landlord is required to incur or incurs any Service Cost that was not anticipated when determining the Estimated Service Charge for any Service Charge Year, the Tenant must pay to the Landlord on demand any sum that the Landlord reasonably requires from the Tenant in respect of that Service Cost.

6.2 Any sums paid by the Tenant pursuant to this paragraph 6 shall be treated as Estimated Service Charge paid by the Tenant for the purposes of paragraph 9.1 of this Part of this Schedule.

7. **Service Charge Statement**

7.1 As soon as reasonably practicable and in any event no later than four months after the end of each Service Charge Year, the Landlord must prepare and send to the Tenant:

(a) a Service Charge Statement for that Service Charge Year (in such form to enable the Tenant to compare it with the previous Service Charge Statement) together with appropriate explanatory commentary; and

(b) an apportionment matrix that shows the basis of calculation and the apportionment of Service Costs across the Building.

7.2 The Landlord must, so far as reasonably practicable, endeavour to ensure that the form and content of the information provided pursuant to paragraph 7.1 of this Part of this Schedule reflects the principles contained in the RICS Statement.

7.3 If any Service Cost is omitted from the calculation of the Service Charge in any Service Charge Year, the Landlord may include it in the Service Costs Budget and Service Charge Statement in [any **OR** the] following Service Charge Year.

7.4 The person giving the certificate in the Service Charge Statement shall be appropriately qualified, competent and non-partisan, and shall have experience in dealing with service charges. The Service Charge Statement shall state the name and role of the person giving such certificate.

7.5 Subject to paragraph 7.5 and paragraph 12 of this Part of this Schedule and except in the case of manifest error, the Service Charge Statement shall be conclusive as to all matters of fact to which it refers.

8. **Tenant's inspection and audit**

8.1 Within the period of four months from and including the Tenant's receipt of a Service Charge Statement, the Tenant may:

(a) inspect all relevant paperwork and any supporting documentation relating to that Service Charge Statement by appointment with the Landlord or its agents; and

(b) may raise enquiries in respect of the Service Charge Statement and the Landlord must respond promptly and efficiently to any reasonable enquiries of the Tenant.

8.2 On request by the Tenant and at the Tenant's cost, the Landlord must agree to an independent audit of the Service Costs.

9. **Balancing payments of Service Charge**

9.1 If the Service Charge (or, where applicable, the apportioned amount of the Service Charge calculated in accordance with paragraph 3 of this Part of this Schedule) payable by the Tenant for a Service Charge Year is:

(a) more than the Estimated Service Charge paid by the Tenant during that Service Charge Year, the Tenant must pay the difference to the Landlord within [ten] working days of demand; or

(b) less than the Estimated Service Charge paid by the Tenant during that Service Charge Year, the Landlord must [credit the difference against the Tenant's next instalment of Estimated Service Charge (and, where the difference exceeds the next instalment, the Landlord must credit the balance of the difference against each succeeding instalment until it is fully credited). Except that, for the Final

Service Charge Year, the Landlord must] repay the difference to the Tenant within one month of the date on which the Service Charge Statement for that Service Charge Year is certified.

9.2 The provisions in this paragraph 9 shall continue to apply notwithstanding the occurrence of the Termination Date but only in respect of the Tenant's obligation to pay the Service Charge for the period up to and including the Termination Date.

10. Alternative annual accounting period

10.1 The Landlord may from time to time stipulate and notify to the Tenant an alternative annual accounting period as the Service Charge Year.

10.2 If the Landlord stipulates and notifies to the Tenant an alternative annual accounting period in accordance with paragraph 10.1 of this Part of this Schedule, the Landlord must:

(a) at the same time notify the Tenant of its decision to change the end date of the Service Charge Year current at the date of that notification to either increase or decrease the length of that Service Charge Year to a period that is more or less than an annual period to accommodate that alternative annual accounting period;

(b) act reasonably in the interests of good estate management when deciding whether to increase or decrease the length of the Service Charge Year pursuant to paragraph 10.2(a) of this Part of this Schedule; and

(c) as soon as reasonably practicable after notifying the Tenant of its decision pursuant to paragraph 10.2(a) of this Part of this Schedule, prepare and send to the Tenant a revised Service Costs Budget and a revised statement of the Estimated Service Charge for that Service Charge Year which includes:

(i) a statement of the amount of Estimated Service Charge payable by the Tenant for that Service Charge Year;

(ii) a statement of the amount of that revised Estimated Service Charge payable by the Tenant for the remainder of that Service Charge Year taking into account any payments of Estimated Service Charge already made by the Tenant during that Service Charge Year; and

(iii) explanations of how the amounts in paragraph 10.2(c)(i) and paragraph 10.2(c)(ii) of this Part of this Schedule have been calculated.

11. Landlord's general rights and obligations

11.1 In performing its obligations in this Schedule, the Landlord must have regard to the aims, core principles and best practice recommended in the RICS Statement except where there are sound reasons not to do so and the Landlord can justify and explain those reasons.

11.2 The Landlord must apportion the Service Costs between the Lettable Units and the Property on a fair and reasonable basis, using a recognised method and consistent basis reflecting the availability to, benefit from and use of the Services by the occupiers of the Building.

11.3 The Landlord must provide the Services on a value for money and cost effective basis. The Tenant acknowledges that this may not necessarily mean doing so at the lowest price.

11.4 The Landlord must ensure that the range, standard and cost of the Services are relevant to the Building (including its location, size, use and character) and the occupiers of the Lettable Units.

11.5 The Landlord must review regularly the range, standard and cost of the Services to ensure that they:

(a) remain relevant; and

(b) still represent value for money (either by benchmarking the cost against the market cost or by requiring submission of competitive quotations or tenders as appropriate).

11.6 The Landlord must ensure that the Service Charge Account is a discrete or virtual bank account in accordance with the RICS Statement.

11.7 The Landlord must ensure that the Management Fee is transparent and is not linked to a percentage of expenditure on the Services.

11.8 The Landlord must credit to the Service Charge Account:

(a) all payments of Service Charge; and

(b) any interest paid on any instalment of Service Charge which is paid late.

11.9 The Landlord must ensure that the interest earned on the Service Charge Account (or a fair and reasonable proportion of such interest, if the account relates to other properties in addition to the Building) is credited to the Service Charge Account (after deduction of bank charges, tax and any other appropriate amounts).

11.10 The Landlord must not include any of the Excluded Service Costs within the Service Costs and no sums payable by the Tenant under this Schedule shall include any Excluded Service Costs.

11.11 Where the Site Management Staff provide Services to the Building and to other properties, the Landlord must include in the Service Costs only a reasonable proportion of the costs set out in paragraph 1.3 of Part 2 of this Schedule.

11.12 The Landlord must credit the Service Charge Account with any Service Charge apportioned to any unlet Lettable Units.

11.13 [Where barrows and kiosks situated from time to time within the Common Parts (not being Lettable Units) derive a benefit from the Services, the Landlord must set off or credit the Service Costs with an amount which reflects a notional fair and reasonable charge for the benefit so derived, but the income otherwise derived from them shall belong to the Landlord.]

11.14 If requested by the Tenant, the Landlord must provide the Tenant with evidence to justify the cost of replacement pursuant to any of paragraph 1.8(a) to paragraph 1.8(c) (inclusive) of Part 3 of this Schedule.

11.15 Where the Landlord believes that the expenditure is justified pursuant to paragraph 1.9 of Part 3 of this Schedule, the Landlord must provide the Tenant with evidence to support and explain its decision before the expenditure is incurred.

11.16 The Landlord must use reasonable endeavours to notify the Tenant promptly in advance (and within the relevant Service Charge Year) of any likely material or significant variation to the Service Costs set out in a Service Costs Budget of which the Landlord becomes aware, together with an explanation of how this variation may be mitigated (if appropriate).

11.17 At the Tenant's request, the Landlord must give the Tenant access free of charge to inspect any report where the cost of obtaining this information is included in the Service Costs, and the tender documents for any tender. If the Tenant requires copies, the Landlord is entitled to charge a reasonable sum for the cost of copying and posting such documents and the time spent arranging this.

11.18 Where the Landlord is required to comply with any obligation contained in this clause such obligation shall, where relevant, include, in the alternative, an obligation on the Landlord to ensure that its managing agent complies with that obligation.

12. Tenant's general obligations

12.1 The Tenant must:
  (a) co-operate fully with the Landlord and its managing agent in order that the Landlord and the managing agent may administer the Service Charge in accordance with the provisions of this clause; and
  (b) disclose to the Landlord details of the brief (and fee basis) for any consultant appointed by the Tenant to assist in resolving any service charge disputes.

13. Disputes

13.1 Any dispute between the Landlord and the Tenant that arises in connection with the provisions of this Schedule 7 may, in the absence of agreement, be referred at any time by either party for determination by an Expert under clause 63.]

Part 5 [Service Charge Cap

1. Definitions

1.1 The following definitions apply in this Part 5 of this Schedule:

Base Index Value:

[[the value of the Index for [MONTH AND YEAR] OR [FIGURE]].

OR

is:

(a) for the first occasion on which the Indexed Service Charge Cap is calculated pursuant to this Part of this Schedule, [the value of the Index for [MONTH AND YEAR] OR [FIGURE]]; and

(b) for each subsequent occasion, the Current Index Value that applied for the previous Service Charge Year.]

Base Service Charge Cap: £[AMOUNT].

Current Index Value: the value of the Index for the month which is [three] months before the month in which the relevant Service Charge Year commences.

Index: the [All Items OR [OTHER INDEX]] index of the RPI.

Indexed Service Charge Cap: a sum calculated in accordance with the following formula:

(A/B) x C

Where:

A = the Current Index Value;

B = the Base Index Value; and

C = the Base Service Charge Cap [for the first occasion on which the Indexed Service Charge Cap is calculated pursuant to this Part of this Schedule and, for each subsequent occasion, the Service Charge Cap that applied for the previous Service Charge Year].

RPI: the Retail Prices Index or any official index replacing it.

Service Charge Cap: is:

(a) for the Current Service Charge Year, the Base Service Charge Cap; and

(b) for each subsequent Service Charge Year, [the higher of] the Indexed Service Charge Cap for that Service Charge Year [and an amount equivalent to the Service Charge Cap that applied for the previous Service Charge Year].

2. Service Charge Cap

2.1 Subject to paragraph 2.2 of this Part of this Schedule, neither the Estimated Service Charge nor the Service Charge payable by the Tenant for each Service Charge Year shall exceed the Service Charge Cap for that Service Charge Year except that:

(a) for the Current Service Charge Year, neither the Estimated Service Charge nor the Service Charge payable by the Tenant shall exceed [a sum calculated by apportioning the Base Service Charge Cap on a daily basis for the period from and including [the date of this lease **OR** [DATE]] to and including the last day of the Current Service Charge Year **OR** £[AMOUNT]]; and

(b) for the Final Service Charge Year, the Service Charge payable by the Tenant shall not exceed a sum calculated by apportioning the Service Charge Cap for the Final Service Charge Year on a daily basis for the period from and including the first day of the Final Service Charge Year to and including the Termination Date.

2.2 If the Landlord increases or decreases the length of any Service Charge Year pursuant to paragraph 10.2(a) of Part 4 of this Schedule neither the Estimated Service Charge nor the Service Charge payable by the Tenant for that Service Charge Year shall exceed the sum calculated by apportioning the Service Charge Cap for that Service Charge Year on a daily basis to reflect the revised length of that Service Charge Year except that:

(a) for the Current Service Charge Year, neither the Estimated Service Charge nor the Service Charge payable by the Tenant shall exceed the sum calculated by apportioning the Base Service Charge Cap on a daily basis for the period from and including [the date of this lease **OR** [DATE]] to and including the last day of the Current Service Charge Year; and

(b) for the Final Service Charge Year, the Service Charge payable by the Tenant shall not exceed the sum calculated by apportioning the Service Charge Cap for that Service Charge Year on a daily basis for the period from and including the first day of the Final Service Charge Year to and including the Termination Date.

3. Changes to the Index

3.1 Subject to paragraph 3.2 of this Part of this Schedule, if there is any change to the methods used to compile the RPI, including any change to the items from which the Index is compiled, or if the reference base used to compile the RPI changes, the calculation of the Indexed Service Charge Cap shall be made taking into account the effect of this change.

3.2 The Landlord and the Tenant must use reasonable endeavours to agree within a reasonable time an alternative mechanism for setting the Indexed Service Charge Cap if either:

(a) the Landlord or the Tenant reasonably believes that any change referred to in paragraph 3.1 of this Part of this Schedule would fundamentally alter the calculation of the Indexed Service Charge Cap in accordance with this Part of this Schedule and has given notice to the other party of that belief; or

(b) it becomes impossible or impracticable to calculate the Indexed Service Charge Cap in accordance with this Part of this Schedule.

3.3 The alternative mechanism referred to in paragraph 3.2 of this Part of this Schedule may (where reasonable) include, or consist of, substituting an alternative index for the RPI.

3.4 The alternative mechanism for setting the Indexed Service Charge Cap shall be agreed between the Landlord and Tenant or may, in the absence of agreement, be referred at any time by either party for determination by the Expert in accordance with clause 63.]

Schedule 8 Guarantee and indemnity

1. **Guarantee and indemnity**
   1.1 The Guarantor guarantees to the Landlord that the Tenant shall:
       (a) pay the Rents and observe and perform the tenant covenants of this lease and that if the Tenant fails to pay any of those Rents or to observe or perform any of those tenant covenants, the Guarantor shall pay or observe and perform them; and
       (b) observe and perform any obligations the Tenant enters into in an authorised guarantee agreement made in respect of this lease (the **AGA**) and that, if the Tenant fails to do so, the Guarantor shall observe and perform those obligations.
   1.2 The Guarantor covenants with the Landlord as principal obligor and as a separate and independent obligation and liability from its obligations and liabilities under paragraph 1.1 of this Schedule to indemnify and keep indemnified the Landlord against any failure by the Tenant:
       (a) to pay any of the Rents or any failure to observe or perform any of the tenant covenants of this lease; or
       (b) to observe or perform any of the obligations the Tenant enters into in the AGA.

2. **Guarantor's liability**
   2.1 The liability of the Guarantor under paragraph 1.1(a) and V1.2(a) of this Schedule shall continue until the Termination Date, or until the Tenant is released from the tenant covenants of this lease by virtue of the LTCA 1995, if earlier.
   2.2 The liability of the Guarantor shall not be reduced, discharged or otherwise adversely affected by:
       (a) any time or indulgence granted by the Landlord to the Tenant;
       (b) any delay or forbearance by the Landlord in enforcing the payment of any of the rents or the observance or performance of any of the tenant covenants of this lease (or the Tenant's obligations under the AGA) or in making any demand in respect of any of them;
       (c) any refusal by the Landlord to accept any rent or other payment due under this lease where the Landlord believes that the acceptance of such rent or payment may prejudice its ability to re-enter the Property;
       (d) the Landlord exercising any right or remedy against the Tenant for any failure to pay the Rents or to observe or perform the tenant covenants of this lease (or the Tenant's obligations under the AGA);
       (e) the Landlord taking any action or refraining from taking any action in connection with any other security held by the Landlord in respect of the Tenant's liability to pay the Rents or observe and perform the tenant covenants of the lease (or the Tenant's obligations under the AGA) including the release of any such security;
       (f) [a release or compromise of the liability of any one of the persons who is the Guarantor, or the grant of any time or concession to any one of them;]
       (g) any legal limitation or disability on the Tenant or any invalidity or irregularity of any of the tenant covenants of the lease (or the Tenant's obligations under the AGA) or any unenforceability of any of them against the Tenant;
       (h) the Tenant being dissolved, or being struck off the register of companies or otherwise ceasing to exist, or, if the Tenant is an individual, by the Tenant dying or becoming incapable of managing its affairs;
       (i) without prejudice to paragraph 4 of this Schedule, the disclaimer of the Tenant's liability under this lease or the forfeiture of this lease;
       (j) the surrender of the lease in respect of part only of the Property, except that the Guarantor shall not be under any liability in relation to the surrendered part in respect of any period after the surrender; or
       (k) any other act or omission except an express [written] release [by deed] of the Guarantor by the Landlord.
   2.3 Any sum payable by the Guarantor must be paid without any set-off or counterclaim, deduction or withholding (other than any deduction or withholding of tax as required by law) against the Landlord or the Tenant.

3. **Variations and supplemental documents**
   3.1 The Guarantor must, at the request of the Landlord, join in and give its consent to the terms of any consent, approval, variation or other document that may be entered into by the Tenant in connection with this lease (or the AGA).
   3.2 The Guarantor shall not be released by any variation of the rents reserved by, or the tenant covenants in, this lease (or the Tenant's obligations under the AGA) whether or not:
       (a) the variation is material or prejudicial to the Guarantor;

(b) the variation is made in any document; or

(c) the Guarantor has consented, in writing or otherwise, to the variation.

3.3 The liability of the Guarantor shall apply to the rents reserved by and the tenant covenants in this lease (and the Tenant's obligations under the AGA) as varied except to the extent that the liability of the Guarantor is affected by section 18 of the LTCA 1995.

4. Guarantor to take a new lease or make payment

4.1 If this lease is forfeited or the liability of the Tenant under this lease is disclaimed and the Landlord gives the Guarantor notice not later than [six] months after the forfeiture or the Landlord having received notice of the disclaimer, the Guarantor must enter into a new lease of the Property on the terms set out in paragraph 4.2 of this Schedule.

4.2 The rights and obligations under the new lease shall take effect beginning on the date of the forfeiture or disclaimer and the new lease shall:

(a) be granted subject to the right of any person to have this lease vested in them by the court and to the terms on which any such order may be made and subject to the rights of any third party existing at the date of the grant;

(b) be for a term that expires on the same date as the end of the Contractual Term of this lease had there been no forfeiture or disclaimer;

(c) reserve as an initial annual rent an amount equal to the Annual Rent payable under this lease at the date of the forfeiture or disclaimer or which would be payable but for any abatement or suspension of the Annual Rent or restriction on the right to collect it [(subject to paragraph 5 of this Schedule) and which is subject to review on the same terms and dates provided by this lease]; [and]

(d) [be excluded from sections 24 to 28 of the LTA 1954; and]

(e) otherwise be on the same terms as this lease (as varied if there has been any variation).

4.3 The Guarantor must pay the Landlord's solicitors' costs and disbursements (on a full indemnity basis) and any VAT in respect of them in relation to the new lease and must execute and deliver to the Landlord a counterpart of the new lease within one month of service of the Landlord's notice.

4.4 The grant of a new lease and its acceptance by the Guarantor shall be without prejudice to any other rights that the Landlord may have against the Guarantor or against any other person or in respect of any other security that the Landlord may have in connection with this lease.

4.5 The Landlord may, instead of giving the Guarantor notice pursuant to paragraph 4.1 of this Schedule but in the same circumstances and within the same time limit, require the Guarantor to pay an amount equal to [six] months' Annual Rent and the Guarantor must pay that amount on demand.

5. [Rent at the date of forfeiture or disclaimer

5.1 If at the date of the forfeiture or disclaimer there is a rent review pending under this lease, then the initial annual rent to be reserved by the new lease shall be subject to review on the date on which the term of the new lease commences on the same terms as those that apply to a review of the Annual Rent under this lease, such review date to be included in the new lease.

5.2 If paragraph 5.1 of this Schedule applies, then the review for which it provides shall be in addition to any rent reviews that are required under paragraph 4.2(c) of this Schedule.]

6. Payments in gross and restrictions on the Guarantor

6.1 Any payment or dividend that the Landlord receives from the Tenant (or its estate) or any other person in connection with any insolvency proceedings or arrangement involving the Tenant shall be taken and applied as a payment in gross and shall not prejudice the right of the Landlord to recover from the Guarantor to the full extent of the obligations that are the subject of this guarantee and indemnity.

6.2 The Guarantor must not claim in competition with the Landlord in any insolvency proceedings or arrangement of the Tenant in respect of any payment made by the Guarantor pursuant to this guarantee and indemnity. If it otherwise receives any money in such proceedings or arrangement, it must hold that money on trust for the Landlord to the extent of its liability to the Landlord.

6.3 The Guarantor must not, without the consent of the Landlord, exercise any right or remedy that it may have (whether against the Tenant or any other person) in respect of any amount paid or other obligation performed by the Guarantor under this guarantee and indemnity unless and until all the obligations of the Guarantor under this guarantee and indemnity have been fully performed.

7. Other securities

7.1 The Guarantor warrants that it has not taken and covenants that it shall not take any security from or over the assets of the Tenant in respect of any liability of the Tenant to the Guarantor. If it does take or hold any such security it shall hold it for the benefit of the Landlord.

7.2 This guarantee and indemnity is in addition to and independent of any other security that the Landlord may from time to time hold from the Guarantor or the Tenant or any other person in respect of the liability of the Tenant to pay the Rents and to observe and perform the tenant covenants of this lease. It shall not merge in or be affected by any other security.

7.3 The Guarantor shall not be entitled to claim or participate in any other security held by the Landlord in respect of the liability of the Tenant to pay the Rents or to observe and perform the tenant covenants of this lease.

Signed as a deed by [NAME OF **Landlord**] in the presence of:

....

[SIGNATURE OF WITNESS]
[NAME, ADDRESS [AND OCCUPATION] OF WITNESS]

....
[SIGNATURE OF **Landlord**]

OR

Executed as deed by [NAME OF **Landlord**] acting by [NAME OF FIRST DIRECTOR], a director, and [NAME OF SECOND DIRECTOR/SECRETARY], [a director OR its secretary]

....
[SIGNATURE OF FIRST DIRECTOR]
Director

....
[SIGNATURE OF SECOND DIRECTOR OR SECRETARY]
Director OR Secretary

OR

Executed as deed by [NAME OF **Landlord**] acting by [NAME OF DIRECTOR] a director, in the presence of:

....

[SIGNATURE OF WITNESS]
[NAME, ADDRESS [AND OCCUPATION] OF WITNESS]

....
[SIGNATURE OF DIRECTOR]
Director

Signed as a deed by [NAME OF **Tenant**] in the presence of:

....

[SIGNATURE OF WITNESS]
[NAME, ADDRESS [AND OCCUPATION] OF WITNESS]

....
[SIGNATURE OF **Tenant**]

OR

Executed as deed by [NAME OF **Tenant**] acting by [NAME OF FIRST DIRECTOR], a director, and [NAME OF SECOND DIRECTOR/SECRETARY], [a director OR its secretary]

....
[SIGNATURE OF FIRST DIRECTOR]
Director

....
[SIGNATURE OF SECOND DIRECTOR OR SECRETARY]
Director OR Secretary

OR

Executed as deed by [NAME OF **Tenant**] acting by [NAME OF DIRECTOR] a director, in the presence of: ……………………… [SIGNATURE OF WITNESS] [NAME, ADDRESS [AND OCCUPATION] OF WITNESS]	……………………… [SIGNATURE OF DIRECTOR] Director
Signed as a deed by [NAME OF **Guarantor**] in the presence of: ……………………… [SIGNATURE OF WITNESS] [NAME, ADDRESS [AND OCCUPATION] OF WITNESS]	……………………… [SIGNATURE OF **Guarantor**]
OR	
Executed as deed by [NAME OF **Guarantor**] acting by [NAME OF FIRST DIRECTOR], a director, and [NAME OF SECOND DIRECTOR/SECRETARY], [a director OR its secretary]	……………………… [SIGNATURE OF FIRST DIRECTOR] Director ……………………… [SIGNATURE OF SECOND DIRECTOR OR SECRETARY] Director OR Secretary
OR	
Executed as deed by [NAME OF **Guarantor**] acting by [NAME OF DIRECTOR] a director, in the presence of: ……………………… [SIGNATURE OF WITNESS] [NAME, ADDRESS [AND OCCUPATION] OF WITNESS]	……………………… [SIGNATURE OF DIRECTOR] Director

Annex A Property Plan
Annex B [Storage Area Plan]
Annex C Building Plan
Annex D [Schedule of Condition]
Annex E [Tenant's Plant Area Plan]

APPENDIX 5

Specimen Authorised Guarantee Agreement

THIS DEED IS DATED . . . .

Parties

- [FULL COMPANY NAME] incorporated and registered in England and Wales with company number [NUMBER] whose registered office is at [REGISTERED OFFICE ADDRESS](Landlord).
- [FULL COMPANY NAME] incorporated and registered in England and Wales with company number [NUMBER] whose registered office is at [REGISTERED OFFICE ADDRESS](Tenant).

Background

1 This agreement is supplemental and collateral to the Lease and to the Licence to Assign.
2 The Landlord is entitled to the immediate reversion to the Lease.
3 The residue of the term granted by the Lease is vested in the Tenant.
4 The Tenant intends to assign the Lease and has agreed to enter into an authorised guarantee agreement with the Landlord.

1. Agreed terms

1.1 The definitions and rules of interpretation set out in this clause apply to this agreement.

Assignee: the person or persons defined as assignee in the Licence to Assign.

Lease: a lease of [ADDRESS/DESCRIPTION OF THE PROPERTY] dated [DATE] and made between [PARTIES], and all documents supplemental or collateral to that lease.

Licence to Assign: a licence to assign the Lease dated [DATE] and made between [PARTIES].

Property: [ADDRESS/DESCRIPTION OF THE PROPERTY] as [more particularly described in and] demised by the Lease.

[1954 Act: Landlord and Tenant Act 1954.]

1.2 References to the Landlord include a reference to the person entitled for the time being to the immediate reversion to the Lease.

1.3 The expression Tenant Covenants has the meaning given to it by the Landlord and Tenant (Covenants) Act 1995.

1.4 References to the Completion of the Assignment are to the date on which the deed of assignment to the Assignee is dated and not to the registration of that deed at Land Registry.

1.5 Unless otherwise specified a reference to a particular law is a reference to it as it is in force for the time being taking account of any amendment, extension, application or re-enactment and includes any subordinate laws for the time being in force made under it.

1.6 A Person includes a corporate or unincorporated body.

1.7 Except where a contrary intention appears, a reference to a clause or schedule is a reference to a clause of, or schedule to this agreement, and a reference in a schedule to a paragraph is to a paragraph of that schedule.

1.8 Clause, schedule and paragraph headings are not to affect the interpretation of this agreement.

2. Consideration and effect

2.1 The obligations on the Tenant in this agreement are owed to the Landlord and are made in consideration of the Landlord's consent granted in the Licence to Assign.

2.2 The provisions of this agreement shall take effect on the date the Assignee becomes bound by the Tenant Covenants of the Lease, and are to continue until the end of the term of the Lease (however it may end) and during any agreed or statutory continuation of it, or until the Assignee is released from the tenant covenants of the Lease by virtue of the Landlord and Tenant (Covenants) Act 1995, whichever is earlier.

2.3 If the Tenant is more than one person, then each of those persons shall be jointly and individually liable for their respective obligations arising by virtue of this agreement or the assignment. The Landlord may release or compromise the liability of any one of those persons or grant any time or concession to any one of them without affecting the liability of any other of them.

3. Guarantee and indemnity

3.1 The Tenant guarantees to the Landlord that the Assignee will pay the rents reserved by the Lease and observe and perform the Tenant Covenants of the Lease and that if the Assignee fails to pay any of those rents or to observe or perform any of those Tenant Covenants, the Tenant will pay or observe and perform them.

3.2 The Tenant covenants with the Landlord as a separate and independent primary obligation to indemnify the Landlord against any failure to pay any of the rents reserved by the Lease or any failure to observe or perform any of the Tenant Covenants of the Lease.

4. Tenant's liability

4.1 The liability of the Tenant shall not be affected by:

4.1.1 Any time or indulgence granted by the Landlord to the Assignee (or to any person to whom the Assignee has assigned the Lease pursuant to an assignment that is an excluded assignment under section 11 of the Landlord and Tenant (Covenants) Act 1995); or

4.1.2 Any delay or forbearance by the Landlord in enforcing the payment of any of the rents or the observance or performance of any of the tenant covenants of the Lease or in making any demand in respect of any of them; or

4.1.3 Any refusal by the Landlord to accept any rent or other payment due under the Lease where the Landlord believes that the acceptance of such rent or payment may prejudice its ability to re-enter the Property; or

4.1.4 The Landlord exercising any right or remedy against the Assignee for any failure to pay the rents reserved by the Lease or to observe or perform the tenant covenants of the Lease; or

4.1.5 The Landlord taking any action or refraining from taking any action in connection with any other security held by the Landlord in respect of the Assignee's liability to pay the rents reserved by the Lease and observe and perform the tenant covenants of the Lease (including the release of any such security); or

4.1.6 A release or compromise of the liability of any one of the persons who is the Tenant, or the grant of any time or concession to any one of them; or

4.1.7 Any legal limitation or disability on the Assignee or any invalidity or irregularity of any of the tenant covenants of the Lease or any unenforceability of any of them against the Assignee; or

4.1.8 The Assignee being dissolved or being struck off the register of companies or otherwise ceasing to exist; or

4.1.9 Without prejudice to clause 6, the disclaimer of the liability of the Assignee under the Lease; or

4.1.10 The surrender of part of the Property, except that the Tenant shall not be under any liability in relation to the surrendered part in respect of any period after the surrender; or

4.1.11 Any other act or omission except an express release of the Tenant made by the Landlord under seal.

4.2 Any sum payable by the Tenant under this agreement is to be paid without any deduction, set-off or counter-claim against the Landlord or the Assignee.

5. Variations and supplemental documents

5.1 The Tenant shall, at the request of the Landlord, join in and give its consent to the terms of any licence, consent, variation or other document that may be entered into by the Assignee in connection with the Lease.

5.2 The Tenant is not be released from liability under this agreement by any variation of the rents reserved by, or the Tenant Covenants in, the Lease, whether or not:

5.2.1 The variation is material or prejudicial to the Tenant; or

5.2.2 The Tenant has consented to the variation.

5.3 The liability of the Tenant under this agreement shall apply to the rents reserved by and the Tenant Covenants of the Lease as varied except to the extent that the liability of the Tenant is affected by section 18 of the Landlord and Tenant (Covenants) Act 1995.

6. Tenant to take a new lease

6.1 If the liability of the Assignee under the Lease is disclaimed and the Landlord gives the Tenant written notice within six months after the Landlord receives notice of that disclaimer, the Tenant shall enter into a new lease of the Property on the terms set out in clause 6.2.

6.2 The rights and obligations under the new lease are to take effect from the date of the disclaimer and the new lease shall:

6.2.1 Be granted subject to the right of any person to have the Lease vested in them by the court and to the terms on which any such order may be made and subject to the rights of any third party existing at the date of the grant;

6.2.2 Be for a term that expires at the same date as the end of the contractual term granted by the Lease had there been no disclaimer;

6.2.3 Reserve as an initial annual rent an amount equal to the rent which is payable under the Lease on the date of the disclaimer (subject to clause 7) and which is subject to review on the same terms and dates provided by the Lease; [and]

6.2.4 [Be excluded from sections 24 to 28 of the 1954 Act; and]

6.2.5 Otherwise be on the same terms as the Lease (as varied if there has been any variation other than a variation in respect of which and to the extent that the Tenant is not liable by virtue of section 18 of the Landlord and Tenant (Covenants) Act 1995).

6.3 [The parties confirm that:

6.3.1 the Landlord served a notice on the Tenant, as required by section 38A(3)(a) of the 1954 Act, applying to the tenancy to be entered into by the Tenant pursuant to clause 6.1 [not less than 14 days] before the authorised guarantee agreement was entered into (a certified copy of which notice is annexed to this agreement); and

6.3.2 [the Tenant] [[NAME OF DECLARANT], who was duly authorised by the Tenant to do so], made a [statutory] declaration dated [DATE] in accordance with the requirements of section 38A(3)(b) of the 1954 Act (a certified copy of which [statutory] declaration is annexed to this agreement).]

6.4 The Tenant shall pay the Landlord's solicitor's costs and disbursements (on a full indemnity basis) and any VAT on them in relation to the new lease and shall execute and deliver to the Landlord a counterpart of the new lease within one month after service of the Landlord's notice.

6.5 The grant of a new lease and its acceptance by the Tenant shall be without prejudice to any other rights which the Landlord may have against the Tenant or against any other person or in respect of any other security that the Landlord may have in connection with the Lease.

7. Rent at the date of disclaimer

7.1 If at the date of the disclaimer there is a rent review pending under the Lease, then:

7.1.1 the relevant review date in the Lease shall also be a rent review date in the new lease;

7.1.2 the rent to be first reserved by the new lease shall be the open market rent of the Property at the relevant review date as agreed or determined in accordance with the new lease;

7.1.3 until the rent is agreed or determined the rent under the new lease shall be payable at the rate that was payable under the Lease immediately before the disclaimer; and

7.1.4 the provisions in the new lease relating to the payment of any shortfall and interest following agreement or determination of a rent review shall apply in relation to any shortfall between the rent payable and the rent first reserved, in respect of the period after the date of the disclaimer.

7.2 If at the date of the disclaimer there is any abatement or suspension of the rent reserved by the Lease, then, for the purposes for this agreement, that rent shall be deemed to be the amount which would be payable under the Lease but for the abatement or suspension, but without prejudice to the provisions relating to abatement or suspension to be contained in the new lease.

8. Payments in gross and restrictions on the Tenant

8.1 Any payment or dividend that the Landlord receives from the Assignee (or its estate) or any other person in connection with any insolvency proceedings or arrangement involving the Assignee shall be taken and applied as a payment in gross and shall not prejudice the right of the Landlord to recover from the Tenant to the full extent of the obligations that are the subject of the guarantee and indemnity in this agreement.

8.2 The Tenant shall not claim in competition with the Landlord in any insolvency proceedings or arrangement of the Assignee in respect of any payment made by the Tenant pursuant to the guarantee and indemnity in this agreement. If it otherwise receives any money in such proceedings or arrangement, it shall hold that money on trust for the Landlord to the extent of its liability to the Landlord.

8.3 The Tenant shall not, without the consent of the Landlord, exercise any right or remedy that it may have (whether against the Assignee or any other person) in respect of any amount paid or other obligation performed by the Tenant under the guarantee and indemnity in this agreement unless and until all the obligations of the Tenant under the guarantee and indemnity in this agreement have been fully performed.

9. Other securities

9.1 The Tenant warrants that it has not taken and covenants that it will not take any security from or over the assets of the Assignee in respect of any liability of the Assignee to the Tenant. If it does take or hold any such security it shall hold it for the benefit of the Landlord.

9.2 This agreement is in addition to any other security that the Landlord may at any time hold from the Tenant or the Assignee or any other person in respect of the liability of the Assignee to pay the rents reserved by the Lease and to observe and perform the tenant covenants of the Lease. It shall not merge in or be affected by any other security.

9.3 The Tenant shall not be entitled to claim or participate in any other security held by the Landlord in respect of the liability of the Assignee to pay the rents reserved by the Lease or to observe and perform the tenant covenants of the Lease.

10. Costs

On completion of this agreement the Tenant is to pay the reasonable costs and disbursements of the Landlord's solicitors and its managing agents in connection with this agreement. This obligation extends to costs and disbursements assessed on a full indemnity basis and to any value added tax in respect of those costs and disbursements except to the extent that the Landlord is able to recover that value added tax.

11. Indemnity

The Tenant will indemnify the Landlord against all costs and claims arising from any breach of the terms of this agreement.

12. Notices

Any notice given pursuant to this agreement shall be in writing and shall be delivered by hand or sent by pre-paid first class post or recorded delivery or by any other means permitted by the Lease. A correctly addressed notice sent by pre-paid first class post shall be deemed to have been delivered at the time at which it would have been delivered in the normal course of the post.

13. Contracts (Rights of Third Parties) Act 1999

No term of this agreement shall be enforceable under the Contracts (Rights of Third Parties) Act 1999 by any third party.

APPENDIX 6

Extracts from the Landlord and Tenant Act 1954, Part II

SECURITY OF TENURE FOR BUSINESS, PROFESSIONAL AND OTHER TENANTS

TENANCIES TO WHICH PART II APPLIES

23. Tenancies to which Part II applies

(1) Subject to the provisions of this Act, this Part of this Act applies to any tenancy where the property comprised in the tenancy is or includes premises which are occupied by the tenant and are so occupied for the purposes of a business carried on by him or for those and other purposes.

(1A) Occupation or the carrying on of a business—
   (a) by a company in which the tenant has a controlling interest; or
   (b) where the tenant is a company, by a person with a controlling interest in the company,
   shall be treated for the purposes of this section as equivalent to occupation or, as the case may be, the carrying on of a business by the tenant.

(1B) Accordingly references (however expressed) in this Part of this Act to the business of, or to use, occupation or enjoyment by, the tenant shall be construed as including references to the business of, or to use, occupation or enjoyment by, a company falling within subsection (1A)(a) above or a person falling within subsection (1A)(b) above.

(2) In this Part of this Act the expression 'business' includes a trade, profession or employment and includes any activity carried on by a body of persons, whether corporate or unincorporate.

(3) In the following provisions of this Part of this Act the expression 'the holding', in relation to a tenancy to which this Part of this Act applies, means the property comprised in the tenancy, there being excluded any part thereof which is occupied neither by the tenant nor by a person employed by the tenant and so employed for the purposes of a business by reason of which the tenancy is one to which this Part of this Act applies.

(4) Where the tenant is carrying on a business, in all or any part of the property comprised in a tenancy, in breach of a prohibition (however expressed) of use for business purposes which subsists under the terms of the tenancy and extends to the whole of that property, this Part of this Act shall not apply to the tenancy unless the immediate landlord or his predecessor in title has consented to the breach or the immediate landlord has acquiesced therein.

In this subsection the reference to a prohibition of use for business purposes does not include a prohibition of use for the purposes of a specified business, or of use for purposes of any but a specified business, but save as aforesaid includes a prohibition of use for the purposes of some one or more only of the classes of business specified in the definition of that expression in subsection (2) of this section.

Continuation and Renewal of Tenancies

24. Continuation of tenancies to which Part II applies and grant of new tenancies

(1) A tenancy to which this Part of this Act applies shall not come to an end unless terminated in accordance with the provisions of this Part of this Act; and, subject to the following provisions of this Act either the tenant or the landlord under such a tenancy may apply to the court for an order for the grant of a new tenancy—
   (a) if the landlord has given notice under section 25 of this Act to terminate the tenancy, or
   (b) if the tenant has made a request for a new tenancy in accordance with section twenty-six of this Act.

(2) The last foregoing subsection shall not prevent the coming to an end of a tenancy by notice to quit given by the tenant, by surrender or forfeiture, or by the forfeiture of a superior tenancy unless—
   (a) in the case of a notice to quit, the notice was given before the tenant had been in occupation in right of the tenancy for one month; . . .
   (b) . . ..

(2A) Neither the tenant nor the landlord may make an application under subsection (1) above if the other has made such an application and the application has been served.

(2B) Neither the tenant nor the landlord may make such an application if the landlord has made an application under section 29(2) of this Act and the application has been served.

(2C) The landlord may not withdraw an application under subsection (1) above unless the tenant consents to its withdrawal.

(3) Notwithstanding anything in subsection (1) of this section,—
   (a) where a tenancy to which this Part of this Act applies ceases to be such a tenancy, it shall not come to an end by reason only of the cesser, but if it was granted for a term of years certain and has been continued by subsection (1) of this section then (without prejudice to the termination thereof in accordance with any terms of the tenancy) it may be terminated by not less than three nor more than six months' notice in writing given by the landlord to the tenant;
   (b) where, at a time when a tenancy is not one to which this Part of this Act applies, the landlord gives notice to quit, the operation of the notice shall not be affected by reason that the tenancy becomes one to which this Part of this Act applies after the giving of the notice.

24A. Applications for determination of interim rent while tenancy continues

(1) Subject to subsection (2) below, if—
   (a) the landlord of a tenancy to which this Part of this Act applies has given notice under section 25 of this Act to terminate the tenancy; or
   (b) the tenant of such a tenancy has made a request for a new tenancy in accordance with section 26 of this Act,
   either of them may make an application to the court to determine a rent (an 'interim rent') which the tenant is to pay while the tenancy ('the relevant tenancy') continues by virtue of section 24 of this Act and the court may order payment of an interim rent in accordance with section 24C or 24D of this Act.

(2) Neither the tenant nor the landlord may make an application under subsection (1) above if the other has made such an application and has not withdrawn it.

(3) No application shall be entertained under subsection (1) above if it is made more than six months after the termination of the relevant tenancy.

24B. Date from which interim rent is payable

(1) The interim rent determined on an application under section 24A(1) of this Act shall be payable from the appropriate date.

(2) If an application under section 24A(1) of this Act is made in a case where the landlord has given a notice under section 25 of this Act, the appropriate date is the earliest date of termination that could have been specified in the landlord's notice.

(3) If an application under section 24A(1) of this Act is made in a case where the tenant has made a request for a new tenancy under section 26 of this Act, the appropriate date is the earliest date that could have been specified in the tenant's request as the date from which the new tenancy is to begin.

24C. Amount of interim rent where new tenancy of whole premises granted and landlord not opposed

(1) This section applies where—
   (a) the landlord gave a notice under section 25 of this Act at a time when the tenant was in occupation of the whole of the property comprised in the relevant tenancy for purposes such as are mentioned in section 23(1) of this Act and stated in the notice that he was not opposed to the grant of a new tenancy; or
   (b) the tenant made a request for a new tenancy under section 26 of this Act at a time when he was in occupation of the whole of that property for such purposes and the landlord did not give notice under subsection (6) of that section,
   and the landlord grants a new tenancy of the whole of the property comprised in the relevant tenancy to the tenant (whether as a result of an order for the grant of a new tenancy or otherwise).

(2) Subject to the following provisions of this section, the rent payable under and at the commencement of the new tenancy shall also be the interim rent.

(3) Subsection (2) above does not apply where—
   (a) the landlord or the tenant shows to the satisfaction of the court that the interim rent under that subsection differs substantially from the relevant rent; or

(b) the landlord or the tenant shows to the satisfaction of the court that the terms of the new tenancy differ from the terms of the relevant tenancy to such an extent that the interim rent under that subsection is substantially different from the rent which (in default of such agreement) the court would have determined under section 34 of this Act to be payable under a tenancy which commenced on the same day as the new tenancy and whose other terms were the same as the relevant tenancy.

(4) In this section 'the relevant rent' means the rent which (in default of agreement between the landlord and the tenant) the court would have determined under section 34 of this Act to be payable under the new tenancy if the new tenancy had commenced on the appropriate date (within the meaning of section 24B of this Act).

(5) The interim rent in a case where subsection (2) above does not apply by virtue only of subsection (3)(a) above is the relevant rent.

(6) The interim rent in a case where subsection (2) above does not apply by virtue only of subsection (3)(b) above, or by virtue of subsection (3)(a) and (b) above, is the rent which it is reasonable for the tenant to pay while the relevant tenancy continues by virtue of section 24 of this Act.

(7) In determining the interim rent under subsection (6) above the court shall have regard—
    (a) to the rent payable under the terms of the relevant tenancy; and
    (b) to the rent payable under any sub-tenancy of part of the property comprised in the relevant tenancy,
but otherwise subsections (1) and (2) of section 34 of this Act shall apply to the determination as they would apply to the determination of a rent under that section if a new tenancy of the whole of the property comprised in the relevant tenancy were granted to the tenant by order of the court and the duration of that new tenancy were the same as the duration of the new tenancy which is actually granted to the tenant.

(8) In this section and section 24D of this Act 'the relevant tenancy' has the same meaning as in section 24A of this Act.

24D. Amount of interim rent in any other case

(1) The interim rent in a case where section 24C of this Act does not apply is the rent which it is reasonable for the tenant to pay while the relevant tenancy continues by virtue of section 24 of this Act.

(2) In determining the interim rent under subsection (1) above the court shall have regard—
    (a) to the rent payable under the terms of the relevant tenancy; and
    (b) to the rent payable under any sub-tenancy of part of the property comprised in the relevant tenancy,
but otherwise subsections (1) and (2) of section 34 of this Act shall apply to the determination as they would apply to the determination of a rent under that section if a new tenancy from year to year of the whole of the property comprised in the relevant tenancy were granted to the tenant by order of the court.

(3) If the court—
    (a) has made an order for the grant of a new tenancy and has ordered payment of interim rent in accordance with section 24C of this Act, but
    (b) either—
        (i) it subsequently revokes under section 36(2) of this Act the order for the grant of a new tenancy; or
        (ii) the landlord and tenant agree not to act on the order,
the court on the application of the landlord or the tenant shall determine a new interim rent in accordance with subsections (1) and (2) above without a further application under section 24A(1) of this Act.

25. Termination of tenancy by the landlord

(1) The landlord may terminate a tenancy to which this Part of this Act applies by a notice given to the tenant in the prescribed form specifying the date at which the tenancy is to come to an end (hereinafter referred to as 'the date of termination'):
Provided that this subsection has effect subject to the provisions of section 29B(4) of this Act and the provisions of Part IV of this Act as to the interim continuation of tenancies pending the disposal of applications to the court.

(2) Subject to the provisions of the next following subsection, a notice under this section shall not have effect unless it is given not more than twelve nor less than six months before the date of termination specified therein.
(3) In the case of a tenancy which apart from this Act could have been brought to an end by notice to quit given by the landlord—
   (a) the date of termination specified in a notice under this section shall not be earlier than the earliest date on which apart from this Part of this Act the tenancy could have been brought to an end by notice to quit given by the landlord on the date of the giving of the notice under this section; and
   (b) where apart from this Part of this Act more than six months' notice to quit would have been required to bring the tenancy to an end, the last foregoing subsection shall have effect with the substitution for twelve months of a period six months longer than the length of notice to quit which would have been required as aforesaid.
(4) In the case of any other tenancy, a notice under this section shall not specify a date of termination earlier than the date on which apart from this Part of this Act the tenancy would have come to an end by effluxion of time.
(5) . . .
(6) A notice under this section shall not have effect unless it states whether the landlord is opposed to the grant of a new tenancy to the tenant.
(7) A notice under this section which states that the landlord is opposed to the grant of a new tenancy to the tenant shall not have effect unless it also specifies one or more of the grounds specified in section 30(1) of this Act as the ground or grounds for his opposition.
(8) A notice under this section which states that the landlord is not opposed to the grant of a new tenancy to the tenant shall not have effect unless it sets out the landlord's proposals as to—
   (a) the property to be comprised in the new tenancy (being either the whole or part of the property comprised in the current tenancy);
   (b) the rent to be payable under the new tenancy; and
   (c) the other terms of the new tenancy.

26. Tenant's request for a new tenancy

(1) A tenant's request for a new tenancy may be made where the current tenancy is a tenancy granted for a term of years certain exceeding one year, whether or not continued by section twenty-four of this Act, or granted for a term of years certain and thereafter from year to year.
(2) A tenant's request for a new tenancy shall be for a tenancy beginning with such date, not more than twelve nor less than six months after the making of the request, as may be specified therein:
Provided that the said date shall not be earlier than the date on which apart from this Act the current tenancy would come to an end by effluxion of time or could be brought to an end by notice to quit given by the tenant.
(3) A tenant's request for a new tenancy shall not have effect unless it is made by notice in the prescribed form given to the landlord and sets out the tenant's proposals as to the property to be comprised in the new tenancy (being either the whole or part of the property comprised in the current tenancy), as to the rent to be payable under the new tenancy and as to the other terms of the new tenancy.
(4) A tenant's request for a new tenancy shall not be made if the landlord has already given notice under the last foregoing section to terminate the current tenancy, or if the tenant has already given notice to quit or notice under the next following section; and no such notice shall be given by the landlord or the tenant after the making by the tenant of a request for a new tenancy.
(5) Where the tenant makes a request for a new tenancy in accordance with the foregoing provisions of this section, the current tenancy shall, subject to the provisions of sections 29B(4) and 36(2) of this Act and the provisions of Part IV of this Act as to the interim continuation of tenancies, terminate immediately before the date specified in the request for the beginning of the new tenancy.
(6) Within two months of the making of a tenant's request for a new tenancy the landlord may give notice to the tenant that he will oppose an application to the court for the grant of a new tenancy, and any such notice shall state on which of the grounds mentioned in section thirty of this Act the landlord will oppose the application.

27. Termination by tenant of tenancy for fixed term

(1) Where the tenant under a tenancy to which this Part of this Act applies, being a tenancy granted for a term of years certain, gives to the immediate landlord, not later than three months before the date on which apart from this Act the tenancy would come to an end by effluxion of time, a notice in writing that the tenant does not desire the tenancy to be continued, section twenty-four of this Act shall not have effect in relation to the tenancy unless the notice is given before the tenant has been in occupation in right of the tenancy for one month.

(1A) Section 24 of this Act shall not have effect in relation to a tenancy for a term of years certain where the tenant is not in occupation of the property comprised in the tenancy at the time when, apart from this Act, the tenancy would come to an end by effluxion of time.

(2) A tenancy granted for a term of years certain which is continuing by virtue of section twenty-four of this Act shall not come to an end by reason only of the tenant ceasing to occupy the property comprised in the tenancy but may be brought to an end on any day by not less than three months' notice in writing given by the tenant to the immediate landlord, whether the notice is given after the date on which apart from this Act the tenancy would have come to an end or before that date, but not before the tenant has been in occupation in right of the tenancy for one month.

(3) Where a tenancy is terminated under subsection (2) above, any rent payable in respect of a period which begins before, and ends after, the tenancy is terminated shall be apportioned, and any rent paid by the tenant in excess of the amount apportioned to the period before termination shall be recoverable by him.

28. Renewal of tenancies by agreement

Where the landlord and tenant agree for the grant to the tenant of a future tenancy of the holding, or of the holding with other land, on terms and from a date specified in the agreement, the current tenancy shall continue until that date but no longer, and shall not be a tenancy to which this Part of this Act applies.

29. Order by court for grant of new tenancy or termination of current tenancy

(1) Subject to the provisions of this Act, on an application under section 24(1) of this Act, the court shall make an order for the grant of a new tenancy and accordingly for the termination of the current tenancy immediately before the commencement of the new tenancy.

(2) Subject to the following provisions of this Act, a landlord may apply to the court for an order for the termination of a tenancy to which this Part of this Act applies without the grant of a new tenancy—

(a) if he has given notice under section 25 of this Act that he is opposed to the grant of a new tenancy to the tenant; or

(b) if the tenant has made a request for a new tenancy in accordance with section 26 of this Act and the landlord has given notice under subsection (6) of that section.

(3) The landlord may not make an application under subsection (2) above if either the tenant or the landlord has made an application under section 24(1) of this Act.

(4) Subject to the provisions of this Act, where the landlord makes an application under subsection (2) above—

(a) if he establishes, to the satisfaction of the court, any of the grounds on which he is entitled to make the application in accordance with section 30 of this Act, the court shall make an order for the termination of the current tenancy in accordance with section 64 of this Act without the grant of a new tenancy; and

(b) if not, it shall make an order for the grant of a new tenancy and accordingly for the termination of the current tenancy immediately before the commencement of the new tenancy.

(5) The court shall dismiss an application by the landlord under section 24(1) of this Act if the tenant informs the court that he does not want a new tenancy.

(6) The landlord may not withdraw an application under subsection (2) above unless the tenant consents to its withdrawal.

29A. Time limits for applications to court

(1) Subject to section 29B of this Act, the court shall not entertain an application—
(a) by the tenant or the landlord under section 24(1) of this Act; or
(b) by the landlord under section 29(2) of this Act,
if it is made after the end of the statutory period.

(2) In this section and section 29B of this Act 'the statutory period' means a period ending—
  (a) where the landlord gave a notice under section 25 of this Act, on the date specified in his notice; and
  (b) where the tenant made a request for a new tenancy under section 26 of this Act, immediately before the date specified in his request.
(3) Where the tenant has made a request for a new tenancy under section 26 of this Act, the court shall not entertain an application under section 24(1) of this Act which is made before the end of the period of two months beginning with the date of the making of the request, unless the application is made after the landlord has given a notice under section 26(6) of this Act.

29B. Agreements extending time limits

(1) After the landlord has given a notice under section 25 of this Act, or the tenant has made a request under section 26 of this Act, but before the end of the statutory period, the landlord and tenant may agree that an application such as is mentioned in section 29A(1) of this Act, may be made before the end of a period specified in the agreement which will expire after the end of the statutory period.
(2) The landlord and tenant may from time to time by agreement further extend the period for making such an application, but any such agreement must be made before the end of the period specified in the current agreement.
(3) Where an agreement is made under this section, the court may entertain an application such as is mentioned in section 29A(1) of this Act if it is made before the end of the period specified in the agreement.
(4) Where an agreement is made under this section, or two or more agreements are made under this section, the landlord's notice under section 25 of this Act or tenant's request under section 26 of this Act shall be treated as terminating the tenancy at the end of the period specified in the agreement or, as the case may be, at the end of the period specified in the last of those agreements.

30. Opposition by landlord to application for a new tenancy

(1) The grounds on which a landlord may oppose an application under section 24(1) of this Act, or make an application under section 29(2) of this Act, are such of the following grounds as may be stated in the landlord's notice under section twenty-five of this Act or, as the case may be, under subsection (6) of section twenty-six thereof, that is to say:—
  (a) where under the current tenancy the tenant has any obligations as respects the repair and maintenance of the holding, that the tenant ought not to be granted a new tenancy in view of the state of repair of the holding, being a state resulting from the tenant's failure to comply with the said obligations;
  (b) that the tenant ought not to be granted a new tenancy in view of his persistent delay in paying rent which has become due;
  (c) that the tenant ought not to be granted a new tenancy in view of other substantial breaches by him of his obligations under the current tenancy, or for any other reason connected with the tenant's use or management of the holding;
  (d) that the landlord has offered and is willing to provide or secure the provision of alternative accommodation for the tenant, that the terms on which the alternative accommodation is available are reasonable having regard to the terms of the current tenancy and to all other relevant circumstances, and that the accommodation and the time at which it will be available are suitable for the tenant's requirements (including the requirement to preserve goodwill) having regard to the nature and class of his business and to the situation and extent of, and facilities afforded by, the holding;
  (e) where the current tenancy was created by the sub-letting of part only of the property comprised in a superior tenancy and the landlord is the owner of an interest in reversion expectant on the termination of that superior tenancy, that the aggregate of the rents reasonably obtainable on separate lettings of the holding and the remainder of that property would be substantially less than the rent reasonably obtainable on a letting of that property as a whole, that on the termination of the current tenancy the landlord requires possession of the holding for the purpose of letting or otherwise disposing of the said property as a whole, and that in view thereof the tenant ought not to be granted a new tenancy;
  (f) that on the termination of the current tenancy the landlord intends to demolish or reconstruct the premises comprised in the holding or a substantial part of those premises or to carry out

substantial work of construction on the holding or part thereof and that he could not reasonably do so without obtaining possession of the holding;

(g) subject as hereinafter provided, that on the termination of the current tenancy the landlord intends to occupy the holding for the purposes, or partly for the purposes, of a business to be carried on by him therein, or as his residence.

(1A) Where the landlord has a controlling interest in a company, the reference in subsection (1)(g) above to the landlord shall be construed as a reference to the landlord or that company.

(1B) Subject to subsection (2A) below, where the landlord is a company and a person has a controlling interest in the company, the reference in subsection (1)(g) above to the landlord shall be construed as a reference to the landlord or that person.

(2) The landlord shall not be entitled to oppose an application under section 24(1) of this Act, or make an application under section 29(2) of this Act, on the ground specified in paragraph (g) of the last foregoing subsection if the interest of the landlord, or an interest which has merged in that interest and but for the merger would be the interest of the landlord, was purchased or created after the beginning of the period of five years which ends with the termination of the current tenancy, and at all times since the purchase or creation thereof the holding has been comprised in a tenancy or successive tenancies of the description specified in subsection (1) of section twenty-three of this Act.

(2A) Subsection (1B) above shall not apply if the controlling interest was acquired after the beginning of the period of five years which ends with the termination of the current tenancy, and at all times since the acquisition of the controlling interest the holding has been comprised in a tenancy or successive tenancies of the description specified in section 23(1) of this Act.

(3) ...

31. Dismissal of application for new tenancy where landlord successfully opposes

(1) If the landlord opposes an application under subsection (1) of section twenty-four of this Act on grounds on which he is entitled to oppose it in accordance with the last foregoing section and establishes any of those grounds to the satisfaction of the court, the court shall not make an order for the grant of a new tenancy.

(2) Where the landlord opposes an application under section 24(1) of this Act, or makes an application under section 29(2) of this Act, on one or more of the grounds specified in section 30(1)(d) to (f) of this Act but establishes none of those grounds, and none of the other grounds specified in section 30(1) of this Act, to the satisfaction of the court, then if the court would have been satisfied on any of the grounds specified in section 30(1)(d) to (f) of this Act if the date of termination specified in the landlord's notice or, as the case may be, the date specified in the tenant's request for a new tenancy as the date from which the new tenancy is to begin, had been such later date as the court may determine, being a date not more than one year later than the date so specified,—

(a) the court shall make a declaration to that effect, stating of which of the said grounds the court would have been satisfied as aforesaid and specifying the date determined by the court as aforesaid, but shall not make an order for the grant of a new tenancy;

(b) if, within fourteen days after the making of the declaration, the tenant so requires the court shall make an order substituting the said date for the date specified in the said landlord's notice or tenant's request, and thereupon that notice or request shall have effect accordingly.

31A. Grant of new tenancy in some cases where section 30(1)(f) applies

(1) Where the landlord opposes an application under section 24(1) of this Act on the ground specified in paragraph (f) of section 30(1) of this Act, or makes an application under section 29(2) of this Act on that ground, the court shall not hold that the landlord could not reasonably carry out the demolition, reconstruction or work of construction intended without obtaining possession of the holding if—

(a) the tenant agrees to the inclusion in the terms of the new tenancy of terms giving the landlord access and other facilities for carrying out the work intended and, given that access and those facilities, the landlord could reasonably carry out the work without obtaining possession of the holding and without interfering to a substantial extent or for a substantial time with the use of the holding for the purposes of the business carried on by the tenant; or

(b) the tenant is willing to accept a tenancy of an economically separable part of the holding and either paragraph (a) of this section is satisfied with respect to that part or possession of the remainder of the holding would be reasonably sufficient to enable the landlord to carry out the intended work.

(2) For the purposes of subsection (1)(b) of this section a part of a holding shall be deemed to be an economically separable part if, and only if, the aggregate of the rents which, after the completion of the intended work, would be reasonably obtainable on separate lettings of that part and the remainder of the premises affected by or resulting from the work would not be substantially less than the rent which would then be reasonably obtainable on a letting of those premises as a whole.

32. Property to be comprised in new tenancy

(1) Subject to the following provisions of this section, an order under section twenty-nine of this Act for the grant of a new tenancy shall be an order for the grant of a new tenancy of the holding; and in the absence of agreement between the landlord and the tenant as to the property which constitutes the holding the court shall in the order designate that property by reference to the circumstances existing at the date of the order.

(1A) Where the court, by virtue of paragraph (b) of section 31A(1) of this Act, makes an order under section 29 of this Act for the grant of a new tenancy in a case where the tenant is willing to accept a tenancy of part of the holding, the order shall be an order for the grant of a new tenancy of that part only.

(2) The foregoing provisions of this section shall not apply in a case where the property comprised in the current tenancy includes other property besides the holding and the landlord requires any new tenancy ordered to be granted under section twenty-nine of this Act to be a tenancy of the whole of the property comprised in the current tenancy; but in any such case—
   (a) any order under the said section twenty-nine for the grant of a new tenancy shall be an order for the grant of a new tenancy of the whole of the property comprised in the current tenancy, and
   (b) references in the following provisions of this Part of this Act to the holding shall be construed as references to the whole of that property.

(3) Where the current tenancy includes rights enjoyed by the tenant in connection with the holding, those rights shall be included in a tenancy ordered to be granted under section twenty-nine of this Act except as otherwise agreed between the landlord and the tenant or, in default of such agreement, determined by the court.

33. Duration of new tenancy

Where on an application under this Part of this Act the court makes an order for the grant of a new tenancy, the new tenancy shall be such tenancy as may be agreed between the landlord and the tenant, or, in default of such an agreement, shall be such a tenancy as may be determined by the court to be reasonable in all the circumstances, being, if it is a tenancy for a term of years certain, a tenancy for a term not exceeding fifteen years, and shall begin on the coming to an end of the current tenancy.

34. Rent under new tenancy

(1) The rent payable under a tenancy granted by order of the court under this Part of this Act shall be such as may be agreed between the landlord and the tenant or as, in default of such agreement, may be determined by the court to be that at which, having regard to the terms of the tenancy (other than those relating to rent), the holding might reasonably be expected to be let in the open market by a willing lessor, there being disregarded—
   (a) any effect on rent of the fact that the tenant has or his predecessors in title have been in occupation of the holding,
   (b) any goodwill attached to the holding by reason of the carrying on thereat of the business of the tenant (whether by him or by a predecessor of his in that business),
   (c) any effect on rent of an improvement to which this paragraph applies,
   (d) in the case of a holding comprising licensed premises, any addition to its value attributable to the licence, if it appears to the court that having regard to the terms of the current tenancy and any other relevant circumstances the benefit of the licence belongs to the tenant.

(2) Paragraph (c) of the foregoing subsection applies to any improvement carried out by a person who at the time it was carried out was the tenant, but only if it was carried out otherwise than in pursuance of an obligation to his immediate landlord, and either it was carried out during the current tenancy or the following conditions are satisfied, that is to say,—
   (a) that it was completed not more than twenty-one years before the application to the court was made; and

(b) that the holding or any part of it affected by the improvement has at all times since the completion of the improvement been comprised in tenancies of the description specified in section 23(1) of this Act; and

(c) that at the termination of each of those tenancies the tenant did not quit.

(2A) If this Part of this Act applies by virtue of section 23(1A) of this Act, the reference in subsection (1)(d) above to the tenant shall be construed as including—

(a) a company in which the tenant has a controlling interest, or

(b) where the tenant is a company, a person with a controlling interest in the company.

(3) Where the rent is determined by the court the court may, if it thinks fit, further determine that the terms of the tenancy shall include such provision for varying the rent as may be specified in the determination.

(4) It is hereby declared that the matters which are to be taken into account by the court in determining the rent include any effect on rent of the operation of the provisions of the Landlord & Tenant (Covenants) Act 1995.

35. Other terms of new tenancy

(1) The terms of a tenancy granted by order of the court under this Part of this Act (other than terms as to the duration thereof and as to the rent payable thereunder), including, where different persons own interests which fulfil the conditions specified in section 44(1) of this Act in different parts of it, terms as to the apportionment of the rent, shall be such as may be agreed between the landlord and the tenant or as, in default of such agreement, may be determined by the court; and in determining those terms the court shall have regard to the terms of the current tenancy and to all relevant circumstances.

(2) In subsection (1) of this section the reference to all relevant circumstances includes (without prejudice to the generality of that reference) a reference to the operation of the provisions of the Landlord and Tenant (Covenants) Act 1995.

36. Carrying out of order for new tenancy

(1) Where under this Part of this Act the court makes an order for the grant of a new tenancy, then, unless the order is revoked under the next following subsection or the landlord and the tenant agree not to act upon the order, the landlord shall be bound to execute or make in favour of the tenant, and the tenant shall be bound to accept, a lease or agreement for a tenancy of the holding embodying the terms agreed between the landlord and the tenant or determined by the court in accordance with the foregoing provisions of this Part of this Act; and where the landlord executes or makes such a lease or agreement the tenant shall be bound, if so required by the landlord, to execute a counterpart or duplicate thereof.

(2) If the tenant, within fourteen days after the making of an order under this Part of this Act for the grant of a new tenancy, applies to the court for the revocation of the order the court shall revoke the order; and where the order is so revoked, then, if it is so agreed between the landlord and the tenant or determined by the court, the current tenancy shall continue, beyond the date at which it would have come to an end apart from this subsection, for such period as may be so agreed or determined to be necessary to afford to the landlord a reasonable opportunity for reletting or otherwise disposing of the premises which would have been comprised in the new tenancy; and while the current tenancy continues by virtue of this subsection it shall not be a tenancy to which this Part of this Act applies.

(3) Where an order is revoked under the last foregoing subsection any provision thereof as to payment of costs shall not cease to have effect by reason only of the revocation; but the court may, if it thinks fit, revoke or vary any such provision or, where no costs have been awarded in the proceedings for the revoked order, award such costs.

(4) A lease executed or agreement made under this section, in a case where the interest of the lessor is subject to a mortgage, shall be deemed to be one authorised by section ninety-nine of the Law of Property Act 1925 (which confers certain powers of leasing on mortgagors in possession), and subsection (13) of that section (which allows those powers to be restricted or excluded by agreement) shall not have effect in relation to such a lease or agreement.

37. Compensation where order for new tenancy precluded on certain grounds

(1) Subject to the provisions of this Act, in a case specified in subsection (1A), (1B) or (1C) below (a 'compensation case') the tenant shall be entitled on quitting the holding to recover from the landlord by way of compensation an amount determined in accordance with this section.

(1A) The first compensation case is where on the making of an application by the tenant under section 24(1) of this Act the court is precluded (whether by subsection (1) or subsection (2) of section 31 of this Act) from making an order for the grant of a new tenancy by reason of any of the grounds specified in paragraphs (e), (f) and (g) of section 30(1) of this Act (the 'compensation grounds') and not of any grounds specified in any other paragraph of section 30(1).

(1B) The second compensation case is where on the making of an application under section 29(2) of this Act the court is precluded (whether by section 29(4)(a) or section 31(2) of this Act) from making an order for the grant of a new tenancy by reason of any of the compensation grounds and not of any other grounds specified in section 30(1) of this Act.

(1C) The third compensation case is where—
  (a) the landlord's notice under section 25 of this Act or, as the case may be, under section 26(6) of this Act, states his opposition to the grant of a new tenancy on any of the compensation grounds and not on any other grounds specified in section 30(1) of this Act; and
  (b) either—
    (i) no application is made by the tenant under section 24(1) of this Act or by the landlord under section 29(2) of this Act; or
    (ii) such an application is made but is subsequently withdrawn.

(2) Subject to the following provisions of this section, compensation under this section shall be as follows, that is to say,—
  (a) where the conditions specified in the next following subsection are satisfied in relation to the whole of the holding it shall be the product of the appropriate multiplier and twice the rateable value of the holding,
  (b) in any other case it shall be the product of the appropriate multiplier and the rateable value of the holding.

(3) The said conditions are—
  (a) that, during the whole of the fourteen years immediately preceding the termination of the current tenancy, premises being or comprised in the holding have been occupied for the purposes of a business carried on by the occupier or for those and other purposes;
  (b) that, if during those fourteen years there was a change in the occupier of the premises, the person who was the occupier immediately after the change was the successor to the business carried on by the person who was the occupier immediately before the change.

...

(8) In subsection (2) of this section 'the appropriate multiplier' means such multiplier as the Secretary of State may by order made by statutory instrument prescribe and different multipliers may be so prescribed in relation to different cases.

37A. Compensation for possession obtained by misrepresentation

(1) Where the court—
  (a) makes an order for the termination of the current tenancy but does not make an order for the grant of a new tenancy, or
  (b) refuses an order for the grant of a new tenancy,
  and it subsequently made to appear to the court that the order was obtained, or the court was induced to refuse the grant, by misrepresentation or the concealment of material facts, the court may order the landlord to pay to the tenant such sum as appears sufficient as compensation for damage or loss sustained by the tenant as the result of the order or refusal.

(2) Where—
  (a) the tenant has quit the holding—
    (i) after making but withdrawing an application under section 24(1) of this Act; or
    (ii) without making such an application; and
  (b) it is made to appear to the court that he did so by reason of misrepresentation or the concealment of material facts,
  the court may order the landlord to pay to the tenant such sum as appears sufficient as compensation for damage or loss sustained by the tenant as the result of quitting the holding.

38. Restriction on agreements excluding provisions of Part II

(1) Any agreement relating to a tenancy to which this Part of this Act applies (whether contained in the instrument creating the tenancy or not) shall be void (except as provided by section 38A of this Act) in so far as it purports to preclude the tenant from making an application or request under this Part of this Act or provides for the termination or the surrender of the tenancy in the event of his making such an application or request or for the imposition of any penalty or disability on the tenant in that event.

(2) Where—

(a) during the whole of the five years immediately preceding the date on which the tenant under a tenancy to which this Part of this Act applies is to quit the holding, premises being or comprised in the holding have been occupied for the purposes of a business carried on by the occupier or for those and other purposes, and

(b) if during those five years there was a change in the occupier of the premises, the person who was the occupier immediately after the change was the successor to the business carried on by the person who was the occupier immediately before the change,

any agreement (whether contained in the instrument creating the tenancy or not and whether made before or after the termination of that tenancy) which purports to exclude or reduce compensation under section 37 of this Act shall to that extent be void, so however that this subsection shall not affect any agreement as to the amount of any such compensation which is made after the right to compensation has accrued.

(3) In a case not falling within the last foregoing subsection the right to compensation conferred by section 37 of this Act may be excluded or modified by agreement.

38A. Agreements to exclude provisions of Part 2

(1) The persons who will be the landlord and the tenant in relation to a tenancy to be granted for a term of years certain which will be a tenancy to which this Part of this Act applies may agree that the provisions of sections 24 to 28 of this Act shall be excluded in relation to that tenancy.

(2) The persons who are the landlord and the tenant in relation to a tenancy to which this Part of this Act applies may agree that the tenancy shall be surrendered on such date or in such circumstances as may be specified in the agreement and on such terms (if any) as may be so specified.

(3) An agreement under subsection (1) above shall be void unless—

(a) the landlord has served on the tenant a notice in the form, or substantially in the form, set out in Schedule 1 to the Regulatory Reform (Business Tenancies) (England and Wales) Order 2003 ('the 2003 Order'); and

(b) the requirements specified in Schedule 2 to that Order are met.

(4) An agreement under subsection (2) above shall be void unless—

(a) the landlord has served on the tenant a notice in the form, or substantially in the form, set out in Schedule 3 to the 2003 Order; and

(b) the requirements specified in Schedule 4 to that Order are met.

40. Duties of tenants and landlords of business premises to give information to each other

(1) Where a person who is an owner of an interest in reversion expectant (whether immediately or not) on a tenancy of any business premises has served on the tenant a notice in the prescribed form requiring him to do so, it shall be the duty of the tenant to give the appropriate person in writing the information specified in subsection (2) below.

(2) That information is—

(a) whether the tenant occupies the premises or any part of them wholly or partly for the purposes of a business carried on by him;

(b) whether his tenancy has effect subject to any sub-tenancy on which his tenancy is immediately expectant and, if so—

(i) what premises are comprised in the sub-tenancy;

(ii) for what term it has effect (or, if it is terminable by notice, by what notice it can be terminated);

(iii) what is the rent payable under it;

(iv) who is the sub-tenant;

(v) (to the best of his knowledge and belief) whether the sub-tenant is in occupation of the premises or of part of the premises comprised in the sub-tenancy and, if not, what is the sub-tenant's address;

(vi) whether an agreement is in force excluding in relation to the sub-tenancy the provisions of sections 24 to 28 of this Act; and

(vii) whether a notice has been given under section 25 or 26(6) of this Act, or a request has been made under section 26 of this Act, in relation to the sub-tenancy and, if so, details of the notice or request; and

(c) (to the best of his knowledge and belief) the name and address of any other person who owns an interest in reversion in any part of the premises.

(3) Where the tenant of any business premises who is a tenant under such a tenancy as is mentioned in section 26(1) of this Act has served on a reversioner or a reversioner's mortgagee in possession a notice in the prescribed form requiring him to do so, it shall be the duty of the person on whom the notice is served to give the appropriate person in writing the information specified in subsection (4) below.

(4) That information is—

(a) whether he is the owner of the fee simple in respect of the premises or any part of them or the mortgagee in possession of such an owner,

(b) if he is not, then (to the best of his knowledge and belief)—

(i) the name and address of the person who is his or, as the case may be, his mortgagor's immediate landlord in respect of those premises or of the part in respect of which he or his mortgagor is not the owner in fee simple;

(ii) for what term his or his mortgagor's tenancy has effect and what is the earliest date (if any) at which that tenancy is terminable by notice to quit given by the landlord; and

(iii) whether a notice has been given under section 25 or 26(6) of this Act, or a request has been made under section 26 of this Act, in relation to the tenancy and, if so, details of the notice or request;

(c) (to the best of his knowledge and belief) the name and address of any other person who owns an interest in reversion in any part of the premises; and

(d) if he is a reversioner, whether there is a mortgagee in possession of his interest in the premises and, if so, (to the best of his knowledge and belief) what is the name and address of the mortgagee.

(5) A duty imposed on a person by this section is a duty—

(a) to give the information concerned within the period of one month beginning with the date of service of the notice; and

(b) if within the period of six months beginning with the date of service of the notice that person becomes aware that any information which has been given in pursuance of the notice is not, or is no longer, correct, to give the appropriate person correct information within the period of one month beginning with the date on which he becomes aware.

(6) This section shall not apply to a notice served by or on the tenant more than two years before the date on which apart from this Act his tenancy would come to an end by effluxion of time or could be brought to an end by notice to quit given by the landlord.

(7) Except as provided by section 40A of this Act, the appropriate person for the purposes of this section and section 40A(1) of this Act is the person who served the notice under subsection (1) or (3) above.

(8) In this section—

'business premises' means premises used wholly or partly for the purposes of a business;

'mortgagee in possession' includes a receiver appointed by the mortgagee or by the court who is in receipt of the rents and profits, and 'his mortgagor' shall be construed accordingly;

'reversioner' means any person having an interest in the premises, being an interest in reversion expectant (whether immediately or not) on the tenancy;

'reversioner's mortgagee in possession' means any person being a mortgagee in possession in respect of such an interest; and

'sub-tenant' includes a person retaining possession of any premises by virtue of the Rent (Agriculture) Act 1976 or the Rent Act 1977 after the coming to an end of a sub-tenancy, and 'sub-tenancy' includes a right so to retain possession.

40B. Proceedings for breach of duties to give information

A claim that a person has broken any duty imposed by section 40 of this Act may be made the subject of civil proceedings for breach of statutory duty; and in any such proceedings a court may order that person to comply with that duty and may make an award of damages.

42. Groups of companies

(1) For the purposes of this section two bodies corporate shall be taken to be members of a group if and only if one is a subsidiary of the other or both are subsidiaries of a third body corporate or the same person has a controlling interest in both.

(2) Where a tenancy is held by a member of a group, occupation by another member of the group, and the carrying on of a business by another member of the group, shall be treated for the purposes of section twenty-three of this Act as equivalent to occupation or the carrying on of a business by the member of the group holding the tenancy; and in relation to a tenancy to which this Part of this Act applies by virtue of the foregoing provisions of this subsection—

   (a) references (however expressed) in this Part of this Act and in the Ninth Schedule to this Act to the business of or to use occupation or enjoyment by the tenant shall be construed as including references to the business of or to use occupation or enjoyment by the said other member;

   (b) the reference in paragraph (d) of subsection (1) of section thirty-four of this Act to the tenant shall be construed as including the said other member; and

   (c) an assignment of the tenancy from one member of the group to another shall not be treated as a change in the person of the tenant.

(3) Where the landlord's interest is held by a member of a group—

   (a) the reference in paragraph (g) of subsection (1) of section 30 of this Act to intended occupation by the landlord for the purposes of a business to be carried on by him shall be construed as including intended occupation by any member of the group for the purposes of a business to be carried on by that member; and

   (b) the reference in subsection (2) of that section to the purchase or creation of any interest shall be construed as a reference to a purchase from or creation by a person other than a member of the group.

43. Tenancies excluded from Part II

(1) This Part of this Act does not apply—

   (a) to a tenancy of an agricultural holding which is a tenancy in relation to which the Agricultural Holdings Act 1986 applies or a tenancy which would be a tenancy of an agricultural holding in relation to which that Act applied if subsection (3) of section 2 of that Act did not have effect or, in a case where approval was given under subsection (1) of that section, if that approval had not been given;

   (aa) to a farm business tenancy;

   (b) to a tenancy created by a mining lease;

(2) This Part of this Act does not apply to a tenancy granted by reason that the tenant was the holder of an office, appointment or employment from the grantor thereof and continuing only so long as the tenant holds the office, appointment or employment, or terminable by the grantor on the tenant's ceasing to hold it, or coming to an end at a time fixed by reference to the time at which the tenant ceases to hold it:

Provided that this subsection shall not have effect in relation to a tenancy granted after the commencement of this Act unless the tenancy was granted by an instrument in writing which expressed the purpose for which the tenancy was granted.

(3) This Part of this Act does not apply to a tenancy granted for a term certain not exceeding six months unless—

   (a) the tenancy contains provision for renewing the term or for extending it beyond six months from its beginning; or

   (b) the tenant has been in occupation for a period which, together with any period during which any predecessor in the carrying on of the business carried on by the tenant was in occupation, exceeds twelve months.

44. Meaning of 'the landlord' in Part II, and provisions as to mesne landlords, etc

(1) Subject to subsections (1A) and (2) below, in this Part of this Act the expression 'the landlord', in relation to a tenancy (in this section referred to as 'the relevant tenancy'), means the person (whether or not he is the immediate landlord) who is the owner of that interest in the property comprised in the relevant tenancy which for the time being fulfils the following conditions, that is to say—

　(a) that it is an interest in reversion expectant (whether immediately or not) on the termination of the relevant tenancy, and

　(b) that it is either the fee simple or a tenancy which will not come to an end within fourteen months by effluxion of time and, if it is such a tenancy, that no notice has been given by virtue of which it will come to an end within fourteen months or any further time by which it may be continued under section 36(2) or section 64 of this Act,

and is not itself in reversion expectant (whether immediately or not) on an interest which fulfils those conditions.

(1A) The reference in subsection (1) above to a person who is the owner of an interest such as is mentioned in that subsection is to be construed, where different persons own such interests in different parts of the property, as a reference to all those persons collectively.

(2) References in this Part of this Act to a notice to quit given by the landlord are references to a notice to quit given by the immediate landlord.

(3) The provisions of the Sixth Schedule to this Act shall have effect for the application of this Part of this Act to cases where the immediate landlord of the tenant is not the owner of the fee simple in respect of the holding.

APPENDIX 7

Use classes prior to 1 September 2020

Class A1: shops

Use for all or any of the following purposes: retail sale of goods other than hot food; post office; ticket or travel agency; sale of cold food for consumption off the premises; hairdressing; direction of funerals; display of goods for sale; hiring out of domestic or personal goods; washing or cleaning of clothes on the premises; internet cafe. In all cases, however, the sale, display or service must be to visiting members of the public.

Class A2: financial and professional services

Use for the provision of financial services, professional services (other than health or medical services) or any other services which it is appropriate to provide in a shopping area, where the services are provided principally to visiting members of the public. In the case of solicitors' and other professional offices, the crucial question is whether the firm principally serves visiting members of the public. In *Kalra v Secretary of State for the Environment* [1996] JPL 850, CA, the Court of Appeal held that the introduction of an appointment system did not of itself prevent a solicitor's office falling within Class A2.

Class A3: restaurants and cafes

Use for the sale of food and drink for consumption on the premises.

Class A4: drinking establishments

Use as a public house, wine bar or other drinking establishment.

Class A5: hot food takeaways

Use for the sale of hot food for consumption off the premises.

Class B1: business

Use for all or any of the following purposes, namely as an office other than a use within Class A2, for research and development of products or processes, or for any industrial process (being a use which can be carried out in any residential area without detriment to the amenity of that area.)

Class B2: general industrial

Use for the carrying out of an industrial process other than one falling within Class B1.

Class B8: storage or distribution

Use for storage or as a distribution centre.

Class C1: hotels

Use as a hotel or boarding or guest house where no significant element of care is provided.

Class C3: dwelling houses

Use as a dwelling house whether or not as a sole or main residence by: (a) a single person or by people to be regarded as forming a single household; or (b) not more than six residents living together as a single household, whether or not care is provided, other than a use falling within Class C4.

Class C4: houses in multiple occupation

Use of a dwellinghouse by not more than six residents as a 'house in multiple occupation' (known as an 'HMO').

Wales

Note that separate secondary legislation applies in Wales. Class A3 covers use for the sale of food and drink for consumption on the premises or of hot food for consumption off the premises. Classes A4 and A5 do not exist. Class B8 in Wales does not include use of a building or land for the storage of, or as a distribution centre for, radioactive material or radioactive waste.

APPENDIX 8

Use classes from 1 September 2020

B2 General industrial

Use for industrial process other than one falling within class E(g) (*previously class B1*) (excluding incineration purposes, chemical treatment or landfill or hazardous waste)

B8 Storage or distribution

This class includes open air storage.

Class C1: hotels

Use as a hotel or boarding or guest house where no significant element of care is provided.

Class C3: dwelling houses

Use as a dwelling house whether or not as a sole or main residence by: (a) a single person or by people to be regarded as forming a single household; or (b) not more than six residents living together as a single household, whether or not care is provided, other than a use falling within Class C4.

Class C4: houses in multiple occupation

Use of a dwellinghouse by not more than six residents as a 'house in multiple occupation' (known as an 'HMO').

Class E - Commercial, Business and Service

E(a) Display or retail sale of goods, other than hot food

E(b) Sale of food and drink for consumption (mostly) on the premises

E(c) Provision of:

E(c)(i) Financial services,

E(c)(ii) Professional services (other than health or medical services), or

E(c)(iii) Other appropriate services in a commercial, business or service locality

E(d) Indoor sport, recreation or fitness (not involving motorised vehicles or firearms)

E(e) Provision of medical or health services (except the use of premises attached to the residence of the consultant or practitioner)

E(f) Creche, day nursery or day centre (not including a residential use)

E(g) Uses which can be carried out in a residential area without detriment to its amenity:

E(g)(i) Offices to carry out any operational or administrative functions,

E(g)(ii) Research and development of products or processes

E(g)(iii) Industrial processes

Class F - Local Community and Learning

F1 Learning and non-residential institutions

Use (not including residential use) defined in 7 parts:

F1(a) Provision of education

F1(b) Display of works of art (otherwise than for sale or hire)

F1(c) Museums

F1(d) Public libraries or public reading rooms

F1(e) Public halls or exhibition halls

F1(f) Public worship or religious instruction (or in connection with such use)

F1(g) Law courts

F2 Local community

Use as defined in 4 parts:

F2(a) Shops (mostly) selling essential goods, including food, where the shop's premises do not exceed 280 square metres and there is no other such facility within 1000 metres

F2(b) Halls or meeting places for the principal use of the local community

F2(c) Areas or places for outdoor sport or recreation (not involving motorised vehicles or firearms)

F2(d) Indoor or outdoor swimming pools or skating rinks

Source: Mostly taken from <www.planningportal.co.uk/info/200130/common_projects/9/change_of_use>

Index

adjudication 170
administration 371
  administrator
    appointment 377–8
    powers and duties 378
  covenants 391
  moratorium 378–9
  rent 390
advertising 277
agreement for lease
  completion date 189
  damage before completion 190
  deducing title 192
  defects in work or materials and 190
  example 188–92
  force majeure clause 189–90
  form of lease 191
  incorporation of conditions of sale 191–2
  incumbrances 192
  landlord's obligations 188
  liability for delay 190
  merging with lease 192
  penalties for delay 190
  practical completion 189
  premises 191
  requested modifications 188–9
  responsibility for damage 190
  supervision 189
  when used 187
airspace 215
alienation 253–64
  see also **assignment of leases; subleases**
  notice of 263–4
  protocol 263
  restrictions on 255–9
    consent 260–3, 315–16
    covenants 255–6
alterations
  see also **improvements**
  alterations clause 274–6
  Code for Leasing Business Premises 2020 266, 278–9
  covenants against
    absolute covenants 274–5
    compensation for improvements 278
    fully qualified covenants 275
    landlord's concerns 273–4
    need for 273–4
    other lease clauses 276–7
    qualified covenants 275
    tenant's concerns 273
  landlord's consent 275–6
  lease controls 274–7
  nature of premises 273
  protocol 279
  restrictions outside lease 277–8
  term 274
  type 274

alterations – *continued*
  withholding consent 275–6
alternative accommodation
  offer of 354
appeals
  certificates of lawful use or development 84
  contaminated land 126–7
  enforcement notices 94–6
    costs 95
    documentation 95
    effect 95
    fees 95
    forum 95
    further appeals 95–6
    grounds 94
    procedure 95
    time limits 94–5
    who may appeal 95
    written representations 95
  planning obligations 69
  planning permission 59–63
    appeal form 60
    challenging appeal decision 63
    costs 63
    hearing 62–3
    initial procedure 60
    inquiry 62
    statement of case 60
    statement of common ground 60
    types 60–3
    who may appeal 59
    written representations 61–2
  refusal of certificate of lawful use or development 84
arbitration 170
architects 153
asbestos 116, 141–3
  Control of Asbestos Regulations 2012 142–3
  duty to manage 142
  dutyholder 142
  enforcement 142
  landlord and tenant issues 143
  non-domestic premises 142
assignment of leases 253
  see also **authorised guarantee agreements**
  assignee's guarantor 213
  consent
    applications for 260–1, 315–17
    avoiding disputes 317
    consent not to be unreasonably withheld 261–2, 316–17
    delays in obtaining 262–3
    failure to obtain 315
    reasonable response time 316
    refusal 263
    restrictions on charging for consent 263
    superior landlord's consent 317
  covenants against 255–6

assignment of lease – *continued*
  remedies for breach 331
  covenants and 206–7, 315–16
  detailed provisions 257–9
  excluded 208
  guarantee agreements 208, 211, 212, 257, 258–9
  indemnity and 206, 207, 208
  licence to assign 317–18
  privity of estate and 206–7
  virtual assignments 264
assignment of rights
  construction projects 167
authorised guarantee agreements 208, 212, 257, 258–9, 318
  Code for Leasing Business Premises 2020 260, 318
  content 318
  LTA 1954 considerations 318
  specimen 489–92

bankruptcy 372, 376
  covenants 391
  effect 376–7
  forfeiture and 301
  guarantee for lease and 212
  non-payment of rent and 328
  rent 389–90
  restrictions 377
  trustee in bankruptcy 376, 391
    powers 377
blight notice 98–9
  counter-notice 99–100
  'material detriment' 100
  'qualifying interest' 99
  service 98–9
  'specified description' 98–9
boundaries
  lease of part 305
breach of condition notice 86
breach of covenant
  default notice 327
  landlord's breach 333–5
  landlord's remedies 327–33
  obligation not to derogate from grant 334–5
  other covenants 331–2, 354
    forfeiture 298–300
  quiet enjoyment 334
  remedies for landlord 327–33
  repairing covenant 329–31, 333–4
  tenant's breach 327–33
  tenant's remedies 333–5
break clauses 201, 220–2, 338
Brexit
  compulsory purchase 97
  environmental law and 117–18
building
  definition of 199
building contractors 151–2
building operations 35
  see also **construction projects**

call options 23
case law
  change of use 36–7

certificates of completion 189
certificates of lawful use or development 82
  appeals 84
  effect 83
  existing development 83
  general provisions 84
  issue 83
  offences 84
  onus of proof 83
  proposed development 83–4
change of use
  case law 36–7
  Code for Leasing Business Premises 2020 266, 278–9
  non-statutory guidance 36
  statutory clarifications 37–8
charges
  fixed 15, 255
  floating 15, 255
  priority 15–16
  registration 15–16
  restrictions 255
clawback *see* **overage**
climate change 115–16, 136
  'cap and trade' principle 137
  Climate Change Act 2008 137
  European Union Emissions Trading Scheme 136–7
  Kyoto Protocol 136
  Paris Agreement 136
  UK Emissions Trading Scheme 137
  UN Framework Convention on Climate Change 136
Code for Leasing Business Premises 2007 194
Code for Leasing Business Premises 2020 193–5
  alterations 266, 278–9
  assignment of lease 259–60, 318
  change of use 266, 278–9
  charging 259–60
  forfeiture 302
  group company sharing 257
  guarantee agreements 260
  insurance 285–6, 287, 289
  rent 324
  rent review 229
  rent suspension 291
  repairs 248–50
  sharing 259–60
  sub-lettings 255, 257, 259–60
  tenant's concerns 248–50
  termination 293, 294
  terrorism 287
  text 427–37
collateral warranties 165–7
commercial developments
  value added tax 173, 174–5
commercial property
  meaning 3
  purchasers 4–5
  value 3
commercial rent arrears recovery 328
  Covid-19 situation 328
common parts 199
commons registration search 147
Community Infrastructure Levy 65–6
  area subject to charge 71–2

Community Infrastructure Levy – *continued*
   charging authorities 70
   charitable exemption 74
   charitable reliefs 74
   date rate payable 73
   enforcement 75–6
   exceptional circumstances relief 75
   exemptions 74–5
   figure payable 73
   fundamentals 69–74
   interest 76
   liability 72
   management of liability 75
   payee 72
   payment 73–4
   penalties for non-payment 76
   planning obligations and 76–7
   procedure 76
   proposed reform 66
   rate payable 71
   reliefs 74–5
   social housing relief 74
   surcharges and interest 76
company voluntary arrangements 371, 373
   approval 373–4
   covenants 390
   moratorium 374
   rent 389
compensation
   compulsory purchase 104–8
   development potential 105–8
   disturbance 110–11
   exclusion 201
   failure to obtain new tenancy 358–9
   improvements 278
   injurious affection 108–9
   inverse compulsory purchase 98
   market value 104–5
   penalties for delay 190
   purchase notice 101
   stop notices 92–3
completion certificate 189
completion notice 53
compulsory purchase
   acquiring authority 97
   blight notice 98–9
      counter-notice 99–100
      'material detriment' 100
      'qualifying interest' 99
      service 98–9
      'specified description' 98–9
   challenging order 102
   compensation 104–8
      betterment 105
      development potential 105–8
      disregards 105
      existing use value 104
      hope value 106–7
      market value 104–5
      marriage and ransom values 104–5
   Covid-19 situation 98, 102
   development potential 105–8
   disturbance *see* **disturbance**

compulsory purchase – *continued*
   expropriation 103–4
   general vesting declaration 103
   hope value 106–7
   injurious affection 108–9
   inquiry 102
   inverse 98–101
      blight notice 98–100
      compensation 98, 101
      purchase notice 98, 100–1
   judicial review 103
   market value compensation 104–5
   notice to treat 102–3
   notification 102
   objections 102
   order 101–2
   overriding third party rights 97
   planning permission 105–6
   procedure 100–1
   purchase notice 98
      characteristic of land 100
      compensation 101
      'incapable of reasonably beneficial use' 100
   s17 certificate 107–8
   stages 101–2
   temporary possession 97–8
   valuation rules 104–5
conditional agreements 20–3
   condition 21–2
   time for performance 22–3
   types 21
consent
   alterations 275–6
   assignment of leases
      applications for 260–1, 315–17
      consent not to be unreasonably withheld 261–2, 316–17
      failure to obtain 315
      reasonable response time 316
      refusal 263
      restrictions on charging for consent 263
      superior landlord's consent 317
      virtual assignments 264
   delay in obtaining 262–3
   disclaimer 392
   subleases 322
      consent not to be unreasonably withheld 261–2
      refusal 263
      restrictions on charging for consent 263
conservation covenants 140–1
construction management 161–2
construction projects 151–70
   adjudication 170
   agreement for lease and
      completion date 189
      damage before completion 190
      deducing title 192
      defects in work or materials 190
      example 188–92
      force majeure clause 189–90
      form of lease 191
      incorporation of conditions of sale 191–2
      incumbrances 192

construction projects – *continued*
  landlord's obligations 188
  liability for delay 190
  merging with lease 192
  penalties for delay 190
  practical completion 189
  premises 191
  requested modifications 188–9
  responsibility for damage 190
  supervision 189
  when used 187
 arbitration 170
 construction management 161–2
 contract types 154–62
 design and build contract 157–9
 dispute resolution 169–70
 duties owed to third parties 162–5
  legislation 163
  liability for economic loss 164–5
  liability for physical damage 164
  tort liability 163–5
 litigation 170
 management contracting 159–60
 pricing 162
 principal designer 153
 protection for other parties
  assignment of rights 167
  collateral warranties 165–7
  declaration of trust of rights 167
  defect liability periods 169
  forced enforcement of remedies 169
  latent defects insurance 167–8
  limiting repair covenants 168–9
 reconstruction as ground for opposition to new tenancy 355–6
 traditional procurement 155–6
 who is involved
  architect 153
  building contractor 151–2
  costs consultant 153
  employer 151
  engineers 153
  project manager 153
  quantity surveyor 153
contaminated land 116, 120–30
 appeals 126–7
 apportionment of liability 125–6
 appropriate persons 121, 123, 124–6
 asbestos *see* **asbestos**
 case law 126–7
 contaminant linkage 122
 contamination definition 121–2
 DEFRA guidance 121
 determination of liability 123–4
 enforcement 127–8
 exclusion tests 124–5
 harm 121–2
 landlord and tenant issues 129
 liability 125–6
 local authority duties 121
 planning and 128–9
 Practice Note 121
 regime 121

contaminated land – *continued*
 review 129–30
 remediation notice 123, 127–8
  appeals 128
 responsibility 123
 risks 120–1
 sanctions 128
 searches and enquiries 147
 special sites 123
contracts
 conditional agreements 20–3
  condition 21–2
  time for performance 22–3
  types 21
 construction projects 151–2, 154–62
  duties owed to third parties 162–5
 estate contracts *see* **agreement for lease**
 guaranteed maximum price 162
 insolvency 372
 joint ventures 7
 lump-sum 162
 measurement contracts 162
 option agreements 23–4
  put and call options 23
  terms 24
  uses 23–4
 overage *see* **overage**
 privity 203, 205–6, 207, 210
 for sale 19–20
 searches and enquiries 145
  enquiries of seller 147
  investigation of title 148
  local 145
 types 20–5
contractual control agreements 27–8
Corporate Insolvency and Governance Act 2020 368–70
costs
 appeal against enforcement notices 95
 appeals 63
 value added tax on 178
county planning authorities 31
courts
 application under LTA 1954 351–2
  renewal lease 359–61
covenants 200, 203
 administration 391
 against alterations
  absolute covenants 274–5
  compensation for improvements 278
  fully qualified covenants 275
  landlord's concerns 273–4
  need for 273–4
  other lease clauses 276–7
  qualified covenants 275
  tenant's concerns 273
 against assignment 206–7, 255–6, 315–16
  remedies for breach 331
 against dealings 255–6
 against subletting 255–6
 assignee liability 208
 bankruptcy 391
 conservation covenants 140–1
 direct 207

covenants – *continued*
    liability of parties on covenants in lease 184–5
    limiting repair covenants 168–9
    liquidation 391
    named tenants 267–8
    negative 268
    permissions and prohibitions 256–7
    positive 268
    quiet enjoyment 281–2
        remedies for breach 334
    receivership 391
    remedies for breach
        landlord's breach 333–5
        landlord's remedies 327–33
        non-payment of rent 328–9
        obligation not to derogate from grant 334–5
        other covenants 331–2, 354
        repairing covenant 329–31
        tenant's remedies 333–5
    repairing
        covenant to yield up in repair 250
        decoration 250–1, 277
        definition of subject matter 244–5
        enforcement 250
        insured risks 289–90
        landlords 251
        remedies for breach 329–31, 333–4
        tenant's 244
        tenant's concerns and amendments 248–50
    subleases 325
    successors and 204–5, 208–9
    to pay rent 223
    user
        ancillary clauses 269–70
        competition legislation and 270–1
        extent of landlord's control 268–9
        need for 265–6
        permitted use 267–8
        remedies for breach 331–2
    variation 208–9
    voluntary arrangements 390
    which touch and concern 207
Covid-19
    commercial rent arrears recovery 328
    compulsory purchase 98, 102
    forfeiture for non-payment of rent 329
    impact on commercial property 3, 6
    insolvency 368, 379–80
    winding up proceedings 379–80
criminal offences
    certificates of lawful use or development 84
    Japanese knotweed 143
    non-compliance with enforcement notice 90–1
    obstruction of right of entry 85
    stop notices 92

damage
    construction projects 164
    insurance and 289–91
    termination of lease 292–3
damages
    breach of covenants 329–30, 331–2, 333
        leave to sue 330

damages – *continued*
    measure of damages 329–30
    quiet enjoyment 334
dealings with part 254–5
death
    guarantee for lease and 211–12
debt finance 12
    due diligence 13
    loan agreements 13–14
    security
        further advances 16–17
        need for 15
        perfection 15–16
    term sheet 12–13
Debt Relief orders 372
declaration of trust of rights
    construction projects 167
decoration
    covenant to repair and 250–1, 277
    forfeiture 301
    lease of part 307–8
    subleases 325
default notice 327
defects
    see also **repairs**
    agreement for lease and 190
    inherent defects 245–6
    latent defects insurance 167–8
    liability periods in construction projects 169
defences
    non-compliance with enforcement notice 91
demolition 36
    conservation areas 52
    grounds for opposition to new tenancy 355–6
derogation
    obligation not to derogate from grant 334–5
design and access statement 55
design and build contract 157–9
developers
    planning obligations 78
    as purchasers 5
development
    certificates of lawful use or development 82–4
    compulsory purchase 105–8
    demolition 36
    disturbance 110
    material change of use 36–9
    operations not constituting development 35
    permitted
        GPD Order 39–44
        resumption of previous use 39
    use classes 38–9, 267
development plans
    definition 32
    importance 34–5
    regional planning 32–3
    weight given 33–4
disclaimer
    consent 392
    effect 393–4
    meaning 391–2
    persons able to disclaim 391
    property disclaimed 392

disclaimer – *continued*
   timing 392–3
Display Energy Certificates 138
dispute resolution 169–70
   adjudication 170
   arbitration 170
   litigation 170
distress remedy 224, 328
district planning authorities 31
disturbance 97
   adaptation of new premises 111
   basic loss payment 112
   claimant 110
   compensatable losses 111
   development potential 110
   goodwill 111
   home loss payment 112
   interest and charges 111
   legal costs 111, 112
   loan for new premises 112
   mitigation of losses 110
   occupier's loss payment 112
   part acquisition 110
   profits 111
   type of loss 110
doctrine of waste *see* **waste**
drafting of leases
   commencement 197
   covenants 200
   definitions section 197–9
   exceptions and reservations 200
   execution 202
   forfeiture clause 296
   habendum 200
   interpretation clauses 199–200
   Land Registry prescribed clause leases 197
   lease of part 305–13
   letting 200
   Model Commercial Lease 195–6
   operative words 200
   parcels clause 200
   prescribed clauses 197
   principles 196–7
   provisos 200–1
   reddendum 200
   schedules 201–2
   structure 197–202
   subleases 323–6
   testimonium clause 202
   value added tax 177
drainage
   searches and enquiries 146

easements
   compulsory purchase 102, 103
   lease of part 306
economic loss
   construction projects 164–5
employees
   lease of part 308
employers
   construction projects 151
energy performance 116, 137–41

energy performance – *continued*
   air conditioning assessments 138–9
   enforcement 139
   Future Buildings Standard 139–40
   Future Homes Standards 139–40
   minimum energy efficiency standard (MEES) 139
Energy Performance Certificates 138
enforcement
   asbestos regulations 142
   contaminated land 127–8
   energy performance 139
   environmental regulation and permitting 134
   forced enforcement of remedies 169
   notice *see* **enforcement notice**
   nuisance 132
   planning control 81–96
      definitions 81–2
      time limits 82
   planning law
      appeals 94–6
      breach of condition notice 86
      injunctions 93–4
      planning contravention notice 85–6
      right of entry 84–5
      stop notice 91–3
      time limits 88
   planning obligations 67–8
enforcement notice 87–91
   action by LPA 91
   appeals 94–6
   challenging 88
   contents 88–9
   defences 91
   effect 90
   invalidity 90
   issue 87–8
   non-compliance 90–1
   nullity 89–90
   offences 90–1
   service 89
   time limits 88
   validity 89–90
   variation 90
   withdrawal 90
engineering operations 35
engineers in construction projects 153
entry
   for repairs 250
   right of 84–5
      subleases 325
Environment Agency
   contaminated land 129
Environmental Impact Assessment 55–6
environmental law
   domestic law 118
   effect of Brexit 117–18
   EU law 117–18
   international law 116–17
   overview 115–16
   sources 116–18
environmental regulation and permitting 116, 133–6
   enforcement 134
   hazardous substances 135–6

environmental regulation and permitting – *continued*
  offences 134–6
  permit requirement 133
  transfer of permits 134
  waste 135
  water 134
environmental risk management 116, 118
  desktop study 119
  enquiries of consultants 119
  enquiries of seller 119
  insurance 120
  pre-contract searches 118–19
  searches and investigations 119
environmental statement 55–6
equity funding 12
estate contracts *see* agreement for lease
European Union Emissions Trading Scheme (EU ETS) 136–7
expiry of leases 337
expropriation 103–4

finance
  debt finance
    due diligence 13
    loan agreements 13–14
    security 15–17
    term sheet 12–13
  equity funding 12
  forward funding 11–12
  methods 11–12
  sale and leaseback 4, 12
  share capital 11
fixtures 215–16
  removal 216
  repair 216
flooding
  insurance 288
  risks 143–4
  searches 147–8
force majeure clauses 189–90
forfeiture 295–302
  breach of other covenants 298–300, 332
  breach of repairing covenant 300–1, 331
  clause 296
  Code for Leasing Business Premises 2020 302
  decoration 301
  express reservation of right 295–6
  insolvency and 301, 388–9
  non-payment of rent 296–8, 329
    Covid-19 situation 329
  particular premises 301
  reform 302
  s146 notice 298
  subtenants/mortgagees and 302
  waiver of right 296
forward funding 11–12
frustration 224, 292
Future Buildings Standard 139–40
Future Homes Standards 139–40

gender
  in deeds 199

goodwill
  rent review and 238
green leases 116, 136, 140
'Grey Belt' 29
guarantees
  see also **authorised guarantee agreements**
  guarantors of leases 209–13
    assignee's guarantor 213
    bankruptcy or liquidation of tenant 212
    death of tenant 211–12
    discharge or release 210–12
    drafting points 213
    extent of guarantee 210
    giving time 211
    release of co-guarantor 211
    variations 210–11

habendum 200
hazardous substances 135–6
hearings
  appeals 62–3
heating
  lease of part 308
highways
  searches and enquiries 146
hope value 106–7

improvements
  compensation for 278
  rent review and 238–9
  repairing covenants and 247
indemnity
  assignment of leases and 206, 207, 208
individual voluntary arrangements 371, 373
  approval 373–4
  covenants 390
  moratorium 374
  rent 389
Infrastructure Levy 66
injunctions 93–4, 332
injurious affection 108–9
  compensation 108–9
  McCarthy rules 108–9
inquiry
  planning appeals 62
insolvency
  see also **liquidation (winding up)**
  administration 371, 377–9
    administrator appointment and powers 378
    covenants 391
    moratorium 378–9
    rent 390
  bankruptcy *see* **bankruptcy**
  'breathing space' regime 372
  company moratorium 368
  compulsory liquidation 372
  contracts 372
  Corporate Insolvency and Governance Act 2020 368–70
  covenants 390–1
  Covid-19 and 368, 379–80
  Debt Relief orders 372
  disclaimer 391–4
  forfeiture and 301, 388–9

insolvency – *continued*
  guarantee for lease and 212
  identification of contract type 372
  importance 367–8
  insolvency official 367, 372
    requirement to observe covenants 390–1
    requirement to pay rent 389–90
  liquidation
    compulsory 372, 379
    covenants 391
    moratorium 380
    powers and duties of liquidator 380
    rent 390
    voluntary 371–2, 379
  non-payment of rent and 328
  preferences 380–2
  receivership 371, 374–6
    breach of repairing covenant 334
    covenants 391
    rent 389
  reducing perceived risk 370
  regimes 370–2
  rent 389–90
  restructuring plans 368–9
  setting aside transactions 380–2
  tenant, landlord's remedies 382–8
  transactions at an undervalue 380–2
  vesting orders 394
  voluntary arrangements 373
    approval 373–4
    company 371, 373
    covenants 390
    individual 371, 373
    moratorium 374
    rent 389
  voluntary liquidation 371–2
insurance
  additional provisions 294
  breach of covenant to insure 331
  by landlord 286
  by tenant 294
  Code for Leasing Business Premises 2020 285–6, 287, 289
  compliance with terms 289
  damage to premises 289–91
  environmental 120
  excess payable 289
  flood 288
  latent defects insurance 167–8
  lease of part 312
  loss of rent 288
  losses covered 287
  payment 288–9
  reinstatement 289–91
    impossible 293
  retention of monies 293
  risks covered 198, 287
  subleases 325
  sum insured 288
  terrorism 287–8
  uninsured risks 293–4
  what insured 286
  in whose name 286–7

interest 198
  disturbance and 111
  rent and 224–5
interim rent 223, 352–3
interpretation clauses 199–200
inverse compulsory purchase 98–101
  blight notice 98–100
  compensation 98
  purchase notice 98, 100–1
investors
  as purchasers 4–5

Japanese knotweed 143
  impact 143
  liability 143
joint and several liability 199
joint ventures 5–6
  contractual 7
  limited liability partnerships 8–9
  partnerships 8–9
  special purpose vehicles 7–8

Kyoto Protocol 136

Land Registry
  prescribed clause leases 197
landlord
  breach of covenant by 333–5
  drafting points 212–13
  party to lease 203–5
  remedies for breach 327–33
latent defects insurance 167–8
leases
  agreements for *see* **agreement for lease**
  assignment *see* **assignment of leases**
  compulsory purchase 103–4
  covenants 200
    assignment of lease and 206–7
    liability of parties on covenants in lease 184–5
    limiting repair covenants 168–9
    successors and 204–5
    variation 208–9
  distinguished from licences 183–4
  drafting
    commencement 197
    definitions section 197–9
    execution 202
    interpretation clauses 199–200
    lease of part 305–13
    letting 200
    Model Commercial Lease 195–6
    principles 196–7
    provisos 200–1
    schedules 201–2
    structure 197–202
    subleases 323–6
    value added tax 177
  future developments 362–3
  office blocks 439–87
  options to renew 222
  parcels clauses 200, 215–17
  of part
    boundaries 305

leases – *continued*
    demised premises 305–6
    easements 306
    insurance 312
    repairs 306–7
    service charges 307–12
    sinking and reserve funds 312
  parties
    guarantors 209–13
    landlord 203–5
    successors 204–5
    tenants 205–9
  rent *see* **rent**
  security of tenure *see* **security of tenure**
  stamp duty land tax and 179
  term 198, 219–20
    renewal lease 360
    subleases 323–4
  termination *see* **termination of leases**
  value added tax and 177, 198
  variation of terms 208–9
Levelling-up and Regeneration Act 2023 29
licences
  distinguished from leases 183–4
  licence to assign 317–18
liquidation (winding up) 212, 328
  see also **insolvency**
  compulsory 372, 379
  covenants 391
  moratorium 380
  powers and duties of liquidator 380
  rent 390
  types 371–2, 379–80
  voluntary 371–2, 379
local authorities 31
  contaminated land 121
  development plans *see* **development plans**
  enforcement and *see* **enforcement**
  planning obligations *see* **planning obligations**
  planning permission *see* **planning permission**
local development frameworks 32
local development orders 45
local plans 32, 33
local searches and enquiries 145
London 31
  development plans 32

McCarthy rules 108–9
management contracting 159–60
managing agents
  lease of part 308–9
market value compensation 104–5
merger
  agreement for lease 192
  termination of leases 339
minimum energy efficiency standard (MEES) 139
mining operations 35
Ministry for Housing, Communities and Local Government
  administrative powers 30–1
  circulars 30
  guidance 30
  legislative powers 30
  quasi-judicial powers 31

misrepresentation 201
Model Commercial Lease 195–6
mortgages
  compulsory purchase 103
  forfeiture and 302
  legal mortgage 15
  restrictions 255

National Planning Policy Framework (NPPF) 30–1, 33–4
  draft revision 29
  enforcement 87
  sustainable development 33
nationally significant infrastructure projects
  planning permission 53–4
neighbourhood development orders 45–6
neighbourhood development plans 32–3
neighbourhood forums 32
notice
  of assignment/subleases 263–4
  blight *see* **blight notice**
  enforcement *see* **enforcement notice**
  purchase *see* **purchase notice**
  s146 notice 298
  service *see* **service of notices**
  stop *see* **stop notice**
  to quit 337–8
  to treat 102–3
  under LTA
    counter-notices 350
    prescribed forms 415–25
    s25 notices 348–9
nuisance 116
  enforcement 132
  environmental permitting and 131
  immunity 131
  planning permission and 131
  private 130–1
  public 131–2
  rule in *Rylands v Fletcher* 132–3
  standing 130–1
  statutory 132
  trespass 133

occupation
  occupation by landlord as ground for opposition to new tenancy 356–7
  purchase by occupiers 4
offences *see* **criminal offences**
office blocks
  lease of floor(s) 439–87
operations
  definition 35
  not constituting development 35
option agreements 23–4
  pre-emption agreements 25
  put and call options 23
  terms 24
  uses 23–4
options to renew 222
overage 25–7
  bond 27
  drafting considerations 26–7
  freehold right of re-entry 27

overage – *continued*
  guarantee 27
  meaning 25
  mortgage or charge 27
  negative 25
  payment
    amount 26–7
    security for 27
  positive 25
  positive covenant 27
  ransom strips 27
  restrictive covenant 27
  securing payment 27
  seller's lien 27
  trigger event 26

parcels clauses 200, 215–17
  airspace 215
  fixtures 215–16
  rights granted and reserved 217
  underground 215
Paris Agreement 136
part, lease of
  boundaries 305
  demised premises 305–6
  easements 306
  insurance 312
  repairs 306–7
  service charges 307–12
  sinking and reserve funds 312
parties to leases
  guarantors 209–13
    assignee's guarantor 213
    bankruptcy or liquidation of tenant 212
    death of tenant 211–12
    discharge or release 210–12
    drafting points 213
    extent of guarantee 210
    giving time 211
    release of co-guarantor 211
    variations 210–11
  landlord 203–5
    drafting points 212–13
    successors 204–5
  tenants 205–9
parting with possession 254
permitted development
  checklist 44–6
  GPD Order 39–44
  resumption of previous use 39
permitted use 267–8
planning contravention notice 85–6
planning law
  enforcement 81–96
    appeals 94–6
    breach of condition notice 86
    definitions 81–2
    enforcement notice 87–91, 94–6
    injunctions 93–4
    planning contravention notice 85–6
    right of entry 84–5
    stop notice 91–3
    time limits 82, 89

planning law – *continued*
  reform 29
  sources, legislation 30
planning obligations 65–79
  Community Infrastructure Levy and 76–7
  developer 78
  enforceability 67–8
  formalities 67
  Government policy 68
  LPA 77–8
    enforcement by 68
  meaning 65, 66–7
  modification and discharge
    appeals 69
    applications 69
    determination of applications 69
    powers 69
  reform 66
  unilateral undertakings 68
  when used 67
Planning Performance Agreement (PPA) 55
planning permission
  abandonment 51
  Agricultural Holdings Certificate 56
  amendments 57–9
    s96A 59
  appeals 59–63
    challenging appeal decision 63
    costs 63
    form 60
    hearing 62–3
    initial procedure 60
    inquiry 62
    statement of case 60
    statement of common ground 60
    types 60–3
    who may appeal 59
    written representations 61–2
  application for
    action by planning authority 56
    certificates with 56
    covenants against 277
    decision 57
    fee 56
    full or outline 46
    notification 56
    preliminary steps 54–5
    procedure 55–7
    submission 55–6
  article 14 certificate 56
  basis for decision 47–9
  completion notice 53
  compulsory purchase 105–6
  conditional 49–51
    Central Government guidance 50–1
    judicial restrictions on power 49–50
    Section 73 and Section 73A applications 58
  contaminated land 128–9
  deemed refusal 57
  design and access statement 55
  discrimination 48
  duration 52
  effect 51–3

planning permission – *continued*
  environmental considerations 48
  environmental statement 55–6
  full 46
  hybrid applications 47
  implementation 52–3
  material planning conditions 48
  modification 52
  nationally significant infrastructure projects 53–4
  nuisance and 131
  outline 46
  planning register entry 57
  power to decline to determine 56–7
  in principle 47
  procedure after decision 57
  refusal, deemed 57
  renewal 53
  reserved matters 46
  revocation 52
  searches and enquiries 145–6
  time limit for decision 57
  when required 35–46
Planning Practice Guidance (PPG) 31
  enforcement of planning control 87
  guidance on planning conditions 50–1
pollution *see* **contaminated land**
pre-emption agreements
  options 25
preferences 380–2
premises
  definition 198
privity of contract 203, 205–6, 207, 210
privity of estate 206–7
project manager 153
promotion agreements 27
purchase notice 98, 100–1
  characteristic of land 100
  compensation 101
  'incapable of reasonably beneficial use' 100
put options 23

quantity surveyors 153
quiet enjoyment
  breach of covenant 282
  covenant for 281–2
  remedies for breach 334

rack rent lease 4
railways
  searches and enquiries 146
receivership 371, 374–6
  breach of repairing covenant 334
  covenants 391
  rent 389
reddendum 200
Regional Development Agencies 32
registered property 17
  contractual control agreements 27–8
  future developments 27–8
remedies
  see also **damages; forfeiture**
  breach of covenant
    landlord's breach 333–5

remedies – *continued*
  landlord's remedies 327–33
  obligation not to derogate from grant 334–5
  other covenants 298–300, 331–2, 354
  quiet enjoyment 334
  repairing covenant 329–31, 333–4
  tenant's breach 327–33
  tenant's remedies 333–5
 distress 224, 328
 forced enforcement 169
 injunctions 93–4, 332
 non-payment of rent 224, 296–8, 328–9
 right to overriding lease 332–3
 self-help 330–1, 333
 specific performance 331, 332, 333
renewal lease 359–61
 duration 360
 premises 360
 rent 360–1
renewal of leases
 options to renew 222
rent 198–9
 amount 224
 Code for Leasing Business Premises 2020 324
 covenant to pay 223
 delay in payment 354
 insolvency and 328, 389–90
 interest charged 224–5
 interim 223, 352–3
 non-payment 224, 328–9
  collection from sub-tenant 328–9
  commercial rent arrears recovery 328
  Covid-19 situation 328, 329, 379–80
  forfeiture for 296–8, 329
 other payments reserved as 224
 premiums and 233
  reverse premiums 233
 reddendum 200
 renewal lease 360–1
 rent-free periods 177–8, 223
 review *see* **rent review**
 subleases 324
 suspension 201, 224, 291–2
 time for payment 224
 value added tax 225
rent review
 assumptions 231–8
  duration of lease 233–4
  fitting out 235–6
  landlord's obligations 236
  premiums 233
  rent-free periods 232–3, 234–6
  restoration of damage 237
  reverse premium 233
  sub-tenancies 232
  tenant's obligations 236
  terms of lease 234–5
  use of premises 234, 236
  vacant possession 232
  VAT 237–8
  whole or part 231–2
  willing parties 231
  work diminishing value 237

rent review – *continued*
  dates 230
  disregards 238–9
    goodwill 238
    improvements 238–9
    occupation 238
    statutory restrictions 239
  fixed increases 227
  index-linked 227
  late 241
  mechanics 239–41
  need for 227
  open market revaluations 228–9
    comparables 231
    defining 230–1
    instructions to valuer 231
    upwards only 228–9
    upwards/downwards 229
  penultimate day 230
  recording 241
  regularity 230
  time of essence 239–40
  turnover 228
  types of review clauses 227–9
  valuer
    appointment 240
    capacity 240–1
    costs 241
    instructions 231
repairs
  access for 250
  agreement for lease and 190
  covenants
    definition of subject matter 244–5
    enforcement 250
    insured risks 289–90
    landlord's 251
    limiting repair covenants 168–9
    remedies for breach 300–1, 329–31, 333–4
    tenant's 244
  decoration 250–1, 277
  extent of liability 245–8
    reducing 249–50
  failure to repair 353–4
  fixtures 216
  inherent defects 245–6
  lease of part 306–7
  meaning 245–6
  multi-occupied building 243
  scope 246–7
  standard of 247–8
  subleases 325
  whole building 243
  yielding up in repair 250
reserve funds
  lease of part 312
reserved matters
  planning permission 46
reserved rights 217
residential property
  value added tax on development 173, 174
resumption of previous use 39

reverse premiums
  value added tax and 177–8
RICS Professional Statement: Service Charges 312–13
Rylands v Fletcher, rule in 132–3

s25 notices 348–9, 362
s26 requests 349–50
sale and leaseback 4, 12
searches and enquiries
  access land 147
  commons registration search 147
  contaminated land 147
  drainage 146
  enquiries of seller 147
  flood searches 147–8
  highways 146
  investigation of title 148
  local 145
  planning permission 145–6
  rights of way 147
  survey and inspection 148
security of tenure
  business tenants 184, 201, 341–63
    application of LTA 1954 341–3
    competent landlord 343–4
    continuation tenancies 347
    contracting out 344–7
    definitions 343–4
    exclusions 343
    holding 344
    order for new lease 361–2
    protection 341
    renewal lease 359–61
  interim rent 223, 352–3
  termination of leases under LTA 1954 347–51
    application to courts 351–2
    compensation for failure to obtain new tenancy 358–9
    counter-notices 350
    grounds of opposition to new tenancy 353–7
    LTA 1954 text 493–506
    prescribed forms of notice 415–25
    s25 notices 348–9, 362
    s26 requests 349–50
    service of notices and requests 350–1
self-help remedies 330–1, 333
seller
  searches and enquiries 147
service charges 224
  definition 199
  landlord's covenant to perform services 309–10
  payment
    advance payments 311
    certification of amounts due 311–12
    final payments and adjustments 311
  RICS Professional Statement 312–13
  services to be provided 307–9
  tenant's contribution 310–11
service of notices 201
  blight notice 98–9
  compulsory purchase 102
  default notice 327
  enforcement notice 89
  stop notice 92

service of notices – *continued*
    under LTA 1954 350–1
services
    definition 199
share capital 11
sharing possession 254
signs 277
simplified planning zones 45
sinking funds
    lease of part 312
spatial development strategies 32
special development orders 45
specific performance 331, 332, 333
stamp duty land tax 179, 222
statement of community involvement 32
stop notice 91–2
    compensation 92–3
    contents 92
    offences 92
    service 92
    temporary 93
    withdrawal 92
structure plans 32
subcontractors
    construction projects 151, 152
subleases 253–4
    alienation 325
    break clauses and 221
    consent 322
        consent not to be unreasonably withheld 261–2
        delays in obtaining 262–3
        refusal 263
        restrictions on charging for consent 263
    covenants 325
    covenants against 255–6
    dealings with part 254–5
    decoration 325
    disclaimer effect 393–4
    drafting points 323–6
    forfeiture and 302
    grounds for opposition to new tenancy 354
    head landlord liability 323
    head-lease and 325
    insurance 325
    liability of subtenants 323
    licences to sub-let 322
    nature of 321
    non-payment of rent 329
    reasons for subletting 321–2
    rent 324
    repair 325
    restrictions 259, 322
    rights of access 325
    sub-tenant's concerns 326
    term 323–4
succession
    landlords 204–5
surrender of leases 178, 338–9
surveys 148
sweeper clauses 309

taxation
    stamp duty land tax 179

taxation – *continued*
    transfers of going concerns 178
    value added tax
        commercial developments 173, 174–5
        on costs 178
        drafting points 176–7
        option to charge 175–7
        rent and 225, 237–8
        rent-free periods and 177–8
        residential developments 173, 174
        reverse premiums and 177–8
        surrenders and 178
term of lease 198, 219–20
    renewal lease 360
    rent review and 233–4
    SDLT impact 222
    subleases 323–4
termination of leases
    damage to property 292–3
        landlord 293
        tenant 292–3
    expiry 337
    forfeiture *see* **forfeiture**
    merger 339
    notice to quit 337–8
    operation of break clause 338
    restriction on *see* **security of tenure**
    surrender 178, 338–9
    under LTA 1954 347–51
        application to courts 351–2
        compensation for failure to obtain new tenancy 358–9
        counter-notices 350
        grounds of opposition to new tenancy 353–7
        prescribed forms of notice 415–25
        s25 notices 348–9, 362
        s26 requests 349–50
        service of notices and requests 350–1
terrorism
    insurance 287–8
time for performance
    conditional agreements 22–3
    liability for delay 190
    penalties for delay 190
time limits
    agreement to extend 352
    appeal against enforcement notices 94–5
    defect liability periods 169
    enforcement of planning law 82, 89
title
    agreement for lease and 192
    investigation 148
tort liability
    construction projects 163–5
transactions at an undervalue 380–2
transfers of going concerns
    value added tax and 178
trespass 133
trust of rights
    construction projects 167

UK Emissions Trading Scheme 137
UN Framework Convention on Climate Change 136
underground 215

unilateral undertakings 68
uninsured risks 293–4
unitary councils 31
unregistered property 17
use
   certificates of lawful use or development 82–4
   covenants *see* **user covenants**
   material change of use 36–9
   permitted 201
   resumption of previous use 39
   use classes 38–9, 267
     after 1 Sep 2020 509–10
     before 1 Sep 2020 507
user covenants
   ancillary clauses 269–70
   competition legislation and 270–1
   extent of landlord's control
     absolute covenants 268
     fully qualified covenants 269
     qualified covenants 269
   need for 265–6
     landlord's concerns 265–6
     tenant's concerns 266
   permitted use 267–8
   planning 265
   remedies for breach 331–2

utilities
   searches and enquiries 146–7

value added tax
   commercial developments 173, 174–5
   on costs 178
   drafting points 176–7
   leases and 177, 198
   option to charge
     how election made 175
     should election be made 176
     who or what is affected 175–6
   rent and 225, 237–8
   rent-free periods and 177–8
   residential developments 173, 174
   reverse premiums and 177–8
   surrenders and 178
   transfers of going concerns 178
vesting orders 394

Wales 31
   regional planning 32
warranties
   collateral 165–7
waste 135, 276
water 134
winding up *see* **liquidation (winding up)**